Edo (Jeddo)

Kyoto

Osaka

KOREA

Peking

Tsushima

Hirado
Nagasaki

Tanegashima

EAST CHINA
SEA

Nanking

Ningpo

RYŪKYŪ

CHINESE EMPIRE

Fukien

Amoy

Pescadores

TAIWAN

Kwangtung

Tayouan

Canton

PACIFIC OCEAN

Macao

TONGKING

Chiang-mai

Manila

Pegu

Tourane

PHILIPPINE
ISLANDS

SIAM

ANNAM

Faifo

Ayuthia

CAMBODIA

SOUTH
CHINA
SEA

MOLUCCAS

CELEBES
SEA

Singora

Ternate
Tidore

Patani

Achin
(Acheh)

Amboina

CELEBES

Banda Islands

Malacca

BORNEO

Boeton

SUMATRA

Macassar

SUNDA SEA

Batavia
(Jacarta)

Timor

Bantam

JAVA

A WORLD ELSEWHERE

A WORLD ELSEWHERE

*Europe's Encounter with Japan in the
Sixteenth and Seventeenth Centuries*

Derek Massarella

YALE UNIVERSITY PRESS
NEW HAVEN AND LONDON 1990

TO THE MEMORY OF MY FATHER AND MOTHER

The Publication of this book has been generously assisted by a subsidy from The Japan Foundation.

Set in Linotron Bembo by Best-set Typesetter Ltd, Hong Kong. Printed and bound at the Bath Press, Avon, Great Britain.

Library of Congress Cataloging-in-Publication Data

Massarella, Derek, 1950–
    A world elsewhere: Europe's encounter with Japan in the sixteenth and seventeenth centuries/Derek Massarella.
      p.   cm.
    Includes bibliographical references.
        1. Europe – Foreign economic relations – Japan.   2. Japan – Foreign economic relations – Japan.   3. East India Company – History.   4. Nederlandse Factorij in Japan – History.   5. Hirado-shi (Japan) – Industries – History.   6. Europeans – Japan – History – 16th century.   7. Europeans – Japan – History – 17th century.   I. Title.
    HF1532.19.J3M37 1990
    337.4052'09'031 – dc20   89-22639
                                                                                      CIP

Contents

Acknowledgements

My debts in writing this book are many. Imai Hiroshi first suggested to me the importance of worlds elsewhere during an early stage of my stay in Japan and encouraged me to explore the subject with the attention it deserves. The late Iwao Seiichi readily shared his formidable knowledge of Japanese and European sources. Leslie Le Clair, the Librarian of Worcester College, Oxford, has taken a keen interest in my work since my days as a research student. She provided the essential link in the chain of events which made this book possible for which I am grateful.

I would also like to thank a number of friends and colleagues whose encouragement, support and help over the years has been invaluable: C. R. Boxer, Alexander Bruce, Michael Cooper, Guy Faure, Leslie and Susan Fearns, Sheelagh Fullerton, Geneviève Guth-Kitts, Philip Healy, Christopher Hill, Robert and Sunae Hinton, Kanai Madoka, Ōba Tōmō, Geoffrey Parker, Ivan Roots, Michael Strachan, Tamaura Hideo, Mariko Yandell and Austin Woolrych. My colleagues in the Faculty of Economics at Chuo University have been generous in their support; my students have taught me more than they realise. My editors at Yale, Robert Baldock and Elaine Collins, have been immensely supportive. Robert suggested that the seed of the original idea for the book should grow into something bigger and has nurtured the project to see that it did. Elaine cast a sharp, objective eye over the final typescript and saved me from a number of infelicities and unclear modes of expression.

Thanks are also due to the Japan Foundation for awarding a grant under its Publication Assistance Program and the staff of the various archives and libraries where the research was undertaken, in particular the India Office Library and Records, especially the Deputy Director, Anthony Farrington, the British Library the Public Record Office, Chuo University Library and the Shiryō Hensan-jo of the University of Tokyo.

My obligation to my father who many years ago crossed the seas which figure so largely in this book is evident from the dedication.

Finally I would like to acknowledge the huge debt I owe to Gerald Aylmer. Although this book is about a subject removed, but not entirely so, from army politics during the English Revolution I have tried to maintain the standards which he would expect. Any short-coming is entirely my responsibility.

Glossary

bakufu	'tent government', the shogun's government or shogunate
daikan	deputy. The Nagasaki *daikan* was appointed by the bakufu and governed Nagasaki. The English referred to him as the Nagasaki governor or *bongew*, a corruption of *bugyō*, magistrate.
daimyo	feudal lord
godown	warehouse
itowappu	or *itowappu nakama*, silk yarn allotment guild, established in 1604; regulated the purchase price of silk brought by the Portuguese to Nagasaki. The Portuguese called it the pancado.
jitō	land steward
jurabasso	interpreter, from the Malay *jurubahāsa*, language master
mestizo	a Eurasian
nanbanjin	southern barbarian, original name for the Europeans who arrived in Japan in the sixteenth century. During the course of the seventeenth century it was used only for the Roman Catholic Europeans, that is the Portuguese and Spanish.
náo	*náo do trato*, great ship of commerce, or carrack as the English styled these Portuguese ships which varied between 600 and 1,600 tons.
nihonmachi	name applied to the communities of Japanese who formed the Japanese diaspora in southeast Asia.
pancado	see *itowappu*
pangeran	Javanese prince

rōjū	elders, the senior councillors of the shogun
shuinjō	vermilion seal document, important documents bearing the shogun's official seal.
shuinsen	vermilion seal vessels, Japanese authorised to sail overseas because they carried a *shuinjō*.
VOC	*Vereenigde Oost-Indische Compagnie*, the Dutch East India Company.
wakō	Japanese pirates or bandits, the term applied to Japanese pirates who attacked the coastal areas of China and Korea from the thirteenth to the seventeenth centuries; from the Chinese *wo-k'ou*.

Notes for Readers

Currency and Money of Account

Most of the accounting of the Hirado factory was recorded either in reals or taels of silver. The Spanish real (rial-of-eight) was the commonest and most sought after European coin in the Indies. The value of the real in Japan, as elsewhere in the Indies, fluctuated but was worth between 3s 6d (17.5p) and 4s 6d (20.5p) during the factory's existence. It never fetched the 5s (25p) which the Company set as the official rate of exchange for the portion of its factors' salaries payable in the Indies. The tael was solely money of account and was subdivided into 10 mas and 100 candereen. Its value in Japan was 5s. In Siam its value in the 1610s was between 8s (40p) and 9s 8d (48p). The Dutch kept their accounts in florins or guilders (*f.*). The guilder consisted of 20 stuivers and the stuiver of 16 penningen. Until 1636 the tael was worth 3 guilders 2 stuivers 8 penningen, from 1637–66, 2 guilders 17 stuivers, and after then 3 guilders 10 stuivers. In English money the guilder was worth 1s 8d (just over 8p). Silver in Japan was exchanged according to weight. The momme (3.75 grammes) was the standard unit and the tael was reckoned at 10 momme.

Weights

The pecul (picol) contained 100 catties and was used for accounting purposes for weighing goods such as silk, lead or sappan wood rather than Japanese weights. The pecul was equivalent to 133 1/3 lbs avoirdupois, 125 Dutch ponds or 1 Japanese kin.

Measure

The English made linear measurements in Japan in 'tatami' which
was not in fact a Japanese unit of measure. In Japanese buildings the
distance between two architectural supports was a ken. The ken was
equivalent to the length of a tatami, the matting used to cover floors
in more affluent Japanese housing, and the English and Dutch
assumed, incorrectly, that the Japanese measured in tatami rather
than ken. The length of the ken, which was not standard in Japan,
and hence of the tatami, can be taken as 2 yds (1.82 m).

Capacity

The *koku*, on which land productivity, tax assessments and daimyo
stipends were determined, was equivalent to *c*.5 bushels or 182 l.
The above is based upon Oskar Nachod, *Die Beziehungen der Nieder-
ländischen Ostindien Kompagnie zu Japan in siebzehnten Jahrhundert,*
Leipzig, 1897, pp. CXCIV–CXCV, CC–CCI; Ernest M. Satow (ed.), *The
Voyage of Captain John Saris to Japan, 1613,* London, 1900, p. 96, n. 1;
C. R. Boxer, *The Great Ship from Amacon,* Lisbon, 1959, pp. 335–42;
John E. Wills, Jr, *Pepper, Guns, & Parleys: The Dutch East India
Company and China, 1662–1681,* Cambridge, Massachusetts, 1974,
p. 10; *Kodansha Encyclopedia of Japan,* 8, pp. 239–40; and information
contained in the original sources.

Spelling

Citation from English MS sources retains the original spelling
although punctuation has been added. Japanese has been romanised
according to the Hepburn system. Japanese personal names are given
in the Japanese style, that is family name first except where authors
have published in foreign languages and have used the Western
convention. The romanisation of Chinese is according to the Wade-
Gilles system, although I prefer the Portuguese Macao to the English
Macau. I have left the most frequently cited Indonesian and Malay-
sian place names in their pre-1972 English forms (e.g. Bantam
instead of Banten, Moluccas instead of Maluku). This is purely for
the convenience of readers.

Dating

The English continued to use the Julian calendar (Old Style) until
1752 although most of continental Europe had switched to the

Gregorian calendar (New Style or NS) in 1582. Unless otherwise stated, all dates are given Old Style (OS) which was ten days behind the Gregorian calendar in the seventeenth century. The new year is taken to begin on 1 January. The correspondance between the Japanese lunar and the Western calendar is based on the tables in Paul Yachita Tsuchihashi, *Japanese Chronological Tables from 601 to 1872 AD*, Tokyo, 1952.

Introduction

Our knowledge of the history of European overseas expansion and our approach to the subject have travelled far since J. C. van Leur attacked the Eurocentric views of Dutch colonial historians prevalent in the later nineteenth and early twentieth centuries. Van Leur charged them with viewing the Indies 'from the deck of the ship, the ramparts of the fortress, the high gallery of the trading house'.[1] The reaction against Eurocentrism flourished against a background of withdrawal from empire and a backlash of attacks, sometimes virulent, on the erstwhile colonial rulers by their former subjects. The bitter denunciations of the economic and cultural rape visited by imperialism, and an ensuing sense of guilt among the European intelligensia, helped produce numerous works which, in varying degrees, were critical of empire. Such works constituted a form of intellectual reparation. Some writers denounced full-bloodedly the whole elaborate enterprise of empire; others questioned the assumptions and were mildly apologetic about the excesses. But the dialectic of reaction engenders a counter reaction and the forward march of 'discovery', expansion, settlement and empire is dismissed by some scholars as marginal to European economic development and which, had it not occurred, would not have retarded the crowning glory of the European achievement, industrialisation. The experience of empire can thus be disowned as the deviant stepchild of European history. However, we cannot escape so lightly from our past. We cannot write it out of our collective consciousness. Nor should we want to; but neither should we allow ourselves to become a victim of it.

For Professor Immanuel Wallerstein, drawing heavily upon the dependency theory of André Gunder Frank and others, the era of European expansion is synonymous with the emergence of a modern world system in which the peripheral areas, first in Europe and then overseas, were increasingly subordinated to the economic supremacy

of the metropolitan, or core, states of western Europe and their
offspring across the Atlantic, the United States. In Professor Wallerstein's words this amounted to 'an appropriation of surplus of the
whole world-economy by core areas'.[2] For those who subscribe to
the notion of a modern world system, Europe's expansion was a
malignant, unsolicited intrusion into the affairs of others. Without
that intrusion, so the logic proceeds, the other two great areas of
world civilisation, China and India, propelled by endogenous economic and cultural strengths, might have achieved a spontaneous
industrialisation, thus freeing them from the stigma of having failed
to unbind Prometheus.

It is a seductive theory, rich in implications for academic debate
and for polemics about the contemporary relationship between core
and periphery, or 'north' and 'south'. But it is a theory which has
difficulty passing the test of rigourous empirical analysis. Dr
Leonard Blussé has exposed the tenuous underpinnings on which
Wallerstein's discussion of east Asia rests, and advocates of the
theory have a problem fitting the rise of modern Japan into the
model and doubtless will have similar difficulties accommodating
the economic success of other Asian countries, especially South
Korea and Taiwan.[3]

A major onslaught against the idea of a modern world system is
contained in the writings of Professor Paul Bairoch and Dr Patrick
O'Brien. Bairoch argues that in 1700 European consumption of
non-European products amounted to between 2 and 10 per cent of
total European consumption and that the value of non-European
products amounted to between 2 and 3 per cent of European GNP.
In 1800 only 4 per cent of Europe's exports went to Asia as opposed
to 74 per cent exchanged in inter-European trade, while in 1830, 12.5
per cent of Europe's imports came from Asia, 63 per cent being
exchanged within Europe.[4] O'Brien goes further, and suggests that
non-European trade accounted for less than 1 per cent of Europe's
aggregate output in 1800 and that non-European trade accounted for
only 10 per cent of the gross investment available in Europe at the
time. For O'Brien trade with the rest of the world mattered little
for the genesis and sustentation of the industrial revolution: 'for
the industrial revolution in Western Europe, the periphery was
peripheral'.[5]

It is a salutory argument but one that skirts close to defining a
neo-Eurocentrism, albeit an inverted one. Even if the economic
impact of the first encounter between Europe, the Indies and the rest
of the world was not as great as has sometimes been imagined, it was
not as inconsequential as Dr O'Brien suggests.[6] Industrialisation was
made possible by the successful application on a grand scale of the
technological breakthroughs of the late eighteenth century. But this

could not occur without the requisite institutions and organisational forms. These did not emerge spontaneously; they owed much to previous development. In this respect the mature English and Dutch East India Companies made a significant contribution to the evolution of the institutions of capitalism, in particular to the money market and, because of the companies' success, to the adoption of business firms as the appropriate structure whereby capitalist enterprise could take advantage of the opportunities created by the industrial revolution. In Professor K. N. Chaudhuri's words: 'The most powerful and revolutionary impact of the Companies lay in the public acceptance of the notion that the corporate financial liabilities were someone else's assets. Investment and capital accumulation were at once affected through this mechanism.'[7] Professor Niels Steensgaard's insistence that the companies were not an essential link in the evolution from medieval forms of business enterprise to the modern business corporation is not incompatible with Professor Chaudhuri's view. Steensgaard acknowledges that it was the ability of the mature trading companies to compete successfully in the market rather than any other advantage they enjoyed, notably their association with government and their monopoly status, which gives them their special character.[8] Success breeds imitation and adaptation. In other realms too, such as the rise of marketing skills to create demand for new, often exotic products, the impact of the companies, and therefore of Euro-Asian trade, should not be overlooked.[9]

European expansion was hardly irrelevant either for the individual countries involved, for the continent as a whole, or for the people (Europeans and non-Europeans) who came into contact with each other for purposes of trade, to say nothing of those who had the misfortune to live in places where the Europeans chose to settle, and those others who survived the transatlantic crossing to work in the plantations of the Americas. (It should be remembered, however, that the Europeans had nothing to teach the world about violence or the exploitation of their fellow-men except perhaps testing the limits of what could be achieved by employing such means.) For better or worse, the experience of European expansion has helped define the world in which we live. It also helped define Europe, a continent, a culture and a civilisation. The discovery of new worlds and old civilisations provided plenty of evidence of 'otherness' and eventually created a sense of Europeanness in much the same way as the earlier threat from the 'otherness' of Islam had helped define Christendom. There remains much to learn from this and historians still have far to travel and hard to labour before, if ever, they will have harvested 'all the tea in China and all the quinine in Peru'.[10]

However, when the Europeans moved from the Atlantic to the

Indian Ocean and then on into the China seas to establish a direct
trade with the Indies on a scale far greater than the indirect trade
Europe enjoyed through the Levant and Mediterranean, the value-
laden notion of the Orient, and the Orientalism which Professor
Edward Said has described, had yet to be invented.[11] The Europeans
did not voyage to the Indies, to quote the older, simpler, and
untenable view of Sir George Sansom, 'in a spirit of determination to
succeed that was stronger than the will of the Asiatic peoples to
resist.'[12] Nor did they have an exalted view of themselves (except the
Spanish in the Philippines, but even there conquistador rhetoric
remained largely that, words unsupported by action). Europeans did
not gaze at the societies in which they worked and lived from the
deck, the rampart or the high gallery. They mixed, jostled and
hustled with the other merchants against whom they were
competing and within whose ranks they were living. They sought
favours from local rulers by bribery and flattery. In some places they
took advantage of local conflicts or weak, unstable regimes to secure
an advantage for themselves. Away from the littoral society of the
Indonesian archipelago they encountered formidable polities and
civilisations as old as and even older than their own. There they were
witnesses to, sometimes participants in, but seldom initiators of, the
momentous events that were shaping those polities. This was the
case in their relations with Japan where the English East India
Company maintained a factory or trading post from 1613 to 1623.

The story of the English, or more strictly speaking British, for
men from other parts of the British Isles were present in Japan, has
been told before, notably by Ludwig Riess in the nineteenth century
and in a number of books on William Adams, the 'first' Englishman
in Japan.[13] But it has never been told adequately or completely, that
is, within the larger context of the new relationship between Europe
and the Indies, of the ambitions and policy of the East India
Company and its Dutch rival (which also maintained a factory in
Japan), of developments in Europe, and of those within and around
Japan's east Asian setting. It is such a lacuna which this book seeks to
fill. The richness of the sources, many previously untapped, and the
harvest of new research on closely related subjects make it possible to
present a fresh and comprehensive study of the Company's factory in
Japan at a time when the country was in the last stages of a
momentous transformation which secured the Tokugawa shogunate
firmly in power, where it remained, impregnable, until it was
overthrown in 1867. Viewed from the broader perspective and
stripped of the nineteenth-century romantic gloss of heroic voyages
of discovery, the stuff of which novels are made, the history of the
factory provides a fascinating case study of the evolution of

England's, indeed of Europe's, newly established presence in worlds elsewhere.

The history also provides a better vantage point for an understanding of the contemporary relationship between the West and Japan which has emerged in the late twentieth century as one of great importance in a manner inconceivable in the sixteenth and seventeenth centuries. Looking forward from these centuries rather than taking up the story in the early 1850s with the arrival of Commodore Matthew Perry and the establishment of the treaty ports or with Japan's defeat in 1945, the relationship is free of the twin shadows of European and Japanese imperialism. It can be seen as having returned to what it was originally, a trading relationship, if, nevertheless, a troubled one. But just as in the sixteenth and seventeenth centuries trade did not, and could not, exist in a vacuum, so today trade cannot be stripped of its geopolitical implications. This makes it all the more imperative to return to the beginning. Without a firm anchor in historical understanding such a relationship becomes an orphan in a storm; it drifts helplessly and dangerously, a hostage to the powerful forces of misunderstanding and perversion. We should all ponder seriously John Dos Passos's poignant observation that '[i]n times of change and danger when there is a quicksand of fear under men's reasoning, a sense of continuity with generations gone before can stretch like a lifeline across the scary present.'[14] The fact that Dos Passos was writing in 1941 when the world was indeed scary does not detract from the wisdom and pertinence of his advice.

The book adopts a narrative approach. An examination of the unfolding of events, rather than an analysis of their outcome judged with the benefit of hindsight, seems to me appropriate and gives one a better measure of England's, and more generally Europe's, efforts to drive a direct trade with the Indies. There was no straight road to success in these efforts. The way was littered with false starts, lost opportunities, misjudgements, and unrealistic ambitions. These have to be appreciated in any assessment of the outcome. This does not mean that analysis has been neglected. To do so would be to return to an earlier, insufficient narrative which left too many questions unanswered or unasked. Rather the analysis has been incorporated into the discussion. For one is writing a history not a pathology, to borrow R. H. Tawney's telling phrase.[15] There is no doubt in my mind which is the more exciting.

CHAPTER 1

First Encounters with Japan

(i)   Earliest Contacts

Contact between the extremities of the great Eurasian land mass had existed for hundreds of years before Vasco da Gama's successful voyage across the Indian Ocean in 1497–8, the overture to regular maritime contact and a permanent European presence in Asia. However, in the apposite words of Sir Henry Yule 'the *fluctuation* of knowledge in regard to geographical truth in general, and to the Far East in particular, is very noticeable'.[1] This was the case during the earliest period of trade between the Indies and Europe and remained so well after the earliest Portuguese voyages of exploration.

The geographers of antiquity were trying to piece together a map of the world derived from knowledge brought back by explorers to Tyre and Alexandria. These eastern Mediterranean cities served as information centres in much the same way as the Italian city states of Genoa and Venice and the capitals of Portugal and Spain, the countries in the vanguard of European overseas expansion, did later.[2] Most of the established knowledge of the ancients was clearly inadequate and often fancifully embellished, but in an age in which science and technology were in their infancy, it was impossible to separate fact from fiction. Ptolemy, the most influential of the ancients for later generations, writing in AD 150 based his estimates of the earth's circumference on those of Pondonius rather than Erathosthenes's more accurate ones, thereby overstating the length of a degree. This helped convince Columbus that the eastern extremes of Asia were closer to Europe than had been imagined previously. Ptolemy also considered that the Indian Ocean was an enclosed sea, bound on its eastern extremity by a huge *terra incognita* and to the south by a continuation of eastern Africa stretching out from the Horn to meet the projection of China.[3] Yet even with these limitations and the errors incorporated into academic knowledge, it is remarkable what was known to the ancients and how much progress was made (for example, the grid system of mapping, the representation of a sphere on a plain surface) to the advancement of academic geographical knowledge.[4]

More obvious and immediate to many contemporaries than the development of academic geography was trade, especially the commodities and manufactured goods eagerly sought by merchants and consumers and carried along the routes which linked the distant civilisations of the ancient world. Trade stimulated greater curiosity about other civilisations and created the thirst for information, geographical, cultural and, eventually, social, political and economic.

For the ancients China was differentiated into the territories of the Sinae and the Seres. The former, whose name was known to the Greeks as well as the Romans and was derived from Arab sources, were said to border on the shores of the Indian Ocean and were considered to live at the edge of the habitable world. The Seres were of commercial importance to the Roman world where their goods and commodities were much in demand. The Romans thought of them as a civilised people and, as their name implies, silk was one of the principal commodities traded.[5]

In addition to silk, which began to reach Rome during the reign of Augustus (27 BC to AD 14) and which was mostly brought raw to be manufactured by the weaving industries of the Roman orient, furs, lacquer-ware and possibly iron work were imported from China. The Chinese imported wool and linen textiles, coral and pearls (from the Red Sea) and glass and amber (from the Baltic).[6] It was essentially a luxury trade and was conducted overland and by sea, explaining the division of the Chinese into the Sinae and Seres.[7] Overland, in caravans of 50, 100 or even 1,000, trade moved along the silk road, in reality a number of roads or routes, which spread out from the western frontiers of China crossing deserts and mountain passes before reaching the eastern edge of the Mediterranean at Antioch, or further south near the textile and dying centres of Tyre, Sidon and Gaza.[8] The route had come into use around 200 BC and its importance fluctuated in accordance with the cataclysmic power struggles that periodically shook the peoples and territories along its great length. Its apotheosis came after the Mongol conquest of China during the thirteenth and early fourteenth centuries when northern Asia, from the Pacific coast to the eastern European plains, was united under the empire of the Khans. The sea route, which also brought spices, much in demand for their medicinal value, from the Indonesian archipelago, became the major conduit of trade after the Parthian war of AD 162–5, which had broken the Parthian monopoly of trade with China. Goods were sent by sea from southern China

usually in Chinese vessels, transported overland across the Malay
peninsula at the Isthmus of Kra and loaded on to Indian ships
operating from the southern Indian states which took them across
the Bay of Bengal. From India they were taken in Arab boats to Red
Sea or Persian Gulf ports where further overland journeys brought
them to the shores of the Mediterranean and from there, except for
goods needing manufacture, by sea to the heart of the empire and
beyond.[9] Trade was also conducted along the silk routes to Bactria,
then down to the Indus port of Barbaricon where goods were loaded
on to ships for the voyage west.[10]

Of the Chinese themselves little was known and as it is improbable
that any Chinese arrived in Rome; that which was known owed
more to fable than to fact. Pliny suggested that the Chinese had
red hair, blue eyes, hoarse voices and no common language.[11] Not
surprisingly there was no knowledge of China's neighbour, Japan,
which during the first hundred years of the Christian era was well
advanced in its transition from a mainly hunting and fishing society
to a more settled rice culture. Japan was already sending tributary
missions to China and by the third century AD was receiving embassies from the middle kingdom.[12] Japan was in Ptolemy's *Terra
Incognita*, which was 'full of marshes and lagoons in which great
canes grow, and that so densely that people are able to cross the
marshes by means of them.'[13] Ptolemy rejected the previous con-
jectures of Mela and Pliny that an ocean existed beyond the eastern
extremity of Asia.

To the Chinese, knowledge of places in the distant West also came
along the silk road to northern China and to the Han capital,
Chang'an, in the Wei valley. From the southern provinces came
knowledge of the 'western sea'. By the end of the first century AD the
Chinese were aware of the existence of the Roman world which they
called Ta-ch'iu, meaning 'Great China', possibly assuming that the
Roman world was a mirror image of the middle kingdom. Ta-ch'iu
referred to Rome's oriental provinces in the middle east and by
extension other countries in the region with which the Romans
conducted trade. The Chinese believed that 'the precious and rare
objects of all foreign countries come from [Ta-ch'iu].'[14] In AD 166 a
number of merchants made their way to the Chinese court claiming
to be legates of the emperor Marcus Aurelius Antonius (161–180).
They were accepted as such by the Chinese but were not an official
embassy and like others who may have made their way to China
probably came from the scattered Roman communities that had
grown up beyond the formal boundaries of the empire, especially in
Arabia, southern India and down the east coast of Africa. They were
citizens of Rome, either Egyptian Jews, Hellenised Egyptians or
some other Levantine people, but certainly not 'Italians'.[15]

By the third century AD, trade between the two empires tapered off. Gradually the Roman empire was engulfed by civil war and the Han empire collapsed under a welter of economic and political problems in AD 220 leading to a fragmentation of power in China which did not have central government restored until the establishment of the Sui (581–618) and T'ang dynasties (618–907). The two empires whose commerical needs had complemented each other had provided 'imperial umbrellas over most of the trade between China and the Mediterranean'.[16] The fall of the Han empire enabled the 'barbarian' nomads on the northern boundaries, previously kept at bay by means of the Great Wall (really a series of walls), to push into the heart of the old empire in search of pasture and plunder. The collapse of law and order, a recurrent theme in Chinese history, caused many people to escape from the troubled areas and flee to the south. There, as in the north, a succession of dynasties rose and fell. However, the relative stability of the southern kingdoms which were cut off from access to the northern overland routes (which by the fourth century were under the control of 'barbarians', themselves adept at profiting from them) was an important factor in stimulating sea trade between China and the lands to the southwest in the Nan-yang or 'southern ocean', that is, southeast Asia. This had an important influence on the evolution of the Chinese world order which the Portuguese were to enter in the sixteenth century.[17]

The demand for luxuries in the southern Chinese dynasties, especially by the nobility, who were eager to recreate the splendid life-style of the Han, contributed greatly to the political and economic growth of the western parts of the Indonesian archipelago, which by the fifth century was already eclipsing southern Indo-China as the major crossroads of international trade between the China Seas and the Indian Ocean. By the time the Portuguese arrived in the early sixteenth century its ascendency had long since been established.

The rise of the archipelago was based on maritime trade and trade was intimately connected with the development of early southeast Asian states.[18] Rulers controlling the main trading emporia actively sought and encouraged trade. These emporia were: Funan, on the southern coast of present-day Vietnam, the major entrepôt for shipping from China from the first to the fifth centuries AD; Jambi and Pelambang, part of the kingdom of Śrīvijaya in Sumatra whose influence extended into Java and exercised hegemony over the strategically important Straits of Malacca until its demise in the late fourteenth century; and Malacca (c.1400–1511), successor state of Śrīvijaya, the thriving, cosmopolitan port which the Portuguese found when they first moved across the Indian Ocean to the Malay archipelago in 1509. Trade provided money and prestige, but an open and secure trading environment was required in order to attract merchants. The ability to guarantee such an environment, for example, against rivals or pirates, in part determined the rise and fall of the successive trading emporia in the region.

As with other historical periods, including the present, the lure of the China market was great, certainly compelling enough to stimulate the Sumatran Malays, who became the principal carriers of goods (Sumatran resin, benzoin, camphor all much in demand among Chinese aristocrats) from the second half of the fourth century. By the late seventh century, with two strong empires existing again in East and West (the T'ang and the Umayyad caliphate), Persians and Arabs sailed to China via the Malaccan Straits circumventing the Isthmus of Kra, to trade directly with various ports in southern China, including Canton, the main destination and itself an important commercial centre since the Former Han dynasty (206 BC to AD 8). The extent of Canton's cosmopolitan character can be gauged by the massacre of 120,000 people in 879, mostly foreign merchants from southeast Asia, the Indian subcontinent, Persia and Arabia (Muslims, Nestorian Christians and Jews), by the rebel warlord Huang Ch'ao. The carnage contributed to the cessation of direct Arab and Persian trade with China. Henceforward the Arabs and Persians preferred to use ports in the Malay archipelago, including those of Śrīvijaya, then in its ascendency.[19]

It was from this period that the first notice of Japan reached the western parts of Asia, but not Europe. In his *Book of Roads and Provinces*, compiled between 844 and 886, the Persian writer Ibn Khurdadhbih wrote: 'To the east of China are the lands of the Wakwak which are very rich in gold which the natives make into chains for their dogs and the collars of their monkeys. They wear tunics stitched with gold. Ebony of excellent quality is also found there.... Gold and ebony are exported from Wakwak.' He estimated the distance from Jazia, north of Suez, to the land of the Wakwak as 4,500 parasanges (leagues). Despite the obvious inaccuracy of Ibn Khurdadhbih's description, Persian merchants are known to have traded with the Silla kingdom of Korea where they would have heard about Japan, and it is conceivable that some found their way across the straits which separate the two countries. The name Wakwak comes from one of the Chinese names for Japan, *wa-koku*, which in its Cantonese rendition is pronounced *wo-kwok*. Ibn Khurdadhbih's account of a land rich in gold is no more fantastic than the later one of Marco Polo and, unlike the latter, it did not suggest that Japan was commercially isolated.[20]

Under the Sung (960–1280), whose power base lodged south of the Yangtze river, there was a greater inclination to develop the trading contacts which had already been established by the earlier southern dynasties and the Chinese themselves emerged as major traders in the southern ocean. The expansion of foreign trade was encouraged by an increase in domestic demand which took place against a background of remarkable economic growth, especially in iron and coal production, which in turn encouraged a greater degree of urbanisation, commercialisation and monetisation. Cities became centres of exchange rather than merely administrative locations. Spices and aromatics from Arabia and ivory products from east Africa were imported. Ivory, much in demand for making the subtle handicrafts still greatly admired today, was trans-shipped via Oman and the Persian Gulf. The major Chinese exports in return were porcelain and silk. The goods were carried in Persian or Arab ships to southern India and transferred to Chinese junks which took them across the eastern Indian Ocean *en route* to China. Foreign trade became an important source of government revenue, and efforts were made to regulate the trade by establishing government offices in various ports, although such measures proved incapable of preventing illegal trade. In addition, foreign trade enabled the Chinese to develop a greater awareness of the Indian Ocean and east Africa. Knowledge of these areas was brought together in the *Chu-fan chih*, compiled in 1225. During the Sung period numbers of Chinese from the southern provinces made voyages overseas for trade and a Chinese diaspora was established in southeast Asia.[21]

Trade was also bound up with diplomacy. China had long since developed a sophisticated and flexible concept of international relations to give substance to its pretensions as the middle kingdom and to serve its defensive and offensive requirements, the tributary system. The system, which perhaps only merits this characterisation after the establishment of the Ming dynasty in 1368, had evolved over the centuries and had become institutionalised with various rituals and protocols. At the heart of the tributary system lay the assumption that China was the middle kingdom surrounded by inferior states who periodically acknowledged the supremacy of the celestial ruler on the Dragon throne by sending embassies and tributes. Like all mechanisms for conducting international relations it provided benefits to both the 'superpower', China, and to the smaller states on its periphery, and it was intimately bound up with trade. Ideally the tributary system aimed to provide stability among the polities within its geopolitical orbit even though the traumas of the Mongol conquest showed that this was impossible to realise in practice. Stability was a prerequisite for a thriving trade. If the tributary states did the necessary policing on the empire's borders there was no reason, except in extreme circumstances, for the Chinese to commit armed forces or even possess strategic bases abroad. The Chinese entertained the notion of cultural superiority, a belief by no means unique to them, although, wisely, under the Sung they treated their restive neighbours to the north as equals. The tributary system benefited the polities within its orbit. This was true of countries like Japan and Korea. Both made heavy cultural borrowings from China and were greatly influenced by the civilisation and statecraft of their giant neighbour, even if Japan's incorporation into the tributary system was more ambiguous than Korea's. It was also true of smaller, distant polities. In such polities the rulers valued the trade that flowed from the tributary system. It created wealth which had a tremendous symbolic value in legitimising power and gave rulers the means with which to influence their neighbours. For example, the power of Śrīvijaya was at its height from the seventh to the eleventh centuries during the T'ang and Sung dynasties but declined with the disintegration of the Sung.[22]

The defeat of the Southern Sung dynasty in 1279 and the inauguration of the Mongol Yüan dynasty (1280–1368) as rulers of China ushered in a period when strong unified power was imposed from the Pacific edge of Asia to the borders of Christendom. The Mongol sweep west across Asia followed on the triumphs of Chingiz Khan and his son Ögedei which had led to the conquest of northern China by 1234. The defeat of the armies of Poland, Moravia and Silesia at the battle of Liegnitz in 1241 was not followed by further Mongol advances westwards. Much to the relief of Christendom, the Mongols retreated into Asia to deal with the succession crises that followed Ögedei's death and fears of invasion subsided. In 1255 the Mongols turned their attention to Christendom's traditional enemy, the Muslim Abbasid caliphate, whose capital, Baghdad, was conquered in 1258.[23]

The reaction in Christendom to this first 'yellow peril' was the launching of an effort to convert the Mongols, although if the Mongols had been inclined to embrace Christianity other than just superficially, it would likely have been the Nestorian strain rather than the Roman one. In 1245, just before the Council of Lyons, called to discuss ways to deal with a possible renewed Mongol advance, Pope Innocent IV decided to send an emissary to the court of the Khan to attempt a conversion. This was the first step towards direct contact between Europe and China. It was made possible by the fact that the 'pax Mongolica', a convenient but misleading description of the status quo that followed the Mongol trail of conquest, death and destruction, gave a temporary unity to northern Asia.[24]

The missionaries were the earliest Europeans to leave accounts of their travels and descriptions of the lands they reached. It was from their reports, especially that of the Franciscan William of Rubruck (Willem van Ruysbroeck), that an image of 'Cathay', as China was first known, was formed in Europe.[25] The missionaries were quickly followed by merchants, although their numbers should not be exaggerated. The most famous were the Polos who travelled to Cathay in the late thirteenth century and it was from Marco Polo's record of his travels and sojourns in China that knowledge of Japan, Chipangu (a corruption of the Chinese Jih-pen-kue, kingdom of Japan) was first introduced to Europe.[26]

Marco himself never visited Japan and his comments were very vague and largely erroneous, especially concerning its distance from China:

> Chipangu is an Island towards the east in the high seas, 1500 miles distant from the Continent; and a very great Island it is. The people are white, civilised, and well-favoured. They are Idolaters, and are dependent on nobody. And I can tell you the quantity of gold they have is endless; for they find it in their own Islands, [and the King does not allow it to be exported, Moreover] few merchants visit the country because it is so far from the main land, and thus it comes to pass that their gold is abundant beyond all measure.

He added that the emperor's palace was 'entirely roofed with fine gold' and the floor and windows of its rooms made of gold 'so that altogether the richness of the Palace is past all bounds and all belief', and that there was also an abundance of pearls in the country.[27]

The Polos were followed by others and during the first half of the fourteenth century overland trade with China was conducted mainly by Genoese merchants, the most ambitious and enterprising, and by Venetians and Florentines.[28] The Florentine merchant Francesco Balducci Pegolotti, described the overland route as 'entirely without danger'.[29] He was greatly exaggerating. However, use of the route was encouraged by other factors: a papal prohibition against trade with the Egyptian sultanate, which like all such sanctions could be, and was, broken; the existence of colonial outposts of the Italian city-states in southern Russia and the Crimea, and in Asia Minor and Persia at the western end of the overland route; and by Egyptian policy which endeavoured to keep the sea route firmly under the sultan's control by excluding foreign merchants seeking trade with India and China from crossing Egyptian territory. As with the papal embargo this could not be rigidly enforced either. Unfortunately, the Genoese, jealous of their commerce, have left precious little indication of their involvement in the trade and no personal accounts whatsoever to match Marco Polo's. Like the trade of the Roman Empire, silk, initially marketed in Europe with the exotic cachet 'Cathay silk', was the commodity most in demand. Profits were high, but so too was the investment required to bring it westwards and most of the European demand for silk continued to be satisfied by Turkestan and Persian producers.

Knowledge of paper money, printing and gunpowder also filtered back to Europe across the overland route along with the impressions of the people who travelled it, accounts which were supplemented by those of fictitious travellers, notably Sir John Mandeville, which enjoyed great popularity and fed the imagination of a still credulous European audience at this time.[30] The promising beginnings petered out with the collapse of the Mongol empire as quarrels between rivals for succession turned to fighting. In the west, the Persian khanate began to disintegrate from 1338 leading to a pogrom of European merchants and missionaries and a closure of the overland route to China. The last recorded crossing was made in 1342.[31] In the east, the Chinese began to reassert their independence, which they achieved in 1368 with the explusion of the Mongols and the inauguration of the penultimate Chinese imperial dynasty, the Ming, which survived as a unified dynasty until 1644.

It is easy to exaggerate the importance of the overland route. The Silk Road has acquired a legendary status quite out of proportion to its true role in China's overseas trade. However, its eclipse increased the importance of the sea passage. This route had already carried westerners to India in the twelfth century in search of the tomb of St Thomas, and from there, in the late thirteenth century, some missionaries, or at least Christianised Arabs from the Levant, had sailed on to China. It is even possible that the enterprising Genoese, who were asked to build two galleys for the Persian Khan in 1290, operated their own ships in the Indian Ocean. More probably they used indigenous vessels. Even under the Yüan dynasty the sea route had remained the main outlet for Chinese foreign trade. The Yüan had established Bureaus of Trading Junks at the ports of Ch'üan-chou (Polo's 'Zayton'), Ningpo, Canton and elsewhere. The Yüan assertion of the tributary system stimulated trade, carried in Chinese and foreign vessels, which the Yüan, like their Sung predecessors, tried (unsuccessfully) to control. However, it was an increasingly expensive system to operate because it occasioned hospitality and impressive return gifts, thereby stretching Chinese fiscal resources.[32]

In the west, the Genoese had already gone out into the Atlantic and on to the west African coast in the twelfth century where a settlement was established in 1253 and had rediscovered the Canaries, islands known to the Romans, in the early fourteenth century. The lure of a possible sea route to the east (whether westwards across the Atlantic or round Africa is unclear) had led to the ill-fated voyage by the Vivaldi brothers, unfamiliar with and therefore uninhibited by Ptolemaic geography, in 1291, some two hundred years before Columbus. The purpose, so far as any can be detected, seems to have been the hope that the discovery of a sea route to Asia would open up new commercial opportunities. Others were of the opinion that Mongol rule over northern Asia made such efforts redundant.[33] However, it was only during the fifteenth century that real progress towards opening a direct sea route to Asia was made when the Portuguese, who assumed the mantle of exploration that had been only partly donned by the Genoese, began to take an interest in the sea and lands to the south of the Algarve, an interest that led Portuguese ships and merchants down the coast of Africa and eventually round its southern Capes, and beyond into the vibrant trading worlds of the Indian Ocean and Arabian and China Seas.

(ii)   The Portuguese reach Japan, 1543

The existence of a Portuguese maritime empire in Asia in the sixteenth century in which a number of enclaves were scattered at strategic points along established trade routes, wherever possible protected by a fort, and supported by naval power superior in that it was more effective than anything that Asian polities were able to muster, was not the consequence of a Portuguese master plan. Nor was it the result of superior geographical knowledge or higher technical and commercial ability *vis-à-vis* the competitors the Portuguese encountered in Asian waters. Portugal's sea empire evolved out of a very tentative, haphazard series of voyages undertaken from the fourteenth century, and from motives that were both commercial and geopolitical in origin. Skill, determination and foresight led the Portuguese down the west African coast to the Capes at the southern extremity of the continent, and Vasco da Gama out into the Atlantic and then round the Capes and across the Indian Ocean in 1497–8. But these positive qualities were tempered by stubbornness (the dogged, misguided pursuit of an easy way to reach the Indian Ocean overland across Africa and the futile quest for the mythical northeast African Christian monarch, Prester John) and bad judgement (the dismissal of Christopher Columbus as 'very talkative and vain' when he requested financial backing for his bold proposal to sail westwards to discover Chipangu, a project described as 'nonsense' by King João II's advisers).[34] The character of the era, as Europe, or more accurately, the countries on the continent's western seaboards, expanded overseas in the sixteenth and seventeenth centuries, fully deserves to be styled the 'age of reconnaissance'.[35]

In 1415 the Portuguese captured the northwest African enclave of Ceuta. This encouraged them to look southwards as a means of outflanking Muslim control of north Africa and eventually attacking the area from the rear. This strategy had been anticipated in the early fourteenth century in the Dominican William Adam's bold recommendation that the Genoese should build four galleys for the Persian

Khan for service in the Indian Ocean as a first step towards strang-
ling Egyptian commerce by blocking the Red Sea thereby choking
Egypt's commercial lifeline. The proposal was reiterated more modestly by Jourdain de Severae in 1324.[36] By 1434 the Portuguese had
rounded Cape Juby and over the next few years expectations of
lucrative trade in slaves and gold on the coast of Africa (another
powerful reason for moving further down the African coast) were
fulfilled. In the mid fifteenth century a *feitoria*, or factory, was
established at Arguim (south of Cape Blanco). Factories were established throughout Africa and Asia as the Portuguese crown attempted to assert a monopoly over the new trade.[37] They also served as a
model for the English and Dutch although the organisation of their
trade in companies was different from the Lusitanians.

After the Portuguese and Castilian wars of succession 1475–9,
Portuguese exploration took on a new zeal and vigour, especially
during the reign of João II (1481–5). João fully appreciated the
strategic and commercial value of voyages of exploration. In 1488
Bartolomeu Dias succeeded in rounding the southern tip of Africa.
This hammered a nail into the coffin of Ptolemaic geography, which
had already been called into doubt anyway in the 1457 Genoese map
of the world and by Fra Mauro's planisphere of 1459, which had
been commissioned by the Portuguese crown and incorporated
information from Arabian sources and Portuguese voyages. Both the
map and the planisphere suggested that the Indian Ocean was not
landlocked and Mauro even included a boat from the Indies, the
exact provenance of which is unknown, rounding the Cape with the
date '1420'. The planisphere also mentioned 'Zimpagu', possibly
Polo's Chipangu, but positioned to the north of Java.[38]

After a gap of some nine years, the reasons for which modern
historians fail to agree upon,[39] the Portuguese finally decided to
exploit the potential of a circumnavigable Africa. Enthused by the
possibility of securing spices, a fleet of four vessels under the
command of Vasco da Gama set sail for India in July 1497. Vasco da
Gama moved out into the Atlantic, rather than down the African
coast, skilfully taking advantage of the prevailing trade winds and
ocean currents, rounded the Capes and sailed up the east coast of
Africa to encounter the western rim of the trading world that
encompassed the Indian Ocean and the China Seas. At Melinda on
the east African coast, Da Gama was able to procure the services of
an Arab pilot, possibly the famous Ibn Ahmed Madgid,[40] who
guided the fleet across the Indian Ocean, waters unfamiliar to
European ships. On 20 May 1498, Da Gama reached Calicut.

'Christians and spices' was the riposte Vasco da Gama made to the
question a Tunisian Arab posed in Castilian as to why he had come
from Portugal (although probably he meant the hope of finding

Christian communities) and a connection between trade and religion persisted throughout the subsequent history of the Portuguese in Asia. This should be kept in perspective, however, for it was only from the 1540s when the Counter Reformation was gathering steam in Europe and at a time when the Portuguese maritime empire in Asia was passing its peak economically that the major proselytising effort got under way. Contrary to the proud assertion of Camões in *The Lusiads*, who criticised the indolence of the French for failing to spread the faith and the Germans and English for persecuting it in their countries, Portuguese missionary activity was never to be on the scale of the Spanish in the New World.[41]

Pepper was a much sought after commodity in Europe. The Romans had imported it from the East but after the fall of Rome and the rise of Islam in the Mediterranean supplies had been cut off. By the twelfth century it was again in demand and used for various purposes, as a seasoning, a way of disguising old meat and, when mixed with salt, as preservative for meat.[42] Great profits could be made in the Mediterranean world from importing pepper from the Levant. Venice, which had almost cornered the market in bilateral trade with the Levant, exercised considerable influence over the import and distribution of pepper. By the end of the fifteenth century the Venetians were investing about 580,000–730,000 ducats per annum in their Levant trade.[43] The Portuguese had been tempted to break this control since the 1480s and the triumph of the Vasco da Gama voyage, even if in financial terms the commodities he brought back were of little value, transformed thought into determined action to beat the Venetians, outflanking them and acquiring the pepper at one of its major sources, India – William Adam's geo-political argument in commercial dress. It was a struggle that sapped Portuguese energies during the sixteenth century and proved un-winnable.

Within a few short years of Vasco da Gama's return to Lisbon in 1499, the Portuguese had defeated a combined Gujarati-Egyptian fleet, the only naval force then in a position to challenge their armed merchantmen, at Diu in 1509, and seized Goa the following year, making it the principal Portuguese base in India and destination of the voyages of the *Carreira da Índia* (the voyage to India) mono-polised by the Portuguese crown. From Goa the Portuguese sailed eastwards across the Indian Ocean and down the Malay coast to seize Malacca in 1511, and four years later they stormed Ormuz, at the entry to the Persian Gulf. But they did not meet with success everywhere. The great empire builder Afonso de Albuquerque was repulsed at Aden in 1513, thus failing to gain control of the Red Sea. This failure dashed all hopes of bringing Venice to its knees by cutting its access to pepper supplies because the Red Sea passage for spices had already eclipsed that of Ormuz and the Gulf as the transit route to the Mediterranean.[44] But too much should not be made of this failure. In the words of Professor Niels Steensgaard, it was in the interests of the Portuguese to 'control, not blockade' the Red Sea, to ensure that trade was directed through Portuguese customs houses,[45] for at its economic peak the financial strength of the Estado da Índia (the 'State of India', or Portugal's maritime empire in the Indies) was not based on the direct trade in pepper with Europe. Its strength lay in Portuguese country trade, customs exactions in the Indies, and the sale of *cartazes* or safe-passes (safe, that is, from Portuguese attack but not for example, from pirates) issued to local shipping. This was plain extortion, predicated on intimidation and if need be the use of force.[46] However, the other Portuguese successes, together with a number of lesser acquisitions in India and previously acquired places on the east African coast and the overwhelming sense of national purpose with which the enterprise was pursued, laid the foundations for Portugal's maritime empire.

Consciously or not, the Portuguese, especially under the bold (and at times brutal) leadership of Albuquerque, were emulating the Venetians and Genoese who had pioneered a 'maritime trading-post empire' in the eastern Mediterranean and Black Seas. This involved control of a number of carefully chosen centres through which the sinews of trade passed, obviating the need for territorial conquest.[47] However, regardless of the originality of Albuquerque's vision, a number of factors ensured that the pretensions inherent in the grandiose titles of King Manuel (1495–1521), 'Lord of the Conquest, Navigator and Commerce of Ethiopia, Arabia, Persia, and India', fell far short of reality. First, there was the vastness of the area to be controlled. The possession of strategically-located centres could not offset the emergence of strong continental powers, the Mughals in India, the Safavids in Persia, and the Ottomans in Iraq, Syria and Egypt, which were more important for the subsequent development of west and southwest Asia than the arrival of the Portuguese. Second, there were the inadequate resources for the job and the quality of the men who were to develop and administer the empire, men more adept at turning their hand to personal gain than advancing the national cause, unless, of course, the two coincided. Third, there were the prevalent attitudes in Portuguese society where a premium was placed on men of noble blood (*fidalgos*). Seafarers were considered socially inferior, a major handicap for a maritime power. Fourth, there was the diversity of the trade and the impossibility of eradicating local competition. Fifth, the Portuguese faced competition from the English and Dutch from the seventeenth century. Finally, Portugal's aspirations were tempered by the economic assumptions underpinning the organisation and conduct of her trade. The Estado da Índia functioned as a redistributive enterprise, consuming or redistributing the profits from the revenues it gathered from existing supply and demand rather than creating additional demand by devising ways to increase supply. The Portuguese forced their way into an established trading world; they did not revolutionise Euro-Asian trade. Portuguese power was derived from strength at sea; it did not rest on the conquest of large areas of territory. The striking innovations in the conduct of European trade in the Indies which the mature English and Dutch East India Companies represented lay far in the future.[48]

Of Portugal's early achievements, the seizure of Malacca is rightly said to have been 'by far the richest prize that the Portuguese had attempted to take in Asia or Africa'.[49] In little over a hundred years since its foundation, Malacca had become the major emporium of the trade routes that united the Indian Ocean and China Seas; open, international and prosperous, a glittering, enticing jewel. Its cosmopolitan character and extensive trade covering an area from east Asia to the eastern Mediterranean are vividly described in the famous account of Tomé Pires, written shortly after its seizure by the Portuguese.[50] It was here that the Portuguese became familiar with the thriving trade between east Asia and the Indonesian archipelago.

Chinese vessels carried some of this trade, in defiance of Ming prohibitions against overseas trade. Such bans had originally been decreed during the reign of the first Ming emperor, Hung-wu (r. 1368–98), but the second emperor, Yung-lo (r. 1403–24), had pursued a vigorous maritime policy with ambitious foreign relations and commercial goals. The voyages organised by the eunuch admiral, Cheng-ho (c.1371–1435), which took place between 1403 and 1433, on a far greater scale than anything the Portuguese attempted (the first comprised 28,000 officers and men and 63 ships), ventured into the Indian Ocean to Ceylon and beyond, touching the east African coast at Mogadishu and Malindi. The voyages were intimately related to a spectacular, and when necessary, ruthless, reassertion of the tributary system. But commercial objectives were also conspicuous. On their voyages the Chinese exported silk, porcelain, lacquer-ware, art objects, copper coins, and Buddhist sutras. They imported camphor, tortoise shells, coral, pepper and spices, sandal wood, incense, dyes, cottons, sugar, ivory, various animals including elephants, horses and giraffes, and precious stones. Business factors and accountants went on the third expedition. The memory of the voyages lived on, at least in India, where the Portuguese were told of 'certain vessels of white Christians, who wore their hair long like Germans and had no beards'. The Portuguese did not equate them with Chinese, doubted they were Germans, and thought that they might be Russians.[51] The voyages

were impressive feats of seamanship and there is no doubt that
Chinese naval technology and maritime skills would have enabled
the Chinese to achieve in reverse what the Portuguese were
beginning to undertake from the other side of Africa. But official
policy, unlike that of the Potuguese crown, provided no logic for
sending ships beyond the frontiers of China's world. The voyages
were broken off abruptly at a time of renewed threat from the
Mongols in the north and coastal incursions by the wo-k'ou, literally
'Japanese' or 'dwarf pirates', and the prohibitions against maritime
trade were reimposed.[52]

Ming disdain for trade owed much to the ascendancy of neo-
Confucianism in the bureaucracy where the antipathy towards
eunuchs and merchants (in classical Confucian thought the latter
were at the bottom of the status hierarchy) and its belief that the
voyages soaked up precious financial resources that could be better
spent at home. Moreover, as a major territorial power China
depended more on taxes from land than on duties from commerce.[53]
In practice the proscription against Chinese involvement in private
overseas trade remained a dead letter in the southern coastal provinces of Kwantung and Fukien which continued, as they had done
for centuries, to view the seas lapping their shores as a gateway to
opportunity. Merchants, aided and abetted by local officials and
encouraged by the existence of the Chinese diaspora, traded with
southeast Asia and, closer to home, with Korea and Japan and Japan's
southern neighbour, the Ryūkyū kingdom (present-day Okinawa),
the archipelago stretching from Japan to northeastern Taiwan.[54]

The Portuguese had become aware of the Chinese, or 'Chijns' as
they called them at first, during their earliest voyages in the Indian
Ocean. In 1508 a fleet under the command of Diogo Lopes de
Sequeira was dispatched for Malacca and was specifically instructed
by King Manuel to 'inquire about the Chijns', from where they
came, where they traded and with what commodities, the design of
their ships, and whether they were Christian.[55] Sequeira's squadron
reached Malacca in 1509 where it sighted three or four Chinese junks
in the harbour.[56] Two years later, Chinese junk masters provided
Albuquerque with assistance in the capture of the town from its
ruler, the sultan Mohamed, a tributary vassal of China. This diplomatic nicety carried no weight with the junk masters, especially
as Mohamed was heavy-handed in his dealings with the merchant
community, nor ultimately with the imperial government in Peking
which did not come to the assistance of its tributary vassal even
though the Portuguese attack threatened to create disorder on the
periphery of the Chinese world.[57]

In Malacca the Portuguese became familiar with another people
whom they called the Gores. The Gores visited Malacca between

January and April, and their country was said to be around forty days' voyage from Malacca and to have extensive gold mines. It was not clear whether their homeland was an island or not. The etymology of the word and the identity of these people have long been controversial. A number of hypotheses have been advanced suggesting that they were either Japanese from southern Kyushu or the Gotō Islands off northwest Kyushu, Ryūkyūans based on Taiwan, indigenous Taiwanese, or Koreans based on Ryūkyū. The name itself was picked up by the Portuguese in Malacca and may be from the Arab *Al-Ghur*, a possible rendering of the Chinese for Korea, *Ko-ryo* or *Kao-li*, which the Arabs might have confused with Ryūkyū. The Arab references to the Gores as traders clearly refer to people from Ryūkyū and it was this identification which the Portuguese adopted, although after 1514 they tended to use the word Lequios (which the English and Dutch later adopted) from the Chinese *Liukiu*, meaning Ryūkyū. The Ryūkyūans, ethnic Japanese whose language and culture had developed distinct from that of the main islands, had been active traders in east and southeast Asia since the early fifteenth century. Naha, the principal port of the kingdom, was cosmopolitan, though less so than Malacca, and Japanese lived and traded there. However, it is stretching the evidence too far to argue that the Ryūkyūans whom the Portuguese met at Malacca and later on the China coast were mainly Japanese. This stems from a misplaced logic which equates Pires's description of them as being 'great draftsmen and armourers' with the Japanese.[58] It is possible that some of the Gores were Japanese for the Ryūkyū kingdom played an important role in the country trade or inter-Asian trade not only with southeast Asia, but also with China, Japan and Korea, although by the time that the Portuguese reached Malacca the golden age of Ryūkyū's overseas trade was fast fading.

One fact that emerged explicitly from the earliest reports from Malacca, especially Pires's, was that the Chijns and the Gores conducted an extensive trade which appeared to be highly profitable.[59] Pires did not equate China with Marco Polo's Cathay, although a reference by an Italian, Giovanni da Empoli, in Portuguese service in Malacca, and a member of the first Portuguese voyage to China (an unofficial one which travelled in Chinese junks in 1514), mentions that the 'Grand Khan who is called the King of Cathay' resided in 'Zeiton' (Ch'üan-chou). But in official circles no connection between China and Cathay was made and it was not until the early seventeenth century that the two were shown conclusively to be the same.[60]

Not much attention was paid to the other northeast Asian country which the Portuguese heard about in Malacca–Japan. Pires described '[t]he island of Japan (*Jampon*)' briefly in two paragraphs.

This was the first European usage of the name and itself a corruption of the Malay word *Japun* or *Japang* (derived from Chinese coastal renderings of *Jipengo*). He was uncertain as to whether or not the Japanese themselves actually traded, but mentioned that Japan was about seven or eight days' voyage to the north of the Ryūkyūs. The 'king' of Japan was said to be 'more powerful and greater' than the Ryūkyū sovereign but 'not given to trading, nor [are] his subjects. They do not often trade in China because it is far off and they have no junks, nor are they seafaring men'. Pires added that the Japanese traded gold and copper with merchants from Ryūkyū. The tone and brevity of the discussion, like that of the Lucoes (the Philippines) suggests that not much was expected of Japan, certainly not as much as China, which became the focus of attention over the next thirty odd years, or even the Ryūkyū kingdom itself, to which a mission was dispatched, but failed to reach, in 1518.[61]

Portuguese ambitions in the region were more modest and fuelled by far less energy than those marking their first advance into the Indies. They were also less official. The last of the great Portuguese voyages commissioned by the crown to seek and make contact with new lands, commanded by Martim Afonso de Mello Coutinho, and charged specifically with negotiating a treaty of friendship and securing permission to establish a fortress in the Pearl River estuary, ended in a battle with Chinese warships near Canton in 1523. After this, attempts to establish official relations ceased until the 1550s and Portuguese trade on the China coast was conducted covertly. The Portuguese feared a Chinese attack on Malacca, whose ruler had appealed to China for help to drive out the Lusitanians, an appeal which the Portuguese embassy to Peking, headed by Pires, believed the Chinese were studying seriously. Indeed fleets were fitted out from 1523 to 1527, but these were intended for defensive purposes in case the Portuguese should return to Chinese waters. In fact the Lusitanians had already reached the limits of their geographical ambitions in Asia; the focus of empire was to remain firmly in the Indian Ocean.[62]

In trying to establish trade with China, the Portuguese found themselves confronting the first major territorial power since their overseas voyages had begun. The Chinese imperial institution considered its extensive southern seaboard as unstable, difficult to control and vulnerable to attack from pirates, still called *wo-k'ou* but by the sixteenth century no longer exclusively Japanese.[63] Local officials and trading families were anxious to profit as much as possible from foreign trade which the central authorities could not stamp out. The Portuguese adapted remarkably well to this situation. After the events at Canton they quickly appreciated that on the China coast they could not blast their way into the dominating position they had won for themselves in Goa or Malacca. Instead, they conformed to local practice, plying the coast trading in contraband while taking advantage of accommodating officials and shifts of policy as best they could. Their position changed for the better in 1557 when the Cantonese authorities decided to regularise Portuguese trading activity and granted them the right to settle near the mouth of the Pearl River at *Ao-men*, which the Portuguese corrupted to *A-ma-gao*, or Macao. The concession was made without the knowledge of the imperial government in Peking which did not understand what had been granted and to which particular barbarians, until the early seventeenth century.[64]

During their insecure, peripatetic trade on the coast the Portuguese deepened their knowledge of trade and international relations in the region and it is certain that they came into further contact with the Ryūkyūans and probably with Japanese (the Japanese sent two tributary missions to China in 1523 and 1539). Fernão Peres mentions seeing Japanese junks in the Pearl River estuary in 1517, although these could have belonged to Chinese based in Japan.[65] At first sight it appears rather puzzling that the Portuguese did not follow the leads of harbour gossip and make for Ryūkyū and Japan. However, there is no need to attribute their failure to reach the Ryūkyū Islands, much less Japan, until the 1540s to a deception perpetrated by the Ryūkyūans to protect their trade.[66] The China coast was a frontier area for the Portuguese. They had limited financial resources and manpower available and no overall strategy, certainly not an official one. Trading activity took place in junks manned by international crews. Profit, not 'discovery' or exploration was the motive. Trade was private in character, quite uncoordinated and free from government interference. If profits were good on the coast there was no compelling reason to venture to other as yet unfamiliar places until new opportunities made the risk attractive. The Portuguese involved in these activities would not have appeared a threat to Ryūkyū's trade. If individuals did venture further afield from the China coast (as is possible) they have left no records and it is highly unlikely that there was a deliberate cover-up by the Portuguese of visits to Japan before 1543.[67] More detailed commercial, geographical and maritime knowledge was built up gradually. By 1536 the Portuguese knew that the Ryūkyūs were three days' voyage from the Fukienese coast and were said to be rich in gold, copper and iron.[68] But it was to be at least another six years before they reached the island kingdom.

In this context it is not surprising that the first recorded Portuguese to reach Japan (António da Mota, Francisco Zeimoto and António Peixoto) were private traders who had set out from the capital of Siam, Ayuthia, for the China coast but who arrived instead in Japan after they were blown off course in a typhoon in 1543. They

landed on Tanegashima just off the southern coast of Kyushu on 23
September, according to Japanese sources, which add that there were
one hundred men from various parts of the Indies aboard.[69] They
were treated well by the locals who were 'whiter than Chinese, but
with small eyes and scanty beards' and they were informed that the
islands were '*Nipongi* which we usually term *Japão*'. The people were
kind and treated them well, repaired their junk 'and exchanged their
merchandise for silver, since their is none other [item for exchange]'
before they left for Malacca.[70]

The promising first encounter on Tanegashima developed into a
flourishing trade for the Portuguese and became the cornerstone of
their activity beyond Malacca, and until the late 1630s, the life-blood
of Macao. Japan also held great promise of becoming a fertile ground
for missionary work. Francis Xavier, shortly after his arrival in
Japan in August 1549, remarked, in oft-quoted words, that 'the
people whom we have met so far, are the best who have yet been
discovered, and it' seems to me that we shall never find among
heathens another race equal to the Japanese'.[71] But in what manner of
country had the Portuguese unexpectedly found themselves?

(iii)   The Empire of Japan

As had happened in medieval Europe, Japan's medieval age was
characterised by a struggle between competing interests to possess,
control and regulate land and simultaneously to establish procedures
to guarantee rights to its use, possession and transfer. It was only
when new sources of power and wealth created by a monetary
market economy took deep, permanent root that the more modern
obsession with exploiting the fruits of the soil rather than merely
possessing it triumphed. By the mid sixteenth century such a
monetary market economy was developing in Japan.

When the Portuguese first arrived in Japan the country was in the
last stages of the *sengoku jidai* (era of the country at war, or, more
evocatively, warring states).[72] There was an emperor in Kyoto, a
nominal locus of central power, and a shogun, also in Kyoto. In
reality, however, the country was torn between different factions of
feudal lords (daimyo) each trying to enhance their power and
prestige at the expense of the other. But even in the absence of any
central authority capable of exercising control, the *sengoku* period
was far from one of featureless anarchy. The reasons for this lie deep
in Japanese history.

By the end of the seventh century when the old-English kingdoms
were still in the process of unification, Japan had already established a
central polity which drew inspiration and practical example for its

culture and institutional structure from China. The absorption of Buddhism in the sixth century accelerated the phenomenon of borrowing from the continent and Japan began more consciously to imitate Chinese institutions. In 604 it adopted a centralised bureaucratic system of government (the Shōtoku constitution), modified, by the Taika reforms later in the century. Chinese architecture and city planning greatly influenced the building of the first permanent capital, Nara (710), and its successor Heian-kyō, or Kyoto, established in 794, which remained the capital until 1868.

The imperial institution provided legitimacy for the rule of an aristocracy comprising the heads of families, monasteries and shrines which ensured that legal codes were respected, mostly in its own interest. After 1000 this arrangement, which had provided the stability for the flourishing of a splendid, vigourous culture in the imperial capital, began to come unstuck. Central authority and the institutional framework on which it rested was challenged from within by competing elements of the imperial–aristocratic ruling class. A naked power struggle over the control of land rather than a quarrel over more abstract philosophical issues about the nature of government ensued.

Central authority could no longer adjudicate between the competing interests and by the end of the eleventh century was itself one of those interests as the imperial court tried to safeguard its own position. Legal proceedings could no longer be trusted to provide i npartial decisions nor could those decisions be enforced as factions within the ruling élite recruited armies of *bushi* (samurai or warriors) to protect their own interest. New leaders emerged from among the *bushi*, the most important of whom were the Taira and Minamoto families, the former based in the western part of Japan, the latter in the eastern. As frequently happens in such situations, those called upon to save the *ancien régime* end up by pushing out the old rulers and establishing themselves in power. The initial conflicts which called the *bushi* into existence were soon turned into a struggle among the *bushi* themselves as the Taira and Minamoto fought each other to achieve supremacy. By 1185, with the destruction of the Taira house, the Minamoto had won.

Professor John W. Hall has remarked that the triumph of the Minamoto, in the person of Minamoto Yoritomo, marked one of the two occasions in Japanese history when it might have been possible to overthrow the existing polity and create an entirely new one (the other was Oda Nobunaga's triumph in the sixteenth century).[73] However, a recurrent theme in Japanese history, both at the national and at the local levels, is the quest for legitimacy. Thus, while the new regime established by Yoritomo made a symbolic break with the past by establishing its capital in the eastern part of Honshu, at

Kamakura, it did not eliminate the imperial institution nor purloin the imperial title for itself. Instead Yoritomo chose to clothe himself in the mantle of legitimacy provided by the emperor's grant of the title 'shogun' in 1192.[74] This ushered in a period of renewed central government known as the Kamakura bakufu (literally 'tent government') or shogunate. Bakufu rule, albeit with subsequent transformations and even a brief intermission at the end of the sixteenth and beginning of the seventeenth centuries, became the hallmark of Japanese government until the restoration of imperial rule in 1868. Professor Hall has further remarked that: 'There are obviously certain features of the process of élite competition in Japan that made it most difficult for any group to acquire the superior force necessary to establish a totally new polity.' This suggests that change was built on a foundation of continuity, although as with all such transitions the precise mix between continuity and innovation is open to debate.[75]

The Kamakura shogunate (1192–1333) attempted to consolidate its rule by securing the allegiance of existing landholders while interspersing its own vassals as jitō (land stewards), who acted as intermediary officials between the regime and private landowners, and shugo (constable or military governor). The latter in particular developed into a new landed class in its own right and came to view its own interests as more important than those of the central authority. The Kamakura structure of government proved incapable of accommodating the demands of the new élite with those of the old, and the regime collapsed in the 1330s during an attempt by the imperial court to reasert its right to rule following a dispute within the court between rival claimants to the throne which the shogunate failed to settle.

During this dispute one of the shogunate's principal vassal families, the Ashikaga, originally sent to destroy the imperial revolt, turned against the shogunate, ensconced a new emperor on the throne in 1338 and established its leader Ashikaga Takauji as the new shogun with his headquarters in the Muromachi area of Kyoto. As with its predecessors, the concern for legitimation and continuity shaped the style and institutions of the second era of bakufu rule, the Muromachi age which was to last until 1573.

The imperial succession struggle was resolved in 1392. Meanwhile, the Ashikaga had been able to extend their rule throughout most of the country, although not quite securely on the periphery, especially in the west, in Kyushu. Although they were not themselves major territorial landholders, unlike the Tokugawa who established the third period of shogunal government from 1603–1867, the Ashikaga sought to consolidate their power by relying on vassals (shugo, family and kinsmen and a shogunal military guard) and by implementing policies that gave the *shugo* remaining from previous regimes increased powers over their own holdings. These were not concentrated in one territorial unit but were scattered over different areas. The Ashikaga, however, were unable to thrust themselves forward successfully, although under the shogun Yoshimitsu efforts were made to establish an independent economic base by developing foreign trade and exploiting the commercial expansion of the Kinai area (the provinces around the capital, Kyoto), and to devise a system of government and bureaucracy capable of dominating the coalition of élites which had to be accommodated within any power structure. Again, in Professor Hall's words: 'It was as much the effort of the shogun to dominate this balance of power as it was the growth of independent *shugo* ambitions that destroyed the Muromachi political system.'[76] In the absence of adequately developed institutions to provide a balanced tension between competing interests, the conflict between central and local power (a conflict not without its parallels with Europe's transition from medieval to modern) remained unresolved.

It was this conflict which tore the regime apart after the outbreak of the Ōnin war in 1467.[77] The war or rebellion was as much a revolt *within* the provinces as it was a revolt of the provinces *against* the centre.[78] The shogun came under attack from those below especially the samurai, many of whom were ambitious to enhance their powers and extend their landholdings, some of which had been granted by the shogunate itself in a rather reckless effort to check possible *shugo* ambitions. Over the next 100 years, the *sengoku jidai*, the shogunate ceased to function as an independent agent. Much as the imperial institution had been used by previous competitors for power to screen their own ambitions, the shogunate became an important symbol of legitimacy and national unity. Together with the offices which its authority sanctioned, especially that of *shugo*, it was the supreme political prize which the most ambitious warriors coveted.[79]

The *sengoku* period, especially in its later stages, is usually characterised as one of *gekokujō* (those above toppling those below). But it was not a dark age of unbridled anarchy; the arts (*bun*) and the sword (*bu*) flourished together. Besides being a manifestation of centre/local conflict, the *sengoku* age was also driven by its own social, economic and cultural logic which generated enough momentum to reshape fundamentally the Japanese polity and society. The destruction of Kyoto during the ten years of the Ōnin War and the period of protracted warfare that ensued, far from destroying or even inhibiting cultural life, led to a diffusion of what was to become a very distinctive Muromachi culture to the provinces.[80] In contrast with the Heian period, when culture had been the preserve of the

court, the Muromachi age witnessed the emergence of rich, but
more widely diffused, forms of culture which helped fill the vacuum
created by the disintegration of central authority and contributed to
the preservation and enhancement of a sense of national identity.
Such national self-awareness had existed from an early stage in
Japan's evolution and during the Muromachi period it gained greater
currency, although how far and how deeply within the general
population is unclear.

In religious matters too there were considerable changes. Zen
Buddhism provided the samurai with a religion that emphasised
self-discipline and action as a source of merit. Among the masses
more popular forms of Buddhist religion became influential. It was
an age of religious diversity. The monasteries, which had always
been important landholders, and therefore members of the political
nation, also participated in the battles raging throughout the country. Militant religious organisations joined the ranks of the competitors for power, a development which was to have important
repercussions for Roman Catholic missionary activity in the
sixteenth century.

In its efforts to consolidate power, the Ashikaga shogunate tried to
manipulate various symbols and institutions inherited from previous regimes. It was compelled to do so because it lacked a strong
territorial base of its own from which it could secure a sizeable
independent income. It also tried to take advantage of new sources of
power and patronage created by economic changes in medieval
Japan. One of the most important of these was trade, especially trade
with China. Trade was both a source of tax revenue and a vehicle for
profitable investment.[81]

Contact between China and the various minor Japanese states located
in the south and west of the main islands of the archipelago had
existed from the later Han period, and the first Japanese embassy to
the Chinese imperial court is recorded in AD 57. Embassies between
the middle kingdom and its island neighbour took place fairly
regularly. The Japanese were greatly interested in acquiring knowledge from China, especially about religion and philosophy, and they
did this with an intensity that would be repeated in the late
nineteenth century when modernisation and industrialisation were
pursued this time with the Western model as guide. Originally, the
relations were tributary in character, the Japanese receiving tokens of
investiture from the Chinese. However, from the fourth and fifth
centuries the Japanese became uncomfortable with such a status and
began to assert their independence while at the same time using
Chinese tributary concepts to define their own relations with
neighbours much closer – Korea and the petty states on the periphery

of the main island. The adoption of the title 'emperor' for the Japanese sovereign, a deviation from Chinese nomenclature and a challenge to Chinese assumptions of superiority, is one indication of this. The manner in which embassies from the Korean peninsula were received until the late eighth century is another.[82]

Japanese embassies to the Sung and T'ang capitals became confident enough, even if Japanese navigational skills were little more than rudimentary, to sail directly from Japan from the early eighth century to various destinations along the Chinese coastal province of Kiangsu, including the mouth of the Yangtse which provided good access via the grand canals to the Chinese court.[83] By the middle of the ninth century trade between China and Japan had also mushroomed with the ports on the Fukien and Chekiang coasts serving as terminal points. As has been mentioned, these ports were already frequented by Arab and Persian traders, hence the possibility that these west Asians met with Japanese. The Japanese were mainly interested in religious artefacts, for example, Buddhist texts, images, incense, and luxury goods like herbs, perfumes, fabrics, damask, brocade and silk, but items such as musical instruments, furniture and ornaments originating from central Asia also found their way to Japan. Although some of the ships which crossed the East China Sea were Japanese, most of the trade was conducted in Chinese and Korean vessels, often with Japanese merchants on board. The Chinese sailed from the Chekiang and Fukien ports, the Koreans from the Hua river via the western and southern coasts of Korea, making for Kyushu and the port of Hakata where the trade was centred and regulated.[84]

By the early tenth century, the Japanese government had restricted trading contacts with continental Asia, mainly in order to curb conspicuous consumption among the nobility. In 894, Japan, worried by Korean pirate attacks in waters and islands off the Kyushu coast, and aware of the troubles in China that were contributing to the disintegration of the T'ang court, terminated embassies to China. Early in the next century, Japanese traders were forbidden to voyage overseas, although Buddhist priests continued to sail for China. Trade gradually passed into Chinese hands after the fall of the Korean Silla dynasty, an event which gave rise to the outburst of Korean piracy. However, its own stricture notwithstanding, the Japanese government found it impossible to regulate trade and eradicate private commerce.[85]

The expansion of trade, especially by non-government traders under the Sung dynasty, had repercussions for Japan. Chinese merchants from Ch'üan-chou and other Fukienese ports traded with Japan as well as the Korean kingdom of Koreyo, bringing silk, porcelain, sandal wood, ambergris, copper, cash and other goods sought by the *shōen* estate holders of Heian Japan.[86] Many of the *shōen* bypassed the official government supervision of foreign trade by encouraging the smuggling of goods into their domains. One result of this was that ports in the west of Japan, including the island of Hirado, lying just off the northwest coast of Kyushu where the Dutch and English established themselves in the early seventeenth century, became important centres for contraband. By the end of the eleventh century Sung merchants were settled in Hirado and at Hakata.[87]

From the latter part of the eleventh century relations between Japan and Korea improved. Japanese merchants on Japanese vessels and representing *shōen* lords made the relatively easy passage from western Japan to Korea. However, when the Koreyo dynasty itself began to flounder, the Japanese made straight for China where the first recorded arrival of a Japanese vessel specifically for trade is 1175, although, as has been mentioned, Japanese merchants had travelled there on Chinese vessels before then. Direct Japanese trade with China was greatly stimulated by Taira Kiyomori who dominated the government from the late 1150s before the establishment of the Kamakura bakufu in 1192. Kiyomori permitted foreign ships to trade beyond northern Kyushu into the Inland Sea up to the coastal area near the capital. The principal Japanese import from China was copper coins, which were used as currency in Japan, and the principal exports from Japan were gold and wood. In 1226 Chinese coins were accepted as legal tender in Japan, reflecting the beginnings of a monetary economy.[88]

Japan had not escaped the attention of the Mongol rulers of China who were determined to force tributary states to submit to their rule. Korea was forced into submission in 1258 and the Mongols, exploiting advances in Chinese naval technology achieved by the Sung, attempted to invade Japan on two occasions (mentioned by Marco Polo) in 1274 and 1281. Both attempts came to grief as a result of fortuitous storms which the Japanese regarded as evidence of divine intervention, and these *kamikaze* or divine winds came to occupy a place in Japanese mythology more enduring than the so-called Protestant wind of 1688 which was supposed to have prevented James II's fleet from leaving port to attack William of Orange. The Mongol Yüan dynasty was not discouraged by these and other setbacks in southeast Asia, including an abortive invasion of Java in 1293, and continued to plan for an invasion of Japan until the end of the thirteenth century.[89]

After the establishment of the Ashikaga shogunate, trade with China was re-established on a small scale and conducted with official permission by the Tenryū temple in Kyoto which the first Ashikaga shogun had built to mollify the spirit of his rival, the emperor

Go-Daigo. The temple was no stranger to commerce and became an important location for usury and sake breweries, businesses which had accumulated enough capital to diversify their activities into money lending.[90] The Tenryū trade (in which other monasteries were allowed to participate) conducted by the *Tenryūji bune*, Tenryūji ship, lasted until the fall of the Yüan dynasty in 1368, but its volume was slight. After the Ming were securely settled on the Dragon throne, Sino-Japanese relations were ripe for expansion, although initial efforts in this direction were soured by squabbling.

The early Ming emperors were as concerned as their predecessors to establish their position as the focus of loyalty of the tributary states in China's world order. However, they developed a more sophisticated conceptual framework on which to set out their demands for submission to that order. The Sung had depended on moral 'virtue' (*te*) to provide the compelling reason for tributary states to submit. The Mongols had relied on excessive brute force, or material 'power' (*wei*). The Ming considered it more prudent to emphasise and reassert *te* to impress upon their tributary vassals the innately superior qualities of the institutions and governance of the middle kingdom. *Wei*, the steely counterpart, was kept in abeyance, to be employed if circumstances demanded, as the voyages of the eunuch Cheng Ho under the Yung-lo emperor demonstrated. Japan and other tributaries were to be brought back within the fold or encouraged to join it, enticed by the prospects of peace, tranquility and prosperity that would inevitably flow to them upon paying tribute at the resplendent court of the Ming emperors.[91]

In addition to these lofty calculations intended to establish a Chinese hegemony in east Asian international relations, the Ming were concerned in their early dealings with the Japanese to have the Japanese authorities stamp out piracy in the waters of the East China Sea. Piracy, which was nothing new in these waters and was to continue to infest them over the centuries, is a somewhat misleading term with which to label the activities of those seafarers who operated beyond the laws of the respective polities of northeast Asia. The energies of these men were directed more at Korea than at China and were not confined solely to acts of pillage. Often they represented the pursuit of trade by other means. Misleading too is the original word which was used to describe them, *wo-k'ou* (in Chinese, *wakō* in Japanese), for the pirates were not exclusively Japanese, although in the fourteenth-century phase of wakō activity most of the participants were Japanese. Koreans had pillaged parts of Kyushu in the ninth century and Koreans were involved in the wakō attacks of the fourteenth and fifteenth centuries, while many of the fourteenth century wakō groups included numbers of Chinese. Piracy flourished in conditions of political instability when the central authorities in Japan and Korea were either weak or notional. In the case of China it became endemic because Peking neglected the economic interests of the provinces on the southeastern seaboard, refusing to create conditions that would give them officially sanctioned access to the overseas markets that so neatly complemented their economies.[92]

Relations between China and Japan were further complicated by the fact that until 1392, when the Ashikaga shogun Yoshimitsu finally succeeded in wearing down adherents of the 'southern court' (the supporters of the emperor Go-Daigo who attempted to reassert imperial rule after 1331), Japan lacked a unified central authority. While the country was divided into the southern and northern courts, the early Ming missions to Japan dealt with both. The result was unsatisfactory. The Japanese for their part retained suspicions about Chinese motives after the Mongol invasions. This together with Chinese impatience over Japanese indifference to overtures from the middle kingdom made for an uneasy relationship.[93]

Relations were transformed by the shogun Yoshimitsu. In 1403, two years after he had made proposals to the Ming court about re-opening relations, Yoshimitsu dispatched a mission to China with a letter for the emperor which he concluded, 'Your subject, the King of Japan, submits'.[94] In 1404 an agreement between the two countries was reached which permitted 'official trade' under the guise of tribute missions to the Chinese court. The agreement, in accordance with those governing relations with other tributary states, detailed exactly how many missions would be permitted and how many members could accompany it, the protocols to be followed, and specified Ningpo as the port of entry. To ensure that the trade was conducted officially and not by 'pirates', tallies to check on the authenticity of the missions were introduced. (These were applied to other states as well but failed to discourage sham missions, anxious to use fraudulent diplomacy as a cover for profitable trade.) Over the next 150 years until 1547 when the last ships were sent to Japan, seventeen trips involving eighty-four ships were made. In return the Japanese received eight missions from China, seven between 1433 and 1499 and one in 1434.[95] During the six years following the signing of the agreement, Japanese missions to China were frequent, ignoring the stipulation that they should occur only once every ten years. The Chinese, convinced that yet another tributary state had been won back, were satisfied with Yoshimitsu's submission. An imperial rescript of 1406 declared: 'Our heart rejoices that in the lands east of the sea, since antiquity there has never been a ruler so wise and accomplished as you, and thus we deeply praise and laud you.'[96]

Intriguing as it may be, the question of whether Yoshimitsu's decision to style himself 'King of Japan' (a new departure in Sino-Japanese relations) and his conformity with Chinese diplomatic practice by using Ming year names rather than Japanese ones, compromised Japanese sovereignty, overemphasises the niceties of diplomatic protocol and obscures other, perhaps more significant, aspects determining the choice of nomenclature. Foreign trade was one of the strong cards Yoshimitsu could play to secure his regime and generate an independent income for the shogunate. Trade provided a certain degree of shogunal patronage enabling the bakufu to decide who would participate and benefit from the immense profits that could be realised, although the shogunate's freedom to manoeuvre was to be constrained by the very nature of the Japanese polity, especially the persisting tensions between central and local interests. Moreover, Yoshimitsu's use of the title 'King of Japan' established a shogunal authority independent of the emperor, competent to deal with foreign powers and to dispatch and receive missions, a precedent whose significance was not to be lost on the rulers Oda Nobunaga, Toyotomi Hideyoshi and Tokugawa Ieyasu who pulled the country together during the second half of the sixteenth century, ending the divisions and instability of the *sengoku* period.[97]

After Yoshimitsu's death, relations between the two countries were interrupted. Once again Japan preferred to distance itself from its neighbour. The reasons for the break included Japanese reluctance to be integrated into the Chinese tributary system. Relations were not resumed until 1432 when both sides appreciated that the advantages to be gained from a restoration of relations far outweighed protracted arguments over principles, no matter how deeply these were held. The Chinese hoped that the Japanese would help curtail continuing wakō activity, and the Japanese were attracted by the profitability of the trade that was encompassed by the missions. The shogun Yoshinori accepted the title of 'King of Japan' and the Chinese permitted an increase in the number of merchants included in a single mission.[98]

By this time any political bonus accruing to the bakufu from its role in the China trade had run its course. The bigger temples and some of the more powerful *shugo* daimyo had edged their way into the trade. They co-sponsored ships and shared the profits. More enduringly, the China trade stimulated the growth of a monetary market-economy in Japan. The import of currency helped to increase the number of transactions between the capital, where both the shogun and the *shugo* daimyo had their residences, and the provinces, by encouraging greater demand for goods and services.[99] Chinese coins were widely used in Japan in the absence of a unified Japanese currency to meet the extensive monetary transactions that the greatly expanding Japanese medieval economy demanded. The importance of coin imports declined rapidly during the sixteenth century as Japan, which had fairly extensive gold, silver and copper deposits of its own, was able to harness new technology to exploit its own resources and itself became a major exporter of these commodities, bringing the country into the broader international economy of the sixteenth and seventeenth centuries.[100]

For those more interested in commerce than in the politics of international trade, the most attractive aspect of the missions to China was the supplementary trade the Japanese participants could undertake. The Japanese missions divided their goods into three types: tribute for the Ming court, supplementary articles for sale to Chinese officials, and supplementary goods that could be sold on the open market. In addition, individual members also carried goods for private sale. The tributary articles remained much the same until 1549: horses, fans, screens, suits of armour, ink slabs and cases, sulphur, agate, swords and lances. The main goods in the supplementary category were swords (for example 7,000 in 1478, 37,000 in 1483) in which the Japanese had attained an outstanding level of craftsmenship, sulphur, copper (the 1453 mission carried 150,000 catties of copper and 364,000 catties of sulphur), Japanese craft goods such as fans, lacquer-ware, screens and inkstones, and sappan wood (a high point of 105,000 catties was sent in 1453). The sappan wood came from southeast Asia. In China it was used as a dye and for medicinal purposes. It was brought to Japan via the Ryūkyū kingdom in Ryūkyūan ships which called at the Japanese ports of Hyōgo and Sakai, located near Kyoto. Sakai in particular benefited greatly from the China trade and for a time after the outbreak of the Ōnin war the city's merchants sent their own ships to Ryūkyū, a trade the shogunate attempted to curb.[101] The principal Japanese imports from China were silk, some of which was also brought from southeast Asia on Ryūkyūan ships, porcelain and Chinese coins. Silk could be bought cheaply in China, as the Europeans had discovered in the thirteenth century, and resold for a high profit in Japan where it was very much in demand.[102]

Japanese trade with Korea also flourished during the middle ages. As the Ashikaga bakufu extended its control into the west and into Kyushu, it became easier to suppress wakō activity in Korean waters. This led to a transformation of relations between Japan and Korea. During the fourteenth century the wakō had taken advantage of the acute instability of the Koryŏ dynasty and plundered the Korean coastline, contributing to the fall of the dynasty. More stable relations between the two countries were also fostered by the emergence of a strong new dynasty in Korea in 1392, the Yi, which for its part sought to suppress the wakō by diplomatic means and by strengthening coastal defences.[103]

Once the wakō had been brought to heel a vigorous trade between the two neighbours developed. Of the western daimyo involved in this trade, the Sō domain on Tsushima, the island between Japan and Korea, was especially important. Geography favoured the Sō and enabled them to survive an attempted Korean invasion in 1419 to wipe out the wakō, then using the island as a base for attacks on Korea, and the *sengoku* wars. Tsushima's pivotal role in Japan's trade with Korea was strengthened by a treaty in 1443 initiated by the Korean king, Sejong (1418–50), similar to that governing Japan's trade with China. The arrangement specified the size of ships, number of participants, number of trips and diplomatic protocols, and was regulated by the Sō. Japanese were allowed to continue to reside in the ports of Pusan, Naep'o and Yompo' which had been opened to them in 1426. The number of Japanese living in these ports peaked at 3,105 in 1494. Trade between Japan and Korea boosted the commercial importance of northern Kyushu, in particular the port of Hakata. The Japanese were mainly interested in importing Korean textiles, especially cotton (used as a medium of exchange under the Yi), and to a lesser extent hemp and silk pongee, and Buddhist artefacts and texts; Japanese exports to Korea were similar to those to China, except that swords did not figure as much, and they included goods brought from southeast Asia via Ryūkyū and re-exported to Korea. (There was also a direct trade between Ryūkyū and Korea.) Once the Japanese had developed their own strength in cotton production to satisfy domestic demand, trade with Korea declined and increasingly fell under the monopoly of the Sō.[104]

Thus when the Portuguese arrived in Japan in the early 1540s the country was already well-incorporated into the trading world of east Asia and indirectly through Ryūkyū with that of southeast Asia, a world which the Portuguese themselves had first encountered after they reached Malacca.

(iv)   The Portuguese in Japan

The arrival of Portuguese merchants in Japan and that of Jesuit missionaries hard on their heels, together with the publication of Jesuit accounts from Japan in Europe which, amongst other things, stressed the possibilities for successful missionary work, has given rise to the convenient but inaccurate label for the century between the 1540s and 1640s as Japan's 'Christian Century'.

In reality Christianity touched Japan but superficially during these years. Japan was considered the most promising find in the Indies for new souls, but regardless of their expectations and the diligence and courage displayed by individual missionaries and some of their converts, the missionaries reaped a disappointing harvest. At the height of their proselytising efforts the fathers managed to win over about 300,000 souls, about the same rate of success as in India.[105] Christianity remained marginal rather than central to the transformation of the Japanese polity from *sengoku* competition to the early modern arrangement in which the centripetal tendencies of Japanese feudalism were exploited by Oda Nobunaga, Toyotomi Hideyoshi and Tokugawa Ieyasu to recreate a central authority.[106] Moreover, in the sixteenth and seventeenth centuries, the Japanese were not confronted with a rational, scientific West. The Europeans had been successful in harnessing advances in naval and military technology to overseas expansion (especially the solid, full-rigged ship and the ability to fire a cannon from the deck of a ship without compromising the stability of the ship or its function as a cargo vessel, a feat which Asian ship-design and construction failed to match, thereby giving the Europeans maritime superiority in Asian waters).[107] However, as Professor Jacques Gernet has observed of China, on some points 'the missionaries' psychology was at one with that of the milieux they were seeking to convert. They, too, believed in the reality of demonic possession and in the powers of sprinkling with holy water.' In seventeenth-century Europe, magic and science 'advanced side by side'.[108] So long as the Jesuits, who remained the largest Roman Catholic order in Japan, held a monopoly of information about Europe, the Japanese were presented with a one-sided picture of contemporary European politics and society.

The Jesuits were constantly at pains to screen out any aspect of the Western intellectual tradition, such as the contribution of the pagan ancients or the contemporary reality of Protestantism, which did not fit in with the image of a unified Catholic Christendom they wished the Japanese to accept.[109] In pursuit of this end they enjoyed a limited success and even before the Protestant northern European maritime powers established themselves in Japan, the Japanese were confronted with a Catholic church which was far from united about the best way to further its missionary objectives in Japan. In 1593 the Franciscan mendicants arrived in Japan, much to the consternation of the Jesuits who had lobbied hard in Europe for Japan to remain their exclusive province. The Jesuits were anxious to avoid giving the Japanese the appearance of a divided Church quibbling over interpretations of canon law and to prevent the dissipation of energies in petty controversies about the most effective policy to spread the gospel. Such divisions, they feared, would debase the image of Christianity and destroy the appearance and possible appeal of a united Christian church which contrasted with a deeply divided

Buddhism.[110] The Franciscans, for their part, had great expectations about their chances of success in Japan and wrote enthusiastically that the conversion of Japan would make up for what the Church had lost in France, Germany, Flanders and England.[111] Nevertheless, Japan's first brush with Christianity provides a fascinating study in cross-cultural contact and the misunderstandings that followed.

If the notion of a Christian century in Japan is more apparent than real, in terms of foreign trade Japan's first contact with the West was rather more central to developments within the country, although even here it is necessary to maintain a sense of balance and not exaggerate unduly the Western role.

After the outbreak of the Ōnin war and the collapse of central authority during the *sengoku* period, Japanese overseas trade with China and Korea and involvement in the trade between east and southeast Asia via the Ryūkyū kingdom continued. But it underwent considerable modification. Economic imperatives on both sides of the East China Sea ensured that trade could not remain an appendage to official relations, especially when these relations were jeopardised by other factors. Official relations fell into abeyance as bakufu power was neutralised in the sixteenth century and the Hosokawa (whose domain included Sakai) and the Ōuchi (at the western end of Honshu) families struggled against each other to control missions and trade to China. The Ōuchi emerged as the winners, gaining control of the inland sea and sent the last two 'official' missions to China in 1538 and 1547. This was only a pyrrhic victory, for the Ōuchi themselves were finally toppled by the Mori in 1558. For their part the Chinese had their own misgivings about the more mundane aspects of the tributary system, the drain on imperial coffers issuing from the need to give gifts to tributary missions and the costs of providing transport and hospitality to them during their stay in China. From the second half of the fifteenth century the Chinese attempted, without success, to restrict the number of delegates allowed to proceed to Peking and the amount of supplementary trade that could be conducted.[112] While Peking tolerated and encouraged trade within the context of tributary missions, official disdain for commerce remained deeply ingrained in Ming political culture. There was no recognition of the benefit of overseas trade to the Chinese economy, other than as a source of luxury goods for the imperial court, and no appreciation of its role in the economy of the southern provinces.[113] Under such circumstances overseas trade, which in China, and increasingly in Japan, was no longer a phenomenon that could be turned on or off according to government fiat, sought new outlets. Smuggling was one such vent.

Smuggling had already emerged by 1457–65, around the same

time as official relations declined, and it had picked up briskly by the
1520s by which time it was transformed into a new phase of wakō
activity.[114] However, unlike earlier phases of this phenomenon, in
the sixteenth century activity, which reached its high point during
the middle decades of the century especially from 1553–5, Japanese
played a secondary role despite the fact that official Ming documents
referred to the marauders on the Fukien and Chekiang coasts as
wo-k'ou. The ringleaders were Chinese, some operating from bases
in Japan, including Hirado, exploiting coastal disaffection with various aspects of government policy among the gentry families, local
officials and the common people but in particular resentment against
government restrictions on trade. Some of the merchants and gentry
ran up debts with the smugglers and could not discharge them and
defaulted. To try to get themselves off the hook, they appealed to the
local authorities to enforce prohibitions against foreign trade. The
smugglers countered by applying pressure and resorted to violence
to salvage what they could of their investment and to protect
themselves. Dissident elements were attracted to the fray which
spread over a long coastal stretch north and south of the Yangtze
delta, a highly populated area easily accessible from the sea with a
thriving agricultural and manufacturing base.[115]

In Japan foreign trade was greatly stimulated by an increase in the
country's silver output, made possible by improvements in mining
and smelting technology, especially a new cupellation method (haifu-
ki) learned from Korea which enabled silver to be extracted from ore.
Silver production increased dramatically during the sixteenth century reaching its peak during the early seventeenth century. Silver
acquired its prominence in east Asian trade because the ratio of gold
to silver in China was lower than in Japan. In China it varied from
1:6 to 1:7.50 in 1596 and 1:8 in 1620. In Japan the ratio fluctuated
between 1:7.37 in 1571 to 1:10.99 in 1604 and 1:14 in 1622. By the
late 1620s, however, the ratios in the two countries were almost
even. While this differential existed it was highly profitable to export
the plentiful supply of Japanese silver to China where demand was
great (taxes were collected in silver and silver production was in
decline) in return for Chinese gold. In spite of fairly rich deposits in
Japan, gold was much sought after, especially in the later sixteenth
century when money was required to finance the military campaigns
of the three rulers, including Hideyoshi's invasions of Korea in the
1590s, and to help pay for an ambitious programme of castle
building and urban development in which many structures were
decoratively embellished with gold. Such ostentation was designed
to impress visitors with a sense of power and authority. Gold was
also used in the minting of coins to cater for the increasing monetisation of the economy.[116]

Bullion was by no means the only commodity involved in this exchange. Chinese silk, especially raw silk ('Nanking' silk to the Europeans) which was later woven in Japan, silk wadding used for winter clothing, and silk and cotton mixtures were also much in demand together with cotton cloth, crimson thread used for theatrical costumes, and a variety of other manufactured wares, including iron products and porcelain, art works and medicines. A measure of the increased demand for silk can be had from the comments of the Jesuit João Rodrigues who lived in Japan from 1577–1610, and perhaps the ablest of the early European writers on the country. Rodrigues noted that until the mid-sixteenth century the use of silk was rare and ordinary people never wore it, only the daimyo occasionally. 'But since the time of *Taikō* [Hideyoshi] there has been a general peace throughout the kingdom and trade has so increased that the whole nation wears silk robes; even peasants and their wives have silk sashes, and the better off among them have silken robes.'[117] The profits from silk sales in Japan were high. But it was Japan's capacity to export its natural resources of gold, silver and copper, and its strong internal demand for raw and wrought silks that was to lie at the heart of the country's foreign trade until the early eighteenth century. The rewards for participants in this trade, including the carriers, were high, but at no time in its eventful history did any one group or nation monopolise it.

The Portuguese entrepreneurs who traded on the China coast from the 1520s adapted well to the fluid situation they found. Often they sailed on Chinese junks, which were manned by international crews, and some were involved in wakō activity. During their early years in Japan they followed the example of major Chinese smugglers such as Wang Chih, known as Goho Ochoku in Japanese, who had established his headquarters at Hirado around 1542 and who had made a considerable fortune from overseas trade between China, Japan and Siam. He used Japan as a base for smuggling to China. The Portuguese traded at Amoy (close to the ports of Ch'üan-chou and Chang-chou) and at other places along the Fukien and Chekiang coasts, bringing pepper, armaments, sulphur, furs and silver in return for silk, rice, cloth and saltpetre, although by the end of the 1540s they were forced back towards the Pearl River estuary. There are only the briefest glimpses of this profitable, irregular, speculative and, from the Chinese government's point of view, illegal trade.[118] It is not surprising that detailed records of this individual activity do not exist.[119]

By 1550 the Portuguese Viceroy at Goa had made the Japan trade a royal monopoly and the free-for-all came to a halt. From then the Japan trade was exclusively held by the *Capitão-mór de Viagem da China e Japão* or Captain Major of the Voyage of China and Japan,

known simply as the Japan voyage. The position of captain major
was awarded at the discretion of the Portuguese crown or its
representative in Goa to a distinguished or worthy *fidalgo* and carried
both prestige and profit. But in its last years it was sold off to the
highest bidder. At times, it was also milked as a source of revenue
to pay for defence.[120] The institutionalisation of the Japan trade was
further abetted by the founding of Macao. The Portuguese were
no longer classified as smugglers but instead became officially recognised traders. They were willing to help the local Chinese authorities
suppress smuggling and piracy. Gradually the Chinese became more
inclined to see the benefits of relaxing trade restrictions as a way to
wipe out these evils, but this relaxation was not applied to Japan with
whom official relations were cut in 1548. This new situation proved
highly advantageous to the Portuguese.[121]

Over the following years Macao, where until 1623 the captain
major of the Japan voyage acted as interim governor during his stay,
flourished as the starting point of the Portuguese voyages to Japan
which lasted until 1639 when the Lusitanians were expelled and
prohibited from trading with Japan. The Portuguese *não do trato*
(great ship of commerce), which averaged about 1,200–1,600 tons
by the end of the century (they were replaced by smaller more easily
manoeuvrable galliots in 1618 to avoid attacks from the Dutch)[122]
were made welcome by daimyo in Kyushu who sought to attract the
ships to their own ports, because of the additional revenue they
created. In Hirado, where at least fifteen ships called between 1550
and 1569, their presence attracted merchants from Sakai and Kyoto,
no doubt in much the same way as the vessels of Wang Chih, who
brought the Portuguese to Hirado, had done before.[123] From 1571
the newly established city of Nagasaki became the Japanese terminus
of the *não*, although on occasion the ships called at other Kyushu
ports. In 1580 Nagasaki together with the smaller port of Mogi was
formally ceded to the Society of Jesus by Ōmura Sumitada (Don
Bartolomeu) a Christian convert. This was neither an act of piety
nor of submission on Ōmura's part. The cession appealed to the
self-interest of all concerned. For the Portuguese merchants it made
commercial sense to establish a regular safe haven where business
could be transacted and where more enduring relationships with
their Japanese counterparts could be cultivated in order to sell goods
and procure cargoes for the return voyage to Macao.

The Jesuits, in particular the formidable visitor, Alessandro
Valignano, would have preferred the ships to continue rotating their
ports of call in Japan in order to use commerce as bait to hook new
converts among the daimyo. (Valignano believed Japan to be the
most important missionary ground in the Indies, especially because
the Japanese were willing to convert 'of their own free will'.) But
such arguments were far outweighed by the Jesuit need for a base,

secure from the shifting alliances and fortunes of the *sengoku* warfare, where displaced Japanese converts suffering persecution in lands belonging to daimyo opposed to Christianity could seek refuge. Moreover, desperate for money to finance the running of their mission (by 1582 the mission employed some five hundred personnel and had a number of residences to support), the Jesuits recognised that a regular port for the náo would work to their advantage because of their role in the Macao trade as middlemen between the Portuguese and Japanese (their linguistic skills and contacts were valuable) and they imported silk themselves. Valignano did not mince words in his explanation to Rome in June 1580 about the cession of Nagasaki and what it would mean to the finances of the mission: 'If we lose this finance, we have no way of maintaining ourselves in Japan' – a theme that recurs constantly in his writings. The ceding of Nagasaki satisfied immediate and strategic needs of the Ōmura as well. It provided the daimyo with a regular income from the dues paid by the náo (Valignano estimated them at between 700 and 1,000 ducats for a stay of six months) and from the customs dues paid by the Japanese merchants for using the port, which brought in an additional 3,000 ducats. In Valignano's opinion this was a considerable sum for a daimyo of his rank. Moreover, it considerably strengthened Ōmura's hand in his local *sengoku* struggles against Ryūzōji Takanobu, the ambitious but stronger daimyo of neighbouring Saga, who could not lay claim to the port and its revenues if it was in the hands of the Jesuits. Nagasaki could also be used as an asylum if other Ōmura territory were attacked. The town was, therefore, a valuable asset.[124]

The ceding of Nagasaki did not involve a permanent grant of Japanese territory. Nor was it a precursor of the nineteenth-century treaty ports. Valignano insisted on the grant being revocable; if the náo trade declined or was reorganised in such a way that Nagasaki became superfluous then the grant would lose its *raison d'être*.[125] More controversial is the view that the Jesuit visitor viewed the cession as laying the foundation for a 'military colony'.[126] A start was made on building fortifications but whether, as Valignano later argued, these were intended for defensive purposes only, or whether, as Professor Elison implies, they symbolised a more provocative agenda to forward missionary goals remains unclear.[127] In 1588 after his successful campaign in Kyushu, the final in his efforts to unite the country, Hideyoshi annulled the grant (and the later one of neighbouring Urakami) and vested the Ōmura and another Christian daimyo, Arima Harunobu, with power to administer Nagasaki as possessions on his behalf. This arrangement lasted until 1592 when Hideyoshi established the office of Nagasaki *daikan* (deputy) who acted as governor.[128]

For the Jesuits, missionary activity and the náo trade were

inseparable. But this was not the case for the merchants who came on
the ships nor for the citizens of Macao who invested in the silk trade.
Regardless of professions to the contrary, the propagation of the
faith was never allowed to compromise the pursuit of profit. This
was demonstrated in 1619 when the fourth bishop-designate of Japan
was stopped from proceeding to his see by the Macao government in
case his arrival resulted in trade reprisals by the Japanese government
which in 1614 had issued a decree proscribing Christianity and
expelling all missionaries.[129] Nor was the spread of Christianity of
interest or relevance to the Chinese merchants who invested in the
trade, nor for the many Japanese who expected the Jesuits to act on
their behalf in arranging for the sale of silver in Macao.[130] However,
the linguistic skills of its members made the Society valuable to the
Portuguese merchants. According to an agreement of 1578 with the
city of Macao, the Jesuits were permitted to send fifty peculs of silk
for their own account to Japan and occasionally, if the market was
depressed and the Portuguese could not sell all their silk, an additional forty peculs at cost was allowed.[131] Acute financial problems
meant that individual fathers carried on an illicit trade of their own
despite Valignano's prohibition. In 1613, a year after a further
instruction against illicit trade has been issued, some fathers were
said 'to be immersed in moneymaking leaving hardly any time for
other much more important works.'[132] However, after the promulgation of the 1614 edict, which forced the fathers underground,
Jesuit private trade declined. The Jesuits may have been valuable but
they were not indispensable to the Japan voyage.

Jesuit involvement in trade, and the controversy that this aroused,
was not limited to Japan. Such involvement existed in other parts of
Asia as well as in Spanish and Portuguese possessions in America and
Africa.[133] Despite their attacks on the Jesuits, the Franciscans experienced similar difficulties in financing their mission. They soon
discovered that daimyo made them welcome because they believed
that merchants would come after the missionaries rather than the
reverse.[134] The same was to be true of the Dominicans who followed
the Jesuits, Franciscans and Augustinians in the early seventeenth
century. Dominican attempts to proselytise in the Satsuma domain,
which had long been involved in foreign trade with the Ryūkyū
kingdom, came to an abrupt end in 1609 when they were expelled
from the Kyushu domain because their presence had not been
followed by the coming of a náo. Their protests that they had no
influence over the sailing orders of ships from Manila were brushed
aside.[135]

During the 1570s Portuguese trade with Japan was further regulated to ensure that no middle ranking merchants shared in the
profits. The *Armação*, or corporate agreement drawn up with the

help of the Bishop of Macao, detailed exactly how the trade in silk, which made up the bulk of the cargo to Japan, was to be organised. The authorities in Macao were determined to ensure that as far as possible the trade remained the monopoly of the náo and was not diverted into privately chartered vessels. As a concession the shares (or *baque*) in the amount of silk exported to Japan on the náo were also alloted to Chinese and other nationals. It was strictly forbidden, and considered a blot on one's honour (at least as far as the élite merchants were concerned) to send goods to Japan on private ships via third countries (especially the Philippines, with which Japanese vessels traded) or to import Japanese silver on account of individual Japanese.[136] There was nothing unusual about aiming for a monopoly. Attempting to enforce a monopoly in Macao was one thing, outside the territory in Nagasaki and Manila it was impossible, a shortcoming which highlights the limits of Lusitanian-Spanish co-operation in the East Indies. Regardless of the taboos of the *Armação*, Portuguese participated in Japanese voyages from Nagasaki to Manila in which silver, armaments and other goods were exchanged, mainly for raw silk and sappan wood.[137]

As the number of participants in Japan's overseas trade increased, the Portuguese were powerless to prevent silk, available elsewhere in the Indies, from reaching Japan by means other than the náo and voyages overseas by Japanese vessels and the arrival of the Dutch and English in east Asia bit into the privileged position the Portuguese had enjoyed in their trade with Japan in the sixteenth century. The Portuguese had not created a need in the east Asian trading world; they had been servicing one.

No matter how intimately the realities of their precarious financial situation required the Jesuits to involve themselves in commerce, there were, of course, other dimensions to their work in Japan. Serious efforts were made to understand the Japanese language, culture and society, although mainly that of the upper levels with a view to easing the process of conversion. The point was well made in the important Consultation of 1580, held in Bungo, to discuss policy. The Consultation decided on the need to establish a strong native church. It declared that 'never will the Church merge with the Japanese..., enter into their spirit, strike roots among them, command respect and influence, or be assured of material support save through the Japanese themselves, else we shall always be regarded by them as suspect foreigners.'[138] The Consultation discussed in great detail possible ways to achieve this and how far to proceed in accommodating Japanese custom and practice. But time, resources, circumstances and attitudes were against the Jesuits in 'this vast enterprise' as Valignano referred to the mission.[139] By 1614 only fourteen Japanese priests had been ordained.

In his analysis of the reasons for what he sees as the inevitable rejection of Christianity by the Japanese, Professor Elison questions the depth of the commitment to establish a native church and the ability of the missionaries to break free of the constraints of their own mental world to achieve their goal. He argues that by instigating and encouraging temple and shrine burning the fathers 'were engaged in a wholesale destruction of the Japanese tradition' and even goes so far as to speak of the Jesuit mission as 'a heroic effort to westernise' Japan.[140] Elison overstates his case and by referring to 'westernisation' introduces an anachronism. Jesuit missionary activity in Japan was no different from other places in the Indies where the fathers sought to make converts. It suffered from the same limitations and contradictions. This was inevitable as one strong cultural tradition engaged another equally so in an age when relativism − at least to Europeans − was unknown. In Goa, where the Church Militant had a freer hand than it ever enjoyed in Japan, the destruction of temples and attempts by ecclesiastical councils to eradicate the rites and ceremonies of the Hindu and other religious communities, as well as efforts to convert the local population to Christianity, met with no more success than in Japan. Christians remained a minority and the church tolerated non-Christian ceremonies so long as these were performed privately at home.[141] Besides, it is difficult to know what constitutes 'the Japanese tradition' during the *sengoku* wars in which Buddhist temples, notably Mt Hiei near Kyoto, were wilfully destroyed, and the Japanese themselves had no clear-cut concept of the 'West' (nor indeed did the Europeans) to juxtapose with whatever they imagined constituted the Japanese tradition. Nevertheless, despite the stated aims of creating an indigenous clergy, there were indeed reservations about such a policy among the fathers who voiced concern about native ability and commitment to a vocation. The dilemma about whether or not to admit natives to holy orders presented itself again in South America and in China, while in Goa, where local people were made priests, they were not given positions of responsibility for reasons that were only partly connected with alleged incompetence; the European clergy were also determined to enjoy the income from their parishes.[142]

More convincing as an explanation of the failure of Christianity to take root in sixteenth-century Japan is Elison's argument that the doctrine clashed with and appeared to challenge the assumption of emerging centralism. The Japanese experience with Christianity was in sharp contradistinction to the previous importation of a foreign religion, Buddhism, which had been a successful transplant because its basic doctrinal tenets and the flexibility of its application could be used by the rulers of early Japan to justify and extend their hold on power. Catholic Christianity, however, could make a man the servant of two masters, God and the secular ruler. To complicate matters, God's representatives came to be seen as the possible vanguard of a foreign power.[143] The parallels with earlier struggles in Europe, for example, in England between Henry II and Becket, to define the border between the spiritual and the secular jurisdiction are obvious. The analogy with recent experience in Japan of militant, armed Buddhist sects, the religious *ikki* or leagues, seeking to maintain their independence by military means in the *sengoku* struggles, were obvious to Hideyoshi and later to Ieyasu. The Buddhist sects and temples which resisted the imposition of the political structure initiated by Hideyoshi and firmly set in place by the Tokugawa were crushed, although Hideyoshi preferred to depoliticise Buddhism by bloodless methods.[144] Moves to suppress Christianity were slower, partly because it took longer to grasp that no matter how important the Macao trade was for the Jesuit mission in Japan no umbilical chord linked merchants and missionaries. But by 1614 the Tokugawa shogunate could expel the missionaries secure in the knowledge that trade would not suffer. The emergence of Japan's own official overseas trade from the late sixteenth century and to a lesser extent the arrival of the Dutch and the English in the seventeenth century helped generate this confidence.

Suspicions about an ulterior, political motive for the missionary presence in Japan are reflected in Hideyoshi's decision in 1587 to expel the Jesuits, although no steps were taken to enforce the expulsion decree.[145] They were raised once again, this time with disastrous consequences after the shipwreck off the coast of Shikoku of the Manila galleon, the *San Felipe*, bound for Acapulco with a cargo valued at $1\frac{1}{2}$ million pesos, in October 1596. The incident brought to a head the bitter division among the Christian missionaries which had emerged after the arrival of the Franciscans whom the Jesuits had tried unsuccessfully to have excluded from Japan. This was not a simple doctrinal or policy difference between Jesuit and friar, it also reflected Portuguese–Spanish imperial rivalry. The Jesuits in Japan had never been exclusively Portuguese (Valignano was Italian) but they aligned themselves with the Portuguese merchants to protect their mission and its trade privileges from the intrusion of the Spanish friars and merchants from Manila. The *San Felipe* incident unfolded against a background of foreign policy failure – the grand design to conquer China was bogged down in Korea – and Hideyoshi's concerns about the succession. There are also hints of mental instability creating an outlook whereby any possible threat to Hideyoshi's achievement and his hopes of seeing it advanced by his young son, Hideyori, invited harsh retaliation.[145] While Hideyoshi contemplated seizing the cargo from the *San Felipe*, the friars interceded on behalf of the Spanish merchants for restitution of the goods. However, what should have been a straight-forward dispute over cargo was transformed into an issue striking at the heart of national security concerns.

The spark was a casual remark allegedly made by the ship's pilot major that the overseas conquests of the king of Spain (since 1580, king of Portugal as well, a fact known to the Japanese) had been facilitated by using friars to soften the native population before the arrival of the conquistadores. The Jesuits feared that Hideyoshi already nurtured such beliefs. In January 1588 Francisco Pasio wrote that since Hideyoshi 'cannot believe that our mission is to save souls for life eternal because he does not recognise the immortality of the soul, he is ready to believe that we have no other goal but to prepare the conquest of his kingdom'.[147] Hideyoshi ordered the arrest of all missionaries. The Jesuits were able to negotiate their own release with the exception of two catechists who joined the hapless members of the Fransiscan house in Kyoto and seventeen of their converts, all of whom were sent down to Nagasaki and executed in February 1597. In the post mortem which followed, the friars believed they had been betrayed by a Jesuit plot, while the Jesuits countered that Fransiscan arrogance and an ignorance of Japanese custom had brought disaster to the mendicants. However, contrary to Professor Elison's view that 1597 marks a decisive turning point in the fortunes of Christianity in Japan after which the missionary presence became a question of survival, not acceptance, there was no high road towards the final extirpation of Christianity from Japan. Hideyoshi backed down from his orders to expel all missionaries and his death in 1598 raised the prospect that the tide might turn in favour of missionary activity. There were to be many twists and turns before Christianity was finally outlawed in Japan.[148]

It should be emphasised that rivalry and mistrust between the religious orders was not confined to Japan. It manifested itself in China where many of the problems of preaching the gospel were similar to those in Japan – what level of society should be targeted, the Jesuits accusing the friars of debasing the status of Christianity by mixing too much with the lower orders and of making no efforts to understand the native culture, the Franciscans attacking the Jesuits for their preoccupation with élites; the existence of an intellectually formidable local clerisy which, according to one father, was capable of asking questions 'which even Aquinas and Scotus could not answer satisfactorily'; and the hostility of the Chinese authorities to what was perceived as a threat to the political, social and moral order posed by the activities of the missionaries.[149]

One important consequence of Portuguese contact with Japan was the publication in Europe of information about the country, most of it based on Jesuit accounts. The Portuguese merchants tended to stay on the coast and mixed with Japanese merchants. Unlike the Jesuits, they knew little of the aristocratic culture of Kyoto and their published accounts are virtually non-existent.[150] Jesuit accounts published in the sixteenth and seventeenth centuries were censored in Rome, for if the Jesuits in Japan were selective about what they told the Japanese about Europe, their superiors in Rome did not believe in a free flow of information about Japan within Europe.[151] Nevertheless, the Jesuits helped put Japan both literally and metaphorically on the map. As with China and Cathay, no connection was made initially between Japan and Chipangu. After Balboa's discovery of the Pacific had shown that the West Indies were not Polo's Chipangu, contemporary scholarship placed Japan either in the region described by Ptolemy as *Aurea Chersonesus*, or Golden Chersonese (the Malay peninsula), or south of the equator, some 9,000 kilometres from the actual location of the country.[152] Francis Xavier, writing from Cochin in India to his superiors in Europe on the eve of his voyage to Japan on 20 January 1548 (NS), mentioned 'some big islands recently discovered in these parts called the islands of Japan'.[153] This was the first mention of the 'discovery' to reach Europe, but Xavier, who may have read Polo, did not equate it with Chipangu. It was only in 1557 that the first connection between the two was suggested by Antonio Golvão, although his account was not published in Lisbon until 1563. The suggestion was repeated by the official historian of the Portuguese Indies, Diogo do Couto, and Xavier's biographer, João de Lucena. Finally, in the seventeenth century the connection was established authoritatively by João Rodrigues.[154]

The Jesuits were also responsible for sending the famous embassy comprising four young Kyushu samurai to Europe. The boys left Nagasaki in February 1582, arriving in Lisbon in August 1584. They spent almost two years travelling in Europe before returning to Japan in July 1590. The embassy was carefully stage-managed (the boys were not allowed to get so much as a whiff of Protestantism) and was intended to drum up support among Catholic rulers, especially Philip II and the pope, for the Jesuit mission in Japan. In so far as the Jesuits were rewarded with the papal bull restating that Japan was their exclusive missionary territory, even though subsequent developments made the bull ineffectual, the visit was a success. The embassy heightened consciousness of Japan in Europe, especially in Catholic Europe and on its periphery, but it was not an official embassy from the Japanese government although the regent of Portugal, Philip II, Pope Gregory XIII and his successor, and the doges of Venice and Genoa received the boys as legates of an important foreign potentate. Quite whom these rulers believed that potentate to be is an interesting question. It certainly did not run against the interests of the Jesuits to let them imagine that the boys represented the ruler of a unified Japan but there is no evidence to suggest that the Jesuits perpetrated any fraud in this respect.[155]

The boys and their two servants were not the first Japanese to reach Europe. In 1553 one of the earliest Japanese Christian converts, a young Kagoshima man from a poor samurai background who took the Christian name Bernardo, arrived in Lisbon. He became a Jesuit and died in Portugal in 1557.[156] Almost contemporaneously with the arrival of the Kyushu boys in Europe, two other young Japanese Christians were brought to Europe, to England. They were taken off the coast of lower California in November 1587 from a Spanish Manila galleon, the *Santa Anna*, which had been attacked by Thomas Cavendish during his voyage of circumnavigation in the *Globe*. Francis Pretty's account of the voyage, printed in the first edition of Hakluyt's *Principall Navigations*, described them as 'two yong lads borne in Japon, which could both wright and reade their owne language, the eldest being about 20 yeers olde was named Christopher, the other was called Cosmos, about 17 yeeres of age both of very good capacitie.'[157]

Christopher and Cosmos caused a stir after they reached England and were objects of wonderment. Robert Parke's translation of Juan González de Mendoza's *The historie of the great and mightie kingdome of China* mentioned the two 'young fellows of good capacitie, borne in the mightie lland of Iapon',[158] and in the epistle dedicatory to the first edition of the *Princiapll Navigations*, Hakluyt, with unintentional irony one imagines, drew attention to them and to the three Filipino boys also brought back by Cavendish: 'Is it not as strange that the borne naturalles of Japan, and the Philippinaes are here to be seene, agreeing with our climate, speaking our language and informing us of the state of their Easterne habitations?'[159]

Christopher and Cosmos provided further evidence to support the argument of his great compilation, that the English, then beginning to strike out overseas, should gird themselves and move forward more resolutely to play their part in the age of reconnaissance, seizing the opportunities that came their way and reaping their share of the bounty beyond Europe's seaboards.

CHAPTER 2

Striking Out: The English and the Age of Reconnaissance

(i) From Privateering to Trading Company

The arrival of the Japanese boys Christopher and Cosmos was not the first occasion on which Japan became familiar in England. Ninety years before, John Cabot had secured the backing of Henry VII for his second voyage across the Atlantic in 1498 by claiming that a voyage westward from Bristol would bring him to the island of Chipangu 'where he believes that the spices of the world have their origin as well as the jewels'. However, by the mid-point of Elizabeth's reign there existed among the educated classes interested in these matters an awareness of Japan as a real country with a fixed geographical location. This was quite the opposite of the projection of fantastic expectations conjured up by the term 'Chipangu'. Cabot had read his Marco Polo but he lumped together Chipangu and the Spice Islands of southeast Asia and believed that the spices were shipped from Chipangu to the Asian mainland and from thence by caravan across Asia to the Levant and Mecca.[1] The Columbian chimera, which so much influenced Cabot, that Asia lay westwards, directly accessible across the Atlantic, did not outlast the Cabot voyages. Englishmen soon realised, as had other Europeans, that a huge, new world lay in the way and that those who wanted to reach the Indies by sailing westwards would have to negotiate the Americas rounding them either to the north or to the south, although a long time was to pass before men would shed the belief that there was an easy passage round the new continents.

These ninety years also witnessed a fundamental change in English attitudes to the question of overseas expansion. The English believed that they too had a role to play in the age of reconnaissance. It was even possible to contemplate English shipping entering the Indian Ocean to challenge Portugal's supposed hegemony of the East Indies trade, a myth that was gradually debunked as the century wore on.

As with the Lusitanians, there was no carefully researched and meticulously executed plan guiding the English towards the East Indies. Nor was there much that was heroic about the process itself. During the Elizabethan age, when the foundations of overseas trade and colonial expansion were laid, there were plenty of examples of men driven by bold, selfless courage to undertake voyages of exploration which added to the stock of European knowledge, especially about the New World. But voyages of exploration *tout court* did not provide the motivation much less the money to finance English trade in the Indian Ocean and beyond. Nor, despite the marriage of Protestantism and patriotism (encouraged by the defeat of the Spanish Armada in 1588), did ideological motives *per se* fire the enthusiasm of those who went to sea and those who provided them with the funds to do so. A nascent nationalism and the religious beliefs that buttressed it were inadequate in themselves to build ships and man them for such an undertaking.

The reasons for English overseas expansion, first into the Atlantic and later into the Indian Ocean, spring more obviously from economic and geopolitical factors and are closely related to the major upheavals on the continent. The continental power struggles never resulted in the actual invasion and occupation of England but they were uncomfortably close and threatening enough to make such an outcome seem disturbingly possible. England was a minor power in relation to the two major powers Valois France and Habsburg Spain, which in the second half of the sixteenth century was not just a European but a world superpower. However, because of its strategic location, and, after the accession of Elizabeth in 1557, its strongly Protestant character, England was able to play an important role in continental rivalries, especially in the revolt of the Netherlands which preoccupied Spain for almost eighty years from the 1560s, sapping her strength in an unsuccessful war to recontrol what was fast becoming one of Europe's areas of high economic grow.

England had its own quarrel with Spain. By mid century English trade with the Iberian kingdom was booming. The English share of the carrying trade between Spain and other parts of Europe was considerable, although in the trade between Spain and northern Europe the English later faced competition from the United Provinces. Spain was an important market for a number of leading London merchants. But England's flourishing trade with Spain and English cloth exports to the Antwerp staple market (still under Spanish control) which the Spanish, erroneously, assumed to be the life-blood of English trade, could not exist in a vacuum, isolated from political realities and the shifting pattern of events which determined the structure of international relations. For one thing, Anglo-Spanish relations were souring. The English became embroiled in the Dutch revolt, the Spanish began to meddle in English politics on behalf of Mary Queen of Scots, and in the 1560s there was an increase in the number of English incursions into the Spanish and Portuguese overseas empires. The most striking incursions were the Hawkins voyages in which the queen and some of her courtiers had invested. The aim of the voyages was to break into the profitable trade in African slaves in the Caribbean. Not surprisingly the Spanish resented this presence and reacted accordingly. From 1568–73 Spanish and Portuguese ports were closed to English vessels. Tension ran high and war almost ensued.

By the mid sixteenth century it was obvious that the New World was not only vast but that large parts of it were not under Spanish dominion. Even in parts nominally possessed by the Spanish monarch, control was not absolute. The Hawkins voyages reflected the spirit of pride and a sense of confidence in England's ability to challenge Spanish power in the New World. This spirit found literary expression in the writings of the two Hakluyts and other propagandists of empire. These writings did not create such sentiment but reflected it and by trumpeting recent achievements helped inspire further efforts. In addition to investment by the court, the Hawkins voyages drew on the finance of London and outport merchants who did not depend on trade with Spain. A number of prominent courtiers, whose preference was for a policy of taking the offensive against Spain, were happy that such capital should be employed in a manner that satisfied both commercial interests and their own foreign policy aims.[2]

However, the involvement of the court was not matched by any grand design sponsored and promoted by the queen. There always remained a gap between the rhetoric of the propagandists and the ambitions of courtiers such as Raleigh who sought to realise them, and the more limited, pragmatic policy concerns of the queen who would have preferred accommodation with Spain. Had this been achieved (the chances were slender) the character of English overseas expansion might have been altered.[3] Nor was the entire merchant community in favour of a policy of confrontation with Spain, a formidable imperial power enriched, or so it was thought, by plentiful bullion from the New World. Those who opposed confrontation were concerned not to let slip the opportunity to share the profits that could be made in the European country trade by carrying the goods and commodities that reached Seville and Lisbon from the New World, East Indies and Levant to northern Europe. In 1577 these merchants organised themselves into a regulated company, the Spanish Company, which despite a heavy weighting in favour of London merchants, who conducted most of the trade with Spain, did not overlook representation of the outports whose merchants formed an important political constituency whose interests could not be ignored.[4]

Drake's return from his three-year voyage of circumnavigation in 1580, the second such European voyage round the world, opened up the fissure in the merchant community between those merchants whose profits were derived either directly or indirectly from the trading opportunities created by the Spanish empire and those who favoured a more aggressive stance against the Spanish. By the time the expedition left England in December 1577, Drake's mission had changed radically from its original and more modest goal of exploring the western coast of South America. It set forth with a double purpose: a voyage of reconnaissance especially to explore the Peruvian coast near the Potosí silver mines, whose riches flowed east across the Atlantic to Spain and west across the Pacific to Manila, and as a voyage of plunder and piracy. On the Peruvian coast Drake intended to investigate the possibility of establishing an English colony in lands close to the mines where it was hoped he would find terrain blessed with similar silver deposits. The voyage had the queen's backing. It coincided with an anti-Spanish twist in her foreign policy prompted by developments in the Netherlands and symbolised the beginnings of an expansionist English policy overseas. It was also a considerable navigational achievement. However, after Drake's triumphant homecoming, the Spanish Company merchants, fearing for their investments in Spain, urged the Privy Council to take steps to return the plunder to the Spanish. They were supported by other City merchants and by a faction at court which opposed the policy of brinkmanship in Anglo-Spanish relations pursued by the Walsingham faction. (Walsingham and his associates had invested heavily in Drake's venture and stood to profit from it.) Their protests were not entirely in vain. Some booty was returned but Spanish indignation was brushed aside and relations between the two countries did not improve. This had little to do with Drake's voyage itself, which was a minor thorn in the Spanish king's side, but stemmed from broader geopolitical considerations, especially England's continued support for the Dutch revolt and the concern with which the triumph of Protestantism in England was viewed in Madrid. The emergence of a more hawkish Spanish foreign policy towards England in the early 1580s and an increase in English reprisal actions against Spanish ships for damage suffered in the Spanish New World snuffed out any flickering hopes that the two countries would enjoy a peaceful resolution of their differences. By 1585 England and Spain were *de facto* in a state of war; the formal declaration came two years later. During the war, merchants of the Spanish Company, which ceased to operate from the spring of 1588, quickly changed their tune and fell resolutely in line behind the anti-Spanish adventures of those who had favoured war. They soon appreciated that war, far from killing off trade, created new opportunities. Spanish Company merchants were to be among the most important suppliers of capital for the innovative method by which a financially hard-pressed government was able to finance and fight the war – privateering.[5]

A further consequence of Drake's voyage of circumnavigation had been to demonstrate that the Portuguese monopoly in the East Indies was not as complete as some had imagined. During his stay in the Moluccas, Drake had been invited by the sultan of Ternate, Kechil Babullah, to participate in the island's clove trade. The Portuguese had enjoyed influence but not control in Ternate and they faced a challenge from the Spanish who had their own designs in the Spice Islands and who had allied themselves with Ternate's nearby rival, Tidore. Portuguese captains general and their subordinates had administered the island, located far from the watchful eyes of Lisbon or Goa, corruptly and often cruelly, but in 1576 the Ternateans reacted and expelled the Portuguese. No matter how Drake interpreted the sultan's invitation, the English were not being asked to replace the Portuguese. Nor were they being promised exclusive rights over the disposal of cloves. The Portuguese had not enjoyed such rights nor were they within the sultan's gift. The invitation was part of a shrewd policy to bring another outside player into the game to help redress the balance of power in the sultan's favour and secure Ternate's independence.[6] At least the sultan's offer suggested that attractive commercial possibilities awaited the English in the East Indies and various proposals were put forward about how best to exploit trade beyond the 'Equynoctyall Lyne'. These included a petition drawn up by Walsingham advocating the creation of a new body modelled on the Spanish Casa de la Contratacíon at Seville – that is, a body to regulate the Indies trade rather than raise capital and create a structure to conduct it and therefore not a prefiguration of the East India Company itself – and for Drake to return to the Indies. The proposals conveniently dovetailed with the Privy Council's support for the pretender to the Portuguese throne, Dom António. In 1582–3 a voyage was dispatched to the Indies under the command of Edward Fenton in order to establish trade with the Moluccas. Some of its backers, including the Earl of Leicester, even hoped that it might do the same in China.[7]

Fenton failed to reach the Indies either by way of the Cape or, as Drake had done, by way of the Straits of Magellan, a route which his instructions had specifically ruled out because of the presence of a Spanish fleet in the area. (The Spanish, concerned about the possibility of an attack on Peru via this route after Drake's successful voyage, attempted to fortify the Straits, but these efforts were quickly abandoned.)[8] His failure reflected the lack of consensus about how best to exploit the first encouraging signs of a possible trade with the Indies. It was symbolic too of English inability to decide on which way to sail to the Indies, either east or west. In this respect Drake's circumnavigation and that of Cavendish in 1587–8, while boosting national morale and suggesting that a viable trade might exist, had a negative effect on the efforts to establish the trade itself by highlighting one of the least accessible routes, southwest via the Straits. A lot of energy was to be expended and lives lost, even though geographical knowledge was furthered, in seeking sea routes to the Indies by a northwest, northeast or southwest route, every direction that is except the proven one, round Africa.

So long as merchant capital, particularly that of the London mercantile elite including those merchants whose business had depended on peaceful Anglo-Spanish trade until the outbreak of hostilities, was tied up in privateering voyages, the pursuit of direct English trade to the East Indies and the beginnings of a colonial empire in the New World were relegated to the margin of English concern. It was more profitable and the risks smaller to plunder Spanish and Portuguese shipping in the Atlantic and Caribbean than to venture to the East Indies regardless of what the propagandists of overseas expansion had to say about the benefits that would flow from establishing a trade there.[9] However, privateering also served a national purpose. In a sense merchants who invested their money in privateering ventures were national benefactors. The Elizabethan government's limited national finances (Elizabeth's annual revenue was approximately £300,000) prevented the building of a large royal navy. In a different respect privateering resembled wakō activity in the seas around Japan and China (that is, trade under a different guise). But the analogy is not really apposite. England enjoyed a strong central government administering a nation united against a common enemy seeking to impose what was by then an alien creed, and the government was able to direct this activity in ways that benefited national policy goals. Privateers were not outlaws nor were they pirates like those who had flourished along the southern coast before the war. They acted as instruments of state policy though their motivation was far removed from that of selfless patriots. Pay, for example, was higher on merchant ships than in the queen's navy during the Spanish war and consequently the royal navy suffered from a shortage of manpower. Men were attracted more by the possibility of riches from privateering voyages than serving for a cause.[10]

Privateering represented a mutually advantageous fusion of private and public interest and it provided English naval personnel with invaluable navigational experience and nautical skills, the benefits of which were to be reaped in the following century. On average more than one hundred ships per annum sailed on privateering voyages during the Anglo-Spanish war and there was a marked increase in the number of English ships in excess of 200 tons. But whatever the virtues of privateering as an applied lesson in naval technology and as a school for mariners there was a negative aspect to the voyages as well. They acted as a drag on efforts to establish colonies in the New World and their highly individualistic nature and the short-term, selfish conduct implicit in their goals impeded the development of an effective naval organisation and strategy that could sustain an offensive against Spanish forces.[11] Nevertheless, the great London merchants invested heavily in the privateering voyages. They acted in concert promoting voyages on a joint-stock basis and they put up the money for other types of privateering undertakings. They were also active in the purchase and sale of prize goods brought back to England. Not only were these merchants responsible for funding the majority of new ships built between 1581–97, but among the privateers they made the biggest profits, profits which were available for reinvestment in new business ventures, including those of the future East India Company.[12]

However, capital investment and the experienced personnel to man the vessels and staff the factories that would be set up in the Indies were also forthcoming from the more conventional business activity that characterised English trade with the Levant. English merchants had been resident there during the first half of the sixteenth century but from the 1550s to the 1570s, for reasons that remain unclear, trade was conducted indirectly. From the early 1580s a thriving direct trade was restarted. In 1581 the Levant Company was established by letters patent and remained a joint stock organisation until 1592 when it was given a new charter and operated as a regulated company with a monopoly covering the overland trade routes east of the Levant to India. Some of the prime movers in the establishment of the Company were merchants involved in privateering ventures who combined this orthodox form of trade activity with the unorthodox but profitable opportunities available in the Atlantic. These individuals provided a major link with the future East India Company.[13] The terms of the Levant trade were unfavourable to England, which imported a variety of goods including currants (the most profitable item), pepper, spices, cotton wool, yarn and flax, carpets and even Chinese porcelain in return for English cloth (some of which reached the Levant by way of Venice thus competing with cloth carried by the Levant Company itself), tin, rabbit skins and other goods.[14] However, English cloth did not sell particularly well. The market for cloth and other English goods was limited and purchasers were selective. This was a lesson that the directors of the future East India Company failed to appreciate. They made the same assumption about high demand for English or other European goods in the Indies and met with no better success than the Levant merchants in selling these goods. The Levant trade provided another perhaps more challenging opportunity than was available elsewhere in Europe, with the exception of Muscovy, for English merchants to acquire or sharpen their commercial skills in foreign markets. Moreover, the trade furnished invaluable experience in the conduct of diplomatic relations with non-Christian potentates. The representative of the Company at Constantinople also served as English ambassador to the Ottoman emperor and appointed consuls to serve in various Levantine ports.[15]

The presence of pepper among English imports from the Levant is significant for, as has been mentioned, the Cape route did not eclipse the Red Sea and Persian Gulf routes as the entrée to Europe in the sixteenth century. Europe continued to receive many of its imports from Asia along the latter routes, although this arrangement changed decisively with the establishment of the English and Dutch East India Companies.[16] Trade with the Levant gave English merchants indirect access to Asian goods and for many merchants it was sufficient to have such indirect access to pepper from the Indies. The risks and expenses involved in establishing and driving a direct trade were avoided. After all the arrangement worked well for Venice.

Others thought differently, however. In October 1589 a petition (the promoters were probably Levant merchants) was presented to the Privy Council about the setting out of a small fleet to sail to the Indies by way of the Cape with ambitious and fanciful plans to trade at Calicut, and in China and the Philippines. The petitioners were confident of finding good markets for English cloth and expected 'Great benefitte will redound to our contrie as well for the anoyinge of the Spaniards and Portingalls (now our enemyes)'. The project failed to materialise. However, in 1591 three ships left England in a voyage under George Raynard. One ship, the *Edward Bonaventure* commanded by James Lancaster, reached Penang island off the Malay peninsula (one of the other ships was sent back at Table Bay because of sickness and death among the crew and the other was lost in the Indian Ocean). The ships had not carried much cargo and the voyage was in fact a privateering one, attacking Portuguese shipping in the Indian Ocean and seizing a consignment of Portuguese cargo from some ships from Pegu while at Penang. The voyage had had an inauspicious beginning and ended in disaster as the ships struggled home via the West Indies where they were obliged to call in order to obtain desperately needed victuals. Lancaster made it back to England from the West Indies in May 1594 aboard a French ship. His own ship was taken by the Spanish.[17] The affair did little to promote the idea of direct investment in voyages round the Cape to the Indies.

Predating this fiasco but of more consequence was the attempt by the London merchant John Newberry to explore trade possibilities beyond Aleppo by proceeding overland to Baghdad, Basra, Ormuz and eventually to Goa. Newberry left England in 1583 accompanied by five merchants, including Ralph Fitch, and two other men. The project was undertaken with the backing of the two men most responsible for establishing the Levant Company, Sir Edward Osborne and Richard Stoper, and the group carried several letters from Queen Elizabeth, including one to the 'king of China'. The group was arrested by the Portuguese, who took them to be spies, at Ormuz and they were taken to Goa where they were briefly incarcerated. The men were released after the intercession of, among others, the English Jesuit, Thomas Stevens, who had been acquainted with Richard Hakluyt at Oxford and had served in Goa since 1579.[18] They convinced Stevens that they were Catholics, and were permitted to trade. However, in 1584 the viceroy ordered that the Englishmen were to be sent back to Europe, a move which Newberry, Fitch and one of the other merchants pre-empted by fleeing from Goa. They eventually split up. Over the next few years Fitch travelled extensively in India and across to Pegu and Malacca. (Newberry died while trying to return to Europe overland.) Fitch arrived back in England in April 1591 and was debriefed about his experiences. His account provided valuable information about trade and gave some impression of the countries in the Indies. His rich treasury of information mentioned the profitable Portuguese Macao–Japan trade. Fitch commented that the Portuguese took to Japan

much white silke, golde, muske, and porcelanes: and they bring from there nothing but silver. They have a great caracke which goeth thither every yere, and she bringrth from thence every yere above sixe hundred thousand crusadoes: and all this silver of Japan, and two hundred crusadoes more in silver which they bring yeerely out of India, they imploy to their great advantage in China.[19]

Fitch's account of his travels was not published until 1599 in the second edition of Hakluyt's *Principal Navigations*. However, his travels provided some of the impetus for the extension of the Levant Company's monopoly to cover overland trade with those countries which he had visited when the Company's charter was renewed in 1592.[20] The enhanced jurisdiction existed on paper only. There was no intention of seeking to extend it in practice for the whole episode had demonstrated that whatever small-scale trade the Portuguese had allowed Newberry and the others to conduct at Ormuz and Goa, there was absolutely no likelihood of the Lusitanians, who as part of the Habsburg crown were at war with England anyway, permitting the English Levant Company to gain a footing in the Indies.[21] No matter how remarkable Fitch's achievement, his peregrination provided no encouragement to ideas of extending England's Levantine trade overland from the eastern shores of the Mediterranean to the Indian Ocean and beyond.

Had not some unexpected external factor galvanised English merchants into action, forcing them to think seriously about participating directly in trade with the East Indies, the English would have remained content to receive their supplies of East India goods and commodities via the Levant, supplemented by the odd windfall from privateering, so long, that is, as war with Spain provided opportunities for them to engage in privateering. The English would also have dissipated more of their maritime resources and energies in projects to find a northwest passage to the Indies, a project which continued to cast a spell over mariners and merchants alike. Even Lancaster had brought back unsubstantiated gossip that the Portuguese had 'lately discovered the coast of china to the latitude of nine and fiftie degrees...giving great hope of the Northeast or Northwest passage'.[22]

The event which shook the English out of their complacency and provided merchants with the resolve to embark on the challenge of finding a commercially viable way of trading directly with the Indies, was the return of Cornelis de Houtman with three of his four vessels to Amsterdam on 14 August 1597 (NS), after a two-year voyage, well-planned but poorly led, round the Cape to Bantam on Java. De Houtman returned with a cargo of pepper which more than covered the costs of the voyage when sold. Suddenly and irrevocably the East Indies emerged into the spotlight as an area of major trading importance for the northern European Protestant powers and, regardless of the enthusiasm of Hakluyt and others for a northwest passage, the Cape became the preferred route.

(ii)   Establishment of the East India Company

Dutch shipping strength and maritime expertise had grown consistently throughout the sixteenth century. A petition to the Emperor Charles V from the States of Holland in 1548 insisted that 'the main business of the country must needs be in shipping and related trades'.[23] The Dutch had been the major carrier between the Baltic and the rest of Europe since the late middle ages and by the end of century their share of the carrying trade between northern Europe and the Mediterranean was also increasing. In the Mediterranean trade, the Dutch achieved a higher ratio of cargo space to tonnage than their competitors, the English or the Portuguese. The foundations of their shipbuilding industry, which was to be the envy of Europe in the seventeeth century, were already firmly in place.[24]

Their commercial and shipping skills made them indispensable even to their Habsburg enemy during the war of independence. Spain relied on Dutch shipping for naval supplies (timber, tar and pitch from the Baltic), grain and manufactures, and in return the Dutch had access to bullion from the New World. The Dutch were impervious to the bitter criticism of the English who felt that they had come to the assistance of their Protestant brethren only to find themselves faced with competition in their own profitable Mediterranean trade. Spain's recapture of Antwerp in 1585 paved the way for the emergence of Amsterdam as an international trade and financial centre (merchants who chose to leave Antwerp and move to Amsterdam could take their capital with them but their individual and collective experience was in itself capital enough). By the end of the sixteenth century the Dutch had turned their attention overseas to the Atlantic, particularly Brazil, and to the East Indies as the Spanish belatedly and futilely tried to sever the economic cord which still tied them to their rebellious provinces.[25]

The Dutch had been fortunate to acquire a fairly detailed overall impression of Portuguese trade in the East Indies thanks to Jan Huyghen van Linschoten. Linschoten was born in northern Holland but his family, who were Roman Catholics, had business interests in the Iberian peninsula and at the age of thirteen he moved first to Seville and then to Lisbon. From 1583–8 Linschoten served in Goa as clerk to the archbishop and during these years he met with Newberry and his associates and even helped secure their release. After his return to the Netherlands in 1592 he compiled an account of his experiences and travels which was published in Amsterdam in 1595–6 under the title *Itinerario: Voyage ofte Schipvaert van Jan Huygen van Linschoten naer Oost ofte Portugaels Indien.* This volume, which drew upon Maffei's *Historica Indica*, provided a first-hand account of the Portuguese maritime empire in Asia, its strengths and weaknesses, and confirmed what Drake's voyage had demonstrated previously, that much of the area, especially the spice-producing islands of the Indonesian archipelago, was not under any form of Portuguese control. *Itinerario* also presented a picture of the diversity of the lands in the Indies.[26]

After Houtman's return in 1597 other fleets were dispatched by rival groups of Dutch merchants from different parts of the provinces – the *voorcompagnie* voyages. (The Dutch *Vereenigde Oost Indische Compagnie*, United East India Company, or VOC as it was more generallly known, was established in 1602, two years after the English company.) Mostly they sailed by way of the Cape and they confidently threw down the gauntlet to the Portuguese by leaving factors at various ports in the Indies.[27] However daring these voyages were, they lacked co-ordination but they constituted the prelude to an enduring Dutch presence in the East Indies trade. The Portuguese maritime empire in the Indies lay exposed; the Portuguese themselves had already realised that they lacked the financial resources to defend it. The problem grew worse in the early seventeenth century after the arrival of the northern Europeans as Portuguese trade in the Indies shrank, reducing the customs revenues on which the empire depended.[28]

The return of the *voorcompagnie* voyages, especially that of Jacob van Neck in July 1599, and the highly profitable sale of their cargoes caused alarm bells to ring in English mercantile circles, particularly among the Levant merchants. The more pessimistic among the merchants feared for the very survival of the trade. It became clear that English merchants would have to organise themselves and carve out their own niche in the East Indies trade if they wished to counter not only the most alarmist scenario (the Dutch ruining the Levant spice trade) but the more immediate threat of the Hollanders undercutting English prices. Besides, the more astute merchants sensed that the peace negotiations with Spain underway in late 1599 would, if successful, spell the end of privateering ventures.[29] It was time to think to the future.

By September 1599 over 100 individuals, a third of whom were Levant merchants, had agreed to venture £30,133 6s 8d towards the establishment of a new company to trade with the East Indies. Fifteen directors were elected, seven of them Levant Company members. A petition to the Privy Council was to be drafted in the hope of obtaining letters patent for the Company, permission to export bullion, and exclusion from customs duties for the six voyages that were contemplated initially. The drafting committee was instructed to inform the Privy Council that the merchants were 'induced by the success of the viage [Van Neck's] pformed by the Duche nation [who] beinge informed that the duchemen prepare for a newe viage and to that ende have bought divers ships in England, were stirred vp wth noe lesse affection to advaunce the trade of ther native Cuntrey then the duche merchaunts were to benefite ther Comon wealthe'.[30] In reality the motives behind the Company's formation owed more to mundane commercial considerations than to the higher ideals of patriotism. The objectives of the Company were correspondingly modest. In the words of Professor Chaudhuri, the rise of the East India Company should be viewed 'not as an independent commercial venture, but as an attempt to separate the spice trade from the main body of the Levant trade and to drive it by a new route'.[31] The merchants who advanced their money had no intention of involving themselves in anything revolutionary. In spite of the wider world in which they were obliged to operate they were generally men of limited horizons and concerns. They were not planning to lay the foundations for a future commercial empire in Asia. It was only in the eighteenth century that the Company evolved into a proto-multinational corporation. This was far from the intention of the original adventurers and well beyond their imagination and ability to realise.

The initial panic caused by the return of Van Neck's ships soon subsided after cooler reflection. The Aleppo-based merchant William Clark noted that if the Dutch stuck to pepper and spice imports and did not touch nutmeg and indigo all was by no means lost for the Levant trade.[32] Moreover, foreign policy considerations intervened to delay the establishment of the Company and the dispatch of its first voyage. In October 1599 the Privy Council informed the merchants that priority should be given to the peace negotiations with Spain 'thincking it *more* beneficiall for the generall state of mchaundize to enterteyne a peace' and that a voyage to the East Indies at this juncture would jeopardise such prospects.[33] The Spanish crown claimed a monopoly over the East Indies but the English peace negotiators countered this with documents, based on information provided by the merchants, showing that large parts of the Indies were not subject to Spanish or Portuguese rule and were therefore open to all.[34] Preparations for the voyage had resumed by September 1600, by which time the peace negotiations with Spain had collapsed. By the end of October a charter had been drawn up and submitted to the Privy Council. The final version was dated 31 December and read to the subscribers early the following month. It gave '[t]he Governor and Company of Merchants of London trading into the East Indies', as the Company was formally known, a monopoly over the trade for fifteen years and various privileges exempting it from customs duties on imports and exports plus the right to export bullion. (A new charter was granted on 31 May 1609.) On 13 February 1601 a fleet of five ships, some of which had been privateering vessels, under the command of James Lancaster, himself a veteran of privateering voyages, left Woolwich for the Indies, the Company's First Voyage.[35]

In retrospect it is easy to pick out the factors that were to make the East Indies trade successful and profitable for England before the Company itself was transformed into a territorial power in India in the later eighteenth century: the export of bullion and, of much lesser importance, European goods to the Indies, and the successful penetration of the Asian country trade to provide the means to acquire Asian goods for England, most of which were subsequently re-exported to Europe.[36] But this was not at all obvious during the Company's infancy.

In its early years the Company was concerned (understandably so given the circumstances of its foundation) to get hold of pepper. By the 1620s some six to seven million tons were being imported into Europe, a sizeable part carried by the Company.[37] Pepper was relatively easy to acquire, was ideal as a bulk cargo to fill up the Company's ships, and was profitable. The First Voyage had called at Achin in northeast Sumatra and while made welcome by its ruler, Iskandar Mudah, who was opposed to the Portuguese, found Bantam a more promising source of pepper and a more suitable emporium for other products. Lancaster established a factory there in 1602 and instructed its members to proceed to the Spice Islands to procure spices in anticipation of the Company's next voyage. Lancaster himself returned with 1,030,000 lb of pepper but the Company had difficulties in disposing of it; English and Dutch imports together had glutted the market at home and abroad. To complicate matters, the crown, concerned not to have the value of its own stock of pepper undercut, intervened to hinder sales. Generally speaking, however, and quite unlike the Portuguese crown, which viewed the Estado da Índia as a tax gathering institution, the English crown kept out of the Company's affairs. Yet the Company's role in English foreign policy is somewhat ambiguous. Most of its activity was in the East Indies, a world which impinged only indirectly on the foreign policy calculations of English governments in the early seventeenth century and constituted a grey area for the application of international law.[38] Professor Steensgaard's view that from its foundation 'the Company's policy was dictated by its own not by England's place in the international system' needs modification. In comparison with the Estado da Índia, the Company enjoyed a free hand from the English crown and it never functioned directly as a foreign-policy tool of the English crown. Nevertheless, it aimed to keep on the best possible terms with the crown, not always an easy task. For example, in 1604 James I granted a licence to Sir Edward Michelbourne, in blatant disregard of the Company's monopoly, 'to discover the coutries and domynions of Cathaia, China, Japon, Corea and Cambaia' and to trade in places not yet frequented by the Company. In 1618 the king again ignored the Company's monopoly by granting letters patent to Sir James Cunningham for the formation of a Scottish East India Company. In both cases James was showing who was master in foreign affairs. Nevertheless, the Company had its uses for the crown as an indirect weapon in foreign policy as was apparent in the conduct of James's relations with the Dutch.[39]

Pepper had its ups and downs as an import but it remained the Company's staple import during the first forty years of its activity.[40] But an almost exclusive concentration on pepper and spice imports, even after the government had given permission for their re-export from England to the continent, could not justify the capital expended in building and fitting out the ships, manning them and lading them with goods and bullion, to say nothing of the risks involved in sending them on the long, unpredictable and often dangerous voyage to the Indies and back. By 1606 the Company was fully aware of the importance of the country trade between northwest India and the Indonesian Archipelago and of the role of Indian cloth piece goods in this trade. Lancaster had sold calicoes from a captured Portuguese vessel for a good profit in Bantam and intelligence acquired from Portuguese sources drew attention to the market for Cambay cloth in the Spice Islands and to the fact that they were much cheaper to procure near their place of manufacture than at Bantam where they were also available. In December 1608 one of the Company's factors at Bantam wrote that '[i]t would prove very beneficial to our trade here...to have this place continually furnished' with cloth from India.[41]

From the Third Voyage, the Company tried to establish a presence in the extensive country trade between northwest India and the Red Sea. Its aim was either to set up a factory at Surat (eventually achieved in 1613) or to gain access to the ports of Aden and Mocha in the Gulf of Aden and the island of Socotra near the entrance to the gulf, where Gujarati ships and merchants, long established in this trade and still a major force in other theatres of the Asian country trade, called. Surat was the most important entrepôt of northwest India and a major hub of regional commerce, with the Gulf of Aden as one of the spokes. The founding of an English factory there was not an option: it was a necessity.[42] With the Sixth Voyage, which was intended to establish a factory at or near Surat, the Company showed greater determination to enter the country trade. The chief factor was instructed to explore the possibilities of involvement in the local trade rather than let a capital investment lie idle.[43] (Idle stock was decried as bad business management in the seventeenth century. It was judged the same as a loss.)[44]

The Seventh Voyage was more ambitious. Factories were established at Masulipatan on the Coromandel Coast, two years before the Surat one was opened, Patani (in present-day Thailand but then a small Malay tributary state of Siam ruled over by a queen) and Ayuthia, the Siamese capital, until its destruction by the Burmese in 1768. The idea for this voyage came from two Dutch merchants, Peter Floris and Lucas Antheunis. Both men had served in the VOC on the Coromandel Coast and were well acquainted with the Indies trade. Floris and Antheunis invested £1,500 of their own in the stock of the voyage, a not unusual practice, and sailed to the Indies as principal factors.[45] Tucked away towards the end of the commission for the Seventh Voyage was an instruction to the factors to 'take the opportunitie (from the most conuenient place you shall arriue att) to send one or twoe of o^r factors in such conuenient shippinge as [yo^u] may procure to carrie his Mats lres vnto the kinge of Iapan together wth such stocke of Marchandize & Comodities as wee haue appointed o^r said principall Marchaunts to prouide for that purpose'.[46] Both Floris at Patani and Antheunis at Ayuthia made efforts to garner information on Japan, but Floris's first impression was 'that the trade for Japan is butt of small importance'.[47]

The decision to examine the possibilities of direct trade with Japan was not the first such one. In 1580 the Muscovy Company attempted to send two small vessels of forty and twenty tons under the command of Arthur Pet and Charles Jackman to seek a northeast passage to Cathay. Their instructions included advice by the cosmographer Dr John Dee on how to behave themselves should they reach China. Dee added that '[y]ou may also have opportunitie to saile over to Japan Island where you shall finde Christian men, Jesuits of many countreys of Christendome, and perhaps some Englishmen, at whose handes, you may have great instruction and advise for your affaires in hand'. While the Jesuits in Japan were of differing nationalities there were in fact no English Jesuits among their number. The expedition, in which Jackman and his crew perished, reached no further than the Kara Sea.[48]

Thirteen years later an expedition under the command of Richard Hawkins set sail from Plymouth 'for Ilands of Japan, of the Philippineas and Molucas, the Kingdomes of China and East Indies'. However, this claim was probably added in the 1620s, in deference to the pro-Spanish faction at court, in order to play down the true purpose of the voyage, a grandiose privateering venture, attempting to repeat Drake's circumnavigation. It was handicapped by inadequate ships and poor leadership and reached no further than the coast of Peru.[49] In 1602 and 1606 joint voyages of the East India and Muscovy Companies (the latter claimed a monopoly right to explore for northeast and northwest passages) were sent to investigate the chances of a northwest route to Japan. The commander of the 1602 fiasco, George Weymouth, was promised £500 if he could furnish proof that he had reached China or Japan.[51] These efforts are not the mere footnotes to the story of England's quest for trade in the Indies they are usually judged to be. They reflect a strong intellectual bias in the writings of the influential propagandists of English overseas expansion in favour of a northwest passage as a way to outflank the Portuguese and reach the Indies. Compensation for the risks involved, it was argued, would be forthcoming from sales of English cloth in the northern areas of the Indies including Japan. An additional attraction was the knowledge that, if found, a northwest passage lay in lands and waters over which neither Spain nor

Portugal had any dominion. In so far as there was concern for the niceties of international law, the discovery of a passage would strengthen the legal arguments for an English presence in the Indies. Such was the *raison d'être* for Dutch voyages in search of a passage in the 1590s. Experience was to prove otherwise.[51]

In 1577 Richard Willes, one of the most enthusiastic exponents of a northwest passage, published *The History of Trauayle in the West and East Indies*. This was a new and expanded edition of Richard Eden's *Decades of the new worlde*, a second edition of which Eden was working on when he died. Willes' was an advocate of a northwest route, existence of which he did not doubt. This was a conviction which owed more to faith than to any scientific evidence, but he expected Frobisher's voyage of 1576–7 would place the matter beyond doubt. The northwest passage would enable the English to avoid the Portuguese in the Indian Ocean where he believed they 'doe hold as the Lords of those seas' and reach 'these fruitfull and wealthie Islands, which wee doe usually call Moluccaes'.[52] However, his *History of Trauayle* has the distinction of containing the first published account of Japan in English, predating the English edition of Marco Polo's *Travels* by two years.

Willes was well read in the continental literature about European expansion. He had studied at Winchester and at Oxford, Mainz and Perugia universities and had entered the Society of Jesus but had renounced his Catholicism when he returned to England in 1574. He had read the published Jesuit letters from Japan, 'the Japannish letters' as he termed them, and Barros's history of Portuguese exploration, *Da Asia*, published in Lisbon in 1552. The account of Japan in the *History of Trauayle* was based on letters by Xavier and other Jesuits and a letter by Louís Frois from Kyoto dated 19 February 1565 (NS), which had been published by 'my old acquaintaned friend' Giovanni Pietro Maffei in Naples in 1573. Willes's book clearly served as the inspiration for Dee's recommendation to Pet and Jackman to try to reach Japan. It was republished by Hakluyt in the second edition of *Principal Navigations* in 1599.

Willes added freely to the Jesuit letters and his synthesis is largely a mishmash of poorly digested borrowings. He wrote that

> the noble Iland of Giapan, written otherwise Japon and Japan...standeth in the East Ocean, beyond all Asia, betwixt Cathayo and the West Indies sixe and thirtie degrees Northward from the Equinoctial line, in the same clime with the south part of Spaine and Portugall, distant from there by sea sixe thousand leagues the travaile thither, both for civill discord, great pyracie and often shipwracks is very dangerous.

There then followed a general description of the country which was said to be 'hillie and pestered with snow, wherefore it is neither so warme as Portugall, nor yet so wealthy'. It was rich in silver mines and the people 'tractable, civill, wittie, courteous, without deceit, in vertue and honest conversation exceeding all other nations lately discovered'. The government was said to consist of '3 estates'. At the top was a high priest responsible for all religious matters, public and private, who had 'so large a Dominion and revenues so great, that eftsones he beardeth the petie Kings and Princes there'. The 'second principal Magistrate' was called 'Vo' who was 'made by succession and birth, honoured as a God'. He could not set his foot on the ground without losing his office but had grown so rich 'that although hee may have neither land nor any revenues otherwise, yet may he be accounted the wealthiest man in all Japan' because of the bribes he received from eager solicitors seeking positions of honour. The third officer is a 'Judge' who discharges the executive and judicial functions of government. He has the right to command the nobility to support him in applying the laws but in practice many matters 'are ended rather by might and armes, then determined by law'. Japan is also portrayed as a land of great cities with six universities. The Frois letter itself corresponded more closely to the reality. Frois described Japan as a land rich in silver, plagued by typhoons and earthquakes where the summer was hot and the winter cold although the author erred in suggesting that the Japanese 'never had greatly to doe with other Nations'. Most of the letter was concerned with Japanese religion and religious practices but Frois shows more understanding of recent developments in Japan than Willes's garbled account. Frois wrote of a polity formally united but presently wracked by rebellion and civil war, causing it to shatter into sixty-six kingdoms. The emperor – clearly meaning shogun – enjoyed little beyond the respect accorded him by the nobility, while a 'high Priest' lived on in Kyoto 'maintained by almes', honoured as a god but forbidden to set foot on the ground.[53]

Robert Parke's translation of Juan González de Mendoza's *Historie of the great and mightie kingdome of China*, which appeared in 1588, added no new facts about Japan but speculated that the Japanese 'who in their bodies & faces differ very little fro[m] the *Chinos*' were originally Chinese who had been banished to the archipelago after participating in a failed plot to topple the 'king of *China*'. This accounted for the hatred that existed between the two people. Once settled on their islands the Japanese had developed their own culture and language. However, their 'wittes (although they be good and subtill) are naturally knowne to be inclined unto warres, robberies and doing of evill'. Fortunately, these tendencies had been tempered somewhat by the Jesuits who were credited with sterling achievement in making the Japanese 'much better Christians then those of the Orientall or East Indians' even if their further success was hampered by the paucity of missionaries. González de Mendoza was sceptical about reports that the Japanese traded with the Amazones Islands, said to lie to the east of the archipelago and said to be inhabited entirely by women. The *raison d'être* for the publication of the translation was made clear by Parke in the epistle dedicatory to Cavendish. It was, he wrote, to give Cavendish encouragement to undertake a voyage to China, 'the rich Iland of Iapon' and the Philippines by way of the northwest 'for proofe whereof there bee many infallible reasons, and diverse great experiences to be yeelded', in order to sell English goods, especially cloth. Parke hoped that Christopher and Cosmos 'may serue as our interpreters in our first traficke thither' and was confident that 'many worshipfull and wealthie marchants of this citie and other places would most wilingly ioyne their purses with yours'.[54] He did not mention any names but it is certain that his translation and that of Cesare de Fedrici's *The Voyage and Trauaile of M. Caesar Frederick, merchant of Venice, into the East India, the Indies, and beyond the Indies*, which appeared in the same year, influenced the signatories of the petition to the Privy Council in October 1589 and the sponsors of Lancaster's voyage in 1591.

Fedrici had travelled for eighteen years in the East Indies visiting the sub-continent, Malacca, Siam and Pegu. His book provided information about commercial practices, trade flows (he mentioned the profitable trade in silk and silver which the Portuguese enjoyed with Japan) and gave some general impressions of the geography of the lands there. The English translation was made by Thomas Hickock, who was himself probably a London Levant merchant. Hickock claimed the purpose of his translation was 'the Profitable Instruction of Merchants and all Othere Travellers for their Better Direction and Knowledge of These Countreyes'.[55]

In the first edition of Richard Hakluyt's *Principall Navigations*, which appeared in 1589 and became the most influential publication in English about the worlds the Europeans were encountering on their voyages overseas, there were a few scattered references to Japan: the mention of Christopher and Cosmos; Willes's comment (from the *History of Trauayle*) that 'the Giapans...be most desirous to be acquainted with strangers'; the pilot John Davis's observation that the Japanese and Tartars were 'small eyed' like the eskimos; and a note derived from a map brought back by Cavendish that in Fukien province the Chinese had two great garrison cities 'that keepe watch upon the *Iapons*'.[55] In the second edition, which appeared in three volumes from 1598–1600, Hakluyt included Willes and Federici and published, for the first time, Fitch's account of his travels including his brief discussion of the Japan voyage from Macao. Fitch's only other mention of Japan was that '[a]ll the Chineans, Japonians and Cauchin Chineans do write downwards, and they do write with a

fine pensill made of dogs or cats haire'.[57] Hakluyt added new letters
by Frois, written between 1590 and 1594, under the title 'Three
Severall Testamonies Concerning the mighty kingdom of Coray,
tributary to the king of China, and bordering upon his Northwest
frontier', and 'A briefe note concerning the extreme Northern
province of Japan called Zuegara, situated thirtie degre jorney from
Miaco which argueth the Isle of Japan to be of greater extension
Northward, then it is ordinarily described in maps, or supposed to
be', from a letter by Frois written in 1596. The letters were taken
from the Italian edition published in Rome. The letter about Korea
gave an extensive account of the 'resolute determination of
Quabacondono [Hideyoshi] the great Monarch of all Japan, to
invade and conquere China by the way of Coray'. In his 1594 letter,
Frois wrote that '[t]he whole Empire of Japan is now in the handes
of this king Quabacondono' and that the country was at peace.
Hideyoshi was credited with establishing an enduring framework for
strong but fair government. Frois's assessment was both accurate
and inaccurate (he overestimated the permanence of the Hideyoshi
succession) but he shows familiarity with some of the principal
measures that Hideyoshi had used to strengthen his rule, including
the sword hunt (*katana gari*), the 1591 edict rigidly defining the social
order and forbidding mobility between its constituent parts and his
limited use of what evolved into the system of alternate attendance
(*sankin kotai*).[58]

In the same year as the first volume of the second edition of the
Principal Navigations came off the presses in 1598, Linschoten's
Itinerario was published, at Hakluyt's suggestion, in an English
translation. (Some of Linschoten's material had already appeared in
the *Principal Navigations*.) Linschoten surveyed the countries of the
Indies but his pen portrait of Japan was derived from the usual Jesuit
sources although at Goa he had met some Japanese and, attracted by
the possibility of making money on the Japan voyage, had contemplated going there himself. He described the country as 'cold and
proceeding of much rayne, Snow and Ice'. It had 'some mines of
silver, which from thence is by the Portingals yearly brought vnto
China, and there bartered for silke, and other Chinish wares which
the Japeans have neede of'. The Portuguese 'doe greatly profit' from
this trade. Linschoten mentioned that three sorts of silk were carried,
the best consisting of white Lankin (Nanking) silk, and he gave
details of prices and local weights and currencies. He estimated the
profits which the captain major of the Japan voyage could expect as
ranging between 150,000–200,000 ducats. The people themselves
were described as courteous. They were talented craftsmen 'and
cunning workmen in all kind of hardie workes, they are sharpe
witted and quickly learne any thing they see'. They esteemed fine

pieces of pottery ('the earthen cups which they drinke [tea] in') 'as we doe of Diamants, Rubies and other precious stones'. Their government was quite different from that of China (although he repeated González de Mendoza's story about the founding of Japan), the country being divided into a number of kingdoms in some of which the Jesuits had made progress. These kingdoms were further subdivided into what the translator said were the equivalent of earldoms and dukedoms, lordships and lord lieutenantships. All men were bound to serve their superiors in peace and war and live in a style corresponding to their rank. Responsibility for maintaining law and order was devolved throughout the society right down to the family level. Linschoten mentioned the visit of the young Kyushu nobles to Europe which gave him an excuse to launch into an extended attack on the rapacious greed of the Jesuits not only in Japan but elsewhere in the Indies, perhaps a reflection of the views of his former employer, the Archbishop of Goa, a Dominican.[59]

In 1601 Giovani Botero's *The travellers breviat, or an historicall description of the most famous kingdomes in the world* described Japan as comprising sixty-six islands, similar to the Maldives or Hebrides. Botero's account was a travesty of Jesuit letters, contadictory and confused. The soil was said to be barren, the people hunters, yet the considerable wealth of the present ruler, 'Fassiha' (Hideyoshi), was reported to be derived from rice. Botero implied that Japan was gripped by political instability but his comment that Hideyoshi resembled 'the shadow rather then the king of the ancient & magnificent Monarchs of Japan' does not square with his assertion that Hideyoshi was building many palaces, temples and towns 'the like whereof are nowhere to be seene'. Botero mentioned Hideyoshi's invasion of the continent but alleged (presciently, but unknowingly so) that he was about to receive his nemesis from a new enemy coming from the eastern part of Japan.[60]

Of greater practical consequence for English efforts to break into the Indies trade was the publication in the third book of Linschoten's *Itinerario* of numerous sea routes to the Indies used by the Portuguese, culled from their rutter books (*roteiros*). The rutters, detailed sets of sailing directions, included a number of routes betwen China and Hirado and Nagasaki. One, by the Spanish captain and pilot major for the viceroy of New Spain, Francisco de Gualle, described Japan as 'a country full of Rice, Corne, Fish, and Flesh' and the Japanese as 'an indifferent and reasonable people to Traffick with and that there they haue much siluer', and was reprinted by Hakluyt. Two others were provided by the Dutchman Dirck Gerritsz, who had made voyages from Macao to Nagasaki on the náo *Santa Cruz* as a master gunner in 1585 and 1586. Linschoten met him at Goa and like Linchoten he provided invaluable information to Dutch merchants about Portuguese activity in Asia after his return to the Netherlands in 1590.[61]

The Portuguese rutters printed by Linschoten had the virtue of describing tested, proven and established routes to the Indies. It is not surprising, therefore, that regardless of Hakluyt's personal enthusiasm for a northwest passage and the Company's later flirtation with the possibilities of discovering a northern route, the directors placed their hopes for a successful trade with the Indies on the Cape route.

By the eve of the departure of the Eighth Voyage for the Indies with instructions to set up a factory in Japan, more information about Japan was available in English than had been the case after the arrival of Christopher and Cosmos. But it was of very uneven quality. Readers of Hakluyt's second edition of the *Principal Navigations* or of Linschoten, even discriminating readers such as the directors of the East India Company who read these works for guidance in reaching their commercial decisions, would have been hard-pressed to form a clear picture of Japan. Yet these two collections were without question the most important sources of information about the Indies and other parts of the world in English. On 29 January 1600, Hakluyt himself had been requested by the court of the Company in connection with the First Voyage 'to sett downe in wryting a note of the principall places in the East Indies wher Trade. . .*is* to be had to thend the same may be vsed for the better instrucon of o^r factors'. He was paid £10 for these services plus 30s for maps he provided.[62]

A careful reader would be able to reconcile Linschoten's description of the Japanese polity as a number of kingdoms with Frois's portrayal of Japan in the second edition of the *Principal Navigations* as a recently re-unified country. But it would be impossible to have any clear idea about the country itself and the people. Confusion existed over such elementary yet essential matters for commerce as climate (Frois says it was hot in summer but cold in winter, Linschoten that it was cold, although he mentioned that the 'common Corne is Ryce').[63] And while it was interesting to have such anthropological detail about the use of chopsticks, religious practices and the treatment of children, the random manner in which it was presented lacked context and therefore meaning. Besides, there was not the pressing need for people in England to understand Japan at the same deep level that the Jesuits were attempting in order to further their missionary work. Nevertheless, the general impression created by the various accounts published in English was of a civilised society, well ordered and governed, militarily strong with an administrative system that was as sophisticated as that of contemporary England. It was a society which stressed the rule of law, even if warfare had temporarily weakened central government, and one in which degree or hierarchy was the cornerstone of the social order. These were attributes the English were familiar with and admired. They were among the hallmarks of what was thought to constitute a civilised, wealth-creating society. Japan was no frontier society, its people neither barbarians nor savages, ignorant nor slothful nor negligent about husbanding and utilising their natural resources in order to create national wealth, unlike the Irish or the American Indians of Virginia whose neglect in this respect was used to justify colonisation. A sixteenth-century MS volume based on Jesuit letters and intended to give 'the state of the mightiest princes that now liue in the worlde' included a description of 'The Kinge of Japonie'. Among the criteria for inclusion in the select group was excellence in government. Japan, then, was well to the top of the scale of social development. The Japanese were not a people without a history.[64] Japan's apparent openness to Christianity was a bonus but not a factor of major importance to the English.

To the directors of the East India Company whose interests lay in commerce rather than in the subtleties and complexities of religious or child rearing practices, Japan had the virtue of appearing as a strong and important country, open to trade, in which the Portuguese participated reaping handsome profits for themselves. Reports about the climate suggested a promising market for English cloth. A voyage of reconnaissance seemed well worth the effort, particularly as the directors had concrete information at last of the presence of an Englishman in Japan, William Adams.

(iii)   William Adams and the Dutch in Japan

William Adams is usually accredited with being the first Englishman to reach Japan. More accurately he was the first *recorded* Englishman to arrive there. It is possible that other Britons preceded him. Portuguese ships like those of other European maritime nations at this time had international crews. For example, a Scots pilot in Portuguese service in the East Indies in the early 1540s may have sailed as far as the Ryūkyū kingdom.[65] As with the French Foreign Legion in modern times, country of origin and personal belief mattered less than a willingness to serve. Adams's story has been recounted numerous times both as fact and fiction, and has even been made into a television mini-series. But his life was neither unique nor his position in Japan quite as influential as he himself liked to suggest or as others have subsequently made out.

Adams was born in 1564 at Gillingham in Kent.[66] He had at least one brother and from the age of twelve until twenty-four served as an apprentice to the shipbuilder Nicholas Diggens at the Limehouse

on the Thames. Diggens was a first-rate shipwright and later undertook a lot of repair work for ships of the East India Company. He
was also a luminary in the local parish of Stepney where Adams was
married in August 1589 to Mary Hyn. The fact that he served an
apprenticeship and with a man of Diggens's stature, suggests that
Adams came from a fairly comfortable social background.[67] Adams
completed his apprenticeship on turning twenty-four, the normal
practice as stipulated in the Statute of Artificers of 1563 which
regulated apprenticeship, at around the time of the Spanish Armada
and he participated in the action against the Spanish possibly as
master of the *Richard Dyffylde*, a small supply ship of 120 tons.[68] Like
many of his contemporaries his service did not necessarily stem from
patriotic motives alone. As Professor Andrews reminds us, even
Drake could not desist from a measure of privateering in the midst of
the Armada campaign.[69] Adams later served in the Barbary Company which had been established in 1585 with a charter for twelve
years (which was not renewed) to conduct trade with Morocco.
Adams probably served on one of the ships chartered by the Company which, unlike the East India Company in its infancy, did not
build its own vessels.[70] These ships, usually of 100 tons, took
advantage of their course which fortuitously crossed the homeward
path of Spanish galleons and Portuguese carracks, to engage in
privateering, often with specific instructions to do so from their
owners.[71] According to the Portuguese chronicler of the East Indies,
Diogo do Couto, writing in 1611, Adams, whom he suggests was
a good cosmographer with some knowledge of astronomy,
mentioned to the Jesuits sometime after his arrival in Japan that he
had served on Dutch voyages in search of a northwest passage from
1593–5. Adams himself does not mention such service but says that
he remained in the Barbary service 'about 11 or 12 years...until the
Indian traffic from Holland [began], which Indian traffic I was
desirous to make a little experience of the small knowledge that God
had given me.'[72] His entry into the service of a Rotterdam
voorcompagnie voyage came through Hans Broers who traded with
Morocco. The Dutch were keen to take advantage of superior
English maritime skills at this time. The distinguished navigator
John Davis sailed with Cornelis de Houtman's second fleet round the
Cape to Achin in 1598 and Adams was not the only Englishman to
join the Rotterdam company's voyage.[73] Some thirteen other
Englishmen, including Adams's brother Thomas, thirty English
musicians and a Scot went along as well. The voyage, commanded
by Jacques Mahu, was yet another attempt to repeat Drake's success
by sailing through the Straits of Magellan and attacking Spanish
settlements in South America before setting off across the Pacific for
the East Indies.[74]

The five ships comprising the voyage (the *Hoop*, 250 tons and 130 men; the admiral's flagship, the *Geloof*, 160 tons and 109 men; the *Liefde*, 150 tons and 110 men; the *Trouw*, 110 tons and 86 men; and the *Blijde Boodschap*, 75 tons and 56 men) left Rotterdam on 27 June 1598 (NS) under the command of Jacques Mahu.[75] Adams was pilot of the *Hoop* but he later transferred to the *Liefde* under the command of the vice-admiral Simon de Cortes who died on the voyage. One of his shipmates on the *Hoop* was the gunner Dirck Gerritsz, the veteran of Japan. Their course took them down the Barbary and Guinea coasts where in December on the island of Annobon they attacked a Portuguese settlement after being refused permission to land to care for their sick.[76] The Portuguese fled into the interior of the island and the Dutch crew were able to disembark and refresh themselves with plentiful supplies of fruit. On 2 January 1599 the ships set out across the Atlantic to Brazil, which they reached on 22 January, and edged down towards the Straits where they arrived on 6 April. These proved impassable because of the onset of winter necessitating a forced rest until the following September. During this time many men died as food stocks became depleted. On 3 September the ships finally passed through the Straits with the intention of sailing up the western coast of South America and raiding the territories claimed by the Spanish and planting the Dutch flag. As was to be expected in the treacherous waters where two mighty oceans clashed, the ships became separated. However, arrangements had been made for a rendezvous at latitude 46°, off the Chilean coast. Only two ships made it to the rendezvous, the *Liefde* and the *Hoop*. The *Geloof*, with Gerritsz now aboard, turned back and sailed for the Netherlands. The *Trouw* and the *Blijde Boodschap* may have tried to make the rendezvous and failed. The *Trouw* succeeded in crossing the Pacific with its crew reduced to twenty-four, including the Scot, Willem Loyen (presumably William Lyon), and four Indians taken aboard off the South American coast. They were all arrested by the Portuguese when they made landfall in Tidore and only three or four made it back to the Netherlands; Lyon was still a prisoner in Goa in 1608. The *Blijde Boodschap* was seized by the Spanish at Valparaiso in Chile. Eleven men, including Gerritsz, eventually made it back to the Netherlands.

It was only by chance that the *Liefde* and the *Hoop* found each other. The *Liefde* arrived first, spending twenty-eight days at the rendezvous. The crew found it difficult to establish contact with the local people who brought them food in return for trinkets but would not engage in any trade with the Dutch for fear of Spanish reprisals. Accordingly the *Liefde* moved up the coast to the island of Mocha and then approached the mainland near the island of Sta María. Short of victuals, they attempted to land but were repulsed by hostile natives firing arrows. A landing party finally reached the shore and tried to convince the natives of their peaceful intentions. This met with some initial success and the natives brought wine and potatoes in exchange for iron, silver and cloth. However, the crew tested their luck too far. On 9 November, hoping to secure more provisions, another landing party of twenty-three men including the senior officers and Thomas Adams, went ashore and were ambushed by a large force of Indians. The remaining crew weighed anchor and withdrew to Sta María where a joyous reunion was had with the crew of the *Hoop*. The *Hoop*'s pilot was Adams's friend Timothy Shotten, veteran of Cavendish's circumnavigation, and her crew had been similarly devastated by native attacks at Mocha.

At this stage it was decided (wisely) to abandon any idea of molesting Spanish settlements, especially when they learned from some Spanish whom they met at Sta María that the authorities were aware of the presence of Dutch ships on the coast and that the *Blijde Boodschap* had been seized. Instead of transferring all goods and men to one ship and burning the other, a sensible proposal given the much reduced manpower, it was decided that both ships, with Hudcopee in command of the *Hoop* as admiral and Jacob Jansz van Quaeckernack, the captain of the *Liefde*, as vice-admiral should, in Adams's words, 'direct our course for Japan, having understood that the cloth was there good marchandise', a supposition encouraged by Geeritsz who, before his transfer to the *Blijde Boodschap* from the *Liefde*, had reported that 'woolen cloth was in great estimation in that Iland'. In setting their course for Japan the ships were relying on what turned out to be a false latitude for the position of Japan. All available maps and globes were wrong. Even Linschoten's *Itinerario* gave the southern point of the archipelago as 30°31'. On 27 November the two ships 'stood away directly for Iapan'. After crossing the equator they reached some islands, probably the Hawaiian group, and had a brief skirmish with cannibals in which they lost eight men who, preferring to take their chances ashore, jumped ship. Around 23 February 1600 the two ships were separated in a fierce storm (the *Blijde Boodschap* perishing) and after a voyage of four months and twenty-three days from Sta María, the *Liefde* sighted land around mid-April at Sashio near Usuki in the province of Bungo, Kyushu.[77] During the arduous and debilitating voyage the crew had been further whittled down to twenty-four or twenty-five survivors, many having been wiped out by disease contracted on the trans-Pacific crossing. Only about six were able to stand on their feet. The rest including the captain were sick or exhausted and another six soon died. Nevertheless, the first non-Iberian vessels had reached Japan.

In the records of the Matsūra family (the lords of Hirado),

compiled long after the event, there is a tantalising suggestion that a Dutch ship visited Hirado in 1597. This is highly unlikely. The most plausible explanation is that the ship was Portuguese. There was no Japan voyage from Macao in that year but a Macao junk owned by Francisco de Gouveia made an unofficial voyage, possibly with the approval of the Macao authorities. All that is known about this voyage is that it left Nagasaki to return to Macao early in 1598. It is possible that De Gouveia's junk called first at Hirado before proceeding to Nagasaki. The Japanese sources refer to 'Frans Golvernados' (presumably a garbled version of De Gouveia) and one Hector Kars, who could have been a Hollander in Portuguese service like Gerritsz and others before.[78]

The arrival of the *Liefde*, a seemingly innocuous event, was to have important repercussions on Japan's foreign relations and the conduct of its foreign trade. But this was not apparent at the time. At first the survivors were treated well by the daimyo, who must have believed that good fortune had blown a náo to his shores. The men were given a house to rest in. The arrival of the *Liefde* quickly became known to the Portuguese. Two Jesuits who lived nearby had gone to the distressed ship's help when it first appeared but quickly turned back when they recognised that it was Dutch. They reported the news to their colleagues at Nagasaki who informed the *daikan* (the Nagasaki deputy) that the new arrivals were Lutheran pirates. While the epithet 'Lutheran', if it really was employed, would have meant nothing to the *daikan* and his officials, the description of the new arrivals as pirates would have registered and he went himself to Bungo where he ordered that the ship be brought into port and an inventory made of its goods. These consisted of some eleven chests of cloth, coral, glass beads, mirrors and spectacles, nineteen large pieces of ordnance and some small ones, 500 muskets, 5,000 canon balls, and other weaponry. Two of the Dutch crew, Gisbert de Coning and Jan Abelszoon van Oudewater, tried to ingratiate themselves with the Japanese and the Portuguese, one of them claiming that he was captain of the ship. These were trying days, especially after the hardships of the trans-pacific crossing, and the linguistic confusion could only have created misunderstanding and reinforced fear.

The Jesuits were instinctively jealous of their position in Japan. They had resented the arrival of the Franciscans in the 1590s and the last thing they wanted was the presence of heretics from the rebellious Netherlands encroaching on their missionary territory. On the face of it they seemed to have a couple of good cards to play against the Protestants: they could portray them as pirates and as rebellious subjects of the Iberian king. The attitude of Portuguese merchants is more complex. Clearly those who were directly connected with the official Macao–Nagasaki trade shared Jesuit misgivings about a possible Protestant intrusion into the trade, but on commercial rather than theological grounds; they did not want new competition. Individual Portuguese trading on their own account would not have been so hostile. For all the acts of aggression that were committed in Asian waters by the English and Dutch against the Portuguese and Spanish, an undercurrent of friendship and a sense of common culture that transcended political and religious differences or commercial rivalry existed as well. Van Noort's near contemporary round-the-world voyage met with many individual Portuguese who were both friendly and helpful, and Cavendish on his circumnavigation in 1588 met two Portuguese in Java who were welcomed with 'no small joy' as fellow Christians, even allies. The two men had strong political views of their own: they resented the unification of the Portuguese and Spanish crowns and were supporters of the pre?tender to the Portuguese throne, Dom António.[79]

The Nagasaki *daikan* did not need any promptings from the Jesuits and Portuguese merchants to view the new arrivals with suspicion. The memory of the wakō and Hideyoshi's efforts to suppress them were still fresh in mind, and pirates had been active in the waters off Bungo in the past. The *Liefde* did not appear like a mission from a foreign potentate. The circumstances of its arrival were unorthodox, its cargo small and unconventional compared with what the *nanbanjin*, or southern barbarians as the first Europeans in Japan were styled, usually brought and it was well armed and its cargo included a lot of weaponry.[80] The problem of how to deal with the newcomers was referred to higher authority, at this time the interim government that had been established by Hideyoshi before his death in 1598. This consisted of the *go tairo* or Five Elders, among whom Tokugawa Ieyasu was the pivotal figure. Almost one month after the arrival of the *Liefde*, Adams, the fittest of the senior crew members, was transported to Osaka accompanied by an impressive escort and found himself before Ieyasu. He was interrogated and placed in detention. However, it was not a naïve curiosity which prompted Ieyasu's questions. The *Liefde* had arrived in a Japan quite different from that which the first Portuguese had encountered when they were blown on to Tanegashima in 1543.

In 1600 Japan was in a transition from *sengoku* warfare to the strong, united and stable polity whose foundations Hideyoshi had laid in the later sixteenth century. The stewardship of this polity was to fall into hands different from those Hideyoshi had envisaged, the Tokugawa, who re-established the shogunate in their own line and survived in power until 1867 when they themselves were swept aside by forces they could no longer control.

Hideyoshi, a parvenu, had sought to buttress his position by gathering to himself and his family tokens of legitimacy, especially titles conferred by the imperial court. The court was forthcoming in granting such titles to the Toyotomi, as it had been to Nobunaga before, hoping thereby to regain lost prestige and political influence for the nobility.[81] In 1585 Hideyoshi was promoted to the post of *kampaku*, or imperial regent, and in 1591 when his then heir (his nephew Hidetsugu who was later ordered into exile in 1595 and then forced to commit suicide) was elected to this post, Hideyoshi became *taikō*, retired imperial regent, the title by which he is best remembered. He made conspicuous displays of his power, rebuilding the capital in which he located his Kyoto headquarters, the Jūrakutei or residence of Gathered Peace (which he had demolished after Hidetsugi's death), the construction projects reported in European accounts. In 1591 he surrounded the city with a wall. Some historians have explained the grandiose projects of his last years – the brutal deaths of Hidetsugu and the tea master Sen no Rikyū, the crucifixion of the Franciscans and Japanese Christians in 1597, and the activist foreign policy which sought to impose tributary status on the Philippines and the *folie de grandeur* of the invasion of China through Korea – as signs of madness. Questions of definition aside, this can never be settled conclusively and like all such explanations is at best an oversimplification.[82]

Hideyoshi was a great warrior and a great statesman, not only restoring order but pursuing policies which ensured that his achievements, even if fragile during his lifetime, would outlast him. Commenting on his death, a Spanish observer in Manila, where the customary conquistador self-confidence was put on the defensive by anxiety about Hideyoshi's aggressive posturing in foreign affairs, wrote that with the death of 'the lord of Xapon, the state of some affairs may be changed, but not the government – for this, they say, is well conducted'.[83] This was a shrewd assessment. Hideyoshi's justification for appointing his young son Hideyori, born in 1593, as his successor was rooted in the firm belief that bonds of obligation tying lord and vassal proved most enduring and he pinned his hopes for a peaceful transition on the Five Elders, all sworn to uphold the settlement. But a peaceful transition was not forthcoming. The regents were divided over adherence to the testament and their support for Hideyori was not unanimous. These divisions were reflected among the regional daimyo. The challenge to the settlement was led by the most powerful of the regents, Tokugawa Ieyasu. Conspiracies were hatched and tensions mounted leading to open war and the decisive battle of Sekigahara in October 1600, in which the Tokugawa and their supporters were victorious.

As Adams stood before Ieyasu in Osaka in May 1600 he was totally unaware of these larger issues. Ieyasu too had other concerns, particularly the intrigues of his fellow regent Uesugi Kagekatsu. Nevertheless, while questioning Adams, Ieyasu was keen to find out where the *Liefde* had come from, why it had come to Japan, and even about the European balance of power. Unfortunately, only Adams's retrospective account of this meeting exists but the discussions with Adams were the first occasion on which the Japanese were able to hear about Protestant Europe at any length, about the profound religious and ideological differences dividing the continent, and the open warfare that existed among the European powers. To this extent it marked the end of the monopoly of information about Europe that the Catholic missionaries had enjoyed. The Jesuits and mendicants may have had their differences over how best to further missionary work in Japan but all parties had realised the importance of providing the Japanese with a picture of a Christendom that was in all essentials united and Catholic. There is no indication as to how the Japanese, whose model for the conduct of international relations remained the Chinese tributary one, or rather their interpretation of it, conceived of inter-European relations, if indeed they thought about such matters other than superficially at this time. It was a slow and painstaking process for the Japanese to piece together the complex interrelations and ideological divisions among the various *nanbanjin* who arrived on Japan's shores, and to begin to appreciate the differences between them. Hideyoshi himself had been intrigued by the character of the Spanish monarch (since 1580 ruler of both Spain and Portugal) even if he may have judged the Iberian presence in Manila as a possible threat. However, such strategic considerations apart, the image of the conquistadors was of a disciplined, tough, fighting-force in the service of a powerful ruler whose pretensions and claims to divine sanction were a match for Hideyoshi's own. However, the survivors of the *Liefde*'s crew were the first concrete evidence that Europe was not united and that even if they were Christians, Adams and his colleagues were of a different 'sect' from the Iberians and Lusitanians and that the two sects did not live in harmony. Adams's eloquence in describing contemporary Europe convinced Ieyasu that the new arrivals were something other than the 'theeues and robbers of all nations' the Jesuits and Portuguese portrayed them as, and the future shogun accepted his explanation that the *Liefde* had come to Japan for trade, a purpose which Ieyasu welcomed wholeheartedly.

Adams was kept in detention until late June when he was allowed to rejoin his shipmates and the *Liefde* at Sakai. Entreaties to the Five Elders for permission to refit the ship so that it could continue its voyage fell on deaf ears. The precedent set by the treatment of the *San Felipe* was followed. The ship was considered a wreck and confiscated along with its goods, although according to Adams, compensation of 50,000 reals (a generous amount) was awarded, most of which was used up in fruitless pleas to be allowed to refit the ship and leave. According to a Japanese source, the *Liefde* was shipwrecked again, this time beyond repair, on its voyage from Sakai (where Ieyasu had viewed her) to Edo (Tokyo) where she was to be examined more closely. Adams only mentions a storm on this journey and provides little clue about any damage sustained.[84] But even if the ship was damaged irrevocably the crew could still have left Japan on either Chinese or Japanese vessels bound for southeast Asia. (They would not have wanted to leave on Portuguese or Spanish shipping and face detention and possibly death in Macao or Manila; after all, the Dutch were still at war with Spain.)[85] The exact reason for Ieyasu's prohibition against the crew leaving Japan is unknown but his determination to improve Japanese maritime and shipbuilding skills and to develop mining technology clearly influenced the decision. The arrival of the *Liefde* was a fortuitous occurrence as some of its crew possessed the very skills Ieyasu was seeking: such men were valuable assets.

Ieyasu had already made indirect overtures to the Spanish in Manila through the medium of the Franciscan missionary, Jerónimo de Jesús. Jerónimo informed Manila that Ieyasu sought master shipwrights and workmen to help construct ships capable of carrying Japanese as far as New Spain. When the request reached Manila it caused alarm. The Spanish felt that 'the Islands greatest security...has always been that the Japanese have no ships and are ignorant in matters of navigation', an inaccurate assertion. To comply with the request 'would be equivalent to giving them the very weapons they needed to destroy the Philippines'. The Spanish decided to stall and sent a message to Ieyasu advising him that such an important matter had to be referred to New Spain and eventually to the Spanish king himself. This they expected to take three years. Unfortunately, the ship carrying the Japanese ambassador who received this letter was wrecked off Taiwan on the return voyage. In view of the Jesuit–mendicant rivalry, Jerónimo de Jesús had a vested interest in creating the impression in Manila that Ieyasu's intentions were peaceful – De Jesús cited Ieyasu's withdrawal of Japanese forces from Korea and his firm opposition to any invasion of Taiwan which the Spanish feared might be the prelude to an invasion of the Philippines themselves – and that he favoured the promotion of Christianity even if this was pure invention on the missionary's part. But unlike Hideyoshi's missives, Ieyasu's intentions were indeed unambiguously peaceful and in his letter to Manila De Jesús noted that Ieyasu had also invited the Spanish to trade with Japan hoping to attract galleons to call at Uraga near Edo on their way to and from Acapulco. After one galleon, the *Espiritu Santo*, was seized in Tosa in 1602 after being blown off course, he sent eight safe-conduct passes to Manila extending his protection to any future galleons that might find themselves in Japan. In 1609 Ieyasu took advantage of the presence in Japan of Rodrigo de Vivero y Velasco, the former governor of the Philippines, to draw up a treaty. De Vivero was *en route* to New Spain to become interim governor there, when his ship, the 1,000 ton *San Francisco*, had been wrecked on the coast of Chiba, and was himself in favour of improved relations with Japan. The treaty gave the Spanish the right to set up a factory at a location near Edo where churches would be permitted and granted them freedom to call at any Japanese port. In return, the Spanish were to send one or two hundred mining experts from New Spain to teach the Japanese about the latest mining techniques and receive a share of any increased output. Ieyasu also mentioned the possibility of an official embassy to the Spanish court. However, Hispano-Japanese relations did not take off nor in any way fulfil the bright hopes of the treaty. The miners never came from New Spain – no loss to the Japanese who managed to exploit fully their natural resources without Spanish assistance – and trade between Japan and the Iberian empire was minimal. The Spanish were unable to shake off the suspicion that their activities in east Asia were expansionist and relations between Spain and Japan, such as they were, were broken off by the shogunate in 1624.[86] De Vivero at least was able to leave Japan on a vessel of 120 tons, one of two ships whose construction Adams had supervised.[87]

For three of the *Liefde*'s crew at least, Adams, Jan Joosten Loden-steiyn and Melchior van Santvoort, the *Liefde*'s purser, life in Japan provided new opportunities which they grasped eagerly. Adams and Joosten were both treated as informal advisors, of whom there were a number, to Ieyasu. They gave advice about foreign countries, and in Adams's case, instruction in geometry and mathematics, although this almost certainly had the character of a cultural or recreational pastime rather than of a formal, educational pursuit for Ieyasu. The two were made *hatamoto* (bannermen) and granted small estates. Adams's, which he described as like a lordship in England with eighty or ninety husbandmen at Hemi on the Miura peninsula near Edo, was valued at 150 or 250 koku of rice. Richard Cocks who visited the estate in September 1616 said that it included over one hundred farms and households and that Adams 'hath the power of life & death over them, they being his slaues & he absolute authorities over them as any tono [lord] in Japaon hath over his vassals'.[88] Joosten's estate at Nagasaki was smaller, approximately 100 koku.[89] Both men had houses in Edo, areas which still bear their familiar names in Japan, Adams, *anjin*, in Anji-machi (pilot area, now *anjin-cho*), Joosten in Yayoso-gashi (now Yaesu near Tokyo station). Adams, Joosten and van Santvoort became involved in Japan's flourishing direct trade with southeast Asia and its coastal sea trade. Adams also took a Japanese consort by whom he had two children and later kept a mistress at Hirado by whom he had another child. In Adams's words, God 'hath provided for me after my great misery'; life in Japan worked out for the best.[90]

There are few references to the lives of the survivors in Japan. In 1605 Adams declined an offer from a Jesuit, possibly João Rodrigues (Tçuzzu, the interpreter) another of Ieyasu's informal advisors, of a safe conduct from Nagasaki for Adams and the other *Liefde* crew if they left Japan. Adams and the Jesuit engaged in an impromptu theological exchange and Adams, described as an 'obstinate heretic', cited scripture, erroneously according to the Jesuit, to justify his case. He rejected the offer on the grounds that Ieyasu had refused to grant them permission to leave, although this was no longer the case at least for some of the *Liefde*'s former crew.[91] Adams did not trust the value of such a safe conduct. The incident is an indication of how unwelcome the small Protestant presence was to the missionaries. Adams's fear for his safety at Manila makes it unlikely that he ventured there in 1608 on a mission on behalf of Ieyasu.[92]

News of the arrival of a Dutch vessel in Japan did not take long to reach Europe. It was brought back by Oliver van Noort who had left Rotterdam some three months after the Mahu expedition. Van Noort's voyage, in which Englishmen also participated, encountered similar problems as Mahu's in passing through the Straits of Magellan where one of the three surviving ships got lost. Two ships crossed the Pacific and challenged the Spanish in Philippine waters before sailing on to Borneo. One ship, the *Endracht*, was lost in the fight and the survivors were garotted by the Spanish. Near the Borneo coast on 3 January 1601 (NS), Van Noort's ship met with a Japanese vessel bound for Manila which had been blown off course. (He had already encountered another Japanese vessel near Manila the previous December from whose master, with whom he got on well, he acquired useful general information about Japan and intelligence about Portuguese trade there.)[93] The pilot, a Portuguese, Emanuel Luiz, had previously lived and worked in Malacca and Macao. He told van Noort about the arrival of a Dutch ship of around 250 tons with fourteen survivors in Japan which led Van Noort to assume that it was Mahu's *Hoop*. Van Noort issued the junk with a safe conduct pass made out in the name of the Prince of Orange and urged Luiz to assist the Dutchmen on his return to Japan. Van Noort continued his voyage via Java and round the Cape, arriving home in August 1601 thereby completing the first Dutch circumnavigation. An extract of Van Noort's account was published in September 1601, mentioning the presence of men from Mahu's ships in Japan and the full account of the voyage was published the following year in Rotterdam with subsequent editions in other languages.[94] After Van Noort's return, details of his voyage would have filtered back to England possibly giving rise to expectations that the survivors might include the *Hoop*'s pilot, Adams.

News of the Dutch presence in the East Indies soon reached Japan, conveyed either by Japanese vessels trading in southeast Asia or by the Portuguese. In 1605 Ieyasu gave permission for Jacob Jansz Quaeckernaeck, the captain of the *Liefde*, and Melchior van Santvoort, to sail for Patani where Jacob van Neck had established a factory in August 1602. They carried an offer of generous trading privileges from Ieyasu to the Dutch. The two men travelled on a junk belonging to the daimyo of Hirado carrying a *shuinjō*, or vermilion seal pass.[95] At Patani the two established contact with the Dutch and provided them with accurate information that it was the *Liefde* not the *Hoop* which had reached Japan. However, the VOC had more important matters to contend with. A Dutch fleet under the command of Quaeckernaeck's cousin, Cornelis Matelieff de Jonge, was attempting to storm Malacca. The fleet had left Holland in May 1605 with instructions to sail for China and Japan and seize Malacca. Unable to find a passage home, Quaeckernaeck travelled down the Malay peninsula and made contact with Matelieff's fleet in the midst of the unsuccessful attack on Malacca. He passed on the information that twelve of the *Liefde*'s crew were still alive in Japan and volunteered for service in the Dutch fleet but Quaeckernaeck was killed in a later action in October. Van Santvoort returned to Japan preferring to continue trading on his own account rather than joining the VOC. He remained in Japan until 1639.[96]

After his failure to take Malacca, Matelieff sailed on to Ternate. In 1607 the fleet reached the south China coast where it encountered some Japanese pirates (they were called pirates but were probably illegal traders) who informed the Dutch that they 'knew of Jaep Quaeck [Jacob Quaeckernaeck] and [mentioned] that there were still in Japan eight other Dutchmen, who were building ships for the Emperor'. But Matelieff did not proceed to Japan considering that '[t]he trade of Japan since it subsists upon China goods and a few European cloths, is not to be entered upon nor thought of, until we have first a firm grasp of the trade of China' – a shrewd assessment. Unfortunately, its implications were not grasped by his superiors.[97]

However, in February 1608 the Dutch factor at Patani, Victor Sprinckel, entrusted Van Santvoort, who was by then a regular trader between Japan and southeast Asia, with a letter for the shogun dwelling on the VOC's engagements against the Portuguese and explaining that these had prevented the Dutch from taking up his offer of trade. The letter referred to Matelieff's bloody seige of

Malacca, providing further evidence for the Japanese about the divisions within Europe. Sprinkel also sent a letter to Adams, thanking him for his part in securing the offer of trading privileges for the Dutch, commenting that it was especially pleasing to hear of 'the good favour, love, inclination which Your Honour, with some others, show towards the Fatherland' and asking him 'in friendly wise (since Melchior tells me that your Honour is held in great favour by His Majesty) personally to give His Majesty this letter, with the little gift'. The gift consisted mostly of glassware and cloth and was worth *f.* 112 12st[98]

It was not until 1609 that VOC ships, the *Roode Leeuw met Pijlen* and the *Griffioen*, reached Japan. They were part of a thirteen-vessel fleet under Pieter Williamsz Verhoeven (or Verhoeff) that had left Holland in December 1607. This occurred at a crucial stage in the conflict between the Netherlands and Spain. From 1606 representatives of both sides had been involved in delicate peace negotiations. To secure peace, Johan van Oldenbarnevelt, advocate of Holland, contemplated accepting the heavy price the Spanish demanded for peace, the abolition of the VOC. The plan was quickly scotched by Oldenbarnevelt's advisors. But Spanish arguments that Dutch losses in Asia and elsewhere overseas, including the West Indies (moves to establish a West Indies Company were underway in 1606 until halted by Oldenbarnevelt), would be more than offset by the economic gains to be reaped from the re-opening of Spanish, Portuguese and the southern Italian ports, struck a responsive chord in the United Provinces where overseas enterprise was felt by many to benefit only a small number of towns and their controlling oligarchs. However, as Oldenbarnevelt knew, these oligarchs were extremely influential. Dutch resolve not to give way to Spanish insistence on a complete withdrawal from the Indies stalled the negotiations and the prospects for an immediate truce evaporated. Once the VOC directors, or the Heren XVII, realised that the very existence of the company had been called into doubt and that the Dutch negotiating stance had been altered to aim for a peace in which existing Dutch possessions in the Indies would be recognised by the Spanish, they stepped up their aggressive policy in Asia in the hope of grabbing what they could in case such a peace treaty became operative. The aims and progress of Verhoeven's fleet reflected this policy.[99]

The voyage of the *Roode Leeuw* and the *Griffioen* was intended to test the prospects for trade with Japan and to plunder Portuguese shipping *en route*.[100] Had the ships succeeded in their attempts to waylay the náo, the *Nossa Senhora de Graça* (also known as the *Madre de Deus*), they would have settled for this richly laden prize and left Japan for another occasion. Nicholas Puyek, the commander of the ships, took the precaution of calling at Patani to procure 'some silk, pepper and a small quantity of lead, in order that if we failed to capture the carrack, we might have some evidence that we wished to establish commerce and found a trading factory'.[101]

The ships reached Japan at the beginning of July 1609, picking up two Japanese pilots off Nagasaki who led them directly to Hirado where the Dutch understood, from their Linschoten, that there were no Portuguese.[102] Concerned that the Portuguese would waste no opportunity to denounce them as pirates, two of the Dutch merchants journeyed up to what they believed was the imperial court taking Van Santvoort as their interpreter. In fact they visited Ieyasu at Sunpu (present day Shizuoka) to where he had retired in 1607 as ōgosho (retired shogun), leaving his son Hidetada as de jure shogun in the rapidly expanding Tokugawa capital of Edo. De facto power remained firmly in Ieyasu's hands.[103] The Dutch called only on Ieyasu: they did not visit Edo. A Korean embassy which had visited Japan in 1607 had been strongly requested to proceed to Edo to pay its respects to Hidetada in order to underscore his position as shogun before the world.[104] At Sunpu, Ieyasu granted the Dutch trading privileges, including the right of free trade in Japan, the right to set up a factory and freedom from the itowappu, and a shuinjō giving them the right to call at any Japanese port. Freedom from the itowappu, to which the Portuguese were subjected (they called it the pancada) was an important concession for the future course of VOC trade in Japan. The itowappu-nakama, or silk-yarn allotment guild, had been established in 1604 to bring some order into the market for high quality Chinese raw silk brought to Japan by the Portuguese. From 1604 the Portuguese had to sell all their silk (after the shogunate had bought the supplies it wanted through the Nagasaki daikan) to a guild of merchants from Sakai, Kyoto and Nagasaki (Edo and Osaka were included later). The guild set the price which the Portuguese often claimed was unfair. The Dutch, and later the English, and of course the Chinese were free from this requirement. This did not always work to their advantage. If prices began to rise too steeply the shogunate could release some of its own stock, which could be as high as one-third of annual imports, on to the market to bring down prices.[105]

The privileges granted to the Dutch were set down in a letter from Ieyasu to Prince Maurice of Nassau whom the letter described as 'King of Holland', a fiction perpetrated by the VOC employees to enhance their status. The Dutch were well satisfied with the visit, claiming that the privileges annoyed the Portuguese 'intensely, and the more so because their envoys reached the Emperor's court five days before ours, but were not received' even though they 'reviled us saying that we were pirates and not merchants at all'.[106] It did not occur to the Dutch that the Spanish had received similar privileges (although not exemption from the *itowappu*) and that the Japanese had hoped they too would set up a factory. Nor did they give much thought to the Chinese trade in Japan. Whatever their initial optimism, a long time was to pass before the Hollanders were able to supplant the Portuguese as the major European traders in Japan and when they did it was for reasons largely beyond their control.

A factor, Jacques Specx (a native of Dordrecht in his early twenties who had come to the Indies in 1607 and was to serve two terms as chief factor in Hirado from 1609 to February 1613 and from September 1614 to January 1621) plus three assistants and a youth were left at Hirado, where accommodation was rented, to establish VOC trade in Japan. One of the survivors of the *Liefde*, Jan Cousyns, was employed as a book-keeper at a salary of *f.* 20 per month. The stock consisted of raw silk (worth *f.*15,231 4st 6p lead, pepper (both unrated) and 300 reals to tide them over until the arrival of another Dutch ship on the next monsoon which it was hoped would carry English broadcloth (for which it was believed the market was good) iron and lead. In the absence of a direct link with China to acquire silk, Puyck expected the factory to involve itself in the country trade and in particular with Cambodia. Adams did not have any part in securing the Dutch trading privileges, even though the Dutch were impressed by the high regard in which he was held by Ieyasu and the Nagasaki *daikan* and with the easy access he appeared to enjoy to Ieyasu. He was judged 'a friend of the Netherlands [who] holds it in the same esteem as his fatherland', a not altogether unusual sentiment for a man of Adams's generation. Specx was instructed to keep on good terms with Adams whose contacts the Dutch sought to cultivate, although Puyck foresaw that it would not be long before news of Adams's presence would induce the English to come to Japan and that when they arrived they would also be admitted because of Ieyasu's open-door policy in overseas trade.[107] Puyck offered a free passage home to the survivors of the *Liefde* (including Adams) but they turned it down even though not all were thriving as well in Japan as Van Santvoort, Joosten and Adams. One, described by Richard Cocks as a 'canker, a pore fellow', begged for employment with the English factory having failed to secure a job with the Dutch one.[108]

Ieyasu's snub to the Portuguese came during a difficult stage in Lusitaniàn–Japanese relations. Luis de Cerqueira, the Jesuit bishop of Japan, was alarmed that the arrival of the Dutch would damage both the trade of Macao and Manila. Some senior Tokugawa councillors, including the Nagasaki *daikan*, Hasegawa Sahyōe Fujihiro, who was anti-Christian, favoured imposing restrictions on the Portuguese. Relations had deteriorated after an incident at Macao in 1607 in which some Japanese, including some of the crew of a vessel belonging

to the daimyo of Arima, Arima Harunobu, were killed after a
riot. The acting governor and captain major of the Japan voyage,
André Pessoa, forced the survivors to sign an affidavit, which he
took with him to Japan in 1609, declaring their responsibility for the
episode. Unfortunately for Pessoa, the surviviors returned to Japan
seeking redress. Arima Harunobu argued their case before Ieyasu
who decided to send for Pessoa and have him arrested. The latter,
sensing danger, refused to comply, and on 3 January 1610 (NS) the
Japanese launched a four-day attack on the *Nossa Senhora de Graça*
(the náo the Dutch had hunted in vain on their way to Japan) which
was eventually set on fire and destroyed in a spectacular explosion
caused by Pessoa igniting the ship's magazine.

Ieyasu's decision to have Pessoa arrested was not occasioned by the
Dutch presence in Japan. He did not contemplate a complete break
with the Portuguese and certainly was not operating on the assumption that the Dutch would conveniently replace the Portuguese in the
case of a rupture of relations with Macao. The workings of the
Macao/Nagasaki trade were too complex to permit any simple
substitution. The bakufu and some daimyo invested in the Macao
trade and after more than sixty years Japanese merchants had evolved
strong business relationships with the Lusitanians. Moreover, the
voyage was regular. The Dutch, on the other hand, were new
arrivals and untested. Specx himself realised this, noting that the
Portuguese were popular in Japan because they brought goods that
people wanted – especially silk – and they were generous with gifts
and spent freely. He estimated that the merchants and crew of the
náo spent between 250,000 and 300,000 reals in Nagasaki during
their stay.[109] The order for Pessoa's arrest and the attack on his náo
was intended to serve as a sharp lesson to the Portuguese to take care
how they treated Japanese, including those overseas, who enjoyed
the shogun's protection. Both sides soon put the incident behind
them and in 1611 cordial relations between the Japanese and the
Portuguese were re-established, and the following year a náo returned to Nagasaki.[110]

Specx was frustrated that no ships arrived from Bantam or Patani
in 1610 and worried that this might lead to a loss of the privileges he
sent two of his assistants to Patani in October with a lading of silver
and lacquer-ware. Shortly after he himself went to Patani, probably
on a Japanese *shuinsen* vessel, to acquire some stock for the factory.
He returned in July 1611 with a cargo of cloth, lead, ivory, damask,
taffetas and raw silk; he proceeded to Sunpu to deliver a present to
Ieyasu which included broadcloth, five Nuremberg carpets, ten
glass bottles and 2,000 catties of lead, the most valued item, and to
apologise for the two-year absence of Dutch ships from Japan.[111]

On this occasion Specx and a fellow VOC merchant who had

come with him from Patani visited Hidetada in Edo and gave him similar presents. Adams acted as interpreter and for the first time learned conclusively about the English East India Company's presence at Bantam. On 22 October 1611 (NS) he wrote to his countrymen there. The Dutch could not have kept him entirely ignorant of English activity in the Indies but they almost certainly would have tried to keep information to a minimum and to play down the extent of the English Company's trade. In August 1612 the *Roote Leeuw* arrived in Hirado once again, this time bringing a reply from Prince Maurice to Ieyasu and orders from the Heren XVII confirming the Japan factory. Its cargo of cloves, muscat and pepper was not of great interest to the Japanese. A second vessel, the *Hasewint*, which had called at Patani, followed with goods that were more in demand: silk and wax. A visit was made to Sunpu where Maurice's letter was presented to Ieyasu. This time Adams acted as interpreter and advisor on court protocol. The Dutch, anxious about these matters, received confirmation that they were indeed free from the *itowappu* and enjoyed an unrestricted right to unload their ships without any interference from the Japanese authorities.[112] Thus reassured, Hirado was decided upon as the sight of the new factory. Contrary to Adams's wild, inaccurate boast to the English at Bantam that he had obtained for the Dutch such 'priuilledg as the Spaynnards and Portingalles could neuer gett in this 50 or 60 yeares in Japan',[113] there is no question of the Englishman securing anything other than what the Dutch wanted and, more importantly, than what the Japanese authorities were prepared to offer. Adams acted only as an intermediary. He did not initiate anything.

The *Hasewint* brought letters for Adams from Peter Floris at Patani, from the Company, and from his acquaintances in England. These were not handed over to him for six weeks. (Adams was not at Hirado when the ship arrived although he did complain that the Dutch did not forward his own letters to England and that they had not passed on previous ones from England including letters from his wife.) One of the letters was from Sir Thomas Smythe and mentioned the Company's intention to send a ship to Japan to establish a factory. Adams wrote to Bantam on 12 January 1613 (NS) enthusiastically endorsing the idea, saying that he had mentioned it to Ieyasu who 'was very glad, and rejoiced that strange nations had such good opinion'. Adams undertook to use his favour with Ieyasu to make the English 'so welcome and free in comparison as in the river of London'. He gave an overview of the trading prospects, arguing that cloth would not sell because it was brought in abundance by the Dutch and by the Spanish from New Spain, but suggesting that if the English could get 'the handling or trade with the Chinese, then shall our country make great profit here, and your worshipful Indian Company of London shall not have need to send money out of England, for in Japan is gold and silver in abundance' to finance trade elsewhere in the Indies. Operating costs were low but he recommended that the English should set themselves up near the shogun's capital at Edo. He concluded with a brief mention of the stable political conditions in Japan, some words on Japanese culture and enclosed a sketch of the country.[114] It was an optimistic, encouraging picture.

Adams's letter reached Bantam on 23 April, carried by a Dutch ship, and was delivered to the English by another Englishman in Dutch service, Thomas Hill. However, just over three months previously, on 14 January, the Clove, of the Company's Eighth Voyage, had already left Bantam for Japan.[115]

CHAPTER 3

The East India Company reaches Japan

(i)   The Eighth Voyage

The *Clove* had already been absent from England for almost two years by the time it sailed from Bantam for Japan. The three ships of the Eighth Voyage, the *Clove* (527 tons), *Thomas* (342 tons) and *Hector* (800 tons) left the Downs with a total of 262 men, including eight 'Indians', some Scots and a Frenchman, on 18 April 1611. A boy of eighteen was added to the crew of the *Thomas* without wages three days before the departure. The *Clove* had ninety-three men aboard, the *Hector*, one hundred and fourteen, and the *Thomas*, fifty-five. Christopher and Cosmos and the Philippine boys were not the only Asians to have come to England. Some came as servants to voyage commanders, most were employed as crew to compensate for the high mortality rates on Company voyages. For example, almost 29 per cent of the Eighth Voyage's complement had died by January 1613 when the ships were in Bantam, some within weeks of leaving England.[1] The Asians who came to England included two Chinese, almost certainly picked up at Bantam, Gujarati, renowned for their maritime skills, and Malays, also referred to as 'Indians'. The directors consulted the 'Indians' brought back on the *Dragon* in September 1603. They were interested in their skills and any useful information they could supply to the Company.[2]

The size of the ships of the Eighth Voyage was about average for the Company's shipping at this time. The Portuguese náo may have been a magnificent sight and given an awesome impression of overwhelming power but ships in excess of 1,000 tons, which the náo generally were by the beginning of the seventeenth century, were less manoeuvrable and more vulnerable to shipwreck as the Portuguese discovered to their cost. Economies of scale were in inverse proportion to the size of ships employed on voyages to the Indies.[3]

It is impossible to know exactly the details of the planning for the voyage and how the personnel were recruited because the minutes of the Court of Committees, the Company's governing body, from late January 1610 to November 1613 are no longer extant. The minutes for 1609 show that the Court chose its factors after a screening process from amongst a wide variety of candidates who either petitioned directly or were recommended by members of the Company or other influential people. In late 1609 and early 1610 the supply of candidates far exceeded the available jobs and some aspirants were prepared to accept positions lower than the ones they originally sought. In one instance a candidate made his application more memorable by putting it 'in verse'. By mid January 1610 the Court was able to stop recruiting factors until new voyages were in preparation.[4]

Factors were divided into three grades, of which the principal or cape merchant, who was responsible for running the Company's factories, was the most senior.[5] Ideally candidates would have had experience of living abroad working as a factor or agent for a merchant or syndicates of merchants in England. Such people were usually former apprentices and sometimes apprentice factors in the fifth or sixth year of training. Their job was to buy and sell commodities for whomsoever they represented, at the most favourable prices and to send them home. This required knowledge of local markets and trading conditions, foreign exchange matters, book-keeping and foreign languages.[6] Other qualifications such as Nathaniel Courthorp's skill in 'Calicoes and Naugacon', John Griffen's knowledge of silks, or John Fowler's willingness to provide cordage, could be advantageous to potential candidates depending on the Company's particular needs. Direct recommendation by members of the Court or 'friends' of the Company could help but could not in itself secure employment. One such connected individual was found unsuitable because of his age. A willingness to advance money in stock was greatly appreciated. All candidates had to state their place of abode, education and status and their application was referred so that enquiry could be made of their 'sufficiencie and fitness', a process that was normally conducted with speed.[7] The court minutes for 1609 do not often record the reasons why a candidate was considered 'unfit' but the most likely grounds were insufficient experience of living and working overseas, suspicion of financial impropriety, poor health, uncertain personal circumstances, an inability to pay the surety or bond required of voyage commanders, factors, masters, pursers and pursers' mates, and, above all, any suspicion that a prospective servant was seeking employment solely to feather his own nest by pursuing private trade.

The senior positions on the Eighth Voyage went to men already in the Company's employ or possessing wide commercial experience. The commander or captain of the voyage (the terminology was loose), John Saris, who sailed on the *Clove*, was the younger son of a London merchant from an armigerous Yorkshire family and was aged thirty-one. Saris, an ambitious man determined to advance his career, already had experience of the Indies. He had gone out in the Second Voyage under Sir Henry Middleton in March 1604 and had resided in Bantam for five years as one of the factors and had learned Malay before returning to England in May 1610. In 1608 he wrote an informed, comprehensive paper on the trade of the Indonesian archipelago highlighting the importance of the country trade and drawing attention to the trade between Gujarat and Siam and from China to the archipelago and to the Philippines. He noted that the Chinese exported silk to Manila in return for bullion and that the trade was carried in some forty junks a year (a pretty accurate assessment) whose 'force is nothing so that you may take them with your ship's boat'.[8]

Regardless of the naval connotations of the title, the captain or commander of a voyage (the titles were interchangeable) at this time was a merchant with final responsibility for the selling and buying of goods on the voyage. Navigational matters were in the hands of the master.[9] The master was inferior in rank to both the commander and the other factors aboard, a recurring cause of resentment and conflict. To assist the commander on commercial and strategic matters concerning the voyage, provision was made for a council consisting of the senior factors. There was likewise a council for navigational matters in which merchants were not supposed to meddle, although some did. On the Eighth Voyage the council 'of trade & Marchandiseinge' consisted of Saris; Gabriel Towerson, chief merchant of the *Hector* who had sailed in the Second Voyage and had served as the Company's first chief factor at Bantam from 1605–8 and was to serve the Company until his death in the infamous massacre of Amboina in 1623; Tempest Peacock, chief merchant of the *Thomas*, who served in the Japan factory; Richard Cocks, second-in-command on the *Clove* and the future head of the Japan factory; Ambrose Arnenay (or Arnevy) who died in November 1611; Richard Wickham, who also served in Japan; Edward Camden, appointed chief factor at Bantam for the Eighth Voyage in 1612 but who died there soon afterwards; and George Ball, later president at Bantam, an unscrupulous individual and friend of Wickham who was sent home in disgrace in 1620 for private trading and subsequently charged with embezzlement and serious neglect of duty.[10] The council did not reflect the chain of command. In the event of Saris's death, Towerson was to take command, and if he died the duty fell to Cocks. The name of the next in line was kept in a sealed box in Saris's possession.[11] With so many imponderables about what might happen during the voyage and the scant information available on which to base instructions, it was inevitable that the final decisions had to be delegated and referred to the 'discretion' of the commander and his council. For this reason alone it was absolutely necessary to have able men in charge.

Of the crew little is known. There was still no sharp distinction between officers and men although the master was clearly differentiated in terms of status, prestige and pay from the other crew. Even if some tasks at sea required specific skills and greater responsibilities than others, the crew, with the exception of the master, was classified by the vague term 'mariner'. From what is known of mariners in other undertakings at this time the background and ages of the crew would have varied. Geographically they would have come from all parts of the country. Some would have served as apprentices studying the art of navigation, others would have learned from raw experience. There was a plentiful supply of labour for the Company to recruit from in the early seventeenth century and it must be supposed that there was considerable leeway to pick and chose from among the candidates who applied to serve on the Company's ships. Nevertheless, there were shortages of certain skills. Men were attracted to the Company's service despite the greater uncertainties and dangers involved, especially when compared with the relatively straightforward coastal and continental routes. The jobs offered security, comparatively good wages (certainly better than those in the king's navy: the common sailors received £5 per annum, a master £10 per month, more than most factors) and free board and lodging while serving aboard, albeit in cramped, crowded, unsanitary conditions. There was also the possibility of making extra money from the private trade officially permitted by the Company, and the chance of illicit private trade often in Company goods obtained by pilfering.[12] Other men signed up to escape legal proceedings, or to escape from family or personal problems and some were no doubt attracted by the sheer adventure involved in a voyage to the Indies even if there was nothing romantic about the sea or even foreign travel at this time. The crew on the Eighth Voyage included veterans of the Company's Second Voyage under Sir Henry Middleton, which had visited the Spice Islands in 1605. Two men, John Bowles and Christopher Evans, who jumped ship in Japan, had served in Spanish galleys after alledgedly betraying their ship in the West Indies.[13]

No complete figures survive for the value at which the Company rated the cargo loaded on the three ships of the Eighth Voyage. However, at Bantam Cocks drew up an 'inventory general' of goods and monies received out of the ships. This appears to be his own note of what was loaded in England. It is not an official inventory. Copies of the inventory would have been kept by the pursers but at least Cocks's inventory provides a valuable guide to the original lading. The goods were rated in reals with a value of 4s to the real. According to Cocks the total value of the cargo on the ships was 88,364 7/24 reals, of which 54,486 1/4 reals was in real coins except for a small amount in gold, and 33,878 1/24 reals in goods either for trade or as stock for new factories or for the supply of existing ones. The goods consisted mainly of cloth (both broadcloth and kerseys, a thick cloth used to make up all kinds of warm clothing), iron, tin, lead, fowling pieces and ivory.[14] The cloth consisted of 216 1/2 broadcloths, mainly long cloth (that is, between 29 and 33 yards long and 78 and 84 pounds weight). A large proportion was 'Worcester' cloth, a generic, which at the top end of the quality range was considered (rightly so) 'the finest cloth in the worlde'. The cloth had been bought over a period from 15 September 1610 to 20 March 1611, not long before the departure of the voyage, and was purchased either directly from individual merchants or at Blackwell Hall in Barryhall St where sales were held from Thursday to Saturday. The cost was £2,414 18s 6d and a further £270 13s 4d was spent on dyeing and dressing (a job that turned out not to have been well done). Additional charges, including painted billets and buckram underlay, carriage to the ships, the procuring of customs seals (cockets) and tips (vale) came to £221 18s 9d. A further seventy pieces of kersey were purchased at a cost of £234 3d, including dressing and additional charges. The total cost of buying, preparing for export and loading the cloth on the ships came to £3,141 10s 10d, just over half the total value of goods carried.[15]

Cloth figured so prominently in the cargo because it was England's major export. The Company was confident it would sell well in the Indies and could be sold profitably to pay for the purchase of Asian goods, especially pepper. Cloth exports also helped deflect criticism from the influential body of opinion in government and in the country that the Company's bullion exports (essentially silver) were detrimental to the nation's economic health. The Company was attacked for acting as a drain for the outflow of what was judged a precious national asset. In 1611, for example, when both the Seventh and Eighth Voyages left for the Indies, bullion worth £17,675 was exported as opposed to £10,000 in goods and for most of the Company's first forty years of operations bullion exports far outweighed the export of goods. The VOC similarly exported more bullion than goods on their outward voyages.[16] In reality, of course, it made sense to export bullion. The price of silver in the Indies was higher than in Europe. This fact alone made English or other European goods too expensive regardless of the perverse logic of sending cloth into hot, sultry climates and the variations and peculiarities of local demand in the Indies. It was, therefore, economically sound to use bullion sent from England to purchase local goods and commodities at advantageous prices for sale in Europe. However, such flawless economic theory was not at all self-evident in the early seventeenth century. A few contemporary economic commentators, the most notable of whom was Thomas Mun, one of the Company's members, had greater insight into the structure and complexities of this emerging global trade and were aware of the economic justifications for exporting bullion, and in practice the directors themselves operated on the basis that it made commercial sense to export bullion. However, the Company's export of cloth and its belief that an extensive market in the Indies existed for English cloth was something other than the 'pious hope' that Professor Andrews suggests. The Company had its roots in the London merchant community and was an outgrowth of an economy in which the manufacture and export of cloth was of vital national importance. Professor Chaudhuri is correct to suggest that cloth was exported to provide additional purchasing power for the Company in the Indies, but his argument that the founders of the Company, and by implication their successors, 'had acquired a fairly accurate knowledge of the nature of the East Indies trade and seemed to have been aware of the scope for exporting English woollen cloth to the Asia markets was at best limited and problematic' does not square with the facts. The directors were neither as cynical as Professor Andrews believes nor as well informed as Professor Chaudhuri credits them as the experience of the Japan factory shows.[17] The expectation that the Indies, including Japan, would provide a vast market for English cloth persisted throughout the seventeenth century.

In the case of Japan, cloth was expected to be much in demand largely because of Hakluyt's advice and his unflagging enthusiasm for a northwest passage. At the end of his notes concerning the availability of spices and other goods in the Indies, which was drawn up in 1601 at the request of the directors to help them prepare the First Voyage, Hakluyt added that he had 'large notes of 20 yeares observation concerning the northwest passage, which your worships shall command yf you shall have occasion to use the same'. Hakluyt believed that Hideyoshi's invasion of Korea had transformed Japan into a strong regional power, and that the country stretched further to the north than had been previously imagined and bordered on the territory belonging to the 'Jezi', a Tartar nation, with whom the Japanese were said to trade selling cloth and other goods. This strengthened his conviction that prospects for the sale of cloth in the region were excellent. Hakluyt was confident that the Jezi would have 'the best utterance of our national and chiefe commoditie of cloth'. The Company was certainly prepared to entertain such a possibility and Linschoten's description of the country as cold offered further 'evidence' that there was a promising market for cloth in Japan.[18]

Saris's instructions for command of the Eighth Voyage included specific orders for a visit to Japan. After consultation with William Adams, 'grounded vpon his large experience in those partes', Saris was to examine the possibility of selling 'Cloth leade, Iron & other of o^r Natiue Comodities as by yor obseruacon yo^u shall finde most vendible there, where-in yo^u are to be spetially carefull both whatt Colors and sortes of Cloth, and for what quantitie will there be vented'. He was then to decide with Richard Cocks and the other senior merchants on the *Clove* whether it 'shall be by yo^u thought convenient for the setlinge of a factorie & mainteyning of a trade att Iapan.' If the decision was against setting up a factory in Japan then the ship was to attempt to sell its cargo in the Moluccas, the Philippines or elsewhere.[19]

As was usual, the commission for the Eighth Voyage painted the objectives of the voyage in broad strokes, defining the contours of the mission. The details were left to the commander and merchants' council to fill in. It was understood that the commander and council could interpret the commission as they saw fit according to the circumstances of the voyage but this had to be within the framework of alternatives sketched by the Court in the commission. One such option was for the ships to sail directly for Surat, preferably calling at Socotra to enquire of Gujarati merchants on their way to Aden and Mocha what had happened to William Hawkins, the quasi-ambassador to the Mughal court who had gone to the Indies on the Third Voyage in 1607. If they missed the monsoon that would carry them across the Arabian Sea, they were to proceed either to Aden or Mocha, sell their English commodites or, if prices were favourable, to buy spices for sale at Surat. If, after arrival at Surat, sufficient lading could be bought then all three ships were to return home, otherwise they were to make for Priaman in Sumatra, to acquire calicoes, and then head for Bantam, the Bandas and the Moluccas where if they could find sufficient cargoes they were to return home. If it was discovered at Surat that Hawkins and the other English merchants had failed to establish a factory or that the English were not made welcome then they were to give up any attempt to trade there and recross the Arabian Sea and try to encourage Gujarati merchants to trade with the English at Socotra and then make for Aden or Mocha, assuming that they had not already done so, and make the best of the trading opportunities afforded there to sell the English goods and acquire husked pepper, spices, indigo, calicoes,

sandalwood and aloes wood for England. Once enough of these
goods had been acquired the ships were to return home, otherwise
the unladed ships were to proceed to Priaman and Bantam as above.
Japan came into the picture only if circumstances took the ships to
Bantam and suitable lading could be found there only for the *Hector*
and the *Thomas*, in which case these ships were to return home and
the *Clove* was to proceed to Japan. Japan was an option, not the *raison
d'être* of the voyage. Surat was 'the maine and principall scope of this
o^r voyadge', and before long Surat and Bantam were to emerge as
the two hubs of the Company's trade in the Indies, known respectively as 'northwards' and 'southwards'.[20]

Other stipulations in the commission were very much as in
previous ones: strict accounting, morning and evening prayers 'for
that religeous gourm^t doth best bind men to pforme their duties', no
blasphemy, swearing, theft, or drunkenness, and peaceable and civil
behaviour towards people who provided them with water and
provisions on the voyage. Copies of the works of William Perkins
and Foxe's *Book of Martyrs* were provided, and for more leisurely
reading, but still to help focus the mind, Hakluyt's *Principal Navigations*. Individuals were free to take their own books. Cocks had St
Augustine's *City of God* with him in Japan and the inventory of
Wickham's goods in 1618 records that he had '58 bookes great and
small', although these probably included Japanese almanacs which
intrigued the English. Saris was given a copy of Linschoten's *Itinerario* by the directors and found its rutters reliable. The commission
emphasised that full records of the commercial and navigational
aspects of the voyage were to be kept. Most of the information for
the history of the Company's early years comes from such records as
have survived as well as those kept by the factors in the Indies, their
letters home and the few extant ones they received from England.
Another key stipulation in the commission related to the vexatious
problem of private trade, the spectre of which constantly haunted the
Company.[21]

The Eighth Voyage weighed anchor from the Downs on the first
part of its long journey to the Indies on 18 April 1611, but the
immediate preparations had started well before then. These probably
included consultations between the commander and his senior
colleagues.[22] On 3 April as the ships lay at Gravesend, Dr Wood
came aboard the *Clove* and in the presence of the governor and
directors preached a sermon. The following day saw the official start
of the voyage. On that day Sir Thomas Smythe and the directors
came aboard the *Clove* again. The men were mustered, and the
governor 'gave order for their entrance into whole wages from this
day'. The king's commission was read aboard the three ships and
volleys were fired on the departure of the governor and his entour-

age. The ships moved down to Tilbury where customs officials were displeased that they had done so without the dockets that Saris had to request be sent down from London.[23]

Over the next few days Saris was kept busy with a myriad of managerial and disciplinary problems. On 8 April he received James I's commission for command of the *Clove* and letters from the king to the 'Great Moghul of Surat and Cambay', the emperor of Japan, the king of Hirado and the king of Bantam plus one blank, all pro forma, and letters to the Company's factors in the Indies. Further letters, including the king's commission for command of the voyage and a 'Booke of Wayes of the East Indyes' (that is, Linschoten) were delivered on 15 April. On 7 April one Captain Potter of Whitechapel came aboard to ask the whereabouts of William Chapman, a cooper on the *Thomas*, on suspicion that Chapman had burgled his house and stolen goods and money to the value of £27. Saris was determined to keep Chapman on the payroll and suggested that the £27 be stopped out of Chapman's wages. Potter rejected this and had Chapman arrested but Saris managed to secure his release by claiming that the latter had been aboard ship on the night of the robbery but that his presence had not been recorded because the purser had kept an imperfect muster roll.[24] There were attempts by other individuals to have crew members arrested for unpaid debts which Saris managed to settle or stall, in one case by hiding the man from his creditors.[25] The lengths to which Saris was prepared to go to keep men whom he judged experienced or those possessing useful skills that would be difficult to replace suggests that while the pool of available labour to man ships may have been great its quality was uneven.

Discipline problems quickly surfaced. On 10 April Towerson reported that the crew of the *Hector* had tried to break into the hold overnight to pilfer what they could of the ship's cargo and sell it locally. Saris doubted Towerson's ability to enforce discipline and warned him not to become overfamiliar with his men. On 7 April Edward Camden informed Saris that the pass of the Ottoman emperor which he had brought down from London had been stolen while he was 'making merrye' with his friends the previous night; more probably it had simply been lost during the drunken binge. Saris was furious and displeased 'beyond measure' because of the importance of the letter for the success of the voyage. Camden was sent back to London to obtain a copy, although Saris urged the Company to overlook the factor's negligence. Camden returned the following day with a new letter. On 12 April the *Thomas* was almost set ablaze due to the carelessness of the quartermaster while cooking, an incident which Saris took as another indication of Towerson's laxness. There were further complications at Sandwich where the

ships arrived on 14 April. A meeting of the marine council determined that the ships were overmanned in relation to the amount of
victuals they carried. The victuals had been calculated to supply 220
men rather than the 288 then aboard. It was decided to discharge
thirty-four men. There were problems trying to arrange transport to
carry the discharged men back to London. A man who had agreed to
take them overland changed his mind fearing that the men might
run away with his wagons and the men went by water transport.
Overmanning was not at all unusual at this time and on voyages to
the Indies was judged necessary to compensate for the mortality
inevitable on the voyage. Even after the thirty-four had been discharged and some extra supplies taken aboard, victuals remained
tight.[26] Finally on 18 April the ships were able to set sail from the
Downs and after a brief stop off Dover, to put ashore Saris's brother
and Richard Mountney, the Company's husband, whose responsibilities, rather like those of a modern shipping agent, were to prepare
the ships for the outward voyage and clear them when they returned,
the voyage proper commenced.[27]

The first leg of the voyage was routine. The three ships sailed out
into the Atlantic down towards the Canaries and Cape Bojador, and
from the Cape Verde Islands out across the open sea, skirting Brazil
and back across the southern Atlantic, sighting land some thirty
leagues north of the Cape of Good Hope at the end of July. After a
short sojourn for refreshment, Africa was rounded and the ships
proceeded into the Indian Ocean heading northwards towards Mada-
gascar. They ran into bad weather but managed to reach Moheli in
the Comoro Islands safely, which Cocks later reported to be 'the best
place of refreshing betwixt England and the East Indies'.[28] They
were well treated by the sultan and remained there until 3 November. From Moheli they continued northwards, usually within sight
of land, coming to anchor off Socotra on 18 February 1612. Here
they learned of an attack at Aden (then under Turkish control) on Sir
Henry Middleton, commander of the Sixth Voyage, in which eight
men had been killed and Middleton and some others briefly imprisoned. This news occasioned the first review of the voyage instructions. On 26 February the mercantile council met to assess the
options. One was for the ships to split up and for the Clove to make
for Bantam and Japan, hoping to catch the tail end of the southerly
monsoon by sailing up the China Sea rather than proceeding via the
Moluccas, the preferred route. This is the first indication that Japan
had become a major objective of the voyage, and one that Saris
personally was keen to pursue. After discussion it was decided not to
deviate from the Company's instructions and that all three ships
should stick together. Confident that the Ottoman emperor's pass
would save them from a fate similar to Middleton, the ship pro-

ceeded to Mocha to try to open trade over the summer until the September monsoon could take them across the Arabian Sea to Surat. If no trade were forthcoming the merchants were confident of forcing Mocha to open one either by military action or by spoiling the existing trade by not permitting the Gujarati merchants, who were expected around early March, to land.[29]

They left Socotra on 1 March and arrived in Mocha on the 16th where, contrary to expectation, they were made welcome by the new governor, a Greek turned Muslim. However, this auspicious beginning, made all the more so by the arrival of two Gujarati ships well laden with India goods and carrying some 400 passengers, mostly pilgrims, 'who carried much wealth about them',[30] was cut short with news of the arrival of Middleton in the Red Sea in late March seeking revenge for his earlier treatment and bringing news that Surat was closed to the English. Hawkins, a man of indifferent diplomatic qualities, had failed in his mission. The Portuguese opposed the admission of the English, the merchants for commercial reasons, the Jesuits on religious grounds, and Mughal officials, who were trying to manage foreign trade for their own benefit, all intrigued against him.[31] Middleton's return to the Red Sea marked the beginning of a bitter and acrimonious conflict with Saris which unfolded over the following months. Richard Dawes noted that 'ther was great and open hatred between the two generalles', possibly compounded by Middleton's resentment of his erstwhile subordinate's new position.[32] Disagreement centered on the tactics to be employed against the authorities at Mocha and how their respective voyages should proceed once Middleton had settled his score. The episode illustrates perfectly the weakness of the Company's policy of sending out separate voyages and the lack of co-ordination and wasteful competition which resulted. Each commander, especially such strong-minded, stubborn, ambitious individuals as Saris and Middleton, acted as he saw fit in the interests of his own voyage even if this did not necessarily advance the interests of the Company as a whole. The local authorities at Mocha also suffered from the feuding between Saris and Middleton. Saris had got on well with them and had received encouraging signals about the possibility of opening a factory. But once the English had seized the cargoes on the Gujarati and other Indian vessels that had the misfortune to sail into the area, Mocha was deprived of its full customs exactions. The merchants and passengers, many pilgrims on their way to Mecca, on these vessels, one of which, the *Rehemi*, 1,200 tons, belonged to the Mughal emperor's mother and two others to senior Mughal officials, came out worst of all. The presents they proffered to avoid seizure of their goods availed them little and they were forced to sell their goods at prices arbitrarily fixed by the

English at between 10 and 20 per cent above cost in exchange for English goods, which they did not want and which on, Saris's own admission, were not in much demand in Mocha anyway, at prices between 50 and 100 per cent above cost. The goods from the Indian ships, which included Cambay cloth, indigo, silk and damask, gold, silver and pearls (the more precious items were 'kepte close with stones') were then divided, according to an agreement reached between Middleton and Saris after much haggling, two-thirds for the Sixth Voyage and one third for the Eighth. The Gujarati had to pay an additional ransom in lieu of the restitution Middleton sought for the deaths of his men from the Turks who refused to pay up. This was divided three quarters for the Sixth Voyage and one quarter for the Eighth, the Eighth receiving 8,000 1/4 reals.[33] There was no consideration of the longer term benefits likely to accrue from establishing contacts and promoting friendly relations to advance the Company's prospects of setting up a factory in an area of considerable commercial importance. For example, Dawes provided detailed advice on how best to lay a trap for Gujarati ships in the Red Sea and how to carry out a thorough search of their ships for prizes, including the places 'a man would lest susspecte their greatest treasuer or Riche thinges' – he mentioned the ships' 'cesternes of watter'. The Company's participation in the Red Sea trade had to wait anyway until it was securely established at the other end of the trade in India, which only happened after the successful conclusion of Sir Thomas Roe's embassy and the definition of more consistent policies in London.[34]

Towards the end of May, Saris dispatched the *Thomas* for Socotra to procure aloes and to trail the *Darling*, which Middleton had sent ahead to Sumatra to secure pepper on 19 May. The *Hector* left for Sumatra on 8 August. The most powerful state on the island was the sprawling maritime sultanate of Achin whose ruler at this time was Iskandar Mudah (r. 1607–36). Iskandar had restored Achin's position as a major regional power after a period of forty years of acute internal instability. He had to contend with rivalry from the Portuguese at Malacca whose encroachments he successfully resisted but whose control of the city he could not break even with his large navy, and from the sultan of Johor, the successor to Malay Malacca. Achin controlled much of the pepper export trade in the lands under its sway, exacting a tribute of 15 per cent from producers and fixing prices for the rest. The same applied to gold, another major resource. However, Achin's grip over its hinterland remained tenuous and its food supply unstable. Foreign merchants were permitted to trade and reside in the capital, an impressive city, wooded, spacious and populous, but on terms dictated by the sultan.[35] Neither the *Hector* nor the *Thomas* was able to secure much pepper at the ports of Tiku or Priaman. In fact they were lucky to get any at all because only the favoured Gujarati merchants were free to buy pepper and other goods. Other merchants required a licence from the sultan.[36] Nor could the two ships cajole it from the *Darling* which had enjoyed slightly better success at Tiku but was in distress because of a leak, its men sick and surviving on dwindling victuals. The two voyages remained rivals.

On 13 August the *Clove* herself left Mocha for Bantam where it arrived on 24 October, the *Hector* having arrived the previous day.[37] Bantam was another major port in the western Indonesian archipelago. Its influence extended across the Sunda Straits which it controlled, and into the pepper producing areas of southern Sumatra. Its ruler at this time, Abdul Kadir, was a minor, and power was exercised by a formidable regent, Pangeran Ranamanggala, who owed his position to a judicious marriage to the sultan's mother and astute management of the commercial life of the small state. In Bantam's rich market, pepper, cloves, nutmeg and mace from the Moluccas and Bandas, Cambay and Coromandel cloth, Chinese silk, porcelain and copper coins jostled for the attention of merchants. It was a thriving city, little trace of which remains today, surrounded by brick walls and much more open to trade than Achin where Iskandar Mudah's political absolutism dictated a ruthless determination to control trade. Foreign merchants were welcome in Bantam, much more so than in Achin, and, as was the case in other major cities of the Indies, lived in their own settlements outside the city walls which enclosed the regal and aristocratic quarters. The most important group among the resident foreign merchants were the Chinese, the most prosperous of whom lived in houses built of brick which protected them from fires, a constant threat. Less prosperous Chinese used brick, timber and cane, while the Javanese and other ethnic groups built in cane and wood or other less permanent materials. The Chinese purchased pepper from the producers upcountry from where it was transported to the coast by boat. The strong economic power of the Chinese middlemen in Bantam had been transformed into political power, symbolised by the location of the Chinese quarter near the royal palace. The Chinese were represented on the sultan's council and held important administrative posts.[38] The English and Dutch came to resent bitterly the Chinese domination of the state's commercial life; the Dutch sought to break it.

During his stay in Bantam Saris was preoccupied with a number of problems. He had to procure a lading for the *Hector* and *Thomas*, which arrived on 18 November, and make ready the *Clove* for Japan. He also had to resolve differences with Augustine Spalding, who had been left as chief factor by William Keeling in 1609 and who wanted to throw in the job and return for England. Adding to his worries were further problems with Middleton who arrived on 9 November.

Spalding was uncooperative over the pepper stored in the English house, claiming that most had been set aside for Middleton and what remained was for the use of the Third and Fifth Voyages. He also refused to allow Cambay cloth from the *Hector* to be discharged and stored in the house and failed to hand over a letter from William Adams for Saris to examine until the 28th.[39] When Saris finally got hold of the letter he read it to his merchants 'that they might not be ignorant of ye hoape of that place [Japan]'.[40] Nevertheless, Saris urged Spalding to remain in Bantam and manage the Company's affairs but he refused. At one stage Saris entreated Cocks 'to staye heare in ye charge of ye Comanye's busines but he [Cocks] earnestly intreatedd to pceede [proceed] to ye furthest of ye voyage hoping to doe ye Companye good service in Japan'. Finally, with Towerson's and Cocks's approval, Saris appointed Camden to take charge of the Eighth Voyage's business at Bantam. Saris had attempted to pressure Spalding to stay in spite of his belief that Spalding had operated a racket with Chinese merchants to buy up cloves before the ships came at 16 reals per pecul and sell them to the Company at 38 reals after their arrival. This was reported back to London which began proceedings in Chancery against Spalding. After further inquiry Camden's successor, as chief factor, John Jourdain, wrote that Spalding was not guilty of the charges although he had bought cloves for some private trade but had lost out on this deal because the cloves were garbled and not worth the investment. By the time the Company learned of this it had decided to drop its proceedings against Spalding and kept him in employment; his experience was too valuable to lose.[41]

From a letter by Sir Thomas Smythe, brought on the *James*, the sole vessel of the Ninth Voyage which had arrived on 23 October, Saris learned that pepper was now in greater demand in England than mace or nutmegs and after a mercantile council on 28 October it was decided to find a lading of pepper for the *Hector* at Bantam rather than sending her to the Moluccas and Banda Islands where Saris believed, wrongly, that 'the flemmings' were 'stronge and allmost sole Commanders [of the islands]'. The pepper was procured mainly through the Chinese middleman, Kewee, who acted on behalf of the English, at prices ranging from 1.25 to 1.6 reals per sack. With the arrival of so many English and Dutch ships the price had risen from 1 real per sack. Even so, it was less than previous prices. In 1607 the price of pepper had fallen from 4 reals to 2.[42]

Saris found time to take a break from his busy schedule for relaxation and to enjoy a reunion with some old Javanese friends from his earlier stay. Relations with the pangeran, to whom a present of broadcloth, gunpowder and other goods worth just over 131 reals was offered, were good despite the fact that 'oʳ Swarts brought out of England' had made allegations that 'we had stolne oʳ cloath' from the Gujarati and holy men of Mecca. This allegation did not cause trouble with the authorities who were content to exact their usual custom of 3 per cent on cloth.[43] There were inevitable problems of maintaining discipline among the men and the price of excessive venery was exacted with a vengeance on John Scott the boatswain's mate of the *Clove* who died on 22 December 'his gutts eaten with the pox in the space of 8 or 10 dayes. God helpe the rest, manye of them infected by yᵉ report of the surgion.'[44]

Middleton did his best to make life as unpleasant as possible for the Eighth Voyage. At one meeting with Cocks, who had been sent by Saris to confer about Company business, Middleton so 'reviled the ould man, ptesting to make his boye beate him' that 'the honest man bewaled his hard fortune to haue liued to this yeares to be so abused without remedye'.[45] Middleton contemplated taking charge of the *Solomon*, the only vessel of the Company's Eleventh Voyage, 'purposing to be at Japan before we'[46] and tried to prevent the Eighth Voyage's share of the Cambay cloth seized in the Red Sea from being stored in the English house. He recommended that Saris follow his own example and rent a warehouse but had to back down. When it started to rain Cocks swiftly mobilised various onlookers and the cloth was put safely in the house.[47] Saris accused Middleton of collaborating with a servant of the pangeran to scupper his plans to buy the house next to the existing English one, which like the Dutch was located in the Chinese quarter. Saris hoped this arrangement would rid him of further interference from Middleton although he intended that the two houses should be managed as one. The pangeran eventually decided that the house would go to neither and ordered it to be pulled down.[48] Middleton also refused to recognise Camden as chief factor. Instead he proposed that Alexander Sharpie (Sharpleigh) who had previously commanded the Fourth Voyage become consul for the English, and he nominated John Jourdain as chief factor. Saris refused to recognise Sharpie as consul or to accept Camden's displacement, and the latter remained in charge of the Eighth Voyage's interests, although he died shortly thereafter and was succeeded by George Ball. However, Middleton was posturing from a position of weakness. He accepted 173 3/4 reals for provisions from the Eighth Voyage, 'hee hauinge great want ther of'.[49] The problem of voyage rivalry ceased to be of consequence after the creation of joint-stock voyages according to which a chief factor for Bantam was appointed by London, and later with the establishment of presidencies at Surat and Bantam. As a report dating from the 1650s put it, a compelling non-financial reason for setting up joint-stock voyages was

> ye inconveniences wch befell ye trade by having severall factories in Bantam for severall acco^{ts}. Each endeavouring to prosper ye interest of their distinct employments, they grew up to such an hight of disservice that they became as enemies one against another, making protests each agaynst ye other wch was a great disturbance to ye benefitt of ye trade.[50]

Meanwhile Saris had continued to make preparations for the voyage to Japan. Additional crew were taken aboard, mostly men reassigned from the other ships. But five Englishmen (recruited from men who had come out on different voyages but had remained in Bantam) who were living in the house, 'leaudlye [lewdly]' with local women, according to Saris, were also employed. They held out for their wages, non-payment of which lay at the heart of their complaint.[51] Five 'swarts', including a Gujarati resident in Bantam, were hired along with a Japanese and a Spaniard. The Japanese, another Bantam resident, was hired as a linguist and nicknamed John Japan and later translated from Japanese into Malay for Saris's benefit after the *Clove*'s arrival in Japan. The Spaniard, Hernando Ximenes, who spoke the 'Mallaye tonge verye perfect', had originally been assigned to help Camden but the pangeran, who was incensed against Ximenes for some unknown reason, urged Saris to take him on the *Clove*.[52] Saris was lucky with the ease with which he was able to redeploy men from other ships. Many sailors who came out to the Indies had had enough by the time they reached Bantam and were reluctant to serve on the next stage of the voyage. Those who did agree to continue usually regretted their decision. Jourdain argued that it was necessary to make an agreement in England with the sailors to ensure that they did not try to catch the first available ship home from Bantam.[53]

On 5 December, 133 barrels of lead, three chests and a remnant of tin, considered good commodities for Japan, were transferred from the *Hector*. Two days later six pieces of ordnance were removed from the *Hector* and the *Thomas* (four culverns and two slavers plus shot, valued at £108 13s 6d) on the recommendation of a Dutchman, recently come from Japan. He reported that ordnance was much in demand there and had contributed greatly to the Japanese granting the Dutch permission to set up a factory and had even been requested on the VOC's arrival. There was also a conference about suitable presents that could be spared from the cargoes of the two other ships.[54] A final problem occurred at the end of December when the *Thomas* sprang a leak. At first there was uncertainty about how serious it was. Saris was worried that if the ship had to be abandoned or laid up for a long time it would 'overthrow the voyage'. The crew were unmoved by reassurances that the leak was of no consequence and there were mutinous rumblings. However, the problem was quickly overcome and on 12 January 1613 the *Thomas* left Bantam to join the *Hector* on the voyage home. Two days later the *Clove* departed for Japan with a complement of eighty-one, stopping briefly along the coast at Jacarta for water and provisions and itself experiencing a leak which was quickly put right.[55]

Saris decided to use the voyage to Japan for a reconnaissance of the Moluccas to assess Dutch strength and see how easily spices could be obtained. The voyage to the islands was straightforward and uneventful although there were plenty of indications of the thriving country trade which criss-crossed the archipelago. On 9 February they met Richard Welden who had originally gone to the Indies on the *Expedition* in the Fifth Voyage in 1609. He had stayed on and was now working for the ruler of Boeton. Welden refused to join the *Clove* claiming 'it would be his vndoing, having nothing to live on in his counterye, and [was] in the waye of doing himself good here', a reminder that Adams was by no means the only Englishman prospering in the Indies. Welden also had a native consort.[56] On 24 February the *Clove* anchored off Bachan in the Moluccas. There followed just over five weeks of cat and mouse as the English attempted to defy the Dutch and thwart their efforts to exclude the English from access to the supply of cloves on the island and on the island of Makyan to the north, by far the richest of the clove-producing islands in the Moluccas.[57] Saris showed considerable resourcefulness and a determination not to be intimidated by constant Dutch harrassment as the *Clove* moved around the islands with local pilots acting as guides. The inhabitants ignored Dutch threats not to sell cloves to the English 'vpone there liues', but the Dutch were on their guard to prevent sales wherever possible. On one occasion, at Makyan, Saris met with a kinsman of the sultan of Ternate who reminded him that 'our natyon haue beene heare before, whose demenor they did genrally affect' and this Englishman (Drake) had promised to return 'yet [the Ternateans] could neuer see more then one at a tyme'. The man claimed that if the English would send more ships the Ternateans would rise up against the Dutch and Spanish (the Portuguese were no longer active in the Moluccas), much the same proposal as had been made to Drake. Unfortunately, by the second decade of the seventeenth century the Ternateans' freedom to manoeuvre had been greatly circumscribed. Saris was content to play the man along and the English managed to sell gunpowder and some broadcloth to the sultan.[58] Whatever the sense of achievement in making light of Dutch threats to seize and make a prize of the *Clove*, it was the

Hollanders, whom Cocks later claimed 'used us much worse then either Turks, Moors or any other heathen since our departure out of England',[59] who held the better cards. The Dutch were superior in numbers and had constructed fortifications, which Saris judged not to be impregnable. On more than one occasion, Saris's steadfastness notwithstanding, the English were lucky not to have been blown out of the water or at least have had their ship irredeemably crippled. Yet the VOC had its weaknesses in the Moluccas. The Dutch were still in the early stages of countering Spanish influence and establishing what was to become a brutal hegemony over the islands and they could not even take for granted the loyalty of their own men. Low morale bred discontent and some men deserted to the English. In an important coup for Saris, the VOC cape merchant at Bachan, who was thoroughly disaffected with his treatment by his employers, talked freely with the English commander about 'the hole state of there [the VOC's] business heare in the Mollocos and at Japan' and gave him valuable notes about the trade. The Hollander even contemplated going over to the English but was discouraged from doing so by Saris.[60]

The Dutch followed the *Clove* to Tidore (where they had seized the Spanish fort at Marieko the previous February) making good their promise 'to dogge vs tell we weare out of the Mollocos' but even at Tidore, where the Spanish still controlled a fortress on the eastern side of the island, cloves were not forthcoming, even if the Spanish were friendly. After pausing briefly before the Spanish fort at Ternate (the Dutch had also established themsleves on the island in 1607) the *Clove* set course for Japan on 14 April. The energy expended in the quest for cloves had resulted in the purchase of 3,690 lb at a cost of 273 reals, paid for in reals and Cambay cloth.[61]

On this final stage of the voyage, the *Clove* passed to the east of the Philippines, crossing the Tropic of Cancer at the beginning of June, and skirted Miyakojima, one of the southern islands of the Ryūkyū chain. They attempted to land but were prevented by strong winds and headed on to Kyushu where they arrived on 9 June, to the south of Nagasaki. On the 10th they bore north and at the entrance to Nagasaki Bay met four Japanese fishing boats. Two of the masters were hired at 30 reals each plus rice to take the *Clove* to its destination, Hirado, to the northwest. One of the boats was owned by a Portuguese from Nagasaki and its crew was Christian, but realising the *Clove* was not the Macao náo they retreated back to Nagasaki to report the new arrival. The following day, some two years and two months after her departure from England, the *Clove*, with seventy-one men aboard, anchored before the town of Hirado.[62] The East India Company had reached Japan.

(ii) The Establishment of the Hirado Factory, 1613

The reception at Hirado, or Firando as the English and Dutch called it, was friendly and encouraging. The daimyo, Matsūra Takanobu, and his grandfather, Shigenobu, came out with a flotilla of forty vessels to meet the ship and exchange formal greetings. The Matsūra were *tozama*, or outside, daimyo who had been in possession of the small domain since the eleventh century. The English, with customary confusion, at first referred to Shigenobu as the 'king' and to his grandson as his 'governor' (Takanobu's father had acceded in 1601, on Shigenobu's retirement, but had died the following year). Saris entertained them to a banquet with 'a good consort of Musicke' and the letter from James I was handed over. Later the head of the Dutch factory, Hendrick Brouwer, who had taken over from Specx in February, paid a courtesy call. Contrary to what Saris wrote long after his return to England, the Japanese had almost no idea of the English or England and it was preposterous for Saris to write that they sang a song about English *kurofune* (black ships) to terrify their children 'as the French sometimes did theirs with the name of Lord Talbot'.[63] This was pure fabrication written to titillate a readership that delighted in exaggerated opinions of English fame throughout the world.

As has been mentioned, Hirado was no stranger to overseas contacts. The domain, some 30 km long and 8 km across at its broadest, had been open to trade since the eleventh century and wakō had earlier found it a useful base from which to operate. Hideyoshi had recognised the strategic importance of northwest Kyushu and in 1591 had ordered the Matsūra along with other daimyo to provide a sea guard against possible Chinese incursions. Hirado had also attracted legitimate trade. The earliest Portuguese náo had called there between 1550 and 1564 during which time the domain was locked in fierce rivalry with the neighbouring domain of Ōmura, which had ceded Nagasaki to the Jesuits in 1571. One of the principal causes of this rivalry was the Matsūra's determination to have the náo call regularly at Hirado, a quest in which they were unsuccessful.

The domain had a large number of Christians. The Jesuits, by their own admission, had met with astonishing success in their missionary work in Hirado. Under the patronage of a few Matsūra vassals who were among the earliest converts in Japan, Christianity flourished. In 1580 Valignano estimated the number of Christians on the island and the small adjacent ones as 4,000, a figure which may well be exaggerated as the population of the town of Hirado alone was estimated at 2,000 in 1584. Jesuit success had been achieved despite the opposition of the daimyo, Matsūra Takanobu, who had retired in

1568 but who remained active behind the scenes, living for another
thirty years. Takanobu was described by the fathers as an 'astute
abhorrer of the Christian religion, a gentile to the bones'. He was
prepared to tolerate the new religion because of the strong personal
debt he owed to the faith's most important practitioner in his
domain, Jerónimo Koteda Yasumasa. Koteda had guaranteed the
Matsūra succession by caring for Takanobu from the age of thirteen
when the youth's father died, a perfect illustration of the fortuitous
but fragile circumstances which helped the spread of Christianity in
Japan. But in common with other daimyo, Takanobu also hoped
that Christianity would continue to bring commerce in its wake and
according to the first mendicants, who reached Hirado in 1584 from
Manila, he was reported to be willing to let the Augustinians set up a
convent if it resulted in trade with Manila for the domain. The debt
to Koteda was carried over to the next generation and Shigenobu,
whom the Jesuits called an 'old fox' odious to the Christians,
continued to tolerate the religion in the domain. He even did not act
against his daughter-in-law, an offspring of the Ōmura, who had his
grandson, the second Takanobu, baptised although the latter did not
grow up as a Christian and eventually became a persecutor of the
faith.

In addition to having enjoyed visits from the náo and encouraging
trade with Manila, the domain continued to have important but
unofficial links with China through the resident Chinese, and with
Korea where Shigenobu had served under Hideyoshi. The daimyo
had provided 3,000 men in each of the invasions and had attracted
sufficient attention from the Chinese to be included among a small
number of Japanese who had a reward of 5,000 ryo of silver put on
their heads, half of what the Chinese were offering for Hideyoshi and
Hidetsugu.

The Matsūra thirsted after foreign trade and, taking advantage of
the delicate state of national unity that existed into the early Tokugawa era, thrust themselves forward as best they could. The presence
of the Dutch had been welcome, the arrival of another set of
foreigners seemed to provide further confirmation of the domain's
fortune and that the Matsūra rather than their erstwhile rivals the
Ōmura had come off best after the arrival of the southern
barbarians.[64]

Saris wasted no time in getting down to business. A letter was sent
off to Adams, understood to be at Edo. It was sent with a letter from
the daimyo informing the bakufu of the arrival of the Clove. The
following day Saris received a letter from Adams which had been left
in the custody of his host at Hirado, Yasimon, nicknamed Zanzibar
by the English, for the first English ship that should arrive and Saris
sent off another letter to Adams. Much was expected of Adams who

had stressed his readiness to serve his native country and his letters had been positive about trade prospects in Japan.

On 12 June, with the Matsūra's assistance, the search for a house ashore was started so that the ship's cargo could be unloaded, inspected and stored. The decision to establish a factory came later. A choice was soon made and on the 16th an agreement was drawn up with the landlord, a man who was to figure prominently in the history of the factory, the head of the local Chinese community, Li Tan, or Andreas Dittis, the China Captain as the English referred to him. Li, who personified Hirado's historical connections with China, had extensive business interests both locally and overseas and agreed to prepare the house for the English and furnish it with Japanese tatami mats. The rent was fixed at 95 reals per month. The house was located in Kibikida, where the Chinese were settled (some distance from the Dutch). On 18 June Cocks moved ashore to supervise the preparations and by 1 July the house was ready for occupation and Saris ordered the merchants to transfer their beds and personal chests from the *Clove* to the house. He moved ashore himself the following day and a number of mariners were assigned to assist in the running of the house. The unloading of cargo did not begin until the 14th.[65]

The English tried to learn what they could about the VOC's activities. The Dutch themselves gave away nothing but Saris gleaned some information by bribing the Japanese waterman employed by the Hollanders.[66] But the Dutch did not have much to hide. They were still only piecing together the various strands of Japan's overseas trade. Their knowledge remained elementary and they were in no position to stand back and laugh cynically at the English even if they might relish the spectacle of the English repeating some of their own earlier mistakes. The extent of Dutch knowledge by 1613 was that the market for cloth was not as great as the Heren XVII imagined, although black and red of the right cut regardless of quality would sell, that ivory was not much requested while sappan wood from Patani and Siam would fetch handsome profits, and that manpower and cheap victuals were available in Japan to help further Dutch ambitions in the Spice Islands. The Dutch had realised the importance of silk imports to Japan from the opening of their factory. Brouwer noted that its selling price fluctuated according to supply. Nevertheless, Brouwer commented, as had Matelieff, that without access to a regular supply of Chinese silk Japan could not realise its full potential for the VOC. To avoid confronting the Portuguese and to evade Chinese customs duties Brouwer recommended establishing a factory on Taiwan. This suggestion was not acted upon; its time had not yet come and until the 1620s, certainly for as long as the English traded in Japan, the

Dutch shied clear of importing and selling silk in Japan to any significant extent. The market seemed unpredictable.[67]

On 29 June news reached Hirado of the arrival of Jan Joosten's and Melchior van Santvoort's junks from Ayuthia carrying cargoes of sappan wood and deer hides, another much sought-after good in Japan. Van Santvoort visited Hirado on 11 and 12 July with a letter for Adams from Antheunis and yet another letter from James I addressed to the 'King of Japan', the one carried by the Seventh Voyage. Saris found Van Santvoort friendly and forthcoming and was impressed by his competence in Japanese and his willingness to share his extensive knowledge of regional trade. Van Santvoort emphasised the importance of trading Chinese silk and Siamese goods such as sappan wood and deer skins in Japan, much as Adams had in his letter to Augustine Spalding. He mentioned that the Portuguese obtained silk in Macao, and the Spanish bought stocks in Manila while the Dutch procured silk at Patani where there was a plentiful supply as well as an availability of Siamese goods.[68] Van Santvoort's comments about goods that could be bought at Patani and Ayuthia were true so far as sappan wood and deer hides were concerned but were misleading in respect of silk which was only intermittently available. Most of the silk that was obtainable at this time was snapped up by the thriving local Chinese and Japanese communities. In fact Chinese merchants trading overseas were cautious about their investments and preferred to trade with places closer to home where the risk of loss at sea was less. As a result Japan and Manila were more usual destinations. The heavy exactions demanded by the authorities at Patani was another reason to dampen Chinese enthusiasm for voyages thither.[69] Unfortunately, Saris took Van Santvoort's advice at face value. There was no question of Van Santvoort deliberately deceiving Saris. The Dutch too erred in believing that raw and wrought silk and other Chinese goods were available in great quantities in Patani and Ayuthia. In 1611 and 1612 Specx and Brouwer commented that there was an oversupply of silk in Japan because of cargoes brought on Chinese junks from Patani and the *Hasewint* had brought 40 peculs 8 1/2 catties of white raw silk from Patani in 1612. The prospects for silk purchases seemed good. On 1 January 1614 (NS) Governor General Coen wrote to the Heren XVII about the good stock of silk that could be bought at Ayuthia and Patani to satisfy the VOC's needs.[70]

During these first days a start was made at selling some of the *Clove*'s cargo. Pepper and spices were sold to Matsūra Takanobu on credit, a foretaste of how most payments would be made in Japan.[71] Relations with the Dutch, who, as was to be expected, resented the arrival of the English but who could not harrass and threaten them as they had done in the Moluccas even had they wanted to, were

decidedly cool. It was made clear that both companies were competitors. Saris suggested that the companies fix a price for the sale of
cloth which they would both support 'to auance our Natiue Comodities'. But Brouwer demurred. The Dutch had a large supply in a
market that was already well satisfied and promptly slashed their
own prices in order to keep market share. This stymied the English
whose own cloth had become wormeaten during the voyage, a result
of poor dyeing and dressing, and was therefore more difficult to
sell. Matters were not helped by a squabble over the sappan wood
brought by Joosten from Ayuthia. At first Brouwer said that the
wood had been sent for the account of the English, an assertion he
subsequently withdrew. He claimed that Antheunis had in fact sold
the consignment to Joosten on the understanding that the English
factory at Ayuthia would receive back its capital plus 100 per cent
interest when Joosten or an agent (presumably Adams or Van
Santvoort) returned there. Saris doubted this story and demanded
documentation. When Joosten himself showed up at Hirado with a
letter for Adams he claimed that he was indeed the owner and had
purchased the wood on the terms mentioned by Brouwer. The
matter was not cleared up by the time of Saris's departure from
Japan. Joosten sold the wood, valued at £700, to the Dutch who
promptly resold it for a handsome profit. In 1614 Joosten paid the
English factory 748 taels although this turned out to be only a part of
the money owing. Joosten, whose business ventures frequently ran
into trouble, was considered a bad conduit for investment by many
Japanese. This did not stop the English from using his services at the
shogunal court when Adams's were unavailable. However, the
English had not been cheated. Antheunis had imagined he was
making a good deal by purchasing the wood with six months credit
from the Siamese king thereby confining the risk of the investment
only to the voyage. It would have been more profitable to have
followed the Dutch factor in Ayuthia and paid freightage for the
wood, for which Joosten charged 45 per cent of the cost, and have
someone sell it in Japan on the Company's behalf. The affair should
have been a salutary lesson for it illustrated that while the trade with
Siam was profitable, a good measure of co-ordination was needed
between the various factories engaged in the country trade if profits
were to be fully realised.[72]

Soon after their arrival, the English set aside presents to be divided
equally between the daimyo and his grandfather. These consisted of
broadcloth and Cambay cloth, gunpowder, aloes and two gilt-plated
cups, worth 340 3/8 reals. The bestowing of presents in Japan served
as a substitute for customs levies. It was essential for goodwill and
besides was a practice widespread in the Indies even in places where
customs dues were exacted, as Saris knew. Presents of lesser value

were given to other members of the Matsūra household. On one
occasion Shigenobu took a fancy to a gold ring belonging to Cocks.
After a council meeting it was decided to give it to the former
daimyo, although Cocks was allowed to charge it to the Company's
account.[73]

On 29 July Adams arrived at Hirado, much to the relief of the
English who had gained the impression that he had been deliberately
taking his time, an unfair assumption as he did not have the use of
speedier transport to bring him down from Edo. He was greeted
with a salvo from the *Clove* and was received with much honour by
Saris. A lot was expected of Adams and Saris, as usual, wasted no
time in getting down to business. However, the first meeting
turned out to be an anti-climax. Adams was quizzed about the trade
situation in Japan and replied that 'it was not allwayes alike, but
somtymes better somtymes worse, yet doubted not we should doe
as well as others, saying he would doe his best, giuing so admirable
and affectionated commendaytons of the Counterye as it is generally
thought emongst vs that he is a naturalised Japanner'. Adams's
refusal to lodge at the English house but to stay instead at his own
lodgings, with his mistress, where he hung out an improvised Cross
of St George, was taken as a snub by the English. The impression of
rudeness and indifference to the English was reinforced by his
comments that he could be contacted at his lodgings or at the Dutch
house and by his refusal to allow any of the English to accompany
him to his rooms. Adams's account of the meeting records that there
was a discussion of the cargoes brought in the *Clove*, all of which
with the exception of tin and lead he felt would provide little profit
'to requite such charge' (that is, the voyage from England). He noted
that the Dutch and the Spanish imported broadcloth and that this in
itself had led to a fall in prices and that local cotton textiles were a
match for Cambay cloth and were cheap. There was not much
demand for spices and the market for ivory, such as it was, had been
satisfied by the Dutch who were sending their excess supply to Siam
and places in China (presumably through Chinese intermediaries).[74]
Saris was not unduly discouraged by these comments. More suitable
cargoes could be sent by future shipping. He remained eager to
proceed to Sunpu and procure a charter of trading privileges from
Ieyasu and to pay his respects to Hidetada at Edo. Preparations for
the visit were set in motion.

On 7 August, after deciding on suitable presents for Ieyasu,
Hidetada and shogunate officials (here Adams's advice on the persons and the appropriate gifts was invaluable), arranging for transport, which was supplied by the Matsūra, and providing for the
government of the English house and the *Clove* during his absence,
Saris set off for Ieyasu's court at Sunpu, accompanied by Adams and

two of his servants, ten 'English', including Hernando Ximener, a tailor, cook and surgeon's mate, and John Japan. Besides making available a barque, the daimyo of Hirado provided a retainer and three men, one to carry Saris's pike.[75]

The journey followed the established 'westerly route' for the time: Hirado to Hakata, rounding the north coast of Kyushu through the straits of Shimonoseki and up the inland sea to Osaka where they disembarked and proceeded overland along the Tōkaidō, the road linking the imperial capital with the Tokugawa stronghold of Edo. Saris's description of the journey is interspersed with asides (inacurate in detail and added later) about recent Japanese history. At many places en route the party encountered groups of people, mainly children shouting 'Coré, Coré, Cocoré Waré' (probably something like 'Here, here! We're here!', but certainly not, as was imagined, 'You Coréans with false hearts').[76] In trying to get a measure of Japan, Saris's comparisons (added after his return to England) were inevitably with what was familiar in England. Osaka, where they arrived on 27 August, was estimated to be 'as great as London is within the walls with many faire Timber bridges of a great height, seruing to passe ouer a riuer there as wide as the Thames at London', and the castle, where Hideyoshi's son Hideyori resided, was very impressive with its huge stone walls 'cùt so exactly to fit the place where they are laid, that no mortar is vsed, but onely earth cast betweene to fill vp voyd creuises if any be.' At Osaka goods that had been brought from Hirado, including examples of the Cambay cloth, gunpowder, tin and steel, were left in the care of the innkeeper where they lodged, a usual practice in Japan. The English were to make extensive use of the innkeepers, or hosts as they styled them, during their stay in Japan. Saris found the castle of Fushimi, which Ieyasu used to overawe the Kinai region, impressive and admired the discipline of the soldiers, commenting favourably as a man from a country with no standing army, that their means of supply did not impose a burden on the surrounding countryside. From Fushimi, by order of Ieyasu, the party was provided with pack horses and a palanquin for Saris. This was borne by six men on level ground and by ten when going up hills. The party was treated as a quasi-embassy and awarded the same free passage along the Tōkaidō as was permitted to high officials of the shogunate, court nobles and official foreign embassies. The journey to Sunpu took about a week. Saris noted that the road was clearly divided at intervals of approximately 2 1/2 miles by small hills crowned by a pine tree so that 'the Hacknie men [the palanquin bearers], and those which let out Horses to hire, should not make men pay more then their due, which is about three pence a league'. The road was much travelled and passed by farms, villages, towns where the corpses of executed criminals were displayed on crosses, and temples in groves. On 6 September they arrived at Sunpu, where the sight of many heads upon a scaffold and more exposed corpses 'caused a most vnsauorie passage to vs', although it was the number of corpses exposed which Saris found distasteful not the practice.[77]

A day was spent preparing the gifts for Ieyasu. These included a gold basin and ewer, both marks of honour and respect in England, a roll of broadcloth, one of kersey, Cambay cloth, a telescope and 40s worth of fine English coins. The total value of the presents was just over 349 reals. A smaller selection of presents for Hidetada (worth 175 reals) and other shogunate officials was also made.[78] Saris tried to familiarise himself with court etiquette. The audience with Ieyasu was held on 8 September. The presents, plus some extra ones added on Adams's recommendation and given as if they were personal ones from Saris (they included a large satin quilt and '3 very faire holland napkins'), were laid out in the audience chamber for Ieyasu to view. According to protocol, which Saris questioned and felt unhappy with, Honda Masazumi, Ieyasu's secretary, took the letter from James I and passed it to Ieyasu who touched his forehead with it and, Adams interpreting, thanked Saris and bade him withdraw. Adams remained behind to translate the royal letter, embellishing it somewhat to make it sound more personal than the more general tone of the English original. Ieyasu instructed Adams to have Saris write a draft of his requests for consideration. Adams added, in his own version of the meeting, that Ieyasu asked whether Saris also intended to discover a northwest passage, in which case he offered his assistance both to that end and for any attempt the English might want to make to reach Yezo, which Ieyasu reported to be a great land. Adams was personally enthusiastic about such a scheme and sent a sketch (it would not have been accurate) of the area around Yezo to England. His enthusiasm was not shared by Cocks but Saris recorded some comments about Yezo which he had heard from a Japanese who had been there, describing the inhabitants, the Ainu, correctly, as 'very hairy', and mentioning that, contrary to Hakluyt's earlier assertion, the economy was little more than a barter one.[79]

Saris's original petition was found to be too long and the petition was rewritten and abridged and presented to Ieyasu on 10 September. An inventory of the goods that were to be offered for sale to Ieyasu (lead, tin, ivory, ordnance, gunpowder, aloes and fowling pieces) and the prices sought was left with Gotō Mitsutsugu, the master of the *kinza* and *ginza*, the officer in charge of the gold and silver mints and an important advisor to Ieyasu on foreign trade and diplomacy, who was given a suitable present.[80]

On 12 September the party left for Edo, again with horses and men provided by Ieyasu. They passed the huge copper *daibutsu* of

Kamakura 'in the likenesse of a man kneeling vpon the ground, with his buttockes resting on his heeles, his armes of wonderfull largenesse, and the whole body proportionable' which some of the men went inside and 'made an exceeding great noyse' and, following local custom, scratched some graffiti on the body. Saris also reported the custom of appeasing 'Tencheday' (Tenshodaijin, or Amaterasu Ōmikami, the sun goddess) at the Ise shrine, then becoming a place of pilgrimage, by offering 'one of the fairest Virgins of the whole countrey' once a month who was able to act as an intermediary between the priests and the goddess (Saris confused the deity's gender) after the latter had 'known her carnally'. The story was to be repeated in later descriptions of Japan with even more titillating embellishments.[81]

On 14 September they arrived at Edo, which Saris judged bigger than Sunpu. The castle with its gilded tiles and doors was more impressive and had many guards to protect Hidetada, whom Saris referred to as the king. Saris met Hidetada in audience on 17 September, proffering him a letter from the British king (another of the blanks with the name filled in) and presents. During their stay at Edo, Adams was very much in the background, if indeed he was present and had not gone on to his home at Uraga. He does not mention the audience in his letter to Sir Thomas Smythe and does not appear to have taken part in it. Adams's influence, such as it was, lay more with Ieyasu.

From Hidetada, Saris received presents (two lacquered suits of armour, one of which survives in the Tower of London) for James I and some small gifts for himself. On 21 September he went down to Uraga to examine the harbour as a possible location for the English factory and to look over the hull of a wrecked Spanish ship to see if it could be salvaged for use by the English but Saris thought Adams was asking too much for it and declined the offer. Saris stayed at Adams's house until 25 September before returning to Sunpu with Adams to receive the trading privileges and a letter from Ieyasu for James I on 8 October.[82]

The privileges gave the English permission to trade throughout Japan without hindrance, although the shogunate reserved the right to buy goods from newly arrived ships according to its require-ments. The English were to be given ground in Edo to set up a factory if they so wished (an option much favoured by both Ieyasu and Adams), were to be free to leave Japan as they wished and had the right to dispose of deceased Englishmen's goods. Moreover, the head of the English, the taishō, was to have the right to try his men for all offences committed. (Cocks believed that this authority extended to Japanese employed by the factory.)[83] This vaguely worded concession was not extraterritoriality according to

nineteenth-century practice. There was no question of immunity
from the law of Japan. The English were given the right to administer justice in conformity with the laws of Japan – a convenient
arrangement for the bakufu which had no interest in involving itself
in squabbles among non-Japanese and did not want to devolve any
prerogatives to the Matsūra. In practice the privilege was more
circumscribed than the English, or for that matter the Dutch,
imagined. Once again Adams had secured for the English no more
than the Japanese were willing to grant.[84]

The audiences with Ieyasu and Hidetada raise intriguing questions
about the status of the mission in Japanese eyes. At this time the
Tokugawa shogunate lacked fully developed protocols for the conduct of international relations to which countries wishing to participate in Japanese trade had to adhere. By the late seventeenth century
such protocols did exist and reflected a hierarchical perception of
state-to-state relations. Korea was considered an equal; Ryūkyū an
inferior. The Dutch and the Chinese fell into a different category.
The Dutch represented a company; the Chinese were individual
traders, although the Dutch were permitted the privilege of an
audience with the shogun but did not exchange official letters or
greetings. Their position reflected status distinctions that existed
within the Japanese hierarchy where some samurai had the right of
audience and others did not.[85] When the English, and the Dutch
before them, first arrived such refinements had yet to occur. Nevertheless, it is clear from the way Saris describes the reception by
Ieyasu (Adams's description is less specific and intended to emphasise
his own importance and the good relationship he enjoyed with
Ieyasu) that a certain protocol had to be observed. He mentions
being shown 'the Emperour's Chair of State, to which they [court
officials] wished me to doe reuerence', but none of the accounts of
the actual meeting with Ieyasu mention that the commander had to
lie prostrate, the manner in which daimyo were received, and the
manner in which Sebastián Vizcaíno, the Spanish ambassador from
New Spain, claims he was requested to greet Hidetada in 1611.
Vizcaíno refused on the grounds that the Spanish monarch was the
greatest ruler on earth and that it would be lèse-majesté to prostrate
himself before an inferior. He had been told that Rodrigo de Vivero
y Vasco had done so in 1609, but according to the latter's account he
did not.[86]

Saris too had his own ideas about protocol. He had insisted on
handing the letter from James I personally to Ieyasu, contrary to the
correct procedure, but it was snatched out of his hands before he
could do this by Honda Masazumi and tendered to Ieyasu.[87] Such
concern for niceties was not simply the product of an obsession with
ritual; flagrant breaches of protocol such as Vizcaíno's at Edo and

Sunpu, including the wearing of swords and the firing of guns,[88] undermined the prestige of the shogunate, demeaning it before those whom it sought to impress. Adherence to protocol implied respect for the shogun and was, therefore, *de rigueur*.[89] The Japanese did not consider the visit, nor that of the Dutch before, as official. The shogunate had not solicited an official relationship with England – or the Netherlands – although Ieyasu's letters to James I and to the 'king of Holland' (i.e. Prince Maurice) show that the visits and presents were both welcome and appreciated. But the shogunate did not choose to manipulate relations with the English and Dutch in the same manner as it did those with China, Korea and Ryūkyū. Nevertheless, the visit had its uses. The fact that Saris proceeded – as was required on this occasion – from Sunpu to Edo to the nominal shogun's court was a mark of recognition for the Tokugawa succession, sending another signal to the political nation about the regime's permanence.[90] The letter from James I, a distant, foreign ruler addressed in fraternal and respectful tones, accorded well with fledgling notions of a Japan-centered order of international relations and the concept of shogunal control over foreign relations. But neither the English nor the Dutch, unlike the Koreans and Ryūkyūans, became visible actors in the process of Tokugawa legitimisation by furnishing embassies on the occasion of successions within the Tokugawa line (no official ambassadors from either European country were sent to Japan until the nineteenth century). In this respect the Protestant nations were marginal players in the emergence of Japan's world order. Saris was, of course, ignorant of these considerations. He viewed the alien, and to him bothersome, details of court etiquette as a formality that had to be endured in order to secure the trade privileges.

The party returned to Hirado by way of Kyoto where they had to wait three days to collect ten painted screens which they had been promised by Ieyasu as a present for James I. Saris considered Kyoto 'the greatest Citie of Iapan' and appreciated many of the fine buildings, including the now-destroyed Hōkōji temple ('as long as the Westerne end of Saint Pauls in London, from the Quier, being as high arched and borne vpon pillars as that is,'), built by Hideyoshi, with its mound enclosing the ears and noses of Korean prisoners brought back to Japan, and where the last horse that Hideyoshi had ridden was kept. Saris mentioned the 'stately' Jesuit college which he believed contributed greatly to the success of the order's missionary work in Japan. He estimated that there were five or six thousand Christians in the city. He was impressed with the commercial life of the great city and commented on the distribution of tradesmen in locations according to their occupation and trade rather than being intermingled as was the case in English towns and cities. The party reached Osaka on 21 October and three days later boarded the daimyo of Hirado's barque, which had remained at their service during their visit to the courts, another indication of how hard the Matsūra were working to secure the English factory for Hirado. Saris finally returned to Hirado on 6 November.[91] The cost of the journey was 1,026 3/8 reals. The budget for expenses, excluding presents, had been set at 500 reals before departure, a gross underestimate. Saris had had to borrow 526 3/8 reals from Adams to meet the costs on the journey.[92]

Cocks's record of events, which was published by Purchas, provides information about what happened in Hirado during Saris's absence. The process of familiarisation with Japanese customs continued. Some customs, such as the spreading of gravel before the house and the compulsory hanging of paper lanterns during the August *bon* festival in honour of the spirits of ancestors, seemed a bother; others were puzzling. At a dinner in the Dutch house for Matsūra Shigenobu, Cocks noted that Brouwer served the Japanese dignitaries himself, pouring drinks for them on his knees. Brouwer later informed him that this was the custom of the country. Aspects of life in Hirado such as the constant danger and frequent occurrence of fire (some of which were arson) and the noise of the fire-criers throughout the night were irksome while the force of a typhoon, common in Japan in late summer, alarmed Cocks greatly. Cocks even introduced the first recorded example of English cooking in Japan, providing a meal of English beef, a stew of pork, onions and turnips, white bread and wine which was greatly appreciated by the Matsūra and cooked again after Saris's return.[93]

There were plenty of business matters to attend to during the commander's absence. Saris, was frequently in touch with Hirado and had instructed Cocks to try to sell all the pepper, cloves, ivory, broadcloth and striped Cambay cloth he could to various Kyoto and Nagasaki merchants who were expected in Hirado. On Adams's advice, the powder and other Cambay cloth which were expected to be sold to the shogunate, were not to be touched. Saris was not optimistic about the prospects for the 'evell-condytyoned' broadcloth.[94] On 12 September some Kyoto merchants visited the English house and looked over the goods. It became apparent that Japan was a buyer's market and that besides the glut the Dutch tactic of selling cloth at low prices had worked all too well. The merchants looked over two pieces of broadcloth, the best they could find, and offered £1 15s per yard, not bad in relation to what the Dutch had been selling cloth for after the arrival of the *Clove* (16–20 reals per tatami or approximately £1 12s–£2 per yard) but well below the prices Saris claimed they had fetched before their arrival (approximately £4 per yard) and the prices the English had imagined

broadcloth would sell for. The merchants upped their prices marginally a few days later but nothing was transacted.[95] Later Saris tried
to rationalise the lack of success as a consequence of poor English
sales technique. He alleged that he was told after his return from
Sunpu and Edo that 'you commend your Cloath vnto vs, but you
your selues weare least therof, the better sort of you wearing Silken
garments, the meaner Fustians, etc'. He added that 'I wish that our
Nation would be more forward to vse and spend this naturall
commoditie of our owne Country, soe we shall better encourage and
allure others to the entertainment and expence thereof'.[96] During
Saris's absence broadcloth, Cambay cloth, gunpowder, pepper and
cloves worth 594 5/8 reals had been sold to the Matsūra, and some of
the Cambay cloth left at Osaka had fetched 42 1/2 reals.[97]

The main headache for Cocks during Saris's absence arose from
the drunken and licentious behaviour of the crew when ashore where
they were able to take advantage of the plentiful supply of strong
liquor and women. Cocks sought to control excess and was able to
persuade the daimyo to issue a proclamation that no Japanese were to
receive any English into their houses after sunset and that Cocks
could enter any house especially the 'whoore house' run by one
Bastian to seek out offenders, a restriction which obviously caused
grumbling and protests from the men. Unruly behaviour threatened
to get out of hand after two men fought a duel ashore to settle an
argument and one man died from his wounds. The incident caused
problems with the Matsūra. The daimyo warned Cocks that after
any future such incident the offenders would be executed according
to Japanese custom. On 2 October Cocks was informed by the
master of the *Clove* that seven of the crew, including the Dutchman
who had deserted to the English in the Moluccas, had run away.
They made for Nagasaki and despite great efforts to have them
returned, including a promise to the Nagasaki *daikan* that they would
not be executed if they returned, they eventually left Japan, some on
a Portuguese ship for Macao, others for Manila. Cocks was afraid
that the desertion might set a precedent and was able to secure a
proclamation from the daimyo, who was willing to comply with the
English request, forbidding local people from transporting any of
the English from Hirado without informing the authorities. Cocks
and Saris suspected Miguel, the jurebasso and Adams's servant, of
complicity. They were also convinced of Spanish and Portuguese
involvement orchestrated by the Jesuits at Nagasaki despite protesta-
tions to the contrary.[98] After his return to England accusations were
made against Saris for 'scantinge of his people' on the voyage but the
Court rejected the charges, commenting that he had 'brought home
good store of victuals without any want vnto the men in the voyage'.
Such complaints were common and Saris does not appear to have

been particularly stinting.[99] It took little to provoke men to desert. The grass always seemed greener elsewhere. The real losers were the deserters' wives and families in England. They later pleaded to the Company for payment of the wages due the men at the time of their desertion. The Court dismissed their pleas outright although the directors took pity at the plight of the father of one man who had petitioned the Court for relief and awarded the old man 40s from the poor box.[100]

Saris's final month in Japan was taken up with preparations for the voyage home and establishing the factory. A merchandising council approved the decision to set up the factory. Saris cited several reasons for going ahead: first the intelligence received from the VOC servant in the Moluccas; second, the fact that the Dutch were already settled at Hirado; third, the trading privileges granted by Ieyasu; fourth, hopes of trade with Siam and Patani (it was obvious from Adams's and Van Santvoort's advice, and from observations while in Hirado, that participation in the country trade would be an absolute requirement for the success of the factory, and a letter had already been sent to Lucas Antheunis at Ayuthia on 9 November most probably informing him of the successful visit to Sunpu); fifth, the fact that the stock brought specifically for Japan remained to be sold. The staff was to comprise eight merchants, three Japanese jurebassos, and two servants with Cocks as head of the factory. Adams was taken into the Company's service for two years. The conversations with Melchior van Santvoort, the friendly relations with the Matsūra, the information acquired second-hand about the Dutch trade, the encouragement received from the Nagasaki *daikan* on his visit to Hirado in early October, and the invitation from Terazawa Hirotaka, daimyo of Karatsu, who came aboard the *Clove* on 20 November, and with whom the English were to enjoy good relations, to trade in his domain, reinforced the view that the trade was worth a try. The question of the poor market for broadcloth seemed surmountable if, as was intended, Hirado was used as a base to reach Korea through Tsushima and better quality cloth, properly dressed and laden, were sent from England. Further investigation might lead to the discovery of markets elsewhere. The alternative – everyone to return to Bantam or London – would have been tantamount to failure and would have reflected badly on Saris, laying him open to charges of poor judgement and irresponsibility for spending so much time and money with no results.[101]

The decision to set up a factory at Hirado (rather than at Uraga, close to Edo, as Ieyasu hoped and Adams had recommended, and where the Spanish had originally been given the right to call before they were given access to all Japanese ports in 1609) followed from the same reasoning that had led the Dutch to turn down a similar offer from Ieyasu to open their factory at Uraga. The Hollanders had realised that Uraga, near the entrance to Edo Bay, was a safer haven for ships than Hirado and Saris noted this during his visit there, describing it as 'a very good harbour for shipping, where ships may ride as safely as in the Riuer of Thames before London,' with easy access to the open sea. Its only disadvantage he felt was that it was 'not so well replenished with victuall and fleshmeat as Firando is'.[102] Brouwer had rejected Uraga as a site for the VOC factory because the Dutch had already established themselves at Hirado, enjoyed good relations with the local people, and had invested a lot of money to gain the goodwill of the Matsūra.[103] The English too had found the local people hospitable and the Matsūra had made great efforts to impress the English and make them feel welcome. They had done the same for the Dutch upon their arrival, making land available to the VOC.[104] For the Matsūra the presence of another group of *nanbanjin* at Hirado could not but enhance the domain's prestige and, more importantly for such a small territory, generate additional income. There were other points in Hirado's favour. It was more convenient as a first port of call for ships arriving from Bantam and had long been open to the trade of the China Seas. Moreover, the English could keep an eye on the Dutch in much the same way as the companies shadowed each other elsewhere in the Indies. Both were rivals in the Japan trade, but novices as well; much could be learned from watching each other. Over the course of the years there were to be ups and downs in the relationship between the English and the Matsūra and Cocks eventually contemplated moving the factory to Nagasaki or to the Gotō Islands in the Karatsu domain to escape from what he felt had become the intolerable exactions at Hirado. But he failed to realise that in their dealings with the *nanbanjin* the Matsūra did not have a free rein either. They were subject to pressures from Edo, pressures which became more exacting as the shogunate altered its policies regarding foreign trade. The decision to set up the factory at Hirado cannot be counted among the reasons for the factory's ultimate failure.

Death and desertion had taken their toll on the crew of the *Clove* and made it necessary to recruit new crew members before the ship's departure. An approach was made to the Matsūra for a dozen or so Japanese who could make the voyage to England and they undertook to help find suitable men other than the 'vagrant people' who hung about the town. The Dutch had employed their first Japanese sailors and artisans in February 1613 to man a barque which had accompanied the *Roode Leeuw* on its return voyage to Bantam in February 1613. Brouwer found the men wholly suitable, willing to serve for modest pay and easily satisfied with a simple diet of rice and salted fish which reduced victualling costs. Fifteen Japanese were added to the *Clove*'s payroll bringing its complement to sixty-nine, marginally less than that on the voyage from Bantam to Japan, and 246 1/24 reals was allocated for them. Another new crew member was George Peterson, a Fleming from Flushing and an acquaintance of Adams, returning home with his life savings after twenty-four years' service in Spanish ships, including a stint as a master's mate in the voyage from Acapulco to Manila.[105]

The *Clove* was victualled and the goods that were not to be left in Japan were loaded aboard. These included 47 3/4 barrels of gunpowder which remained unsold (some of which might be needed anyway), two chests containing 4,000 reals apiece, and two broadcloths which were to be used to make clothes for the men as 'could weather [was] Cominge one'. The presents for James I were also loaded and a selection of Japanese goods bought from Adams. These were mainly Japanese writing tables and chests, probably *tansu*, purchased for 628 3/4 reals, and were to prove fashionable in England. An additional 5 5/8 reals had been spent to pack them.[106] Once such trivial matters as bar bills had been settled by the purser (the money was to be abated from the men's wages), the ship was ready to begin the return voyage to Bantam. On 5 December Cocks and the other members of the English factory took their leave, and the ship departed from Hirado heading out into the China Sea and down the China coast, passing the Pescadores and Macao before crossing the Gulfs of Tongking and Siam. On 30 December, some miles short of Bantam, they met the *Darling*, bound for the Coromandel Coast, and learned of the death of Sir Henry Middleton. On 2 January 1614 they encountered the *Expedition* en route for England and transferred a number of letters and four chests to her. The following day the *Clove* sailed into Bantam road. The letters carried by the *Expedition* were read to the Court on 1 July and mentioned the establishment of the Hirado factory 'wth great priuiledges from the Empero^r for trade' and 'the hope of venting Guzarratt Comodities and pcuringe store of China silks, Brasil wood and Skynes wch will yield greate pffitt at Japan.'[107] It was the first news the Company had of the Hirado factory, and both optimistic and misleading: Gujarati cloth was not much in demand in Japan and silk would be difficult to procure in any significant quantity.

At Bantam Saris found that no cargo had been provided for the *Clove*'s homeward lading. The factors of the Eighth Voyage had assumed Saris would not return from Japan until later, and then by way of the Moluccas in order to pick up cloves, and had not bothered to find pepper for the ship. This was something Saris had been afraid might happen before leaving Japan where nevertheless he had left most of the money brought out from England as part of the Hirado factory's stock, taking only the two chests of reals and leaving the *Clove* short of ready cash at Bantam. Once again, the practice of managing voyages separately became self-defeating for the pursuit of the Company's overall interests. After Middleton's death in May 1613, resentment over his appointment of Jourdain as chief factor over the heads of some of the other merchants flared up and almost caused a fight. Jourdain was denounced as 'a neuter' rather than a Company employee and one of the merchants threatened to put him in the bilboes. Tempers were cooled with the arrival of Thomas Best, commander of the Tenth Voyage and a friend of William Adams, from Surat in November where he had succeeded in establishing a factory. At Bantam Best tried to bring some order into the Company's affairs considering it 'a greate disgrace...to our nation and the Honorable Companie our employars to have soe many houses in one place, sepeerated both in qualitie and friendshipp'. With the consent of a mercantile council he persuaded Jourdain to act as chief factor pending a more thorough reorganisation when orders came from London. Separate accounts were still to be kept for each voyage.[108]

On his return to Bantam, Saris was greatly annoyed to learn of Jourdain's appointment and chastised him for not having come out personally to welcome him. Saris threatened to have Jourdain repatriated, a threat that did not alarm Jourdain because Saris had no authority to rescind Best's appointments. Another butt of Saris's temper were the merchants of the Eighth Voyage who had been left at Bantam but whose numbers had been reduced by death. Saris felt they had not been sufficiently attentive to their duties. However, his anger was quickly spent and relations with Jourdain improved as the latter agreed to use money from other voyage accounts to purchase a cargo for the *Clove*. As had happened with the lading for the *Thomas* and the *Hector*, prices rose when it became obvious that the ship was in a hurry. Kewee, the Chinese supplier, told Saris that the price had been 1.2 reals per bag. Saris offered 1.25 but had to settle for 1.3 with some small discount per bag, the weighing of which Saris carefully observed. Saris ordered further changes in the organisation of the factory. The factors were instructed to live together in one house, instead of the present 'upper' and 'lower' ones, thus reducing food and lodging costs. Jourdain supported the move believing that it would

> be fitting both for the profit of the Worshipful Company and not scandalize our nation as formerly it hath been in keeping so many houses, to the glory of the Hollanders, who in their trade are our mortal enemies, and to the profit of the Chinese and Javas, which doth look for such opportunities to have one to cross another that they may the better encroach upon us in the sale of their commodities.

The number of warehouses was to be reduced and the goods better stored to cut costs, and renewed efforts were to be made to get the pangeran's permission to build a new house. This was finally secured after a payment of 1,500 reals. In February 1615 one of the Company's factors speculated that the better health enjoyed by the merchants at Bantam might be attributable to the new house 'having a better air...than formerly we had at our old house'.[109]

By 27 January the *Clove* had her lading aboard and on 13 February passed through the Sunda Straits to begin the homeward voyage. A stop of twenty-three days was made at Table Bay in May for victualling and refreshment. Here the *Clove* found the *Concord*, which had left England in January, the first ship sent out after the establishment of the joint stock in 1613. Saris received letters from the Company informing him that it was planned to send a ship and pinnace for Japan with orders to call at Bantam to receive any instructions that he might have left. (These vessels were part of the first joint stock voyage proper under Nicholas Downton which left the Downs in early March 1614, reaching Table Bay shortly after Saris's departure.) But Saris had left no memorandum about trade in Japan. He had paid little attention to the role of Bantam in the Japan trade emphasising rather the importance of Ayuthia and Patani. This was a surprising omission. After reading the letters, Saris drafted a report of the voyage to Japan and the setting up of the factory, recapitulating the orders he had left with Cocks. This, together with a letter for Cocks, was carried on the *Concord* to Bantam where she arrived on 8 September. Saris justified his omission on the grounds that letters brought to Bantam by Best on the *Dragon* and by the *Expedition* of the Twelfth Voyage, which had left England on 7 January 1613, implied that the Company was awaiting his return before doing anything further about the Japan trade. All that Saris had left at Bantam concerning Japan was an invoice of the goods unloaded at Hirado.[110]

The *Clove* continued her voyage home and arrived at Plymouth on 27 September. This was not quite the end of the Company's longest, most expensive, and, as it turned out, most profitable voyage so far. Violent storms, 'more tempestuous...and our liues more endangered, then vpon the whole Voyage', delayed the ship in Plymouth for some time and it was not until 6 December that the *Clove* finally arrived at Blackwell, where her condition was described to the directors as 'sweete and cleane and a very good shipp'. On 10 December the directors went aboard to supervise the unloading of the cargo. In the weeks before there had been a burst of frenzied activity. Preparations were begun for the sale of the cargo and steps taken to find out what had happened during the voyage. The Court was immediately suspicious about the reasons for the delay at

Plymouth. In a standard clause, Saris's instructions had specifically forbidden any of the ships under his command to put into Falmouth, Plymouth or Dartmouth on the outward or homeward voyage. The directors tended to assume the worst about the motives of their employees, and were determined to prevent any illicit discharge of cargo for private trade. The Court had got wind of this possibility from letters Saris had sent to his brother and cousin who worked in the customs house. Saris asked his brother to send a lighter and two watermen. The Company suspected that Saris 'had vsed very greate priuate trade for himselfe and purposed to conveye away his goods out of the ship'. Concerned to protect its own market it acted quickly. Still expecting the speedy arrival of the *Clove* at the Downs, the Court resolved to send two directors to secure the intervention of customs officials to prevent any private trade. They were to be given £300 to provide necessities for the ship and to buy up goods brought by the mariners 'to preuent ther sale to any other for marringe of the marketts here'. Steps were taken to intercept private letters, including Saris's, and an official was sent to make enquiries 'at the Starre in Bredstreete, the place where Westerne men doe resorte' in case any surreptitious deals were being made for the sale of goods with merchants from the outports or their representatives. Saris was to be asked to surrender his own goods for storage in Sir Thomas Smythe's house but he was to be assured that he would be dealt with in a 'freindlie and kindlie' manner.[111]

Opinion was divided in the Court as to whether Saris should be sent for overland immediately. The majority felt that such an order would be tantamount to disgrace and would ruin his career and that 'his fower years seruice should nott be soe slenderlie respected, which may proue as beneficiall a discouery to this Company and land as euer any was made'. Besides it would hardly have induced him to be co-operative. Finally, it was felt that his presence was needed aboard ship to maintain order and to do what he could to prevent the men from going ashore to sell goods. Still, the Court was anxious to learn in greater detail about the Japan factory. Gradually news filtered up to London. On 12 October a letter from William Adams to Best, dated 1 December 1613, was read, presumably obtained by intercepting the mail (the Court suspected that Adams and Best were in cahoots over private trade). On the 14th the Court requested Saris to send a copy of 'such instructions as he framed and sent by the *Concord* for Iapan, as alsoe the coppie of such as he lefte at Iapan and Bantam'. Saris obliged and eleven days later a detailed letter was received containing information about his stay in Japan and an assessment of the trade prospects there. The following day more information was received including a copy of the privileges (in reality a paraphrase of Saris's original petition to Ieyasu), which were thought to be 'as ample as can be required in that kinde'. Finally on 12 November Saris himself, having come overland, probably of his own volition, appeared before the Court and gave a very full verbal report of the voyage's achievements. Unfortunately, there is no record of what he said. Two days later a full debate was held about whether or not the newly established trade with Japan should be pursued. In addition to Saris's written and verbal reports the Company had received letters from Cocks, Tempest Peacock, Richard Wickham and Adams containing opinions about the trade.[112]

Saris's views were the most detailed. He described the goods that could be sold in Japan and what was available there, gave prices and made a few general observations. He was optimistic, excessively and unjustifiably so, about the chances for the sale of broadcloth, 'of all sortes' adapted for the local market by being low shorn, which he suggested had been in far greater demand than silk or velvet before they arrived and was used by 'the better sorte in vests, coueringe for ther saddles and cases for ther Cattans [swords]'. He suggested broadcloth would fetch between 30 and 50 taels per tatami (that is, between approximately £3 15s and £6 5s per yard) and felt confident that despite Brouwer's attempts to flood the market by reducing the price from £8 per tatami, or approximately £4 per yard, after the arrival of the English 'Mr. Cockes and the Fleminge are agreed and haue aduanced the price againe', a supposition he had no justification for making. (Ironically, the Spanish viceroy of Peru had written to his royal master in 1612 informing him that wool was not suitable to be sent to Manila because of the heat and that in Japan where the cold might make woollen goods attractive 'they cost very little, for the natives cloth themselves with the taffetans of that country, and use cotton quilts'.)[113] English cloth such as bays, velvets, satin, damasks and taffetas would find a ready market, as would Cambay cloth. Other principal commodities in demand in Japan included China silk, especially raw silk, 'whereof there cannot be too much carryed', pepper, which would yield two for one, cloves, sappan wood, deer hides, copper (he meant red copper), lead, tin, iron, steel, ivory, and sugar. In addition he supplied a list of miscellaneous items ranging from paintings, 'som laciuious, others of stories of warrs by sea and land, the larger the better' (Saris had brought back 'certaine lasciuious bookes and pictures' which were judged 'a greate scandall vnto this Companye' and were publicly burnt in January 1615), to glassware, gilt mirrors, table-books, wax and honey. Saris reported that the main exports available in Japan were a blue dye 'allmost as good as Indico' (a commodity in which the Company was beginning to take an interest), rice, brimstone, saltpetre and, most important of all, silver, which could be freely exported and used to pay for the purchase of commodities in the Indies 'whereby the scandall for transportinge siluer from hence will bee taken awaye'. (Gold was available, he said, but was too highly priced.) Saris outlined the organisation of the factory as he had left it and the tasks he had set the merchants, especially that of breaking into the country trade from Japan to Ayuthia and Patani. He mentioned the friendly reception from the Matsūra for whom a small present would be in order (he suggested cloth, a kit for falconry, and some dogs) and that victuals and crew were readily available in Hirado for English ships. He added that Japan would make an ideal base for the discovery of a northwest passage, mentioning Yezo (about which he wrote a separate piece) as a promising market for the sale of cloth and pepper and as a source of gold, silver and fur, a commodity increasingly in demand in England. Saris was convinced that the English would have the support of the 'emperor' for such an undertaking, suggesting that the Dutch had failed to seize this opportunity because of their struggle against the Spanish in the Moluccas. In short, he felt that 'Iapan will proue by the next returne more profittable to you then it may be you expect' and that the Court should act on his 'slender aduise...for it is trwe'.[114]

Unfortunately, 'true' was not the correct label to describe his advice which was misleading on some points and plain wrong on others. China silk was not available in abundance at either Ayuthia or Patani, and Saris was quite wrong to suggest that silver could be refined cheaply at four per cent and then used to buy goods else-where in the Indies, and that bar silver, of which he brought back a specimen, could be 'quined [coined] into Rialls, without refininge' and used as currency throughout the Indies.[115] The Company took these assertions at face value. It trusted the judgement of its com-mander. Experience was to prove otherwise. The only Japanese goods brought back on the *Clove* for the Company to examine were writing desks, the trunks bought from Adams, screens, pottery, and lacquer-ware, which Saris felt was a good adventure recommend-ing that in the next voyage 1,000 or 2,000 reals should be invested in these 'trinkets'. (He had forgotten to bring back a sample of the indigo dye *ai*, which was indeed available in Japan from indigo plants, *tadeai*, in which the Company was interested.) The screens, 'biobee', that is *byōbu*, were sold off at between 3 guineas and £10, the best having been exchanged for the ones intended as a present for James I from Hidetada, which had been damaged on the voyage. Perhaps the most surprising item that Saris listed as being in demand in Japan was copper, which was already well established as a Japanese export. However, Saris was not alone in making this bizarre recom-mendation. Specx, who had drawn up a list of items suitable for trade with Japan together with their prices to which Saris's own list bears an uncanny resemblance,[116] had advised the VOC to send coarse red copper to Japan. Unlike Saris he included white or finer copper among the commodities that could be exported from Japan and believed (correctly) that there was a market for it elsewhere in the Indies, for example on the Coromandel Coast. But it was only from the 1620s, and thanks to the persistence of their factors in Japan and Batavia, that the Heren XVII took an interest in Japanese copper for the European market and began to appreciate the potential profits.[117]

The other factors wrote more generally. Cocks agreed about the availability of silver but was more sanguine about the prospects for cloth, which he judged would sell well but at low prices, adding, with his own unflagging optimism, that as yet the Japanese 'are so addicted to silks that they do not enter into consideration of the benefit of wearing cloth; but time may alter their minds, and in the meantime we must seek out other matters'.[118] Peacock stressed that any profits to be made from trade with Japan would have to come from breaking into the country trade with Ayuthia and Patani. He was pessimistic about the outlook for cloth sales, especially about the worm-eaten supply brought out on the *Clove*.[119] Wickham shared this downbeat assessment, mentioning that the Dutch and the Spanish had already glutted the market, but hoped that discoveries to the north of Japan would yield better results.[120] The Court had three letters from Adams, including one brought back on the *Expedition*, dated 12 Janauary 1613 and addressed to Augustine Spalding at Bantam. It was read to the Court on 5 July and gave the impression that Adams was 'the onlie Instramt that the Holland[rs] haue to mediate for them wth the Empero[r]'. His letters emphasised that English cloth was not a suitable commodity for sale in Japan and repeated his blunt statement to Saris that the goods brought in the *Clove*, including the pepper and cloves, were not worth the investment involved. Adams enthusiastically endorsed the idea of a reconnaissance to the north of Japan, recapitulating his own shipbuilding experience and stressing that ship's stores, victuals and crew were readily available in Japan. He emphasised the importance of the country trade to the Dutch and suggested that the Hirado factory was strategically important to them as a supply point for men, munitions and victuals to fight their war against the Spanish in the Moluccas, an assessment that Cocks and Wickham shared.[121]

Such was the information available to the Court on which the directors could base their decision about the Japan trade. But other considerations had a bearing as well. Saris had made the voyage a success. It had yielded a 200 per cent profit, mainly from the sales of pepper, and the Court was pleased. After a thorough consideration of his management of the voyage, reservations about his unauthorised opening of Company letters during the outward voyage, disapproval of his private trade and criticism from some of the directors that he had spent too much on presents in Japan were swept aside. (He deflected the criticism by answering that the presents, including some from his own goods, had been approved by the mercantile council – a valuable insurance – and had been made 'for the honnour of his Countrye, and the grace of this Companie'.) The Court decided 'to giue [him] his bond and pardon his freight' (that is, he did not have to pay freight charges for the goods he had brought back).[122]

Saris's achievement seemed all the more outstanding when compared with that of Best, who had established the factory at Surat and who had been given a hero's welcome on his return home and an audience with James I. Best himself expected a knighthood and the Company did not object to seeing another of its servants added to the gallery of national heroes. (Lancaster had been knighted after his return from the First Voyage.) But Best quickly fell from grace. The Court began proceedings against him accusing him of negligence in carrying out his instructions and of taking advantage of the confused arrangements at Bantam, 'makinge good use of fishinge in that troubled water' by conspiring with others, including Ball of the Eighth Voyage, to maximise his private trade and returning from a voyage that was 'one of the meanest that hath bene made for the Companye' and which would have been 'the worste voyage for the Companye that ever any had done which retorned saufe' had he not helped himself to some of the cargo salvaged from Middleton's flagship the *Trade's Increase*.[123] Saris's stock was riding high and his employers were inclined to take his views seriously. An additional argument in favour of proceeding with the Japan trade was the belief that the Dutch had invested about £1,500 in building their house in Hirado which, it was conjectured, they would scarcely have done if they did not expect a good return. In fact the Dutch had spent just over *f.* 14,619 on clearing a site (twenty-two houses were demolished) and building a warehouse and accommodation.[124] Dutch reticence over many aspects of their trade and the English belief that they were trading extensively was wrongly interpreted as a mask to hide a profitable trade. On 14 November after hearing all the arguments for and against the trade and disregarding inconsistencies in Saris's testimony (in his oral account to the Court he had recommended purchasing pepper at Bantam for Japan, while in his written testimony he suggested that the two pinnaces, then being prepared for the Indies, should call at Patani and Ayuthia to procure silk, sappan wood and deer hides and pepper from Patani 'which is much fayrer [in price] than Bantam pepper') it was concluded 'that the place is very hopefull'. Steps were to be taken on Saris's advice to procure cargoes for Japan, including cloth, stone pots and steel, to be sent on the pinnaces, the *Advice* and the *Attendant*.[125]

Saris's words had been as sweet music to the ears of the directors.

He had encouraged them with the same great expectations as had his VOC counterpart, Abraham van den Broeck, who in 1610 had reported on the first visit of the Dutch to Japan and urged the Heren XVII to confirm the trade. Brouwer later complained to his employers that Van den Boeck had exaggerated both the market for European goods and the prices that could be obtained for those in demand – a distortion which 'will cause your Excellencies pain'.[126] It was not to be long before similar complaints against Saris were to be heard from the English factors in Japan. The prevailing optimism of the Court was tempered by dissenters for whom the idea of a direct trade with Japan was unpopular on the grounds of the high costs involved. These doubts, which echoed Adams's, had been expressed even before Saris's arrival in London on the grounds that direct trade between England and Japan 'will not answere the chardge'. They had been countered by arguments that the country trade would be an important way of furnishing goods for the factory.[127] Nevertheless, the doubts persisted. On 14 February 1615 the Court resolved 'not to be discouraged by the supposcons of some whoe haue noe opinion at all of that trade' and set up a committee to advise on the purchase of goods to be bought for the trade. In the face of continued opposition, the following week it declared the authority of the committee to be absolute and instructed it 'not to let slipp any opportunities, nor neglect any time' and to procure cloth from the draper, have it dyed and dressed if necessary, according to former practice. Although not a member of the committee, Saris was the single most important influence in determining which goods were suitable.[128]

The decision taken in Hirado in December 1613 to set up a factory had been approved by the directors. Japan, or at least places within striking distance of the factory, were thought likely to provide a good market for broadcloth and other European goods. The Hirado factory's participation in the country trade, from which silk was expected to furnish the rest of the Company's operations in the southwards area with silver, would reduce the need for bullion exports from England and thereby undermine criticism of the Company as a drain on the country's store of silver. These were high expectations indeed.

CHAPTER 4

First Years in Japan

(i) The Trading World of Japan and the Organisation of the Factory

By the time that the Dutch and the English reached Japan the structure and extent of the country's overseas trade was on a completely different footing from that of the early 1540s when the Portuguese first arrived. Both Hideyoshi and Ieyasu had actively encouraged the expansion of foreign trade, partly for political reasons and partly in response to the changing nature of the economy. Hideyoshi had taken steps to curb the activities of the pirates around the western end of the inland sea and, as a man determined to eliminate or bring under control opponents or competitors for power, he favoured bringing the wakō to heel. The suppression of the wakō was one of the consequences of his pacification of Kyushu in 1586–7 and its incorporation into the Toyotomi settlement. Gradually the harbours frequented by the wakō in northern Kyushu were eradicated. Hideyoshi's measures neatly complemented moves to stamp out piracy on the China coast although there was of course no co-ordination of policy between China and Japan and wakō activity on the China coast had fallen off considerably since the 1560s.[1] However, it was impossible to stamp out piracy completely in the China Seas. As an astute observor wrote at the end of the sixteenth century, many of those sailing the seas were 'merchants by the light of the sun and pirates in the dark of the night'. Some of the activities of the Dutch and the English, especially when they operated the joint fleets of defence in 1620–2, were little more than acts of piracy no matter how they were dressed up in the rhetoric of the pursuit of geopolitical ambitions, and when the Portuguese did not have to contend with the outrages of the northern Europeans, vessels from Macao were prone to attack by Chinese pirates. Piracy continued throughout the seventeenth century with European marauders, the most notorious of whom was Captain

Kidd, joining the fray and it persisted into the following century and beyond.[2] Those Chinese and Japanese pirates who did not transform themselves into peaceful traders, taking advantage of the increased opportunities for trade between China and Japan from the second half of the sixteenth century (still an illegal trade as the Ming decrees forbidding trade with Japan had not been revoked) had to move further afield to southeast Asia to secure a living. It was one such band of Japanese wakō who attacked Sir Edward Michelbourne on his interloping voyage in December 1605 near Patani, killing, among others, the pilot, John Davis. The tenacious Japanese, save one who briefly sought quarter before leaping overboard, fought to the death.[3]

Hideyoshi encouraged foreign trade but his aggressive tone, reflected in his threats to invade the Philippines,[4] and pretensions to regional supremacy were at odds with this objective, even if one argues that among the motives for invading Korea in the 1590s (albeit a perverse one) was a desire to reopen official trade with China.[5] One way in which Hideyoshi sought to encourage foreign trade was by granting licences to merchants for trade overseas. These licenses had precedents, notably in the Satsuma domain's trade with Ryūkyū in which vessels carried an authorisation from the daimyo.[6] They were issued under Hideyoshi's official vermilion seal, a practice continued by the first three Tokugawa shoguns. Such documents were issued for other important business as well and were called simply *shuinjō*, literally vermilion seal documents. The vessels which were so permitted to make voyages were called *shuinsen*, or vermilion seal vessels. The *shuinjō* not only gave permission for an overseas voyage but was intended to protect its bearer from hostile acts on the high seas. In this sense they were similar to the Portuguese *cartaze* or the passes issued by the English and Dutch. The *shuinjō* also made clear the distinction between legitimate Japanese foreign traders and the wakō.

The first *shuinjō* were issued by Hideyoshi in 1592 to merchants from Nagasaki, Kyoto and Sakai for voyages to Qui-nam (in the central Vietnamese kingdom of Annam), Cambodia, Tongking, Patani, Ligor (present-day Nakhorn Si Thammarat in peninsular Thailand), Taiwan, Luzon (Manila), Macao and Ayuthia. Other *shuinjō* were undoubtedly issued over the following eight years until 1604 when, under Ieyasu, more detailed records become available, although by no means all Japanese vessels sailing overseas during these years carried *shuinjō*.[7] From 1604 until the shogunate completely forbade voyages overseas by Japanese vessels in 1635, some 356 licences were issued. They were granted to Japanese, Chinese and Europeans, including the servants of the English and Dutch companies and individuals such as William Adams, and Jan Joosten. Of the *shuinjō* issued to Japanese, the majority were given to merchants. Daimyo could obtain *shuinjō* for overseas voyages until 1612 when the shogunate banned daimyo from constructing ships for overseas voyages, although the ban did not prevent daimyo, especially those in northern Kyushu, from investing in *shuinsen* voyages. The geographical origins of the Japanese *shuinsen* operators were concentrated on Kyushu and the Kinai; operators from other parts of Japan were numerically insignificant. For example, only one *shuinsen* owner was from Edo. This reflects the historical and commercial importance of western Japan in overseas trade. The *shuinjō* themselves were prepared by Zen monks in Kyoto who compiled registers of individuals to whom the documents were granted. Cocks referred inaccurately to the monks as clerks or 'griffers' of the privy seal. The *shuinjō* were only issued after a letter of authorisation had been received, usually from Honda Masazumi or Hasegawa Sahyōe Fujihiro to whom applications for the documents were generally made, although other senior bakufu officials occasionally gave authorisation. A small payment was made as well. The *shuinjō* were non-transferable and were issued for the specified voyage only and were supposed to be returned on completion of the voyage together with some presents from the cargo. In practice these rules were sometimes broken and *shuinjō* were sold to a third party[8].

The major destinations of the *shuinsen* were Cochinchina (71), Patani (56), Luzon (54), Cambodia (44), Tongking (37) and Taiwan (36).[9] The *shuinsen* exports included silver, copper, iron, sulphur, lacquer-ware and other manufactured goods, and they imported into Japan raw and wrought silk, cotton fabrics, deer hides, sharkskins (used for sword hilts), sappan wood, lead and sugar – the same range of goods that the English and Dutch aspired to import to Japan.[10] The ships themselves varied in size. The smallest recorded was of 70 tons, the largest 800 and they carried anything from 50 to 470 people aboard.[11] On the earliest *shuinsen* voyages, Chinese pilots were employed but after this European, especially Portuguese, pilots were used. There were of course Japanese pilots too.[12] The *shuinsen* carried 'passengers', most of whom were merchants investing their own capital in the voyage. A voyage to Patani in 1626 by a *shuinsen* vessel owned by the leading Kyoto merchant family, Suminokura, carried 397 people of whom 80 were crew. There were 300 merchants aboard each paying 50 taels for passage and freightage, a total of 15,000 taels, which covered most of the owner's capital investment.[13] The crew of the *shuinsen* were permitted to carry goods for private trade and their quota could add up to about one third of the whole cargo and possibly more.[14] The structure of the *shuinsen* trade was quite different from that of the English and Dutch in the Indies. The Japanese *shuinsen* merchants did not unite to form a joint-stock company employing salaried employees to live and work abroad on a contractual basis. Nor did they become involved in the pursuit of national strategic goals overseas. Indeed the *shuinsen* trade was finally abolished because it was judged incompatible with the bakufu's political agenda in the 1630s. The *shuinsen* quickly established themselves as the major conduit for Japan's increasing overseas trade during the early seventeenth century. They were effective and highly competitive with the other participants in Japan's foreign trade at this time. The Dutch did not understimate them. In February 1620, Specx informed his superiors that any thoughts of encouraging *shuinsen* to trade in the Moluccas should be discontinued on the grounds that they did not venture there anyway and it would be difficult for interested parties to obtain *shuinjō*, but more importantly because he feared they would eat into Dutch profits if they did go.[15]

There was nothing new about Japanese living or working abroad. Japanese had resided in Korea from the fifteenth century and in Ryūkyū as well. However, during the course of the sixteenth century the numbers of Japanese making their way overseas, whether as pirates, peaceful traders or as bondsmen, increased. Bondsmen, or slaves as the Europeans generally called them, were one of the first 'exports' the Portuguese acquired from China and Japan. Servitude had a long history in Japan, and throughout the Indies, and by the time the Portuguese arrived it took the form of selling people, Japanese as well as non-Japanese (prisoners of war, of which there were many after Hideyoshi's invasion of Korea, captives seized by the wakō, criminals, deserters from daimyo households, people in hardship, including children and wives), as indentured servants. The Portuguese merchants were taking advantage of an existing practice and one which provided them with a regular supply of servants and concubines for their possessions in the Indies. The extent of this trade alarmed the Japanese authorities and even hurt Japanese pride, although it was never opposed in principle. The Japanese themselves were happy to buy bondsmen, especially blacks, from the Portuguese. One of Hideyoshi's question's of the Jesuit Gaspar Coelho in 1587, just before issuing his order banishing the missionaries from Japan, was why the Portuguese bought so many Japanese and exported them as slaves to which Coelho replied that it was the Japanese themselves who sold the people and the Japanese could stop the practice if they so wished. This is exactly what Hideyoshi attempted to achieve with a decree issued in July 1587 outlawing the sale of Japanese overseas although the measure did not eradicate such sales completely.[16] Japanese who were sold to the Portuguese ended up as far away as Malacca and Goa but most were sent to Macao. Not all the Japanese who went to southeast Asia did so as a result of becoming slaves or bondsmen. In the aftermath of

the *sengoku* wars and Hideyoshi's campaigns in Korea, many displaced soldiers sought an outlet for their energies as mercenaries in
the service of Asian potentates. During the 1610s younger men who
had seen no such military service were employed by the English and
Dutch.

The anti-Christian policies of Hideyoshi and the Tokugawa
bakufu added to the outflow of Japanese but it was the *shuinsen* trade
which contributed to the establishment of permanent Japanese
settlements in key southeast Asian emporia, the *nihonmachi*. These
were in effect diaspora, promoting trade between the mother
country and the adopted country. In this respect they were similar to
the Chinese diaspora which had been established in southeast Asia
since the ninth century. Such diaspora had long existed in the Indies
and in Europe. They afforded a secure means of conducting international trade through the trusted medium of one's own people
who could be relied upon to provide accurate information about
markets, make business and official introductions and generally help
overcome the myriad problems that arose from trading in a distant
country such as ensuring that customs duties, presents for officials,
loans, packing and loading charges were set at the right level. By the
sixteenth century diaspora were on the decline in Europe. For
example, in London during the sixteenth century the functions of the
Italian diaspora were increasingly taken over by local agents paid on
a commission basis. In the Indies, however, trading dispora remained common. Ethnic groups lived together in cities in their own
quarters and had their own leader who mediated on behalf of the
diaspora with the host authorities. The Europeans adapted to such
arrangements in Bantam and Ayuthia, for example, but where they
believed that they could realise their more ambitious goals, they
overthrew the existing rulers and established themselves as a new
élite, as the Portuguese did in Malacca in 1511 and the Dutch in
Jacarta in 1619. However, the essential pattern of cities with distinct
ethnic quarters was retained even as the Europeans transformed their
presence in the Indies from a trading relationship to one of dominion. Imperialism in its wake created new diaspora, the repercussions
of which are still felt today. It is even possible to argue that the
northern European trading companies were in fact diaspora.[17] This is
valid only in a limited sense. By pooling their investments in a
joint-stock, merchants created a corporation, an abstract body demanding loyalties that transcended the ties of family, kinship, religion, language or culture which held together other diaspora. The
salaried factors employed by the trading companies were expected,
even bound, to apply their energies to further the interests of the
corporation, not to advance their own interests by indulging in
private trade, nor that of individual adventurers to whom they might

be related or obliged by ties of kinship or patronage, especially in London's close-knit mercantile community.

Of the early *nihonmachi* that of Manila was perhaps the largest. The first mention of a Japanese quarter with permanent residents, in Dilao on the edge of Manila near the Chinese settlement, dates from 1585. Over the years the number of Japanese residents increased. In the early 1620s the number was estimated at 3,000, not all congregated in Dilao. The Japanese involved themselves in trade and some entered the religious orders. As a result of Hideyoshi's invasion threats, the Japanese were not completely trusted but they began to work their passage to acceptance by assisting the Spanish to quell an uprising by the local Chinese, or Sanglay, in 1603. Some of the Japanese themselves rebelled in 1606 and 1607 against attempts to expel them from Manila but the Japanese were pacified and the expulsion was not carried out. After the 1630s and the shogunal restrictions on Japanese voyaging overseas, the Japanese *nihonmachi* in Manila was obsorbed into the local society.[18]

Evidence of resident Japanese in the Siamese kingdom of Ayuthia dates from the early seventeenth century, although a Siamese ambassador had visited Japan to establish official relations in the late fourteenth century. Some 200 Japanese were recruited as mercenaries to repulse a Dutch attack on Patani in 1602, and Japanese along with Chams and Malays were employed as guards for successive Ayuthian kings. As a result, the Japanese diaspora in Siam became deeply involved in local politics. The monarchy employed them as a shield to secure the throne's independence from competing local élites. On a number of occasions this policy backfired and the Japanese themselves became major power-brokers, opposing and even deposing kings. In addition to this praetorian guard there was an important group of resident Japanese merchants. One of the first *shuinjō* issued by the Tokugawa shogunate in 1604 was to a Japanese merchant residing in Ayuthia, Yo-emon and in 1606 Ieyasu wrote an official letter to King Naresuan. This marked the beginning of a period of cordial relations that lasted until 1630 when the *nihonmachi* at Ayuthia was sacked during one of Siam's recurrent bouts of dynastic turmoil. The Japanese broke off official relations, although once the situation in Siam had stabilised the Siamese made several attempts to restore relations. Cut off from contact with the motherland from the 1630s, the Japanese community, like that in Manila, gradually disappeared through absorption although there are still references to it in the early eighteenth century and merchants of Japanese origin engaged in overseas trade can be identified from Dutch sources in 1690.[19]

There were other *nihonmachi* in southeast Asia at Faifo (Hoi Ar) and Tourane (Da Nang) in central Vietnam, and at Cambodia at

Phnom Penh and closeby at Pinhalu, all, except for the last place, important destinations for *shuinsen* voyages. There were also places which did not have *nihonmachi* but nevertheless acquired Japanese residents, notably Batavia where Japanese originally found employment as soldiers and sailors with the VOC. The Japanese in Batavia married with other Asians and some Japanese women married Europeans. Many were successful in business activities quite independent of the *shuinsen* which did not visit Batavia.[20]

The English factory at Hirado found itself operating in a Japanese trading world which was already extensive and varied and in which merchants were rationally pursuing profit from the available trade flows. Their activity was certainly more successful than the Company's own efforts in the country trade from Japan which were directed towards *shuinsen* destinations. The English were to become familiar with all aspects of the *shuinsen* trade during their stay sometimes finding it beneficial to their interests, at other times exasperating.

Before his departure from Hirado, Saris had left written instructions, a 'remembrance', about the factory's organisation and its immediate goals. The first objective was the purchase of a junk for a voyage to Ayuthia and Patani early in 1614 when it was believed junks from China would be trading there. The junk was to carry broadcloth, Cambay cloth, ivory and reals and procure silk, deerskins and sappan wood, and, if there was insuffucient lading, then it was to carry 'passengers', merchants travelling with their goods. Secondly, sub-factories were to be set up at Sunpu (Saris assumed that close proximity to Ieyasu would increase sales), the Kinai and at Tsushima which it was hoped would be the launching pad for trade with Korea.[21] A blank letter fom James I was left behind for this purpose. Cocks had learned about Tsushima during Saris's absence from Hirado from some of the Dutch who had been there, ostensibly at the prompting of William Adams, to sell pepper and other commodities, and he suspected that the Dutch carried on a secret trade with Korea, or at least were about to start one. Brouwer's refusal to answer any question about the matter appeared to confirm his hunch.[22] The subfactories could be relocated if Cocks thought fit and accordingly it was decided to open a branch at Edo, the bigger market, instead of Sunpu. Saris counselled the factors to nurture friendly but businesslike relations with the Dutch and to hold 'good correspondency' with the Matsūra, but warned against being 'too bountiful' with them for 'they crave much but give little'. He singled out Sagawa Nobutoshi (Semi-dono), a senior member of the Matsūra household, as someone who would quickly run up debts if the factors were not careful.

The broadcloth was to be sold off at 130 mas per tatami, the price the Dutch had begun to sell their cloth at after the arrival of the English. Saris reckoned this a good enough price given the amount of stock held by the Dutch and the poor condition of the English cloth. Because of the Company's heavy investment in the voyage and the expense involved in obtaining the privileges, all succeeding voyages (at this stage Saris was unaware that joint-stock voyages had been established) were to contribute to costs and if any future voyage commander who called insisted on managing his own affairs while in Hirado, Cocks was to ensure that he at least contribute to the running of the house. In any case 'frugality' was the watchword in husbanding the factory's expenses, 'the place requiring great charge and our knowledge as yet producing little profit'. Saris's mistrust of Adams was made explicit in the remembrance and seems to have been prompted by disappointment that contrary to (undue) expectations, he had not thrown himself more enthusiastically into the service of the English. Adams was not to be given any major role in the running of the factory but was to be used to pilot the junk and for his linguistic skills at the shogunal court. His handling of Company money was to be supervised carefully. Saris's mean-spirited reservations were not entirely unjustified. The fact that Adams, Van Santvoort and Joosten were running their own businesses meant that it was prudent to assume a possible conflict of interest even if, as it turned out, Adams was not so stinting in his attention to the Company's service as Saris believed.[23]

The invoice of the stock discharged from the *Clove* to set up the Hirado factory was not officially rated at the departure of the ship but Saris was confident 'it is sufficient for trial of what may be done in these parts'.[24] However, the so-called 'Firando Ledger B' provides much of the missing detail.[25] For this reason it is difficult to give exact figures for the value of the general stock left in the Hirado factory. The Ledger B gives two figures, although the difference between them is small, almost 500 taels. The amount of goods was given as 11,812 taels 6 mas 2 4/21 candereen, and the amount in cash and plate as 11,302 taels 1 mas 4 1/3 candereen, producing a total stock of 23,114 taels 7 mas 6 11/21 candereen, or just under one third of the total stock of the three ships of the Eighth Voyage.[26] The factory had already dipped into the four chests of reals which Saris left even before the *Clove* departed in order to cover costs, including Saris's trip to Sunpu and Edo, and for various household and shipboard expenses. Total sales had amounted to 637 1/8 reals, much of which remained to be collected when the factory was formally established, and it was credited with 80 taels, the £20 received from Adams in payment for a bill of exchange drawn on the Company for his wife in England. On the debit side the factory owed cash (195 taels 6 mas) to the Matsūra for money lent by them.[27] The stock of goods consisted mainly of broadcloth, '50 whole pieces and 6 remnants in all 1,755 1/2 yards', valued at 3,847 taels 8 mas 8 candereen, Cambay cloth and silks, procured in the Red Sea, valued at just over 2,484 taels, 238 cwt 3 qtr 6 lbs of lead in bars valued at 597 taels 5/6 candereen, ivory valued at 2,123 taels 7 mas 5 candereen, 315 peculs 14 1/2 catties of Java pepper worth 739 taels 2 mas 7 1/7 candereen, 46 barrels of gunpowder worth 651 taels 6 mas 6 candereen, and the ordnance and shot received from the *Hector* and *Thomas*, valued at 434 taels 7 mas. In addition there were small amounts of gold tableware, Priaman gold, tin, and some amounts of galls, wine, aqua vitae and olive oil.[28] The English factory was starting with more capital and stock than had the Dutch in 1609.

Saris laid down a line of succession among the men left in Japan which ran Cocks, Tempest Peacock, Richard Wickham, William Eaton, Walter Carwarden and Edmond Sayers. Jobs were also specified: Peacock and Carwarden were to be employed on the junk to Siam, Peacock because of his mercantile experience, Carwarden because of his knowledge of gold and silver; Wickham was to establish the Sunpu subfactory, Eaton the Kinai one; Sayers was to go to Tsushima. The seventh man, William Nealson, was to remain in Hirado with Cocks as house manager and bookkeeper.[29]

There was nothing surprising about this chain of command. In Saris's view, Cocks was the only candidate for the headship of the factory, having shown his mettle on the outward voyage. Cocks had been sent ashore to make contact with the sultan at Socotra and at Mocha, with Bolton the linguist, he had gone ashore to request permission to trade, a courageous act in view of what had happened to Middleton. He had played an important part in the subsequent negotiations to secure permission to set up an English factory there. He was very much privy to Saris's deliberations during the contretemps with Middleton and dealt directly with Middleton's deputy, Nicholas Downton, in the discussions concerning Middleton's demands for restitution from the Turks, and had been similarly active in the voyage from Bantam to Japan.[30]

Of all the factors left at Hirado, there is a substantial amount of information about Cocks which sheds light on the type of people the Company employed. Cocks was forty-five when he left England, fourteen years senior to Saris and one suspects that on occasion Saris deferred to the older man's opinions. He was born in January 1566 at Stalbrook in Staffordshire, the third of four sons and two daughters. His father had been a bailiff on Lord Stafford's Derrington estate and the family had been in possession of two manors of crown land since the fifteenth century, an upwardly mobile family on the margin of gentry status.[31] As a younger son in later Elizabethan England Cocks

was at a disadvantage in a society in which, in the words of his future
patron, Sir Thomas Wilson, the keeper of the records (like Cocks,
and Saris, himself a younger son), the condition of the 'great
younger brother' was 'most miserable' for the elder brother 'must
have all', leaving his younger sibling little option but 'to apply
ourselves to letters or to arms'.[32] But Cocks, unlike Wilson, did not
come from a 'great gentry' background and had less opportunity to
apply himself to letters or arms. However, he did apply himself to
another avenue open to many younger sons, including those from
more comfortable backgrounds than himself: business.

He was apprenticed in London to the clothworker William
Hewett, an influential London merchant, introduced or recommended (the usual means by which apprentices were selected) possibly by the Dorrington family, kinsmen of the Cocks, whose ranks
included important London merchants.[33] Cocks was made free of the
Clothworkers' Company in 1597 when he was thirty-one, a not
unusual age as apprenticeship could begin in one's late teens or early
twenties in the sixteenth century.[34] During his seven-year apprenticeship Cocks would have acquired wide experience of the business
operations of his master and become familiar with the panoply of
technical skills an apprentice was expected to master. In addition he
would have learned the art of business-letter writing. This consisted
of referring to all recent communications with a particular recipient
to enable the latter to check that all previous letters had been
received; summarising briefly the contents of recent 'out' letters; and
making copies of all letters sent. Cocks's surviving letters show that
he had fully mastered such techniques and conventions and was able
to incorporate them into a fluent, confident and individual style
which could give due expression to his well-developed powers of
observation.[35]

From sometime before March 1603, probably shortly after gaining
his freedom of the Clothworkers' Company, until May 1608 Cocks
was resident in southwest France, at Bayonne, working as 'a factor
for others'.[36] This was a common employment for new freemen and
gave them a chance to put their training to use buying and selling
goods for the London-based merchants they represented on the most
favourable terms and shipping them to England. This required
familiarity with local markets and trading conditions. However, like
many other merchants resident overseas, Cocks worked as an informal intelligence agent for the English government, watching movements into and out of Spain along a road which functioned as the
vital artery of Spain's communications with northern Europe where
its armies were fighting the Dutch. A steady stream of English
Roman Catholic exiles also passed through Bayonne on their way to
Spain where many of them had unrealistic hopes of influencing

Spanish policy and securing Spanish intervention to depose Elizabeth. Their movements were of considerable interest to the English government.[37] Cocks was recruited as an intelligence writer by Wilson, a client of Robert Cecil, one of the most powerful figures in late Elizabethan and early Jacobean England, in Bayonne early in 1603.[38] This was their first meeting and later Wilson was to describe Cocks as 'one of the beter sort of merch[ts] resyding in those parts', more astute than most of the merchants working there who were 'rawe, vnexperionced and vnlanguaged' and easy prey to Spanish harrassment of English merchants attempting to re-establish official trade with Spain following the conclusion of peace between England and Spain in 1604. Wilson felt that Cocks would be a suitable candidate for the position of consul in northwest Spain, one of five consuls intended to represent the interests of the resurrected Spanish Company, which was rechartered in May 1605 and which the English government hoped would restore order to the Spanish trade. Despite his good connections with key individuals in the Spanish Company, notably John Dorrington, one of the company's directors, and chief counsellors, and at court through Wilson, who in the autumn of 1605 formally entered Cecil's service, Cocks did not become consul for northwest Spain. He was not even short-listed. The appointment went to James Wyche, son of another influential member of the Spanish Company, Richard Wyche, who like many other members of the ill-fated Company, which was dissolved in May 1606, circumvented both the Company's monopoly and English customs duties by shipping goods directly to Spain from the Baltic and Muscovy.

Cocks, who sympathised with those who argued in favour of monopolies, rarely lost an opportunity to attack such practices whereby 'the king's majesty is conzened of his customs and a whole kingdom hindered for the particular benefit of four or five such currmudges'.[39] But even after the Wyche appointment had been judged a mistake both locally and in London, Cocks, who received encouragement from Wilson and Sir Charles Cornwallis (the English ambassador to the Spanish court), did not secure the post of consul. There was little enthusiasm among the merchants for such a post anyway and the English government was unconvinced of the need for it. Disappointed by the outcome, Cocks returned to England in June 1608 to face possible legal proceedings and imprisonment because of debts outstanding to various individuals. The money in dispute was in turn owed to Cocks by a Portuguese confidence trickster and had already involved him in a legal case in France. Cock's worst fears came close to realisation for he was almost arrested after his arrival. Thanks to the intervention of the Privy Council, his creditors were ordered to stay their action on the

grounds that Cocks was ready to satisfy all parties. The order noted
that 'the said party is one that hath done His Majesty good service in
foreugn parts'.[40] Cocks went back to Staffordshire where he worked
on behalf of the Court of Wards but the fallout from his legal
problems blackened his reputation and 'hath been an occasion to
hinder me from one or two good marriages, for men judge I owe
him [Sir Gilbert Wakering, his main creditor] great matters, when it
will be found that account will owe much to me'.[41] The repercussions from the affair continued to be felt. In November 1609, in his
last surviving letter before his departure on the Eighth Voyage, he
confided to Wilson that he was 'awery of the country' and was
thinking 'to go over again out of England about the Spring'.[42]
Restlessness, failure to find a wife, and resentment over the uncooperative attitude of his creditors helped make up his mind and given
the path of his earlier career, the East India Company was an obvious
progression. Cocks's solid commercial experience, linguistic ability
(he spoke French and Spanish), and excellent connections were
attractive to the Company, even if at forty-five he was somewhat old
to enter its service. Nevertheless, he successfully passed the screening
process and had no difficulty in posting the bond. Saris had no reason
to doubt the wisdom of his choice as head of the Hirado factory and
felt confident that he had left the business of the factory in capable
hands when he sailed from Japan in December 1613.[43]

     Unfortunately, not so much is known about the other members of
the factory. Tempest Peacock was employed as chief merchant in the
Thomas and was one of the merchandising committee on the Eighth
Voyage, but on the way to the Indies he lost Saris's favour for passing a copy of the voyage's cargo list to Middleton, carrying letters on
Middleton's behalf, and constantly informing the rival commander
of matters which Saris would have preferred remained privy to the
Eighth Voyage. For Saris such behaviour represented a betrayal of
confidence. Peacock's actions came to light at Bantam and he was
censured by the merchandising council for behaviour prejudicial to
the voyage, resulting in the poor cargo of pepper acquired from the
northern Sumatran pepper ports. Given the nature of Iskandar's
control over pepper-production this was a charge of which he was
wholly innocent. He apologised for his actions. Jourdain, then cape
merchant on the *Darling* in the Sixth Voyage, gives a less damning
version of Peacock's behaviour. He stated that 'although the heads
[Saris and Middleton] did not agree yett without them we had
correspondence one to another [i.e. between the *Darling* and the
Thomas] from Diamon [Priaman] to Teco, because we would not
spoile one anothers markett', a sensible policy in view of the scarcity
of pepper. Jourdain confirms that Peacock brought a letter from
Middleton from the Red Sea but that he had taken pains to open,

copy and reseal it, which the *Darling*'s merchants 'perceived by his owne speeches'. Whatever the nature of the information he passed on to Middleton, it did not harm the interests of the Eighth Voyage and the affair is redolent of a storm in a teacup. But Peacock had lost the trust of his commander and after being censured at Bantam, Saris noted that 'I propose to be more warye of him heare after' and urged Edward Camden to observe how he 'doth carry himself to the knight [Middleton]' and to make it clear to Peacock that 'the less familiarity he hath that way the more it will be for his preferment'.[44]

About Wickham more is known. He was probably a Wiltshire man, for in his correspondence from Japan he refers to his mother 'a poor widow...dwelling in Wiltshire in the Vise [Devizes]' and he had two sisters living in Ludlow. He had two brothers, William, who also served on the Eighth Voyage on the *Hector* but who died on 2 April 1612, and Lewes. He was a man of some education and clearly had served an apprenticeship. He had a connection with the governor, Sir Thomas Smythe, who was one of the executors of Wickham's will (a connection that was to serve his widowed mother well in the future) and was originally employed by the Company in December 1607 as a factor aboard the *Unicorn* in the Fourth Voyage which left England in March 1608 under the command of Alexander Sharpie. The Court considered him 'verie honest and as fitt as a man' and employed him at £20 per annum for six years. In February 1609 at Zanzibar on the outward voyage, where the *Unicorn* hoped to rendezvous with the Sharpie's flagship, Wickham and the purser were seized by the Portuguese while taking soundings and taken prisoner to Goa. A third man was killed. Wickham was described by the French traveller François Pyrand who met him at Goa as 'a man of proud and noble bearing, like a captain'. He was brought back to Lisbon along with other prisoners in late August 1610 on a náo bringing an ambassador from Persia to the Spanish court. The Persian showed 'great affection' to Wickham who was lodged at his house and from whence he was able to escape and make his way back to England in time to offer his services for the Eighth Voyage. Before leaving he took the precaution of drawing up a will in which his mother was the main beneficiary. By the time the *Clove* arrived at Bantam Wickham had acquired a reputation with Saris as 'somewhat capricious', a view with which Middleton appeared to concur, and during the voyage to Japan Saris suspected him of improper behaviour over the disposal of the goods of one of the dead crew members, John Craulye, which Saris, according to the procedures for men who died intestate, had ordered to be sold before the mast. Wickham challenged the sale, producing a written document with only a dubious signature of the deceased appended, claiming that Craulye had left him his estate of £12 3s 9d in cash and £58 8s 5d in goods. The purser claimed that Craulye had in fact drawn up a proper will which could not be found and Saris decided to leave the matter to be settled in England although he believed that Wickham had unduly pressured Craulye to leave him his estate. Wickham's preoccupation with making money was obvious to his colleagues, and he made no efforts to conceal it. In 1616 he wrote to Cocks from Kyoto about a nobleman, Matsudaira Tadanao, Ieyasu's grandson, who had carried off a prostitute paying 10,000 taels for the privilege. Wickham commented that 'I would I had the money, and it make no matter who hath the woman etc.' On this occasion Cocks agreed. His behaviour over his claim for a wage increase just before the departure of the *Clove* did not endear him to Saris who advised Cocks to let him leave Japan on the next English ship that called if Wickham so wished. The antipathy between Saris and Wickham was mutual. Both Saris and Cocks felt that Wickham was someone who had to be treated warily on account of his prickly temperament and intractable nature. Yet because of his connection with Smythe they sought to appease him. Regardless of his unattractive qualities, Wickham was an able merchant and had shown great courage and resourcefulness in escaping from the Portuguese, which had given him an aura of respect. He had shown his worth in the Company's service and he had learned how fragile life could be in that service. As a result he had made up his mind that on this voyage he was out for himself as much as for the Company and that neither Saris, a young, pretentious commander, nor Cocks, a 'parvenu' to the Company's employ, were going to get in the way of his ambition.[45]

Neither Peacock nor Wickham lived to see England again. Nor did William Nealson, short-tempered and quarrelsome when drunk, and Walter Carwarden, who had probably trained as a gold or silver-smith. About Carwarden's early life nothing is known. In his will, made in Hirado in May 1620 shortly before his death, Nealson is described as 'merchant & practitioner in the Mathematics in his lifetime'. He does not appear to have had any family in England, or if he did they were not acknowledged in his will for he left everything to Cocks.[46] Of the remaining two factory members, William Eaton was young and had come out as purser's mate on the *Hector*. He may have been a Staffordshire man like Cocks for the cape merchant refers to him as 'my cuntryman'.[47] In commercial matters the purser was the most important man on voyages after the factor. With his deputies or mates he was responsible for keeping exact accounts and records of all victuals and stores aboard ship, including cordage and rigging, munitions and general tools, and was responsible for calling sailors to work, keeping records of their wages and of all monies received aboard the ship for the Company's account. The Company further instructed pursers to 'vse their best endeuor to learne out, and accordingly to aduise the Gouernor, Deputy, and Committees, concerning all private trade in the Compnies Ships, to and from the Indies, and in those parts from port to port.'[48] They were men of fairly high general education and from the crew's perspective well worth cultivating. Eaton was initially appointed manager of the English house's routine affairs in July 1613, but Saris was impressed with his ability and promoted him to factor and Nealson took over his old job. He had an attractive personality and, until the final year of the factory's existence, got on well with Cocks, who described him as a 'true honest man, and a friend to his friend'.[49] The most junior, inexperienced member of the house, Edmund Sayers, was possibly a kinsman of Saris and Cocks felt that he needed time to learn his trade. Tsushima was judged a suitable training ground for this purpose.

The Englishmen left at Hirado were representative of the range of men the Company employed in its factories in the Indies. Men of solid commercial experience jostled with raw recruits. All were ostensibly untied in their professed commitment to advance the East India Company's business, yet all were determined to make a little extra (in Wickham's case a lot) for themselves. They were men of differing and sometimes incompatible temperaments who had to live together, and sometimes apart, far from home, relatives or friends and cut off from physical contact with their fellow countrymen in the Indies for long periods while facing the twin challenges of adapting to an alien culture, society and language and putting the Company's capital to good and profitable use.

(ii)   First Steps, 1614

After Saris's departure on 5 December 1613 little time was wasted in taking steps to carry out his instructions for probing the market in Japan by establishing branches of the factory and preparing for the factory's first venture overseas in the country trade.

On 28 January Wickham, accompanied by Adams, left for Edo with instructions from Cocks to find lodgings and suitable storage for the Company's goods that he took along with him. Cocks urged him to stay with a Japanese rather than in lodgings with Europeans or other foreigners, although Cocks advised him to remain on good terms with all business associates in order to learn what he could. However, he was to remain circumspect about his own affairs. Wickham had the services of a jurebasso and Portuguese was to be used to conduct business. The jurebasso was either to be hired from Nagasaki or else locally in Edo or Sunpu. Adams foresaw no problem in this respect. In the meantime Wickham was urged to use

the services of Adams's brother-in-law whom the English called
Andreas. Cocks urged Wickham to attempt to sell what he could at
Ieyasu's court in Sunpu.

Wickham and Adams were accompanied by Eaton as far as the
Kinai where he was to set up the second subfactory (in fact Eaton
moved between Kyoto, Osaka and Sakai). Both the Kinai and Edo
subfactories were to co-ordinate their activities as far as possible. The
fact that Wickham, the more senior and experienced, was put in
charge of the Edo subfactory suggests that Edo and in particular
Ieyasu's court at Sunpu were thought likely to provide the best sales.

A barque, loaded with the stock for the subfactories, went with
the party. The stock for Edo consisted of fifteen of the broadcloths
discharged from the *Clove*, including pink, dark blue, Venice red
and black, Cambay cloth (part of the spoils from the Red Sea), nearly
10,900 lb of Bantam (Java) pepper, 6 cwt of tin broken down into
some 1,200 pieces, ten barrels of gunpowder, the five pieces of
ordnance loaded at Bantam plus shot, 600 bars of lead, galls (used for
tanning leather) and 100 taels in silver bars. Some stock had been left
by Saris at Edo in the care of Adams's Japanese brother-in-law, and
at Sunpu with Stibio, Saris's host there. According to the Firando
Ledger 'B', the stock was valued at 2,887 taels 1 mas and 2/3
candereen or 12.5 per cent of the total stock.[50] The Kinai factory was
furnished with eight of the broadcloths, four of which were black,
and a selection of the same kind of goods sent to Edo. This stock was
valued at 1,433 taels 6 mas 2 candereen, 6.2 per cent of the total.[51]
Cocks emphasised to both Wickham and Eaton that additional stock
would be sent from Hirado if required. He firmly opposed holding
out for high prices and urged Wickham to sell even at the low prices
they had received so far and to 'turn all into ready money before any
other shipping come out of England that it may not be said we lie
still and do nothing but eat and drink'. The aim at this stage was to
sell off as much of the unsuitable stock as possible and to generate
cash for more promising investment elsewhere, a policy that would
have met with the approval of the Company. As has been mentioned, idle stock was deemed not simply bad management in the
seventeenth century but as bad as a loss.[52] One other instruction
from Cocks merits attention. Wickham was to be prepared to receive
a bill of exchange from the daimyo of Hirado for 1,000 taels if the
latter should come to Edo. Wickham was to honour the bill, Cocks
being assured by Adams that, as had been the case with the Dutch, it
would be honoured in Hirado and the loan repaid. Despite their
considerable misgivings about lending money and their regrets
shortly after that they had not followed the Dutch example and given
the daimyo goods rather than money, even if this would have made
him a competitor in the market, the English had no alternative but to

comply with the request on this and on subsequent occasions, no matter how reluctantly.[53] They needed the daimyo's favour and protection. Besides, the Matsūra had lent the English money shortly after the *Clove*'s arrival.[54] It was not possible to conceive of such loans as simple business transactions. From the Matsūra's perspective, merchants, whether foreign or domestic, existed to serve their betters.

The party used the same sea route as Saris from Hirado to Sakai and reached Osaka early in February. After a short delay to help Eaton set himself up, Wickham continued overland to Edo by way of Sunpu. At Edo he took up lodgings with a merchant called Mikumoya, whom the English called Migmoy or Mickmoy and later 'Nicolo Machiavell', although Wickham's first impression was that he was trustworthy and helpful. He was also indispensable in providing storage for the English factory's goods, making introductions to other merchants and providing other services to help Wickham transact his business. At Ieyasu's court at Sunpu Wickham was able to sell three of the six pieces of broadcloth he had brought with him for 665 taels 5 mas (the rest was rejected because it was moth-eaten) and a price of 6 taels per pecul was settled for the lead, a good price (the lead discharged from the *Clove* was rated at 2 taels 9 mas 7 candereen per pecul).[55] Sale of the ordnance, gunpowder and shot required more negotiation. Adams 'promised to doe his vtmost' to lobby Ieyasu and towards the end of May returned to Sunpu to negotiate for its sale. The price eventually settled on for the ordnance was 1,400 taels, less than the 1,500 taels offered when Wickham himself had done the negotiating but even so a good profit on the £86 8s 0d for which it had been invoiced and Wickham was satisfied. The powder sold for 2 mas 3 candereen the catty and the shot for 6 candereen the catty.[56]

Unfortunately, Wickham had become separated from the bulk of his stock on the journey to Edo. Most of the goods had been sent by sea on a barque belonging to Ieyasu. The barque got as far as Toba, in Shima, where bad weather delayed its progress to Edo until 15 May, well after Wickham's arrival.[57] Wickham, was furious at this delay – Cocks too when he found out. Wickham confided to Nealson that the problems with the barque 'hath so wearied my mind that I haue hade no time to gather matter to write vnto you', and blamed Adams for not sending the goods overland from the Kinai. According to Wickham, Adams had advised against such a route on the grounds that it would be expensive and take too long.[58] It did not help matters that the Dutch had sent their broadcloth overland from Osaka to Edo. Wickham was quick to charge Adams with deliberately giving the English bad advice and was even more furious when he discovered that the Dutch never sent their goods by sea.

Other merchants who traded between Nagasaki and Edo agreed that the advice had been bad.[59] The incident reinforced the doubts the English merchants had about Adams's true loyalties and increased their apprehensions that he was more attentive to Dutch interests than those of his compatriots On this occasion Cocks (rightly) gave Adams the benefit of the doubt over his behaviour. Adams was considered too important an intermediary with Ieyasu to alienate. To counter what he felt was Adams's undue influence over the affairs of the factory, Wickham suggested that a Fleming, Gisbert de Coning, be employed by the factory. De Coning was another member of the *Liefde's* crew and one of the two men whom Adams accused of trying to betray the survivors after their arrival in Japan by ingratiating themselves with the daimyo at Bungo. Wickham understood that there was no love lost between De Coning and Adams, and recommended De Coning for the job because his house at Uraga had recently burnt down and he had a wife and children to support. The Dutch were said to dislike him, another point in his favour, and he had experience having worked for Señor Lorenzo, the agent for the Dutch in Edo. De Coning was hired at £20 per annum. Cocks justified the addition to the factory's personnel on the grounds that De Coning was fluent in Japanese and had access to Ieyasu. The irony of employing a Hollander to counterbalance an Englishman did not occur to anyone, and whatever, if any, access De Coning had to Ieyasu it did not measure up to that of Adams.[60]

Wickham also discovered that the lead that reached Edo was about 1,356 catties or 40 bars short. Some had been lost from the barque during the storms at Toba, although the barquemen claimed that they had failed to retrieve only three bars, a figure with which Adams agreed. According to Wickham, the divers were ordered 'to cutt theyre Bellyes' for their failure to retrieve all the lead but were spared when the master of the barque was told that the authorities did not know as yet the exact weight of the lead sold to Ieyasu. Adams was sure there had been no short-measuring by the Japanese because the lead had been weighed by an impartial weigher, 'which yf he should do wronge eyther vnto vs or the Emperor were without Redemption to die for the same'; Wickham, unsure of Japanese weights, left the matter to Adams to settle, confident that there would be no cheating, lead being a commodity 'that no man else dare b[u]y if the Emp[eror] once Refuse them'.[61] In reality the bakufu did not have a monopoly over the purchase of lead although it bought up as much as possible to prevent others acquiring too great a stock of this strategically important commodity.

The delay in sending the goods from Osaka proved a setback for sales of broadcloth. Demand in Edo for broadcloth was said to be exceptionally high because of a meeting of the daimyo concerning the construction of Edo castle. (Most of the cloth was sought after by the nobility and their servants.) The Dutch were able to beat the English to market and dispose of their cloth, even to buyers who had previously approached Wickham. They also provided their subfactory in the Kinai and agent in Edo with extra supplies. (The Dutch did not have resident factors in the Kinai at this time although two of their factors, Elbert Woutersen and Matthys van den Broecke, visited the Kinai and Edo periodically. They were greatly assisted by Van Santvoort and Joosten.)[62] Wickham believed that the Dutch were greatly concerned to ward off any possible English threat to their market share even though the quality of their cloth was superior to that of the English, which was 'generally soe course & so ill dressed besides the worm holes', and sold as much as they could 'at very meane prices' – 12 taels per tatami he learned from their agent.[63] This was not strictly true. The Dutch had appreciated from their earliest days in Japan that the quality of the cloth mattered little to the Japanese so long as it was of the correct length and was not worm-eaten, and their 'meane' prices were not set with the simple objective of undercutting the English. Regardless of the extra demand generated by the meeting of the daimyo, the market remained oversupplied with broadcloth so much so that Wickham himself commented that 'yf any other shipping come this year with any more Japoan wilbe ouer glutted & no man will looke after it'.[64]

Eaton, facing competition from the Dutch as well as from the daimyo of Hirado and the cloth the latter had received in lieu of a cash loan from the Dutch, had to settle for just over 11 taels per tatami for broadcloth in Osaka but sold four tatami at 15 taels in Kyoto, less than the price of just over 16 taels which cloth had fetched in Hirado and the 15–16 taels Wickham obtained at Sunpu.[65] Wickham wrote to Cocks that he would be glad if they could dispose of all their cloth for 10 taels per tatami and commented on what he saw as a bizarre paradox about the market: '[f]or the nature & Condition of these Japaners (especially of the better sort whoe are most commonly marchants for our Comodytyes) is to buy those Comodytyes that are most Rare & at the time when they are most dearest.' The Spanish had sold broadcloth at 30 taels per tatami but when the price dropped to 25 taels the Japanese stopped buying.[66] Such was to be expected of a commodity for which demand was inelastic, even though Wickham reported that there might be a market for broadcloth in 'Yechingo', eight days' journey to the north of Edo. Cocks suggested he pursue this lead using 'your own discretion, but deal upon sure grounds'.[67] The outlook would be quite different if the factory could get hold of the commodity of which demand was more elastic – silk. On 3 June Wickham wrote to Cocks mentioning the good market for raw and wrought silk 'wch is

the only Comodity sought after not only here but all the kingdome
ouer'.[68] The problem, one that haunted the Hirado factory
throughout its existence, was how to get hold of it.

If broadcloth in general did not sell well there was a particular
demand for coarse, black broadcloth. This was used to make livery
for retainers of the daimyo. Wickham requested Eaton to send up
any black or dark colours he could spare from the Kinai and an
additional supply of six blacks and three of the 'saddest Cullers' was
sent up from Hirado on 25 July. As for the other goods, there was
difficulty in disposing of the Java pepper which was not in much
demand either in Edo or the Kinai. Its sales prospects had been
greatly diminished anyway because refuse had been added to some
sacks to make up weight which 'much disgraced the Rest'.
Nevertheless what was sold made a gross profit of between 200 and
300 per cent. Sales of the Cambay cloth, with the exception of certain
striped varieties, were indifferent 'for that this Cuntry doth afford
almost the like sorts and at very cheape rates'.[69]

Wickham's views on sales policy differed from those which Cocks
intended to adopt. Wickham appreciated that without credit there
could be few sales. He questioned an earlier order from Cocks,
himself influenced by his own unfortunate experiences in Bayonne,
not to permit credit. Wickham contended:

> that yf I eyther deny any marchant of creditt to forbeare him 10 or 20
> dayes I must of necessity keepe the goods & not sell [a] mas thereof. The
> duch doth and hath vsed the marchants of this place to help him to put
> of[f] his cloth by letting them haue a cloth or twoe in theire shoppes to
> sell allowing them some small profitt wch is a continuale custome.

He ignored Cocks's instruction. Later he argued that 'these Japanners
are so slowe in payment that though sure enough that they tire me
with Importuning them ffor money & yet yf I should not trust them
I should not sell for 6^d of goods in ayeare, as Captaine Adams well
knoweth'.[70] Sympathising with Wickham's predicament and appreciating that if Wickham refused credit he would 'lie still and doe
nothing while other men sell', Cocks retracted his prohibition and
urged Wickham to follow 'the Hollanders' course in putting their
cloth into merchants' (or brokers') hands to make sale thereof; it is a
good course so they be men sufficient to be trusted'.[71] This was
indeed the sales practice the Dutch had had to adopt and continued to
employ. It becomes more evident after 1620 when the extant account
books for the VOC's Hirado factory begin. Credit was given to their
regular customers, the wealthy merchants of the Kinai, Nagasaki and
Hirado, with whom it was necessary to develop long-term relationships. These merchants made the biggest purchases of the goods the
Dutch imported, including silk, and were in a position to provide the

goods the Hollanders wanted to export. The merchants were allowed to pay for their purchases in instalments, settling their accounts on an agreed date. The procedure was already there in embryo in the 1610s. The Dutch were no more enamoured of the practice than the English and resented the delays in payment. Only gradually did the Hollanders increase the volume of their cash sales[72] Wickham understood the need to allow credit, believing it a necessary evil, but he mistook the delays in paying as evidence of a desire to evade payment and failed to appreciate that credit was a standard Japanese business practice. In spite of Cocks's initial opposition, sales on credit became the norm. The English, like the Dutch, had no choice in this matter.

By July 1614 Wickham, who had not settled down well in Edo and had been ill for some of the time, was anxious to return to Hirado. In Edo he was on his own and missed the companionship of his fellow countrymen. Besides, he felt that under the circumstances he had accomplished all that could reasonably be expected. Cocks, willing to accommodate Wickham's wishes, had made it clear that he would not object if Wickham went as commander of the Siam voyage that was planned for the end of the year. Wickham considered the offer 'a speaciall kindnes', tartly adding that he expected 'Mr Peacocke to Contrast me herrin whoe esteemeth no man in Japan able to doe the Comp[any] so good service as himself'. Cocks had suggested that the goods that remained unsold should be left in trustworthy hands and Wickham settled on Mikumoya, whom he had no reason to doubt would look after the Company's business honestly. The Siam voyage offered Wickham not only a welcome change from the isolation of Edo but opened up possibilities for private trade. By 23 August Wickham was back in Hirado. Eaton had returned from Osaka on 21 July and remained until 16 September.[73] This enabled some accounts to be drawn up, although given the state of the accounts and the fact that we have to rely on Pratt's selective quotes from the Firando Ledger B it is impossible to give accurate figures about the factory's finances.

Pratt quotes a figure of 4,472 taels 5 mas 5 candereen for gross sales as of 12 September when the accounts of the Edo subfactory were made up.[74] However, the figures do not tally. The sales price of the pepper on the basis of the prices given should amount to 351 taels 6 mas 2 candereen, not 330 taels 9 mas 5 candereen, while the sales price of lead is left blank and should increase the sales by a further 3,453 taels, making a new total for gross sales of 7,235 taels 6 mas 2 candereen.[75] The incidental expenses for the subfactory which included petty charges, transportation, food, and the jurebasso's wages amounted to 317 taels 6 candereen. Presents, to Mikumoya, in lieu of rent (20 taels 8 mas 4 candereen) and to the shogunal barqueman (4 taels 3 mas 5 1/4 candereen), further reduced the gross sales figure. In addition Wickham generously allowed himself 179 taels for wages. Thus the total charges amounted to 521 taels 2 mas 1 1/4 candereen producing a net sales figure of 6,714 taels 4 mas 3/4 candereen. Considering that the value of the stock sent up from Hirado (including the additional cloth and a small quantity of moiré silk in the same consignment) was rated at 3,523 taels 5 mas 2/3 candereen, this was not a bad return. The lead, ordnance and pepper in particular had produced good returns even though they were not staples in Japan. Even after taking into consideration the cash loan made to the daimyo of Hirado (repayable in January 1615) and the fact that many goods were sold on credit, the Edo subfactory injected some 3,131 taels 4 mas into the main factory's coffers. How much of the stock remained unsold and what additional supplies had been sent from the Kinai is unknown, making it impossible to hazard a figure for the profit.[76]

The Kinai subfactory's accounts were made up at the end of July. The total stock received from Hirado (the original shipment plus two additional batches of baftas and broadcloths) was valued at 1,795 taels 3 mas 3 candereen, of which gunpowder, tin and Cambay cloth of various sorts to the value of 284 taels 2 candereen were returned to Hirado for want of sale, reducing the value of the stock to 1,511 taels 3 mas 1 candereen. Gross sales amounted to 1,950 taels. Eaton's expenses were less extravagant than Wickham's, 8 taels 7 mas 4 1/2 candereen in presents for lodging (less than half of Wickham's), and 189 taels 5 mas 9 candereen for petty expenses, producing net sales of 1,752 taels 6 mas 6 1/2 candereen.[77]

The attempt to establish a third subfactory on Tsushima met with no success. Sayers had gone to the island domain at the beginning of January 1614 accompanied by John Japan and a stock of goods much the same as that sent to Edo and the Kinai (broadcloth, Cambay cloth, gunpowder, pepper and lead), valued at 793 taels 7 mas 3 5/6 candereen, 3.5 per cent of total stock. It soon became apparent that there was little business to be done and no likelihood of Tsushima providing the opening to Korea. Sales were slow and the daimyo failed to take up an option on the broadcloth. Sayers decided to follow the tip of a visiting merchant from Hakata that the English should trade there and headed for northeast Kyushu. This turned out to be another dead end. Nothing was sold and Sayers returned to Hirado with goods and cash worth 675 taels 7 mas 1 5/6 candereen unsold. At Tsushima he had been able to make some sales, mainly pepper, worth 265 taels 5 mas 2 candereen. His expenses amounted to 69 taels 7 mas 4 candereen bringing the net sales to 195 taels 7 mas 8 candereen and producing a small profit of 77 taels 7 mas 6 candereen.[78] Another attempt at Tsushima was made in January 1615 when Eaton took along a consignment of broadcloth, 95 bags of pepper, and some Cambay cloth valued at 280 taels 1 mas 2 1/2 candereen. Again, pepper proved best for sales. Twenty-six bags, cost-rated at 72 taels 1 2/10 candereen were sold for 199 taels 5 mas 5 candereen which, after the deduction of presents (the broadcloth and Cambay cloth) and expenses, yielded a paper profit of 56 taels 7 mas 8 4/10 candereen. The balance of the pepper, 69 bags, was left in storage in anticipation of future sales.[79]

Regardless of Wickham's optimistic report from Edo the previous June that 'here I am giuen to vnderstand that there is great hope of that place [Korea]',[80] it was clear that the English were not about to secure admission to the land of morning calm. Even if they had their expectations would have proved fanciful. In November 1614 Cocks wrote to the Company that the Japanese were confined 'into one little town or fortress' in Korea and that although big cities existed in Korea in which Chinese goods were available they were separated from the coast by vast stretches of marsh which could only be crossed by 'waggons or carts which go upon broad flat wheels under sail as ships do...observing monsoons', a preposterous statement. Korea remained *terra incognita* for the English.[81] Tsushima, under the lordship of the Sō, whom Cocks mistakenly thought to be independent of Japan,[82] remained pivotal in the relations between Japan and Korea. These had been officially re-established in 1607, audaciously rekindled by the Sō in 1606 who had forged a letter from the 'king of Japan', Tokugawa Ieyasu, to the Korean monarch. The Tsushima economy was dependent on this intermediary role in the official trade between the two countries, the manner and volume of which was again strictly regulated on the Korean side. There was no place for outsiders.[83] The Dutch had already discovered this. In March 1610 Specx had sent pepper to Tsushima in an effort to secure Sō help in obtaining trade with Korea. The overture led nowhere but Specx, hoping to procure Chinese goods in Korea, did not rule out some future attempt.[84] It is unlikely that the Dutch deliberately misled the English by encouraging them to pursue the chimera of trade with Korea but they would not have objected to seeing the English waste energy on a rerun of their own futile attempt. At least the English had limited themselves to a small investment in Tsushima and even then there were problems in obtaining payment for the pepper already sold, as well as for that left in the custody of Sayers's host there. The latter even came to Hirado in January 1616 offering the English merchandise in lieu of money to settle accounts, claiming that the money of the island was not good for the purpose. By then Cocks's patience had worn thin and it was decided to recall Eaton from the Kinai '& goe to Tushma, to cleare in that place.'[85] In his report to the Company at the beginning of 1617 Cocks concluded that 'the trade of Tsushima is not worth looking after' and Tsushima and Korea were effectively erased from the agenda of the factory's objectives.[86]

Sales in the subfactories during the first few months had been sluggish and disappointing but time had not been wasted and some returns had been made, even in Tsushima. Wickham and Eaton in particular had both acquired first-hand information about the markets, especially what sort of goods were in demand. They had become familiar with weights and measures and the various types of currency in circulation, local trading practices, notably the prevalence of credit and the possibility of dealing through agents, and they had made important business contacts.

During the absence of Wickham and Eaton the Hirado factory had not been idle even though it did not transact as much business as the subfactories. After debts owing to the Matsūra had been repaid, the factory had sold goods worth 618 taels 6 mas 3 candereen to the Matsūra and to Li Tan over a period from 5 December 1613 to 25 March 1615. The most valuable items were fifteen barrels of gunpowder and one piece of ordnance with shot and ladle. There is a gap in the surviving accounts from April to December 1614, but from 3 December 1614 to 22 March 1615 a total of 1,405 taels 3/4 mas 1 candereen worth of goods, mostly broadcloth and Cambay cloth in small lots was sold. Of this 516 taels 6 mas 9 candereen was sold on credit to various members of the Matsūra household, the neighbouring daimyo of Karatsu and Ōmura, and (over 50 per cent) to Li Tan. The buyers of the 888 taels 6 mas 2 candereen worth of goods sold for ready money are not identified but an overlap with those who bought on credit seems likely.[87] By the spring of 1615 Cocks had understood that his stricture against credit was impracticable. The sales made in Hirado must be set beside the amount spent in presents from 22 September 1614 to 25 February 1615 (130 taels 7 mas 7 20/51 candereen), the cost of buying the house and enlarging the factory's premises (by the end of December 1614 this amounted to 1,159 taels 4 mas 1 candereen), the cost of running the house (for which figures do not exist) and the costs involved in preparing the factory's entry into the country trade, to which the energies of the factors remaining in Hirado were devoted.[88]

Almost immediately after Saris's departure, Cocks, accompanied by Adams and Edmund Sayers, had gone to Nagasaki to purchase a junk for the voyage to Siam. In accordance with Saris's instructions the voyage was to be undertaken by Peacock and Carwarden and set out in time to catch the northwesterly monsoon. However, in Nagasaki they found no junks for sale. All available shipping was being used by Japanese *shuinsen* operators who were prepared to offer the English space on board, although not to Ayuthia or even Patani, the destinations Saris had specified, but to Cochinchina, the central Vietnamese kingdom of Annam, one of the two major kingdoms then holding sway over what is today Vietnam. To its north lay its historical rival Tongking, with its capital at Hanoi, and to its south the petty kingdom of Champa, all that remained of the once glorious kingdom, another of the contestants for supremacy in Vietnam. Most of Champa's territory had come under the control of Annam by the seventeenth century. The two *nihonmachi* were situated on the coast just to the south of the Annamese capital, Hué, at Faifo (Hoi An) and Tourane (Da Nang). After due consideration and on learning that Joosten had made a profitable voyage to Cochinchina some two years previously, and no doubt also receiving favourable reports on the trade from the Japanese involved in it, Cocks decided that a voyage to Cochinchina should be undertaken and that space should be hired on one of the *shuinsen*. It was expected that Peacock and Carwarden would return to Japan in time to catch the next monsoon for Ayuthia by which time, it was hoped, a suitable junk for the factory's needs would have been found.[89] On 14 February 1614 Peacock and Carwarden left Hirado for Nagasaki and just over a month later on 18 March they joined a *shuinsen* belonging to a Chinese called Roquan and left for Faifo. Cocks, pleased with the progress in this first English initiative in the country trade, wrote smugly to Wickham in February that 'Captain Brower doth send goods for Cochinchina because we do, for that the States [General] shall not tax him of slothfulness, they having been here so long before us.'[90] The stock was valued at 2,983 taels 9 mas, 13.3 per cent of the entire stock, and consisted of eight broadcloths, half the ivory inventory, Cambay cloth and 1,000 reals in cash.[91] The two Englishmen carried a letter signed by James I (one of the standard blanks) and a present for the king.

What exactly happened to Peacock and Carwarden after their arrival in Cochinchina was to puzzle their compatriots in Japan over the years. Two facts were quickly established: both men were dead, Peacock murdered, Carwarden drowned at sea, and the goods had been lost. News of the disaster reached Hirado in July when it was reported that Peacock and the Dutch with whom he had gone up to Hué had been murdered, allegedly out of revenge for a Dutch attack on Annam in 1601. Carwarden was believed to have escaped in the junk and there was hope, soon dispelled, that he would make it back to Japan.[92] Over the next few years other stories emerged about what had transpired. In July 1615 Li Tan told Cocks that Peacock and Carwarden had been murdered not by the Annamese but by Japanese residents and that the king had known nothing about it and had even offered to make restitution for goods he had purchased. Nothing came of this alleged offer, ostensibly because the Japanese persuaded the king that if he made restitution to the English he would have to do the same to the Dutch, and this he was not prepared to do. A year later a Spanish merchant resident in Nagasaki, Alvaro Muños, informed Cocks that the two Englishmen had been murdered by a gang consisting of two Japanese, two Annamese and a Chinese. He was confident that restitution could be obtained and Cocks was willing to let him act on behalf of the Company. In December a completely different version was given by a mestizo who had been on the junk itself. According to his story there had been a collision with another vessel and Peacock had drowned, dragged under by the weight of the money in his pockets. His body had been recovered and buried and Carwarden had remained in Annam for a month before returning for Japan on a vessel which subsequently met with disaster at sea.

An opportunity to clear up the affair came only in 1617 when Adams (trading on his own account) and Sayers made a voyage to Annam to try to secure trading privileges for the English and to get to the bottom of the Peacock–Carwarden affair. From the information they managed to uncover from the Annamese officials, Adams and Sayers pieced together a full and plausible account of what had happened. Peacock, lured up river towards the capital, had been murdered by the Japanese host with whom the two Englishmen were staying. The Japanese was acting on orders from a group of officials who had been riled, it was alleged, by Peacock's drunken, arrogant, disrespectful behaviour towards the Annamese and his tearing up and trampling upon the trade privileges recently granted them and his boasts that the English could blockade all Annamese overseas trade if they wanted. Carwarden, who had remained on the coast, fled but was killed in a storm. This was largely the account that had been furnished by Li Tan. One of the officials involved in the affair stood his ground and none too subtly made it clear to Sayers and Adams that they should not attempt a visit to the court in order to speak directly with the king. This at least seemed to confirm that the monarch had known nothing of the affair. It is equally possible, however, that Peacock had fallen victim to the factional politics of the court which had caused the Dutch to beat a hasty retreat in 1601. The shogunate refused to become involved in the matter, declining Cocks's request, while on a visit to Edo in September 1616, that Hidetada should write a letter to the Annamese king on behalf of the English. Cocks continued to explore ways to salvage what he could of the missing cargo from the voyage. In April 1621 he followed a lead that he hoped would result in the recovery of a good portion of the lost goods, offering a Chinese trading between Nagasaki and Annam a reward of half the value of the goods he could recover belonging to the ill-fated voyage and from the goods stolen from Sayers ('for better something then nothing'). In any event nothing was recovered.[93] The first venture in the country trade had ended in disaster with the loss of two men and a sizeable portion of the factory's stock.

Even before news of the fate of Peacock and Carwarden reached Hirado, Cocks had been pressing on with preparations for the second overseas voyage, this time to Ayuthia. However, the Siam voyage ran into difficulties of a different kind. On this voyage the factory employed its own junk, the *Sea Adventure*, bought for 2,000 taels and refitted at an additional cost of 2,312 taels 9 mas 5 candereen. It carried a *shuinjō* which Adams had procured at Sunpu. The cargo consisted of 5,000 taels in silver and 129 taels 4 mas 5 candereen in ready money (with which it was intended to purchase sappan wood, deer hides, silk and other suitable goods for Japan). An assortment of Cambay cloth, Japanese weapons and armour for presents and for sale was also included. The total value of the cargo was 5,829 taels 7 mas 8 1/2 candereen (25.2 per cent of the original stock), by far the largest investment so far. The junk took letters for the English factors in Ayuthia and Patani and letters to be forwarded to England via Bantam as well as 748 taels relating to the account outstanding between Jan Joosten and the Seventh Voyage. Adams was designated master, Wickham cape merchant, assisted by Sayers. In the commission Cocks urged Wickham to do his best to avoid conflict with Adams and advised against putting into Cochinchina if Ayuthia could not be reached. Besides buying the specified goods in the Siamese capital, they were to look out for other goods such as shark skins (for sword scabbards and handles), and buffalo horns which would sell well in Japan. Wickham was to use his discretion in this but was to ensure that the junk returned on the next monsoon even if she was not fully laden with cargo. Purchases were to be made for the account of the Eighth Voyage but if space was left over then priority was to be given to goods belonging to other Company voyages, for which freightage was to be charged. Any remaining space was to be made available to other paying merchants. This stipulation conformed with *shuinsen* practice as did Cocks's instruction to let the Japanese crew load merchandise for their own account, in the hope of fostering goodwill for future voyages. On the outward voyage the junk also carried Japanese merchants and their goods for which freightage was charged.[94]

A lot of money had been spent in fitting out the vessel, and yet the *Sea Adventure* was barely seaworthy when she left Hirado on 28 November with a complement of 120 to 130 including the Japanese merchants. Nor did it have a reliable crew. The voyage proper did not start until 17 December when the junk left Kōchi (Kawachi), to the southeast of the town of Hirado and the place where, because of its bigger road, English and Dutch ships usually made their final preparations for departure. Within three days, she hit bad weather to the south of the Gotō Islands and sprung a leak. Rather than return to Hirado, Wickham, Adams and Sayers decided to make for the Ryūkyūs in order to repair the vessel. On 27 December the *Sea Adventure* reached Naha, and what was expected to be a short layover turned into a stay of almost five months during which time the vessel lost the monsoon and had to put back to Hirado.

By this time the golden age of Ryūkyū's overseas trade had long since passed and after 1609, when the Shimazu, daimyo of Satsuma, with the sanction of the bakufu, had invaded the islands, the Ryūkyū kingdom had all but lost its independence. The islands to the north of the main island of Okinawa were incorporated directly into the Satsuma domain and the rest of the kingdom became a tributary vassal of Satsuma. Ryūkyū was allowed to maintain its tributary relationship with China and thus continued to function as an entrepôt between China and Japan. The precise relationship with Satsuma was left purposely vague. Ryūkyūan embassies were sent to Satsuma (enhancing the domain's prestige) and Edo (they continued until the mid nineteenth century) and the kingdom provided yet another outlet for Japanese overseas trade.[95]

The Europeans aboard the *Sea Adventure* were unaware of such larger considerations when their vessel docked at Naha. Adams, who considered the place to be 'vnder the gouerment of Japan', regarded the attitude of the Ryūkyū officials as hostile and outrageous, and threatened to report their behaviour to the shogunal authorities on his return. Unperturbed the officials demanded that the junk should leave Naha as quickly as possible even before Adams was satisfied that repairs had been completed for fear that the Chinese would discover it. Wickham, who believed that Ryūkyū had lost its trade with China since the Satsuma conquest, shared Adams's irritation. He felt that the delays in providing 'those necessarys that our Jonke wanteth' caused the *Sea Adventure* to loose the monsoon.[96] In fact the Ryūkyūan officials' reasons for wanting to be rid of the *Sea Adventure* can be accepted at face value. One reason for the kingdom's ambivalent status *vis-à-vis* Satsuma was the Shimazu's desire not to discourage the Chinese from sending missions to Naha. The *Sea Adventure* was obviously a Japanese vessel even if its owners were Europeans. Moreover, the presence of the vessel infringed the 1611 agreement with Satsuma which stipulated that Satsuma authorise all foreign trade and ships entering or leaving Ryūkyūan waters, although this lapse did not appear to trouble an official from Satsuma in Naha at the time who politely offered his assistance to the stricken vessel.[97]

Another factor that contributed to the long delay of the *Sea*

Adventure at Naha was the vessel's 'mutinous Comp[any]' as Wickham described the crew. Towards the end of January, some of the crew, led by the boatswain and carpenter, refused to proceed any further on the voyage until they received half their wages. Adams, under pressure from Wickham, was inclined to discharge the boatswain and those who supported him but the Japanese merchants interceded on their behalf and Adams and Wickham had no alternative but to relent, keep the men and give in to their demands or face the prospect of being stranded at Naha. The crew's demands were contrary to the usual *shuinsen* practice whereby wages were paid after the vessel had reached its destination. In March arguments between the crew and the merchants erupted (the cause is unknown) and almost culminated in violence. Tension was defused with the mediaton of a Ryūkyū official. Towards the end of April when the *Sea Adventure* was ready to leave Naha and return to Japan, her departure was held up because the men would not come aboard, preferring to linger ashore and demanding extra money from Adams to settle their bills. Wickham put the blame for recruiting such a poor crew on Yasimon-dono, also known as Zanzibar, Adams's host in Hirado (possibly Yasuemon Senzaburo). He wrote to Cocks saying that Yasimon 'hath made a liuinge of the English' and criticised the cape merchant for being too trusting of the Japanese. He recommended his superior to 'Conceaue not well of any Japoners' except those in the employ of the factory. He added, with false humility, that his advice was offered 'not...to teach you whom I know can do better then my selfe' but 'to assist & aduiz you for the good of our Imployers & our owne creditts wch must annswer to what so euer shall be layed against vs, ffor the comp. hath not sent vs ffor Cifers into the ffarthest parts of the earth.'[98] The problems arising from the delay at Naha did nothing to improve relations between Wickham and Adams, the former accusing the latter of looking after his own interests rather than those of the Company, a charge which Adams denied. Wickham even tried to exclude Adams from negotiations with the Ryūkyū officials. Finally on 21 May the *Sea Adventure* left Naha, reaching the Gotō Islands on the 29th where she was careened (permission to do this at Naha had been refused). Wickham proceeded ahead to Hirado, where Cocks had been informed of events in Naha by letters sent via Satsuma, and the *Sea Adventure* herself arrived in Kōchi on 10 June.[99]

The voyage had been a fiasco and it had been expensive to boot. Repairs, lodging and presents, including a 'suit of English Apparel' given to King Shō Nei, had come to 556 taels 7 mas 6 1/4 candereen, easily wiping out the small profit of 128 taels 5 mas 6 candereen gained from sales of 233 taels 6 mas worth of duttis (they had cost 4 mas 8 candereen and 7 mas apeice and fetched 12 mas and 10 mas

respectively) and other Cambay cloth at Naha.[100] But the voyage
had not been a total failure. Wickham was convinced that he could
have sold a further 1,000 duttis had they been available (he gave no
evidence for this assertion and he had sold only 177 pieces). He had
purchased 2 catties of ambergris, a commodity in demand in England, for 128 taels, and he claimed that the Ryūkyū stuff was 'the
best...that the world affordeth and the whitest'. Wheat was also
available and the *Sea Adventure* brought back 1,200 sacks costing just
below 1 mas per sack. (It was difficult to sell the wheat because the
main Japanese supply from Manila had not yet reached Nagasaki and
traders were not prepared to put a price on the Ryūkyū wheat until
after the junks had arrived from the Philippines.)[101] Regardless of the
frustrations of the stay at Naha, which would have been more than
offset by a generous abundance of Ryūkyūan hospitality, Wickham
was convinced that a subfactory should be established in Ryūkyū to
sell duttis, for which he estimated the market at 3,000 pieces per
annum, sappan wood and Japanese products in return for ambergris.
This was a project for which he was to lobby hard over the following
months, failing to realise that the uncooperative attitude of the
Ryūkyūan officials was a clear signal that a regular trade would not
be permitted.[102]

A glimmer of optimism appeared to shine in June 1615 but it was
unwarranted and could not disguise the fact that the Hirado factory's
first efforts to break into the country trade had been unsuccessful, no
matter how mitigating the circumstances. Still, there was no question of giving up. Another effort was to be made and the *Sea
Adventure*, chalking up even more expenses, was overhauled and
made ready over the summer to catch the next monsoon for second
voyage to Siam.

(iii)   The Changing Situation in Japan

During its first year of operations the factory had not been deprived
of news from colleagues elsewhere in the Indies. Communication
was sporadic and arrived in chronological disorder and depended on
the goodwill of Dutch, Chinese or Japanese vessels for conveyance.
For example, a letter from Saris written in Bantam just before his
departure for England in February 1614 and a letter from Ball written
in March 1614 only reached Hirado at the end of June 1615.[103] But it
was not until the end of August 1615 that the English received their
first visit from an English ship, the *Hosiander*, a vessel of some 213
tons.

The *Hosiander* had been laid up at Bantam, but with the arrival of
David Middleton's joint-stock fleet in February 1615 it was decided

to put her to use and follow up Saris's instructions from Saldonia Bay, which had been brought by the *Concord* the previous September, and send her on a voyage to Japan via Patani and Ayuthia. Her departure was delayed until 11 April and her crew, largely provided from Middleton's fleet, included a Japanese and a Chinese who had previously been to Hirado. The cape merchant was Ralph Coppindale, who had joined the Company in March 1614, and was described as 'a very sufficient yet a peacable and quiet, honest man' and 'very pffect [perfect] in accounts'. He had good references from his former master and experience of working abroad in Denmark and the Treceras Islands. The master was John Hunt. The *Hosiander*'s departure from Bantam had been left late and rather than aborting the voyage to Japan the ship made only one stop *en route*, at Patani, where she arrived on 17 June. She sailed again on 10 July, reaching Kōchi on 31 August. As Adams remarked, the ship was lucky to have made it, for the monsoon was usually spent by then.[104] The *Hosiander* was towed into Hirado on 4 September and Cocks, who had been informed of her voyage by two Dutch ships which arrived in early August, counselled haste in proceeding to Sunpu, especially as the Dutch had already gone up. This was to be the first English visit since Saris's.[105]

During the two intervening years the Tokugawa had continued to work towards an enduring settlement that would consolidate their power. The regime, not yet entirely confident of its hold over the country, was determined to gather and secure firmly the reins of power in its hands and to establish the credentials of legitimacy both at home and abroad.

To guarantee any permanent settlement at home, it was absolutely vital for the bakufu to define its relationship with the daimyo and wipe out, or at least neutralise, any posssible focus of opposition. The most important step towards defining the relationship with the daimyo during Ieyasu's life was the *buke shohatto* of 1615, a code of regulations which reasserted the Tokugawa shogunate's primacy over the daimyo, who were deemed to hold their power from the shogun but who were confirmed as authorities within their domains with the right to confer samurai status on their own retainers. The *buke shohatto* also forbade the construction of new castles and laid down rules covering dress, marriage and residence, and articulated the ethos to which the daimyo were expected to adhere. The code drawn up under the guidance of the Zen monk Sūden and the influential Confucian scholar Hayashi Razan, spelt out the assumptions on which Tokugawa rule was based. Ieyasu's successors added other measures which strengthened the position of the bakufu within the Japanese polity. The most notable of these was the establishment of the *sankin kōtai* (alternate attendance) whereby the daimyo had to alternate their residence between their domains and Edo where they were obliged to build an extra residence at their own expense to house their wives and children who were left there as permanent hostages to guarantee loyal behaviour. The system had its origins in earlier feudal practice and it only became a requirement after 1633, during the reign of the shogun Iemitsu, but it was in use earlier on a voluntary basis as Cocks recorded.

The Tokugawa had won a battle at Sekigahara, not a final victory. Hideyoshi's son Hideyori remained ensconced at Osaka with a domain of 650,000 koku, a visible symbol that the Tokugawa had established their ascendency by subverting the Toyotomi settlement, a settlement from which many of the daimyo had benefitted. Osaka itself was also a physical embodiment of Toyotomi ambitions. Hideyoshi had aimed to develop the city as a major commercial centre at the expense of the neighbouring seaport of Sakai which had the arteries of its commere – its canals – filled in, thereby emasculating its role as the port of entry to the Kinai region, although it still remained an important city for commerce. Like the young offspring of Edward IV in the Tower of London, Hideyori was an alternative source of political legitimation, and the Toyotomi past was still capable of casting a spell over those nursing grievances or grudges against the Tokugawa. Another focus of potential opposition, and one physically close to Hideyori, was the imperial court in Kyoto, which was not quite the inconsequential religious institution the English, like the other Europeans in Japan, imagined. On previous occasions the court had tried to take advantage of national upheaval to reassert its own claims to power, notably at the establishment of the Muromachi bakufu and even in the aftermath of Hideyoshi's Korean invasion. Hideyoshi had nipped this in the bud but during the early years of the Tokugawa shogunate the court retained a potent symbolic value and, by virtue of the offices it was able to bestow, remained central to any quest for legitimacy even though it no longer had any independent power, nor even influence, in shaping national politics. Ieyasu preferred to manipulate the court for his own ends rather than to abolish it. He exploited every opportunity to interfere in court affaris. In the process the imperial court was isolated from society but was provided with the resources it had lacked during the *sengoku* period to live comfortably and enact the ancient rituals that made it the fount of legitimacy and embodiment of tradition in the Japanese polity. A lesser source of opposition, at least in terms of numbers, was Christianity, an alien creed which nevertheless posed a threat to the domestic social order, and, because of the Spanish presence on the periphery of Japan's world of international relations, a possible threat to national security as well. Conscious that Ieyasu's advancing age raised serious questions about a peaceful transition for the dynasty, the Tokugawa struck both against the Christians and against Hideyori.[106]

The non-implementation of Hideyoshi's order in 1587 expelling the missionaries was a pyrrhic victory for the progress of Christianity in Japan but it served notice on the missionaries, warning them that there were limits to their proselytising activity. The Jesuits had been allowed to remain in Japan and small numbers of Franciscans, Dominicans and Augustinians had been admitted subsequently. However, in the 1610s the Tokugawa began to assert an anti-Christian policy of their own. In July 1612 Ieyasu wrote to the viceroy of New Spain granting his request, conveyed by Vizcaíno, for trade with Japan. But Ieyasu boldly stressed that Japan did not want trade to be a cover for propagating an alien subversive doctrine: 'The laws of your country are completely different and have no affinity with ours.' He emphasised that in the Japanese polity bonds between lord and vassal were sacrosanct, guaranteed and enforced by the power of the ruler. The Christian religion had no place in such a schema.[107] Vizcaíno's behaviour at Edo (where his men had worn swords and fired off their arquebuses in Edo castle, interpreted as signs of grave disrespect by the Japanese) and his demands that the Japanese expel the Dutch as a precondition for establishing formal relations with New Spain, accounts for Ieyasu's, change of tone from the treaty made with De Vivero y Velasco in 1609, which would have permitted the Spanish to build churches if they chose to settle near Edo for trade.[108]

But no matter how it appeared to the Jesuits in retrospect, Vizcaíno's behaviour was of minor importance in leading to the 1614 edict. It was more than outweighed by the near contemporaneous scandal involving Okamoto Daihachi, a Christian and one of Honda Masazumi's secretaries. Okamoto was involved in forging documents which would have increased the size of the Christian daimyo Arima Harunobu's domain at the expense of the neighbouring Matsūra. His action was discovered and, as a Christian, he refused to commit *seppuku*, and was burnt at the stake. The affair tainted all Christians by association.[109] The role of William Adams was likewise of minor importance in shaping the decision. The Jesuits grossly exaggerated his influence at court, attacking him for encouraging the Japanese to expel the missionaries. According to Jesuit sources, he had warned Honda Masazumi in 1611 that the Spanish had come to Japan not to sound out the ports for future trade but as a prelude to invasion. Adams's assertion was disregarded by the bakufu and the Spanish were permitted to carry out their survey.[110] The following year Adams was reported to have bragged to the ambassador from the Philippines that 'Your Honour will see that within three years there won't be a single padre in Japan'.[111]

Even more marginal was the influence of the English, whom Cocks says the Jesuits held responsible for their banishment, and the Dutch.[112] The English mistrusted the Roman Catholic clergy from their earliest days in Japan, suspecting that they had played a major part in spiriting deserters from the *Clove* out of Japan in 1613. In Wickham's words 'upon demand, as occasion offered, we have done the Jesuits little credit here' and Cocks accused them of spreading misinformation about Adams's death in 1614.[113] Cocks may have despised the Catholic clergy, describing them as 'these villainous papistical rabble at Langasaque,' – his antipathy and that of the other English and Dutch in Hirado was against the Catholic clergy and did not extend to Portuguese and Spanish merchants with whom the Protestants enjoyed good relations – but in Hirado he was far from Sunpu and Edo, and Wickham in the Edo subfactory had no influence at all on bakufu policy.[114] Whatever opinions about the Catholic clergy the English voiced at Hirado or elsewhere, hoping to ingratiate themselves with the bakufu, they counted for nothing in shaping the decision to expel the missionaries and no matter how highly the English and Dutch evaluated their importance, the shogunate did not see them as alternative conduits for foreign trade to the Portuguese. The aim of the bakufu was to get rid of the missionaries not the Lusitanian or Iberian merchants. The Japanese made it clear that the Portuguese merchants who arrived in July 1614, after the edict's promulgation, on the náo, *Nossa Senhora da Vida*, were to be treated with 'all favour and kind usage'.[115] The náo, despite the contribution of *shuinsen* and Chinese vessels remained important in Japan's overseas trade. The shogunate did not contemplate a rupture with the Portuguese. The Japanese wanted to increase foreign trade, not cut it back. The Portuguese were an important ingredient in the Nagasaki economy while the English and Dutch remained unproven as participants in Japan's foreign trade, their record thus far insignificant in comparison with the Portuguese even if their presence was welcome. There was nothing as yet to suggest that they would be able to replace the Portuguese in Japan's foreign trade, especially as they had no comparable access to the Chinese market such as the Portuguese enjoyed at Macao. The Portuguese remained paramount among the Europeans in Japan's overseas trade until the eve of their expulsion in 1639.[116] The anti-Christian policies pursued by the bakufu were part of the broader policy to secure the Tokugawa firmly in power. The Jesuits had an interest in looking for scapegoats for their expulsion for then they could rationalise that neither the message nor the messengers had failed the mission.

The edict proscribing Christianity and ordering all missionaries to leave Japan was proclaimed on 27 January 1614 (NS) (Franciscan churches in the Kinai and at Edo had already been closed in 1613 in the aftermath of the Okamoto affair). Cocks got word of the proclamation by mid February doubting 'the news is too good to be true'. At the beginning of March Eaton reported from Osaka that churches and houses belonging to the friars and Jesuits had been pulled down and, exaggerating, that all local Christians had recanted 'so as now there is no more Christians of Japanners in these parts'.[117] The English were touched by the edict as well. The daimyo of Hirado ordered them to remove the Cross of St George from their house, ignoring their protests that it was only a symbol of English nationhood and had no deeper religious significance.[118] Some missionaries chose to ignore the order and went underground hoping that, as had happened in 1587, the political wind would change. But there was no such change of heart by the bakufu and the policy was ruthlessly implemented with repercussions for the trade of the English and Dutch in Japan. Although the anti-Christian policies of the Tokugawa shogunate were to colour the European image of Japan in terms of domestic politics they were of less significance than the final onslaught against the Toyotomi.

By the beginning of April 1614 Cocks was writing of rumours of 'troubles like to ensue in Japan', one of the reasons, besides the purely commercial consideration of turning goods into cash, why he was concerned that Eaton and Wickham should sell their stock as soon as possible.[119] Wickham reported there was no such trouble in Edo or the Kinai but he had heard the rumours and in June, showing how little he understood of the reality of Japanese politics, he reported that Ieyasu was likely to visit Kyoto in October to visit 'his Goastly father the Dayry' (that is, the real emperor).[120] In fact Ieyasu and Hidetada were preparing for the showdown with Hideyori and it was for this reason that the English ordnance, lead, gunpowder and shot had been avidly sought by Ieyasu. Hideyori's countermeasures accounted for the increased demand for gunpowder in Osaka noticed by Eaton in late October.[121] Anxious to be doing the proper thing, the English gave presents to Takanobu and his party (broadcloth, Cambay cloth and silk) as they left Hirado in December to obey the Tokugawa summons to take part in the siege of Osaka castle. In Osaka, Eaton, unwittingly fishing in troubled waters, assumed that Hideyori as overlord of Osaka would be responsible for protecting the city and gave 50 catties of gunpowder, worth 17 taels 5 mas, as a goodwill present for Hideyori together with a hat for his secretary.[122]

The siege of Osaka castle was staged in two parts, the winter siege lasting from December 1614 to Janaury 1615, and the summer siege from May to June 1615. On 4 June the Toyotomi legacy perished when Hideyori took his own life and his mother, Yodo, had herself killed by a retainer, preferring death to capture. The combined forces

of both sides perhaps numbered 300,000 and the appalling bloodshed
(Cocks heard stories of 100,000–300,000 deaths) had resulted in the
partial destruction of the castle and the burning of most of the city,
including the house where the English factory stored many of its
goods. Sakai had also been burnt to the ground and some of
Hideyori's supporters had attempted to burn Kyoto but had been
seized and crucified before they could do much damage. Fortunately,
Eaton had taken the precaution of returning some of the stock in the
Kinai to Hirado but the English initially reckoned they had lost 155
taels 4 mas 8 candereen worth of goods although this was later
reduced by 21 taels 5 mas, money returned by Eaton's Osaka host for
merchandise which, according to Eaton, he had pretended had been
burnt.[123] The charge was probably unfair. There had been much
confusion and lawlessness during the siege and the English were
lucky to receive anything back. Van Santvoort reported to Specx in
November 1614 that most of the inhabitants of Osaka and Sakai had
fled, and that business activity had come to a halt. Van Santvoort and
Joosten had taken responsibility for the Dutch stock in Osaka which
had been removed from the war zone and entrusted to Joosten for
safe-keeping. After the winter siege Van Santvoort had written to
Specx informing him that the stock in cash would be sent down to
Hirado once the armies 'have returnd to their quarters'. He was
alarmed by the number of 'thieves and robbers' who had taken
advantage of the troubles.[124]

Rumours of the fall of Osaka castle reached Hirado on 2 June,
predating the event itself, although with the start of the summer
campaign it was only a matter of time before the castle fell. On 7
June a destitute Franciscan brought more news. He had been present
in the castle during the siege but had fled before its fall and Cocks, in
an act of Christian charity, gave him 15 mas to see him on his
way.[125] The official news of the fall was announced by the Matsūra
on 20 June. But hard truth was difficult to separate from the welter
of rumours which circulated after the demise of Hideyori. Cocks,
with his experience of intelligence reporting in Bayonne, kept himself informed about the latest news and rumours and insisted on
receiving all reports no matter how wild 'for amongst many lies
something may proceed from truth'.[126] He noted stories that
Hideyori, whose body was never found, had escaped to the
Ryūkyūs, and speculated that the western daimyo would be relocatd
closer to Edo. This was not at all implausible, even if it did not
transpire. Tokugawa power was weakest in the west, where many of
the daimyo had benefited from Hideyoshi's policies, and in northern
Kyushu Christianity was strongest. Cocks also noted such details as
the return of the Hirado forces from the siege at the end of June
(Takanobu and his advisers, like the other daimyo, remained with

Ieyasu) and local compliance with the orders to search for Hideyori's supporters who had escaped from Osaka. Cocks commented that 'in the Sothern parts' people would like to believe in Hideyori's escape 'because they affeckt the yong man more then the ould [Ieyasu]'.[127]

The defeat of the Toyotomi had been achieved at relatively little cost and strengthened Tokugawa power immensely (Osaka castle was rebuilt in the 1620s, a visible and awesome symbol, this time of Tokugawa control over western Japan)[128] but this was not obvious to the English. They continued to pick up rumours and feared that the campaign had merely been the opening shot of a renewed period of civil war, which caused Cocks to worry about the safety of their stock in the Kinai.[129] Fears of war were fuelled by other rumours which abounded, especially of Ieyasu's death. The rumours and the death itself which occurred in June 1616, cast everything into doubt. The Dutch were alarmed as well. Specx, who had already informed Governor General Coen of the disruption to trade in the Kinai and of rumours about a bakufu assault on Nagasaki to destroy the city and its contamination by Chrisitianity, approached Cocks 'to talk with me about the state of Japon, for that he dowbted their might be som alteration by meanes of these reports of the death of the Emperour'. Specx had heard of possible dynastic changes from Woutersen. In early July after the fall of Osaka castle, Woutersen wrote that the 'emperor', Ieyasu, was planning to retire in September or October in favour of Hidetada, who would be given a new name by the 'dairy'.[130]

Against this tumultuous background the factory had tried to press on with its business. In the days after the Hosiander's arrival the English worked hard to unload her, sort out the goods that were to be sent to the Kinai, procure and load a barque to transport the goods and men, no easy matter as most vessels had already been taken for use by the Matsūra and by the Dutch. The one that was hired soon sprang a leak, causing a delay.[131] The Hosiander had also brought news of the establishment of the joint-stock which necessitated changes in the factory's accounting procedures. All existing voyage stock, including goods, money and debt, were to be rated and the accounts sent to Bantam to be incorporated into the joint-stock and in future accounts were to be sent to Bantam, not London. Downton's instructions went further and stated that the factors were to make copies of their journals and ledgers and send them home. Bantam and Surat were to become the chief factories in their respective regions and all other factories were to be subordinated to them. Accordingly, the Firando Ledger B was closed and taken back to Bantam along with other accounts on the Hosiander.[132] Fortunately, another set of accounts drawn up by John Osterwick, who came to Japan on the Hosiander as purser's mate, survives. This

gives an idea of the factory's finances from September 1615 to
January 1617.[133] The stock unloaded from the *Hosiander* was valued
at 8,601 taels 6 mas 3 1/9 candereen, and consisted of various kinds of
Cambay cloth, mercury, pepper, fowling pieces, lead and wax.
There were small amounts of gold leaf, knives, scissors and sugar.[134]
As with the original stock carried on the *Clove*, some goods had not
travelled well. The baftas in particular were spotted, stained or
rotten. Cocks complained that they had been loaded in that
condition, although some were subsequently sold. The wax was 'so
bad that no man will look at it'.[135] The buckshaws were of the
wrong colour (any other colour but red would have sold) while the
allejaes and cajanies sold well. The pepper was of two sorts,
'Bantam' (Java) and 'Patania'. The former was found to sell better, as
it had before, even though the Patani pepper fetched a higher price.
The market for gingham was unknown. After three months in
Japan, Coppindale judged that no profit was 'to be made by any
goods I brought from Bantam and Potania [Patani], and in April
1616, after further sales efforts, Wickham recommended returning
some of the unsold goods to Bantam, tartly adding, lest some factor
there 'hath bin mistaken in sending Chaulke for Cheese'.[136]

After the arrival of the *Hosiander*, Cambay cloth, pepper, lead,
wax and a small amount of Chinese silk were given 'to ye king of
ffirando for a present uppon ye coming of the *Hosiander* accordinge
to ye Custome of ye Countrie'. The goods were rated at 150 taels 4
mas 17/45 candereen and another 126 teals 4 mas 1/4 candereen
worth of goods was given to other members of the Matsūra
household. Together the presents amounted to 3.2 per cent of the
cargo value.[137] Goods to the value of 2,832 taels 7 mas 7 1/3
candereen were assigned to the Kinai subfactory, mostly Cambay
cloth, pepper, qucksilver, fowling pieces, wax and smaller quantities
of other goods such as steel and shark skins. Locally procured
Chinese silk goods worth 345 taels 5 mas were added to the stock.[138]

It had already been decided at Kōchi on 3 September that
Coppindale, Rowland Thomas, the purser, together with Wickham,
Eaton, Adams and Michel, a jurebasso, whose drunken behaviour
Wickham was to complain about, would go up to the court.[139] Eaton
was returning to the Kinai for the fourth time to resume work at the
subfactory. His second visit had been in September 1614 when he
took along a small amount of pepper, Cambay cloth and money for
the subfactory but with the preparations for the siege of Osaka castle
underway he felt it prudent to return to Hirado in December. During
this visit Eaton had sold 523 taels worth of goods, enabling him to
bring down 440 taels in cash.[140] His third visit had been in March
1615 when he took another small consignment of goods worth 185
taels 5 mas 1/6 candereen. Wickham was to continue on to Edo,

which unlike the Kinai had been almost wholly neglected since his departure a year before. The arrangement Wickham had made with Mikumoya for the handling of the subfactory's goods had proven unsatisfactory from the English point of view but with no one available to replace Wickham because of the voyages to Cochinchina and Siam, it had fallen to Eaton to try to sort things out as best he could. In early summer 1615 he had gone up to Edo from the Kinai but had achieved little, although he did bring down a part of the goods from Edo to the Kinai. After his return to Hirado on 13 August he reported to Cocks that Mikumoya and Adams's brother-in-law, Gendoque, had 'dealed Judasly w'th hym at Edo'.[141] It was time to have somebody back in Edo to manage business there and settle accounts.

The party left Hirado on 11 September reaching Kyoto at the end of the month. There they narrowly missed Ieyasu who had left to return to Sunpu. Adams had gone on ahead refusing to wait until problems with the barque, which had begun to leak shortly after the departure from Hirado, were sorted out. His haste was in response to a request from Ieyasu to attend the court. The old doubts about Adams's loyalty resurfaced. Cocks thought that Adams had invented the excuse. He speculated that Adams intended to serve the Dutch, whom he felt Adams 'loveth. . .much better then vs that are of his owne nation', or, alternatively, that because his two-year contract with the Company was coming to an end shortly, he had concocted the story as a pretext to get up to Sunpu to have Ieyasu forbid him from leaving the country so that he would not be able to go on the Siam voyage and thus be better placed to resume his own business activities.[142] In this instance the aspersions were unfounded. Adams had been sent for because of the arrival of a Spanish ship from Acapulco. However, English suspicions were not without foundation. Adams maintained a correspondence with the Hollanders. In the course of 1615 he made it known to them that he remained at their service and in October 1616 he wrote to Specx from Edo informing him of developments there during Cocks's visit. His letter did not breach any commercial confidences, however, and he continued to serve the English until his death in 1620. No matter what his fellow countrymen thought, there was no conflict in Adams's mind about the propriety of serving both the English and Dutch.[143]

The ship from Acapulco was the vessel which had carried Vizcaíno and Date Masamune's embassy to New Spain. Date's representative, Haeskura Tsunenaga, had proceeded to Spain and Rome in the company of the Franciscan, Luis Sotelo, who hoped that the mission would repeat the success of the visit of the young Kyushu nobles some thirty years before and score a similar propaganda coup for the mendicant order. The Japanese, on the other hand, were more interested in trade than in religion or international relations. Date, like other daimyo, could appreciate the benefits that would flow to his domain from trade. The Spanish ship which arrived from New Spain in 1615 brought three Franciscans as ambassadors. Their presence was a clear violation of the edict against Christianity about which the Spanish vice-regal authorities had learned from Manila. The Franciscans did not endear themselves to the bakufu by condemning the destruction of Osaka castle and attacking the 1614 edict. Such meddling only served to underline the bakufu's belief that Christianity was subversive. Anti-Christian sentiment had been further heightened by the presence of seven clergy at the seige of Osaka castle and, in the words of the Jesuit João Rodriguez Girão, the spectacle of 'so many crosses, *Jesus* and *Santiagos* on the flags, tents, and other martial insignia which the Japanese use in their encampments, that this must have made Ieyasu sick to his stomach'. Ieyasu refused to see the ambassadors and Hidetada rejected their presents. Adams was used as an intermediary with the friars who in turn blamed him for sabotaging the mission by spreading false stories about Spanish ambitions in east Asia. The friars finally left for Acapulco in 1617. Religious considerations and the comments of the Franciscans apart, relations between Japan and New Spain could not have developed harmoniously, because the Spanish, concerned about Dutch attacks on their possessions in the New World, had ordered the expulsion of all foreign traders from New Spain and Peru and the closing of the markets to them.[144] It is as a retaliation against this proclamation that the shogunate's ban on Japanese visiting New Spain is to be judged. It did not represent an opening shot on the road to *sakoku*, or the closing of the country. For their part the English were not bothered about the diplomatic purpose of the mission from New Spain but about the unwelcome competition from the stock of broadcloth, kerseys and other cloth which the ship had brought and which Cocks claimed was sold at low rates.[145]

During the brief stopover in Kyoto, the English party set aside goods as presents for 'the Emperor, his sonn & others & for sales if any could be made'. These consisted of Cambay cloth, broadcloth and most of the Chinese silk. Ivory, originally brought on the *Clove*, was added from the Kinai subfactory's stock, bringing the value of the goods taken on to Sunpu and Edo to 808 taels 9 mas 8 5/6 candereen.[141] The party reached Sunpu on 8 October and two days later had a brief audience with Ieyasu which Wickham said was like 'actinge a dome shew for we had only a looke of his Matie & soe we were Comanded out from the presence of the Emperor only smilinge to thinke what paynes we toke and what charge we were at to Come to visit him'. At least they had been granted an audience unlike the Portuguese on that year's náo who had been kept waiting for forty days with their present but were not admitted to Ieyasu's presence. Afraid that the presents might appear paltry, Wickham and Coppindale threw in some camphor and lignum aloes. A few peculs of lead and wax from the Kinai subfactory were added later. As if to emphasise the inadequacy of the goods received from Bantam, the silk purchased in Hirado accounted for 62 per cent of the value of the gift. In return the English received an assortment of kimonos, lance and arrowheads and knives.[147]

In spite of his cynicism, Wickham felt the visit had been successful: the English had been given trading rights in Ryūkyū, subject to the approval of the Shimazu in Satsuma, and Wickham was hopeful that Ieyasu would respond to Adams's entreaties and buy up most of the *Hosiander's* cargo, with the exception of the Cambay cloth. He also thought that both the English company and the Dutch could freely plunder non-Japanese vessels without a *shuinjō* outside Japanese waters because Ieyasu had permitted the Dutch to keep a Portuguese junk, the *San Antōnio*, that they had captured *en route* from Champa to Nagasaki. The vessel did not have a *shuinjō* although Japanese were among its crew.[148] But there was a vast gap between what Wickham thought had been gained and what actually was granted.

Wickham continued on to Edo with the intention of attending to the badly neglected affairs of the subfactory there and trying to gather in as much as he could of the money owing for previous sales. His task was not made easier by the ill-feeling Eaton had caused on his brief visit. On one occasion he had threatened Mikumoya by drawing a sword. Adams urged restraint in trying to recover the debts and cautioned Wickham against resorting to law for their recovery for 'the Jappane merchants, seeing extrmity used, will be afraid to deal with us; therefore for our further credit with them, if it be with some small loss, end with them'. 'Discretion' would rebound to the Company's benefit. This was sensible advice because the Japanese merchants expected to receive rolling credit and legal action, while useful for making debtors jump in England, would only have caused bewilderment and have alienated the merchants who could take their custom elsewhere. Adams's advice did not resolve what Wickham saw as th fundamental problem, the accumulation of long-term debts on some accounts. Given the nature of Japanese business practices, there was, of course, no way round this. Wickham was pessimistic about making further sales, thinking he would be lucky to sell at invoice prices. In fact no sales appear to have been made, and after using some of the stock for presents the rest was sent back to the Kinai.[149]

Coppindale and the others did not accompany Wickham to Edo but returned to Hirado by way of Kyoto, arriving on 28 November. Wickham's jibe about the high cost of the journey was no exaggeration. Coppindale's incidental expenses amounted to 283 taels 8 mas, Wickham's to 219 taels 1 mas 7 candereen, which included 16 taels 7 mas for a saddle and horse trappings. (Both men had received cash advances, most of which were borne by the Kinai subfactory.) Wickham wryly commented that there had been much trouble with the 'hackney men' on the journey in contrast to Saris's 'ffor the wars hath much Consumed the horses but not the hors[e]keepers'. Adams's expenses amounted to 65 taels 1 mas. The cost of barque hire and wages for the sailors to take the party to the Kinai came to 86 taels 5 mas 2 3/10 candereen. In all, the recorded costs of the visit came to over 750 taels (these excluded the expenses of Rowland Thomas and the jurebasso). Coppindale considered the cost of the visit, which was approximately 25 per cent less than the cost of Saris's, and the presents as greater than 'an indifferent custom, especially when a ship cometh with a small capital, and sales so base and slack' and confided to Rowland Thomas that together with the pilfering of cargo from the *Hosiander* by the crew 'he was vtterly vndone in going vpp to the Emperour'. The visit and other pressures got the better of him and sparked off a depression which continued over the next few weeks.[150]

The *Hosiander* did not leave Hirado until 26 February 1616. There were difficulties in careening and sheathing her, exacerbated by the death of two of the ship's carpenters and the stubborn, uncooperative attitude of the master, John Hunt, a man of 'extreme hvmouor' who failed to maintain discipline or help the merchants in matters which fell more obviously within his competence, such as the casting of some ordnance components to be sent to Bantam and London for inspection. Hunt was defying Company rules and his attitude contributed to Coppindale's depression. The extremely cold snowy weather – 'coulder in England at this tyme I think it is nott' remarked Thomas – delayed the loading of the ship. By the time the *Hosiander* sailed from Hirado over 1,300 taels had been spent in making her seaworthy and victualling her, a not inconsiderable burden on the Hirado factory's scarce financial resources.[151] Her cargo consisted of 2,200 taels of Japanese silver and 1,200 taels in reals (easily the most important part of the consignment), ambergris worth 959 taels 3 mas 5 candereen (some brought back from Ryūkyū, some purchased locally and sent at Wickham's insistence) and smaller quantities of musk, iron, copper, Japanese swords, textiles (including some 'Japan Cloath' as samples), and bowls. Brass pulling-wheels for large ordnance and iron shot together with cast iron pieces of ordnance were also included. They were useful for ballast and had been commissioned by the factory. Cocks wrote to the Company that the Japanese 'are not very expert in that faculty [casting of ordnance]...especially in great pieces' but was confident that 'if your Worships do send a man that is an expert [into th]ese parts, he would make ordnance for a third part of that which it costeth in Eng[land]'. The total value of the cargo was 4,668 taels 9 mas 7 candereen. In compliance with the instructions regarding the joint stock, Cocks sent two letters to Jourdain at Bantam 'w'th journall ballance & 4 books petty charges'.[152] The accounts were to cause problems for Cocks later.

Before the *Hosiander*'s departure a general council was held to review the Company's trade in Japan. It was decided that Osterwick, John Coker, and a youth, Richard Hudson, were to be left behind. Osterwick was appointed bookkeeper with a wage of £20 per annum, Coker as cook and Hudson to learn the language. The general council further agreed that Wickham, who had returned to Hirado at the end of January, was to go back to the Kinai to replace Eaton and remain there until final authorisation for the opening of the Ryūkyū factory was obtained. He left for Kyoto in the early spring and remained there until later in the year. Eaton was to be recalled to Hirado and go to Tsushima 'to cleare in that place'. In fact he did not go because he was arrested by the Ōmura and detained for three weeks for slaying a Japanese barqueman. His release was secured by the intervention of the Matsūra who sent an official to the Ōmura domain reminding the authorities there that the English were under the shogun's protection. Cocks attributed the long detention, some of it in solitary confinement, to the influence of the padres determined to get even with the English for their supposed part in the expulsion decree of 1614. This was highly unlikely even if Ōmura had been one of the most successful domains for the missionaries. Coppindale was a keen advocate of reorganisation. On intimate terms with Wickham, he was critical of Cocks's management of the factory, accusing him of being conservative and sticking rigidly to Saris's instructions. However, he did make constructive proposals. The sensible suggestion to reduce costs by covering Edo from the Kinai originated from him during the visit to Ieyasu and it was endorsed enthusiastically by Wickham. The general council also made unilateral wage adjustments.[153] The personnel changes were necessary. Peacock, Carwarden and Gisbert de Coning, the Dutchman employed in 1614, were all dead and Nealson's bouts of consumption and frequent dissipation impaired his performance. Adams, who had left for Siam with Sayers in December 1615, had not renewed his contract with the Company before his departure. He still went on the voyage, but had made it clear to Cocks that he was unwilling to be re-employed. He requested Cocks to instruct the Company to pay £30 or £40 to his family in England which he would repay in Japan with a bill of exchange.[154] Neither Wickham's pessimism about the trade nor his pay grievances were compelling enough reasons for him to avail himself of Saris's authorisation that he could leave on the first English ship that came to Japan. In a letter to Jourdain, with whom he was on friendly terms, he claimed that Saris had left him in Japan because the commander had 'Jealous opinions' of him and accused Saris of a spiteful vindictiveness, thinking that those whom he 'had depressed and wronged' were 'neuer secure enough untile he had eyther made theyre head or feet his Antipodes'. Nevertheless, he claimed that he had not yet been able to put his affairs in order and was not ready to leave Japan.[155] From his correspondence it is evident that his reluctance stemmed from his judgement that although the affairs of the factory were unprofitable at least his own private business schemes were going well, and that with a little more time, including a stint in Ryūkyū, he could amass the nest-egg he sought.

Of the newcomers to the factory, Osterwick, who was half-Dutch, had experience of working at Malaga, spoke French and had served as a clerk in the custom house in London before coming to the Indies in April 1614 on the *Samaritan*. He had been recommended to the Company by John (later Sir John) Wolstenholme, one of the directors and a future farmer of the customs, and when presented to the Court he was described as 'a psonable [personable] younge man'.[156] Hudson was the son of the explorer Henry Hudson who had perished in the 1610–11 attempt to discover the northwest passage. His widowed mother petitioned the Company to employ the boy because she was unable to support him, and the Company, welcoming an opportunity to appear generous and public-spirited, granted her request as her husband had 'perished in the service of the Commonwealth'. Richard left England on the *Samaritan* under the care of the master's mate. A sum of £5 was laid out for his food, clothing and other necessities. At this time the Company had a policy of sending youths to the Indies to various factories so that they could become proficient in Asian languages. The boys were to be educated by the chief factors in the places to which they were sent and were to be brought up free of 'the sins of these lands espetially from that abominable sinne of sodomy and brought up in vertue'. They were to attend prayers every day but if they could not adapt to life in the Indies or became unruly and would not 'reform' they were to be sent home. Boys had gone out on Downton's fleet and went on Keeling's in 1615.[157] Of Coker nothing is known.

In the meantime the *Sea Adventure* had set sail on 7 December in a fresh attempt to reach Siam. She had been made ready for service by mid-October 1615. Adams was master and Sayers cape merchant. The purser and crew were Japanese.[158] The cost of making her seaworthy, victualling her, clearing wages and other expenses, including 4 mas charged for a piece of red zelea cloth for a flag, was

1,696 taels 4 mas 6 candereen, mostly spent on labour and material charges.[159] Cocks complained that the Japanese 'scrivano', or purser, an associate of Adams, had cheated the English of some 50 taels and Adams was suspected of complicity, but Cocks noted that the Dutch were similarly cheated.[160] The *Sea Adventure*'s cargo was valued at 2,949 taels 4 mas 8 1/4 candereen of which 2,400 taels was in money (2,238 taels in reals, the rest in refined silver plate) and 549 taels 4 mas 8 1/2 candereen in goods similar to those carried on the previous attempt (Cambay cloth that could not be sold in Japan, Japanese swords, armour, paper and lacquer-ware).[161] Coppindale objected to the large sum sent in money, arguing that according to information at Patani, the Ayuthia factory had ample cash resources ready to be turned over to the joint-stock. He was overruled. Cocks insisted that ready money was the most suitable lading. He had sent a letter to the Ayuthia factory by Melchior van Santvoort in November informing them of the intended voyage and asking the factors to prepare a return cargo of sappan wood and deer hides. But if for some reason the letter had not arrived or if the *Sea Adventure* did not make it and had to put in to another port such as Cambodia, money rather than goods would prove the more prudent investment.[162]

The voyage was once more operated along *shuinsen* lines. The crew were allowed to take along their own goods. After leaving Kōchi, the *Sea Adventure* skirted down the Fukien coast, catching a glimpse of the Chinese maritime world but did not venture into any of the principal harbours. (Li Tan had given no encouragement to the English to establish contact with members of his coastal network in Amoy.) On 10 January 1616, just over a month after leaving Japan, the junk reached the mouth of the Chao Phraya river and Sayers proceeded upriver in a junk provided by the local governor, arriving in Ayuthia on the 14th.[163]

The circumstances of the Ayuthia and Patani factories had altered greatly since their establishment by Floris and Antheunis in 1612. As with Hirado, Ayuthia had attempted to establish a subfactory, at Chiang-mai in the north of Siam, a place where the Elizabethan Ralph Fitch had visited. The timing, 1613, was unfortunate because of warfare between Ayuthia and the Burmese kingdom of Pegu. One of the factors, Thomas Samuel, was seized by the Burmese in 1615 and taken to Pegu where he died shortly after. He had ignored orders to return to Ayuthia. India cloth worth 2,025 taels 2 mas 2 1/2 candereen had been invested in this venture and 614 taels 2 3/4 candereen received back in gold. Under more favourable circumstances trade might have flourished and even have worked to the Company's advantage, for the gold/silver ratio in Siam was 1:7 – highly conducive to a profitable two-way trade with Japan.[164] The Patani factory had never had much chance to get off the ground. In

1613 Floris and Adam Denton sailed for Masulipatam on the Coromandel Coast of India and the factory was left in the hands of unqualified, inexperienced men. In 1615, after Denton's return, the factors in Ayuthia decided to add another merchant to the factory's roll. Once again the politics of separate voyages damned proceedings. There were quarrels and recriminations over financial responsibility for the godown and house used by the English. Antheunis of the Seventh Voyage charged his fellow merchants of the Ninth Voyage with half the cost of renovating the buildings and threatened to 'make sale of the said godong [godown] to the benfit of the Seventh Voyage and to leave us [of the Ninth] frustrate of means to preserve the goods under hands in places destitute of remedy'. The merchants of the Ninth Voyage had to pay up. They had little choice.[165] The situation changed radically when news of the establishment of the joint-stock arrived. In July 1615 the two factories were reorganised once more. Benjamin Farie was made chief factor at Ayuthia with two assistants and Philip Larkin chief at Patani with one assistant, although John Gurney remained for some time at Ayuthia.[166] Because of their location, half way between India and Japan, the factories looked to both these directions for their trade. Although Antheunis and his assistants had proudly declared that Siam was 'not to be accounted a small limb to the English factory of Japan', the Japan trade was nevertheless crucial for the factories' success.[167]

In addition to inter-voyage rivalry, the warfare between Ayuthia and Pegu and the general instability caused by dynastic problems in Siam, Saris's expectations of acquiring Chinese silk at Patani for Japan had not been realised. The factors attributed this to Dutch success in diverting Chinese junks to Songkla (which they called Sengora), further up the coast, where they claimed the Dutch had a factory. In fact the Dutch had no factory at Songkla but had made a series of agreements with the rulers of the petty territories of Ligor, Songkla and Phattalung from 1612 in which the VOC was recognised as the sole European trade and granted freedom from tolls. Such Chinese vessels as called (except at Phattalung which is inland) were to pay only the required customs duties and be spared the harassment they frequently encountered at Patani. This should have made it attractive for Chinese vessels to avoid the latter port. In practice, however, Chinese vessels preferred to continue to call at Patani and the VOC factory there continued to procure silk, in small quantities, until it was closed in November 1622.[168] The English factories at Ayuthia and Patani were faring no better than the Hirado one, indeed were worse off, when the *Sea Adventure* (cleared by means of an official pass obtained by Sayers) docked in Ayuthia on 16 January 1616.[169]

Sayers wasted no time in procuring his return cargo. To smooth the way, presents, mostly Japanese swords and armour worth 158 taels 5 mas 5 candereen, were given to the king and court officials. Some goods were purchased from resident Portuguese merchants, the rest probably from Japanese and Chinese merchants. For example, the India cloth was sold to 'Jeremy Lee', a Chinese.[170] But it was not until early June that everything was arranged for the return voyage to Japan. A good cargo of sappan wood and deer hides had been obtained but there were problems over cargo space for the Japanese crew who, according to *shuinsen* practice, insisted on their right to lade their own wood for sale in Japan. This took up some 25 per cent of the *Sea Adventure*'s available space, although Farie alleged that it amounted to two thirds and that Adams, who also loaded his own cargo, refused to restrain the crew 'alleging that they were all true men and might lade what they pleased'.[171] Nevertheless, the cargo was too much for the *Sea Adventure* alone and two additional junks, one owned by a Japanese, Shoby-dono, the other by a Chinese, Giquan, had to be freighted. Even then there was not enough space and 30 peculs of sappan wood was left behind. The *Sea Adventure* carried 2,370 peculs of sappan wood costing 7 taels 5 mas per pecul and 3,700 deer hides at almost 1 mas each, inclusive of 'all customs, bribes and duties'. Shoby-dono's junk carried 4,560 hides for the Hirado factory's account and 328 taels payable on a bill of exchange on arrival in Japan. Giquan's junk carried 825 1/2 peculs of sappan wood and a bill of exchange for 1,289 taels payable on arrival at Nagasaki.[172]

The *Sea Adventure* reached Hirado on 22 July and Giquan's junk, in which Sayers returned, was almost lost because of the incompetence of the pilot who led the vessel far off course towards the Philippines. Fortuitously, Sayers managed to save the voyage, making him something of a hero in the eyes of his colleagues, and the junk reached Satsuma on 17 September. Most of the crew, including the owner, were dead. Shoby-dono's junk did not reach Nagasaki until the following June having been forced to winter in Champa. The *Sea Adventure*'s cargo was sold by the end of the year, much of it to the factory's usual customers, Li Tan and the Matsūra. Only a small amount was shipped to the Kinai. The wood from Giquan's junk remained unsold in January 1617, because of the lateness of the season according to Cocks. However, what was sold fetched excellent prices. The sappan wood sold for an average of 25 mas 5 candereen per pecul, over three times its cost, and the hides, which were expected to fetch between 3 and 3 1/2 mas each, nevertheless sold for 2 mas 4 candereen a piece, more than double their cost. They would have fetched more had they not been worm-eaten. These figures gave the factors at Hirado encouragement and caused them to write optimistically about the voyage and the potential for further ones. However, the overheads had been high, a matter that was overlooked in their reports to London. The cost of sending the *Sea Adventure* (repairing and victualling her in Japan, presents and customs exactions in Ayuthia, victualling and loading her for the return voyage, pilotage and mariners' wages) was 2,704 taels 9 mas 6 candereen. Freightage on Giquans's junk was charged at 38 per cent of the cargo (394 taels 7 mas 8 candereen) and that on Shoby-dono's at 24 per cent (113 taels 7 mas 7 candereen) payable in kind in both cases on arrival in Japan. The good relations Cocks had cultivated with the Satsuma daimyo enabled the English to retrieve their cargo from the junk (the Shimazu could have seized the goods had they wished). But the expense of sending Wilmot, the purser of the *Advice* which had arrived in Hirado in July 1616, and Yasimon-dono 'a Japon of respect', to assist Sayers, and give presents to the Satsuma authorities to smooth the way for the release of the cargo, plus the cost of bringing Sayers and the cargo up from Satsuma was 646 taels 1 mas 1 1/2 candereen. Giquan's death created problems over payment of the bill of exchange. In the end the English had to settle for the hulk of the junk which was subsequently sold for 750 taels to Adams who refurbished it for a voyage to Cochinchina. A dispute with the purser over amounts of sappan wood claimed by himself and the English dragged on into the new year and helped sour relations with the Matsūra. There had been other incidental outlays, and payments connected with the voyage continued to be made into 1617, such as a further 30 taels to Yasimon-dono for his expenses. Thus the total cost of the voyage was over 8,200 taels. Nevertheless, the Siam trade had potential and had confounded the doubts of the Ayuthia factors.[173] In his letter to Cocks, Farie had asked for any India cloth that could not sell in Japan to be sent and had undertaken 'with God's assistance' to get hold of 20,000 hides and as much sappan wood as possible before the *Sea Adventure*'s return to Ayuthia. Cocks's decision to send most of the cargo in cash had turned out to be wise for Farie mentioned that the Ayuthia factory had need of money and requested Hirado to send at least 3,000 reals or the equivalent in Japanese plate on the next voyage.[174]

In comparison with the Dutch, whose imports in 1615 amounted to just under *f.* 57,000 and exports to *f.* 194,780 12st 1p, the English did not appear to be doing well in their Japan trade. But figures alone are deceptive. In the country trade the Dutch were not faring noticeably better than the English. In 1615 two VOC ships had brought cargoes from Patani worth *f.* 32,682 13st 7p. The most important items in value (*f.* 30,916 2st 9p) were raw silk (almost 45 peculs, not much more than the *Hasewint* had brought in 1614), poil silk (almost 17 peculs) and silk fabrics. Shark skins (1,190)

Cambodian wax (2,500 peculs), mercury and other odd items accounted for a small percentage of the value. The cargoes of the three Dutch ships which reached Hirado in 1616 (one from Ayuthia, two from Patani) and for which invoices are extant show that the Dutch imported 5,488 shark skins, 37,397 deer hides and 6,114 peculs of sappan wood. There were smaller amounts of wax and other goods plus an important item which the English had failed to procure, lead (135 peculs 3 catties). Moreover, one aspect of the Dutch trade from Japan at this time needs mention. Over 25 per cent of the VOC's imports to Japan in value terms in 1615 consisted of goods seized from the *San Antônio*. This reflected a key aspect of Dutch trade with Japan during the 1610s. Most of the VOC's exports from Japan comprised Japanese silver, copper (for the Indies, not for Europe), construction materials and victuals supplemented by goods captured from Portuguese and Chinese vessels. Among the plundered goods re-exported from Japan, silk, the very commodity which was greatly in demand and highly profitable in Japan, figured prominantly. In short the VOC's knowledge of the Japanese market and success in penetrating it was little different from that of the English, and the Dutch had their share of problems with worm-eaten deer hides. On 26 October 1615, after receiving a cargo from Japan, Governor General Gerard Reynst wrote to the Heren XVII from Bantam that he wished the VOC had never seen Japan for he doubted anything was to be expected from there.[175]

Providence had dealt unjustly with the English in their country trade but there still remained grounds for optimism about the Hirado factory's future.

CHAPTER 5

Hopes, Illusions and Disappointment

(i) *Hirado, Treasury of the Indies*

The years 1615–16 represent the turning point in the history of the Hirado factory. After two years in Japan the factors knew more about the market, the goods in demand (Coppindale, echoing Wickham's earlier comment, had put it well; the goods the English offered were sold not 'so much for cheapness as for strangeness'[1]), prices, business practices and the nature of the competition, and they had appreciated the overwhelming need to break into the country trade.

In the opinion of the Hirado factors there were four strategies worth pursuing to justify the factory's continued existence. First and foremost was the need to acquire silk, the single most profitable import into Japan. Second, the factory had to involve itself in the country trade to procure silk (in the absence of direct access to China) and other goods. Neither Ayuthia nor Patani could supply much silk but sappan wood and deer hides were available and generated profits in Japan. Alternative sources of silk, such as Cochinchina, remained to be explored. Third, was the possible use of Hirado as a base for supplying men and victuals and for the casting of ordnance to realise the Company's ambitions in the Spice Islands. Finally, there was the hope of establishing a subfactory in Ryūkyū, the only seemingly attainable goal within the factory's immediate sphere of operations. Trade with Korea through Tsushima had failed to materialise and the chances of any worthwhile trade to the remote north of Japan were uncertain and were likely to involve expenses the factory could not afford.

There was broad agreement between Cocks and Wickham that the most suitable way to get hold of silk in great quantities other than from southeast Asia was direct access to China. Wickham described the China trade as one 'wch we all sweat for', and believed that the chances of securing admission were good. He wrote that the Dutch were hated by the Chinese for their attacks on Chinese shipping, the source of most of the VOC silk brought to Japan, and the cause of serious disruptions to the flow of Chinese silk by sea to Ayuthia and Patani (a mistaken assumption). Wickham also believed that the Portuguese were mistrusted by the Chinese and were likely to be turned out of Macao. He argued that the absence of the náo from Nagasaki for three of the five years from 1611–16 was symptomatic of Portuguese insecurity there.[2]

In Cocks's view the best way to gain access to China was through the mediation of a third party, the factory's most cherished business associate in Hirado, Li Tan. On the face of it, Li (head of the most important Chinese trading network operating out of Japan with operations in Fukien, where he had a younger brother, southeast Asia and later Taiwan) appeared to have the right connections to secure an entrée for the English. Certainly there was no one else around with such credentials to act for them. In November 1614 Cocks informed the Company about Li's work. He was confident that Li would obtain permission for the English to trade at an island near Nanking (presumably Ningpo) where English factors would be left to manage the trade and that it would not be long before trade on the mainland itself would follow 'for, as the Chinese themselves tell me, their Emperor is come to the knowledge how the Emperor of Japan hath received us and what large privileges he hath granted us'. The Dutch, he said, were detested by the Chinese because of their attacks on Chinese shipping. No matter how much the Hollanders pretended to be English by flying English colours, the Chinese knew that they were not. (This was a common VOC ruse in Asian waters although its impact on local rulers was far less than either the Dutch, or Cocks' imagined.) Cocks asked the directors to send a letter from James I to the Chinese emperor and requested permission to be entrusted with the leadership of any mission to the Chinese court that might ensue. He concluded, 'nothing seek, nothing find'.[3]

Cocks's letter, his first general report to the Company since the departure of the *Clove*, was sent to Bantam on a Dutch vessel and from there was taken on the *Globe* to London where it was read to the Court on 22 September 1615, an unusually speedy transmission.[4] The Court, then in a mood to pursue expansion even though the Company had neither the resources nor the information to fulfil its great ambitions, had been contemplating trade with China anyway. In 1614 the Company had been attracted by the possibility of following the Dutch example and importing Chinese silk, especially the high quality Nanking raw silk. It was less interested in Canton silk, which did not fetch a sixth the price of Nanking silk in England and would not be marketable unless the method of unreeling it to separate the coarse from the fine threads could be learned. Nobody in England had the necessary skills and in November 1614 the directors wrote to Bantam saying that they presumed the method was known to the Chinese and Japanese, 'one or two of whom, if possible, [were] to be induced to visit England to instruct others in the art, in order to bring the Canton silk into esteem and price at home'. After hearing the cape merchant's report, the directors concluded that Cocks had furnished the Company with good intelligence about China and was to be commended for his diligence. They decided that rather than sending someone from London (Edward Connocke had been under discussion for this assignment), Cocks should be authorised to proceed according to his motion and to try to set up a factory in China.[5]

The Company's ambitions in east Asia at this juncture can also be gleaned from the instructions for Downton's voyage. These included orders to study any directions left at Bantam by Saris, and, if things looked encouraging, send a ship to Japan to supply the existing factory, or if none had been established then to set one up. The ship was to attempt trade in the Moluccas both outward and on the return, and to call at Canton to see what goods would sell in exchange for silk and other Chinese goods. At Canton, no mention was to be made of the ship's proceeding to Japan because the two countries 'ar in mortall hatred'.[6]

In securing the services of Li Tan, Cocks was at least acting in accordance with Company policy. However, Cocks, and he was not alone in this respect, had unbounded expectations about what Li could deliver. He exaggerated Li's influence, crediting him, quite mistakenly, with access to the Chinese imperial court. More astonishing was Cocks's belief, mentioned in his letter to the Company, that the Dragon throne was aware of the English presence at Hirado and greatly interested in the Company's proceedings. The late Ming imperial institution, in a state of dynastic decline and facing intrusions from the increasingly Sinicised Manchu under the leadership of Nurhaci, had greater matters to contend with. A few foreign devil merchants operating from a former wakō base in Japan were well beyond the pale of the mandarinate's concern. Li had no influence at Peking nor was he in any position to secure an opening for the English at Nanking. Over the years the Hirado factory poured money both as presents and bribes into the coffers of the Li family to oil what were thought to be the wheels of influence in China.

At first Li Tan and his brother laid out money on their own, or at least claimed to have done so. In August 1615 a deal was struck whereby the Li undertook to procure 'free trade into China' exclusively for the English 'w'th what else shall be thought fiting'. If the trade was not forthcoming the Li were to be liable for the money they spent (a figure of 8,000 taels was mentioned). If the trade did not materialise the Li were to write off the money they had spent.[7] This seemed a favourable bargain for the English, but things were not so simple and in 1621 another contract was made. Cocks advanced 1,500 taels and Li Tan provided matching funds to be sent to China to procure the elusive trade. If this overture failed, Li was to repay the English investment plus interest of 2 per cent per month.[8] There is no question but that the English were being milked.

While there was no possibility of Li Tan securing official trade in China for the English, he could at least have attempted to secure them an unofficial one on the Fukien coast where he did have contacts and some influence even if he was viewed with suspicion by the authorities there. He chose not to; it did not make commercial sense to help possible trade rivals. The deal the English imagined they had made with the Li in 1615 was a dead letter from the first and over the years the Li demanded advances to cover expenses or were given presents in lieu to encourage them in their work. It is impossible to quantify how much was spent by the Hirado factory in its futile effort to trade in China. Wickham, who shared Cocks's faith in Li Tan although with less conviction, wrote to Sir Thomas Smythe in January 1617 mentioning that the Li had spent money on behalf of the English quest in China and was confident positive results would be forthcoming. He believed that unlike Bantam, Patani and Ayuthia 'ther will bee noe want of silke [in China] for to procuer monyes in Japon: or the Rich Comodities of Chena to send for England'. He was also convinced that English goods would sell 'to some purpose' in China, unlike Japan. He claimed the Li were not asking for a penny until the trade was secured, a total misrepresentation of the facts. The sources show that money had already been paid to the Li as loans and to cover expenses. Total recorded payments over the years amount to 4,826 taels 1 mas 1/52 candereen which one suspects was only the tip of the payments. When the English withdrew from Hirado Li Tan was their biggest debtor.[9]

It was not just the China trade which bound the English factory closely to Li Tan. Along with the Matsūra he was the factory's best customer and provided the English with loans at interest lower than the rates at which some Japanese were prepared to advance money. This was another reason why Cocks allowed the Li special favours such as letting them ship goods on English shipping for Bantam, a concession which was condemned by Bantam.[10] Perhaps the most revealing comment about the factory's complex relationship with the Li came from Li Tan's brother, Hua-yü, whom the English called Captain Whaw or Whow, in Nagasaki. In 1618 when the two companies were at war in the Indies, the Dutch humiliated the

English by ostentatiously bringing a captured English ship into
Hirado. Hua-yü informed Cocks 'that till now, they stood dowbtfull
that thenglish and the Hollanders were all one, but now they were
fully resolved to the contrary'.[11] No matter how proudly the
Europeans bragged about their diversity and differing religious
allegiance, the distinctions were lost and of little interest to most
Asians.

Others were not so inclined as Cocks and Wickham to trust the Li.
Coppindale, new to Japan and therefore more detached from the
factory's operations, favoured a more bellicose approach, believing
that if peaceable trade with Chinese could not be had then the
English should 'as the hollanders do, to trade with them per force'.
Cocks disagreed vehemently, arguing that it would be counterproductive because the Chinese emperor had spies everywhere and
would soon be informed of English attacks. Hard-won goodwill
would be wiped out at a stroke and the English brought into the
same disrepute as the Dutch. Cocks was presuming too much. The
Chinese emperor did not have his Cecil presiding over an extensive
intelligence network such as the one Cocks had been a part of in
Bayonne. Wickham, on the other hand, could see the advantage the
Dutch enjoyed from seizing junks and getting hold of silk which
enabled them 'for the better despach of ther shipinge att a daye's
warninge [to] tourne ther Rawe silke into siluer bee ytt for 100,000
tayes at the price Currant wch Cannott soe soddenly bee done by any
other Comodities'. Wickham complained that the Dutch strategy
worked to the disadvantage of those who 'cometh truly by their
goods' but could see the obvious attraction in adopting a similar
policy. Eaton had no reservations about attacking Chinese shipping
and did not share Cocks and Wickham's faith in Li Tan. In December
1616, he wrote to the Company arguing that the English should
follow the Dutch example and plunder Chinese vessels in the China
Seas if trade were not procured within a year, which he doubted
would happen anyway. He noted that the VOC brought 'hither a
good quantitiy of silk and China stuffs the which brings them in
ready money'.[12]

In comparison with the negligible amount of silk and silk fabric
the English factory had to offer for sale, the Dutch seemed better
supplied. But Wickham's comment provides further evidence that
the VOC's policy regarding silk in Japan was limited, dictated by
short-term considerations. A strategy to expand silk sales in Japan to
rival those of the Portuguese was absent from the VOC's agenda at
this stage because silk generated excellent profits in Holland for the
VOC. However, the English factors were correct to notice the
increasing frequency of Dutch attacks on Chinese shipping, especially junks bound for Manila. No matter how sincere Specx himself

may have been when he asserted to Ieyasu in September 1615 that the
Dutch intended to attack only Portuguese or Spanish shipping, on
the grounds that they were enemies of the United Provinces, and not
Japanese or Chinese, citing as evidence the fact that the Dutch had
recently helped a crippled Chinese junk to reach Nagasaki, his
superiors did not subscribe to such a policy.[13] However, as far as the
English company was concerned, the non-belligerent approach to
the quest for trade with China favoured by Cocks was pursued from
Japan until 1620 and the formation of the joint fleets of defence with
the Dutch. The Bantam factory's relationship with the Chinese was
different. There the English, like the Dutch, resented Chinese influence over the pangeran and their control over the supply of
pepper. In 1618 they followed Governor General Coen's example,
stopping Chinese junks in the Bantam road and removing pepper as
part of their efforts to undermine the power of the Chinese middlemen in Bantam's pepper trade.[14]

As for the Company's plans to import Chinese silk into England,
enthusiasm soon waned. Cocks reported that he had not personally
seen Canton silk but that the Chinese in Hirado offered to teach the
method of unreeling it. The offer was not taken up, although some
26 cwt of Chinese silk was auctioned in London in 1614 and the
Company was sufficiently encouraged to consider seriously commissioning silk manufacture in Japan. In April 1615 some patterns for
vests were sent out. Saris opposed such a policy, recommending that
the Company import raw silk directly because it would be cheaper
and supplies were abundant in the Indies. The directors ignored this
suggestion and, afraid that if left to themselves the factors would
make the wrong choice of designs, decided to send the patterns.[15]
However, in November the Court abruptly ordered the factors to
stop buying Chinese silk for England because it believed they had
been cheated by the Chinese at Bantam. Instead the factors were to
concentrate on securing pepper for England and mariners were to be
allowed to purchase silk for their own account, an indication of its
low esteen by the Company as an import to Europe.[16]

This was a surprising decision, for Nanking silk sold well in
Amsterdam. In 1606 the Heren XVII had set a selling price of f. 12
per pond for white raw silk. In 1621 and 1622 quantities of white raw
silk which had been purchased in the Indies for approximately 147
and 154 taels per pecul respectively were sold for 641 taels and 680
taels per pecul. This was more than double the sale price silk fetched
in Japan in a good year. Even after taking into consideration the
additional costs and risks involved in shipping the silk to Europe
rather than disposing of it in Japan it was still a handsome profit. The
20 cwt of silk sold by the English company in 1614 had sold well too
in comparison with Japan, at 462 taels per pecul. In 1617 the Heren

XVII estimated the market in Amsterdam for Chinese raw silk as 72,000 ponds (576 peculs), although in practice this figure, itself an underestimate of the market for raw silk in Amsterdam, was never reached; supplies were erratic. From the 1620s both the English and Dutch companies were able to take advantage of raw silk imports from a different source, Persia, and the VOC – by the middle of the decade more attuned to the possibilities of the Japan market – gave priority to Japan as the destination for Chinese raw silk. Unfortunately, the English prospered no better with Persian silk imports than they had with Chinese; prices fluctuated and demand remained unpredictable. By the end of the 1630s the Company had dissolved its factory at Isfahan in Persia, the source of its Persian silk. The Dutch persisted.[17]

In pursuit of the second strategy for the Hirado factory (participation in the country trade) the merchants had, of course, been active and continued to be so. The 1615–16 Siam Voyage had proved a success, at least in comparison with the two previous southeast Asian ventures, and there was cause for guarded optimism about the future. But there were unresolved questions about how best to operate the trade. Wickham argued that it was best to centre it in Hirado and avoid having ships call at Ayuthia on their way from Bantam. Cocks and Eaton argued that in view of the *Sea Adventure*'s recent voyage and the demands of the Japanese crew to load their own goods, it would be better to send an English ship to Patani to collect Siamese goods and bring them to Japan as the Dutch did although as Cocks admitted, it would be liable to heavy anchorage duties there.[18] However, Cocks's information about the Dutch was misleading. The VOC was not faring much better than the English in its trade with Siam. Their ambition to send a junk from Patani to Ayuthia twice a year to bring down cargoes to Patani for transhipment to Japan came unstuck in 1615 when the junk, with a cargo of 3,360 shark skins, 9,857 hides and 900 peculs of sappan wood, missed the Japan-bound shipping. After this the Dutch employed the captured Portuguese junk, the *San António*, renamed the *Hoope*, on three voyages between Hirado and Ayuthia until 1617.

The third strategy, imitating the Dutch and using Hirado as a supply base for operations in the Spice Islands was in keeping with the Company's overall policy in the southwards region of attempting to secure a share of the spice trade for the English. In a letter to Sir Thomas Wilson in December 1614, Cocks reported his conversations with Spanish and Portuguese merchants in Nagasaki. He said that although the inhabitants had originally detested 'the Intollerable pride of the Spaniard' they preferred them to the Dutch because the Spaniards brought reals 'and in their proud humour were Liberal' with their money, 'but the pore Hollanders wch serue in these parts for Souldiers both by Sea and land haue such base pay that it will hardlie finde them Clothinge to there back and meate for there bellies'. He claimed, with absolutely no justification, that the Dutch 'forces are soe strong at sea that they care not a figg nether for Spannards nor Portingalls' and judged that the Dutch were posing a serious threat to Iberian and Lusitianian interests in the Indies. In another letter, to the Earl of Salisbury, he mentioned that the Dutch dared not fall out with the Japanese or

> they will hardlie hold the molucas very long tyme, for Japon is their storehouse from whence pvid in great abundance as they will viz wheate, Barke, Bemnaes, Rise, Beefe, pork, dried fish, wyne of the Cuntrey and aquavites at a far lower Rate then they arre worth in any part of Chrisendom. And here is Iron & Copp. in greate Abundance to make ordnance & shot [and] skillful workmen to make or cast them.[20]

A year late Coppindale, ever one to adopt someone else's ideas, suggested that the main reason why the Dutch maintained their factory in Japan was because of its excellence as a supply base for their operations in the Spice Islands.[21] Wickham wrote to Jourdain at Bantam in February 1616 saying much the same thing, noting that the Dutch exported copper to make ordnance and victuals. He recommended that the English follow the Dutch example.[22] It was to support such arguments that the specimens of the locally cast ordnance parts had been put aboard the *Hosiander* for examination in London and the factors' enthusiasm for such a policy perhaps accounts why the factory spent 1,112 taels 2 mas 1 1/2 candereen to refurbish a godown as a store for ships provisions and a hospital.[23]

Cocks had first witnessed Japanese casting ordnance at Specx's invitation in August 1615 and had written enthusiastically in his diary that they 'made as formall ordinance as we doe in Christendom, both of brass & iron'. Specx also commented favourably on the quality and the low cost, although the Dutch manufactured and exported only a handful of canons. But Cocks had changed his mind about Japanese skill in casting ordnance by the time the examples were sent back on the *Hosiander* even if the English and Dutch continued to experiment with the casting of firearms in Japan. Yet had the directors shown an interest in commissioning ordnance in Japan there was no chance of weaponry ever becoming a major export from Japan. The shogunate had already taken measures to bring the manufacture of matchlocks under its control and to stave off any possible threat to its own security would not have countenanced the development of ordnance manufacture in outlying domains.[24] Nevertheless, both the English and Dutch exported limited amounts of Japanese weaponry, particularly swords and muskets, and the Dutch employed Japanese soldiers to fight their battles in the Indies. Coen was greatly impressed by them, and made frequent requests for more recruits. However, the VOC was not dependent on Japanese mercenaries. It employed other Asian troops as well as Dutch soldiers sent out from Europe.[25] Japanese also found their way into the English company's service notably at Amboina where a former servant of the Hirado factory, Sidney Miguell, probably a jurebasso, was employed.[26] Any thought of Japan supplying a steady stream of manpower and weaponry to realise the ambitions of the companies was cut short by the shogunate's order in 1621 forbidding Europeans from taking Japanese into service overseas and exporting weaponry from Japan. Besides, Hirado had its limitations as a supply base to advance expansionist goals in the Indies. Governor General Reynst felt that the quality of the victuals received from Hirado was poor even in comparison with food sent from the Netherlands and the invoices of Dutch exports from Japan 1615–17 show that re-exported silk and silver rather than victuals were the most valuable goods sent from Japan. As if to underline the VOC's lack of a consistent policy towards their Hirado factory in this respect, Specx wrote to Governor General Coen in February 1620 saying that with two ships he could furnish the Moluccas, Amboina and the Bandas with plentiful supplies of white rice, arrack, bread, beans, pork and meat.[27] The factory was never the indispensible supply base for the Dutch that the English presumed.

The fourth strategy, opening a subfactory in Ryūkyū, was Wickham's pet scheme. Despite his anger over the Ryūkyūan authorities' indifference to the *Sea Adventure*'s difficulties, Wickham's sales of duttis and the availability of ambergris convinced him that a subfactory should be set up at Naha. In September 1615 he urged Cocks to do all he could to win the favour of the daimyo of Satsuma, arguing that the project would win the Company's approval and rebound to Cocks's credit. At Sunpu the following month he urged Adams to lobby hard to procure a letter from Ieyasu granting the English trading privileges in Ryūkyū, and within two days a letter from Honda Masazumi to the Shimazu had been 'effected'. According to the English, this directed Satsuma to grant the Company permission to set up a factory in Ryūkyū with the same privileges it enjoyed in Japan. Wickham was confident that the new subfactory would be in operation by the following spring and envisaged himself as factor. Both he and Cocks wrote optimistically to Jourdain about the prospects, especially the profitable market for duttis in Ryūkyū. Cocks also informed the Company about the quality and cheapness of lignum aloes available in Ryūkyū which he said were better than anything he had sold in France during his residence there. To smooth the way for the opening of a subfactory, Cocks did what he could to curry favour with the Satsuma authorities. When the daimyo,

Shimazu Iehisa, was passing through Hirado *en route* to Edo in March 1616, Cocks proferred him Ieyasu's letter which he accepted, replying that he would delay answer until his return. No answer was forthcoming, although Cocks claimed to have heard an encouraging report in July that Satsuma would grant the privileges.[28]

The episode is intriguing. However, it is not surprising that Satsuma did not respond to Ieyasu's letter. Neither the bakufu nor the Shimazu were prepared to subvert the regulations that governed the complex role Ryūkyū played in Sino-Japanese relations. The Shimazu did not want another party to edge in on the trade they derived from Ryūkyū's tributary status. Nor did they want to upset the Chinese. From the bakufu's perspective, Satsuma's involvement in Ryūkyū provided a convenient diversion for a powerful domain, which had fought against the Tokugawa at Sekigahara, according it a special status and disinclining it to challenge Tokugawa ambitions. The bakufu also gained from Ryūkyū's status by having more foreign ambassadors to parade through the streets of Edo. The most plausible explanation for the mistaken English belief that they had acquired additional privileges in Ryūkyū is that they misunderstood what had been effected at Sunpu and the true contents of the document they received. It would not be the first time, nor the last, that they did so.

One possible strategy that was unmentioned in Saris's remembrance and scarcely given any attention by the factors, was the use of Japan as a base to explore for a northwest passage, Hakluyt's pet idea. As has been mentioned, Adams was enthusiastic about such a project but Cocks less so. The Company itself was ambivalent. There had been two recent attempts. In neither case had the Company been prepared to act as sole underwriter. The first under the leadership of Henry Hudson and supported by courtiers as well as the East India and Muscovy companies and individual merchant subscribers, left England in 1610 and ended in disaster. The crew mutinied and Hudson, like most of his men severely debilitated, was cast adrift in June 1611. A few survivors made it back to England. In 1612 the Northwest Passage Company was established under the patronage of Prince Henry and the governorship of Sir Thomas Smythe. Most of the members were courtiers or officials and all the directors, with the exception of one, were London merchants. The ordinary members included Richard Hakluyt. It seems that the merchants of the East India Company itself, probably under pressure from Smythe and others, agreed to invest £300 per annum for three years in this Company and that members were allowed to join it for a fee of £10. In April 1612 two ships were dispatched. The backers were optimistic about success and the ships carried a cargo of broadcloth, but the attempt was a failure. There was a distinct unease in the East India Company about diverting scarce capital into such prestigious but fruitless ventures.

On 6 December 1614 the question of adventuring more money in another attempt backed by courtiers was raised. The view was expressed that previous attempts had failed not because the end itself was unrealisable but because of the negligence or ignorance of the commanders. The directors agreed to adventure a further £200, appreciating that because of the passionate commitment of some courtiers to discover the route the northwest passage had become a sensitive matter. On 22 December Sir Dudley Digges, a young courtier, East India Company adventurer, and a zealous advocate and activist in promoting the northwest passage (he stated that North America 'is nothing broad, how ever it be painted') tried to twist the Company's arm further and reminded the directors of the previous commitment to pay up £300 per annum. His tactics paid off to the extent that on a show of hands the directors resolved to adventure £300 from the joint-stock and to extend the privilege for individual members to adventure in the Northwest Passage Company for a £10 fine until the following spring. Again a desire not to offend the court was the likely reason for this decision. By this time the directors had received the reports from Japan brought back on the *Clove* but regardless of Adams's enthusiasm and Ieyasu's willingness to help, they had too much on their plate to bother themselves with risky and commercially untested voyages. Discovery was not their business and many of the directors probably felt that they had already done enough to appease the court. Lack of capital rather than disdain or scepticism lay behind the directors' reservations not to involve the Company in projects to discover a northwest passage. The prospect of such a passage remained tempting and cropped up intermittently in the Company's thinking until the end of the decade when further voyages showed such a way to the Indies to be impracticable. On 15 October 1615 when the Court employed Edward Connocke as factor it considered two places to send him, the Coromandel Coast or Japan as a replacement for Cocks should he have died and to further the discovery of a northwest passage from Japan 'if occasion be'. Occasion was not to be and Connocke ended up in Persia where he performed a more valuable service to the Company than he could ever have done by trying to seek a northwest passage. Cocks himself, ever eager to please his superiors, and aware of the appeal the passage in court circles, wrote to the Earl of Salisbury in December 1614, unaware that he had already died, offering to play his part if the king, privy council or East India Comapny should undertake such a venture.[29] But the northwest passage did not figure in the history of the Hirado factory.

The Hirado factors then were far from bereft of ideas about how to make their factory commercially viable and there was a clear idea about what goods would sell (silk, sappan wood, deer hides, certain colours of broadcloth, particularly black, a colour which Wickham believed the Japanese could not dye for themselves).[30] They believed that the factory, correctly supplied and its activities better co-ordinated with other factories, especially Ayuthia, might go some way towards realising the Company's most optimistic expectation – which was soon to be made known in Hirado – that it would become the treasury of the Company's trade in the southwards region or, as Wickham put it, provide Bantam 'w[i]th soe great quantities of siluer to stuffe all the Factories beetweene this [Hirado] & Bantam that ther neuer should bee any more need to send any more money ovtt of England but hoally depend vppon this ffactory', adding, with a swipe at Cocks, 'the bussines of this place beeinge Carefully & honestly manniged'.[31] It was a tall order and required a degree of planning, organisation and co-ordination that was beyond the Company's, let alone the Hirado factory's, abilities at this time.

If the perspective of the Company's servants in the Indies showed a keener awareness of regional trade flows, as was to be expected, the same was not true of the directors in London. Nicholas Downton had arrived in Bantam in mid June 1615 but as the factory had no suitable commodities for a voyage on to Japan (his own ships had brought mostly reals to purchase a return cargo plus the usual range of goods sent out from England at this time, broadcloth, ivory, lead, mercury, tin and iron) and because the *Hosiander* had not long since left for Hirado he decided against sending a ship there.[32] However, on 10 August the *Advice*, which had newly arrived from England with separate instructions for a voyage to Japan, left Bantam with orders to proceed directly for Hirado. The *Advice*, accompanied by the *Attendant*, had left England shortly after the return of the *Clove*. These were the ships whose outwards cargo had been altered at the last moment by the Court to include the goods for Japan that Saris had recommended and had helped to choose, such as broadcloth and gallipots. At Bantam some cargo was added including 3,000 reals worth of white baftas.[33]

With the arrival of these two ships in the Indies the full implications of Saris's advice to the Company about the Japan trade had become apparent. According to the directors' strategy, the Hirado factory was to be supplied from England with the broadcloth and other goods Saris had recommended (including the gallipots, iron and tin which Cocks had reported to Bantam were not in demand). From Patani and Ayuthia it was to receive Canton silk which the directors believed was 'very vendible in Japan though not in

England'. Thus provided, the factory would be able to furnish the other factories in the Indies with silver. It was also to investigate the prospects of trade with China, and enquire about other goods that might have their use in the Company's inventory such as the dye that Saris claimed would rival indigo. These ambitions were spelled out in the directors' long letter to Bantam and in the instructions for the *Advice*'s voyage which were to bring back silver cast in ingots and 'brought to the height of rialls'. Indeed the Company was so confident about the abundance of silver in Japan that, in Jourdain's words, the directors had been 'so sparing in sending of money in the last fleets that there is scarce a penny in none of the factories, they depending on the great profit and stock of Jappan and other places to be sent in money to Bantam'.[34] The Company thought that in the Hirado factory it had discovered its jewel in the Indies and that the Japanese archipelago was indeed made up of islands of silver.

To confound matters, Bantam faced a liquidity crisis in 1616. The English and Dutch had enjoyed a highly advantageous arrangement with the local Chinese merchants from whom they bought pepper at a price fixed by the Europeans, advancing the money to the Chinese who as middlemen paid the producers up country. In 1615 the Chinese tried to turn the tables and drive up prices by reneging on previously agreed delivery contracts. They demanded more money for the pepper. Complaints to the pangeran got nowhere. The English, desperate to procure a lading for the homeward voayage of the *Gift*, accepted the higher price and paid out more money. The Dutch were in a similar predicament but were saved by the arrival of a fleet from the Netherlands with a supply of ready money. This enabled the Dutch to react more aggressively towards the Chinese and to strike a clever blow against the English as well by seizing Kewee, the Chinese middleman engaged by the English, and holding him as surety for the debts of the Chinese. Kewee was unable to sell any pepper to settle accounts with the English and in early 1616 the Bantam factory reported debts owing in pepper and money of 30,000 reals. The factory had been forced to pawn some of its stock. Jourdain, aware of the misfortunes that had hit the Hirado factory in its country trade, may have been more sanguine about the ability of the factory to generate money in the way the directors imagined, but the Company expected silver to start flowing from Japan and Bantam stood in need of a supply.[35] Could Hirado deliver?

If the Company's plans for the Hirado factory were ill-considered the same was not true of its ambitious plan to restructure the management of its factories in the Indies in an effort to impose order and strengthen co-ordination between them. The man entrusted with executing the Court's radical programme was William Keeling, styled rather grandly the 'commander of the English through out all

India'. Keeling left the Downs in March 1615 with a fleet of four ships, one of which carried the first ambassador to the Mughal court, Sir Thomas Roe. Keeling's brief included powers to assess the performance of all factors, remove incompetent ones, remedy abuses, and audit the books. But central to his task was the proposal to establish four regional directorates answerable to Keeling in Surat, on the Coromandel Coast, and at Bantam and Patani. The letter was to include Japan, Ayuthia, Cambodia, Cochinchina and Borneo within its jurisdiction. Patani itself was described as a place without 'speciall matters of itselfe' but judged an important regional shipping and commercial centre and a source of goods in demand in Japan. (Again one detects the influence of Saris and indeed before he left Keeling requested information from Saris about Japan, 'as well of the manners and disposicons of those people as the Marchandizinge'.) Patani was even considered as a possible springboard for achieving trade with China.[36] The plan itself had its origins in a suggestion to the court by Best after his return from the Indies when he noted that unless the Company followed the Dutch example of appointing a governor general in the Indies (the Dutch had appointed their first in 1609, a post modelled on earlier Portuguese practice) and gave one man full authority in the Indies 'for trade and gouernm^t...their buysines will never bee well carryed'. Best had himself in mind as the person of 'Countenance & sufficiency' for this appointment but his subsequent disgrace thwarted his aspiration.[37] Unfortunately, the Company's ambitious, grand strategy came to nothing. Keeling, greatly distressed by the prospect of prolonged separation from his wife, whom he had unsuccessfully tried to bring with him, even smuggling her aboard ship before being ordered to set her ashore,[38] decided to return to England within days of his arrival at Bantam at the end of August 1616. His mission abandoned, the Company was forced to rethink and scale down its plans.

Nevertheless, Keeling's brief stay in Bantam was sufficient for him to get a measure of the state of the southwards factories and he set down his views in a detailed report. Keeling confirmed the chronic undersupply of the factories and, not mincing his words, criticised the neglect and the misguided policy that had led to this: 'god send some supplies speedie or else yor business lies a bleeding in all theise pts for want of yor foresight and all yor seruants vtterlie disheartened for lack of fondacon to indeavor the building y^{or} pffitt [profit].' The state of the Bantam factory in particular gave cause for alarm. There was 'no want of pepp. [in Bantam] but meanes only to buy yt, that factory being soe bare (soe theire aduice to me) as not onely to haue any valuable meanes left but also to be indebted vnto ye Pangran to or nacion's no small discreditt'. This provided the Dutch 'who await all such opportunities to disgrace vs' with easy ammunition 'to knock vs in the eye of the local people'. As for the Japan trade, Keeling's first impression was that there was 'no likelihood of manie [money] from Japon'. He did not remain long enough at Bantam to acquire greater knowledge about this. However, he left orders with the rather lack-lustre individual he appointed as chief factor at Bantam, George Berkeley (or Barkeley), to send ships to 'Zuaratt and Japan, the former to furnish all places of trade heerabout with comodities [i.e. Cambay cloth], the later to procure money, the nervues [nerves] to all trades and stoppe to scandalous and envious tongues informing against the benefitt of theis trade to our king and state'. From his assessment of the more up-to-date information brought back on the *Hosiander*, he emphasised that Japan should be provided with a good supply of raw silk, 'the onelie comodetie procuring readie money and present payment' to enable the factory to fulfil its projected role.[39]

News of the Company's great expectations of the Hirado factory and Keeling's intended visitation was brought to Japan on the *Thomas*, which arrived in Hirado on 22 June 1616, and was welcomed by the factors, especially as the commander might be sympathetic to their wage grievances. Three weeks later, on 12 July, she was followed by the *Advice*. (The *Advice* had failed to catch the monsoon on its first attempt at Japan and only got as far as the southern China coast with many men sick before returning to Bantam via Ayuthia and Patani.)[40] The factors were stunned by the cargoes brought on the two ships. The *Thomas* carried goods rated at 12,948 taels 3 mas 8 1/3 candereen. These consisted of broadcloth (mainly black, straw-coloured or red) worth 4,004 taels, bays worth 2,778 taels 5 mas 5 candereen and smaller amounts of lawn, Holland and Polish cloth, damask and linen. Over half the value of the cargo was in European cloth. The rest consisted of lead, Muscovy hides, steel, tin, tar, armour (nine corslets and pouldron), coral, gallipots pots (many broken), thread, table books, books 'for Accompt and exersize of Armes', printed books, looking glasses, canvas, and some India cloth. Most amazing, however, was a random collection of pictures and maps worth 329 taels 9 mas. These included maps of Britain, London and the world, views of London, various landscapes, portraits of the kings of England since Brutus, a portrait of the governor of the East India Company, Drake's Cadiz voyage, and, at Saris's instigation, some lascivious paintings including Venus and Adonis and 'Venus Sleeping with two saters'. Many had been damaged because of bad packing.[41] Pictures were much requested as presents at the Mughal emperor's court and the emperor had especially liked one of James I. In 1615 the Ajmere factors recommended that more paintings be sent – pictures of Christ's crucifixion and England's defeat of the Spanish Armada in 1588 for the emperor, and allegorical paintings, scenes of gardens, banquets and novelty pictures for other courtiers. But no such request had been made by the Japanese. The initiative stemmed from Saris's advice to the directors. Fortunately, the Company had sent no overtly religious paintings.[42] The *Advice* carried less than half the cargo of the *Thomas*. It was valued at 5,551 taels 5 candereen and consisted of broadcloth and bays, about 40 per cent of the total, lead and the same ragbag of goods as the *Thomas*, including pictures of James I and parliament. The *Advice* also brought 3 peculs 71 1/3 catties of silk loaded at Bantam which accounted for 12 per cent of the lading.[43] The usual gifts were presented to the daimyo and members of his household, including some of the pictures. The gifts to the daimyo from the *Thomas* amounted to 328 taels 7 mas 4 1/3 candereen or 2.5 per cent of the total value, and from the *Advice*, 78 taels 8 mas 3 13/18 candereen, or 1.42 per cent of the total. Other members of the household received gifts worth 189 taels 6 mas 2 candereen or 1.46 per cent of the total.[44]

Not surprisingly, Cocks was downcast by the cargo. He wrote to the Company at the beginning of 1617 saying that in order to fulfil their ambitions 'greater quantity and better commodities than yet we have had out of England or from Bantam' were absolutely necessary, adding that the sale of all commodities except lead took up to a year. He confided to John Browne at Patani that 'I am aweary of the place' and that were it not for the hope of getting the China trade 'I would rather depart from hence to-night than tarry till to-[morrow]'. He had expressed similar sentiments on various occasions in Bayonne when the going had been rough. The cargo brought on the *Hosiander* could be dismissed as an aberration, hastily put together, but the goods brought on the *Thomas* and the *Advice*, except for some of the broadcloth, the lead and the silk, could not. Cocks found the cargoes an embarrassment and urged Wickham to keep them a secret. Wickham wrote cynically to Jourdain that even 'yf we were lerned alchi[mists] we could not so soone turne mettles into siluer'. But if Cocks wondered where to lay the blame for the selection of such cargo, Wickham was not puzzled. He felt that the Company had been 'deluded' and he was in no doubt by whom, Saris. He agreed with Cocks that it took a year to make any decent sales and told the directors that while he had been in Edo only about 20 per cent of his total sales were of broadcloth and bays. He estimated the market for English broadcloth at sixty cloths per year, about ten more than those brought on the *Clove*, adding that they would fetch 100 per cent profit if they were of the right colour. Lead would also fetch 100 per cent profit he argued. Experience confirmed this. The ludicrous cargo gave him an ideal opportunity to hit back at Saris. He asked the directors who had 'spoken soe largely of this siluer Cuntry' and how many chests of silver the commander had been able to take from Japan as a result of selling goods during his stay.[45] The English were not alone in their complaints about unsuitable cargoes. In October 1616, one of their Dutch counterparts, Leonard Camps, later to be head of the VOC factory at Hirado, wrote to his superiors in less scathing terms than the English about the unvendable cargoes cluttering up the VOC's Hirado godowns.[46]

If the exogenous factors affecting the Hirado factory's activities were unfavourable in 1616, the endogenous ones were to take a downturn as well, as Cocks was to discover during his visit to Hidetada in Edo.

Cocks had already considered a visit to Ieyasu in March but the arrival of the *Thomas* and *Advice* together with Ieyasu's death and persistent rumours of further trouble in the country made a journey to the shogunal court imperative. The Matsūra had informed the English that their trading privileges would have to be renewed by the 'new Emperor', as Cocks referred to Hidetada. Cocks assumed this would be a mere formality but the daimyo warned Cocks that the English must not sell any goods from the ships without permission from Edo, a departure from the existing privileges.[47] The Matsūra's cautions were the first indication that reconfirmation of the privileges would not be a formality.

Cocks's departure for Edo was delayed by the unloading of the *Advice*'s cargo. Meanwhile the *Sea Adventure* returned from Siam enabling Adams to accompany the party, which included Eaton and some of the crew from the ships. They left Hirado on 30 July in two barques loaded with goods for the Kinai factory and presents for the court.[48] The new stock for the Kinai factory amounted to 7,111 taels 2 mas 2 1/3 candereen, almost half of which consisted of broadcloth and bays and the rest comprising lead and tin (both requested by the bakufu), steel, Muscovy hides, amber, gallipots and other goods brought on the newly-arrived ships.[49] The party reached Osaka on 5 August and after a short stay to sort out the goods that were to be left in the Kinai with Wickham and those that were to be taken to Edo (2,988 taels 6 mas 7 candereen worth) the party proceeded to Edo, for the most part along the Tōkaidō, with Cocks jotting down notes about the places they passed and remaining alert for any clues about the political situation.[50]

At first all seemed to go well in Edo, which they reached on 27 August, but if they were inclined to take such things seriously, a severe earthquake on the 30th and the discovery that some of the presents for the shogun had been damaged or stolen on the journey did not augur well for the visit. The audience with Hidetada was held on 1 September, considered an auspicious day, with Cocks, Eaton

and Nicholas Wilson of the *Advice* admitted to see the shogun in his
'pallas' which Cocks described as 'a hvge thing, all the rums being
gilded w'th gould, both over head & vpon the walls, except some
mixture of paynting amongst of lyons, tigers, onces, panthers,
eagles, & other beastes & fowles, very lyvely drawne & more
esteemed [then] the gilding.' (He estimated the size of Edo castle 'far
bigger then the Cittie of York'.) The shogun sat 'alone vpon a place
something rising w'th 1 step...vpon the mattes croslegged lyke a
telier, & some 3 or 4 *bozes*, or pagon pristes, on his right hand in a
rum somthing lower'. Cocks's restrained behaviour and sense of
court protocol, refusing to enter the shogun's chamber, seemed to be
appreciated by court officials. Quite how the presents that were
offered (they included broadcloth, coral, three looking glasses, three
dozen rabbit skins and a posset pot) were received goes unrecorded.
The total value of the presents given to Hidetada and court officials
was 745 taels 3 mas 6 2/3 candereen, or less than 4 per cent of the
combined total of the ships' cargo.[51]

Cocks wasted little time in trying to ensure a speedy dispatch of
his business but it was to take another three weeks before the English
finally received a document which they took to be confirmation of
their privileges, and a new *shuinjō* for the *Sea Adventure*. In the
interim Cocks and Adams badgered officials almost daily. Cocks
suspected that they were being put off 'with fair words'. In reality
the shogunate, prompted by its hard line against missionaries, was in
the midst of a lengthy debate that was to lead to an important change
of policy towards the English and Dutch. In Edo Cocks was made
fully aware of the hardening of opinion against Christianity. Once
again the shogunate probed the differences between the Christianity
of the Roman Catholic missionaries and the Protestantism of the
English and Dutch. Cocks was asked why James I had styled himself
'Defender of the Christian Faith' in his letters to Ieyasu and Hidetada,
a claim made by the Jesuits and mendicants as well.[52] Cocks spared
no opportunity to distance the English from the Catholic missionaries. In a meeting with an assistant to the shogun's chief secretary,
Doi Toshikatsu, he 'took occation to answer hym that he needed
no[t] to dowbt of vs, for that they [the padres] were enemies to vs,
& to the state of England, & would destroy vs all yf they could'. He
was glad the shogun was wary of them 'lest they did not goe about to
serve hym as they had donne the Kinges of England, in going about
to kill & poizen them or to blow them vp w'th gunpoulder, &
stirring vp the subiectes to rebell against their naturall prince, for
w'ch they were all banished out of England.'[53] Later through Adams
and the jurebasso he declared with the voice of a true Protestant
patriot that 'we are no frendes of the Jesuites nor fryres, nether suffer
any of their sect to remeane in England, but punish all them w'ch are

fownd w'th death.'[54] In what appears to have been a spontaneous and
somewhat ill-considered bid to emphasise more concretely England's anti-Catholic credentials he even suggested to Mukai Tadaka-
tsu, son of Mukai Masatsuna, the *bugyō* for maritime affairs, both of
whom he described as 'the trustiest frendes we haue in these p'rtes',
that the English and Dutch would be willing to assist the Japanese in
a conquest of the Philippines. The suggestion was not taken up.[55]
Finally, on 26 September armed with what were thought to be the
renewed privileges and warned not to 'communicate, confess, nor
baptize with them [the Catholics], for then they should hold us to be
all of one sect',[56] a cheerful, relieved Cocks and party left Edo for
Hirado making a brief detour to visit Adams's estate at Hemi.

On the way to rejoin the Tōkaidō, Cocks received the first inkling
that the privileges were not quite in order. On 30 September he was
handed a letter from Wickham informing him that a proclamation
had been issued in the Kinai forbidding Japanese to purchase 'any
m'rchandiz of strangers' and that such 'strangers' were to leave for
Hirado or Nagasaki and take their goods with them 'which notice
from Mr Wickham seemed strange unto me'.[57] It was only then that
the 'privileges' were examined and read with the help of a Buddhist
priest. With the jurebasso's assistance, Adams, who may well have
been seeing them for the first time, translated the priest's rendition
into English. (Adams's knowledge of written Japanese was not of a
level sufficient to read the complex diplomatics of official documents.) It was discovered that the original privileges, far from being
automatically renewed, had been cut instead. The English were
permitted to trade only in Hirado. Shocked and angered, Cocks
decided to return to Edo immediately with Adams and Eaton to seek
clarification and demand a restoration of the original privileges. The
rest of the party were sent on to Hirado with the *shuinjō* for the *Sea
Adventure*'s next voyage. After further delays in Edo, Cocks was
informed that the English and Dutch had indeed had their privileges
curtailed and that in future they would be confined to selling in
Hirado and Nagasaki. Cocks was furious and told Itakura Katsushige
(the bakufu's deputy in Kyoto, or *shoshidai* and one of the shogunate's most important officials whose duties included overseeing the
daimyo in the western part of Japan) 'that the Emperour might as
well banish vs right out of Japan as bynd vs to such an order, for that
we could make no sals at that place, as I had fownd p'r experi. of 3
yeares space & vpwardes'.[58] He was told that the decision could not
be altered. Undeterred Cocks sought out over the next few days all
the people of influence whom he could contact who were prepared to
listen to him. He tried to persuade them of the justness of his case.
He countered the national security arguments which lay at the heart
of the ruling by insisting that unlike the Portuguese and Spanish, the

English and Dutch were only in Japan to trade, not to make Christian converts, and he skilfully appealed to a notion that his Japanese listeners fully appreciated, the bonds between a lord and his servants, stating that 'my sovereign lord King James would think it to be misbehaviours that caused our privileges to be taken from us...and that it stood me upon as much as my life was worth to get it amended, otherwise I knew not how to show my face in England'. He requested three years grace to appeal to England to see if 'our King's Majesty' would accept the new privileges, pretending that James was the final arbiter in these matters and not the Company.[59] Seemingly moved by this appeal, Honda Masazumi appeared to hold out some hope saying that while the decision could not be changed immediately it was not irrevocable and Cocks had the impression that it had been far from unanimously accepted among the senior bakufu officials. If the curtailment had to be accepted in the interim (in Cocks's mistaken but interesting opinion because 'an Emperor's edict by act of parliament being so lately set out could not so soon be recalled without scandal') it still seemed possible that with the right kind of diplomatic footwork it might be revoked in the future. Cocks believed the chances of this were encouraging. Under the compromise thrashed out before Cocks's departure on 17 October, permission was given for the stock remaining in the Kinai to be sold through Japanese agents. The English were to withdraw all personnel to Hirado, and no more stock was to be sent up from Hirado.[60] Permission was also given to leave stock in Edo in the custody of agents. Most of the balance of the stock brought up to Edo which had not been given away as presents remained unsold. This amounted to 2,142 taels 2 mas 7 5/6 candereen and was divided between Neamon-dono, an Edo merchant and Adams, who was exempted from the restrictions and could still operate anywhere in Japan.[61]

At Kyoto and Osaka on the way back to Hirado, time was spent in procuring cargo for the two ships and for the *Sea Adventure*. Loans were raised, debts collected and whatever could be was sold, especially the lead and the steel, which had been promised to the bakufu. The shogunate had first option on both the lead and the steel and in his negotiations with Hasegawa Gonroku, the Nagasaki *daikan* who was acting for the bakufu, Cocks was told that he should not set his prices higher than the Dutch or 'it would be ill taken'. Cocks claimed that the English lead was superior in quality and its market value was currently 7 1/2 taels per pecul but that he would be satisfied with 7 taels. (The Dutch had sold theirs for 5 taels and this was all that Hasegawa said he was permitted to offer in cash.) In the end 100 of the 203 peculs 33 catties of lead brought up to the Kansai were sold to the shogunate, with Cocks reluctantly accepting 5 taels with payment for the rest on credit, although there were the usual quibbles over weight discrepancies. The rest was sold at 7 taels per pecul to Cuemon-dono nicknamed Grub Street (possibly Kubo Kuemon), the Osaka host of the English who paid for most of it in cash. The lead had been rated at 3 taels 6 mas per pecul for the bar sort, most of the sheet at 4 taels 8 mas. It was not a good price. The steel was fixed at 20 taels per pecul (the same price as the Hollanders') and the shogunate took 10 peculs to be delivered at Hirado. It had been rated at 9 taels 9 mas 8 candereen for faggots of steel and 12 taels 1 mas 5 candereen for the gads steel. In these negotiations Cocks had had little room to bargain and had achieved the best prices under the circumstances.[62] In arranging sales, securing loans, refining plate into high quality silver, procuring copper and putting the stock that was to be left in the Kinai into trustworthy hands, the assistance of Hiranoya Tōzaemon (Tozayemon-dono), the English host at Sakai, a merchant and secretary to the governor, Hasegawa Sahyōe Fu-jihiro, was indispensable. Hiranoya helped smooth out difficulties for the English, and lent them 1,000 taels interest free and paid 1,300 taels in cash for lead and other goods to be sent up from Hirado. At one point Cocks mentioned that 'we can do nothing w'thout hym'.[63] The daimyo of Osaka, Matsudaira Tadaaki, gave encouraging words about a restoration of the original privileges in the near future, or so the English understood his words, and in his letter of thanks to Yokota Kakuzaemon, secretary to Doi Toshikatsu, for various favours in Edo, Cocks restated his hope that the restrictions would be removed the following year. Wickham was confident that this would transpire.[64]

Cocks left the Kinai on 25 November taking with him 8,846 taels 8 mas 7 candereen in money and 200 peculs of copper. (Wickham brought down a further 1,830 taels 7 mas 8 2/3 candereen.) Before he left Cocks arranged the affairs of the subfactory as best he could. A further supply of goods had been sent up from Hirado after Cocks's departure for Edo. This included some of the goods received from Siam. The total value of the stock sent up to the subfactory, including that left by Cocks, was 8,675 taels 2 mas. To this should be added a further 353 taels 7 mas 3 1/2 candereen returned at some stage from the Edo visit in the winter of 1615–16 making a total of 9,028 taels 9 mas 3 5/6 candereen. Gross sales had amounted to 12,589 taels 1 mas. The black and red broadcloth, which had been rated at 5 taels 6 mas, fetched between 10 taels 5 mas and 16 taels per tatami. Transportation costs came to 275 taels 8 1/3 candereen and Wickham put in for 763 taels 6 mas 5 1/3 candereen for sundry expenses for himself and Richard Hudson, of which board and lodging were a small part. A sum of 242 taels 5 mas 8 candereen was spent on gifts, producing net sales of 9,896 taels 3 1/6 candereen.[65] A total of 2,672 taels 9 mas 9 5/6 candereen was left in trust with Cuemon-dono, Yechiro-dono (Ichiro), his son, Hiranoya Tōzaemon, Shroyemon-dono (Shiroemon?), an Osaka cloth merchant, Skengro-dono (possibly Sukegoro), son of the English host at Kyoto, Itamiya Magozaemon, and some steel only worth just over a tael with Amanoya Kurobe (Amaco Crobydono or Croby-dono, Adams's and the Hollanders' host at Osaka, an important merchant whom Cocks did not fully trust). All men were well known to the English and in the case of Hiranoya Tozaemon, with whom most of the goods were left, a man of some importance in bakufu affairs. A further 1,367 taels 5 mas 8 5/6 candereen worth of goods was returned to Hirado 'for want of sales', a euphemism for unsellable, and 94 taels 4 mas 3 5/6 candereen was written off to cover various goods, such as broken gallipots and for making clothing for Richard Hudson. Thus net sales of 9,896 taels 3 mas 1/6 candereen had been achieved on a stock of 4,893 taels 9 mas 1/3 candereen, making a profit of 5,002 taels 1 mas 2 5/6 candereen.[66] No wonder there was such despondency about the curtailment of the trading privileges.

On the way down to Hirado it was clear that news of the order confining English and Dutch trade to Hirado had not yet been disseminated fully. A retainer of Fukushima Masanori informed Cocks that the English would be welcome to trade in his master's domain.[67] (The rōjū had already issued its order of 8 September making it clear that this would not be possible.) At last Cocks reached Hirado on 3 December, after an absence of over three months. The cost of the visit had been high, at least 1,202 taels 9 mas 6 1/2 candereen, more than Saris had spent, and only to receive bad news.[68] Any hopes the English and Dutch had of circumventing the restrictions were soon dispelled. On 6 December, Takanobu summoned both Cocks and Specx to show them the instructions from Edo that the two factories were to confine their trade to Hirado and Nagasaki, that they were to inform him of the cargoes their ships brought, and that they were not to sell anything from those cargoes until the bakufu had been informed and permission for sales granted. A few days later the daimyo queried Cocks about the goods sold for cash in advance to Hiranoya. Cocks, resenting the intrusion, replied that this did not contravene the new restrictions as Hiranoya intended to come down to fetch the goods himself. Life in Japan would no longer be the same now that the English, and Dutch, were 'shut...up in such a corner [of Japan] as Firando'.[69]

(ii)   Trade Restricted 1617–1618

Christmas day, when the *Thomas* and *Advice* fired off a number of salvoes, afforded some relaxation from the task of preparing the *Sea Adventure* for her next voyage to Siam, making ready the two ships for their return to Bantam, and preparing the factory's accounts which were to be sent to Bantam. In addition to the cost of setting out the *Sea Adventure* yet again, the Hirado factory had to bear the expenses of careening and victualling the two ships. Most of the money to cover this had been brought down from Kyoto, fortuitously because a request to Takanobu for payment for the 3,000 taels worth of goods sold to him came to nothing. The cost of overhauling and victualling the *Thomas* amounted to 2,093 taels 9 mas 2 candereen, almost half of which was spent on victuals (pork, beef and rice), while a further 927 taels 3 mas 7 candereen was spent on making the *Advice* seaworthy.[70] The *Thomas*'s cargo was mainly in silver and copper and was rated at 11,172 taels 6 mas 6 1/2 candereen including 6,400 taels in silver plate and 200 peculs of copper worth 1,546 taels 6 mas including 'charges'. She took along a 'Japon beame' to convince Bantam of the difference in weights between the Javanese port and Japan. There is no record of what the *Advice* carried but it does not appear to have been much, certainly nothing of value.[71] A decision reached after the *Sea Adventure*'s return from Siam in July to sell her and buy or freight a Chinese junk was not implemented; a buyer could not be found, hardly surprising considering her troubled history. Somewhat reluctantly, Cocks had agreed with the recommendation of Osterwick, Nealson and Sayers that rather than let her lie idle she should be fitted out again and sent on the next Siam voyage. The cost of refitting her was 1,625 taels 7 mas 3 candereen, a little less than that of the previous voyage, and her cargo was rated at 3,085 taels 7 mas 2 1/2 candereen (2,200 taels in silver, the rest an assortment of Japanese goods and India cloth, which had been specifically requested, and a selection of the goods which had been sent on the *Thomas* and the *Advice*). Adams did not sail on this occasion and two men from the *Thomas* and the *Advice* were seconded as pilots, one for the *Sea Adventure* and one to sail a second junk which it was proposed to freight in Siam. This was deemed prudent after Sayers's experience with Giquan's junk. The captain and crew were Japanese and the constant misunderstandings over crew privileges gave rise to problems that almost jeopardised the voyage. However, she finally left on 21 December.[72]

Twenty-five Japanese went on the two ships (the *Thomas* left on 17 January 1617, the *Advice* on 1 February), some in response to a request from Jourdain that they be employed at the English factory in Bantam and some to make up crew numbers on the *Advice*, six men having deserted from the ships during Cocks's visit to Edo. The master of the *Advice,* John Totten, who was severely ill, remained in Hirado and because his replacement was inexperienced and judged unlikely to be able to control the crew, which included a number of impressed men, it was decided that Wickham should make the round

voyage to Bantam and use the occasion to give an account of the
factory's affairs. The previous autumn Wickham had rejected the
possibility of leaving Japan for at least another year. His private trade
had gone through a bad patch and he thought it prudent to await the
arrival of Keeling 'under whose command I had Rather be one year
then a moneth under any Mariner.'[73] But the trade restrictions had
made it impossible for him to continue working in the Kinai and had
scuttled any hopes of a Ryūkyū subfactory. Accordingly, he changed
his mind, preferring to hazard the voyage than pass the time idly in
Hirado. The delivery of a personal report to Bantam about the
factory seemed a sensible idea and Wickham a good choice to present
it. He had a perfect understanding of the factory's condition, had
experience of the Japanese market, was articulate and enjoyed good
relations with the factors at Bantam. But he had no loyalty to Cocks.
He jarred with the cape merchant at the best of times although both
men tried to maintain a show of amicability. Cocks was to have
cause to regret Wickham's mission. The *Advice* reached Bantam on
11 March and Wickham remained there until June.

Meanwhile the *Sea Adventure* had reached Ayuthia on 19 January.
The factory there had been making efforts to co-ordinate trade with
Hirado but faced stiff Dutch competition and was handicapped by a
shortage of personnel. (Although there were three members the third
was 'neither fit nor capable to be employed in any business whatsoever' and Eaton, after his earlier visit, reckoned that at least six
factors were required to supervise the movement of cargoes up and
down the Chao Phraya river.)[74] In May 1616 two factors, George
Savidge and John Facye, were sent to Cambodia to open trade. Their
instructions specifically mentioned that they were to obtain bees'
wax and lignum aloes which 'being well bought ar good Comodit-
tyes for Japon'[75] The Ayuthia factory initiated a country trade with
Champa as well to procure sappan wood, aloes wood, hides, silk,
shark skins and ivory. A small junk was sent in March with two
Englishmen as master and merchant and a Japanese crew from the
Ayuthia *nihonmachi*, whose good behaviour was guaranteed by the
'Umpra Japon' (the *umpra* or headman of the *nihonmachi*), and a
Dutchman employed locally by the factory. The factory was also
optimistic that the military situation in the Chieng Mai region in the
northwest had stabilised after control over the area had passed to
Pegu and that renewed efforts could be undertaken to open trade
there. These were worthy but bold ambitions. The Siam factory was
short of cash and had strapped itself financially by procuring in
advance the cargo for the *Sea Adventure*. This consisted of 2,531
peculs of sappan wood costing 7.23 mas per pecul, 9,000 hides at
1.18 mas each, 10 peculs of silk, costing almost 168 taels per pecul,
and smaller amounts of lead, rattan, and betel nuts. The total cost of

the goods purchased was 4,750 taels 1 mas 5 candereen. The sappan wood had not been easy to obtain. There had been a general shortage and Dutch competition for what was available had exhausted supplies so that there was no surplus cargo to justify the hire of a second junk. Much of the wood was bought from Portuguese merchants but the king provided an extra amount in return for a present of goods from Japan specifically requested by the Siam factors. The factors emphasised that if they had 'neither money nor goods', nor suitable supply of India cloth for which there was a ready market, then they would have to depend on money from Japan if they were to take advantage of any favourable shift in prices to buy up goods for future voyages from Japan. A figure of 10,000 taels was suggested which Cocks dismissed as impossible because available money was needed to supply Bantam.[76]

The *Sea Adventure* left Siam on 28 May and, true to form, ran into difficulties and was driven by storms to Tsushima, her main mast broken and most of the crew dead. Sayers was dispatched to Tsushima to help bring her back to Hirado, which she finally reached early in September. Cocks blamed the misfortune on the vessel's late departure.[77] Nevertheless, sales were good, although the sappan wood did not fetch as much as the previous year, 19 mas per pecul, or almost three times the cost but not enough for Cocks who was worried about its bulk and perishability (it easily broke up), and silk prices were slightly depressed, at 218–229 taels per pecul, because of oversupply from other sources, yet still enough to yield a 100 per cent profit. The hides sold for 2 mas 3 candereen- 2 mas 5 candereen each.[78] But overheads remained high. The *Sea Adventure* had had to be overhauled once more at Ayuthia, and problems with the Japanese crew continued.

The other voyage undertaken by the Hirado factory in 1617 was to Cochinchina where Sayers was sent on a vessel belonging to Adams, the *Gift of God*, in the hope of acquiring silk. Cocks was confident that silk, adequate supplies of which had eluded the factory thus far, was available more plentifully than at Ayuthia, Patani or Bantam, and at cheaper rates. Sayers was instructed to secure the king's permission to settle a factory at some future date and in the interim obtain his 'gooshane' (an interesting corruption of *go-shuin*, great red seal) or safe pass to guarantee the security of the yearly voyages that were envisaged. He was also to clear up the mystery surrounding the deaths of Peacock and Carwarden.[79] The factory sent 1,896 taels 6 mas 4 candereen worth of money and goods. These consisted mainly of broadcloth, India cloth and ivory, copper, Muscovy hides, fowling pieces, table books and other goods which the Hirado factory had been unable to dispose of, including gallipots. The factory had rented cargo space along with other Japanese merchants. After some early problems with the Matsūra official responsible for maritime affairs and some harrassment, the reasons for which are unclear, the voyage went smoothly, leaving Kōchi on 23 March and arriving at Faifo on 20 April. Commercially, the results were mixed. Sayers's accounts show that net sales, mostly to the king, amounted to 1,316 taels 3 mas 4 1/2 candereen with the broadcloth and ivory, which had been lying around the Hirado factory since 1613, producing the best returns, copper little. There was no demand for Muscovy hides or gallipots so that one third of the stock was returned to Hirado unsold. This can hardly have caused much surprise as Cocks knew before the *Gift*'s departure that ready money was the commodity most in demand in Cochinchina. However, overheads had been kept down. The cost of passage to and fro, the payment of jurebassos' wages, and the incidental charges came to 90 taels 4 mas 1/2 candereen while victuals added a further 72 taels 4 mas 4 1/2 candereen and presents 117 taels 9 mas 4 candereen, the latter equivalent to almost 6 per cent of the stock. Other costs such as exchange commissions were also low. For the return cargo, Sayers obtained just over 3 peculs of white silk at a cost of 156–170 taels per pecul (it was sold in Japan for 230 teals the pecul) and he brought back 142 catties of aglaia wood which it was hoped would prove a marketable substitute for sappan wood. As it cost more than the latter (between 8 mas and 1 tael 6 mas 5 candereen per catty) this was unrealistic. Freightage of the silk was charged at 5 per cent of the cost, quite low, and almost the same rate for the wood. The modest success of the voyage was wiped out because on 26 June the hapless Sayers was cheated out of 656 taels 6 mas 6 candereen by a local jurebasso working in cahoots with a Chinese who was supposed to provide the Englishman with an additional amount of silk. Sayers had no one to blame but himself. He was supremely gullible, sheepishly obeying an instruction to put the money for the silk against the wall of the house where he was to meet the merchant and receive the silk. While Sayers patiently awaited the arrival of the merchant, the jurebasso, whose home was adjacent, slipped into his own house and grabbed the money through the flimsy reed wall separating the two houses and ran off leaving the Englishman stunned. Sayers, unwilling to delay his departure, accepted the undertaking of the head of the local Chinese community that the money would be returned and left one of his own jurebassos to retrieve the money before the arrival of the next voyage.[80]

Yet another voyage had failed to live up to expectations even if, as has been mentioned, it had clarified the circumstances of Peacock's and Carwarden's deaths.[81] But the king, whom Sayers was unable to meet because the mandarin implicated in the death of Peacock refused to allow him access to the monarch, made it known that the

English were welcome to return at any time and that if they presented him with a piece of ordnance on their next voyage they would pay no customs duties. The king also issued a safe pass, guaranteeing that 'not any of his Contrey dourste Rounge vs in pane of thayer liues', although judging from past experience this was a pretty hollow guarantee. The Dutch at least believed that the English had gained an advantage and felt inclined to get even.[82]

The *Gift of God* left Cochinchina on 1 July and Sayers reached Hirado on 7 August. Once again silk had turned out to be elusive and Sayers was lucky to procure what he had. He complained that a Japanese *shuinsen* merchant, Bernardo, tried to prevent him from purchasing silk brought by Chinese junks in May, claiming that he had a special commission from the king to divide it among the Japanese but that the Chinese 'ffor some Ronges ofered theme' would not sell to the Japanese.[83]

During the course of 1617 the implications of the curtailed trading privileges became clear to the factors in Hirado. In January 1617 Cocks was accused of sending goods directly to Kyoto instead of selling and delivering them in Hirado and was asked by the Matsūra to inform them of all goods sold and the names of the buyers. He refused, although it is likely that some trade was carried on in this way.[84] The Matsūra even tried to regulate the activities of Adams, who was not affected by the restrictions.[85] The English felt that they were being treated unfairly. They depended on the Matsūra to settle disputes such as that over the sappan wood brought back on Gi-quan's junk and the row with the Japanese crew of the *Sea Adventure* over the goods they insisted on loading on the vessel as their due. But they suspected that the Matsūra officials were prejudiced against them or else acting against them in league with their adversaries so that there was little prospect for justice.[86] In many ways the Matsūra were in an unenviable position. Any breach of the shogunate's orders would create difficulties for them with Edo and as a small domain their influence in national politics was limited. Their hands were tied and Edo was able to make its presence felt through the Nagasaki *daikan*. There were rumours, quickly scotched and certainly without foundation, that the Matsūra wanted the Europeans to quit Hirado and in May an incensed Cocks wrote an official letter of complaint to Takanobu about the treatment the English had received during the previous six months.[87] Nevertheless, the Matsūra covertly purchased goods from Dutch ships which arrived in June and during the daimyo's absence in the Kinai his brother, Matsūra Nobutoki, tried to lay claim to one-third of the goods plundered by the Dutch from Chinese and Portuguese shipping which the local Chinese were trying to recover by an appeal to the shogun. But the risks for

Japanese officials who tried to press their luck too far were brought home dramatically in December when two officials were ordered to commit *seppuku* for illegal trade with the Dutch.[88]

On 2 August the *Advice* returned from Bantam with a cargo more in keeping with what the factors had requested: silk (alas not of the finest quality and badly packed), lead, mercury and broadcloth. Set aside such welcome goods, however, was a stock of rotten lamb skins and rabbit skins.[89] On board the *Advice* too came Wickham and eleven of the fifteen Japanese who had gone to England on the *Clove*. Overjoyed to be home, they promptly demanded additional payment for alleged wage arrears.[90] The value of the cargo is not known but the obligatory presents, broadcloth and other goods, were given to the daimyo and other members of the Matsūra household. The total value of the presents is not clear but Takanobu's present was rated at 182 taels 4 mas 8 5/12 candereen.[91] The *Advice* also carried letters for Cocks from George Ball, the new chief factor at Bantam and a fellow member of the Eighth Voyage. (Berkeley, Keeling's appointment, whose 'knowne fidelitie, diligence and sufficiency to ye Comp^s service', the general had commended, had not lived long enough to make much of an impact beyond leaving the factory's accounts in disarray.)[92] Ball's letters were a savage, uncompromising attack on the cape merchant's character and professional competence. They grew out of an antipathy which had taken root on the outward voyage and a bitter resentment of Saris's preferment of Cocks. One suspects that Cocks was not the intended butt for Ball's outpourings, but a convenient proxy for the real target of Ball's venom, John Saris, a man despised and resented by Ball and, of course, by his friend Richard Wickham. Ball's attack on Cocks does not constitute a reasoned, objective critique of the latter's management of the Hirado factory's affairs. Some of Ball's accusations could be shrugged off as comical. Others could not. Ball charged Cocks with negligence, petty corruption, the promotion of unworthy subordinates, and he implied that Cocks was aiding and abetting the Li family to defraud the Company and that he was possessed by a blind, unshakeable faith in Li Tan's promises to secure trade with China. In a long, rambling, repetitive but pugnacious reply Cocks defended himself, rejecting Ball's attack as the product of an overimaginative mind which governed a man who himself was far from being a shining paragon of shrewd business acumen and solid achievement.

Ball's charges revolved around criticism of Cocks's dealings with the Li (which he considered the source of most of the cape merchant's irregular proceedings), his incomplete and inconsistent accounts of transactions in the Red Sea and at Bantam before his departure for Japan (Ball had not forwarded these accounts to London although Cocks had sent them on the *Hosiander* from

Hirado), his preferment of Eaton and Sayers, and a wanton exaggeration of the effects of the curtailment of the trade privileges on
the factory to cover up his own poor management. The tone and
absurd nature of some of the attack can be gauged from Ball's
comments that Cocks's reports from Japan were 'copious, but not
compendious, large, but stuffed with idle and needless matter,
ill-beseeming one of your place, years and experience'. He recommended that Cocks should '[b]eware of sending home imperfect
accounts; better it were in my opinion to send none. In England a
man may have them perfected for a matter of 10 or 20 l' [that is £10
or £20].' As for the Chinese, they were 'bent to none other end than
to deceive you', which was 'not to be marvelled at, they serving so
faithless and fraudulent a master as is the devil, who being the father
of deceit, cannot but have inspired his disciples with his rules of
perdition'.[93] Cocks denied the charges. He agreed that he had
performed some favours for the Li but for two reasons: one, they
lent money to the factory at more favourable rates than the Japanese;
secondly, they were working to secure access to China for the
Company. In Cocks's view it was necessary to trust them for 'yf wee
macke so many yfs & doubts in the matter' then no progress could be
expected. Cocks suggested that Ball's opinion of the Chinese had
been clouded by his experience in Bantam so that it was impossible
for Ball to be objective and believe that the Chinese did anything
'without a Mr Trick'. He rejected the allegation that he knew that the
Li had shipped copper on the *Thomas* to the detriment of English
sales at Bantam and he suggested, plausibly, that the copper was
loaded with the connivance of others who 'did winke at his [Li Tan's]
littell to Culler ther owne' dealings in larger amounts. Had he known
that Li Tan intended to ship copper he would have prevented him.
As for Cocks's Red Sea and Bantam accounts which Ball had
stayed (an arbitrary action which infuriated Cocks), the cape merchant denied any wrongdoing. Accounting problems had been inevitable considering the hasty manner in which goods had been
transferred from the Indian vessels to English ships. Cocks had
already written to the directors about some of the problems,
although they had already heard of the discrepancies from Saris, and
he convincingly countered Ball's attempts to lay the blame for the
confusion in the accounts, from which some of the other factors had
stood to benefit, at his doorstep. He particularly resented the allegation that there had been a conspiracy on his part to cheat the
Company. Cocks challenged Ball to forward the accounts and let the
directors judge the issue.

Regarding Ball's more damaging insinuation that he could have
sent more of the money he received from Wickham from the Kinai
subfactory to Bantam on the *Thomas* and the *Advice* had he not

siphoned off some of it for his own private trade, Cocks drew attention to the costs of careening and victualling the ships, preparing a cargo for the *Sea Adventure* and for the voyage to Cochinchina, to say nothing of the costs involved in running the household and paying factors' and servants' wages. Cocks considered the charges of favouritism in preferring Eaton and Sayers to be without foundation especially if the implication was that he had advanced them to spite Wickham who 'amongst all men...hath lest Cause to Complayne, for I neuer denyed him anything he asked & was in my power to performe'. Perhaps, he suggested, Ball wanted to elevate Wickham to the post of chief factor. If so, Cocks had no objection and would gladly return to England, adding that 'I doe not speake this for any ill will I haue to Mr Wickham, for god is my Judg I doe nott, only your letters Macke mee to think more then other wayes I would haue done'. Cocks refused to be drawn into the attack on Saris's advice to the Company that Chinese silk could be had easily at Patani and Ayuthia and that Japan could furnish the Indies with silver. He implied that Saris was not responsible for this misinformation. In so doing he was carrying loyalty to a superior to an excess. But if Cocks was prepared to exonerate Saris from the blame, the question arises whom he imagined was responsible. Unfortunately, he remained silent on this point. Ball was on firmer ground in attacking Cocks for his blind faith in Li Tan which had clouded his judgement and closed his mind to arguments that Li's fair promises to serve the English ought not to be taken a face value. It was insufficient to argue that there were good Chinese and bad, and that Bantam had been unfortunate to find itself dealing with unreliable and dishonest Chinese (he had Kewee in mind). Cocks *was* too trusting of Li, even if he was not alone in this respect. His experiences in southwest France should have bred an instinctive caution in his dealings with people like Li Tan who dangled tantalising proposals before his eyes. Unfortunately, he had learned little. Nevertheless, one important revelation from the exchange of letters is the extent to which the English factory had come to depend on Li Tan.[94]

These poisoned arrows apart, the *Advice* had brought the first cargo from Bantam that could realise a profit. Even the Dutch were alarmed. Specx was surprised and expressed his concern to the governor general that the English were turning into more effective competitors of the VOC in Japan.[95] Momentarily, at least, things were looking up. If the original trading privileges could be restored they would do so even more.

The arrival of the ship meant that another visit to the shogunal court was required. The visit would also provide a chance to plead for a restoration of the original privileges. On 16 August Cocks left for the Kinai, where Hidetada was making his first visitation as shogun with a show of power and majesty intended to awe the imperial court and the assembled daimyo, arriving in Osaka on 5 September. He was accompanied by Wickham and took along samples of the goods available for sale. Adams, back from Cochinchina, followed in his own barque carrying his own goods. Cocks, recalling the hints dropped the year before, was optimistic that the restrictions would be lifted, so much so that he wrote confidently to Hirado that they would soon have to send up 'our Comodities'. Adams was sent to Fushimi, where Hidetada was holding court. Once again there were delays and excuses, which the English found irritating. However, the shogun was in the midst of staging the reception of an official and quite magnificent Korean embassy consisting of some 428 people from King Kwanghaegun. The embassy was not simply a spectacle to enthral the populace. It was intended to reinforce the message about the status and international standing of the shogunate. The bakufu saw the mission as bearing felicitations on the Tokugawa victory in Osaka in 1616; the Koreans came because they wanted to negotiate the repatriation of Korean prisoners remaining in Japan from Hideyoshi's invasions. By contrast the English and their complaints were of minor importance. Two sets of presents were given to Hidetada on this occasion, one set in the name of James I with a letter from the British king, a ploy contrived to impress the shogunate with the British king's desire for strong bilateral relations, the other in the name of the Company. The English imagined that a letter from a fellow ruling monarch would flatter the shogun, smooth the way for a restoration of the original privileges and even upstage the Dutch. The presents in James's name consisted largely of broadcloth, kerseys, perpetuanoes and fustians, and an English writing table; those from the Company, 51 catties of raw silk, wax, broadcloth and bays, lamb skins and rabbit skins, and 10 peculs of lead, more than the year before, but less than the Dutch whose present for Hidetada in 1617, largely of silk, amounted to f. 2,127.[96]

Unfortunately, the letter from James I was addressed not to Hidetada but to Ieyasu, a serious breach of protocol. Cocks was informed that because of this blunder no reply or reciprocal present would be forthcoming; it had been a clever gambit, if ineptly executed. Adams's lobbying was also of little consequence. He had no direct access to Hidetada, although interestingly he was present at a dinner given for the Korean ambassadors and the daimyo. As Cocks put it 'we are put to hodgson's Choice to take such previlegese as they will geue vs or else goe w^{th}out'.[97] The shogunate had no intention of changing its policy and was impervious to the special pleading of the English. They were told directly that if they did not like the existing arrangements they could leave Japan. The Japanese were well supplied with foreign goods from *shuinsen*, Portuguese and Chinese sources. Cocks was informed of the rejection on 23 September. The justification for the ruling was once more based on national security considerations that 'no padrese nor prest should walke vp and down Japon in disguise of m^rchants as they were informed they did'. But another explanation was added that 'itt was for the good of Japon mrchants whome strangers did Carry away the profitt & transporting up of goods, which was Agaynst reason'.[98]

It is important to clarify exactly who these merchants of Japan were. Cocks was right to stress that the refusal to restore the original privileges was not simply predicated on the national security threat posed by Christian missionaries but on economic considerations as well. He blamed 'a Company of Rich vserers' for influencing the shogunate's decision and in a letter to the Company in February 1618 claimed they were the '*pancada*' (that is, *itowappu*) merchants who showed up in Nagasaki 'when the Amacon [Macao] shipp cometh' and suggested that the Matsūra aided and abetted this conspiracy to prohibit the English and Dutch from trading directly in the Kinai. Two years later he referred to this 'Company of Ruch userars' once more, describing them as both *pancada* merchants and merchants who 'Com downe to ffirando and Nangasaqe where they Joyne together in Seting out of Juncks for Syam, Cochinchina, Tonkin, Camboja or any other place where they vnderstand that good is to be donne'. He accused them of acting as an oligopoly to sell their cargoes. For Cocks there was no distinction between the *itowappu* and *shuinsen* merchants. He saw only a group of faceless 'ruch men' who 'haue got all the trade of Japan into their hands'.[99]

This was an over-simplification. When the *itowappu* mechanism had been established in 1604 there had been no distinct groups of merchants with conflicting views and ambitions about the structure of Japan's overseas trade. However, by the late 1610s a division between *shuinsen* and *itowappu* merchants is discernible. The *shuinsen* merchants tended to be well connected with the bakufu while the *itowappu* merchants were less established, working on a smaller scale, enjoying less influence with the shogunate and initially not well organised. The former were, of course, able to sell their silk free of the price set for the Portuguese, a privilege much resented by the *itowappu* merchants. By the 1630s, the decade in which Japan's foreign trade was radically altered, resentment had already been transformed into rivalry to secure the maximum share of the profits from overseas trade, and the *itowappu* merchants sought to end the privileged position of the *shuinsen* merchants. When Cocks made his attacks on his Japanese rivals these developments lay in the future but his comments underline the fact that towards the end of the 1610s Japanese merchants did not constitute a solid indivisible group even if the two groups benefited from the shogunate's decision to restrict the trade privileges enjoyed by the companies and its rejection of Cocks's request to have the decision reversed.[100]

The curtailment of the trade privileges made no difference to the shogunal officials who invested in the Portuguese náo and *shuinsen* voyages; they continued to make excellent returns from these investments. The English with their irregular and insufficient shipping and patchy success in the country trade were ill-equipped to attract such investment and the same was true of the Dutch at this stage. As a result, court officials had no interest in the complaints of the companies about their treatment; they turned a deaf ear to them.

The decision not to restore the original privileges was not unexpected. The English had heard from the Dutch on 12 September that the VOC's request had been refused. Even if Cocks fooled himself into believing that the English enjoyed more favour than the Dutch in Japan, he could scarcely have seriously imagined that the English would be treated differently from the Hollanders. In his dealings with the Matsūra in Hirado he constantly tried to cast the English as the older, more powerful nation, a claim the Japanese would not have seen reflected either in the ships, cargoes or personnel the English sent to Japan. The gulf between Cocks's proud boasts and reality was made clear with the arrival in 1617 of the Dutch admiral Jan Dircksz Lam in Hirado, the most senior person yet of either company to visit Japan. Lam had engaged a Spanish fleet near Manila and in a repeat of the 1610 fiasco, the Dutch were trounced. Lam had been lucky to survive. His flagship was sunk but he transferred ship and reached Hirado to join other ships of his fleet which had arrived in Japan bringing a valuable cargo of silk and porcelain, the booty from indiscriminate attacks on Chinese shipping before the engagement with the Spanish. The Spanish, Portuguese and Chinese protested to the shogunate about these attacks but to no avail. The Dutch had not seized any ships in Japanese waters and luckily for them they had restrained themselves from pillaging junks carrying a *shuinjō*. Pending instructions from higher authorities, the Matsūra had imposed restrictions on the Dutch, keeping a careful watch over their house and ships and forbidding contacts with Japanese. The English were not unaffected by the controls and felt themselves dragged unwillingly into a dispute which was none of their making or responsibility. They complained to the Matsūra that 'we were worse vsed then in tyme of Foyn[e] Samme [Ieyasu].' The restrictions were removed by an order from Edo.[101]

Unlike the Dutch, Cocks did not attempt to strengthen his plea for restoration of the original privileges by objecting to the restrictions imposed by the Matsūra on the grounds that it was better 'to be Sylent'. He feared that such complaints might lead to the dispossession of the daimyo who 'oweth our hon'rable employers so much' and a repudiation of his debts. In reality, of course, complaints by the English and Dutch about their treatment had little impact on the bakufu and would never have led to the overthrow of the Matsūra. Open defiance of or conspiracy against the Tokugawa would have been necessary for that to occur and such activities were never likely. Cocks was misguided in thinking that the show of cordial relations with Takanobu at Fushimi, where along with the other daimyo he attended Hidetada, would bring the English additional favours. Once Cocks had been told the news that the English were to be permitted to stay in Japan on the basis of the curtailed privileges he saw little reason to appease the Matsūra any longer and he tried to secure a provision that if relations with the Matsūra deteriorated, the English should be allowed to transfer their factory either to the Gotō Islands, just to the south of Hirado, where the English had always been made welcome, or to Satsuma. If the visit had failed to win a restoration of the original privileges, at least no new restrictions, such as exclusion from trading in Nagasaki which Cocks believed some of the rōjū strongly advocated, had been imposed, and the English were given new shuinjō for voyages to Siam and Cochinchina.[102]

The English party had left the Kinai on 2 November 1617, reaching Hirado on the 17th.[103] Besides lobbying for a restoration of the original trade privileges during the stay in the Kinai, there had been a flurry of business activity. The presence of the Korean embassy presented an opportunity to explore the possibility of an opening to Korea, if not for trade then at least to secure a right of safe haven in case English vessels were blown there. Cocks tried to arrange a meeting with the ambassadors through the offices of the daimyo of Tsushima. Not surprisingly he refused, Cocks commenting that 'the King of Tushma' was 'jelouse we might get trade into Corea w'ch non other are p'rmitted but the Tsuchmeans', asking why the English sought such contact with Korea as the Koreans were 'such barbrous people'.[104] Wickham had been sent to Kyoto with samples of goods available at Hirado to attempt some sales through the Japanese agents of the English. The objective was to raise cash for the *Advice* and for the next Siam voyage. Cocks urged Wickham to sell 'at what price soever; & niow our pr'veleges are lost we must not stay heare to procure orders; & we knew well ther were no m'chandes beloe, so that now is the tyme to goe thorow or never'. The Japanese merchants, realising the desperation of the English, kept their offers low, for example 218 taels per pecul for silk. Cocks accepted, selling 13 peculs 88 catties to Hiranoya Tōzaemon and making a deal to sell the rest at Hirado for the same price to the Osaka merchant, Amanoya Kurobe. Amanoya was supposed to

make an advance payment of 1,000 taels for the silk but sent down
only 500. He also agreed to take broadcloth, sappan wood and deer
hides. The silk price turned out to be a mistake, understandable, but
an error none the less. After the party's return to Hirado the price of
silk rose because the Dutch made no sale of their booty from the
China Seas, and the Portuguese and Chinese merchants held out for
higher prices so that the price rose to over 250 taels per pecul and
eventually broke the 300 mark before the shogunate became alarmed
and opened 'the Emperours magazin of Silk' thereby increasing
supply. Prices fell back to 260 taels per pecul. The best price the
English had received in 1617 was 230 taels (for the silk brought from
Cochinchina) otherwise they had sold for 218–229 taels per pecul.
The silk they had imported in 1616 had fetched 312 taels.[105]

As in Edo, the experience of selling goods in the Kinai through
agents had proved unsatisfactory. Accounting could only be made
on the irregular visits to the court. According to Cocks, in his letter
to the Company in February 1618, the agents exacted a hard bargain
for their services, fixing a price beforehand. There was nothing to
stop them from doubling or trebling this if they could without
bothering to inform the English. Cocks accused the merchants of
fraud. He alleged that they sold cloth but lied about it when the
English came up, borrowing extra amounts from their colleagues in
order to have the requisite stock on hand for accounting purposes.
This was returned after the English had gone. Cocks was bitter that
the same merchants were free to come down to Hirado to buy up silk
and sell it in the Kinai and Edo 'when we sit still heare [in Hirado]
and doe nothing'.[106]

Fortunately there is enough evidence to probe these charges. One
thing stands out: not much was sold by the agents in the Kinai,
hardly surprising in view of the bakufu's orders. Of the goods left
with Itamiya Magozemon, which were rated at 802 taels 5 mas in
1616, 384 taels 6 mas 3 candereen were returned to Hirado. Cuemon-
dono, who had been entrusted with Muscovy hides and steel rated at
626 taels 2 1/4 candereen, returned all the hides, worth 432 taels to
the factory. Yechero, who had received a small amount of goods
rated at 82 taels 8 mas 8 1/3 candereen, returned 65 taels 4 mas 1/2
candereen worth. These goods were brought down to Hirado by
Adams in December 1617. Of the other two merchants with whom
goods had been left in 1616, no information is available about
Shroyemon-dono. He had received a small amount of goods rated
at 97 taels 2 3/4 candereen. The second merchant, Hiranoya
Tozaemon, kept the goods, rated at 1,062 taels 4 mas 7 2/3 candereen, in his custody for another year, and in December 1618 when
Cocks was in the Kinai on his way back to Hirado from Edo, around
50 per cent of the goods were returned unsold and Cocks settled the

account with him. Hiranoya had been the most active of the agents in selling the goods on behalf of the English. He was also the one Cocks trusted most. Information about the goods left in Edo is less complete. Of the 2,142 taels 2 mas 7 5/6 candereen worth left with Neamon-dono and Adams, the bulk of which was broadcloth and bays, only 91 taels 9 mas 3 candereen is mentioned as being returned in 1617. More was sent down the following year. On his visit to Edo in 1618 Cocks complained about the underhand dealings of Neamon-dono and his business associate Yodayo (Yodayu) and he requested Adams to sort them out 'w'thout going to law where I am ashewred we should haue small right, as I haue know[n] p'r experience'. Adams himself was queried about '10 shire maps' left with him in 1616 and resented the implications of any impropriety on his part. The maps were rated at 2 taels 3 mas 3 1/3 candereen. One suspects that as with the goods left in the Kinai most were returned from Edo to Hirado.[107] Cocks's allegation of an elaborate conspiracy among the Japanese merchants to defraud the Company does not square with the facts. The amount of goods left in trust by the English was insignificant in the turnover of these merchants, while language problems, different methods of accounting and the practice of storing goods in several locations were bound to create misunderstandings. There is a clear distinction between the normal business imperative of driving a hard bargain and fraud, but it was in Cocks's interest to make his employers believe that embezzlement was prevalent. This provided another defense against possible suggestions of mismanagement.

By the end of 1617 the strategies that had seemed to point the best way forward for the factory had either progressed little (the country trade), not at all (access to China), had been thwarted (the Ryūkyū subfactory) or, because the policy of the directors was unknown, could only be left to the future (using the factory as a supply base). But the problem of securing a regular flow of suitable goods still remained. In December 1616 Wickham had written to Farie in Ayuthia that 'if wee cannott the next yeare procure this priueledge of free trade agayne yt will be butt a Folly to hould a Factory in Japon'.[108] In February 1618 Cocks was inclined to agree, fearing that the refusal to restore the original privileges would turn the English trade in Japan into a 'monson trade' like that of the Portuguese, who, fenced in by the itowappu, were driven 'offe to the last Cost' because their shipping 'must of force return with the monson'. He resented the fact that trade in Japan was not 'as it is in all places in Christendom wher e[a]ch man that hath money goeth to the mark towne & buyeth for him selfe', an over-simplified interpretation of commercial practice in Europe.[109] But such sober judgements were confounded

yet again by Cocks's naïve optimism. In Bayonne this had led
him to cling to the belief that his connections in high places would
enable him to win the nomination for English consul in northwest Spain. In Japan it led him to take literally Li Tan's promises about the China trade without which 'it will not quite cost
to mentayne a factory in Japon'. Buoyed by the news brought on the
Advice that the Company approved of his efforts to secure trade in
China, he boasted that no one else, including Edward Conocke (he
was unaware that Conocke's mission had been cancelled), could do
so much as he to forward the business, and that Li had told him that
his presence was essential to steer the overtures to a successful
conclusion.[110] If the Hirado factory lacked success, Cocks could at
least contemplate glory in China. A thin line separates optimism
from self-deception and by the beginning of 1618 Cocks was crossing it. One does not have to share Ball's prejudices against Cocks or
the Chinese in Bantam to appreciate why he could write to the
Company that Li's promises were likely to prove 'the plott of a
Nymble brayne to secure his owne turne, which Mr Cocks having
his imaginations leavealled beyond the Moone hath the eyes of his
vnderstanding so blynded with the expectacon of incredible wonders
that it is to be feared he will feel the losse before he will be made to
see his error'.[111] After four years the factory was still living on hope
rather than solid achievement, failure was hanging heavy in the air.

CHAPTER 6

Living and Surviving in Hirado

(i) Private Trade and Private Lives

There were of course other dimensions to the lives of the English in Hirado. They did not spend all their waking hours attempting to sell English broadcloth, bemoaning the poor cargoes they received or dreaming about the China trade. They had a private life and led a full social life which provided a measure of compensation for the frustrations of their job as factors of the East India Company.

The first priority of the English factors after moving ashore from the *Clove* had been to make themselves comfortable. In February 1614 the house that the English had rented from Li Tan for 76 taels for one monsoon, or 6 months, was bought outright or fee simple for 100 taels.[1] It was not in very good condition. Like most Japanese buildings the house was not intended as a permanent construction and its owner would have expected to repair or rebuild regularly. Moreover, as Cocks had noted with alarm during Saris's absence at Sunpu, fires were a common hazard in Hirado, indeed throughout Japan and the Indies. Fire was not so much a threat to life – one could get out of a burning building – but it threatened to destroy the goods. By the end of September 1614, steps had been taken to repair the house, make it more suitable to live in and to reduce the fire risk by surrounding it with walls a yard thick. The cost of these improvements came to 1,159 taels 4 mas 1 candereen. Cocks justified the expense by mentioning that the Dutch were spending even more.[2] The building programme continued into mid 1616. Neighbouring houses were purchased and then flattened. An orchard was laid out and a garden added in which Cocks cultivated the first sweet potatoes in Japan, brought back by Wickham from Ryūkyū.[3] To reduce the fire risk, yards were created to separate the buildings, which besides the residence itself and godowns, included a showroom to display the factory's merchandise, a storeroom for ships' provisions and a small hospital. The aim was to make the factory secure, functional and agreeable for its residents to live in. In February 1616, perhaps alarmed at the costs of building, the factors decided that plans to build a new garden would have to be shelved. By June a total of 3,897 taels 7 mas 3 3/4 candereen, including timber costs (some of the timber was brought down from Kyoto) and carpenters' wages, had been spent on the programme, a not inconsiderable investment considering the state of the factory's finances. It also suggested a long-term commitment unjustified by trading realities but justifiable on the grounds that it was necessary to maintain appearances before the Matsūra and the Japanese merchants and not to allow themselves to be upstaged by the Dutch who continued to expand their factory. The building programme also provided employment for local labourers, especially carpenters and tilers who on some days numbered above fifty.[4]

No detailed description of the English factory exists, but it would have been similar to the Dutch one which was built of wood with whitewashed plaster walls protected against the elements by small wooden boards. The floors consisted of Japanese tatami mats. The house had to be kept scrupulously clean, especially in the rainy season and summer, to counter the effects of high humidity and prevent mildew from forming.[5] The two factories added to what was otherwise a rather drab town architecturally. In March 1637, one of the Dutch factors, Henrik Hagenaar, noted disparagingly that without the VOC factory (then a large compound consisting of four main buildings and annexe) Hirado would be nothing but an insignificant community of fishermen and low-class people, a view which Cocks had expressed earlier.[6] Neither the English nor the Dutch factories at Hirado were in any way fortified, nor was fortification ever contemplated. The bakufu would not have permitted this anyway. Walls may have been a yard thick but they were not several yards high.

Nealson was responsible for the day-to-day running of the house but with his poor health, frequent trips to hot springs to convalesce (and to pursue the pleasures of the flesh) and his bouts of drinking, he was unreliable. The house employed a number of Japanese servants in addition to the jurebassos. Mostly these were young boys indentured to the Company and assigned to one or other of the factors, sometimes on the understanding that they would serve on overseas voyages. Eaton's boy Domingo was indentured for seven years service in Japan, Siam, Cochinchina and Patani, but was not to serve in Bantam or England. The money paid to their parents was small, between 2 and 10 taels and they were bound to serve for a fixed term, with food and apparel paid for by the Company. A written agreement was drawn up in Japanese specifying the details.[7]

The model for these indentures was a mixture of English assumptions about servitude and Japanese custom. The factory also acquired bondsmen, again quite cheaply, from Li Tan and its most important contact at Nagasaki, the Goanese Jorge Durois.[8] Punishment for misdemeanours, as opposed to random beatings meted out on account of the whimsical moods of short-tempered masters like Nealson, were quite severe. One of the bondsmen was flogged by 'all the servants in the howse w'th others apointed' each administering '10 lashes w'th a duble rope over the naked body & buttockes, till all the skin was beaten affe, & after washed him in bryne'.[9] Nevertheless, the Japanese honoured the agreements with the English. Nealson's boy Larrance, whom Cocks considered 'the best boy in the howse', ran away after one of the numerous beatings administered by his master but he was brought back by his parents and entrusted once more to his master. In January 1621 Man, a bondsman bought in 1619 in Nagasaki to serve as a calker, ran away after it was discovered that he had been stealing silverware from the house. Cocks wrote to Nagasaki, where he suspected Man had gone, and was informed that the *daikan* had ordered that Man's parents and brother should be arrested and 'the ten of the streete' (the *go-nin-gumi*) where they lived were to be held responsible under threat of death for finding him or of giving the English satisfaction for what was stolen. Man was returned.[10] The other servants such as Hatchman, the scullion, or Eurque, the butler, who was paid 8 mas 7 candereen per month, were engaged as employees and were free to leave English service when they pleased.[11]

The jurebassos remained the factory's most important links with the Japanese society in which it had to operate (none of the factors appears to have made much effort to learn Japanese); but they were not always dependable. John Japan, who had come on the *Clove* from Bantam, was dismissed in June 1615 because of eccentric behaviour and because he was alleged to be suffering from the French disease (presumably the pox). However, he appears to have been re-employed later, although not as chief jurebasso, a position which passed to Co John. Wickham thoroughly disliked Co John, alleging that he was a cheat, drunkard and an impediment to the satisfactory conduct of the factory's business. He wanted the jurebasso dismissed.[12] The pay of the jurebassos employed by the factory varied. Tome, who acted for Eaton, received 1 tael 6 mas 8 candereen per month, Miguel, 2 tael 5 mas and was employed from May 1616 until February 1618 when he left the factory's employ because of illness which Cocks (probably incorrectly) suspected was the pox. Co John appears to have received more and to have been paid in merchandise which he could later sell on his own account.[13] On visits to the shogunal court Adams served as intermediary with the appropriate officials rather than the jurebassos, but with the accession of Hidetada to full power, Adams's influence waned.

Even after arranging their living-quarters satisfactorily and securing staff to attend to the daily needs of the house, the factors still felt that their wages were inadequate to cover the costs of living in Japan. The question of wages was a recurring cause of complaint, not only at Hirado but elsewhere in the Indies. In November 1609, the Company, fired by a zeal to curb private trade, had ruled that wages, for which there were no uniform rates, were to be paid in England or adventured in the general stock 'as shall be by them [i.e. the factors] required, vnless yt be for some small som to be allowed them in the Indies for their necessary apparell'. The factors were '[t]o be bound and sworne from private trade but what shall be knowne and allowed by the Companie and their wages to begynne from their goinge abourde the shipps at Tilburne hope'.[14] The sum eventually allowed for apparel or living expenses was fixed before the departure of the Eighth Voyage at 1/3 to be paid in reals at an exchange of 5s to the real. The other 2/3 of their wages were to be held until their return or paid to assignees in England. In January 1614 as a further inducement to refrain from private trade the Company declared its willingness to accept factors' wages as adventures in the joint-stock with the rest being allowed them in the Indies 'for their apparell' so that 'they shall labour wth conforte as well for them selues as there M[rs]'. The factors could add to their investment if they wished but adventures were to be solely for their own benefit, not for others.[15] Saris had been sympathetic to the requests of those who were to remain in Hirado for an increase in the allowance paid locally, conceding that the cost of living was high. In particular he acknowledged that the wages of the junior members of the factory (Eaton, whom Saris had promoted from purser, was to get £18, Carwarden and Sayers £12) would not be enough to cover apparel and other necessities. Nevertheless, remembering the Company's displeasure with other commanders who had altered wages without authorisation, Saris was concerned not to fall foul of his employers and refused to concede everything that the factors demanded, especially Wickham. However, he did make concessions and permitted Cocks to pay the factors one half rather than one third of their wages locally pending further instructions from London and promised to make known their requests to the Court and intercede on their behalf.[16]

In their letters to the Company, which were sent back on the *Clove*, the factors, Cocks included, asked for an increase in their local allowance on the grounds that living costs were high, the exchange rate for the real unfavourable, and that they would spend all their wages on apparel with no benefit to themselves. Cocks claimed that he had spent more than £100 fitting himself out for the voyage and was not aware of the fact that most of his salary would be paid in England with only an allowance payable in the Indies until he boarded the *Clove* at Gravesend, a surprising statement considering that the terms of employment were agreed between factors and directors at the time of employment. He also pleaded that he was beginning 'to wax old and two or three years hence...I may be ready to return for my country, I would not return empty handed, and yet not meddle in any matters prejudiciall to your Worships' affairs for God sparing me life to return into my country it will be time for me to take my rest.' In comparison with Wickham (who was on a salary of £20 per annum), Peacock was well paid. He received £50 per annum, increased from £40 at Gravesend for reasons unknown, but still less than the £75 per annum awarded Coppindale. In January 1614 the Company's treasurer presented a motion on Peacock's behalf that £25 of his annual wages was to be put into the joint stock on condition that if he lived it would be for his use but if he died it would be retained by the Company. The Company got the better deal in this case. However, the English were not as well paid as their Dutch counterparts in Hirado. On his reappointment as *opperhoofd* (chief factor) of the Dutch factory in 1614 Specx was given a 'salary of *f.* 126 per month (£121 per annum) while Woutersen was reemployed for a further three years in 1615 with a salary of *f.* 72 per month (*c.* £69 per annum).[17]

The Court was not impressed by the Hirado factors' pleas; such letters were common. The directors were unmoved and took exception to the tone of the letters and the veiled threats of private trade to make up for shortcomings. On 26 October 1614 when the requests were first heard they were 'distasted, supposinge that they were butt pretences and that tyme would either giue them experience to find the countrarye or the Company satisffacon and cause to beleeue otherwise then at pr[esen]t they can be pswaded' and then they would consider some competent allowances to encourage their servants 'to proccede cheerfullie and confortablie in their dutyes and service'. On 15 November when the matter was taken up again and a joint letter from the factors read, the Court, resenting such a collective stance, considered that the factors' true purpose 'pceeded from thyere intent to haue meanes to vse priuate trade' and decided that Keeling was to inform them on his arrival that the Company had never been 'close handed to such as haue deserued well'. He was not to increase their allowances locally beyond the third allowed for in the factors' agreements with the Company, the Court refusing to believe that it was necessary and convinced that the cost of living was low in Japan. However, he was to peg the allowance at the real's local value and was given discretionary authority to award merit pay for any outstanding service performed or in order to encourage such service. The Hirado factors' complaints had produced some results. On 22 November the Court resolved to give factors higher wages in future to encourage them in the Company's service.[18]

There was a major difficulty regarding Wickham's wages. Wickham had been employed in December 1607 for a period of six years with wages of £20 per annum. On Saris's departure he made a point of reminding the general that his time of service was almost up (before the departure of the voyage from England he had been given his wages for three years, to December 1610, and a gratuity of £30, possibly a recompense for his captivity with the Portuguese) and pressed the commander to grant him a hefty pay rise, not simply an increased local allowance. Saris, sensing that appeasement was necessary to ensure Wickham's co-operation (he was after all an experienced factor and valuable member of the factory and, more important, his patron was Sir Thomas Smythe),[19] overcame his reservations and offered £40, which Wickham scorned. His wages remained unaltered at £20. Wickham boldly proclaimed to Cocks that he would 'make himself wages out of such goods as you shall deliver...to make sale for the Company', hence Saris's advice to Cocks to let Wickham leave Japan on the next English ship if he so wished. In his letter to the Company, Wickham claimed that Saris had offered him £60 but the Court could easily see from Saris's remembrance that the figure was only £40. Wickham repeated his pay grievance over the years. In January 1617 he wrote to Sir Thomas Smythe that his present allowance was barely enough to meet six months' expenses and that 'after 10 yeares service I shall be ashamed to looke my ffrends in the face hauing spent my time to little purpose'.[20]

The *Hosiander* brought a letter from the Company reiterating that the allowance on wages should not exceed 1/3 and that the real should remain for wage calculations at 5s. (The orders were sent to the other factories in the Indies as well; they predated the concession made in November 1615 but they undid Saris's concession regarding living allowances). However, in February 1616 at the general council held before the *Hosiander*'s departure for Bantam the factors unilaterally chose to disregard the Company's orders and set an allowance of £20 per annum as the minimum for 'ap'rell & other necessaries' (the amount given to the factory's latest member John Osterwick). Wickham was granted a discretionary allowance of 150 taels per annum, backdated to June 1613 when the *Clove* had arrived in Japan, and an award which Coppindale argued reflected Jourdain's wishes. Wickham had made his grievances known to Bantam where he found a sympathetic ally in John Jourdain. Both men had joined the Company at the same time and had served together on the Fourth

Voyage. Jourdain's wages had been set at £36 per annum but during his stay at Bantam had been augmented to £150, reinforcing Wickham's sense of injustice. However, in June 1616 letters from the Company, brought on the *Thomas*, ordered that there should be no deviation from the wages set in Saris's remembrance and the scales established earlier in the year were annulled pending the arrival of Keeling. Wickham was incensed by this decision, arguing that a council's decision could not be so easily reversed. He claimed, somewhat disingenuously, that the council had passed no resolutions to benefit a particular individual but for 'the sole good of the Honourabell company'. Keeling of course never made it to Japan and so the promised review of the factors' wages never took place, much to the regret of the factors. But, during his stay at Bantam in 1617, Wickham, determined not to be outdone, and with the help of his friend George Ball, obtained an order confirming the pay rise for himself and the others fixed before the *Hosiander*'s departure.[21]

There was also a problem over Adams's wages. Adams had been given permission to leave Japan by Ieyasu after the audience with Saris but he refused the offer of the passage home which Saris had been instructed to make. He gave various reasons for his refusal: he had not yet made enough money to enable him to return home; 'divers injuries done against me' by Saris which he did not elaborate on; and his desire to serve the Company from Japan, especially if it should decide to pursue the hunt for a northwest passage. Whether or not these were convenient pretexts, his decision to remain in Japan made sense as it did for Van Santvoort and Joosten. Adams was forty-nine years old; he had not been in England for fifteen years and had served abroad before joining Mahu's fleet. By 1613 he was comfortably established in Japan with high status, land, a family and opportunities to make money. England, by contrast, must have seemed remote and uncertain, with little likelihood of employment, especially for someone of his age. He was no Drake; no hero's welcome awaited him at home. Adams decided to accept Saris's offer of employment in the factory but found the initial offer (cancellation of the £20 loan the Company had made to his wife in England pending a more formal contract to be drawn up after the *Clove*'s return) demeaning and uncertain. He held out for a better deal arguing that the £20 would be paid by bill of exchange by his friends in London and that he could get better terms elsewhere, including from the Dutch. Finally, it was agreed that Adams would receive £100 per annum for two years or until a ship came from England with news of the *Clove*'s arrival there. He was given the usual advance for apparel and other expenses (£20) and in his letter to the Company requested that a further £30 or £40 be lent to his wife on his account. There was an element of bluff in Adams's demands. He

was not being head-hunted by the Dutch. Moreover, his wages were
generous in comparison with what the Dutch paid Melchior van
Santvoort for his services in 1609, $f.$ 50 per month for two months
which works out at £48 per annum, admittedly on the low side for
the VOC.[22] On his release from the Company's service in December
1616, Adams was paid 1,233 taels 3 mas 3 candereen for three years
and one month's service, as stipulatd in his contract. Adams dutifully
continued to provide for his family in England, behaviour which
Cocks found wholly admirable. The Company also felt some obligation and paid Mrs Adams £15 per annum against his wages, but
when the directors found out that his wages had been settled
in Japan they were reluctant to grant her request for a further payment of £66 sent her in the custody of the master of the *Thomas*
and purser of the *Advice*, arguing that she had already received £80.
The Company decided to appropriate the money itself and made a
token payment of £6 supposing 'her want cannot be greatt' because
of the £15 annuity allowed her. Perhaps anticipating the Company's
parsimony, Adams also sent her money in the custody of the Dutch
via Amsterdam.[23]

The factors' requests for higher pay had a ritual quality to them
and, fully aware of the Company's tight-fisted attitude to money,
they compensated themselves for the likely rejection of their requests
by indulging in private trade. Private trade was not entirely ruled out
by the Company but it was restricted. In 1607 the Court ruled that
factors were permitted to take £25 with them for private trade but
they were not to use it to buy the key commodities of pepper, spices
or drugs 'and all manner of pestering comodities'. They were also to
pay freight and duties on their goods. The amount of trade the crew
could conduct was limited to what would fit into their 'pporcioned
chest', which was carried freight free.[24] In practice the regulations
were ignored and the Company bought up supplies of pepper and
spices which the men brought back illicitly.[25] Private adventures
were carried aboard Company ships as well as on local Asian ones in
the country trade. The extent of this unofficial economic activity is
impossible to determine. It was conducted openly, sometimes too
openly for the comfort of more fastidious colleagues. In 1617 the
factors in Shiraz in Persia were admonished not for engaging in
private trade as such, which it was felt would not damage the
Company, but because 'you profess it to the world in such a manner
public as we all here [Shiraz] know not what or how to proceed'.[26]
Yet everyone in the Company, including the directors and the
governor and his wife, was involved in private trade of some kind.
The latter sent to Japan an English writing desk (escritoire) packed
with gloves, mittens, looking-glasses and silver. Rather than being
sold it was used instead as a present for the shogun as if from James I

in 1617 and Lady Smythe was compensated with Japanese lacquer-ware to the value of the desk.[27]

Frequent denunciations of private trade notwithstanding, the Company had no option but to tolerate it.[28] It could not have manned its ships or staffed its factories otherwise. For example, before his departure in 1615 Keeling requested of the Court that he be allowed to engage in private trade. The Court 'vtterlie distasted' the proposal, fearing the precedent such a concession would make, although some directors admired his frankness. Keeling refused to give up, and insisted that he should not be the first commander whose private trade the directors did not 'winke at'. Not wishing to let him slip from their employment, the Court offered to double his salary (payable on his return after five years) if he gave a firm promise not to indulge in private trade. Keeling stood his ground claiming he could not accept such an offer because he wanted to ensure that his family were provided for should he die. As time was pressing the Court instructed the governor to deal personally with Keeling giving him discretionary powers to offer a pay rise 'Not doubtinge of his care to drawe yt to as lowe a rate as he could'. In the end Keeling's salary was fixed at £400 per annum. This was augmented by £50 per annum for his maintenance in the Indies and a further £100 was to be paid annually to his wife, the balance to be invested in the joint-stock in return for a pledge not to engage in or permit private trade. However, the Court allowed Keeling to export some goods for his own trade, but these were to be kept in a separate account so that the Company could audit it on his return to make sure that he had not sold the goods at a better rate than those of the Company.[29] Conscious of the fact that they were indeed creating a precedent, the directors were required under oath not to reveal the arrangements that had been made with Keeling. For his part Keeling also swore to keep the deal secret. He had scored a victory. Keeling kept his side of the bargain, at least as far as prohibited goods were concerned. During his stay at Bantam in October 1616, Keeling warned Robert Bonner, who was working in league with George Ball, against dealing in spices and cautioned Bonner to flaunt the Company's orders 'at yo[r] perill'.[30]

The Keeling case suggests that there was a tacit assumption that private trade was tolerated, but not encouraged, so long as it did not become excessive and individuals too greedy and preoccupied with pursuing it to the detriment of the Company's trade, especially by attempting to sell goods which competed with the Company's, as happened at Surat in 1617.[31] In October 1617 the English ambassador to the Mughal court, Sir Thomas Roe, wrote to Thomas Kerridge, the chief factor at Surat and *de facto* president of the factories on the sub-continent, warning that the Company's factors should not presume that they enjoyed unlimited licence to send goods to England on their own account for the Company would confiscate them. Roe believed that 'the Company will deal with favour, if men deal with modesty. . . [f]or they intend not that their servants should get nothing but that it should be with their consent, and not to their injury'.[32] Kerridge and the other factors had already written to the Company claiming that '[p]rivate trade is too common to be reformed by us' and that officers and men on ships from England expected the factory to buy up goods they brought from England if they could not sell them themselves. Fearing violence, the factors claimed they had no option.[33] Employees who disapproved of excessive private trade but who lacked Roe's status exposed themselves to ridicule, even to threats of violence. In Persia George Paley was reviled by a fellow merchant as a 'knave, puritan knave', an epithet he took great exception to.[34] The Company did of course seize goods sent home illicitly and examples were made. The directors took action against George Ball (Cocks's tormentor who was sent home in disgrace in 1620) in Chancery and in the Star Chamber, although private trade was only one of the charges against him.[35]

With the exception of Wickham the private trade of the factors in Japan was not great and little effort was made to conceal it. Osterwick, who handled Wickham's private trade during the latter's absence in Kyoto, began one of his letters to Benjamin Farie in Ayuthia in September 1616:

> By the Company's letters we have written unto you jointly concerning such business as the present time affordeth to write of. . .I call it the Company's letter, because it treateth of their business, and where a man cannot so well congratulate with his friend as he desireth.

He then proceeded to give Farie information about how his investments (three pieces of damask, mostly rotten, and some mace which had been entrusted to Osterwick during the *Hosiander*'s stay in Patani *en route* to Japan) were performing. Unfortunately, Farie had made a poor selection. Only one piece of damask was sold, for two reals, and there was no market for mace in Japan. Osterwick sent it to Bantam on the *Hosiander* for Farie's account.[36]

Wickham's private trade was of a different order. It was well-managed and it was highly profitable but in the Company's view it was excessive. His estate was valued at £1,400 on his death in 1618 at Bantam.[37] Wickham had left for the Indies with the intention of indulging in private trade and had not wavered from his declared intention to compensate himself for his low wages by trading on his own account. On the outward voyage while the *Clove* was at Bantam he sold some India cloth to Kewee in exchange for an unspecified commodity which Kewee assured him would sell well in

Japan. Whatever this was, it did not sell and Wickham felt cheated, alleging that he could have made another 60 reals in the Moluccas on the way to Japan from the Cambay cloth he had given Kewee. He returned the commodity on the *Clove*. It was only in October 1615 that he took steps to get back his capital when he wrote to Hernando Ximenes, one of the individuals the factors used as a middleman in their private trade, instructing him to negotiate with Kewee. He also asked Ball and Richard Westby, one of the other factors at Bantam, to send him goods that would sell in Japan such as silk, lignum aloes, even pepper 'or any knowne Comodity that will make me my principal againe'.[38]

Wickham had no qualms about disregarding the Company's pro-hibitions against trade in goods in which the Company itself traded, although he was by no means unique in this respect. On the first attempted voyage to Siam in 1615 he brought back a large amount of ambergris from Ryūkyū in addition to the 2 catties he had bought for the Company's account. The cost had been 64 taels per catty and Wickham sold 198 catties to the Company at 100 taels per catty, a tidy profit for himself. He sold a further 2.5 catties through an agent in Nagasaki, Pasqual Benita, also for 100 taels per catty and sent 1 catty to Jourdain, entrusted to Coppindale (who refused to sell it to the Company's account) on the *Hosiander*.[39] Cocks was incensed by the transaction, not only because the Company was deprived of some '4 or 5 cattis of excellent amber greece' but also by the fact that he had personally adventured 150 taels on the voyage, entrusted to Wickham to whom he had lent another 150, '[b]ut he retorned me my money as I del'd it, & emploid all his owne'. The true extent of Wickham's dealings in the Ryūkyū ambergris did not emerge until April 1616 and then only because Benita came to Hirado, while Wickham was at Kyoto, with money from the sales at Nagasaki.[40] The disposal of the ambergris together with a sum of 420 taels unaccounted for during the stay at Ryūkyū, which Cocks believed Wickham had used for his private trade (Wickham insisted that he had given it to Adams) caused yet another souring of relations between the two men. Wickham rejected Cocks's criticism, testily telling the cape merchant to balance 'if you please my gains made in Japon, or since my coming from England, with my losses and expenses, continually posting from place to place upon the Honour-able Company their business by your appointment'.[41] At least Wickham was candid about his private trade. He informed Oster-wick in the autumn of 1616 that he did not intend to leave Japan on the *Advice* 'by Reason the Macau shipp came not I knowe not howe to Imploy a penny to profitt'.[42] If others had been as single-minded as Wickham in the pursuit of personal gain there would have been anarchy in the Company's affairs.

As a participant in private trade himself, even if his investments were small and lacklustre, Cocks did not consider exposing Wickham's trade to London. Besides, all the factors at Hirado, even Richard Hudson, were making private deals and Wickham acted on behalf of Jourdain, both men sending the other small shipments for trade.[43] Cocks and Wickham kept separate accounts of their private transactions with each other and Wickham an account of his own deals. Eaton and Adams operated a lacquer-ware syndicate which by May 1617 had produced dividends of 27 taels 5 mas each.[44] In March 1616 Cocks ventured 100 taels with Li Tan on a voyage to Ryūkyū to buy ambergris and a further 100 on a voyage to China which Li was to invest 'at his discretion for my best advantage'.[45] He invested 100 taels in the 1616 voyage of the *Sea Adventure* and lent Eaton and Domingo his servant money to invest as well. He adventured a further 100 taels and some coral in the unsuccessful voyage to Cochinchina in 1617 and sold some of the coral on his visit to Edo later that year.[46] The jurebassos Miguel and John Japan made small investments of 17 taels and 30 taels each, Nealson 50 taels and John Totten, the invalid master of the *Advice*, 100 taels in the 1616 *Sea Adventure* voyage. Wickham invested and received hides and silk (it did not occur to anyone to exchange the rotten hides among those on the Company's account for ones in good condition) and Sayers loaded 11 bundles of deer hides, a tiger skin and 12 jars of black varnish on the return voyage for his own account. The following year, while Cocks and Wickham were trying to have the original privileges restored, Sayers illicitly sent up some goods care of a Japanese man for sale on his own account.[47] For the 1617 voyage Eaton requested Wickham to send him saddles and silverware from Kyoto where Wickham had gone with Cocks *en route* to Edo, and Cocks invested 50 taels in Adams's voyage to Tongking in 1619.[48] Sayers received some coral from England from his brother and another man, both goldsmiths in London. The coral was hidden in a hatcase and brought out on Keeling's voyage. Disregarding the request from the Court, Keeling ordered one of the factors at Bantam to send the coral on to Sayers.[49]

None of the other factors did as well as Wickham out of private trade, and his connections served him well. In the late summer of 1621, Mrs Wickham appeared once more before the Court demanding her son's estate be handed over (she was the chief beneficiary). The Court refused, believing she had no case. The directors knew that Wickham had gone out to the Indies in 1611 with only three years' wages and a gratuity of £30 and could not have amassed such a fortune without private trade. They were puzzled as to how Wickham had done so well 'in a place where the Comp. lost all theirs'. The tenacious and determined Mrs Wickham would not be put off so easily and in November 1624 the Court decided to obey the decree in Chancery which she had obtained and hand over her son's estate. However, it made a cutting gesture the following year of accepting Wickham's provision for restitution and put the money in the poor box, pointedly recording in the minutes that Wickham had himself gone out poor to the Indies. The money was to be obtained from Sir Thomas Smythe.[50] This was one case where patrons in high places, in this case the governor, had proved advantageous.

Wickham joined Spalding and Ball in the Company's gallery of rogues who were judged to have greatly overstepped the assumptions about private trade. In 1628, bowing to the inevitable, the Company spelt out what commodities its servants could legitimately and freely trade in and laid down limits on others. It also secured a royal proclamation declaring that transgressors would be dealt with in the Star Chamber.[51] This had a limited effect. Later in the century the Company eased the restrictions on its servants' participation in the country trade in the Indies. The directors came to appreciate the value of private participation in the country trade as a means of absorbing risk and testing possible new markets. The opening up of the country trade to individuals trading on their own account began in the 1660s and by 1674 it was almost entirely free of restriction. In that year the Company ruled that any of the king's subjects under forty could sail for Bombay, but only there, to reside and make their living from the country trade.[52] The following year wages were restructured on the assumption that inadequacies would be compensated for by private trade. The potential for private trade was greatly enhanced by the Company's decision to freight vessels for the country trade rather than to continue using the Company's ships, a policy that was not finally established until 1694. In the eighteenth century almost all country trade in the Indies conducted by the English was private. Nevertheless, the Company continued to restrict private trade on outward and homeward voyages. The privileges granted to both officers and men were increased considerably and they were invariably abused.[53] Wickham's estate is dwarfed by some of the fortunes reported in the 1630s of between £30,000 and £40,000.[54] Private trade never threatened the survival of the Company and was qualitatively different from the corruption prevalent in the Estado da Índia. Indeed it can be argued that private trade not only gave the English an advantage over their rivals but contributed to closer involvement in Indian politics and hence to the evolution of empire.[55]

The English merchants had settled in quickly to their accommodation at Hirado and sought to live, so far as was possible, in the style to which they were accustomed at home. They used tables, chairs, beds, tablecloths, napkins (made from duttis), silver forks, spoons, gold bowls and other tableware, and they slept in beds rather than on futons on the tatami floor over which they would have walked with their shoes.[56] They made their lives even more agreeable by establishing relationships with local women. This was another widespread practice in the Company's factories in the Indies and was well known to the directors in London. Company policy dictated that those factors who were married should not take their wives with them overseas on the grounds that the voyage was dangerous, the climate unsuitable, and the presence of wives would prevent their husbands from carrying out their duties. At this stage the Company had no ambitions to encourage settlement in Asia. The Dutch, on the other hand, especially under Governor General Coen who bluntly stated to the VOC directors that '[e]veryone knows that the male sex cannot survive without women', were keen to settle and as early as 1609 some thirty-six women had left for the Indies on VOC ships, wives of Dutch soldiers and sailors, many ending up in the Spice Islands where Saris records their presence in 1613. In the 1620s more women, married and single, sailed from the Netherlands to form the nucleus of the Dutch settlement at Batavia. The policy did not last long. From 1632 the VOC ended its sponsorship of women migrants to the Indies (one reason was that the presence of women on ships was found to be bad for discipline). The restriction did not apply to the wives of factors and officers. By the early 1650s the VOC favoured recruiting bachelors but permitted its servants to marry local women.[57]

The English company was more conservative than the VOC about allowing women to voyage to the Indies. In February 1614 three 'Indians', who had come to England aboard the *Hector* in May 1610, and their wives petitioned the Court for permission to go to the Indies. The Court refused to allow the women to sail, commenting 'howe inconvenient and vnfitting it is for such weomen to goe among so many vnrulie sailors in a shipp'. The men were offered a pay rise and relief of £5 per annum was provided to their wives during their husbands' absence.[58] More remarkable were William Keeling's efforts to secure permission to have his wife accompany him on his five year mission to the Indies. On 8 November 1614 he petitioned the Court for his wife, Anna, who, it later transpired, was pregnant, to accompany him. Some of the directors, perhaps with qualms about destabilising the institution of marriage by insisting on a prolonged separation of husband and wife,

> approved of the mocon [motion] sapposing yt to be very fittinge in reguarde of the quiet of his mynde and good of his soule w[ch] otherwise could hardlie be setled to liue for longe from his wife; and as a curse befalleth those that keepe a man and wife asunder, soe this Company

cannott butt expect a blessinge in giueinge way for them to contynue together.

Others pointed out the dangers to her person during the voyage and in the Indies, suggesting that as she 'was a weake woman and vnfitt for trauaile' she would insist on staying in the place with the best climate and prevent her husband from fulfilling his mission 'of passing from Porte to Porte'. Over the next few days Keeling repeated his request, arguing that his wife's presence would bring God's 'better blessinge in his labo^{rs} haueinge this meanes to free his mynde from sundrye corrupt thoughts'. The directors remained divided, the opponents fearing to create a precedent, and a consensus was not forthcoming The directors referred the matter to a general court which rejected Keeling's suit, although some members were favourably disposed towards it. On 16 December, in response to a demand from the directors, Keeling informed the Court that he was dropping the request.[59] The Court had insisted on such a statement as there had been rumours that the Keelings might try to force the Company's hand by smuggling Mrs Keeling aboard ship. This is exactly what happened in February 1615 when Mrs Keeling joined her husband on the *Dragon* in spite of earlier undertakings not to do so. This presented the Company with a *fait accompli* and had possibly been encouraged by those directors who were sympathetic to the Keelings' plight. The Court, reluctant to remove a pregnant woman forcibly, threatened to discharge Keeling if his wife was not put ashore. An embarrassing public incident was avoided. The Keelings capitulated, although Mrs Keeling, at her husband's instigation, petitioned the Court for permission to leave for the Indies on the next available ship, a request which was turned down. From Portland, shortly after the official start of the voyage, Keeling wrote to the Company mentioning discussions he had held with his fellow merchants about the desirability of wives accompanying their spouses. The discussion had concluded that for the indivdual's well-being and to prevent 'scandall to o[u]r religion' factors who 'haue speciall place' should be allowed to take their wives to the Indies and that the Company should employ married men rather than bachelors,

affirmeinge confidentlie, though men out of modestie shame to confesse such wants in themselues, yet indeede there are very fewe (not the tieth) whoe are able (notwithstandinge there best endevo^{rs}) to liue w^{t}hout the Companie of woemen instancinge the greate disorder of the facto^{rs} now liuinge at Bantam, and elsewhere growne to an vnsufferable height in this kinde.

The Company was unmoved by this appeal and, as has been mentioned, Keeling's love for Anna triumphed over his duty to the East

India Company. He could not bear separation and returned home after only two years service.[60]

The factors at Hirado never bothered to attempt with 'there best endevo[rs]' to live without the company of women. Within a few months of Saris's departure they had acquired consorts. In Japan marriage represented an alliance between families, although the strength and durability of such arrangements depended on rank. As in other parts of the Indies there were no religious or social sanctions against concubinage, which was viewed as an indication of status, and there was a tolerant attitude towards casual sex. For those unable to support an extra-marital partner, prostitutes were widely available. According to the sixteenth-century account of Francesco Carletti, a Florentine in Portuguese service, when the Portuguese arrived in Nagasaki they were approached by pimps enquiring 'whether they would like to purchase, or acquire in any other method they please, a girl for the period of their sojourn, or to keep for so many months, or for a night, or for a day, or for an hour'. A contract was made 'with these brokers, or an agreement entered into with the girls' relations, and the money put down'.[61] It was a market offering a sliding scale of opportunities and satisfaction according to the contents of an individual's purse. Similar arrangements were available at Hirado and as the English and Dutch factors were to remain in Japan for an extended period, such a contract was the most suitable manner of obtaining a partner to ease the pains of loneliness. The Matsūra would have encouraged such arrangements and the English were not at all unhappy at the opportunity to please their hosts while at the same time satisfying their carnal lusts in an ideal coalition of business and pleasure. Some of the consorts of the English were acquired by arrangement with their parents in return for a fee and a promise to provide accommodation and food. (They did not live in the English house and were not, therefore, concubines as the term came to be understood in the nineteenth and twentieth centuries.) The women were probably Christians. The English had become aware of the existence of Christians on their second day in Hirado when the *Clove* was visited by a stream of people anxious to view her. Some of 'the better sort of women' were invited into Saris's cabin 'where the picture of Venus hung, verye lasiuiously sett out'. According to Saris, the women mistook the picture for the Virgin and fell down to worship it whispering that they were Christians.[62]

The factors enjoyed gossiping about their girlfriends in their letters and sent them presents. In May 1616 Wickham sent Cocks's consort, Matinga, the latest in Kyoto fashions. Wickham referred to Matinga and Nealson's consort as 'tuto[r][s] in the Languadge etc.' and there were jokes about sexual prowess. In May 1614 Cocks wrote about Jorge Durois, the Goanese becoming a father, commenting, '[w]ell fall (or fare) an old knocker'. Wickham replied that the news 'makes me half out of Conceyt with myself, but you old chippes are most dangerous fuell standing neere such tinder boxes etc.'[63] Eaton caused problems for himself early in 1616 by selling a girl called O-man (usually called 'Woman') to Wickham. When her mother complained that Eaton had 'sold away her daughter to one that will carry her out of the land of Japon' and threatened to take Eaton before no less a person than Itakura Katsushige, Eaton became apprehensive but a satisfactory way to appease the mother seems to have been found (probably in the form of a guarantee that the girl would not be taken overseas).[64] O-man was not Wickham's only consort. Another was Femage or Femeine, a Hirado girl. To soothe his loneliness while serving in the Kansai both women were sent up from Hirado at his own request in June 1616, accompanied by O-man's mother.[65]

Not much is known about the social origins of the women although the threat by O-man's mother to take her case before Itakura implies a fairly high status. Matinga's father had been a retainer of the Matsūra and Cocks tried to ensure that she lived in a style befitting such a background. She had a house and her own servants (three boys and two girls) paid for by Cocks who, despite his complaints about poor pay, was generous in bestowing gifts on her.[66] Petty resentment against the consorts may have lain behind the poison-pen letter thrown into the English house accusing Femage of being a whore and for the 'rymes cast abrode & song vp & downe towne against Matinga & other Eng'sh men's women'. Cocks, with no justification, believed the Dutch were responsible for spreading the stories, but as the Hollanders had their own consorts this is unlikely.[67] Jealousies over the women sometimes soured relations between the factors and Nealson was not boasting idly when he wrote to Wickham, somewhat cryptically, in February 1614 that he had slept with Matinga:

> He that hath a high horse may get a great fall;
> And he that hath a deaf boy, loud may he call;
> And he that hath a fair wife, sore may he dread
> That he get other folks' brats to foster and to feed.

By the spring of 1620 Cocks had finally become aware of Matinga's 'villany & that she had abused her selfe w'th vj or 7 p'rsons'. Fond romance gave way to bitterness and the relationship was terminated, adding to his general dissatisfaction with Japan although there are indications that he himself had not always been constant.[68]

Cocks makes no mention in his diary of having to support 'other folks' brats' or indeed of fathering any children himself, but the others were not so chaste. Wickham, Nealson, Sayers and Eaton all had offspring: Wickham a daughter by 'Woman', born after he had left Japan;[69] Nealson, a daughter called Helena;[70] Sayers, a daughter called Joan;[71] and Eaton three children, a daughter, also called Helena, from his consort in Sakai, and two boys, William, who was taken back to England, and another born after the closure of the factory and who was described as being 'plump and round just like his father'. The boys' mother was Eaton's consort in Hirado, Kamezo.[72] In July 1621, a child fathered by the purser of the *James Royal* was christened by Arthur Hatch, preacher on the *Palsgrave*.[73]

The English were not alone in sowing their seed. In June 1620 Batavia gave permission to Albert Woutersen to leave Hirado accompanied by his consort and their three children. Coen gave orders that Woutersen and his family were to be well treated.[74] In December 1627, after a visit to Edo, Pieter Nuyts, the Dutch governor of Taiwan commented that soon Hirado would have 'as many Dutch mestizos as thorough Japanese for inhabitants, an intolerable and ignominious matter' and ordered steps to be taken to stop the lechery which produced such an affront to the Christian religion. Little was done, or indeed could be done. An ordinance against concubinage in Batavia passed in July 1621 included harsh penalties but it failed to stop the practice and by the 1630s the Council of the Indies allowed the ordinance to lapse and ignored such unions.[75] In June 1639, as part of a clamp-down against Christianity, the shogunate ordered that all women who had been consorts of Dutch or Englishmen together with their offspring were to leave Japan for Batavia (consorts of the Portuguese had been expelled in 1636) and that Japanese women were no longer to liaise with the Dutch. Among those recorded as having sailed for Batavia were Maria, Sayers's consort, and Joan, their daughter.[76] In future the only contact the Dutch were permitted with Japanese women was with prostitutes. The bakufu preferred to be rid of people who were tainted with Christianity no matter how indirectly.[77]

Consorts and other girlfriends were not the only female company the factors enjoyed. During visits to Edo and the Kinai their Japanese hosts and officials arranged *kabuki* parties for the English. The 'caboques', or 'dansing bears' as Cocks describes them, whom the English had first observed shortly after their arrival in Hirado, bore little resemblance to the stylised plays performed by male actors much admired today. In the early seventeenth century the 'caboques' were mainly women and in addition to their acting and dancing they provided other favours. On Cocks's visit to Edo in 1616 he reports a dinner at the house of a merchant called Neyen-dono 'where he provided caboques, or women plears, who danced & songe; & when we retorned home, he sent eavery one of them to lye w'th them yt would have them all night'. The troupe was paid 6 taels 4 mas for the extra services. A few days later Cocks reciprocated with a dinner at which the 'caboques', to whom Cocks was always generous, performed once more. One caboque, Tagano, coquettishly wrote to him from Osaka in 1618 that she regretted not having been able to say farewell before he left for Hirado but was greatly looking forward to his next visit.[78] Those who did not have concubines or were not of sufficient rank to be invited to caboque parties had to make do with prostitutes. One of the mariners on the *Hosiander* drank himself into a stupor and stabbed himself in the arm because Osterwick refused to lend him 1s to pay for a whore. On the visit to Edo in 1616, John Hawtrey, whose sexual appetite was insatiable, stole some of the merchandise to pay for his women and the liquor with which to fuel his lust.[79]

When Keeling and the merchants on the *Dragon* had voiced their opinions about allowing wives to join their husbands in the Indies they had made the elimination of 'Disorder' central to their argument. Licentiousness brought disorder to the Company's affairs; marriage fostered a more settled way of life and was therefore conducive to furthering the Company's business. This reflected contemporary social attitudes. In early seventeenth-century England pre-marital sex was not uncommon. For young people it functioned almost as a marriage contract and bridal pregnancy was viewed benevolently even if divines and zealous ecclesiastical and secular court officials sought to stamp it out. Generally speaking, however, sex outside of marriage was not condoned. It was perceived as immoral, a threat to the institution of marriage itself, to the ideal of domestic bliss and to the stability of the social order. Such thinking was not confined to the ruling élite alone but permeated all social groups, although not uniformly. Punishment for fornication and bastardy could be severe (whipping or a spell in a house of correction) but it was not capital, unlike that for sodomy, a felony punishable by death since 1534. Statutes against bastardy were not occasioned solely by a desire to enforce the precepts of Christian theology but by concern about the social implications of the problem, the potential cost to a parish of supporting bastard children, especially in a period of economic downturn. However, the degree to which the statutes were enforced and the severity of punishment varied from place to place, depending on such factors as the zeal of the Justices of the Peace and the intensity of public opinion against sexual misconduct.[80]

In comparison with the moral climate prevailing at home the English factors in Hirado were living in a sexual paradise, free of the constraints of social pressure and far beyond the reach of the laws and courts that sought to regulate sexual behaviour. The possibilities for sex outside marriage certainly existed at home – whatever the prevalent moral climate it was impossible to control people's sexual appetite let alone to legislate against it – but the opportunity to keep consorts and bastard offspring as openly as in Japan, where concubinage was condoned by social convention, or of unashamedly enjoying the pleasures of the 'caboques', was not available in England.

How the factors themselves viewed the relationships with their consorts is impossible to know. Clearly the relationships were not marriages in that they were never solemnised by the Church and none of the factors chose to have them so ordained by the chaplains who reached Hirado on English ships. The relationships were convenient liaisons easily entered into and equally quickly terminated when the English left Japan. But the factors were no proto-Lt Pinkertons, selfishly exploiting the vulnerable femininity of the Orient, any more than the women were blushing, submissive Madame Butterflys, passive victims of an acquisitive, domineering West. The women were given over by their families to the English on the basis of a contractual arrangement from which both parties benefited. The case of Adams, the one Englishman residing in Japan who was already married, is more complex. To the extent that his Japanese marriage had not been solemnised, technically it did not constitute bigamy, while the fact that his Japanese children, for obvious reasons, were not a drain on his parish in England and his English wife, Mary, and their daughter, Deliverance, received regular financial support from him removed what constituted a major social objection to such behaviour in England. In choosing to establish a Japanese family Adams was making his own judgement about the moral questions involved although the fact that he steadfastly made the payments to his family in England shows that a strong sense of duty, perhaps even guilt, troubled his conscience even over a distance of thousands of miles.

The Company itself did not inquire into the sexual lives of its factors so long as venery did not interfere with the conduct of business, and although contemporary thinking held that sexual propriety along with frugality, industry and honesty were the ideal attributes for a merchant, no one was ever discharged from its service for fornication alone.[81] The directors, conscious of the fact that by recruiting single men for prolonged service overseas, they were exposing their employees to the temptations of the flesh, did not encourage marriage with native women as a solution to the moral and disciplinary problems posed by men having to live without the company of women. Quite the contrary, such marriages were discouraged. This had nothing to do with considerations of racial superiority. The directors had been angered by the conduct of

their only servant to have married in the Indies, William Hawkins.
Hawkins had been provided with an Armenian wife by the Mughal
emperor as an inducement to stay in his domain. The Company
believed that his marriage had puffed him up with delusions of
self-importance, causing him to live at Agra as 'a great man, Cour-
tio^r and warrior in great pompe' and at great expense 'to the
Company's damage, the shame of his friends & vtter disgrace and
ruine of him selfe', thereby contributing to the failure of his mission.
In their instructions to Downton in 1614 the directors ordered that
anyone appointed to live at the imperial court should live in a 'frugall
& sparinge' manner and was not to marry even if they were led to
believe it would be beneficial to the Company's business. Any factor
disregarding this order was to be discharged from the Company's
service and repatriated. The same prohibitions against marriage were
to apply throughout the Indies.[82] (The relationships the English
factors enjoyed with their consorts in Hirado were beyond the scope
of these restrictions.) The Hawkins case strengthened the resolve of
those directors who were opposed to Anna Keeling going with her
husband.

One essential difference in character between the Hirado factors'
liaisons with Japanese women, indeed their relationships with the
Japanese in general, and that of the relations between Europeans and
Asians during the years of empire, was that in the seventeenth
century the English were not expectd to sustain a mystique of
superiority towards the Asian people among whom they lived and
worked. Indeed the idea that they formed a superior caste was
beyond their imagination. Sham notions about concubinage and
inter-racial marriages debasing the white colonial race and its man-
date to rule and the hypocrisy that these notions engendered did not
exist in the seventeenth century, at least in the East Indies.[83] The
consorts of the English factors in Hirado were kept openly and were
an integral part of the factors' social lives. In the British Empire
concubines inhabited a twilight world beyond the fringes of official
society and played no part in the community occasions of colonial
society.

In the New World in the seventeenth century, on the other hand,
the English had a reputation for self-denial, preferring not to have
sexual relations with the native population even when there was a
shortage of English women in their colonies. Unlike their fellow
Europeans, they did not keep concubines and forbade intermarriage
with natives. This in itself speaks much about the inferior status the
English accorded the Indians. Asian people were civilised; the American Indians, in Purchas's words, were 'bad people having little of
humanity but shape, ignorant of civility or arts or religion, more

brutish than the beasts they hunt'.[84] Sexual relations, even marriage, was permissable with civilised people; with brutish people such intimacy was tantamount to bestiality.

This is well illustrated by the proposal received from the 'Kinge of Sumatra' (the sultan of Achin, Iskandar Mudah). Iskandar had written to the British king 'desyringe his matie to graunte him one of his subiects for wife wth sundrye proffers of pruiledges to such yssue as God shall send unto them'. The offer had been conveyed by Best who had arrived home on 8 June 1614. The sultan had asked Best to arrange for two white women to be sent saying that 'if I get one of them with child, and it proove a son I will make him King of Priaman, Passaman, and of the coast from where you fetch your pepper, so that yee shall not need to come any more to mee, but to your owne English king for these commodities'.[85] At his audience with James I, Best presented the letter to the king along with presents from Iskandar Mudan.[86] A marriage alliance with the most powerful ruler on Sumatra and the tantalising prospect of English control over pepper was not to be treated lightly and the directors weighed into a full and serious debate about the offer. A 'gent of honorable parentage' offered his daughter, a beautiful, highly presentable girl skilled in music, needlework and conversation. When the sultan's offer was discussed by the directors in November some felt that because the kingdom 'is very emynent for Antiquitye amongst historiographers' and the monarch powerful, a marriage might by 'the secreete puidence of God be a meanes to the ppaagaton of the Gospell and very beneficiall to this Countrye by a setled trade there, seeinge the place is very rich and the people cyvll'. The girl's father was willing to accompany his daughter. A consensus emerged among the directors that such a marriage could benefit the Company, certainly would not do it any harm and should be pursued if the 'learned fathers of the Church' approved and found it lawful.[87] The issue was addressed again later in the month. The girl's father, who was enthusiastic about the project, produced refutations based on scripture to counter the doubts of some directors about the lawfulness of a Christian marrying a Muslim. Others had less canonical doubts and feared that the rest of the king's harem might become jealous and poison the girl. But her father argued that the sultan's love would be her security, imagining, perhaps, that the girl's English beauty would prove irresistible to the sultan and capture his heart at the expense of the other wives. The Court requested the father to secure the king's permission in order to assay the doubters, reaffirming that such a marriage would prove 'a very hon[oble] Action to this Lande and his Ma[tie]'. What happened after this is unknown but the matter was dropped.[88] By way of contrast, when Sir Walter Raleigh proposed a marriage alliance between England and the mythical kingdom of

Manoa in order to forge an alliance that would conquer Peru, the Manoans were to be given English wives but they were to convert to Christianity.[89]

Iskandar's motives for this proposal can only be guessed at. He was capricious but he was not the caricature oriental despot Sir William Foster portrayed him as. He was a shrewd manipulator of power and his offer was serious although far less generous than the English imagined. It is highly likely that he would have expected any bride from England to be a daughter of the British monarch. In Iskandar's eyes this would have implied that the British king was paying a vassal's homage.[90] The prestige to be had from securing a marriage to distant princess was immense. However, his treatment of the Company's servants and his behaviour in August 1617 when he announced that the trading privileges granted to Keeling in 1615 for a factory at Tiku had only been for that voyage and no other and his 7 per cent customs levy were no way to woo for such a marriage.[91] Nevertheless, Iskandar's boldness in international relations once more stands in sharp contrast to the response of the other rulers in the Indonesain archipelago to the European presence.

It was only later in the century, from the late 1660s, that the Company let women sail for the Indies, to Surat and Bombay. In 1667 the Court permitted a number of factors and writers to take along their wives and servants, a time when the Company's committee 'for shipping and plantacon' was looking at ways to encourage English settlements in Surat and Bombay. When the country trade was thrown open in 1674 to all Britons under forty it was ruled that anyone wishing to take advantage of this concession could take their wives, servants and children provided they first obtained a licence from the Company. In 1675 the number of Britons in Bombay was given as 262 men and twenty-six women.[92]

One outlet to relieve the wants of men, homosexuality, was not tolerated, even if it was common and fairly open in the Indies, including Japan. The Jesuits had been shocked by its prevalence and openness and frequently condemned it. Cocks too commented on it. He noted the predeliction of Matsūra Nobumasa (Takanobu's half-Korean uncle and one of the members of the household who frequently approached the factory for loans) for women '& bogering boyes'.[93] Those in the Company's employ suspected of buggery were tried. In March 1624 the boatswain of the *Hart* was arraigned in Batavia by his servant, James Lewes, for buggery. After a trial before the president and council he 'was found guiltless and aquitted contrary to all the expectations of those of the bench considering the evidence and p[ro]babilities of the fact'.[94] The Dutch also tried suspects and if convicted punishment could be merciless and cruel: the offenders were tied together and cast into the sea.[95] Nevertheless, the crime that dared not speak its name and which men at sea preferred not to mention was certainly more common than the records suggest if the eighteenth century is anything to go by.[96]

As for the more general considerations of religious propriety, the Company stressed the need to preserve a moral and religious tone aboard ship and expected the same in its factories. The encouragement of a routine of religious observance had a purpose other than simply spiritual elevation. Prayers were to be said in the presence of ships' companies in the morning and at night, as they were on Spanish and Portuguese ships, 'for that Religious gou^rnm^t and exercise doth best bynde men to pforme their Duties' as the standard phrasing in voyage commissions laid down. Copies of the bible, books of sermons and other religious works were also carried aboard. In an attempt to reinforce religious observance the Company sent preachers to the Indies from the First Voyage. The Company tried to recruit the best available candidates. Approaches were made to the universities, other candidates were recommended but all had to give a sermon before the Court which then judged their suitability. One man was rejected as too young and 'too much in the fashion'. Men of grave countenance and conventional opinions were preferred. But it was difficult to find a steady supply of suitable men, and preachers employed by the Company were not the most able of their generation. In March 1614 the Court resolved to send a preacher to Bantam 'to entrust their people there, beinge the most espetiall meanes to reduce them to a Conssonable and dutyfull respect, both to God and their Masters'; but a suitable candidate could not be found. There were of course exceptions. One was Patrick Copland, one of two divines to reach Japan in the Company's service. He had a successful and financially rewarding career and was able to endow a chair in divinity at Marshall College, Aberdeen.[97]

There is no hard evidence that private trade was the source of Copland's wealth but other preachers proved themselves as adept as some of the factors in feathering their nest. William Leske was sent home in disgrace from Surat in 1617. He had gone to the Indies in Keeling's fleet as chaplain. The Court, satisfied with his qualifications and impressed by the gravity of his demeanour, was confident that he would be able 'to contest wth and hould argument wth the Jesuits that are busyie at Surat'. His surviving letters show an intelligent mind, knowledgeable about the factory's trade and perceptive about its problems. But he alienated his fellow countrymen who seized upon his frequent visits to brothels and his liaisons with an outcast woman to denounce him as 'a most licentious, ungodly liver and one that prefers his epicurian, drunkenness, and intolerable, insolent pride before the divine worship of God' and sent him home. The Court agreed with the factors reviling him 'for his so evil and dissolute carriage' but 'were willing to cover his shame and not complain of him to the fathers of the Church'. He had also brought back cotton and baftas worth £300.[98]

At Hirado the factors could not make any overt show of their religion. None of the factors were inclined to do so anyway. Discreet Christian services were held at burials but otherwise there was little in the way of formal Christian observance. The factors were not excessively godly but nor were they godless. Similarly there is nothing to suggest that their sexual behaviour was inordinate in comparison with other factories in the Indies. The fact that it is better documented is only a matter of chance.

On the whole, the Japanese world into which the English entered and lived for just over ten years left the factors remarkably untouched. Cocks, with his trained eye and natural inquisitiveness about such things, took pains to inform himself of what was happening in the country and to acquire at least a rudimentary knowledge of the country's history.[99] The others for the most part did not bother themselves. But Cocks's descriptions of Japan (and those of Saris), even if they are resonant with a spontaneity that gives them a vital and enduring quality, are incidental rather than central to his purpose, unlike those of the Jesuits who had a compelling need to understand as best and as fully as they could the alien society in which they hoped to reap their harvest of souls. The English factors in Hirado took Japan at face value and made little effort to explore Japanese culture and society beyond the superficial level required to ease the conduct of their business. As a result the contribution of the factors to our knowledge of seventeenth-century Japanese culture and society as distinct from Japan's overseas trade is trifling, especially in comparison with the Jesuit writers on Japan, notably Rodrigues. The age of Sir William Jones and the Asiatic Society of Calcutta lay far over the horizon.

Yet regardless of the great physical distance separating Japan from England and the length of time it took to travel across it, early seventeenth-century Japan would not have seemed so completely strange and foreign as it would to later visitors. Saris, Cocks and their colleagues came to Japan without a stereotype or particular vision of the country firmly lodged in their minds, unlike, for example, eighteenth-century travellers to Greece who were greatly influenced by a Hellenic ideal against which they measured the country and civilisation even before they set foot on Greek soil.[100] Moreover, Japan, like England, was a hierarchical society of which degree, patronage and connection were the foundations. It was also an agricultural society in which the standard of living and the average age expectancy were little different from England. In the vivid words of Professor Holden Furber: 'Cows were kept in the heart of

London just as they were in the center of Delhi and other great Asian cities.'[101] The English had no notions of Europe as the world's most advanced civilisation. The Enlightenment which would engender such assumptions and the Industrial Revolution which appeared to prove them had both yet to occur. The English did not bring along any sense of cultural let alone racial superiority in their mental baggage. In Japan and elsewhere in the Indies the English (and other Europeans) depended on Asians for loans and shipped their goods on local shipping.[102] In fact it was not just in their business affairs that they depended upon Asians, they relied upon them at almost every turn in their daily lives as well. Regrettably, the evidence with which to judge the Japanese response is disappointingly thin but on the whole the relationship, at least on the day-to-day level, appears to have been warm and friendly, perhaps because the participants demanded so little in the way of mutual understanding.

If the English became depressed from time to time in Japan that was understandable. They were after all settling in to a foreign environment far from family and friends and had to contend with the pressure of adjusting to ways of doing business that seemed cumbersome, frustrating and unfair. Adjustment was made no easier by the poor results they achieved. The *mentalité* of such an early seventeenth-century expatriate is best captured in the words of one of the factors in Japan, Wickham, writing to his aunt from Bantam in 1617. In his letter he reproaches his family for not writing once during his absence from England despite having written himself by every possible conveyance:

> Neuerthelesse when I Consider the great mortallyty of men in these long Voyages with the great distance Eng[land] & the farthest p[ar]ts of Japon where most Comonly I Continue for the Affayres of the Honbl Comp[any], my letters being to passe 5 severall Conveyances before they Can eyther Come or goe surely I [am] the better satissfied in wanting the Comfortable Remembrance of my frends for a season.[103]

Stoicism was the essence of survival in the Indies.

(ii)   Years of Drift 1618–1620

The *Advice*, with Wickham aboard once more, finally leaving Japan, sailed from Kōchi in late February 1618 for Bantam carrying the five chests of refined silver plate, cask, lacquer-ware and iron for ballast. Cocks wrote to Ball that more would have been sent had the Hirado factory not had to provide for the Siam and Cochinchina voyages and if debts outstanding (worth 4,200 taels) from the daimyo of Hirado and merchants in the Kinai had been repaid on time. A sum of 1,428 taels 2 mas 3 7/12 candereen had been spent on victuals and ship's stores. The *Advice* took along a batch of correspondence including copies of previous 'out' letters and accounts, and copies of the factory's journal. Cocks apologised that his accounts had fallen behind because of the trip to the Kinai. His letters included one to his nephew, John Cocks, who had joined the Company and who had left England for Bantam in 1616. Cocks requested Ball to 'vse him kyndlie'. Unfortunately, he died at Bantam.[104] Unknown to the factors, the departure of the *Advice* marked the start of a period of isolation for the Hirado factory. The next English ships to come to Hirado were prizes seized by the Dutch in the Spice Islands. It was not until July 1620 that a Company ship from Bantam arrived. The Company's attempt to trade directly with Japan was already a commercial failure; yet the factory was to survive for another five years before it was finally closed in December 1623.

Even had the problems of supply been overcome to any significant degree it had become apparent by 1617 that the ambition of turning the Hirado factory into the treasury of the southwards region would not have been a simple task to achieve. A new problem emerged: the quality of the silver to be exported from Japan. Silver was abundant in Japan but its quality was not uniform and demand in the Indies for Japanese silver varied according to the level of its purity. Bakufu-assayed silver had a high copper content while the currency of some of the domains was purer. The cash from the sales of the English factory at Hirado was generally paid for in inferior bakufu bars, called *bakufu chogin*. These bars were one of the means by which the bakufu sought to establish a uniform national currency and were themselves often coined from the superior domain currency. The English referred to the *bakufu chogin* by a number of names including 'Japon plate' and 'bar plate'. However, because of their high copper content the bakufu bars were not the most suitable form in which to export silver from Japan, as Wickham had observed during his stay in Edo in 1614. He informed Cocks that if *bakufu chogin* were sent on the Siam voyage there would be a loss of 28 per cent when it was exchanged in Siam. He recommended Cocks to ensure that all silver exported by the factory from Japan should be fine silver called 'faybooque' which would only lose 2 1/2–3 per cent in exchange.[105]

What Wickham was referring to was the finest grades of silver produced in Japanese mines, known collectively as *haifukigin*. This together with domain currency was indeed much sought after by those engaged in foreign trade. Although the shogunate had declared the export of *haifukigin* illegal, the prohibition was not easy to enforce and the bakufu made provision for foreign traders to exchange *bakufu chogin* into *haifukigin* by official bakufu assayers. Before the curtailment of the trade privileges the English had sometimes used the Osaka branch of the *ginza*, or silver mint, but after 1614, when another branch was established in Nagasaki, they could either use the official assayers who visited Hirado or have it exchanged at the Nagasaki *ginza* on their behalf by the Li who charged a premium for their services. The Dutch followed the same procedures. The *Hosiander* had carried bullion in reals (1,200 taels) and in 'Japon plate' (2,200 taels) of which 800 taels was in *soma* plate (the finest silver as it was twice assayed). The rest was of unknown quality.[106] The *Thomas* had carried 6,400 taels in *soma*. The *Sea Adventure* had carried 93 per cent of its ready money in reals, the rest in *haifukigin* on its Siam voyage in 1615.[107] In Bantam, Ball was dissatisfied with the silver he was receiving from Japan and complained to Cocks that the *soma* or *goke* (that is, *gokuin*, or hall-arked silver) was too fine and the Japan plate too coarse and lost 20 per cent of its value when minted. He alleged that it had been debased by the addition of tin and accused the Li of corrupting it. Cocks rejected this, stating that it had been refined by the shogun's mintmen and that Kewee had debased it in Bantam when it was being exchanged into reals. Ball's charge was nonsense and Cocks's rebuttal correct, at least about the procedures adopted in Japan. Cocks felt that silver 'with themperours stampe upon it... will...passe in Saffetie'. Ball instructed Cocks either to send silver that had already been coined into reals or at least into long square bars equal in fineness to reals.

Reals were the most widely used currency in the Indies (the silver from the Peruvian mines was purer than that from Japanese mines) and the cash sent on Company ships from England was in reals. English coins had been sent on the First Voyage but were dropped from subsequent ladings as they were not acceptable tender in the Indies. Cocks argued against sending reals minted in Japan to Bantam because he had heard reports that some Chinese at Nagasaki had produced counterfeit reals which had been passed on to the Dutch as payment for the silk they had plundered from Chinese vessels near Manila; if true it was a just revenge. On the *Advice*'s return voyage to Bantam in February 1618 Cocks sent the silver (worth 9,063 taels) in four lots so that Ball could choose which was the most suitable for Bantam's needs. These were *soma* (Cocks added that he hoped there would be no debasement this time at Bantam); thin long bars, which he described as tin-like and the closest in fineness to reals, lozenge-shaped bars, the kind exported by the Portuguese; and finally plate 'melted Rough' or *seda*, which the Dutch exported and which was finer than the long bars and lozenge-shaped ones. All were different grades of *haifukigin*. The cost of refining *bakufu chogin* into *haifukigin*, borne by the Hirado factory, was expensive and Cocks suggested that Ball examine the possibility of refining the silver in Bantam by dependable local Chinese. The charges for refining varied but were far in excess of the 4 per cent Saris had led the Court to believe on his return in 1614. *Soma* was the most expensive. The *soma* sent on the *Thomas* in 1617 had been refined at just over 20 per cent, that on the *Advice* in 1618 at 19 per cent and on the *Sea Adventure* at 23.45 per cent. The long bars sent on the *Advice* that year were refined at 13 per cent and 14 per cent respectively and the 'fibuck' (another form of *haifukigin*) at 12 and 16 per cent. The cost of refining the silver sent on the *Advice* amounted to 1,857 taels 7 mas 8 1/2 candereen, a 20.5 per cent overhead. This, together with the costs of fitting out the ships that came to Hirado, was an expediture Cocks would have preferred Bantam to shoulder.[108] The bickering over what kind of silver should be exported from Japan and who was to pay for exchanging it remained unresolved and was to crop up yet again before the closure of the factory.

Keeling's decision to abandon his mission in Bantam in 1616 and return home meant that an opportunity had been lost to review the factories in the region, restructure their management and determine which should remain in business and which should be closed. He arrived back in England in May 1617, followed by John Jourdain in June. Both men provided the directors with hard truths about the state of the Company's trade in the Indies. In a letter from Lime, Keeling rubbed in the point about the financial deprivation of the Bantam factory, mentioning for good measure that on his departure a Dutch ship arrived in Bantam, part of a fleet of six vessels which together brought '800 Thousand Re^s of 8, a some of enncouragem^t to the managers whence they may acquire some repute'.[109] His figures were exaggerated. Between 1603 and 1617 Dutch money exports to the Indies never exceeded 600,000 reals per annum and in 1614–15 and 1615–16 were 288,000 and 460,000 respectively rising to 544,000 in 1616–17. This was still greater than the English company which sent £113,942 in 1614, £26,660 in 1615 and £54,087 in 1616.[110] However, Keeling had spent his glory and his contribution to the debate about Company policy in the Indies over the next few months went unheeded. There was a great sense of disappointment and anger over his premature return from the Indies. The Court accused him of negligence, which 'griued' Keeling, and refused to give him a gratuity.[111]

On 25 September Jourdain presented a letter to the Court 'as his opinion cocerninge the Contynueinge and prosecutinge of Trade in the Indies and dissolvinge some vnnecessarye and vnprofitable factoryes', and on the 30th he appeared in person before the directors and made such a favourable impression that he was eyed as the most suitable person to take on the demanding job which Keeling had thrown down so selfishly.[112] The directors thus had some sound

up-to-date information on which to act and were convinced of the
need to adhere broadly to the plans they had devised in 1614. The
idea of a grand visitation of the Indies and the establishment of
sub-presidencies, which had been central to Keeling's commission
and had been reconfirmed by the Court in orders sent to Bantam on
the *Swan* in February 1616, was modified in favour of establishing a
regional command, or presidency as it was soon styled, at Bantam
where the president was 'to examine, establish and dissolve factoryes
as occasion shalbee with the advise and counsell of two or more to be
joyned with him'.[113]

However, plans to restructure the southwards region faded into
the background as the problems posed by Anglo-Dutch rivalry in the
Spice Islands, where the English had gained a foothold at Run and
Nailaka in late 1616 and early 1617, emerged centre stage. The
Court, convinced of the righteousness of its cause – according to its
interpretation of existing international law – remained intent on
pressing the Company's claims there despite Dutch opposition and
was prepared to risk a clash with the Dutch. This was not a sudden
decision nor a unanimous one. Nor for their part did the Dutch
wholeheartedly welcome the prospect of armed conflict with the
English. Negotiations for a peaceful resolution of the dispute between the two Companies over trading rights in the Spice Islands
had dragged on for several years, part of a broader economic rivalry
between the two Protestant powers sparked off by James I's proclamation restricting all foreign access to fisheries on the British coast,
a move directed squarely against the Dutch herring fleets. Negotiations for a merger between the two companies had been held at the
instigation of the Dutch in 1610, and in 1613 and 1615 further
conferences tried to iron out all the matters in dispute between the
two countries. The Dutch modified their uncompromising position
that treaties signed with native rulers gave them the right to exclude
the English from the Spice Islands but argued that the English should
pay a share of what they saw as the high investment they had made
and were continuing to make to secure access to the islands in the
face of Spanish and Portuguese opposition. The English countered
with arguments that the Dutch themselves had employed against
Spanish exclusionist claims, drawing upon the notion of *mare librum*,
or open sea, whereby no nation was presumed to have the right to
exclude another from freedom of the seas. The English were being
disingenuous for they were flouting this principle themselves by
trying to prevent Dutch whaling in the northern seas on the grounds
of prior discovery by the English.[114]

News of proposals for a union of the two companies reached the
Indies in 1614. Opinion was divided about the scheme for both
emotional and strategic reasons. In Japan, Cocks heard about the

proposals from the Dutch sometime in 1614 at a time when, like Keeling, he was greatly impressed by what he imagined to be superior VOC strength in the Indies. With only his own vague impressions to rely on, he asserted confidently that the Dutch 'are so strong at sea that they care not a figg nether For Spaniards nor Portingals'. He welcomed the prospect of an alliance to sweep the Catholic powers out of 'these Easterne parts of the worlde'.[115] The following year a Hollander who spoke to him about a possible union of the companies felt that even if the English paid compensation for Dutch pioneering endeavours to take the Spice Islands from the Catholic powers this would not make up for Dutch lives lost in the struggle; to which Cocks replied that for every Dutchman lost in the Moluccas twenty Englishmen had 'lost their lives in driving the Spaniards out of the Low Countries and making the Hollanders a free state. Unto which he knew not well to answer but laughed it out.' In July 1617 Lam, whose experience before Manila had taught him how inter-company rivalry wasted energy and valuable re-sources, told Cocks, with whom he enjoyed amicable relations, that he 'did verily think that their Company and the English were all joyned in one before now, for that the difference, being but a money matter, could not chuse but sowne be decyded'.[116] Some of the English Company's servants also lamented the bleeding of resources in a wasteful rivalry.[117] Others felt more strongly about Dutch harrassment and suspected that whatever the discussions in Europe their experience in the Indies showed that the Dutch were wholly bent on driving the English out of the Spice Islands and from other parts of the Indies to boot. This was the tenor of Keeling's letter to the Company from Bantam in 1616 in which he referred, with some hyperbole, to 'y[e] insufferable wrongs' offered by the Dutch 'to y[e] pson[s] of the English yo[r] servants by beatings, bindings, continuall shootings at their boats wth great ordin: bilborizing them, threaten-ing to cutt their throats'.[118] Other factors commented on Dutch efforts to prevent the local people from trading with the English, something the *Clove* had experienced first-hand on her voyage to Japan, and Dutch unpopularity with the locals, which Cocks had mentioned.[119] Jourdain would have repeated many of these allega-tions and comments before the Court.

In 1617 the Dutch became more obdurate in the quarrel over the herring fisheries and relations between the two countries more strained. Secretary Winwood predicted that because of 'the grie-vances, which our merchants of the East India Company daily do suffer by the intolerable insolencies of their people trading in those parts...an open breach will e'er long ensue between his Majesty's kingdom and their provinces' if no remedies were found.[120] How-ever, the breach did not take place in Europe, it occurred in the

Indies, a more convenient location for a war. In the heady atmosphere of 1618, Keeling's quite different proposal to avert hostilities, a division of the Indies 'twixt both nacons in wch case I think y^t ye moluccas & bandas were whollie left them, Bantam, Japon & ye coast of Coromandell free to both, Zuratt and the wholl Ile of Sumatra sollie to o^r nacon', was brushed aside.[121] The Court, encouraged by Jourdain's assertion that the Dutch would not put up a fight, decided to proceed with its claims in the Spice Islands, overruling the views of a minority of directors who believed that the pursuit of an agreement with the Dutch was still preferable. Preparations for the dispatch of a fleet went ahead.[122]

The idea of appointing a single commander in charge of both naval and commercial operations, as Keeling and previous commanders had been, was dropped. On reflection, Jourdain, inexperienced in naval matters, was considered unsuitable for such a position and with a lack of adequately qualified candidates the Court wooed Thomas Best for the post of commander of the fleet. There were reservations that 'he would nott be rulde, beinge ungratefull, covetous and prowde' and would make the Company pay for his service but the directors were in 'noe doubt butt if his private trade can be changed, hee is the most sufficyent man in the kingdome for this service'. Best, aware of his bargaining power, held out for generous terms, making demands for musicians, trumpeters and '2 suites of apparel', presumably envisaging quasi-diplomatic status for himself, a status which was not necessarily so frivolous and vain as the directors imagined. In the end, however, he overplayed his hand and the Court was unwilling to give in to his demands. Best was dropped and Sir Thomas Dale, the former governor of Virginia who had seen service in the Netherlands, appointed in his place. Jourdain, with an augmented salary, was made 'principall agent', although he was given the authority 'to give direccions to whatt places the shipps shall be employed and soe comand and direct as principall agent for merchandizing'. Dale was to have 'command of the shipps and men', an ambiguous division of duties which led to conflict later at Bantam. Jourdain was also instructed to go in person as 'chiefe marchant to the Moluccaes'.[123] Implicit in this last instruction was an abandonment of the plan for a systematic reorganisation of the southwards factories along the lines proposed in 1615. It had been overambitious and had been greeted with scepticism at Bantam. Ball considered it impractical, informing the Company in January 1618 that the plan for 'quarteryinge the Indies, creatinge of Consulls, Agents, Directors and Councellors' was 'worthy & may (when you shall haue able men to pforme such places) be putt in execution, but at present the number of factors are so fewe & so young in experience that they must of necessity learne before they take vpon them to teach others'.[124]

If the English Company was divided over the most appropriate policy to adopt *vis-à-vis* the rival company so too was the VOC. A number of the VOC's most senior and able servants in the Indies believed that whatever the rights and wrongs of the issues between the two companies, confrontation was best avoided. The Dutch admiral, Steven van der Hagen, believed that the VOC lacked the resources to take on the English as well as the Spanish and Portuguese, a realistic appraisal underscored by Lam's poor showing before Manila in 1617. The Heren XVII themselves sent ambiguous orders to their servants in the Indies which betrayed reluctance and hesitation to order hostile action against the English. This infuriated Laurens Reael who was not inclined to shoulder the responsibility for starting hostilities against the English company without clear instructions from his superiors. Moreover, both he and Van Hagen were less inclined to pursue a policy that bore down heavily on the native populations whose rulers had signed treaties with the Dutch, usually under the threat of force. The treaties were oppressive and in Van Hagen's view only encouraged the population to break them and trade with the English whenever possible. Jan Pietersz Coen, on the contrary, was not at all ambivalent, nor indecisive. Instinctively he did not tend towards compromise nor was he reluctant to apply force either against the English or the native producers of spices and the Chinese middlemen in the pepper trade. Like Albuquerque before him Coen dreamt of dominion. He deprecated the treaties ('There is nothing in the world that gives one a better right than power and force added to right') and held that the English rather than the Iberians were the real threat to the VOC in the Indies. Ironically, just as some of the English were impressed by what they saw as Dutch supremacy in shipping and manpower in the Indies, Coen believed that the English company was stronger. Coen's hand in the Indies was strengthened by the departure of Van Hagen and Reael for Europe in March 1619 and his own elevation to the governor generalship. The ambiguities and lack of clarity in Dutch policy at this time serve as a reminder that the Dutch were far from being the relentless, confident builders of a commercial empire in the Indies that they are sometimes pictured as. The VOC had its share of policy disputes and personality conflicts. If, as Professor Kristof Glaman rightly says, 'Dutch expansion was not only commercial, but also a political and military action against the Iberians' (and, one would add, at times against the English as well), the two objectives were not always compatible nor executed in perfect harmony.[125] By February 1618, when Dale and Jourdain sailed from England, hostilities between the two companies had already broken out in the Bandas (in early 1617) over the English presence on Run. Regardless of Reael's penchant for compromise and negotiation, relations grew steadily worse as the year wore on.[126] If the English were spoiling for a fight with the Hollanders, Coen was the man to give them one. Warfare between the two companies lasted until April 1620 when news of the accords, signed at Westminster on 7 July 1619, reached the Indies. The Dutch captured eleven ships, including one outward from England loaded with silver supplies and the English were only able to capture one Dutch ship. In addition the English house at Jacarta was burned by the Dutch.[127] However, in February 1618, as the *Advice* lay in Kōchi awaiting favourable winds to carry her to Bantam, the prospect of war was impossible to conceive. Cocks had delayed her departure on the 20th so that provisions left behind in Hirado could be fetched and to enable Specx to write a letter to Governor General Coen which he entrusted to Wickham to be carried on the *Advice*, and then forwarded from Bantam. Wickham had even offered to load some goods belonging to the Dutch but Specx, remembering the trouble this had caused before, politely declined.[128]

English energies in Hirado were still directed towards the country trade, not to preparations for war. On 2 January, the *Sea Adventure*, refitted and victualled at a cost of 1,330 taels 3 candereen, had finally put to sea for Siam with a cargo worth 3,374 taels 1 mas 5 candereen in bullion, 3 taels 7 mas 9 candereen in strings of cuttlefish and 461 taels 8 mas 1 3/4 candereen in goods (India cloth, Japanese armour and weaponry and small amounts of paper and fans). In response to a request from the headman of the *nihonmachi* in Ayuthia, a man whom Cocks was anxious to cultivate because of the assistence he was able to give the Company, three Japanese were sent along. There had been problems with the Japanese crew over the number of passengers (that is, merchants) permitted on board. The Japanese officers with the backing of Matsūra Shigetada, the senior *bugyō*, each insisted on carrying two passengers according to *shuinsen* practice, but Cocks, determined to cut down on voyage costs and in particular on the freight the Japanese crew and passengers brought back, was adamant that passengers should not go. He had to make concessions as a sweetener. A backhander was given to the boatswain and a loan of 150 taels to the crew, interest free if they created no trouble on the voyage, to invest in goods. If they mutinied they were to be fined 300 taels. Should they decide not to buy cargo for themselves they were to let the Company use the space, for which it would pay them freightage but under no circumstances was anyone else to be permitted to take up any available space. The crew accepted although there was a last-minute attempt to smuggle passengers aboard which was foiled by Eaton.[129] Ways of reducing if not terminating English dependence on Japanese crews in the country trade had been under consideration since the 1615–16 voyage to Siam when Farie had criticised Adams for allowing the crew to load what they liked on the *Sea Adventure* for the return voyage to Hirado.[130] Cocks and his colleagues had complained to the Matsūra about the matter but they sided with the 'brabling knaues', as Cocks styled the crew, and sent men to observe the unloading and ensure that the crew received their due. Adams also supported the crew, much to Cocks's chagrin. However, as a *shuinsen* operator himself, he was more familiar with Japanese practice. Cocks was astonished by Adams's 'extraordinary humour' in siding with 'villains that have cozened the company' and judged his refusal to support the factory in its protest to the Matsūra as tantamount to betrayal. He confided his frustration to his diary: 'I take God to witnes I do what I can to keepe in w'th this man.' However, the difficulties were not the one-sided product Cocks suggests. Around September 1618 Konomi Seikichirō wrote to Osterwick offering his services on the next overseas voyage to be undertaken by the English. The letter is polite and friendly and refers quite specifically to a contract of employment. The author was no 'brabling knave'. Many of the problems the Hirado factory encountered with its Japanese crews were the result of misunderstanding and poor communication.[131]

One solution to the problem was to cut back on the number of Japanese officers and for this reason Eaton was sent as commander, James Burges as pilot and a third Englishman as steersman on the *Sea Adventure*'s new voyage. Another was for the factory itself to send factors as passengers on *shuinsen* and Chinese vessels as had been the case on the 1617 voyage to Cochinchina. Cocks suggested such a procedure for Siam voyages in his letters to Bantam and the Company in February 1618. Such a policy he argued would cut costs by eliminating the need to give presents to the Siamese king and court officials. He overlooked the point that presents were a way of purchasing good will and that while *shuinsen* were unlikely to be attacked by the Dutch for fear of Japanese reprisals, they were open to attack from others who had no connection with Japan. Besides, *shuinsen* voyages to Ayuthia were not numerous, unlike those to Cochinchina. While Cocks did not favour using English shipping in the country trade, the Company did and in June 1614 had ordered the construction of two small vessels of between 80 and 100 tons specifically for the trade. The directors had even criticised Cocks for buying the *Sea Adventure*. This was unfair. On past experience, the factory could not depend on regular arrivals of any English ships, great or small. In Cocks's view English shipping was unsuitable for the country trade because the crew remained on pay even when there was no voyage and would be a charge to the factory if they stayed in Japan between voyages. At least the crew of the *Sea Adventure* was seasonal and could be paid off after the completion of a voyage. Cocks had other ideas for co-ordinating the country trade between Bantam, Patani, Ayuthia and Hirado, suggesting that while trade between Hirado and Ayuthia could be conducted on junks, ships coming to Japan from Bantam should call at Patani. There they should discharge Coromandel cloth, which was 'as good as money' in Ayuthia, Cambodia and Champa (he based this opinion on Ayuthia's request for the shipment of any surplus India cloth in the Hirado stock), and take on pepper, wax and other suitable goods for Japan as well as Siamese silver. This he argued was freely available and finer than Japanese silver and could be taken back to Bantam together with the proceeds from sales of silk and other goods in Japan.[132]

Cocks was trying to spread the burden of responsibility implicit in the Company's strategy for the Hirado factory and restated in letters recently received, thereby hoping to shake off criticism of the Hirado factory's own lack of success to date. (Attempting to deflect possible charges of mismanagement was not unique to the Hirado factory; the Ayuthia factory had complained to Cocks that Hirado's failure to give advance warning of when cargoes from Japan could be expected in order for Ayuthia to buy up goods had led to a loss of £1,000 in the trading season 1616–17, a charge which Cocks dismissed as foolish.) But Cocks's views on the country trade were poorly thought out. Silver had been mined in Siam since the fifteenth century and manufactured into ticulls, or small balls of a stamped, fixed weight, but Siam's output was easily dwarfed by that of Japan and the Peruvian mines. Even had it been commercially worthwhile to export silver from Siam, the folly of running additional risks by sending bullion from Siam to Japan and then back down to Bantam did not occur to Cocks. The Dutch were more fortunate in their country trade with Ayuthia to the extent that the captured Portuguese junk that they used for the voyage to carry silver, copper, iron, weaponry and luxury goods from Hirado was seaworthy. But even then their results were patchy and it was not until much later in the century that the VOC was better placed to exploit the potential of the trade more fully.[133] The English factory in Hirado remained burdened by misfortune in its efforts to participate in the country trade from Japan.

Cocks had not remained to see the *Advice* put to sea but had gone down to Nagasaki. There he helped Sayers and Robert Hawley prepare for a new voyage to Cochinchina as passengers in a junk owned by a Nagasaki merchant, Shiquan, which after some delay put to sea on 17 March. Adams had been engaged as captain, the reason he gave for declining a passage to England on the *Advice*.[134] The cargo is unknown but its value was certainly far less than the figure of 200,000 taels Cocks mentioned in letters to the Court and the Bantam presidency as being insufficient to procure the silk available in Annam if an English ship were used on the voyage.[135]

Meanwhile, the saga of the China trade continued to unfold. Cocks had received two letters from James I to the Chinese emperor, one friendly in tone, the other threatening. These he had translated into Chinese, presumably from English to Portuguese to Japanese and finally to Chinese. The letters had been brought on the *Advice* from Bantam where the Chinese had refused to translate them, preferring to have nothing to do with them because they were offensive and could cost them or their relatives in China their lives. Cocks ridiculed Ball for accepting these excuses, saying that the Li did not balk at translating the letters although Li Tan recommended that the friendlier letter be sent. However, the Chinese who resided in or traded with Bantam were no more able than the Li to present such letters at Peking even had they wanted to. Their refusal was almost certainly triggered by an instinctive desire to preserve their own trade from English competition. Li Tan was content to play Cocks along. In June he informed the cape merchant that the letter and a covering note by Cocks had been received 'by the noble men in China in good p'rte' and that a mandarin was soon to come from China about the request and to lodge a complaint with the shogunate over the continued Dutch presence in Japan despite their attacks on Chinese shipping. This was complete nonsense; no diplomatic relations existed between the two empires.[136]

The voyages to Siam and Cochinchina both failed, the weather in the East China Sea proving extremely bad. Sayers, Hawley and Adams returned to Hirado, via Nagasaki, on 14 May with the cargo intact. The junk had made it as far as Amami Ōshima to the north of Ryūkyū with a damaged rudder and it was debated whether to proceed to Naha for refitting and to procure a new rudder or whether to abandon the voyage and return to Hirado. Adams finally decided on the latter course. The expenses were listed as 165 taels 3 mas 6 1/2 candereen.[137] The *Sea Adventure* had had troubles quite apart from the stormy weather, and, in a repeat of her first voyage, managed to reach Ryūkyū. This time the reception was good. Eaton decided to remain there, refit and catch the next monsoon for Siam. Cocks, anticipating such a decision, wrote to him by means of Satsuma officials, ordering him to load wheat and return to Hirado (Sayers wrote to him with similar advice from Amami Ōshima), but Eaton, if he received the letters, chose to ignore the orders. He remained at Naha, paying out 500 taels for repairs to the *Sea*

Adventure, before proceeding to Siam. This was another tempestuous voyage. The *Sea Adventure*'s mast broke and near Hainan the hull was found to be taking in some 9 feet of water. Fortunately, the pumps coped with the inundation and disaster was avoided. The *Sea Adventure* reached Ayuthia at the end of December. Eaton judged that this time she was well beyond repair and decided to dispose of her. The sails, cables, cordage and ship's stores that were salvaged from her were rated at 282 taels of Siam and a replacement junk of 250 tons was purchased for 990 taels of Siam (1,584 taels in Japanese reckoning) and later sold in Hirado for 3,100 taels.[138] The *Sea Adventure* had cost £1,000 but through her leaky hull alone much of the factory's precious capital had drained.

These voyages were not the only overseas investments at this time. Li Tan had urged Cocks to invest 1,000 or 2,000 taels in voyages to Taiwan or Takasago as the Japanese called it. Until the early seventeenth century Taiwan, which was not then a part of the Chinese empire, had been a destination mainly for Chinese fishermen and merchants (attempting to sell their goods to the aborigines) and wakō. There had not been much settlement. Peaceful Japanese traders had also gone there and Taiwan was one of the destinations authorised by Hideyoshi's *shuinjō*. Hideyoshi sought to make the island a tributary vassal of Japan and in 1593 sent an envoy to demand submission, an impossible demand as there was no central authority to speak on behalf of the aborigines. In the 1610s, however, Taiwan was emerging as an important emporium in east Asian trade and increasingly as a strategically located island in the geopolitics of the region. (Ieyasu had authorised an expedition in 1609 to find out why Taiwan had not sought official relations, unlike Cambodia or Siam, and in 1616 permitted Murayama Tōan to attempt a conquest, which failed.)[139] Li Tan and other Chinese from Japan traded with junks from the mainland. Li reported that silk was available in Taiwan at half the price in Bantam or Cochinchina. The prospect was attractive but Cocks was worried about the risk of attack from Dutch ships prowling the seas for Chinese prey. Overcoming his qualms, he finally invested 600 taels which was returned (less 100 taels) in August because no shipping had come across the straits from China. The Li, with the encouragement of the Matsūra and the bakufu, continued their trade and almost half of the *shuinjō* issued to the Li were for Taiwan.[140]

The Hirado factory had received a trifling amount of goods in 1618: calambac (aloes wood), silk and fish skins together costing 272 taels 2 mas from Ayuthia, sent on a Dutch vessel (freightage was extra). The silk, weighing 68 1/2 catties (although invoiced as 71 1/2 catties) cost 115 taels 4 mas. At least it made a profit for Cocks reported that the sale price of silk at Kyoto was 300 taels per pecul. However, the amount was negligible in comparison with the silk brought on the four Portuguese galliots which arrived at about the same time.[141] A small amount of wax was also received from Cambodia, brought by two Japanese junks belonging to Jan Joosten. This was in return for some fowling pieces sent from Cochinchina the previous year by Sayers, but there was no word of the state of the factory there.[142]

In comparison with the performance of the English factory, the figures for Dutch trade with Japan in 1618 look impressive. However, this is only superficially so. The tendency of the VOC factory in Hirado to import plunder captured from Chinese vessels which was brought to Japan and then mostly re-exported is much more striking. The Dutch brought *f.* 615,333 14st 5p worth of Chinese goods to Hirado, captured from seven junks, but sent more than half of these goods (*f.* 352,309 8st 9p) and another *f.* 218,917 13st 7p worth of money and Japanese goods on to Coen, who was pleased to receive them. Of the latter sum, *f.* 204,000 consisted of silver and reals, *f.* 7,486 16st 10p of camphor and the rest of lacquer-ware (chests and tables), weaponry, building materials and foodstuffs. (Specx added an extra 800 reals as a subvention for the 'Church of the Indies'.) The silk and camphor were sent back to the Netherlands where, as has been mentioned, raw silk was judged more profitable to sell than in Japan. The same pattern is evident in Dutch trade in 1617 after the arrival of Lam's fleet. At least 69 per cent of the captured raw silk brought by Lam's ships was re-exported. The extent and importance of the VOC's Hirado factory as an entrepôt especially for silk shipments can be gauged from the composition of VOC cargoes sent from Bantam to the Netherlands in 1617 and 1618. In those years the value of the goods sent from Hirado, essentially the plunder from the China Seas, was second only to that of the goods assembled in Bantam and far in excess of those brought from Patani or the Coromandel Coast. However, in terms of cracking the Japanese market, the Dutch remained no more successful than the English and the Governor General was growing impatient. On 25 October 1617, echoing the comments of his predecessor, Reynst, Coen wrote to the Heren XVII that the VOC's Japan trade was one 'of false hope without realisation' and urged his employers to follow the recommendation of the Council of the Indies and terminate it to prevent more good money being thrown after bad. Silk, he argued, could be acquired from Portuguese and Chinese shipping without the cost of maintaining a factory in Japan. (Camps had argued as much from Hirado in October 1616.) But Coen was overlooking one key point. At the end of January 1616 the shogunate had warned the Dutch and the English (who were in no position to contemplate attacking the Portuguese) to let the náo pass freely 'for that the Emperour had much adventure in her'.[143]

Fortunately for the Dutch, Coen's advice was not pursued and Coen later changed his mind about the value of the Japan trade to the VOC. Nevertheless, given the Heren XVII's continuing enthusiasm for Chinese raw silk imports to feed the Amsterdam market the interesting possibility arises that in the absence of Persian silk imports to the Netherlands from the 1620s the Heren XVII might have been forced to choose between bringing all available Chinese silk to Amsterdam rather than supplying the Japanese market as well – not enough Chinese raw silk was available to the VOC to supply both – in which case they might have decided to follow Coen's earlier advice and close the Hirado factory.[144] The consequences of such a move for the development of Japan's overseas trade and its relations with the West are fascinating to contemplate. There was nothing inevitable about the eventual VOC success in Japan any more than there was about failure for the English company.

As the year progressed, Cocks grew increasingly restless and weary. He was troubled, even somewhat paranoid, by the aspersions cast upon his reputation by 'ill wilers wch goe About to bring me in disgrace'. He mentioned Ball in particular and accused him of detaining his accounts in Bantam 'only upon Spleene & not for any default' in them. He believed Ball had doctored his accounts to make him seem 'less then a pore man' but Cocks was confident his many friends in England would speak out in support of him.[145] Cocks had informed the Company of his wish to return home and scotch the allegations personally. Indeed the tone of his letters is remarkably similar to that of his last couple of years in Bayonne when he was worn down and alarmed by the implications of his suit to recover debts. Wickham, free of the responsibility of the cape merchant's position, had calculated that he had milked the Japan trade of all he could and that it was time to enjoy the benefits, although in a letter to his mother he stressed filial duty, and promised to return home within three years. He already had Saris's permission to leave Japan and hoped to secure the Company's permission to return home from Bantam thereby releasing him 'out of the labyrinth and thraldom of General Saris' and others disgraces'. He promised to speak of the 'many disorders and wrongs offered by many within these few years, to the great hindrance of the East India trade and dishonour of our nation by men of divers faculties employed in the best and meanest places'.[146]

This was the spiteful, intemperate voice of thwarted ambition. His death at Bantam deprived him of the opportunity to release his venom and reap the fruits of his private trade. Cocks had no such easy choice as Wickham. He could take some comfort from the most recent letters from the Company, brought on the *Advice*, which supported the overall direction of his management of the factory, especially his efforts to secure access to China and participation in the country trade. However, both he and the other factors could only wring their hands in desperation at the directors' wish 'to be advized we could make dispach of greate quantety of Broad Cloth in these parts'.[147] Moreover, the efforts to break into the country trade were still producing headaches and on present form the returns did not justify the investment. Cocks's heart was no longer in the job. His undiminished optimism about the China trade and his belief that he was central to that project provided some antidote to counter frustration; but the China trade offered hope and nothing more as yet. In some respects, especially the companionship of consorts, life may have been comfortable in Hirado, but if the Company had sent a ship with orders to withdraw the factory in 1618, Cocks and the other factors would have complied willingly. As it was the factory just kept ticking over.

The twenty-three months from August 1618 to July 1620 mark the nadir of the Hirado factory's fortunes. Not only was business bad but the warfare between the English company and the VOC in the Indies spilt over to Japan, disrupting the factory's affairs and also threatening the physical well-being of its personnel as well. Cocks's proud boasts to the daimyo of Hirado that England was a more powerful nation than the Netherlands and that the latter owed their independence to English assistance and continued English patronage were shown to be empty. The claims would not have meant much to his audience anyway.[148]

Anglo-Dutch rivalry in the Spice Islands was of course familiar enough to the factors at Hirado. Those who had come on the *Clove* had experienced it first-hand, but in Japan, regardless of their commercial rivalry, the factors of the two nations had had to live in close proximity. Good neighbourly relations led them to carry each other's letters. The English occasionally charged the Dutch with opening sealed letters (more routine information was sent in open letters) and although there is no evidence to incriminate Cocks and his associates at Hirado of indulging in similar practices these cannot be ruled out absolutely.[149] The English and Dutch reciprocated with presents on the arrival of their respective ships. Cocks was even censured by Jourdain for allowing the Dutch to ship 800 peculs of ebony wood on the *Hosiander* in 1616 as a substitute ballast for stones which were off-loaded at Dutch expense even if freightage was to be charged on the ship's arrival at Bantam. Specx wrote to Jourdain expressing his regret that Cocks's action had met with disapproval and offered the English similar concessions in future. But Ball in his catalogue of attacks on Cocks called the incident 'a haynos offence' and ignored the fact that carriage had been approved by the other merchants at Hirado, including Coppindale.[150] Noticing examples of petty rivalry over status (for example, who should be introduced first to the daimyo of Satsuma on his visits to Hirado), the Japanese were inclined to believe that the two companies 'were frendes but from the tooth outward & not cordially, as neighbours ought to be'. Cocks's reply to this observation of Matsūra Nobutoki in July 1617, appeared to give confirmation. Cocks contrasted 'the mighty and powerfull governm't of the king of England' with 'ther small state govend by a couty [committee]'.[151] As with the Spanish and Portuguese before them, the English and Dutch carried their rivalries overseas. On the whole, however, language problems notwithstanding, relations between the factors of the two companies were generally amicable. Specx wrote to Coen at the beginning of March 1618 that the Dutch were 'good friends' with the English especially singling out Wickham.[152]

News of the confrontation in the Bandas had already reached Hirado in June 1618 and was made known to Cocks by a handful of Englishmen serving under the Dutch in Lam's fleet. Cocks reported to the Company that the Dutch had called James I 'startman' and had whipped the Company's employees on 'their back sides' with their own colours.[153] Any hope that the cordial relations with Lam and the shared grievances over the curtailment of their trading privileges would enable Hirado to remain isolated from the hostilities elsewhere in the Indies was shattered on 9 August 1618 when two Dutch ships escorted the English ship *Attendance* into Hirado 'in a bravado & shot affe many gvns out of her, and out of their other two.'[154]

The daimyo refused to grant Cocks's request for a Japanese official to accompany him in an attempt to board the ship to demand the reason for her seizure. The Dutch in Hirado seem to have been as surprised as the English at this turn of events. Specx came to the English house 'offering the ship & what was in her at my [Cocks's] comand'. Cocks took this as an empty gesture believing that her cargo had already been discharged and rejected the offer. Inevitably tempers were lost. Cocks charged that 'yor m'rsters comand yow to comvne theevs'. Specx, calmer, replied that 'hitherto they had held frendshipp with vs, & still would do, till their comanders gaue them order to the contrary & then they would doe as they thought good'.[155] Cocks had had no intention of accepting Specx's offer anyway for he had made up his mind to go to Edo 'to aske justice against the Hollanders'. To accept custody of the *Attendance* was therefore out of the question. Cocks hoped that representatives of the Chinese with their own grievances against the Dutch would accompany him in this mission but they chose not to. On 10 August Cocks, Sayers, Nealson and Osterwick held a council. It was decided that Cocks and Nealson should proceed to Edo 'to complain against the insolentie of the Hollanders in pr'suming not only to take our ships, but openly to bring them in to our disgrace'. The visit was also to be used as a pretext to transact such business as could be undertaken, to collect outstanding debts, and to bring down any stock remaining in Edo. Adams, who had already left for Edo with a Dutch party in July, was to be contacted and asked as a gesture of solidarity 'to retyre hym selfe from them' and not to go before the shogun on their behalf.[156]

Cocks and Nealson left Hirado on 23 August. They took along fowling pieces, broadcloth, calambac and silk as presents. *En route* to Osaka, Cocks received a letter from Adams. Adams took exception to the earlier letter claiming he was no longer a servant of the Company nor at its beck and call. He advised Cocks not to proceed to Edo and make an issue of the dispute with the Dutch. Cocks felt slighted and questioned Adams's loyalty complaining that he was 'altogether Holandized'. But Adams was simply being realistic. No matter how sensitive they were about their national pride, the English would not be treated any differently from the Spanish, Portuguese or Chinese who had all suffered similar depredations at the hands of the Dutch yet had had their suits dismissed by the shogunate without redress. Nevertheless, Adams, confounding Cocks's suspicions, performed his usual chore of regularly lobbying court officials and requesting a hearing to present a petition (drawn up by a Japanese scribe) on behalf of the English.

The comet that shot across the Edo sky at the beginning of November was not auspicious and as on earlier occasions a dispute between foreign traders was well to the bottom of the agenda of concerns confronting the *rōjū* who in October were visiting Tōshō-gū, the shinto shrine in Nikkō where Ieyasu had been interred in 1617 and deified as Tōshō Daigongen (the great Incarnation, or Avatar, of the East) and which became the focus of a cult from the 1630s. Again Cocks suspected malice on the part of the Matsūra and judged that there were factions within the household, with the daimyo's brother favouring the English while his secretary, Momo-no Tarōzaemon, favoured the Dutch. It would be understandable if there had been partiality towards the Dutch: they had more booty at their disposal and could afford to be more generous with their presents than the English. But the Matsūra were not intent on losing business by driving out the English. Fuelled by these suspicions and the memory of past difficulties with the Matsūra, Cocks tried to secure permission for English shipping to call at Nagasaki. He was unaware that such permission had already been granted, in the *rōjū*'s notification to the various daimyo in September 1616 of the restrictions placed upon English trade in Japan, although one suspects that for obvious reasons the Matsūra had not been keen to pass on this information. However, it was reconfirmed.[157]

Cocks did not secure an audience with the shogun although he was requested to deliver a present to Iemitsu, Hidetada's eldest son. At least the English were considered important enough to play a role, if minor, in the politics of establishing Tokugawa legitimacy. Finally an answer to the English complaint against the Dutch was given (when is not clear). The *rōjū* washed their hands of it and referred it to the Matsūra 'to heare both parties & see justis p'rformed. Yet from that tyme till now, there is nothing donne, although I [Cocks] haue divers tymes very instantly desired it of the kinge, whose best answer I eaver could gett was, that the Hollanders hadd kild no Englishman, but a Japonar, his owne vassale [in a dispute], w'ch yf he were content to pardon, what hadd I to doe therw'th?'[158] The shogunate did not want to involve itself in other men's disputes if these did not affect Japanese or impinge upon matters pertaining to bakufu authority.

Of more concern to the *rōjū*, because it did impinge on that authority, were problems concerning a *shuinjō* issued to Cocks for the voyage to Cochinchina in 1617 which he had sold to Li Tan and Skydayen, a local Hirado trader and entrepreneur who had served as captain on the *Sea Adventure* on its 1616 voyage, for 1,200 taels (the price included Adams's discarded junk). The sale breached the procedure that *shuinjō* were not transferable and should be returned after the particular voyage for which they had been issued. Without Cocks's knowledge, the *shuinjō* had been resold first to Sagawa Nobutoshi who then disposed of it to another individual for 300 taels to undertake a voyage to Cochinchina. The shogunate knew about the transfers because the crew had become involved in disorders in Annam (according to Cocks they had attacked Chinese junks; if so, it was not the first time that the intractable Japanese had caused problems in Annam as Sayers knew from his own voyage). As a result, the king of Annam had written to the bakufu demanding that the intractable Japanese diaspora be compelled to submit to the authority of a Japanese headman. The *rōjū* did not suspect English complicity in the disorders but the investigations into what happened at Annam created delays in the issuing of a new *shuinjō* to Cocks for a voyage to Tongking, and Cocks left for Hirado on 18 November with the matter still pending. Eventually, through the intercession of Chaya Shirojirō, one of the leading Kyoto merchants and himself a *shuinsen* merchant with excellent connections at the shogunal court, the *shuinjō* was obtained and sent down to Hirado. Chaya emphasised that it should only be used for Tongking, the specified destination of the voyage, and was not to be given to anyone else.[159] This did not stop Cocks from attempting to transfer a *shuinjō* issued to Adams for Specx's use in 1621. Chaya, one of Cocks's infamous 'rich men', would not have performed this valuable service if he and his associates were intent on monopolising Japan's overseas trade as Cocks imagined.

Cocks had achieved little although his visit prompted the *rōjū* to address a letter to Matsūra Takanobu and Hasegawa Gonroku, the Nagasaki *daikan*, reminding them that Christianity was strictly forbidden in Japan and that extra care was to be taken to ensure no further diffusion of the pernicious doctrine. The letter reiterated that English ships were permitted to call at both Hirado and Nagasaki.[160] Over the next couple of years Cocks grew increasingly bitter about the factory's relations with the Matsūra. By March 1620 he firmly believed that the factory should be moved to Nagasaki and in his letters to England even suggested (plausibly) that he had secured permission from the *daikan* and had been offered a plot of land on which to build a new house. He argued that Nagasaki would be less expensive in terms of presents than Hirado, having only the *daikan* to satisfy and not the daimyo and his household who 'are allwaies borowing and buying, but sildom or neaver make payment, except it be the king [daimyo] hym selfe'. Moreover, Nagasaki had a bigger, safer, and more easily navigable harbour than Hirado. The suppression of Christianity and the final destruction of the churches and desecration of Christian burial places also favoured such a move, although Cocks added that 'I doe not reioyce herein, but wil all Japon were Christians'; only the banishment of the Jesuits and friars meant that the English could walk the streets without being called 'Lutranos & herejos'.[161] However, the factory remained in Hirado. The Matsūra would not have let the English transfer so easily no matter what encouragement was forthcoming from Hasegawa Gonroku in Nagasaki. Besides, the sums which the Matsūra borrowed from the English and Dutch served as a kind of security to ensure that the companies remained in Hirado. The Dutch factors in Hirado rehearsed similar arguments when they contemplated moving their factory to Nagasaki in 1627. They also found that it was not so simple to escape from the Matsūra and the idea was dropped, although it was suggested on other occasions in the 1630s but failed to win the approval of the governor general.[162]

Cocks and Nealson, who had not helped his consumption by sitting 'in his shert & gowne 2 or 3 howres...on the top of the house' to marvel at the spectacle of a fire in Edo and as a result had developed a fever and a 'bloody fflix', left Edo on 18 November. They travelled down the Tōkaidō to Kyoto, arriving on the 30th, moving on to Osaka and finally leaving the Kinai for Hirado on 21

December, reaching the factory on 8 January 1619. Another Edo
visit had turned out to be fruitless. The reason for the delay in the
Kinai was to enable Cocks to make an inventory of the goods
remaining there (remnants of broadcloth, bays, and 36 Muscovy
hides which had been left with Hiranoya). A few sales were made to
Cuemon. The broadcloth sold for between 10 1/2–14 1/2 taels per
tatami, the black cloth fetching the best price, and a barter deal of
broadcloth and bays in exchange for lacquer-ware to the value of 324
taels was concluded.[163]

In the new year relations with the Dutch deteriorated sharply. The
Hollanders taunted the English with insults, jibes and threats. The
VOC personnel in Hirado was augmented by the arrival of a fleet
of seven ships in October including the *Attendance*, renamed the
Vligende Boode, and the *Swan*, another English vessel captured in the
Bandas (the *Attendance* had been incorporated into the VOC fleet
prowling before Manila in 1618). Cocks alleged that the commander
of the Dutch fleet, Adam Westerwood, secretly offered a reward of
50 reals for anyone who assassinated him and put a price of 30 reals
on the heads of the other English.[164] Had this been carried out the
Dutch would have been in serious trouble with the shogunate; what
happened beyond Japan's littoral was one thing, but disorder within
Japan itself would not have been tolerated. The most serious incident
occurred after three Englishmen escaped from the English prize ships
and sought refuge in the English house. The Dutch demanded their
return, demonstrating in front of the house. Eventually a group of
Hollanders, whether acting on orders or not is unknown, broke into
the house and wounded John Coker. The English decided it was wise
to protect themselves and hired 'a gard of Japons, night and day,
armed, at meate, drink, & wages, to yor Wors. great charge'.[165]
Cocks and Specx were summoned before the daimyo and had to
swear in writing not to 'misvse' each other neither 'in word nor
deed'. This was not an act of sympathy with the English plight on
the part of the Matsūra. They wanted to stamp out disorder. In
August 1619 Cocks again went up to Edo to protest against Dutch
harrassment 'and to demand justice'. He got nowhere. The *rōjū*'s
concern remained the maintenance of order for which they held the
Matsūra accountable.

Yet the reality of these years was almost certainly not as desperate
as Cocks painted it. In his letters he was condensing events which
took place over two years, highlighting the drama of what remained
vivid in the memory. The 'storming' of the English house was
probably a case of men hardened by an overindulgence in alcohol
losing control. Petty intimidation and jeering were probably closer
to the norm and the Dutch would have quickly wearied of that. In
August while Cocks was on his trip to Edo, Eaton wrote that the

Dutch were 'quiett'.[166] It was in Cocks's and the other factors' interest to play up the danger, and project themselves as patient but fearless and dedicated stewards of the Company's affairs; thereby might lie preferment.

For their part the Dutch knew that harrassment had its limits before it invited reprisals from the Matsūra and ultimately the bakufu. Coen, usually unperturbed by such matters, was genuinely alarmed by the news he received from Hirado about the English protests to the shogunate. In January 1619, he expressed his concern to the Heren XVII that the protests, and those of the Portuguese, Spanish and Chinese before, were giving the shogunate the impression that the Dutch were not 'real merchants but more a gang of sea rovers', pillaging at will. He approved Specx's request that a good cargo of merchandise should be sent to Japan to convince the Japanese otherwise. A year later he was still fuming about the English complaints, fearing that they might result in the Japanese cutting off sales of victuals to the Dutch. Coen was determined to procure a copy of the English charges to publicise the English 'calamunies' to the world.[167] Unknown to the governor general, the Spanish in Manila, sensing a chance to strike back diplomatically at the enemy, advocated stepping up their protests against the Dutch to the bakufu with the aim of having the VOC expelled from Japan, thus depriving the Hollanders of what the Iberians believed was an important supply base for their activities in the Spice Islands.[168]

Commercially, however, the English factory's affairs could only be painted in bleak colours. The junk Eaton had bought to return from Siam had been sold because the factory could not afford to set out another voyage.[169] Eaton had brought back 2,100 peculs of sappan wood, 300 peculs of lead, 950 deer hides, 920 leach skins and smaller amounts of oil nuts, betel nuts and hemp from Ayuthia.[170] The factory's stock was increased marginally by the addition of 7 1/2 peculs of white Nanking silk, 450 catties of yellow Cochinchina silk, 143 pieces of cheremies, and smaller amounts of silk fabric brought back by Sayers from Cochinchina.[171] The factory also received 4 peculs 20 catties of yellow silk from its investment of 700 taels in a *shuinsen* voyage to Tongking on which Adams had gone.[172] However, sales were sluggish and prices poor. By March 1620 only 320 peculs of the sappan wood had been sold at 1 tael 8 mas 5 candareen per pecul (it had cost 8 mas 6 candareen per pecul). The hides sold for 24 taels per hundred, over double their cost of 10 taels 7 candareen per hundred. But overall, sales prices had dropped considerably in 1620. Nanking silk slipped from 300 taels in 1619 to 230 per pecul and other sorts by the same margin; sappan wood had dropped from 27 to 30 mas per pecul to 18, hides from 30 taels per hundred and fell further, below those paid for the stock brought back from Siam, to 18 mas and 20 taels respectively. The price of lead fell to 5 taels per pecul but Cocks managed to hold out for 5 1/2 taels for the lead which Eaton had brought from Siam (it had cost 3 taels 9 candareen).[173] The disasters which had befallen the Siam voyage and other incidental costs wiped out the profits from the sales in Japan. In business terms the situation had not remained static; it had become worse. It was hardly surprising that Cocks's letter of 10 March 1620 covers much the same ground as the letter sent on the *Advice* just over two years before. Once more he blamed the fall in prices on the notorious 'ruch vsurars', failing to distinguish yet again between *shuinsen* and *itowappu* merchants.[174] In September 1619 Eaton commented that he was at a loss to know how to generate income for the factory to pay its way. Such was the gloom that any talk of profits had ceased.[175]

To make matters worse the house's running costs had become inflated by the additional personnel stuck in Hirado. The supernumeraries included the prisoners who had escaped from the Dutch. Another three had been brought from Patani on the Dutch ship *Angell* on 12 September 1619, two of whom escaped with Adams's help. The third slipped away on his own.[176] Other newcomers to the factory included James Burges, who had been seconded from the *Advice* to go as pilot on the Siam voyage, and Robert Hawley, the surgeon on the *Advice*, who had stayed to attend the ailing master, George Totten and other individuals (the exact number is unknown) who had stayed behind from previous voyages. Some of these men had interesting *curricula vitae*. John Porteus, a Scot, had served the Spanish, arriving in Japan in 1618 when his ship was driven to Japan by foul weather. He had been sent to Spain as a child and had returned to England before leaving for Spain again, serving in the West Indies, New Spain and the Philippines. He was taken into the Company's service, unwaged.[177] Henry Shankes, another Scot who had served with the Spanish until his ship was forced to make landfall in Satsuma because of contrary winds, was a gunner by profession. He was left behind when the ship and its escort hastily left Japanese waters (the smaller of the two was driven back on to the coast but her crew was saved). Shankes was given asylum in the English house until the next Company vessel could take him home but he decided to stay, although not in the Company's employ. He sailed to Siam on one of Li Tan's junks and was still in Japan in 1621. His knowledge of Spanish was useful but he was a quarrelsome and violent person when drunk, on one occasion throwing a whore out of a window.[178] Thomas Hood had been in the Company's employ but, in the words of Cocks, 'vnbefitting a man of his ranck' he had deserted to the Portuguese and allegedly spent time in the Inquisition House at Goa before coming to Japan by way of Macao and rejoining his countrymen. He sought a passage home. The reference to detention in Goa could have been added to make what was otherwise a simple desertion less heinous in the eyes of the directors.[179]

To ease the burden on the budget of the house, a small junk of 50 tons was purchased for 430 taels and renamed the *Godspeed*, ostensibly to carry men to seek out the English fleet at Bantam or elsewhere and supply them with reinforcements and victuals. Fourteen Britons and nine Japanese sailors left from Nagasaki in March 1620 carrying meal, pork, beef, fish, gunpowder and shot to the value of 1,000 taels.[180] Sayers and John Coker went along, Sayers because he had been ordered out of Japan after an incident in which Eaton and Osterwick were attacked and beaten, without provocation according to Cocks, by servants of Sagawa Nobutoshi. Cocks protested about the attack to the daimyo, but was informed that Sayers had to leave Hirado for Nagasaki and from there Japan and that two of Sagawa's men were also to be banished. In vain Cocks complained of injustice, mentioning that the Dutch had killed a man during one of their contretemps with the English and had not been punished, but the daimyo refused to change his mind. The voyage of the *Godspeed* did not get very far. She missed the monsoon and had to return to Hirado. The order banishing Sayers was revoked.[181]

In March 1620 Nealson had finally died 'being wasted away w'th a consumption'. He died intestate but bequeathed all his possessions to Cocks, a man whom Nealson, on one of his many drunken binges, had called 'ould drunken asse'.[182] Two months later, on 16 May Adams also died. He had been terminally ill since the beginning of the year. His will was drawn up on the day of his death and Cocks and Eaton were made overseers. Half his estate he left to his wife and child in England and half to his son, Joseph, and daughter, Susanna, in Japan, with smaller bequests to various Japanese and English. Cocks sent £100 on the first available English ship, the *James Royal*, to England to be augmented by another £100 later for 'yt was not his mind his wife should have all, in regard she might marry an other hvsband & carry all from his childe'. On 8 October 1621 Mary Adams was made executrix of the will, the estate in England being valued at £165 9s 10d.[183] In his letter to the Company mentioning Adams's death Cocks commented that 'i canot but be sorofull for the losse of such a man as Capt. Wm. Adames was, he having byn in such favour w'th two Emperours of Japon as never was any Christian in these p'rtes of the worlde, & might freely haue entred & had speech w'th the emperours when many Japon kinges stood w'thout & could not be p'rmitted.'[184] It was a generous obituary considering the mistrust and acrimony that had soured relations over the previous seven years. But Cocks was overstating Adams's standing and

subsequently his historical importance has been distorted. Adams
was not a major player in the unfolding of early Tokugawa history;
his influence was at best marginal even if he did enjoy the respect of
the first shoguns. As Cocks noted 'this Emperour [Hidetada] hath
confermed the lordshipp to his sonne w'ch thother Emperour gaue
to the father'[185] and Joseph Adams became an established *shuinsen*
merchant in his own right, inheriting his father's familiar name in
Japan, *anjin*, pilot. For the English and Dutch he was helpful but not
indispensable to their business activity in Japan. The Dutch also had
the services of Van Santvoort and Jooosten at their disposal and both
men were unstinting in their work for the VOC. Adams's career was
not unique among the early Europeans in the Indies even if he did
manage to live a life that was more colourful and certainly more
financially rewarding than would have been the case had he remained
in England or returned from Japan.

   Finally, after two years of isolation, and at times physical danger,
it was with great relief that the members of the Hirado factory
greeted the arrival of the *James Royal* at Kōchi on 23 July 1620. The
commander, Martin Pring, brought news, 'wellcome. . . vnto vs that
live heare', of the Anglo-Dutch accord, concluded in London a year
before.[186]

CHAPTER 7

The Manila Voyages and Withdrawal from Japan

(i)   First Manila Voyage, 1620–1621

Had the factors of the two companies in the Indies any influence over the negotiations they would not have advocated the close co-ordination of the companies' activities envisaged in the accord. Coen for one would have preferred to continue applying force to drive the English out of the Spice Islands. Force was, after all, producing results. The English, lacking reinforcements and supplies from home, had taken a beating and while they welcomed peace they realised its limitations. But the reasons for the conclusion of the Anglo-Dutch accord were closely related to developments in Europe.

By 1618 the Twelve Years' Truce between the Dutch and the Spanish had only three more years to run. In the Netherlands the outcome of future negotiations over whether to renew or abrogate the truce was influenced by the coup of August 1618 in which Prince Maurice of Nassau was the prime mover.[1] Oldenbarnevelt was arrested and his supporters among the regent class ousted from the town councils of the republic. His fall and subsequent trial and execution removed the architect of the truce and one of the principal and most powerful advocates of a negotiated peace with Spain, even at the price of reducing or curtailing Dutch expansion overseas. In Spain, during the same month the Spanish architect of the truce, the Duke of Lerma, also fell from power and was replaced by Baltasar de Zuñiga, a critic of the truce.

The political demise of these two men increased the likelihood of renewed warfare. The Dutch economy had flourished during the truce. Amsterdam had replaced Antwerp as the conduit for trade between northern and southern Europe and the Dutch were contemplating expansion in the West Indies. Iberian critics of the truce, alarmed by such military and economic threats to Spain and her empire, were determined to fight back. There was little room for compromise. Nevertheless, both sides made efforts to prevent renewed warfare. The slim chances of a successful conclusion were further undermined by developments elsewhere in Europe, particularly the Bohemian revolt (against the authority of the Habsburg Holy Roman Emperor in Bohemia) in May 1618 posing yet another, and perhaps the most serious, challenge to Habsburg power in Europe. Victory for the rebels raised the possibility of a Protestant domination of the Empire. Such fears were put to rest with the Habsburg victory at the battle of the White Mountain in November 1620 in which the Bohemians and their allies were defeated. Even if this success did nothing to solve the German question (it was only one of the opening battles of the more general conflict, the Thirty Years War), the victory boosted Spanish confidence, steeled their resolve and swung the government against the idea of permitting the truce with the Dutch to continue. There was no longer any intention of trying to crush the republic, whose existence was now recognised *de facto*; rather the aim was to contain it and weaken Dutch ability and resolve to assist the enemies of the Habsburgs and to prevent the Dutch from making further inroads into Spain's overseas empire. As one of Philip III's generals, Luis de Velasco, Marquis de Beldever, wrote from Flanders, war would enable Spain 'to force them [the Dutch] to guard their homes and lands so that they shall not sail to do us damage in the Indies nor assist our enemies as they do [in Germany]'.[2] If the Dutch could be contained in this manner, Spanish prestige, or *reputación*, another factor weighing heavy in the calculations of Madrid, could also be restored.

England did not commit forces to the Bohemian revolt. Setting aside dynastic loyalties, James I refused to help his son-in-law, Frederick, Elector of the Palatine who had become embroiled in the revolt, championing the cause of the Bohemians by pitting his claim to be elective king of Bohemia against that of the Holy Roman Emperor as hereditary monarch. James was attacked in the House of Commons in 1621 and in the country for failing to uphold the Protestant cause in Europe, although his lack of enthusiasm for the revolt was shared in varying degrees by other Protestant powers, including the Dutch.[3] However, in the immediate aftermath of his coup, Maurice decided that in such uncertain times it was necessary for the republic to improve its relations with England and try to settle the unresolved issues between the two countries, including the conflict in the Indies. Negotiations lasted from December 1618 to early July 1619 when the thirty-clause accord was signed. The main points of the agreement, which was to run for twenty years, stated that the English were to be permitted one third of the import and export trade in the Spice Islands while pepper from Java and elsewhere was to be shared equally between the companies; existing forts were to remain in the possession of the respective companies (a matter of more concern to the Dutch as they held more forts than the English); each company was to furnish ten ships for a fleet of common defence; a joint council of defence was to be set up in the Indies to administer the accord; contentious issues were to be referred back to Europe where the English king and the States General were the final arbiters in any disputes. The thorny question that had led to the recent hostility (whether the English had the right to establish new factories in the Spice Islands) was to be shelved for two or three years.[4]

The Heren XVII who, as has been mentioned, had not been unanimous or enthusiastic about employing force against the English anyway, welcomed the accord. It would help reduce the huge costs of their military operations in the Indies which were draining the profits of their trade. Keeling and the other factors in the Indies had reproached their employers because the Dutch were better supplied than the English but in reality the cost of maintaining forts, garrisons and a battle fleet ate up most of the money sent from the Netherlands and the profits from Dutch participation in the country trade. The VOC had to borrow heavily and ran up debts to finance its ambitions and to pay dividends to its uneasy shareholders (unlike the English company, the VOC paid only four dividends in its first twenty years of operations). But by the 1620s luck was on its side and its past efforts were reaping rewards. Portuguese naval power was considerably weakened, not least because of the high rate of shipwrecks the massive Portuguese carracks suffered on the voyages to and from the Indies, and the finances of the Estado da Índia had sharply deteriorated. VOC finances, on the contrary, were sound while the English company was entering a twenty-year cycle of crisis.[5]

The directors of the English company welcomed the cessation of hostilities but a number questioned the wisdom of allowing the company to become embroiled in military action in the Spice Islands and Philippines, arguing that Surat or Bantam would be better bases for the operations of the fleet of defence and locations more suited to the pursuit of English ambitions.[6] With hindsight it is possible to agree with these reservations. The English did indeed shift their attention to India and Persia while the Dutch attained their monopoly in the Spice Islands. However, at the dawn of the 1620s the English company's policy remained opportunistic, piecemeal rather than visionary in conceptualisation with the directors still inclined to follow the VOC's path. There was no great strategic thinker to match Coen in the Company's employ in the Indies.

English concerns were more immediate: inferiority in shipping and naval organisation and a lack of experience of fighting in the Indies. The overtures for the accord had come from the Dutch and its provisions stipulated equality, but in reality the English, whatever their national pride might dictate, were the junior partners.

In the Indies Coen complained to his superiors that by signing the accord the VOC had been 'so bridled with so hard a bit' and had thrown away the recent hard-won gains at the expense of the English.[7] Outwardly he observed the accord but did his best to undermine its operation, blocking the English wherever possible, and made his views clear to his subordinates in Hirado.[8] Nor did the accord prove popular with the English who complained that hitherto 'The sea hath...beene free for vs butt if our masters will suffer themselues to be debarred of those priuiledges we must p. force suffer for ye hollanders power is so great for vs to contend wth all'.[9] But, regardless of their weaker position, the English, particularly the factors in the Spice Islands which had been in the frontline of the struggle against the Dutch, were not immune themselves from the temptation to break the spirit of the accord. In September 1622 the southern presidency in Batavia reminded its factors in Ternate not to stir up the natives to rise against the Dutch as this was contrary to the Company's orders.[10] Even if the presidency was more inclined to respect the accord and try to hold the Dutch to its provisions (if only because it well understood that the English lacked the resources and confidence of the Dutch to flaunt it) its protests were met with a frosty reception. The Hollanders overawed the English who, because of Dutch 'greatnesse and soueraigne power' in Batavia and 'to auoid further inconveniences and preiudices', judged it prudent to pass over their right to chair joint meetings of the council of defence in alternate months. No matter if the Dutch gave the English plenty of advance warning of their intentions, as the presidency reported to the directors in December 1623, the tone of the relationship was conditioned by the Hollanders' view that 'their m[rs] were not well informed when they made the agreement and we here knowing better will doe as we think good'.[11]

In theory the accord remained in force for its full twenty years, but in the Indies all it achieved was a fragile *modus vivendi* and soon became a dead letter. The English, weary of the struggle, finally abandoned their attempts to secure a share of the trade in the Spice Islands. In the long run this was to the benefit of the English company. The Dutch had to invest heavily in forts, ships and men in order to enforce their hard-won monopoly over the spice trade. The English could still procure spices on the periphery of the islands (notably from smugglers at Macassar where a factory remained until 1667 when the Dutch expelled the English) for so long as it was profitable to send them to England. As a result, the English did not depend on spices to generate profits to the same extent as the Dutch, ultimately to the detriment of the VOC's long-term development. The spice trade together with the VOC's Japan trade may have made the Dutch a powerful force in the country trade in the Indies for much of the seventeenth century but when these trades declined late in the century the Dutch were overtaken commercially by the English, especially in India where English investment and increased involvement in the country trade over the years began to pay off, and the VOC came to depend on Euro-Asian trade for its profits.[12] The way then lay open for the English company's rise to superiority in the Indies.

Three fleets operated in the Indies from 1620–23. One was purely Dutch and blockaded Malacca. Another consisting of seven Dutch and four English ships was sent to attempt a blockade of Goa and disrupt Portuguese shipping in the Indian Ocean. The third fleet was ordered to Hirado, which was intended to serve as a base for operations in the waters around Manila.

The eight-member council of defence stipulated in the accord met in Batavia in May 1620. A decision to send a fleet to blockade Manila and harass Manila-bound Chinese shipping was taken quickly. There were of course no scruples among the English at Batavia about the morality or efficacy of attacking Chinese shipping, which they had been doing anyway since 1618.[13] Unlike Cocks's relationship with the Li in Hirado, there was little love between the English and the Chinese diaspora of Bantam. The fleet was to consist of ten ships, five from each company, and the admiral was to alternate between the commanders of each company. An English admiral was to serve first. The most obvious and best qualified candidate was Martin Pring who, after the death of Dale from illness in August 1619, had become the senior English commander in the Indies. He had wide experience of privateering voyages in the Atlantic, where he had also served with the Dutch, and had joined the Company 1614. However, Pring felt otherwise and refused the command, preferring to undertake only the separate voyage to Japan on the Company's account that was planned in his flagship, the *James Royal*, and then return to England. Robert Adams, commander of the *Bull*, and James Clevenger, commander of the *Palsgrave*, were considered next and Adams accepted.[14] On 26 May (NS) the council decided to send a part of the fleet (the English ships *Elizabeth* and *Bull*, and the Dutch ships *Haarlem* and *Hoope*) in advance to cruise near Macao, Taiwan and Ryūkyū before making their way to the Kyushu coast off Satsuma to entrap the Portuguese galliots arriving from Macao. Another ship, the English *Hope*, was to proceed to Patani to buy

provisions. For accounting purposes she was only to become a part
of the fleet after passing Pulo Condor. However, she never reached
Japan. Cocks feared that the crew had mutinied; in fact the ship was
taken by the Portuguese.[15] The *James Royal* and the *Unicorn*, which
had sailed on 27 April from Bantam road with a cargo of money and
goods (valued at 39,074 reals) to provide some relief for what the
presidency described as Hirado's 'vereie needfull' condition, were
not part of the fleet. The *Unicorn* also failed to reach Japan and was
shipwrecked off the Kwangtung coast near Macao. Some of the crew
and passengers, who included two Englishwomen, one the wife of
Thomas Frobisher, and her maid, were picked up by the Portuguese.
Frobisher, whose skills as a carpenter were valued by the Portuguese,
was taken to Malacca.[16]

The instructions issued to the ships of the fleet had a confident,
agressive tone. Vessels belonging to the Portuguese and Spanish or
their adherents were to be captured no matter where, even in the
road of Macao or off the coast of Japan; inventories were to be made
of all goods seized and the prizes divided upon arrival at Hirado
under the supervision of the respective chief factors there; and two
persons from each company were to serve in ships of the other
company. Pillaging was forbidden. The commanders were given
additional instructions: only Chinese junks bound for Manila were to
be attacked; no harm was to be done to other Chinese shipping,
especially those bound for Japan, or to Japanese, either their persons,
ships or goods (a prudent self-denial); any Portuguese vessels that
attempted to flee were to be chased even into 'any road or port upon
the coast of Japan' and forced out into the open sea.[17]

A valuation of nine of the ten ships of the fleet was also performed
at Batavia. The five English ships, the smallest of which was 400
tons, the largest 800, together with their ordnance, shot and other
weaponry were valued at £47,760 17s 6d; the four Dutch ships,
ranging from 250 last (c.500 tons) to 400 last (c.800 tons) at f. 437,069
12 st.[18] This was a sizeable investment in itself and excluded manpower, ships' stores and victuals. The English ships were to be
careened at Hirado and the costs borne by the factory. (The fifth
Dutch ship, the *St Michiel*, was to join the fleet from Amboina but
was shipwrecked on the way.)

The objectives of the Manila voyage itself, as laid down in the
commission to the admiral and vice-admiral, were stated to be 'the
weakening of the common enemy and to draw the trade of China
unto ourselves'. The first part was self-evident, the disruption of
Spanish trade and communications, in an effort to make life as
uncomfortable as possible for the Iberians; there was no question of
seizing Manila. To this extent the voyage represented an extension of
earlier Dutch operations off Manila, notably that of Lam in 1617,

which had so impressed the English at Hirado. Lam himself had recommended that these operations should be continued despite his own misfortunes and the Batavia council cited them as a precedent.[19] The second part was more germane to the enterprise, particularly for the Dutch. The commission also spoke of forcing the Chinese into friendly commerce with the English and Dutch, which they had hitherto refused, and of drawing Chinese traders away from Manila, where they procured silver bullion from the New World, to Batavia or some other place where the two companies had factories.[20]

In fact this meant Batavia, which the Council of the Indies had been seeking to make the regional entrepôt for Chinese trade, rather than Bantam or Manila, since the founding of the city in 1619.[21] (The schizophrenia of trying to draw Chinese shipping and settlers to Batavia while at the same time attacking Chinese vessels originating from the same points on the China coast trading with Manila did not occur to the Dutch.) In addition to this stated aim the Dutch had a more ambitious agenda of their own. If silk and silver oiled the wheels of trade in the China seas then it was necessary to participate fully in that trade. This meant securing access to China by force or otherwise; spoilers could achieve little. The three years from 1620–23 represent an essential preliminary stage in the process whereby the Dutch transformed themselves from a marginal, disruptive force in east Asian trade, bent on acquiring silk for the Amsterdam market by plundering Chinese and Portuguese shipping, to major, settled participants in the trade, deriving large profits for themselves. The strategy which had first been mooted in 1607 by Matelieff (who had argued that the Japan trade would be worthless without access to China) and more specifically by Brouwer, who in 1613 had shrewdly suggested using Taiwan as a location for acquiring Chinese goods. By then the Heren XVII had lost interest in the China trade although not in Chinese silk and Brouwer's recommendation had not been taken up. But in the early 1620s, thanks to the vision and dogged persistence of Coen, the idea had come of age and because of the availability of Persian silk the VOC did not have to confront the dilemma of choosing between Chinese raw silk for the Amsterdam market or for Japan.[22] The English only slowly woke up to the implications of the VOC's covert agenda but, in spite of intense curiosity about what the Dutch were up to, did not themselves affect a similar transformation, even though the Company's factors in Hirado had advocated the need to gain an entry into the China trade more consistently than their Dutch counterparts.

On 23 July 1620, as the *James Royal* moved from Kōchi to Hirado, the *Moon* and *Elizabeth* arrived along with the Dutch *Trouw*. The *Palsgrave* arrived on 5 August and the *Bull* on the 7th after losing all

her masts in a typhoon. The English ship, the *Expedition*, then in
Dutch service, was lost in another typhoon, sinking in Hirado
harbour in September.[23] The Dutch ships had also brought orders
for Specx's recall to Batavia and his replacement, Leonard Camps,
who had served before in the Dutch factory. Camps succeeded to
the post of chief Dutch factor in January 1621 but Specx did not
leave Japan until October.[24] The ships brought a much-needed
replenishment of money and goods to the English factory. The
largest item was lead of which 2,874 peculs 73 catties was made over
to the account of the factory (the ships kept small amounts on their
own account). The *James Royal* also brought three 'baels' or bundles
of broadcloth, mostly stammel, 1,818 1/2 catties of kensey silk (a
cheap, oily silk), 4,317 catties of pepper and four chests of reals. Each
chest should have contained 4,000 reals but 123 3/4 were missing
(allegedly because of poor packing so that the chests broke loose
during the storms on the voyage although pilfering seems an equally
plausible explanation). A further 10 1/4 were lacking from two
chests of reals brought in the *Moon* and *Palsgrave* so that the factory
received 23,866 reals instead of 24,000.[25]

The arrival of so many English and Dutch ships in waters off Japan
had not gone unnoticed and both Cocks and Specx were alarmed
about the likely Japanese reaction to a presence which could easily be
interpreted as provocative. The bakufu wasted little time in making
it clear that it considered the activities of the fleet a breach of the
shogunal peace. Both the English and Dutch knew that they could
not afford to alienate the Japanese authorities and that there were
limits to what they could do in waters surrounding Japan (they still
intended to conduct their usual business in Japan and they hoped to
win the approval of the *rōjū* for the operations of the fleet). It was
quickly decided to suspend the orders issued at Batavia. The ships
still cruising off Nagasaki in the hope of intercepting the galliots
were called in.[26] The vessels had been prowling in vain anyway for
the galliots had evaded capture and slipped into Nagasaki.

During the voyage to Japan the vessels of the two companies had
had little contact with the enemy. One of the galliots had a narrow
escape from the Dutch, an escape the Portuguese attributed to the
intervention of the Virgin. Efforts were made to adhere to the
instructions issued at Batavia forbidding attacks on Chinese vessels
bound for Japan. A junk from Macao was stopped and issued with a
pass but the unfortunate vessel was stopped again by another ship
belonging to the fleet. The captain refused to allow a boarding party
on his vessel and in the skirmish that followed the junk was pillaged
and set on fire, injuring a number of Chinese, English and Dutch.
John Munden, master of the *Bull*, tore up a pass that was proffered
but the captain produced another confirming the junk's right to

travel unhindered and efforts were then made to restore the pillaged goods. The English participants were greatly concerned to report their version of the events to Batavia 'in regard we know not what the Chinaman may aleadge against vs'.[27]

If the companies were concerned that their activities should not alienate the Japanese authorities then the seizure of a junk captained by a Japanese Christian, Hirayama Jochin, with Japanese and Iberian crew and passengers aboard tested the shogunate's toleration to the full. The junk was seized in the Straits of Taiwan by the *Elizabeth*. At first the distressed vessel was offered assistance, but on searching her, two Europeans were discovered hiding below deck. Immediately, the men were suspected of being priests but the English were more preoccupied with the cargo (Canton silk, deer hides, sugar, porcelain and other goods, including two gold chains and 106 reals) to think about this. After some debate it was decided to take the junk, her cargo and all aboard to Hirado where, once the goods belonging to the Japanese were sorted out and returned to their owners, the spoil was to be divided between the two companies.

However, at Hirado the vessel and its cargo were promptly sequestered by the daimyo pending a decision from Edo about her disposal. (The cargo was not actually unloaded from the junk and the *Elizabeth* until December and was then stored, by order of the daimyo, in the English godown and in other godowns belonging to Japanese, although some small goods were sold including one of the gold chains for 70 reals.) Papers found on the two men confirmed that they were indeed priests, Pedro Zuñiga, an Augustinian who had been in Japan before and whose father, the Marques de Villamanrica, had been a viceroy of New Spain, and Luis Flores, a Flemish Dominican, although at first the English and Dutch mistakenly believed that they were Jesuits. Unwittingly, the *Elizabeth* seemed to have scored a perfect coup for the companies but little did the factors realise that the seizure of Hirayama's junk was to involve them in a protracted case that almost led to the companies' expulsion from Japan.[28]

One of the first decisions of the joint council of the two companies in Hirado was to send a delegation to Edo. Custom dictated it and current strategy demanded it regardless of the costs. The discovery of the two missionaries seemed an unexpected bonus, casting the two companies in the role of upholders of the shogunate's anti-Christian policy. There was considerable optimism about the mission to Edo and expectations ran high that their action in seizing the priests would guarantee them a favourable hearing and that they would be rewarded with the cargo from the vessel. Cocks and Specx were to oversee the selection of the presents and approve what gifts were 'very needful'.[29] In addition to the shogun, the *rōjū* whom the

English and Dutch considered most influential were to receive presents as well as officials who, it was believed, could ease access for the delegation and hasten the despatch of its business. The *Kyoto shoshidai*, Itakura Katsushige, who was described as 'our great frend wch wee haue many tymes founde', and his son Shigemune were also to be given presents. Contrary to Cocks's report to the Company that 'our geavings [are] greater then otherwise' to match the Spanish and Portuguese 'Angling wth goulden hooks' in order to gain influence,[30] the presents were not lavish, consisting mainly of silk, smaller amounts of velvet, satin and other goods. The shogun was assigned 2 peculs 54 catties of white raw silk, which according to Cocks the *itowappu* merchants, in a buyer's market, were purchasing at 130 taels per pecul. Other individuals received amounts corresponding to what the English and Dutch assumed to be their position in the shogunal hierarchy.[31] The gifts were no more impressive than in previous years. They were neither expensive nor rare and their market value not at all great.

The joint council decided that two representatives of each company, a merchant and sea officer should visit Edo. Joseph Cockram and Charles Clevenger were chosen to represent the English and Matias van der Bock and Jacques Le Febure, the Dutch. The party left for Edo on 1 September with three objectives in mind. The first was to present a letter to the shogun from the joint council informing him of the purpose of the fleet of defense. The letter, drafted under the guidance of Cocks and Specx, made great efforts to fan the anti-Catholic sentiment of the shogunate and its suspicions of Spanish imperial ambitions in east Asia. The shogun was reminded that the subjects of the Spanish king had 'entered as firm inhabitants in Leconia [Luzon] and at Macao' and (disingenuously) requested him to judge attacks on Spanish and Portuguese shipping in waters near Japan not simply as an extension of warfare in Europe (the fact that England was not at war with either Spain or Portugal was overlooked) but as a reflection of a policy of 'defending of His Majesty's land and state from the treacherous practices of the Friars'. The shogun was asked to suspend the issue of *shuinjō* for Manila which it was alleged owed much of its prosperity to provisions supplied by Japanese merchants whose ships were often used as cover to smuggle priests into Japan. The shogun was also requested to order his subjects not to carry any Spanish or Portuguese nor their goods on their voyages and that the rules governing the issue of *shuinjō* should be strictly observed, especially to ensure that the destination for which they were issued should be the real one and not Macao or some other place.[32] The second objective was to lobby the *rōjū* to allow the English and Dutch to keep Hirayama's junk and its cargo as lawful prize, and the third, the least controversial, but which nevertheless took a long time to settle, was to set a price for the lead both companies had brought to Japan.[33]

These were audacious requests, and neither the English nor Dutch held any suitable cards to play for such stakes. By raising the spectre of the missionary threat and drawing attention to abuses in the operation of the *shuinjō* system, which the bakufu was concerned to stamp out, their demands cleverly played on bakufu fears. But the companies were deceiving themselves if they really imagined that the shogunate would grant even a fraction of what they wanted. The requests impinged upon important issues of sovereignty, an area of acute sensitivity to the shogunate and one in which it would not tolerate any encroachment from outsiders. Moreover, the English and Dutch did not advance their case by sending 'strangers' on such an important mission rather than the respective heads of the factories with whom the *rōjū* were already familiar. Cocks and Specx, understandably, preferred to remain in Hirado to supervise preparations for the fleet. This was a tactical error. Their presence would not have altered the outcome but it might have reduced the complications they experienced over the seizure of Hirayama's junk and the sale of the lead. The daimyo of Hirado made as much clear to them in August 1621. The demands were given short shrift in Edo. The relationship between Macao and Japan continued as before. The Spanish and Portuguese may have been the 'mortal enemies' of the two companies and the missionaries a threat to the shogunate, but Portugal remained the most important European participant in Japan's overseas trade and a number of influential Japanese, including shogunate officials, benefited from this participation, a factor of greater immediacy for some of these individuals than abstract notions of sovereignty. Consequently, the Portuguese had their own 'well willars' in Edo, even if Cocks consistently overestimated the influence of the Iberians and their efforts to 'Crosse our p°ceedings in all they may both wth greate bribes & trecherouse plotts'.[34] Cocks had to make do with receiving letters of guarantee from the partnership to whom he had lent his *shuinjō* for Tongking or Cochinchina in the spring of 1621 that their vessel would not call at Macao. Just how seriously the Japanese partnership financing his voyage took these letters is unknown and the matter was not put to the test for the vessel, the *Willing Mind*, failed in its voyage.[35]

The sudden arrival of so many ships in Hirado imposed a heavy financial burden on the English factory and the presence of over 1,000 men from both companies created problems of discipline. Hirado was an excellent location for procuring victuals but for ships stores it was not so convenient. The voyage from Batavia had taken its toll on the ships and had been so rough that Edward Lennis, master of the *Elizabeth*, wrote that if he had known the danger of the pasage between Batavia and Japan he would not have undertaken it for '500 liv. more then his wages'. All the ships were in need of repair before they were ready for the Manila voyage and the *James Royal* had to be turned round for the voyage back to Bantam. There was also a timetable to adhere to. The factory had had no warning of the ships' arrival and had been unable to contract for supplies in advance. Inevitably, this pushed up prices as local suppliers sought to take advantage of the situation. The *James Royal* and the *Moon* were sheathed, and the *Bull* provided with new masts. Lennis complained of the indifferent workmanship of the mastmakers and the poor quality of the powder and cordage, commenting, with some exaggeration, that 'except plentie of provisions be sent out of England manie of or ships will never retorne'. The unsuitability of Hirado as a base for overhauling the fleet was a constant refrain during the operations of the Manila voyages. After the first voyage Robert Adams wrote to the Company complaining that the lack of canvas, cordage and especially tar, with which the Dutch were fortunately well-supplied, caused 'much hurte unto or shipps' and Lennis added cable (expensive and 'not serviceable') to his list of insufficiencies.[36] Wood and nails were in plentiful supply.

The cost of fitting out the four ships that eventually went on the first Manila voyage was put at 30,000 reals by the Batavia presidency. This figure excluded provisions. Some 1,110 taels alone was spent on poultry provided by Cushcron-dono, a neighbour of the English. Cocks's estimate of £10,000 for the total cost of preparing the ships plus the *James Royal* was not far out and Batavia had not expected the costs to be low anyway.[37] Part of the cost was met with the money brought from Batavia. Not much was raised from sales. Over the period from 10 March to 12 December sales (small amounts of broadcloth, sappan wood, fish skins and table books) amounted to some 4,177 taels 3 candereen, over 70 per cent of which came from the sappan wood. Most of these sales had probably taken place before the arrival of the ships.[38] To cover the additional expenditure the factory had to borrow heavily. Some of the loans were short term, some with options of repayment in goods. Interest was charged at 2 per cent per month, not much above the rate of 20 per cent offered by Li Tan which Cocks had stressed to Ball in 1618 was generously below Japanese rates. Two thousand taels were lent by Yayemon-dono of Hakata, and 3,500 by Machida Soka (Faccata Soka) also of Hakata but most of the money was raised in Nagasaki from Japanese sources which involved Sayers and Cocks travelling there in December and Janauary. Sayers raised 6,000 taels and Cocks 14,500, some of it from Hiranoya Tozaemon but a request to borrow money from the *daikan*, Hasegawa Gonroku, was turned down. A total of 26,000 taels in loans is recorded, although in a letter to the presidency after the departure of the fleet Cocks put a figure of 11,500 taels at 2 per cent interest per month on the money borrowed. Robert Adams reported to the Company that in the absence of sales and with the factory so unprovided for the fleet could not have been made ready if Cocks's credit had not been so high.[39] The Japanese were in effect banking the English contingent in the fleet.

The influx of so many men posed problems of discipline. Conflicts over jurisdiction between merchants and naval officers, and resentment among the men over their treatment and inadequate provisions, intensified the problems. None of these difficulties were new; nor were they unique to the fleet of defence. Rivalry and lack of co-ordination between the merchants and marine officers continued to plague the Company in the Indies. The Bantam presidency had complained to London at the beginning of 1619 that Henry Pepwell considered himself and his captains senior to the merchants both at sea and on land and usurped the merchants' authority over punishment and ships' movements. The presidency recommended that in future the powers given to principal factors in the Indies should be granted by royal authority under the great seal and that a seal should be created for the presidency.[40] The pursers on the English contingent of the fleet of defense wrote devastatingly about morale and the poor quality of the officers. Robert Turbervill of the *Elizabeth* wrote that the commanders and officers were 'not worth the name of Govnors'. Their laxity caused the men to rebel and 'raile and speake to do what they luste, to strike, mayme and murther one another and may be well termed sea devill, nor the like knowne'. Turbervill thoroughly disapproved of the easy availability of drink and alleged that even if the master, Lennis, would not admit it, for he himself was 'a vearie drunkard', rack was freely sold above deck 'wch hath bin the death of many'. He also noted that the sacrament had only been administered once since the ship left England. Richard Watts, purser of the *Bull*, wrote to Sir Thomas Smythe:

> I pray god all things may goe well for yor pofitts, wch I muche doubt, for here is suche strivinge for greatnes that their is nothinge els alemost regarded. For a man that before he Came into yor wo^rships service Could haue byn Content to haue byn a M[aste]r of a Barque of 30 tunes, now one of your greatest ships is scarse Roome Inoughe to Conteyne him in his greatnesse.

Cocks noted that if any of the merchants, including Cockram, complained 'they are thrust back & somtymes in danger of their Lives'.[41] Turbervill's view of the men as 'sea devills' was shared by Cocks and others, although Watts was more inclined to believe that 'the whipe and other strange punishments now in vse' had made men so indifferent that they would rather serve the Spanish. Bantam had described ships arriving from England as manned 'for the most part with as honest men as are in Newgate, or any other prison of common rogues' and 'more fitter for Bridwell then the employm^t they are put into.'[42]

Such comments reflect the view from above. Unfortunately, the common sailors did not write down their side of the story and it is difficult to gauge how far their complaints about inadequate food were justified. The master's mate of the *Palsgrave* complained about discrepancies between the beef and pork allowance and what was actually supplied before the ships left England; this had led to protests by the men while John New, purser of the *Moon*, reported that thirty casks of beef and pork and other quantities of food and drink remained unused after the ship's arrival at Hirado.[43] The ships would not have acquired many victuals at Batavia where the presidency preached 'good husbandry' of victuals and was itself poorly supplied – a situation which was to deteriorate. The presidency reported that the Dutch were given generous allowances (3/4 lb of beef and 1/2 lb of pork per man per week). Those who sailed in the Company's own ships, at least in the country trade, and they would have included many locals, received nothing like that. Meals with meat were restricted to 2–4 times a week with an allowance set at 'three pounds of flesh waighed out of ye pickle to a messe [i.e. four men]'. Other meals were to consist of sugar and salted fish mixed with rice. All meals were washed down by rack, a quart a day per mess.[44] The presidency had already warned the Company that the inadequate victualling of ships and the poor storage of food (in one case cheese had been ruined by being placed in tar) would lead to discipline problems in the country trade unless it were remedied and continued to make its views known. It criticised the use of blocks and timber for ballast because this took up precious space for victuals. The directors, who were familiar with complaints about the poor quality of the victuals and of too strict rationing by commanders – a charge that had been levelled against Saris after his return – expressed 'surprise' at the complaints about lack of victuals considering the 'plenty' that was to be had at Pulicat and Japan and reminded the presidency that victuals were expensive in England and that it had already received sufficient quantities.[45] Whatever its shortcomings, at least the directors were correct to assume that there was no lack of victuals at Hirado.

The problems of indiscipline and desertion were nothing new and had occurred before in Hirado when previous ships had called, including the *Clove* in 1613. What was different about the fleet of defence was the scale of the problem and the fact that it defied management. Temptations were great, grievances (imagined and real) numerous, and the officers weak and themselves on the make.

Major problems did not begin until after the return of the fleet from the first voyage, although there were indications of what was to come. On 20 December 1620 Robert Adams wrote to the Company describing Hirado as 'a Second Sodamye':

There is neuer a house in the towen butt the basest fellow in the fleete may haue wine and a hoore; if they have it not in the house to fit their Turne they will Send for it out of doores. We have soe much fauor with the king that they shall not Trust our men furder then their money Reacheth vnto; yet they will let them haue drinke and hoores soe longe as they think there Clothes are worth itt and then the Japanns will strip them naked and turn them out of doors. More, when the woomen have Children heere, if they will keepe them alive they may; if they will kill them, they may.[46]

The men needed no enticement to end up in trouble; liquor was the perfect lubricant to induce brawling. One drunk fell into the harbour and drowned, another fell overboard from one of the ships and into a junk 'where he broke his skull, & is meamed in one legg & an arme & in danger to die'.[47] The lure of profit in what had effectively become a frontier town drew people from neighbouring areas, eager to share the bonanza.[48] It is unlikely that many men were stripped naked. The most common procedure was for creditors to detain men, offering to release them when their debts were settled. This led to protests to the Matsūra about infringement of the trading privileges. Lacking ready money to finance their debauchery, the men resorted to extortion to try to secure some. A Scot, James Littel, of the *Elizabeth*, pressed demands for the men to be allowed a 1/5 share of the goods from Hirayama's junk. His efforts to organise the men and involve those on the other ships were quickly cut short. He was arrested and sent to Batavia as a prisoner in February 1621.[49] Not everyone was seduced by the flesh-pots of Hirado; some men deserted, preferring to take their chance, as Watts had said, in Manila or Macao.[50] To make up for insufficient men, the English employed Japanese on their ships, paying them 10 taels each.[51]

By the end of the year the fleet was at last ready for its voyage. Four English merchants, including Sayers, were chosen to sail in the fleet and two men from each company were to serve in the other company's vessels. Strict orders were issued by the joint council prohibiting the men from pillaging junks seized and (expecting the worst) the officers were required to ensure that 'our men doe nott drink them selues drunk'. To make up numbers (because of the failure of the English *Hope* and the Dutch *St Michiel* to arrive) the *Swan*, which had been seized by the Dutch in the Moluccas, was to join the fleet later. Both companies were to share her charges, although the Dutch armed her. Manila (where it was reported that

twenty-four Chinese junks would be met) was the goal of the
voyage, and on 3 January 1621 the fleet of nine vessels set sail from
Kōchi.[52]

The voyage lasted until 29 June when the ships returned. Much
time was spent fruitlessly cruising around Manila Bay. Both companies remained suspicious of each other and a joint council drew up
new rules aimed at preventing pillaging and to ensure that neither
side would cheat by seizing goods for its own account when vessels
were seized. Eight persons of each company, two merchants and six
others known to be 'honest', were to go aboard any captured vessel
and supervise the unloading. All goods seized were to be divided
between the companies' ships after inventories were made, a necessary insurance policy. These measures looked stringent on paper but
were ignored in practice. The English later complained of arguments
and disagreements threatening the success of the voyage and that the
Dutch 'did much abuse our English men'. According to Robert
Adams, the Hollanders behaved like 'so many devells or Raveinge
wolves seekinge after their pray'. Not surprisingly, the Dutch made
similar accusations about the English. Jacques Le Febure, the Dutch
vice-admiral, complained that the English 'had no government over
their people' during the voyage and allowed them to plunder willy-
nilly. Le Febure would have preferred that the Dutch had gone on
the mission alone. Cockram's more level-headed remarks are probably nearer the truth. Writing to Batavia in September 1622, after the
return of the second voyage, he noted that 'in their voyadges [there
are] so many abuses and complaints on eyther syde by wicked and
vnrulie people that it is hard to iudg betwine our two nacons wheare
lyeth the greatest fault for on eyther syde are knaues enough'. He
added that on the second voyage there was 'better order and good
Agreement then was the last yeare' yet 'some tyme a little
Brablinge'.[53]

The defiant language used by the companies in their joint letter to
the shogun was but empty rhetoric. The first Manila voyage was a
mission executed without vigour, courage, or outstanding naval
tactics and was certainly not one to be proud of. It was a far cry from
the Elizabethan privateering voyages. The men were keen to attack
unarmed Chinese vessels but were reluctant to face vessels of the
'common enemy' even when offered a reward.[54] Nevertheless, the
Spanish in Manila, who had received intelligence of the accord and of
the proceedings of the two companies at Edo, were sufficiently
alarmed by the strength of the fleet to send ships to Mexico and an
ambassador to Goa to ask for assistance. Defences were prepared at
Manila against an attack which never materialised, although Spanish
accounts differ as to the degree of readiness achieved. To impress his
superiors, Alonso Fajardo de Tenca was adamant that his prep-

arations for the defense of the city by fortifying Cavite further along the Bay were adequate even with the lack of available manpower. Another report alleged that the Anglo-Dutch fleet, realising how paltry the defenses were, sailed into the Bay 'as if on their own seas and in a safe port', a view quite at odds with English accounts.[55]

Officially the fleet was credited with seizing five junks carrying silk, a poor showing. It failed to prevent Chinese junks from reaching Manila and it missed the arrival of the galleon from Acapulco and the departure of two ships returning to Mexico. Sometime after the ship's return, Cocks heard reports that 14 junks and 6 galliots had evaded the fleet while Le Febure reported to his superiors that the Spanish had been able to warn the Chinese in advance about the fleet's likely activity and many junks remained at home on the China coast until the end of the year. Spanish sources state that a number of vessels were able to slip into Manila when the fleet was cruising away from the Bay.[56] Vessels carrying a *shuinjō* were not seized, nor were friendly ships that had been issued with passes. These friends included Li Tan to whom five passes had been issued, three for Taiwan and two for Manila. A pass was even requested by the Siamese ambassador in 1621 prior to his return home from an embassy to Edo.[57]

Once the ships were safely in Hirado, the captured goods were quickly unloaded and stored in the godowns of both companies. However, the problems that had manifested themselves before the voyage seemed minor in comparison with what happened during the intermission before the next one.

(ii)   Between Voyages, 1621

During the absence of the fleet measures were taken, so far as circumstances permitted, to make Hirado a more suitable base for future operations. The factory was expanded by the addition of a new godown in which to store the expected plunder. The land was obtained by buying neighbouring houses. The wharf was also lengthened by about six yards at a cost of 269 taels. At Kōchi, the land which the factory had been given by the daimyo was measured more exactly to prevent any encroachments from new buildings which were being erected nearby and the quay was lengthened. This was an expensive development programme and lasted from February to June 1621, providing employment to many labourers, another boost to the local economy. The programme also involved the English in a minor dispute with Sagawa Nobutoshi who was concerned that the activity generated by the fleet should benefit the local economy, and himself in particular. He demanded that all stores and materials, including those for the new building, should be bought from local suppliers. However, he was overruled by other members of the Matsūra household. With the increase in the number of men in Hirado and the consequent higher mortality rate the small cemetery was also enlarged. Discreet Christian burial was tolerated. The building programme suggested confidence in the future, an attitude that was not at all justified by cold reality.[58]

While the fleet was away, the factory had been able to make some sales. The largest item was an unspecified amount of silk sold to Hiranoya Tōzaemon for 3,575 taels 2 mas 5 candereen. Otherwise sales were indifferent. Sappan wood as usual sold well, fetching 400 taels for 300 peculs and broadcloth 160 taels. Over this period sales, as recorded in Cocks's diary, totalled 4,199 taels 9 candereen.[59] Both Cocks and Eaton requested Batavia to send more broadcloth, of which only a small quantity had been brought in 1620. Eaton recommended that 40–50 broadcloths (the *Clove* had brought 50) be sent, half stammel and half black. Stammels had been snapped up quickly and most of the cloth had been sold by early December 1620. In 1618 Cocks had informed the Company that the daimyo remained interested in buying cloth for their retainers, noting that while before it had only been worn around the waist, now it was used to dress the men almost down to their feet. He attributed the sudden increase in demand in 1620 to a fire at Kyoto which destroyed a number of buildings where cloth was stored. Early in 1621, when cloth was fetching 30–40 taels per tatami (Saris had informed the Court in 1614 that prices between 30 and 50 taels per tatami could be expected in Japan), Hasegawa Gonroku recommended Cocks to secure another 30–40 tatamis of stammel or red cloth of any shade or quality to sell to the shogunate. Bays and yellow broadcloth, for which there was absolutely no market and which had been in a poor condition when delivered anyway, were given over to the ships' accounts to be used for apparel 'for naked marrenars' who were suffering from the onset of an early winter in December.[60] Regardless of this sudden upsurge in demand, broadcloth remained a risky, unpredictable investment, with the popular colours changing according to fashion. The factory tried to encourage sales by inviting Hiranoya and other merchants to dinner at which the 'dansing beares' were hired to try to loosen their purse-strings. But later in the year demand had fallen off again.[61]

Sale of the lead, the factory's largest inventory, proved frustrating and it was only in August 1621 that the factory managed to dispose of it. In September 1620 Cocks and Specx had gone to Nagasaki, where they had business to do anyway in connection with the fleet. They took presents for Hasegawa who had the responsibility for buying the lead on behalf of the shogunate. The presents, described as 'requisit & necessary', comprised 20 catties of silk, 25 catties of pepper and various kinds of cloth, but Hasegawa was unimpressed and, hoping to beat down the price by wearying the companies into a quick sale, referred the matter back to Edo. Accordingly, the English and Dutch sent additional presents to Edo, care of the representatives whom they had left there to look after their interests, to various officials whom they imagined could speed things up.[62] Hasegawa made it known that the factories should expect no more than 3 1/2 taels per pecul, which Cocks complained 'was not the money it cost in England', and was below previous prices. Even after the factories' representatives in Edo brought news that the bakufu was offering 5 taels, Hasegawa demurred, claiming the price was too high and, using his discretionary powers, continued to try to drive down the price. The English and Dutch were left uncertain about the price they would be given and both Cocks and Specx had to make further trips to Nagasaki. Hasegawa tried (successfully at times) to sow suspicion between the two companies, telling each separately that their lead was superior to the other's and that the rival company had agreed to accept a reduced price. However, the English and Dutch stuck together, displaying a remarkable degree of unity and trust which was not equalled in other aspects of their mutual relations, and the price was finally settled at 4 1/2 taels per pecul, down on the 6 taels given in 1614 and the 5 taels 5 mas in 1620.[63] Hasegawa's behaviour was not simple caprice. He was underscoring his own importance and his dislike of the relative autonomy enjoyed by the companies at Hirado. The weighing of the lead, under the supervision of officials from Nagasaki, began in September. Of the 2,874 peculs 73 catties discharged by the English at Hirado, 2,780 peculs 40 catties were sold to the shogun for 12,511 taels 8 mas, 1,495 were returned to the ships, and 666 taels were sold to Li Tan, also at 4 taels 5 mas per pecul.[64]

The unpleasant memory of such tough bargaining seemed likely to be erased by the profits from the booty brought back from the Manila voyage. Unfortunately, timing and incompetence conspired to cheat the English factory of the rich profits expected. The fleet had not prevented six Portuguese galliots reaching Japan from Macao over the summer months, and had not even tried to intercept them. (According to the Dutch, the English commander had refused to detach any of the ships from the fleet to hunt for the galliots.) The galliots were reported to be carrying up to 1,000 peculs of silk, estimated to be worth 100,000 reals, a plausible figure.[65] The safe arrival of the galliots drove down the price of silk which was especially galling for the English because they had arranged to sell their share of the silk from the Manila voyage to Hiranoya Tōzaemon at 310 taels per pecul for the best Nanking silk. Not surprisingly, Hiranoya changed his mind when he heard of the arrival of the galliots and the English were unable to hold him to the deal because of a faulty contract drawn up by Eaton. This stated that Hiranoya had an option to buy 1 pecul of each type of silk not that he had agreed to buy all the silk.[66] Hiranoya drove down the price to 220 taels (and a further small discount to 219 taels appears to have been made), not a bad price in comparison with other years but still below previous highs. At least the deal enabled the factory to pay off debts owing to Hiranoya.[67]

Profits from sales were further eroded by the private trade conducted by both officers and men, and by the demands of the men for a share of the spoils. In pursuing such demands the men were following the practice of their Elizabethan predecessors. Such extortion could not have been entirely unexpected with so much tempting booty around, and provided a convenient screen to hide the officers' private trade. The men were bought off easily with an offer of one-sixteenth of the takings, well below the one-fifth they had demanded the year before and far short of the one-third allowed the crew on Elizabethan privateering voyages.[68] Once again the ringleader of this campaign was a Scot, John Martin, of the *Bull*, who was reported to have urged the men to mutiny because 'they [the factors and officers] sell away the goods, & yf you suffer them to carry them away, you shall neuer have anything'. The men were attuned to legal niceties. In a letter to the Company, Cocks claimed that they had threatened to withdraw their labour and refuse to serve on a second voyage, protesting that the ships had come out of England without a royal commission to wage war against the Spanish and Portuguese and that they themselves had been employed on merchant ships not on men-of-war and were being kept in the Indies 'against their wills as Slaues'. Adams was said to have been forced to offer the one-sixteenth under duress before anything could be unloaded and opened and the men wanted to place a lock on the godown where the goods were stored until they were paid. Cocks claimed to have stood firm and rejected such demands.[69] In fact, Cocks was distorting the events in order to justify the concessions that were made. According to his diary, the cargo was discharged before the men from the *Bull* and the *Moon* mutinied and they were easily duped because the factors and officers undervalued the cargo by almost 20 per cent, thereby reducing the payout to the men to 1,814 reals. This was converted at a rate of 5s to the real, the rate at which the Company set wages, not the 4s 6d on which sales were calculated, nor the 4s at which the reals brought on the *Peppercorn* (which arrived in Hirado in late July) were rated. The division of the one-sixteenth was of course against Company rules, although the men claimed a provision had been made in Batavia for some form of payment *ex gratia*. To get round this everyone, factors, officers and men, signed papers discharging themselves from liability should the Company disallow the payment, in which case the men were to repay the money from wages owing in England. Knowing the dangers and uncertainties of the voyages that lay before them, the men preferred to run such a risk, chose instant gratification and received their money on 18 October.[70]

This declared outlay was only the tip of the money from the voyage which the Company never saw. There had been plenty of opportunities for pillage so that the volume and value of the goods officially discharged from the fleet fell far below that officially recorded in the accounts for the voyage. In this activity the men were secondary players. Eaton estimated that over 45,000 taels worth of sales were made unofficially in Hirado by the officers and men.[71] If so, then the English company's half share of the voyage, 35,629 taels 8 mas 5 candereen (officially rated, on Batavia's orders, according to its sales value in Hirado) was a poor second, and it had spent over 22,000 taels to prepare the voyage. (The Dutch rated their share at f. 63,817 10st 1p and also commented on the extent of private trade estimating it at f. 120,000). Arnold Brown, master of the *Palsgrave*, was accused of stashing silk in his cabin and having permitted others to do the same. By the time the merchants protested to Adams and demanded a search of the master's cabin the goods had been sold.[72] As Eaton commented, many individuals 'haue made a better voyage then our Imployers haue done'.[73] Richard Watts, purser of the *Bull*, went even further and wrote to the Company that

this house of yo[rs] is more liker a Pinteree [whore house] then a merchant's factory, everie man for the most pr[te] afected to his owne pleasure o[r] his priuate pfitte Rather Respectinge their own priuate then y[or] wo[r]ships bussines as [the] acompts will to yor worships one day appeare of the greate expence and littell gaine.[74]

There was perhaps some exaggeration in these stories. Later the presidency reported to the directors that on Lennis's death 'there was only a small matter found' despite suggestions that he had 'imbezeled great matter in his Manillia voiage'. However, Munden, master of the *Bull*, was thought to have siphoned off profits from the Company by his private trade.[75] Eaton did not implicate the factors in the embezzlement – for which precedents again existed in Elizabethan privateering voyages – and although the factors had themselves on occasion indulged in private trade it seems that even had they wished to, they were unable to participate in this free-for-all to any great extent given the poor relations existing between them and the ships' officers. Private trade at least continued as before. For example, Cockram entrusted some gold beads, valued at 3 taels 7 mas 5 candereen, to Cocks for sale and Cocks lent Osterwick 500 reals 'to accomplish a barge of pepp'r bought p'r hym of marrenars in the Pep'rcorne'.[76] With the increased money flowing into Hirado it is not surprising that the Matsūra were keen to have the English and Dutch remain in their domain even if the presence of the fleet created headaches.

Reports of the voyage and its indifferent takings were carried to Batavia on the *Swan* which left Hirado on 6 October. Batavia with its own experience of acquisitive officers sided with the merchants and put the blame firmly on the shoulders of the officers for their laxity in 'suffringe our people to take and share what they liste, not regardinge at all the excessiue charge which you are att in furnishinge that fleete but euery man serues his owne turne'. But the presidency criticised the granting of the one-sixteenth.[77] Nevertheless, Cocks and the other merchants, who had no love for their sea colleagues, believed the decision had been justified. On 25 September Munden fell between two ships while crossing a plank connecting them. According to Cocks, one of the *Peppercorn*'s crew 'hive[d] vp the plank with his shoulder & threw hym affe' but because the ships were lying close together Munden did not fall into the water 'yet he was sore brused with the falle'.[78]

The distractions of the brothels and drinking dens of Hirado, the high rate of 'the Japan fflux or desease' (dysentery) and a more general disinclination to serve any longer meant that many men 'did lie ashore Continually' and did nothing to ready the ships for the next voyage so that Japanese labourers had to be hired. The maintenance of discipline became a major problem. Non-payment of bills 'for drinke & weomen', theft and violence led to conflict with the Japanese brothel-keepers and liquor suppliers who took the law into their own hands (the legal niceties regarding the trading privileges were lost on them).[79] Two men were detained, one for stealing and one for 'bad handling of a woman great with child, whereby she cast her child'. After pleas from Cocks to the Matsūra the men were released and given exemplary punishment, a heavy laying on of the lash, 'for out of doubt some abuse there was, otherwais the Japons would not hau[e] laid handes on them'.[80] Some of their Dutch counterparts were less fortunate. Jacques le Febure reported another breach of the trading privileges to his superiors at Batavia. In late July (OS) Dutch sailors were cut to pieces and fed to the dogs for wounding two Japanese in a drunken argument after being fleeced in a brothel.[81] Cocks gives a different version of the event saying that the two were seized from a group of Hollanders who had run amok while drinking, riding over children and slashing at Japanese. He says that after their summary execution their heads were sent to the Dutch factory where the Dutch refused to receive them and that their bodies were left in the fields 'to be eaten by Crowes and doggs' until their corpses were discovered by some Englishmen who buried them.[82] The Japanese were not acting arbitrarily even if the punishment appeared to breach the trade privileges. Expecting trouble, the Matsūra had issued orders before the return of the fleet that mariners were not to come ashore with swords.[83]

If the companies could not control their men then other measures might prove more effective. Cocks claimed that some men were kept at Kōchi 'w'th boultes & shakells, other[s] w'th cheanes, other[s] bownd, & pineoned w'th ropes, some owing nothing to the Japaons, & others tormented because they would not confess they owed 4 or 5 times more to Japons then was due to them'.[84] This was not the whole story. Some men conspired with Japanese brothel-keepers to pretend that they were being kept prisoner for non-payment of debts in order to extort money from the factory, claiming that the money should be set against their wages. No doubt they intended to split the money with their hosts and let the good times continue. Cocks refused to give in and many men were set free regardless.[85] Some pushed their luck too far. When the fleet put to sea in late November twelve men remained captive, in spite of what Cocks, who had lodged a protest with the Matsūra, understood to be an order from the daimyo that they should be released. The English and Dutch, who had four men detained, agreed to refuse to pay the men's debts outright for fear of setting a precedent which would only lead to increased exactions in future and even greater irresponsibility and indulgence, but the English, short of men for their vessels, relented and offered to pay just under half the 330 reals claimed, an offer rejected by the men's creditors. The example of men left to languish in detention was not unwelcome to the merchants and officers. Osterwick said that they were left behind 'in the power of the Japons wheare they are soe well handled as I hope it wilbe a warninge to all others how the[y] Come in debt againe'. Adams requested Cocks to send the men in chains to Batavia upon their release 'as villans & traitors to their prince & countrey'.[86] Resolution of the question was not easy. Officials at Kōchi where the men were detained said that if the English did not pay the debts the men would be transported to Nagasaki and sold as slaves or bondsmen. Over Cocks's protests, six of the men were later ordered to disembark from the Dutch ship that was to take them from Japan and were sent to Nagasaki but they were not given to the Spanish, as Cocks thought, but to Jan Joosten who, short of men and looking for cheap labour to supplement his Chinese crew for a voyage to Batavia, intended to put them to good use. The men did have some choice in the matter. They were not, as Cocks charged, sold unwillingly by the Japanese. One returned to Hirado, presumably in the hope of effecting a negotiated settlement. He was immediately detained in the factory and this time sent to Batavia according to Adams's order. The three ringleaders apparently tried to negotiate a deal with the Iberians 'and soe to haue for saken god and theare Cuntrie' in Eaton's words. Hudson and a jurebasso went to Nagasaki to try to get the men back but Joosten refused to hand them over unless the English paid 20,000 taels to buy his junk and compensate him for the provisions he had bought for them. Cocks rejected the demand, commenting scornfully that 'the world knoweth that Yoosen is not worth 20,000 pence'.[87] It is unlikely that Joosten left Japan under a cloud, as Cocks believed, even if he had had trouble paying debts before both to the Dutch and to various Japanese. Eventually, his junk sailed to Bantam, but the voyage was not a commercial success and Joosten died in a shipwreck on his way back to Japan on a subsequent voyage in 1623.[88]

A more serious threat to the functioning of the fleet was posed by deserters, reducing the already inadequate number of crew members. In the autumn of 1621, the Dominican Diego Collado and a number of other 'loyal vassals of your Majesty [Philip of Spain]' made a reconnaissance of Hirado in search of information about the fate of Zuñiga and Flores. Disguised as Spanish merchants, they mixed with the English and Dutch whose numbers ('disgracefully', Collado noted) included Catholics, and informed themselves about the objectives of the fleet. They noted the size of the ships and observed that the English ones in particular were well armed, but that the ships appeared undermanned for their size. Collado was confident that sabotage would not be difficult and there is little doubt that the mendicant and his associates were the instigators of a bungled attempt to blow up the English powder magazine in September. Cocks knew of the friars' presence in Hirado and reported it to the Matsūra who decided to take no action pending a visit of Hasegawa for the trial of Zuñiga and Flores.[89] Cocks suspected the friars had encouraged desertions including that of Richard Short, master's mate on the *Moon*, and one of the key witnesses who could testify that Zuñiga and Flores were priests (he had been to Japan before and had seen Zuñiga say mass in Nagasaki). Short reached Nagasaki from where he was whisked out of Japan. Six other men who tried to desert at the same time were unsuccessful and were returned to Hirado with the help of the Matsūra. At their trial they declared (somewhat too conveniently for the record) that it was not inadequate victuals nor any cruel treatment by their commanders but enticements by a Portuguese, who was seized with them, that had prompted their desertion. The court martial decided that they were traitors 'to o^r most gratious king and Cuntrie by runninge unto the Enemy to betray his ma^{tes} shippes and subjects into there hands' and sentenced four men, including Alex Hixia, a boy servant, to death by hanging, a punishment designed to 'breede terror and feare in the harts of all others'.[90] The fact that England was not at war with Spain was overlooked. Death sentences were also imposed for murder on an Englishman and a German from Hamburg in Dutch service. The Englishman, John Roan of Bristol, was tried by a jury and before his death (by hanging from the yard-arm) contrite and seeking to give his fate some meaning, urged his fellow crew members 'to take example by hym, & to beware of woamen & wine, w'ch had brought hym to that vntymly death'.[91]

In the matter of capital punishment the factors and sea officers at Hirado were less hesitant to proceed than the presidency at Batavia which prevaricated, not because of humanitarian considerations but from fear of possible legal repercussions that might follow in England for sentences carried out with insufficient authority. In 1623 the presidency received the king's charter giving it full authority under the great seal to punish men but the factors remained uneasy. They wrote to the directors that 'being for o[r] owne parts marchants' they were not 'well versed' in the laws of the land especially in matters of life and death and would welcome stricter and clearer guide-lines similar to those used by the Dutch which set down punishments for all offences and offenders 'from the least to the greatest and what fines or bodilie punishn[ts] to be inflicted' for each offence, leaving it to the governor general and council to interpret. Later in the century the directors made it clear that military discipline, as enforced in the king's army and navy, was to be applied to its servants in the Indies and in 1686 sent copies of the relevant martial codes to Surat and Bengal.[92]

On 26 July 1621, the *Peppercorn* arrived from Batavia with a letter from the president, Richard Fursland, dated 20 June, with orders for the fleet to set out again with the Dutch for Manila. She brought a much-needed supply of reals (five chests) and two pieces of broadcloth and had also managed to take some prize goods on the voyage to Japan, worth 1,137 taels 3 mas 8 candareen, which were added to the account of the first Manila voyage. Cocks commented that the ship 'Came in good tyme to bring vs out of debt for money taken vp at Interest'. The *Peppercorn* and the Dutch ship, the *Moyen*, which arrived from Batavia on the 27th bringing some ships' stores for the English, had orders to join the second Manila voyage.[93] In accordance with the joint agreement for the government of the fleets of defence, the Dutch provided the admiral, Willem Janszoon, on this voyage. Robert Adams objected strongly to going on a second voyage, claiming he had permission to return to England as his service with the Company had run out and he nominated Clevenger as his replacement. However, fearing the precedent his action might set, Adams was prevailed upon to serve in the voyage as vice-admiral.[94] On 10 September a joint council decided that the new fleet would consist of ten ships and prepared instructions for the voyage.[95] For his part, Coen, then on Amboina, informed his subordinates in Hirado that he hoped the English would refuse to go on a second voyage in which case the Dutch were to go it alone.[96]

Collado had been correct about the ships being undermanned. In addition to the toll on manpower from 'the Japan fflux', desertions, detentions and executions, the *rōjū*, concerned about Japanese becoming involved in conflicts in which the shogunate had no clear interest, issued orders forbidding the two companies from employing Japanese on their ships. They were also prohibited from taking indentured Japanese overseas, from exporting arms and munition from Japan, were ordered not to attack shipping, especially Portuguese, in waters around Japan (the precise limits were not defined), and were informed that there would soon be a full inquiry into the affair of the two priests seized on Hirayama's junk.[97] News of these orders, which amounted to another revision of the trade privileges, first reached Hirado in July and the full details in September. Both companies were completely taken aback. The Matsūra intended to apply the laws rigorously (the previous December, before the prohibitions were issued they had tried to search the *James Royal* to ensure that no Japanese were aboard but they did not prevent Japanese from serving in the first Manila voyage). On one occasion the Dutch were ordered to unload pikes that were to be sent to Batavia, protests notwithstanding that the weapons had been purchased before the restrictions had been announced. Osterwick reported that the prohibition 'is so strictlie lookt vnto that 3 Japons weare crucified ffo[r] hidinge themselues in the Swan wth intent to passe in her for Jaccarta'. Later there were fears that the restrictions might be extended to forbid the export of victuals and, more seriously, that limits might be imposed on the number of ships permitted to visit Hirado.[98]

The new regulations were an additional headache to add to the reverberations from the seizure of Hirayama's junk. The goods from the junk remained impounded, although stored in the English godown and elsewhere. Zuñiga and Flores, who steadfastly refused to admit that they were priests, had in accordance with local practice been handed over to the two companies to remain in their custody until the case against them was heard. (The Dominican historian, Diego Aduarte considered their refusal 'a lawful artifice' justified under the circumstances.)[99] By mutual agreement between the English and Dutch the men were detained in the Dutch factory along with two other Spaniards from the junk (the English had been given custody of the Japanese crew but they were quickly released). Missionary sources claim that the two priests were brutally tortured on various occasions in order to extract a confession. But as with the horror stories of the Inquisition that Protestants consumed so eagerly, these allegations are not sustainable. Pressure may have been applied, but the stories of torture, such as suspension from a rafter in a small cave with mortars filled with gunpowder dangling from their feet are preposterous. For one thing confinement was not so close. Two Japanese employees of the Dutch factory, one a jurabasso, were able to smuggle correspondence in and out for the priests as well as bring them food and clean clothing (the two were executed by the Japanese in 1622) and Cocks reports that a group of Portuguese merchants from Nagasaki and the erstwhile employee of the English company, Hernando Ximenes, managed to 'steale' one of the captive priests, but he was quickly recaptured.[100]

The rōjū had delegated the investigation of the two priests to the Matsūra and Hasegawa Gonroku. Both companies felt they had a strong case, even if the priests refused to admit their identity, and felt that their stock with the bakufu was running high. The case seemed open and shut to the English and Dutch, but it was far from so to the Japanese. Cocks and his Dutch counterpart were irritated by the long delay over the case. They were also concerned not to create new problems by incurring the displeasure of the shogun and rōjū for failing to make the requisite trip to Edo to pay their respects and give presents after the return of the ships from the first Manila voyage. Accordingly, they were eager to proceed to Edo as quickly as possible even before they heard of the restrictions barring the employment of Japanese overseas and forbidding the export of weapons. Cocks even felt it would be better to cut their losses and write off the junk and the booty 'then encur the Emperours displeasure', by delaying the visit to Edo. However, in September the daimyo, who had returned from Edo in August, insisted that Cocks and Specx stay in Hirado until Hasegawa arrived (he eventually came on 5 November) and the case against Zuñiga and Flores got under way. There had been so much rancour in the past with the Matsūra that Cocks could not believe Takanobu's assertion that 'we had no frend soe sure in Japan to trust vnto as he was'.[101] He believed that the daimyo's insistence that the English and Dutch remain in Hirado was yet another indication of Matsūra perfidy, speculating that the daimyo was in league with Hasegawa and the Iberians. He even claimed (absurdly) that the Matsūra were papist Christians.[102]

To complicate matters further, the Dutch decided that Specx should no longer stay in Japan but should leave for Batavia on the Swan which was ready to depart, in accordance with the orders previously received (he had remained in Hirado to perfect his accounts). Both the Matsūra and the English tried to pressure the Dutch to delay Specx's departure. The daimyo claimed that his experience and familiarity among the *rōjū* made his continued presence in Japan imperative. According to Cocks, Takanobu strongly recommended that Spex 'goe to Edo this yeare in respect he was well knowne to themperour & his Councell, as also thenglish had need to send one that knew the order of Japan, for that we had many enemies at Cort p'r meanes of the Portingales & Spaniardes & their well wishars w'ch were many'. He even threatened to forbid Specx's departure until permission was received from Edo.[103] But Janszoon, the Dutch commander whose authority, unlike that of his English counterpart, Robert Adams, was greater than the merchants', disregarded the Matsūra's advice and the opinion of the Dutch merchants that the former head of the factory should stay. He decided to comply with the orders from Batavia that Specx should leave Japan, which he did on 6 October.[104]

The exact reasons for his recall are unclear. His accounts for the factory, like those of Cocks, were in disorder, and there were rumours of embezzlement, although Janszoon was in no doubt that Specx would be able to counter any charges of wrongful accounting or mismanagement should they be made. After seven years in Japan, Specx, a man of considerable ambition, probably welcomed the opportunity to leave. At Batavia an examination of the accounts for the years 28 November 1614 to 28 December 1620 found them to be incomplete with gaps totalling thirty-four months. But the small sums unaccounted for were deemed to be the result of clerical error and Specx was cleared of any wrongdoing. His ambition carried him up the VOC hierarchy: he became governor general in 1629 and he was replaced by another Japan hand, Brouwer, in 1632.[105] The Matsūra reluctantly accepted the Dutch decision and recommended that two junior members of the respective factories should proceed ahead to Edo to take the presents and pay preliminary respects.[106]

In the event it was just as well that Cocks and his Dutch opposite number, Camps, remained in Hirado to argue their case even if there was reportedly some surprise in Edo, notably with Doi Toshikatsu, that they had not come earlier to counter the arguments of the Iberians who had been in Edo over the summer.[107] The affair of the two padres had acquired an importance greater than either the English or Dutch realised. The seizure of the junk and the Anglo-Dutch activities in the China Seas were threatening to disrupt Japan's overseas trade much to the alarm of certain senior bakufu officials who made investments in the Macao–Nagasaki trade. These men did not want their money put at risk by the English and Dutch fleet. Cocks alleged that Hasegawa, with the backing of the *itowappu* merchants, was sowing the seeds of suspicion about the English and Dutch, damning them before the *rōjū* as 'pirates and theevues [that] live upon the spoile of the Chinas and others', the same argument as the Portuguese and Spanish and, ironically, the English themselves had used previously in their complaints against the VOC.[108]

The Matsūra for their part sensed that the stakes were greater than a simple dispute over a junk. It was not just personal profit from the Macao trade that inclined some bakufu officials to nurture reservations about the English and Dutch. The shogunate was still consolidating its power, trying to tilt the balance of power between the daimyo and the shogunate further towards the latter. Some senior members of the bakufu favoured chipping away at the privileges enjoyed by the Matsūra and the margin of independence (however small this may have been) afforded them by the foreign trade conducted in Hirado. In February 1628 the VOC's chief factor at Taiwan, Pieter Nuyts, wrote to Batavia that Matsūra Takanobu was not much respected by the rōjū members who resented and were jealous of the presents and other profits he received from Hirado's foreign trade and the prestige the trade gave the Matsūra which was out of all proportion to the size of their domain.[109] The Matsūra, even if their anti-Christian credentials were not in doubt, had their ill-wishers in Edo as well.

It is against this background that Hasegawa's apparant partiality towards the padres should be judged. He was not, as Cocks foolishly imagined, a covert Christian. On his visit to Hirado in February 1621, en route to Edo, Zuñiga and Flores were brought before the daikan and denied that they were priests. Hasegawa, who knew Zuñiga was lying, remained impassive and refused to recognise the priest or take much notice of the documents the Dutch handed him and the matter was put on hold until his return from Edo.[110] When the trial proper started in November, Hasegawa tried to influence the case against the two companies by questioning the reliability of their witnesses, drawing out the proceedings as long as possible and trying to have them removed to Edo. If the English and Dutch failed to prove conclusively that the two men were priests then they laid themselves open to the charge of having unlawfully seized a Japanese vessel and sequestering its cargo. Their trade privileges could then be revised, at the expense of Hirado but to the benefit of Nagasaki and the itowappu merchants, who increasingly resented the freedom from the itowappu price which the English and Dutch enjoyed in Hirado – hence the Matsūra's keenness to support the companies. Takanobu insisted on retaining the proceedings in Hirado, outlined the strategy that the northern Europeans should adopt and fed them valuable information and advice.[111] The Matsūra did not want to lose their guests. Their reasons were not sentimental but pecuniary. The presence of the northern Europeans brought prestige t⌐ domain and, more importantly, boosted the local eco⌐ Manila voyages greatly so. It was not so much Zuñiga who went on trial in 1621 but the role of the Matsūra in Japan's overseas trade and beyond that the role of the English and Dutch.

The English and Dutch suspected that there was another dimension to the proceedings. Cocks believed that the protracted difficulties were caused by Hasegawa's scheming in favour of the Portuguese and Spanish. He felt that 'if we prve [prove] these 2 frires to be padres...then all is on our side, yf not all is lost'. In the meantime the cloud of suspicion under which the companies had fallen was 'the utter overthrow of the trade in Japon, noe one dareing to come hither fore feare of us'.[112] The English and Dutch viewed the proceedings as farcical. At one point Cocks, according to Sicardo's account, shouted that the Japanese could cut off his head if it were not true that Zuñiga had said mass in Nagasaki and was lying about his identity. Finally Zuñiga and Flores were shown to be priests largely on the evidence of a Japanese Christian apostate and former Jesuit, Thomas Araki, whose word was held to be decisive.[113]

In mid-December in Kyoto on the way to Edo from Hirado, which he had left on 30 November, Cocks was astonished 'to heare what a Coyle is kept in theese parts about our processe'. People expected that the English and Dutch 'durst never shew our faces before the Emperour, butt now we haue proued them such [that is, Zuñiga and Flores to be priests] makes all astonished'. He was sure that the outcome had boosted the standing of the two allies in Japan and that there were good prospects 'to get other matters redressed', especially the prohibition against taking Japanese overseas and exporting weapons, although he would not 'brag of it till I see the event'.[114] Eaton commented on the 'loue and ffrendship' the daimyo of Hirado had shown the English 'in takeinge our part against our enimies whome haue fought by all meanes possible to haue had vs putt forth of this Cuntrie'. He was similarly optimistic that their role in exposing the priests 'will make the better for us'.[115] Unlike Zuñiga, Flores and Hirayama and his crew, neither the English nor the Dutch were ever under threat of death, although at one point when it was obvious that the proceedings were going in favour of the English and Dutch, Cocks was alarmed to hear a report that Hirayama was demanding that if he were executed either Cocks or Camps should die 'according to the vse of Japon that he w'ch causeth an other man to die must goe the same way hym selfe'.[116] Commenting on the executions of the priests during the 'Great Martyrdom' in Nagasaki on 19 August 1622, (NS), Osterwick wrote that 'had wee not wth great diligence proved them fathers our selues had suffered their punishment' for seizing the vessel.[117] Perhaps he seriously believed this, or maybe he was trying to assuage his conscience. In a letter to the Company, Cocks played up the danger in order to impress his employers saying that if Zuñiga and Flores had not been revealed as priests 'themperour meant to haue put Capt Leonard Camps & me to death & to have Sezed on all we had in the Cvntry, & yf any resistance had byn made, to haue burned all our Shiping & put us all to the Sword. God send vs well out of Japon, for I dowbt it wilbe every day worse then other'.[118] As with Osterwick, one suspects he was trying to still a troubled conscience. Cocks was essentially a tolerant man.

The Matsūra's 'loue and ffrendship' had a price. The daimyo expected a cut from the Manila booty as did other local dignitaries. Takanobu not only expected but demanded and threatened. At first the demands were pitched too high, 20,000 taels from both companies. Cocks's protests that 'it was against reason for vs to take vp money at interest & lend to others for nothing' made little impression on the daimyo but at least Takanobu scaled down his demands, accepting 5,000 taels from the Dutch and 3,000 from the English. No loans were made to other members of the household. As with previous loans this one was paid mainly in goods, rated cheaply and the principal was to be repaid a year later. Cocks emphasised to the presidency that 'if we luve in Japon we must giue Content to the princes wheare we be as well as the hollanders dow or else we must giue ouer all'.[119] The money was eventually returned in 1622. A similar demand for money was made after the second Manila voyage and 4,000 taels exacted, once more under protest. On this occasion other members of the Matsūra household again demanded a share claiming that 'yt Costeth vs nothinge, itt beinge all stolne goods' which prompted another of Cocks's invocations to God to 'send me well from' Japan.[120]

The English and Dutch remained in Edo for eighty-two days (the whole trip took some five months) before finally being given permission to return to Hirado. They received no answer to their petition for the removal of the recent restrictions. At first Cocks accepted the delay as inevitable but once informed that a decision would not be forthcoming until after the daimyo of Hirado arrived, which was not expected until the early summer, he became frustrated and weary of the enforced stay in Edo and the refusal of permission to return to Hirado. He interpreted the fact that the shogun's present was not ready by the time of his departure as a snub prompted by the underhand dealings of the 'papisticall Christeans'.[121] The more irritated and impatient Cocks became the more his judgement became clouded. During his stay in Edo, Cocks had been questioned closely yet again by the rōjū about the puzzling nature of English religious beliefs and whether the English were in fact Christians. Cocks drew attention to James I's letter to the 'emperor' in which he styled himself 'defender of the Christian faith' but added that unlike the Spanish and Portuguese 'we held nothing of the pope of Roome but next & Emmediately vnder God from [the?] kynge', an answer which 'it seemed in som sort to geve them content'.[122]

Before their departure from Edo on 18 March 1622, Cocks and Camps appointed Momono Tarozaemon, Takanobu's secretary, to look after their business and receive the shogun's present on their behalf. News of the *rōjū*'s rejection of their request to have the prohibitions rescinded and orders for the companies to hand over the goods from Hirayama's junk to Hasegawa for the shogun's use were received over the summer. It seemed an unjust reward for doing the shogun's bidding. Coen, who especially welcomed Japanese immigrants in Batavia and Japanese weaponry, was displeased and ordered Camps to continue to lobby vigorously to have the restrictions removed. Cocks believed the rejection reflected the view 'that such a mightie prince as he is will not breake his word, once haueinge sayd us nay to people as wee are'.[123] If so, it was only a formal reason. The exposure of Zuñiga and Flores had not won the companies any accolades from the bakufu nor brought them the rewards they expected for their sterling service. The companies did not suddenly become most favoured foreigners. Rather the English and Dutch were being reminded to watch their behaviour. However, Hirado's foreign trade was guaranteed, at least for the immediate future.

(iii)   The Second Manila Voyage, 1621–1622

Throughout the year preparations for the second Manila voyage had continued. Having been forced to pay for ships' stores and provisions at premium rates in 1620, the factory had made considerable efforts to secure adequate supplies before the return of the fleet. Forward contracts were struck and payments were sometimes made in goods. The stores were procured from a number of sources, and, contrary to Sagawa Nobutoshi's earlier complaint, the lion's share of the material was provided by local suppliers, although timber came from the neighbouring domain of Ōmura, the Gotō Islands, and sheathing nails were bought from Bingo in the western part of Honshu, through the inn where Cocks had stayed on visits to Edo. Indeed, by February 1622 the factory was well stocked with wood suitable for sheathing and for masts, oakum, nails, spikes, iron hoops, pipe staves and yarn for ropes (made from high quality hemp). Most of the materials had been bought at cheaper rates by Eaton when the fleet was absent. Victuals were, of course, bought shortly before the fleet set out. The final cost of setting out the five ships (four were completely careened and sheathed, and the fifth, the

Moon, sheathed where needed) for the second voyage amounted to 22,234 taels 3 mas 7 candereen, hence Cocks's relief at the arrival of the *Peppercorn* with its much needed supply of cash.[124]

The voyage left Hirado in two contingents: the *Peppercorn* and the *Moyen* on 18 October 1621 with orders to cruise along the China coast between Ryūkyū and Taiwan until the rest of the fleet, which left on 23 November, joined them. Once again, factors went on the voyage which meant that only Eaton and Hudson remained in Hirado while Cocks and Osterwick were at Edo.[125] The voyage followed much the same pattern as the first, cruising in or near Manila Bay. There was no inclination to take on the Spanish forces defending Manila at Cavite although there was a token exchange of volleys before Manila. Negotiations with the Spanish for an exchange of prisoners proved fruitless. The English prisoners possibly included men from the *Unicorn*, some of whom were reported to have been taken from Macao to Manila. If so, they might have preferred employment with the Spanish or Portuguese as was the case with eight of the *Moon*'s crew who deserted near Manila; the Spanish would not have objected to the additional manpower. The Spanish and Portuguese prisoners were taken from galliots seized on 20 January. Chinese crewmen seized were generally released after being questioned for information about the whereabouts of other Chinese ships although the fleet was again scrupulous about not molesting *shuinsen* or Chinese vessels with a pass from Dutch factories elsewhere in the Indies. On 9 May 1622 a joint council resolved that four ships (two Dutch and two English) should detach themselves from the fleet and proceed to Macao where they were to cruise until 20 June while the rest of the fleet would patrol near the Pescadores (Peng-hu).[126]

Unknown to the Dutch admiral of the fleet, Janszoon, Governor General Coen had dispatched another fleet of eight ships, all Dutch, from Batavia under the command of Cornelis Reijersen, with orders to attack and seize Macao itself and establish a Dutch fortress on the Pescadores.[127] The English at Batavia had watched this fleet depart, unaware of its exact destination but surmising that it was intended for Macao or somewhere thereabouts in complete disregard of the accord. They knew that it carried equipment to build fortifications.[128] The destruction of Macao had long been one of Coen's ambitions and captured Portuguese documents which suggested that the settlement's defences were poor led him to believe that the task would be simple. The Dutch, or rather the governor general whose proposals had not been endorsed by the Heren XVII because they would entangle the VOC in yet another engagement, were pursuing an independent policy. Fortunately for the future development of the VOC, the Heren XVII's order to cancel the mission reached Batavia after the fleet's departure. Reijersen's orders were explicit. The English company was not to be permitted to assist in the attack on Macao in order to deprive it of any claim to a share of the spoils or right of dual occupation in the event of victory. Efforts to attract Chinese junks to Batavia had not met with success, hardly surprising in view of Dutch attacks on Chinese shipping at Bantam and in the China Seas. As a result, Coen had placed the goal of direct access to the China trade at the top of his list of priorities. One million reals had been set aside at Batavia to pursue this end. Reijersen's fleet carried 213,588 reals worth of pepper, sappan wood and lead; the rest of the account was kept on hold at Batavia. The first objective in Coen's grand strategy was the elimination of the Portuguese from China's overseas trade. Once the Chinese had been convinced of the greater advantages to them of dealing with the VOC rather than the Lusitanians, sixty per cent of available funds were to be spent on procuring goods for Japan.[129]

An attack on Macao was not in itself inimical to the English. Cocks had advocated that the fleet of defence should sack Macao which, if achieved, would destroy 'all the portingalls trade in these pts of the world...both for the Manillias, Malacca, goa & else wheare'. He argued, in much the same way as Coen, that the Portuguese enclave was an easy prey with poor defences and that 'as our frends [the Li] wch p^{r}ure our entry for trade into China tell me...[the emperor of China]...doe say that he wished that we Could drive them [the Portuguese] from thence'.[130] This suggests that a possible Dutch attack on Macao had been a subject for speculation in the factories at Batavia and Hirado for some time. However, Cocks completely misjudged Dutch willingness to undertake a joint attack and after seven years and nothing to show but fair words, his faith in the Li remained undiminished and his ignorance of China as great as ever. Yet there was some truth in the purported words of the Li. By the 1620s Macao's relations with both the Ming court and the Cantonese merchants, on whom they depended for supplies of silk and other goods with which to trade in Japan, Manila, Malacca and Goa, were indeed strained. The Chinese were angered by a number of activities in Macao: Portuguese traffic in Chinese children, who were sold into bondage; the presence of *shuinsen* (after the first decade of the seventeenth century no official *shuinjō* was issued for Macao but this did not stop *shuinsen* from calling at Macao, as Cocks had noted); acceptance of Chinese goods on which duties had not been paid; the avoidance of duties chargeable on incoming Portuguese shipping; and unauthorised building projects.[131] Moreover, the Ming court had even less awareness of the subtle distinctions between the foreign devils from the southern ocean than the Japanese shogunate, something which did not improve as the century progressed. When the Spanish were in the early stages of their occupation of the Philippines, many Chinese believed that they were indigenous Filipinos and in 1638 a paper written by some leading figures in Foochow made no distinction at all between the Portuguese and Dutch. Later, in 1667, during Pieter van Hoorn's embassy to Peking, mandarins believed that the governor general at Batavia was the 'king of Holland', implying that for them Batavia and Holland were identical.[132] Unlike some bakufu officials, the mandarinate in Peking were not involved or greatly interested in overseas trade, except in so far as it posed a threat to the peace of the empire. As a result they were less inclined to favour one group over another as traders on the maritime periphery of the Chinese empire.

Nevertheless, as was the case in Japan, the Portuguese still enjoyed some advantages over the Dutch and the English. Firstly, too many local Ming officials benefited from Macao's trade to wish to see it destroyed. It filled government coffers and lined their own pockets. Secondly, the Christian religion was viewed differently in China than in Japan at this time. It was not yet judged a threat to national security and the Jesuits had scored a success in China, gaining access to the ruling élite and bedazzling them with Western scientific knowledge which was eagerly devoured, although ultimately, the Jesuit achievement in China proved superficial and did not endure.[133] Thirdly, the Portuguese were sensitive to Chinese complaints and tried to remedy perceived abuses. They had to; they often depended on Chinese credit to conduct their trade.[134] As in Nagasaki, a trade rooted in familiarity and conducted according to long-established, mutually recognised procedures had much to recommend it. Yet within the broader context of trade along the southern Chinese coastal provinces the Portuguese could not remain complacent. Commercial rivalry existed between the Kuangtung merchants, who benefited from the Macao entrepôt, and those of Fukien, rivals of the Portuguese in Japan and at Manila. Fukienese traders at least would not have been dismayed by Macao's fall.[135] This wider backdrop was wholly unfamiliar to the English or Dutch, who were pinning their hopes on a decisive military blow against Macao rather than on patient diplomacy to establish themselves as the major European participants in China's overseas trade.

If the English were not opposed in principle to the use of force against Macao, they did object strongly to being treated as super-numeraries in the ensuing action, in blatant disregard of the accord between the two companies. The presence of the *Palsgrave* and the *Bull* during the assault on Macao was ignored and the two Dutch ships that had been accompanying them were reported to have endangered a part of pickings from the Manila voyage when they joined in the action.[136] The assault itself was a failure. Resistance was greater than had been anticipated and a well-placed canon-shot destroyed the Dutch landing party's ammunition. Casualties were high with an official Dutch tally of 136 dead and 124 wounded. The English at Hirado believed they were higher.[137] The débâcle, together with other recent Dutch setbacks, gave the English presidency something to gloat over, even if its elation was tempered by admiration of Dutch resolve in the face of adversity:

> hereby wee conclude that fortune's wheele goe Round and Cmitts not men allwayes to sayle wth full gales in their ambition and prosperryty yett our desembling frinde[s] make light of thes Crosses and losses befallen them w[ch] if truly considerd wee must confesse is Better then to hang ye head.[138]

The Dutch had mounted too high on the wheel of fortune, but the wheel continued to revolve, eventually carrying them to success once more.

After the repulse at Macao, Coen's fall-back orders for the occupation of the Pescadores, the barrren, windswept islands between Taiwan and the mainland known as the gate of Fukien and whose numerous inlets had provided shelter for the wakō in the sixteenth century, were implemented. Supplies were brought in from Japan to strengthen Dutch positions on the islands.[139] Dutch tactics were redirected towards attacks on the mainland at Amoy and the old practice of seizing junks and taking their hapless crews to Batavia. Ming officials feared a new wave of wakō activity was about to burst forth.[140] But the VOC tactics proved counterproductive. A sea-based power with 'barely sufficient force to set ashore unless under the protection of the ships' canon' stood little chance of forcing its will on a huge territorial power.[141]

It was at this stage that the Dutch themselves became involved more closely with Li Tan.[142] Always ready to exploit an opening, Li, on one of his periodic visits to the area in 1623, boldly asked the Dutch on the Pescadores to help him in his own activities off the China coast by lending him some vessels that would sail under Dutch colours. This request was refused although later Li was able to tap the Dutch for a loan of 4,000 taels to purchase silk on the mainland, in spite of a warning from Camps at Hirado to Reijersen that no money should be given to him 'for he is a sly man, with fine manners and several lovely wives and children at Nagasaki and here at Hirado' who owed the English 7,000 taels.[143] Nevertheless the Dutch on the Pescadores fell temporarily under the same spell as had Cocks. Reijersen's successor described Li Tan as 'a man considerably trusted by several high officials in China'. These were presumed to be officials at the Ming court. The Dutch commander was prepared, as Cocks had been, to entertain the belief that Li would open the door to China for the VOC. By August 1624 the Dutch on the Pescadores were themselves under seige, outnumbered ten to one by Ming forces determined to eradicate the potential threat off the Fukienese coast. The Dutch were lucky not to have been wiped out. Instead negotiations were started. Li Tan acted as intermediary, although his precise role in these events defies easy interpretation. However, it appears that he was no longer a free agent but was acting under orders from the Ming authorities who had taken hostage a child of one of his closest associates on the Fukien coast. The negotiations resulted in a Dutch withdrawal to Taiwan where at Tayouan, a sandy islet just off the coast at present day Tai'nan, they established a colonial city, Zeelandia, which they hoped would rival Macao.[144]

The Dutch commander, Marius Sonck, criticised VOC policy on the coast over the previous two years, complaining that it had 'so embittered the whole country against us, that we are universally regarded as nothing but murderers, freebooters, and pirates...Our Proceedings against the Chinese have indeed been very cruel and brutal and in my opinion such that we could never have obtained trade with China by this means.[143] However, the Dutch withdrawal to Taiwan was no defeat. It was the key which unlocked the door to a regular supply of Chinese goods and finally to a stable and profitable VOC trade with Japan.[146] The Dutch procured Chinese silk and from sources which were happy to rival the Canton merchants who supplied the Portuguese. By a supreme irony Li Tan helped turn the lock to Dutch success in east Asia; but he did so involuntarily, under duress. To some extent Cocks's advocacy of peaceful overtures as the best way to secure the China trade had been vindicated, but he had erred badly in making Li Tan the sole instrument.

The English enjoyed only a short-lived gratification from the Dutch setback in 1622. Cocks hoped that the English would be the benificiaries. He was heartened by Li Tan's assurances that he had sent word to Peking to deny that the English were involved in the occupation of the Pescadores. This was pure fabrication. The Ming court was unable to distinguish between the two companies. However, news of the Dutch attack on Macao again raised suspicions in Japan about the true motives of the companies. The last thing the Japanese wanted was a collapse of their trade with Macao.[147]

On 18 June 1622 six ships of the fleet, three English and three Dutch, returned to Hirado. The *Palsgrave* and the *Bull* returned from Macao on 8 July with news of the attack on Macao. The English presidency had made it known that the first voyage was 'not Answerable to [its] good hopes and Expectacon and the worse p.

discorde' between the companies. However, in September Cocks
was able to report that the ships had returned 'haueinge made a far
richer voyadge this yeare then they did the last and wth less skar
Amongst themselues then was the last yeare'.[148] (Dutch behaviour
towards the English before Macao was judged a separate issue from
the other activities of the fleet.) The fleet had captured six junks, a
Portuguese galliot and a number of sampans. It was decided to
ignore orders from Batavia sent in 1621 that goods seized from the
second voyage were to be sent to Batavia for sale there. This
deviation was justified on the grounds that since no Portuguese
galliot had come from Macao that year prices were higher in Japan.
According to Osterwick 'the like price is not to be found in any other
place of our trade' and that ready money 'wilbe as welcome as
comodities'. A further reason was that the Dutch, continuing their
previous practice, were planning to send a ship to Batavia with
silk.[149] The English felt that they would benefit from this. Camps
reported to his superiors in Batavia that he believed the English were
foolish to sell in Japan and should have sent their silk to England
where he believed it would have fetched a better price.[150] Cockram,
on the contrary, was confident that the price would hold because of
the continued Dutch blockade of Macao, even if some Japanese
merchants held back from making purchases in the hope that the
galliots would arrive and drive down prices.[151] By the first week of
September 213 peculs 14 1/2 catties of raw silk and over 2,300 pieces
of silk fabric had been sold or contracted for, with Nanking silk
fetching 320 taels per pecul, a good price.[152] Preliminary estimates
for the total value of the goods seized varied between 300,000 and
400,000 reals. The figure finally realised by the English was 159,405
taels 3 mas 9 candereen.[153]

   The cost of making ready the ships for their next assignment (the
Moon was now careened and fully sheathed, the other ships sheathed)
and stocking them with victuals came to 18,201 taels 2 mas 4
candereen. Once again Japanese carpenters had to be hired because
the crews preferred to stay ashore at 'tippling houses'.[154] Nevertheless, a total of 118,033 taels 7 mas 7 candereen was sent for Batavia in
bar plate, *soma*, *seda* and reals on the *Bull* and the *Elizabeth* (the
cargoes of the other ships are unknown but as they did not return
directly to Batavia their lading cannot have been important). A
further 43,880 taels 5 mas 1 candereen worth of goods, mostly
unsold goods (aloes wood, table linen and 'Sley and Polonia cloth'
and 415 ends of rusting English iron) was sent to Batavia together
with Chinese cotton cloth in various colours seized on the voyage
and victuals, desperately required by the presidency. Hopes of selling
the cotton cloth at Manila were dashed because the Chinese and
Japanese merchants who might have shipped it there refused to

handle it for fear the Spanish would realise its provenance. Some of the cloth was off-loaded at Jappra on the *Bull*'s voyage to Batavia where, because it resembled India cloth in quality, there was a market for it. When the presidency received the silver from Hirado early in 1623 it assumed that this was only an instalment and that money remaining in Hirado plus 'a good remaine of the first voyage' amounted to an additional 'great some'. In fact the balance between the sum sent and the Company's share of the spoil amounted to £8,549 19s, more than half of which had been used to turn round the ships. How much was kept for presents is unknown. There was nothing more to be sent from Hirado and there were no remains from the first voyage unless this meant money still owing for sales on credit. The inadequate accounts kept for the first voyage explain the misunderstanding. How much was traded privately after the second voyage goes unrecorded but on this occasion the men were not allowed one-sixteenth and mutinous behaviour does not seem to have been a problem. However, the presidency was certain that money had been 'sharked and stolen', a not unreasonable assumption.[155] In order to cut costs Cocks sent most of the silver to Batavia in bar plates provided locally in Hirado. To help resolve the still unsettled question of the quality of the silver that should be exported from Japan, two Chinese, supposedly experts in refining silver, were hired by Cockram at Nagasaki through Li Tan to sail on the *Bull* for Batavia to teach the method of refining bar plate into *soma*. They were to be paid 6 taels per month each plus food and 25 taels were advanced to each. Unfortunately, they failed to reach Hirado from Nagasaki before the ship's departure on 23 November but left on the *Elizabeth* at the beginning of January 1623.[156]

Apart from silk, one other good was greatly in demand in Japan in 1622, broadcloth, but the factory had none available to take advantage of the continuing buoyancy in demand despite the earlier requests by Cocks and Eaton. The Dutch had recently been supplied from Batavia and sold theirs for 20–30 taels per tatami, a good price. To rile the English they boasted that they sold more that year than during their whole stay in Japan. The most sought-after colour was stammel although black broadcloth still remained in demand. Osterwick suggested to Batavia that if the Hirado factory were to be maintained a supply should be sent from England. Cocks attributed the demand to rumours of war sparked by a disagreement between the shogun and his uncle. Such rumours had been circulating since the spring. Whatever the reason, the increase in demand was short-lived.[157]

On hearing the first optimistic forecasts of the takings from the second voyage, the presidency felt that it had been 'a Reasonable good voyage' but this welcome news was insufficient to shake off the

gloomy pessimism which gripped it at this time. The presidency
concluded that because of the costs of setting out the fleet 'our
masters can be noe gainers'. Nevertheless, when Batavia finally
received the money early in 1623 the presidency's first response was
relief that it had some liquidity at last to inject into its 'declining
affairs'.[158] Unfortunately, the silver could not be put to immediate
use. In December 1623 the presidency informed the Company that
there was a great store of Japanese silver 'lying by us dead'. Some had
been sent to Masulipatam where it was hoped to exchange it for India
cloth which could be used to purchase pepper and spices in the
Indonesian archipelago. 'But contrary to expectations, wee found
that want of gold or rialls to putt off wth the said silver' had thwarted
this effort. The presidency had tried unsuccessfully to dispose of the
silver in Achin, Jambi and other places and it intended to see if it
could be used on the Coromandel Coast. If this plan failed, as the
presidency suspected it might, the silver would be sent to England.
In any case it sent a chest of bar plate for a trial, a strange twist to the
controversy about bullion exports from England.[159] When a second
try was made to use the silver to obtain cloth in Masulipatam it was
sent along with reals.[160]

The reason why so much 'dead' silver lay on the presidency's
hands was simple. It was unrefined *bakufu chogin*. Why the presidency should have been puzzled by its lack of success in disposing of this
silver is itself astonishing. During Ball's presidency there had at least
been an understanding of the fact that silver minted into reals was the
preferred currency in the Indies. Hence the complaints to Cocks
about the quality of the silver sent from Hirado in 1617. The
presidency's problems were exacerbated by the fact that the two
Chinese sent from Hirado to refine the silver proved to be incompetent. They refined one chest of bar plate but the presidency found
it 'so badly donn that we would not lett them proceede any
further...for they spoile all they take in hand'. The men were sent
back to Japan on the *Bull* in 1623, wages unpaid, and Cocks was
ordered to reach a settlement with them.[161] The unresolved bickering about whether lozenge-shaped *haifukigin* or tin-like, long, thin
haifukugin was the most appropriate form in which to export silver
from Japan and the arguments about who was to pay for refining it –
Hirado or the presidency – bogged the English down and, more
seriously, fostered the impression in London that Japanese silver was
a problem commodity. This perception contributed to the directors'
subsequent negative assessment of their Japan factory. On this score,
at least, the factors at Hirado were not entirely to blame. But the
failure to exploit the availability of silver in Japan meant that the
Company excluded itself from one of the most profitable trades in
the Indies. During the seventeenth century silver coinage gradually

replaced gold as the medium of exchange in the Indies. By the 1640s and 1650s, before its export was banned by the bakufu, the VOC was successfully exporting Japanese silver to Bengal in return for raw silk and silk fabric. Of all the silver they sent to Bengal, Japanese silver returned the highest profit.[162]

After hearing of the poor results of the first voyage, the presidency had already decided to break off the Manila voyages after completion of the second. However, in comparison with the Goa voyage of the fleets of defence, the Manila ones had been a success. The English made a formal complaint to the Dutch about the conduct of the VOC commander of the Goa voyage, Dedell, for ordering his ships to cross the Indian Ocean to Mozambique. The English claimed that this had ruined the voyage and refused to join in a second one. The Goa fleet had netted only 36,591 reals from seizing some Portuguese vessels. As with the Manila voyages there had been 'exceeding grosse pilfering' by the commanders and mariners and the English commander, Green, emerged from the voyage with his reputation in tatters. He was accused of private trade and keeping '2 Portugal woomen (that were taken in the Carracks) in his Cabbin a yeare together' after refusing a 600 real ransom for them at Mozambique. He was alleged to have given them 'Costly apparrell' and more victuals than the ship's company.[163]

On 26 March the presidency sent orders on the Dutch junk *Firando*, which reached Hirado in mid July, for the redeployment of the ships because of their 'little expectation of theis manelia voyages'.[164] The *Palsgrave* and the *Moon* were to sail for Jambi in the Moluccas, the *Peppercorn* to cruise off the China coast to keep an eye on the Dutch proceedings in the Pescadores until December before returning to Batavia, and the *Bull* and the *Elizabeth* were to proceed directly to Batavia. The *Palsgrave* and the *Peppercorn* sailed on 16 October. The *Moon*, 'as sufficient stronge to goe for England as any in our fleet as the commanders and carpenters of our fleet doe giue Creditt', a tribute to the fine workmanship in Hirado and a reversal of earlier negative judgements, sailed on 15 November and the *Bull* on the 23rd with the money from the second voyage. The *Elizabeth* did not sail until the beginning of January because of delays in receiving some money from sales.[165] Along with these instructions the presidency had included orders for management changes to the factory, the first since its establishment.

The initiative for a reorganisation of the southwards factories came from the Batavia presidency itself. Short of cash, goods and victuals, the presidency was forced to examine the benefits of maintaining so many factories. However, the policy of closing down a number of them was not taken suddenly but only after careful review. Again, the decision was made by the presidency itself. The directors'

approval came later. The need for a review of the factories had been
pending since Keeling's aborted mission. When the presidency had
left Bantam in 1619 because of the hostilities with the Dutch it was
intended, in spite of the opposition of Dale, to relocate it temporarily
on the Coromandel Coast while Jourdain conducted a review of 'the
allmost decayed factories' in Jambi, Patani, Ayuthia and elsewhere.
Warfare with the Dutch and Jourdain's tragic death put paid to this
plan. Not only did the Company lose a highly able servant but the
presidency lost papers and accounts which Jourdain had taken with
him. These were seized by the Dutch who steadfastly refused to hand
them back, claiming they had sent them back to Amsterdam.[166]

Once re-established at Batavia, the presidency was aware of the
general state of affairs in the southwards region and fully understood
that all was far from healthy in the factories under its competence.
The hostilities against the Dutch had allowed some to languish even
further into decay. The presidency complained that the 'Accompts of
the Indies [are] Confuzed' blaming this on the factors, most of whom
it alleged were men of low ability who were poorly trained in the
keeping of accounts. It made some poignant recommendations to the
Court for the better management of the presidency itself, reviving
the idea of the need for a man equal in authority and 'sufficiencie' to
Coen to head it and for the presidency to have undisputed authority
over the voyage commanders. It also wanted full power and discretion over wages, a suggestion the Court was unlikely to accept. It
requested a royal commission to carry out the death penalty (which
as has been mentioned was forthcoming) and drew attention to the
need for accountants and for a secretary who could speak Dutch. In
the meantime it took some remedial action of its own and set about
trying to build up a more detailed picture of the state of its subordinate factories.[167]

A number of men at Batavia who were said to have the name of
merchant but not the competence were sent home. These included
Robert Randall who was found to be honest but not fit for employment and Richard Bishop who could not read or write and who was
alleged to have spent 800 reals over seven years in 'whooring and
drinking' (the presidency had spent 100 reals on his account for a
woman he had brought over from Macassar for whom he was
beholden to the sultan). The factor at Patani, Edward Gilman, was
described as a 'malefactor' for having squandered the Company's
resources there while blaming the Dutch for a state of affairs which
was the result of his own incompetence. Not all factors chose to hang
around the Indies until they were forced to return home and not all
were incompetent. Some, dissatisfied with exile, opted to return to
England after serving out their contracts. This meant that there was a
shortage of experienced men in the Indies. The presidency attributed

this to low wages.[168] In October 1620 the presidency ordered Jourdain's predecessor, and Cocks's persecutor, George Ball, to return from Masulipatam with his accounts. All other factors were required to send in a statement of their accounts, although the accuracy of the 'Ballance of the Estate of the Comp[a] in the Indies nowe sent home' is questionable.[169] Gradually a picture of the state of the southwards region emerged and in February 1621 the presidency described Ayuthia as a place of potential if properly supplied, Patani not worth the expense, while 'Ric[d] Coxe his aduise from Japan' was found to be 'vearie abiguous'. It was considered 'verie necesserie' that Cocks should be replaced by someone more able; he was considered one of the factors who had overstayed their usefulness. He was no more remiss than others, including his sometime Dutch counterpart, Specx, in failing to keep his accounts up to date or in an orderly fashion, but he did not inspire much confidence in Batavia by sending 'nothinge but two ould accompts of busines passed longe since' on the *Swan* which reached Batavia in November 1621.[170]

The orders brought on the *Firando* stipulated, as the presidency reported to London in August 1622, that Cocks, Eaton and Sayers 'which haue bene a longe Tyme att Japon [were] to come awaye from there in the ffleete for this place [Batavia]'.[171] Osterwick, assisted by two others was to remain behind as chief factor 'vntill we see what the next yeares bussines may Require, by aduizes which we shall recaue from yo[r] wor[s] in answeare to o[r] letters' or, as it was put in another letter, 'for Reformation of abuses in those pts'.[172] On hearing the news, Cockram reported to Batavia that he was certain Osterwick's 'honest cariedg and good gou[r]ment will Answere suficiently' to the presidency's expectations of sound management of the factory and that he for one had been much impressed with Osterwick's performance over the two years he had spent in Hirado.[173] Osterwick himself was gratified to hear of the promotion and promised to do his best. He wanted Robert Hawley to remain as his number two and Henry Dodsworth, who had come on the *James Royal*, to be an assistant.[174]

The prospect of leaving Japan was not unwelcome to Eaton. He had written to Batavia in February 1622 mentioning that he had been absent from England for twelve years 'w[ch] is a lounge time' and had been eight and a half years in Japan 'w[ch] is a place y[t] hitherto hath yealded butt smale pfitt or benifitt to our Hono[ble] Imployers and butt little to my selfe and others in the ffactory'. He repeated his wage grievances claiming that £18 per annum was not enough to defray 'my Charges of expences, this Cuntry beinge so Chargable as it is'. He requested permission to leave on the first available ship and asked the presidency to write to Cocks '2 or 3 words to lett me depart'.[175] Richard Hudson made a similar plea. He had been so young when he left England that he had been ineligible for wages 'wch doth nott a little discouradge me because I spend the prime of my dayes wthout any bennifit to helpe me in future time' and if he fell sick would have to rely on 'others Curtisies'. He pleaded with Batavia 'to fill vp the measure of my happines fo^r I shall Accompt my selfe happie if it should please god that once againe I should see my frends'.[176] After leaving Japan, Hudson made up for the lost time.

The presidency expected Cocks and the others to comply with its orders and come away on the first available ship from Hirado, the *Bull*, but Cocks, following the example of Specx, stalled and in fact none of the long-serving personnel of the factory left Japan. This was not because of any reluctance to leave the good life of Japan. In spite of the companionship of their consorts, neither Cocks nor any of the others had integrated themselves into Japanese society as had Adams, Van Sanvoort or even Joosten, and the cape merchant had expressed his desire to leave Japan on numerous occasions before. One can only conclude that Cocks deliberately took advantage of any excuse to delay his departure and that his motive for so doing was acute worry over the state of the factory's accounts and fear of being held responsible for the factory's obvious lack of success. The prospect of returning to England if not in disgrace then under a cloud to face the probing questions of the directors and a protracted inquiry into his conduct while his wages were witheld was terrifying and stirred up memories of his return from France in 1609. On that occasion he had been lucky. His connections had intervened to save him. Such luck could not be guaranteed again. Time was needed to put some order into the accounts and to ensure that Eaton, Sayers and Osterwick bore their share of the responsibility for the running of the factory. He was determined not to allow a repeat of the Wickham visit to Bantam in 1617 and the demeaning attack which followed. If he was not yet ready to leave Hirado then none of his subordinates would be permitted to depart either. He was afraid of what they might say in his absence in Batavia about the running of the factory, blackening his reputation and leaving him exposed to charges of incompetence.

Early in September Cocks wrote to Batavia declaring that he intended to reach there shortly but saying that he would not leave on the *Bull*. Instead he proposed to leave on the *Elizabeth* with Eaton. One reason he gave for the delay was the incompleteness of the accounts, which both Osterwick and Eaton were helping him balance. He added jokingly that 'to come away w^{t}out endinge Acco: your worshipp may bid me retorne backe againe like an old foule as I am and doe itt'. Another reason was the need to send mission to Edo with a present for the shogun following the return of the second Manila voyage. Osterwick was the most obvious person to undertake this and it would have enabled him to introduce himself as the new chief factor, but he was still busy with the accounts. It was decided, therefore, that Sayers, accompanied by Hudson, should make the journey. Cocks and Eaton would leave on the *Elizabeth* and Sayers would remain in Hirado until the next monsoon. However, even in this letter Cocks was inventing excuses for staying on. He contended that if the accounts could not be settled 'in short tyme' and if the money for the *Elizabeth* came in quickly the ship should still leave, 'she being a shipp of such great charg', even if 'we staye all 3 till next monson'. This prospect was not at all welcome to the others, a fact which Cocks noted:

> but itt seemeth they will not Condisend vnto me, but [will] goe away and leave all att 6 and 7, Mr Cockaram and Mr Osterwicke giueing them Councell to doe itt, of the wch I thought good to advize your worshipp beseechinge you not to thinke I neglecte your advize and stay here Contrary to your Commission as some tells me I doe if I stay, but I answer before god itt is meare necessitye wch constrand me to doe itt.

Cocks added a final, desperate excuse for the delay, the China trade. He had convinced himself that the Company was on the threshold of receiving permission to trade in China. Li Tan had told him that this would have been granted already and 'had it not beene for the tartar wars' and the death of '3 China kings in one year' (in fact two, the Wan-li emperor, who ruled from 1573 to August 1620, and the T'ai-ch'ang emperor, from August to September 1620) the English 'had beene there 2 or 3 yeares since'. Li had spent 12,000 taels to secure this permission so that 'if I goe away now and leave him he is vndone, offeringe to be our bond man and loose his life if he effects itt not wth a yeare or two to our owne Content'.[177]

The other excuses at least had a ring of plausibility to them. The final one was sheer delusion. Ball's comment that Cocks had had 'his imagginations leuelled beyond the Moone' appeared fully justified.[178] One can fully understand why the Batavia presidency concluded that it was 'neglecte' and not 'meare necessity' which led Cocks to linger in Japan. On 4 January 1623, before the departure of the *Elizabeth*, Eaton wrote bitterly to the presidency complaining that Cocks had had time enough since October to perfect the accounts for which he (Eaton) was responsible but that Cocks 'hath construned your letter to this effect that none of vs shall goe away from heare before he goeth himselfe wch when that wilbe, god knowes'. Eaton felt that he was being 'detayned here by force against my will' and 'intreate your worshipp for gods sake to giue such order in your letter that I may Come away from hence the next monson in the first shipp either English or dutch... for I should be very loth to stay here any longer tyme for Capt Cocks his pleasure'.[179] He could have been speaking for the others as well. Cocks's panic and self-absorption had foolishly lost him the loyalty of his subordinates, none of whom was prepared to stand up to him as Wickham had done.

Meanwhile, the Dutch were delighted at the prospect of the imminent departure of the English. Camps reported to Batavia, in words that echo Wickham's, that rightly supplied 'the Company [the VOC] will neither have had nor [will] have a more profitable place in the Indies than Japan when the English are out of it' and once the Portuguese had been excluded as well. He added that Cockram, whose 'chattering' enabled the Dutch to know what was going on in the English house, and 'all who have been here and those who are still here, have a thorough contempt for Japan, which we try to increase as much as possible, and, if you are inclined towards us, please do the same'.[180]

Hirado was not the only factory where the factors had ignored such orders. The factors at Ayuthia and Patani had similarly refused to come away in 1622. At Ayuthia the factor, Edward Longe, claimed that debts were outstanding and that the king was unwilling to see the English depart and had written a letter to James I (to be delivered by two ambassadors sent to Batavia) extending the hand of friendship once more and offering the English trade privileges throughout his domain. Batavia thought this worth taking up and, if a market for English cloth seemed likely to materialise, would consider reopening the factory. In August 1624 the Roebuck was sent to Ayuthia to buy rice and other provisions and returned the following January with the provisions, a 'kind' letter from the king of Siam and a present.[181] At Patani the factor John Jourdain, a nephew of the deceased president who had come to the Indies with his uncle in 1618, had incurred debts of 4,000 reals and said he could not leave until the money was received. Inspection of his accounts showed that he had not defrauded the Company and that indeed his pay was 'in deep arrearages'. His estate, such as it was, was seized and his refusal to obey orders was referred to London.[182]

The decision to close these factories and the Hirado one was based solely on short-term economic considerations reinforced by the insubordination of the factors. It was not irrevocable. The Batavia presidency under Richard Fursland was more resolute in pursuit of discipline than its predecessors. The lash was freely administered for violent drunken behaviour, fights and absence without leave. Other punishments included a spell in the stocks or in the bilboes, no light punishments under the tropical sun, and docking of pay. One individual was ordered to be ducked three times from the main mast of his ship for wounding a 'black' (a Javanese) in the thigh with a sword while drunk. He was also to pay seven reals as compensation to the man and three reals for his medical treatment. The incident was said to have caused a 'greate scandal'. A tougher approach to pilfering and illicit trade also prevailed. Those caught trading with Chinese below ships' decks were to lose two months pay and could receive the lash. Fursland was intent on establishing higher standards of morality. John Vincente, the Italian 'Commander of the blacks' was ordered to be placed in the stocks and lose three months' pay for fornicating with a Javanese woman 'in his Chamber, uppon his bedd, the light unto and the dore shutt'. This was considered a light punishment because it was Vincente's first offence. The unfortunate woman, on the other hand, was ordered to receive fifty lashes with a rattan 'well lade on by each one of the woomen blacks, being seuen in number'.[183] In this atmosphere it is not surprising that reports about Hirado being more akin to the cities of the plain than to an East India Company factory constituted another argument in favour of recalling the factors. If the stories about life in Hirado were to be credited, the presidency reported to London, 'it is a misery to know that men of such antique yeares should be so miserablie giuen ouer to voluptuousness, regarding not what they consume therein'.[184]

The presidency received word of Cocks's disobedience of its orders when the *Elizabeth* reached Batavia on 4 February but it was not before 25 April that it passed a resolution to close the Hirado factory and withdraw all the factors. (In February the *Bee* had been sent to Patani and Ayuthia to close those factories and bring down the factors 'they being both places of great Chardg and noe way proffitable to or honble Imployers as divers yeares Experience hath manifested'.)[185] Cockram was ordered to return to Japan on the *Bull*, commanded by Mathew Morton, to close the factory and bring to Batavia all remaining men and goods. If debts outstanding could not be collected before the ship was due to return to Batavia, Cockram was given discretionary power to leave two men in Japan to maintain the factory while the debts were collected. They were then to return on a Dutch ship. Under no circumstances were Cocks, Sayers or Osterwick to remain. Friendly, respectful leave was to be taken of the daimyo to whom the Company's house, godowns and other buildings were to be entrusted until the presidency sent someone else to repossess them. If Cockram deemed it unsuitable to leave men behind, then the Dutch were to be given power of attorney to collect the debts. Cockram was also authorised to purchase 10 peculs of camphor which the Dutch, according to information provided by Osterwick, bought in great quantities and which the English presidency wanted to test for sales in England or on the Coromandel Coast. The *Bull*, which was to be sheathed at Hirado, was to take along some India camphor to see if it would sell in Japan, although there was some doubt about the chances of selling the 60 catties that were loaded.[186] The placing of the factory's buildings in trust with

the Matsūra and the instructions to test the market in Japan were
indications that the door to the Company's Japan trade was not being
closed but left on the latch.

The *Bull* was supposed to leave on 20 May and call at Jambi to
procure what goods she could for Japan, but her departure was
delayed for a few days. A terse, uncompromising letter, dated 22
May, addressed to 'Mr Cocks and the rest' was given to Cockram.
The letter expressed surprise that none of the factors had shown up in
any of the returning ships of the defence fleet and doubted that there
was any excuse to explain 'so great disobedience'. Not knowing
who was to blame, judgement and censure would be reserved for the
moment. Cocks was ordered to deliver

> into the handes and custody of Mr Joseph Cockram all such monnies,
> goods, debts, etc., as pertaine to the Honorable Compa. our imployers,
> and boath you, Mr Richard Cock, William Eaton, Edmond Sayers and
> John Osterwick, shall all and every of you come awaye from thence
> uppon the ship Bull for Batavia, herby charging you and every of you to
> fulfill our saide order, as you will answere the contrary at your perelles.

As for Li Tan's fate, Cocks was told that he had 'two long deluded
you through your own simplicitie to give creditt unto him' and the
factors were reminded that they had lived 'long enough in those parts
to be better experienced of the fraudulent practizes of those people'.
Steps were to be taken to secure satisfaction for the money Li Tan
owed the Company. The factors were ordered to adhere strictly to
Cockram's instructions and to make speedy efforts to procure the
victuals and ships' stores Batavia wished to receive from Hirado. The
letter touched on other points, including the quality of the silver to
be sent back. The presidency insisted that no bar plate was to be sent,
only *soma*, *seda* or *fibuck*, provided there were no difficulties in
exporting these grades. (There was, of course, no prohibition against
the export of refined silver so long as it was refined by official
assayers.) The presidency ignored Cocks's previous statements about
the high cost of refining the silver and who should foot the bill,
Hirado or the presidency. The letter closed by restating 'our commission in the conclusion of our letter, least having read itt in the
former part therof, you should forgett it before you come to
thend'.[187] The Hirado factory was ending in disgrace.

(iv)   Closure of the Hirado Factory, 1623

The directors upheld the Batavia presidency's decision to close many
of the factories in the southwards region The reasons are complex
but quite unrelated to the notorious massacre of Amboina in 1622,

news of which reached London in June 1623.[188] In the calculations
of the directors and the presidency, any withdrawal from east Asia
was short-term. Professor Chaudhuri is correct to stress that despite the volley of complaints from Batavia that the presidency was
undersupplied and neglected and the corresponding attacks by the
directors on the laxity of the factors in the southwards region, the
Company had begun to supply the presidency adequately from 1622,
a time when criticism of the Company's export of bullion was at its
fiercest. The volume of pepper imports increased noticeably between
1622 and 1626, especially when compared with the decline evident
from 1619 to 1622. The directors had to increase supply or face the
complete loss of their previous investments. Professor Chaudhuri is
also right to emphasise that the Company had underestimated the
investment required for the southwards factories to yield the profits
that were expected (the Hirado factors knew this from bitter
experience) and that the directors had made a serious error in
believing that the Dutch would make reparations for English losses
in the hostilities of 1619.[189] The scale of the support for the Batavia
presidency can be judged from the figures preserved in the letter
from the court to Batavia, written in the spring of 1623. This records
a startling injection of 428,000 reals sent out on the *Abigail*, *Roebuck*,
Hart, *Coaster* and *Charles*, which left England in April, and mentions
that a further 40,000 reals in bullion and goods had been sent on the
Discovery which had left for Surat and Batavia in 1622.[190]

The degree to which the Company had underestimated its investment requirement can be gauged from the same source which lists
the balances, or rather what the Company presumed the balances
were, remaining in the southwards factories. This provides an
astonishingly healthy picture wholly at odds with the reality. The
Hirado factory alone was listed as having a balance of 87,700 reals
even after the dispatch to Batavia of the 156,000 reals on the *Bull*.
This made it appear the best-provided factory in the region. (The
original stock in 1613 had been 23,114 taels 7 mas 6 candereen or
£5,778 14s).The total capital resting in the southwards region was
put at 1,027,300 reals.[191] In the absence of the Company's account
books it is impossible to know how these figures were reached. The
directors had received enough information about Hirado from letters
brought back by Pring on the *James Royal* (which had reached
England in September 1621) about the factory's unprofitability and
poor condition. In view of the directors' upbeat assessment of the
southwards factories it comes as no surprise to learn that they had no
intention of turning their back completely on Japan. The blame for
the poor showing so far, it was believed, lay with the personnel. (In a
perverse way Wickham's estate, the struggle for which was underway, had shown that profits could be made.) The directors had also

read a report from one of their servants on the availability of bullion
in the Indies, including silver in Japan and gold in Sumatra, which
would obviate the need for exports from England. The author
blamed the Company's poor trade on the hostilities against the
Dutch and advocated participation in the country trade from settled
factories.[192] The directors ordered the presidency to send Cocks
home on the first available ship 'to give vs further relacion of those
places' but added that 'If after wardes yo^u shall haue occason^s to vse
anie factors at Japo^n yo^u may send some other fitt man for that place'.
The directors also noted with approval Batavia's 'resolve to dispose
of vnprofttable & vnnecessary factories' and the removal of incompetent, idle factors, mariners and men and emphasised that they
wanted 'the weeding off them all out'.[193] There was no order from
London to the presidency in the early 1620s to close factories;
discretionary powers were given to Batavia to make decisions as it
saw fit. Indeed far from abandoning east Asia the Court talked of
establishing a presence off the China coast.

At government level there was renewed interest in the Company's
trade with the Indies and matters left unresolved by the 1619 accord
with the Dutch. Such interest was related to the foreign policy
agenda of the English government, especially the tortuous evolution
of its policy towards Spain in the early 1620s. In January 1621, at the
beginning of his first parliament since 1614, James had received
supplications from the Dutch for English help should war break out
between the United Provinces and Spain on the expiry of the Twelve
Years' Truce in April 1621. The Dutch were greatly alarmed at the
prospect of an embargo banning all Dutch shipping from Spanish
ports, a potentially lethal blow to the country's economic survival.
While James did not want to give any guarantees, he was keen to
send a signal to Spain that England was at least prepared to consider
involvement in any hostilities in the hope of pushing Spain towards
peace, thereby avoiding a European conflagration.[194] Even while
pushing his project for a marriage between Prince Charles and the
Spanish infanta, a match which was opposed by some of the privy
Council and widely disliked outside it, there was much to be said in
favour of a negotiating stance which dangled the carrot of marriage
before the Spanish while simultaneously threatening them with the
stick of English assistance to the Dutch. It is against this background
that the treaty between England and the Netherlands, concluded
towards the end of January 1623, should be interpreted. The treaty
dealt mainly with restitution for ships and goods damaged, lost or
confiscated during the hostilities between the two companies prior to
the signing of the accord in 1619 and for a restoration of the island of
Run to the English company. Other matters, such as the construction of an English fort near Batavia and proposals for future co-

operation, including a joint effort to open up trade with China in which both companies would be equal partners, obviously proved more contentious and were set down in a supplement to the treaty. The English company could scarcely have expected the Dutch to be accommodating on these questions and the suspicion exists that the directors were happy to see the accord lapse while hoping to benefit from the concessions on restitution.[195]

The treaty was of little consequence but copies of the text and supplement were sent to the Batavian presidency in the spring of 1623. In their covering letter the directors reported that the future of the fleets of defence was under review and that the king favoured moderating the number of ships involved and using them only 'in merchandise and defence so that our merchant ships can perform as well in Bantam, Manillas & Mollucas as at Surat & Persia'. In the Court's estimation the Dutch were using the accord to further their own ends and cited the Dutch seizure of the Pescadores in 1622 in which the *Palsgrave* and the *Bull* had been mere spectators. The seizure of the islands was interpreted in London as an attempt 'to ingrosse the China trade solely to themselves and exclude vs'. In both Amsterdam and London the Dutch 'doe...make great boasting in expectance of wonderfull proffit thereby'. The Court asserted that the Dutch had unjustly excluded the English from the Pescadores even though it was the English who had made the occupation possible by keeping the Spanish at bay – a distortion of the truth. The Dutch were said to 'haue drawne vs along to make o^r shipping a meanes of their conqueste'. Batavia was given guidelines to extricate itself from the accord, at least as far as the fleets of defence were concerned, while not giving the Dutch 'a playne deniall'. (In other words there was to be no unilateral repudiation of the accord.) The directors were greatly intrigued by what was going on in the Pescadores and instructed the presidency to set out a secret voyage of reconnaissance to find out 'howe comodious it is for them and what trade it produceth'. If the trade looked promising steps were to be taken to set up an English factory in the vicinity, preferably on an island with a good harbour some two leagues from the mainland where the Court had been informed by one of the factors in Batavia that the Chinese would come to trade. (Presumably this meant one of the islands around Amoy, Hsia-men.) This information had been furnished by a Chinese at Batavia who was to accompany the voyage – shades of Li Tan. If the island was found suitable then 'lett them plant upo^n it' and be supplied with all necessities. Additional supplies would be sent from England. The voyage was to be provided with 'a good sum of money to trade there with junks for silk but if they shall refuse to trade wth yo^u then yo^u may make prazis of them'[196] There was no mention of where any of the silk it was hoped to buy on the

China coast was to be sold or what goods should be used by the
English to establish the trade but the only conceivable destination for
the silk was Japan.[197]

The presidency shared the directors' misgivings about the VOC's
attitude towards the accord and drew up a stinging critique of Dutch
violations which was tendered to the Dutch council in Batavia.[198] In
its reply to the Court, the presidency commented that the Hollanders
sought by 'the consumption of yo[r] Shippes and ruine of yo[r] Stocks'
to achieve 'their Soueraignties...[and] turne you out of all Trade at
their Pleasures or els putt such intollerable yoaks uppon yo[u] that you
wilbe forced of yo[r] selues to leaue off all Trade in those parts'.
However, the presidency was doubtful about the chances of slipping
past the Dutch fleet around the Pescadores, which it estimated at
sixteen vessels, and landing near Amoy for the Dutch 'will you haue
no share nor part in their achivem[ts] except uppon such unreasonable
terms that you were better be w[th]out it and so much Generall Coen
declared vnto vs uppon the sending awaie of his first ffleet uppon
those Expolits'.[199] The ambitious plan was quietly dropped. Besides,
the presidency was more concerned with the immediate task of
flushing out Cocks and the others. Once that had been achieved, and
circumstances permitting, Japan and the Company's trade in east
Asia could be looked at with fresh eyes.

The *Bull* arrived at Hirado on 19 July and Cockram, to whom
Cocks, swallowing his pride, had now to defer, set about the task of
closing the factory. On 20 July a letter was sent to Takanobu, then in
Kyoto where Hidetada was visiting to receive imperial authorisation
to hand over power to his eldest legitimate son, Iemitsu, another
important symbolic step in the Tokugawa consolidation of power.
The letter was carried by the jurebasso Co John. It rehearsed the
orders brought from Batavia and stated that the *Bull* hoped to leave
Japan, its mission accomplished, by November. The letter stressed
that the decision to leave Japan did not proceed 'out of any vnkinde
vsage heare in his Mat[ies] Dominions' but from the 'daunger of the
Seas' between Java and Japan. The Company had lost two ships in
recent years on this route (one was presumably the *Unicorn*) and
recently a ship (the *Tryall*), which, it was said, was carrying cargoes
from England specifically for Japan, had been lost on her outward
voyage 'by wh[ch] meanes wee reste alltogether vnprovided of goods
to supplie this factorie'. If 'the next yeare shall produce better
encouradgement [we] (maye then) returne againe'. For this reason
the factory's buildings would not be sold but left 'to Your Highness
intreatinge they maye be kepte for vs and repocessed by vs if wee
shall returne hither againe, of which yo[r] highnes shall haue due
advice everie yeare.' A similar letter was enclosed for the *rōjū* which
Takanobu was requested to deliver if required. There were apologies

for not sending an Englishman to deliver the message (it had been concluded that if any of the English went up to Kyoto they would be unable to return to Hirado in time for the *Bull*'s departure) and for the absence of presents as the ship had not been furnished with anything suitable.[200]

However, protocol could not be sidestepped so easily and within a week the English were informed by Matsūra officials in Hirado that it was necessary to send at least one Englishman to Kyoto with presents in order to secure permission to leave. After consultations, Hudson, the youngest and least likely person to dally in Kyoto, was chosen to fulfil this requirement. The presents selected were of small value 'beinge such as tyme will aford and our abilitie of meanes strech vnto'. The shogun was to receive five pieces of cushion velvet worth 45 taels and various *rōjū* similar gifts, although Doi Toshikatsu's was worth more than the shogun's. The total value of the presents was 269 taels.[201] Hudson left for Kyoto early in August, taking along 'his maiesties Goshen, wi^{ch} was grannted vs for o[u]r free traficke heare in Japon' and which the Matsūra had advised would have to be surrendered in order for the English to have formal permission to leave Japan and return at some future date. Cockram and Cocks requested that the Matsūra retain the document in Hirado to ease such a return.[202] There is no record of Hudson's journey nor of exactly when he returned, but the visit delayed the *Bull*'s departure until late December. In the meantime the factory complied with the other instructions from Batavia. Victuals were bought for the presidency some of which were paid for in goods (mostly silk).[203] However, efforts to secure the payment of debts did not proceed smoothly. The Matsūra were given presents to win their co-operation. The daimyo himself, who had returned from Kyoto by late November, did better than the shogun, receiving presents worth 299 taels 4 mas 5 candereen out of a total of 744 taels 1 mas 5 candereen given to his household. But the Matsūra regarded the presents as their due, the customary ones on the arrival of a ship, not as a prerequisite for additional favours.[204]

By the middle of December, shortly before the *Bull* was ready to leave, the English complained that despite their 'best endeauours, both by curteous meanes and alsoe by complaininge to the Justises' they had failed to recover all debts owing to the factory. A sum of 12,821 taels 8 mas remained outstanding. After deliberation the English decided that as the debts were unlikely to be forthcoming quickly it would serve no purpose to leave anyone to collect them. Accordingly, the Dutch were to be authorised to gather them and send them on to Batavia in *soma* or *seda* plate. The factory's debtors were to be requested to sign papers in Japanese acknowledging the sums owing. On 22 December the papers giving the new *opperhofd*,

Cornelis van Neyenroode, power of attorney to collect the debts and copies of the list of debtors were handed over to the Dutch. Copies in Japanese were presented to the Matsūra. But there was 'much adoe with Tonomon Sama, Semi Dono, Taccamon Dono & others to give vs their bills...& when they didd itt, put in what they list'.[205] Their debts amounted to 417 taels 7 candereen, 670 taels 6 mas, and 437 taels respectively.[206] For the Matsūra the pieces of paper were meaningless, but at least Cockram could take evidence to Batavia that he had done his best to carry out the presidency's orders. Most of the other debts were small and not all debtors evaded their responsibility to pay up. For example, in December Kawabuchi Kuemon (Cawabuch Kewiero-dono), who owed 400 taels, paid back half of the debt leaving 200 taels outstanding, the figure on the list given to the Dutch.[207] The biggest debts were those of Yoshemoro Shojero-dono, 3,218 taels, and Li Tan, 6,636 taels, almost half the total.[208] Li had returned to Japan from the Pescadores in the summer. Surprisingly, the English record of these final months in Hirado makes no mention of his presence although Dutch sources record it. It was only after the Dutch learned of the extent of Li's indebtedness to the English that Camps, before leaving Hirado, warned his colleagues in the Pescadores to beware of lending him money.[209]

The Dutch were concerned to find out what other papers the English had left with the Matsūra and after the *Bull* had departed, Neyenroode approached the daimyo and requested copies of all the letters he had received from the English. Neyenroode was anxious to make sure that no aspersions had been cast against the Dutch and that the Hollanders had not been blamed for causing the English to withdraw. The Matsūra willingly complied. But the Dutch need not have worried themselves.[210] Some goods were also left with the Dutch and stored in a godown. They were placed in five boxes and forgotten about until 8 September 1634 when they were opened by the then *opperhoofd*, Nicholaes Cockebacker. The goods included a number of skins which were found to be damaged and worthless.[211]

The last few days in Hirado were hectic. Presents, 'few exceeding two or three tales', were given to the factory's servants. The *Bull* loaded her cargo: 6,926 taels in silver (according to the Dutch, low-quality bar plate as there had not been enough time to have the silver refined); ships' stores, which the presidency later described as 'trash and lumber', the remains of the sheathing wood procured for the fleet of defence and valued at 800 reals; victuals; and what the presidency termed 'branded wares, mostly worthless'. Household expenses and the sheathing of the *Bull* had eaten up the rest of the money and the goods carried from Batavia had been used for presents. The camphor does not seem to have been sold.[212]

As the day of departure approached there were sad farewells. On 22 December 'many of the townsmen came with their wives and families to take leave of the factors, some weeping at their departure'. The following day the Dutch and many of the 'Japanese friends' of the English came aboard the *Bull* at Kōchi. Cockram was sufficiently moved to deviate slightly from his orders and postponed the departure so that an impromptu party could take place. Cocks and Osterwick proposed leaving 50 taels as a gesture so that a second party could be held after the ship had left, but Cockram overruled them and at noon, on Christmas Eve, the *Bull* set sail for Batavia.[213] The Company's direct trade with Japan had come to an end after ten years, six months and twelve days. It was not until the 1850s that Englishmen once more traded officially in Japan.[214]

The tears that had been shed before the ship's departure were genuine, at least on the part of the Japanese. Some were tears of regret at the passing of a business opportunity; others were more personal and heartfelt. A measure of the sadness about the exit of the English can be read from letters written in Japanese by two of the factory's employees a short time later. One, to Cocks, was from Oto, who had been Matinga's servant. She enquired whether Cocks had arrived safely at Batavia and hoped that he would soon return to Hirado. She thanked him for his 'kindness while you were in Japan and wish to see you once again and offer my heartfelt thanks'. She concluded her brief note by asking Cocks to help her find employment in Batavia.[215] The other letter was addressed to Sayers from 'Mateyasu', possibly Matias who served on the *Bull* on the first Manila voyage. He wrote that 'I cannot forget the friendship you showed me while you were here' and hoped that Sayers would soon come back. He urged the Englishman not to worry about Maria and asked to be remembered to all the English individually.[216] In his letter Mateyasu had asked if 'Uriemon arrived safely'. This was young William Eaton whose mother, Kamezo, also wrote to Cocks rather than to the '*ishikiriba*' (*escrivão*, scrivener, that is, Eaton). She thanked Cocks for the 'kindness you showed me while you were staying here and beseech you to take care of Uriemon. I am relying on you [more] than on my own father, and I have always said this to Uriemon. Please be kind enough to take good and gentle care of him, and I wish you also to be on good terms with Ishikiriban.'[217]

The tensions of the last year in Hirado had not gone unnoticed. Quite why young William was sent from Japan on a Dutch ship after the English had left and who was to be responsible for him is unknown. Perhaps it was thought that at some future date he might return to Japan and reopen the Company's trade in much the same way as Robert Parke had expected Christopher and Cosmos to do. Kamezo seemed to think that Cocks would be responsible for him but when she wrote she was unaware that he was already dead. However, young William Eaton was to distinguish himself, becoming the first Japanese to attend a British university. On 5 February 1639 he was made a denizen of England by which time he was already a student of Trinity College, Cambridge. Some time during 1640 or 1641 as a senior sophister in the college, he petitioned Charles I to intervene with the master and fellows to secure his preferment to scholar, pointing out that in the last election of scholars he had missed his turn 'being by the will of god visited with extremitie of sicknesse'. He described himself as 'borne in Japaon one of the remotest parts of the east Indyes' and 'in his yonnge yeares brought into England where by the charitable dispocion of some and by like well disposed people hath hitherto bene mainteyned in y^{or} Ma^{ts} Colledge in Cambridge'.[218] It is likely that these 'well disposed people' included the governor of the East India Company and possibly Sir Thomas Wilson, himself a graduate of Cambridge, although not of Trinity.

The English may have shed tears as well (they were after all leaving their women and children) but, as Camps had reported before, they were glad to be getting out of Japan. Only Cocks had misgivings but not for sentimental reasons; he did not relish the prospect of the inquiry at Batavia. None, except William Adams, had chosen exile. Trade in Hirado had produced headaches rather than rewards for the factors, apart from Wickham. Japan, with its cold winters, hot, humid summers, its interfering and unpredictable local officials, was no paradise, caboques and consorts notwithstanding.

The *Bull*'s new sheathing did not prevent her from springing a leak on the first night of the voyage to Batavia although she managed to reach Batavia safely on 27 January.[219] Almost immediately the inquest into the recent affairs of the Hirado factory got under way.[220] The presidency, now under Thomas Brockeden, found that the accounts were totally confused, with nothing perfected since 1617 (the time when Osterwick's accounts break off). Of the factory's accounts since then all that existed were two waste books with assorted entries by one or other of the factors. When asked to explain this Cocks replied 'that he was ashamed his acc^{os} were in such disorder' and shifted the responsibility to his subordinates arguing that Osterwick and Eaton had received and delivered all goods from the Manila voyages (there had been very little other trade between 1617 and 1620) and that he himself had taken no charge of them. But as head of the factory and the individual responsible for its management he could not absolve himself so easily. He was told that if he had chosen to delegate matters he should at least have demanded periodic accounts. He said he would answer only to the Company for that and 'doubted not but his acc° be found good and iust'. When questioned about his role, Eaton replied that he had only taken responsibility for the accounting of the goods from the first Manila voyage and that he had presented his accounts for that voyage to Cocks, who never even looked at them. After examining the accounts the presidency found goods to the value of 596 taels unaccounted for; Eaton claimed that they had been stolen. Cockram, Osterwick and the others all agreed that goods had been received in a 'confused manner', attributing this to circumstances beyond their control such as pilfering when the goods were being divided between the two companies. Eaton, they said, was not to blame. The presidency accepted this and left it to the Court to decide whether it wanted to pursue charges against Eaton. As for the second Manila voyage, Osterwick said he could give 'iust accompt' and was granted time to perfect his accounts. Judging from his earlier surviving accounts this would not have been a difficult task for him. It was agreed that all other goods received and handled at Hirado had not been entrusted to the care of a particular individual 'as they all affirme and the wast books show'. This shifted the burden of responsibility back to Cocks,

as principall, yet are not the rest wthout fault for they pceiuing Mr Cox wholie to neglect the hon^{ble} Comp^{as} busines their care ought to haue been the greater and to haue advized thereof in due time: but example is so forceable especially in Superio^{rs} that most comonly those who are vnder Comand doe imitate their good or euill qualities & conditions.[221]

This was not the end of the matter. The counts against Cocks 'collected by orselues and from the advize of others' were failure to keep proper accounts, or at least to supervise delegation satisfactorily, 'suffering all to runn on for many yeares in such Confusion'; ignoring orders from Batavia to leave Japan in 1622; not using the extra time to perfect his accounts or collect outstanding debts 'for wch his staue was pretended'; allowing Li Tan to run up debts in goods 'which might have been sold for readie money', and more seriously for receiving a 400-tael investment from Li at the departure of the *Bull*, as witnessed by Cockram, Eaton and Osterwick and a matter 'unjust & preiudiciall vnto [the Company]'; bringing 'such store of trash and lumber' from Hirado that the *Bull* 'was exceedinglie pestered therewth'; and finally failing to keep a record of consultations and not observing decorum and order. The presidency decided against seizing Cocks's estate for the Company's use. So far as it could discover the estate did 'not exceed 1,500 Rs [reals] wch is not much considering the long time he liued in the Countrie'. It also decided against sending him home in disgrace as a malefactor although it did feel that in view of 'the insufferable neglects and

abuses Comitted to yor [i.e. the Company's] preuidice' there was a
prima facie case for doing so. There were mitigating considerations,
his age, status and especially 'the weake est[ate] of his bodie and his
teastie and waieward disposition'. Too harsh a treatment 'would be
the shortning of his life'. After further deliberation, the presidency
'generally resolued to deale mildlie wth him here and referr him
wholie to yor [the Court's] more iudiciall c[ensure]'. Nevertheless,
his estate was ordered to be seized pending the Company's final
decision and he was forbidden to convey anything to England.[222]

As for the others, the presidency concluded that it could not
charge Eaton and Sayers with anything 'other then aforementioned'
and at the end of its deliberations asked Cocks if he had anything to
say in defence of himself or against the charges of his erstwhile
subordinates. Cocks, now a broken, pathetic figure, answered 'no
and indeed how can hee charge anie one except hee had comitted
especiall trust in pticular to any of them'.[223] It was an insufficient
answer. He was paying the price for his short-sighted, high-handed
behaviour in 1622 in refusing to allow the others to leave and to let
Osterwick take over the management of the factory. His action had
raised suspicions about his subordinates' motives in Batavia and not
surprisingly they were determined to clear themselves. By the time
they had reached Batavia whatever loyalty, respect or affection they
had possessed had evaporated. Cocks had no one to blame but
himself for his final isolation. It was a sad, diminishing end to his
stewardship of the Hirado factory and to what had been a varied and
full career. Yet not all of Cocks's accounting was inadequate. After
Cocks had left for England the presidency in one of its numerous
squabbles with the Dutch had cause to examine the charges for the
Swan which had joined the fleet of defence on terms negotiated by
Cocks and Camps. The presidency found Cocks's negotiations to
have been satisfactory.[224]

The presidency ordered Osterwick to remain behind in Batavia to
write up the accounts of the Hirado factory as best he could, which in
turn would enable those of the Ayuthia factory, which had 'dependence' on Hirado, to be perfected. Cocks expressed no objection.
The others were to leave for England 'for they being able to giue no
reason at all for anie thing that appertaines to the said acc^{os}, it were
needlesse to keepe them here uppon Charge'.[225]

Within a month of arriving at Batavia, Cocks, his health broken
and his spirits depressed, was once again aboard ship, the *Ann Royal*,
bound for England. The vessel left Batavia on 22 February, finally
clearing the road on the 26th. Just over a month later at the end of
March, after passing the Sunda Straits, an unfinished journal kept by
one of the crew noted that 'Captan Cock died, and was buried under
a discharge of ordnance', a small mark of honour for a man who was
otherwise returning home in disgrace.[226]

The other members of the Hirado factory continued to serve the Company. Osterwick was still in Batavia in August 1624 using his acquaintanceship with Specx to glean information from the Dutch. But he did not live much longer and by 1627 he was dead. His affairs were promptly settled by the Company on the intercession of no less a figure than Sir Robert Cotton.[227] Eaton and Sayers sailed on the *Ann Royal* but did not return directly to England. They disembarked at Surat. In November 1625 both men in recognition of their experience were made members of a council of sea captains which was to consider measures to protect the Company's ships from the Portuguese. In March 1626 the sea captains, who included Goodhall, master of the *Ann Royal* and Charles Clevenger, who had served on the Manila voyages, were reminded that the merchant members of the council were to have an equal voice in the deliberations and votes. However, both Eaton and Clevenger soon set sail for England and on 24 November appeared before the directors. Eaton was described as 'a factor from Japan, who went out with Capt Saris 15 yeares since in the *Hector*'. The Court, 'having no leisure to Conferr wth them', they were referred to another time. Their second appearance took place on 2 December. Eaton was questioned about his service in the East Indies and what he knew 'of the Carriage and Condicon of Mr Cox and how he dyed', what number of servants were in the Company's house at Hirado, what entertainment they had had and 'by what meanes so great an estate of the Comp[any']s was spent by Cox & such like', testimony to the directors' own ignorance of these matters. Eaton seemed uncooperative, making 'cold and vncertaine answers' and was dismissed so that he could 'recollect his memory' and from his 'bookes and noates...make a short and briefe Journall of his service done the Companie and how he hath spent his time and bin imploied during his aboad in ye Indies' for the Court.[228] Unfortunately, if prepared, no such document has survived.

The Court had an immediate reason for finding out about the conduct of its affairs in Japan, quite apart from the possibility of an extensive post-mortem. On 24 November Richard Cocks's elder brother John also appeared before the Court to present a petition regarding his brother's estate. John Cocks was told of the

debaust Carriage of his brother and the euill service performed by him at Japan, where he had liued long Contrarie to the Companie's mind and had expended 40ᶜ pounds [£4,000], neuer returning anything to the Comp, but consuming whatsoever came to his hands in wastfull vnnecessarie expences, nay for 3 yeares togeather refused to come away when by expresse order from the Comp. he was called thence, insomuch that at last the President and Councell were inforced to send for him w'th a ship sent purpostlie'.

Richard's estate was said to be 'very little or none at all' at the time of his death and what existed was insufficient 'to answer the Comp. what he ought them, haveing confessed upon foote of his accompt at Jaccatra that he was indebted to the Companie 900*li*'. Unaware that the Court's version of what had happened at Hirado was a travesty of the facts, John Cocks said that he 'was sorry to heare this report of his brother'. He requested the Court to deal favourably with him. The Court recommended him 'to informe himselfe Concerninge the truth of theis things from those that are come home' (that is, Eaton and Clevenger) and because business was pressing suggested that he return to Staffordshire and leave the matter in the hands of the Company.[229] The directors had excelled themselves in their customary heavy-handed tactics to ward off claims by the relatives of deceased employees. Stunned by the gravity of the charges made against his brother and shocked by the allegations of debauchery, John Cocks took no further part in the efforts to secure his brother's estate; he did not even approach Richard's patron, Sir Thomas Wilson, who had intervened before at the request of Richard to help secure a job for his younger brother Walter. Two of Richard's nephews, the sons of Margery Cocks and William Staresmore, the sole surviving executor of Cocks's will, were not so easily cowed and took up the cudgels against the East India Company which was determined not to return the bond Richard Cocks had made on entering its service. The nephews were energetic in their quest, demanding access to their deceased uncle's accounts. After persisting for almost four years John Staresmore was able to settle with the Company for £150, less than half the estimated value of the estate calculated in Batavia.[230]

There were problems over setting accounts with Eaton and with Sayers's executors (his brother and sister; Sayers had died on the voyage to England in 1626). Eaton was still petitioning the Company in 1632 for payment of his wages. His claim was complicated by private trade involving 550 pieces of calicoes brought back by Eaton and another factor for the account of the former chief factor at Masulipatam. Calicoes were not among the goods the Company forbade its employees from trading in but the fact that the cloth had been discharged from the *James* at Rochester to avoid paying freightage irked the Court. The calicoes in question were seized and placed in the customs house and in 1632, when Eaton was petitioning for settlement of his wages, he requested remission from the freight charges on the calicoes.[231] Sayers's executors fared no better. When his brother and sister petitioned the Court for settlement of his estate they were told that this was not possible as no papers or accounts belonging to him had been handed to the Company and that, like Cocks, he had died indebted to the Company. The Court rejected the contention that Saris had doubled Sayers's wages from 20s to 40s a month (it had rejected the similar contention by Mrs Wickham) challenging them to obtain proof from Saris that he had done so, and had even been authorised to do so. In the end the pair were glad to receive £100 in satisfaction of all demands against the Company.[232]

The other surviving long-term member of the Hirado factory, Richard Hudson, joined Cocks, Eaton and Sayers on the *Ann Royal* from Batavia. But after leaving Surat she ran into trouble and by the time she reached the Comoros had lost 90 of her 133-man crew. Rather than proceeding to England she put back to Surat, which she was lucky to reach in October 1625. Hudson decided to return to Batavia where he arrived in October 1626 and requested a new appointment. His new round of service with the Company was in India and in September 1628 he began work as a factor at Masulipatam and on the Coromandel Coast. He soon acquired a reputation for dishonesty and, had there been a suitably qualified successor, would have been repatriated. At the end of the 1630s his luck ran out and he was sent home on 1 December 1639 along with Thomas Clarke, the accountant at Masulipatam, to face the wrath of the Company.

Upon arrival in England, which Hudson had not seen for over twenty-five years, in July 1640 both men were arrested and imprisoned on charges of misdemeanour. The case dragged on for two years. However, the Court, concerned lest the men fell ill and died while in prison, attracting bad publicity for the Company and, more seriously, depriving it of any possibility to recover the sums for which the men were accountable, decided to release them on condition that they attended the Court daily and undertook not to flee abroad. (The Privy Council, before which the Company had brought serious cases against its servants in the past, had other matters to contend with in the summer of 1640.) Hudson and Clarke, anxious to clear their names, agreed to these conditions. The two men hated each other. Clarke, who was said to be unfit for any employment except 'to sitt in a Tapphouse', had overtaxed his liver by excessive drinking and was reported to have become incapable of discharging his duties. More seriously he was accused of collaborating with and receiving money from John Weddel, commander of the first highly ambitious voyage of the Courteen Association, the rival company enjoying royal patronage and attempting to break the East India Company's monopoly in the Indies. Hudson was accused by Clarke of having run up bad debts of 8,000 reals and of alienating the local authorities and merchants by reckless, high-handed behaviour for which his colleagues believed that the local Indian authorities would have been justified in arresting him. He was also said to have seized 1,800 reals together with numerous accounts and papers from Clarke's room without making a proper inventory. This action could have been justified on the grounds that it was necessary to remove the incompetent Clarke but his colleagues no longer trusted Hudson and believed he had behaved solely for his own ends. The Court was incensed by the behaviour of the two men but after a full examination Hudson was found to be indebted to the Company for only £188 10s, considerably less than the 8,000 reals Clarke had alleged, and the 1,800 reals in dispute between the two men was later discovered to have been sold to Hudson by Clarke. The directors were inclined to deal lightly with Hudson. In spite of the allegations of private trade, he was said to be living in poverty and on 4 May 1642, after signing a general release, the Company awarded him £100 on account of his twenty-nine years' service.

Over the next few months Hudson worked under the Company's management, supervising the unloading of homecoming ships. He refused an offer of employment in the Indies, which struck the directors as ungrateful. However, in October 1643 he decided that prospects were perhaps better in the Indies than in a country already divided by civil war and the following month was appointed a factor at Bantam to serve for five years. The Company itself was in no position to be selective and even Clarke was given another chance. After some negotiations, Hudson was awarded a £60 advance on his wages. By this time Hudson was married and his wife was awarded £15 per annum from her husband's salary during his absence. Once in the Indies he served in Masulipatam again and in Bengal, areas which, like Japan, proved disappointing for the Company's trade. He did not live to see England again and died in India before the expiry of his term of service. He had devoted a lot of time and energy to private trade but unlike his erstwhile mentor, Wickham, an East India fortune evaded him.[233]

Neither the factors nor their relatives and friends had any reason to look back on the Hirado factory with nostalgia. Only Wickham had profited from his stay in Japan but he had not lived to enjoy his gains and they turned out to be a poisoned chalice for his mother who had to fight hard to wrench free what she could from the Company's tight-fisted grip. It was an especially rough justice that was meted out to the relatives and friends of the deceased factors after such long service in Japan and the Indies. The directors never blamed themselves for mistakes, only their employees. Service in the Indies was a gamble in a lottery to seek some fortune. But the stakes were high and the dice loaded against the individual. If shipwreck, disease or some other act of nature or violence from his fellows did not take a man's life he survived to face the prospect of an extended struggle with the Company to obtain what he felt was his due. The wonder to the modern mind is that so many men still thought the job worthwhile.

CHAPTER 8

Further Attempts at Direct Trade after 1623

(i)   The Hirado Factory and Knowledge of Japan in Seventeenth-Century England

One aspect of the Hirado factory remains to be considered: its contribution to knowledge about Japan and the East Indies in contemporary England. George Ball may have complained in 1617 that Cock's letters were 'copious but not compendious; large but stuffed with idle and needless matter, ill keeping one of your place, years and experience' but a modern historian obviously would disagree.[1] So too did at least one of the recipients of Cocks's copious letters, Sir Thomas Wilson. Knowing of James I's interest in the world beyond Europe (he had from his days as king of Scotland built up an extensive library of geographical and cosmographical works and was reported to have read Purchas's earlier volume *Purchas his Pilgrimage* six times),[2] Wilson sent one of the cape merchant's letters, written in January 1617, to the king. He included a 'long scrole of fyne paper', which appears to have been a Japanese almanac, and an account of the estates and revenues of the daimyo, 'most of them, equally or exceeding the reuenues of most of ye greates Princes of Christendome'.[3] The two additional items had originally been sent by Cocks to Salisbury in 1614. Unknown to Cocks, Salisbury had died in 1612 and the items had remained with Wilson, who probably felt that Cocks's latest letter provided an ideal occasion to show them to James. Wilson sent a covering note saying that he had received the letter 'from ye most remote part of the world' and described the author as 'not lettered yett a man of honesty, yeares and judgment'. Obsequiously, he suggested that 'it were a good recreation for your Ma^ty (if you had any ydle howres)' and declared that 'nether our Cosmographers nor other wryters have giuen vs true relacion of ye greatnes of the Princes of those parts'. Later he discussed the contents of the letter with the king, which described Edo, the shogun's magnificent retinue as Hidetada led a falcon-hunting party (hunting was a pastime he had in common with the British monarch), the great *daibutsu*, or Buddha, of Kamakura, the sights of Kyoto, including an excellent description of Sanjūsangendō temple, and recent developments in Japan concerning the banishment of the missionaries. But James 'co[u]ld not be induced to believe that the things written are true but desyred to speake with the writer when he comes home' and dismissed the contents as 'the loudest lyes that ever [he] heard of'.[4] Wilson forwarded no more letters to the king.[5]

Regardless of James's scornful dismissal, the extant archive of the Hirado factory is the fullest of the Company's factories in the southwards region; the only comparable one is that of Tongking which operated from 1672 to 1697, a factory which in many ways mirrors the Hirado one. Only a small portion of the letters, journals and other documents sent back from Japan was printed, and then only in Samuel Purchas's *Hakluytus Posthumus or Purchas His Pilgrimes*, published in 1625. There is only one other published reference to the Company's presence in Japan by someone who had been there, Patrick Copland's *Virginia's God be Thanked, or a Sermon of Thanksgiving for the Happie successe of the affayre in Virginia this last yeare*.[6]

The fact that so little of the material found its way into print is unsurprising. Whatever interests some of its eighteenth century servants may have pursued in their free time, the East India Company was a business organisation, not a society dedicated to the creation of a corpus of knowledge about distant lands. It guarded jealously information about its activities, determined to prevent knowledge of its affairs from falling into the hands of competitors or critics who might use it to damage the Company. Both Hakluyt and Purchas were indebted to the Company's first governor, Sir Thomas Smythe, for making material available to them and in February 1622 when Purchas applied for permission to consult some of the Company's journals 'that might give him lighte' to complete his undertaking to produce 'a great volume of there voyages' (he added pointedly that he only wanted to consult 'the historicall voyages, and will medle wth nothinge') his request was granted. However, there were certain restrictions. Nothing was to 'be taken out of their Journalls but that wch is proper to a History not preiudiciall to the Companie and they entreated Mr Deputy that he would take pains to puse the notes before they were carried out of the howse'.[7] Purchas ignored his undertaking to 'sett downe [the rivalry with the Dutch] otherwise then they be in the Journalls' but with the arrival of the news of the massacre of Amboina he could afford to.[8] However, the circumstances which had permitted the easy transformation from manuscript to publication that had greatly assisted

Hakluyt in his undertaking were already changing by the time that Purchas took it upon himself to continue Hakluyt's work. Purchas commented that after the establishment of joint-stock voyages in 1613 access to East India Company material became more difficult and in 1694 the editor of a collection of voyages to the South Seas mentioned that he could provide no information on recent voyages because he had not been able to see any journals relating to them.[9]

Purchas was fortunate that there were other channels through which he could gain access to material and he was able to secure additional material on Japan from John Saris and Sir Thomas Wilson both of whom supplied him with copies of letters from Cocks. Saris also furnished him with the revised version of his journal for the *Clove* and Purchas commissioned Arthur Hatch, who had served as preacher on the *Palsgrave*, to write a description of the country which bears favourable comparison with Cocks's observations. The material on Japan published by Purchas was the most comprehensive account of the country available so far in print in English. Besides the documents relating to the Hirado factory, Purchas published translations of Jesuit and other missionary letters, possibly bought from Hakluyt's executors.[10] Other contemporary or near contemporary publications touching on Japan made no mention of the Hirado factory.[11]

Copland's references to Japan in *Virginia's God be Thanked*, a stirring sermon preached before the Virginia Company on 18 April 1622, not long after his return from the Indies, sought to draw a moral lesson from his experiences intended to further the activities of the Virginia Company. Copland told of the stormy weather encountered on the passage from Bantam to Hirado on the *James Royal* in 1620. It had been 'as if Jonah had been flying unto Thor...an Egypt night of five or six days perpetual horror'. The tempest was only stilled by God's mercy. 'He pitied the distresses of his servants, He hushed the Tempest, and brought us safely to Hirado.' Japan, he commented, 'aboundeth with all things for profit and pleasure, being one of the mightiest and opulentest Empires in the world, having in it many rich mines of Gold and Silver' and because Virginia shared the same latitude, his propagandist logic led him to expect that Virginia would furnish similar riches, much to the profit of the company's backers. Finally, he stressed the need to promote the gospel in the new colony because the Jesuits in the Indies and in Japan had possessed many thousands of native people 'with the Coloquintide of Popery'.[12] Here was one lesson at least from the Hirado factory!

However, it was not simply the Company's reluctance to provide access to the details of its trade to outsiders that inhibited a wider dissemination of information about Japan and other places in the

Indies; there was not much of a market anyway for books on the East
Indies in England. The Company's activities failed to take hold of the
educated public's imagination as had the exploits of Drake,
Cavendish and others in the preceding century. Up to 1614 the
Company's early voyages had inspired only five publications.[13]
Moreover, the connection between overseas adventures and state
policy had become less obvious, less direct even if some of the
advocates of a West Indies Company in the 1620s appealed to the
spirit of the Elizabethan voyagers to support their case for the
establishment of the new company.[14]

Overseas voyages in the pursuit of trade and encounters with
different races, creeds and cultures did not broaden the seventeenth-
century English mind to any noticeable extent. Nor did it lead to a
questioning of accepted interpretations of the origin of man and of
notions of social and political organisation. Such questions had first
been raised after the discovery of the New World, a vivid expression
in itself, but the traditional authority of the Bible and of the ancients
on such matters remained remarkably unshaken by the voyages of
the sixteenth and seventeenth centuries. There was little in the way
of an intellectual voyage of discovery to match what were, from the
European perspective at least, voyages of discovery. In the words of
Professor J. H. Elliot '[t]he possibilities of relativism as a weapon
for challenging long-established religious, political and social assumptions [had] as yet barely been grasped'.[15] At the end of the
eighteenth century the naturalist and geographer Thomas Pen
believed 'HOLY WRIT our safest guide on all occasions' for the
study of Asian history,[16] although he might have added that
scripture was open to different interpretations, as the tremendous
upheavals during the English Revolution had shown.

However, one should not judge the early seventeenth-century
servants of the East India Company too harshly. Even if these men
were almost all without exception intellectually unequipped for such
a task, it was not their purpose to promote the kind of fundamental
enquiry that would lead to a radically different interpretation of
the world. Even after the greater possibilities for travel, work or
residence abroad had been opened up by the process of industrialisation, travel did not broaden the European mind appreciably. The
experience generally served as a mirror with which to look inwards,
either to the self or to society at home. For the Victorians and
Edwardians, travel did not eradicate ignorance nor lead to a greater
understanding of the countries rapidly becoming accessible to
them.[17] At least Cocks and his colleagues elsewhere in the Indies
considered neither themselves nor their society superior to the people
and civilsations in which they worked. The Japanese experience of
attempting to open a window to the West after the Meiji Restoration

in 1868 bears interesting comparison with the West's longer experience of contact with Asia. The Japanese were more intent on acquiring Western scientific and technological knowledge. In this they were, and have remained, successful. Their efforts to understand the essence of Western culture and civilisation have not been characterised by a similar level of achievement.

At a less exalted, more practical level, English geography was not noticeably advanced by the East Indies voyages.[18] After the mid-century the Fellows of the Royal Society were still intrigued by the possible existence of the fabled islands of gold and silver to the east of Japan (islands which Cocks in 1616, although not Vizcaíno and his mission from Acapulco in 1612, nor the Dutch in 1640, had concluded were non-existent), by the likelihood of a northwest passage, and by the question of whether or not Japan was an island, a question which Robert Boyle noted in the early 1690s still needed to be answered conclusively.[19] The distinction between fact and fantasy remained unbreached.

In this respect Ibn Muhammad Ibrahim's account of Japan, based on information he acquired on an embassy from the Shah of Persia to Siam in 1685, bears fruitful comparison with those of the English and other Europeans. Ibrahim's description is an elegant tapestry of truth and poetic invention partly accounted for by the literary conventions of his culture. As with the European accounts, the references for comparing the phenomena of an alien culture and society are those familiar at home.[20] In England the 'travels' concocted by Sir John Mandeville, whom Purchas considered 'the greatest Asian traveller that ever the world had', were republished in 1612 and 1618 and remained influential into the following century.[21] Thus there are strong grounds to doubt Professor Lach's claims for a central role for Asia in the making of Europe.[22] Judging from the remarks of James I, printed and unprinted accounts and descriptions of the Indies failed to have the impact on the educated, literate classes Professor Lach would have us believe.

The information about Japan that was published as a consequence of the Hirado factory did nothing to alter the generally positive, if vague, image of Japan that had existed before the voyage of the *Clove*, that of a civilised society, husbanding its resources, exactly the image that Copland was outlining in *Virginia's God be Thanked*. Pagan it may be, and governed by men determined 'utterly to roote out the memory of Christianitie out of Japan',[23] but these policies came across as anti-papist rather than anti-Christian *tout court* and, therefore, were not necessarily antipathetical to contemporary Englishmen. In 1596 the most articulate spokesman for a military conquest of Ireland, Edmund Spenser, advocated that the leaders of opposition to England rule in Ireland (he had in mind Catholics)

should be cut down by the sword if they refused to submit.[24] No one
contemplated such a policy towards Catholics in England no matter
what threats from Habsburg Spain were conjured up by the
imagination of paranoid Protestant minds. A Protestantism that was
almost entirely non-proselytising in the Indies at this time, even if
advocates of missionary activity were to be found in both England
and the Netherlands, could afford to gloat over the reversals suffered
by papism in Japan, and Protestants, to the extent that they were
troubled by such concerns, could indulge themselves in the
deception that the Japanese were anti-papist not anti-Christian.

The material on Japan published by Purchas remained a major
quarry from which future writers hacked out accounts of the
country, notably the eighteenth-century travel writers who
compiled thick anthologies about distant lands to satisfy the desire
for titillation of their readers. Purchas was later supplemented by
English versions of works by François Caron, Arnoldus Montanus,
Jean de Thevenot, and Engelbert Kaempher.[25] The presence of an
English factory was sometimes mentioned in later works which
touched on Japan but the detail had been forgotten and the facts, even
elementary ones, were often inaccurate.

One of the earliest and most vivid of these works was written by
Sir Thomas Herbert, who had been with those arch-confidence-
tricksters, the Shirleys, in Persia. It appeared in 1638. The preface to
the reader by the Lord Fairfax, Baron of Cameron, defines the
character, scope and purpose of this literary genre:

> Here thou at greater ease than he
> Mayst behold what he did see:
> Thou participat'st his gains,
> But he alone reserves the pains,
> He travell'd not with lucre sotted:
> He went for knowledge, and he got it.
> Then thank the Author; Thanks is light,
> Who hath presented to thy sight
> Seas, Lands, Men, Beasts, Fishes and Birds,
> The rarest that the World affords.

Herbert, who mentions that the English had had a factory at
'Fyrando', plagiarised and embellished Saris's description of the
appeasement of the goddess Amaterasu Ōmikami at the Ise shrine. In
Herbert's concoction, salacious rituals were enacted by the priests in
the 'Fotique' (he follows Saris and makes no distinction between
temple and shrine) to appease the 'Prince of darknesse'. The 'roome
is first made glorios with Lamps a burnisht gold, and a preperation
by incendiating *Lignum vitae*, or other gums and perfumes'. Then the
place is thrown into darkness and a young virgin, carefully selected

for her looks, who has been placed 'right against the Mamada or Idoll' is visited by 'the Devill' whose work has to be seconded by the priests 'who ravish her with songs and pleasant musique'.[26] The priests' more common predilection for sodomising boys, which had caught the attention and censure of Xavier and his successors, escaped Herbert's notice. But Herbert was not writing about Japan as such. Japan was a metaphor for his anti-papist and anti-Laudian sentiments. It was the first time that an imaginary Japan served such a figurative purpose. The genre remains with us reconstructed in the countless books proffering lessons from Japan's economic success. Herbert's yarn was repackaged in Thomas Salmon's *Modern History: or the Present State of All Nations* and is indicative of the use made of the small amount of new information published about Japan whose provenance can be traced back to the Hirado factory.[27]

Ultimately, it is fruitless to dwell at length on the image of Japan that emerged from the published Hirado material. Japan remained undifferentiated from the rest of the Indies in the seventeenth-century mind, remote both physically and in most people's consciousness. There was no reason why this should have been otherwise even if one takes issue with Dr John Harris's dismissal in 1705 of Cocks's account of Japan in Purchas as 'long and tedious and besides intermixt with abundance of vulgar, frivilous, and unprofitable matters'.[28] What is more worthwhile is to examine what use was made of the even greater amount of material that remained in the Company's custody when it looked at the possibility of re-establishing direct trade with Japan at various times later in the seventeenth century, before finally (in 1671) sending three ships from England on a mission to request a resumption of the trade.

(ii) Japan, the Summum Bonum of the Indies

The question of what use the directors made of the Company's extensive archive of the Hirado factory can be answered easily: none. Contrary to Professor K. N. Chaudhuri's view, the East India Company did not possess a 'highly developed sense of corporate history' by the mid seventeenth century.[29] Such a sense implies a conscious policy of preserving its records for consultation in order to provide information to improve the decision-making process. This was not the case; the Company did not treat its records either with care or respect. Like most business organisations its time horizons were short. One organisation which did place a high premium on maintaining proper archives was the Society of Jesus. Loyola himself had recognised the importance of records and in the Indies the

provincial archive in Goa, modelled on the Society's archives in
Rome, was established in 1583.[30]

From its earliest years when it had more the character of a group of
individual merchants united for a particular purpose, a single
voyage, the East India Company was quite the opposite in its
attitude towards the preservation of records. In 1604 when certain
documents were sought for consultation they could not be found.
The Court ordered that in future records should be better preserved,
but it is clear that this sensible order met with little success. In July
1608, the Court ordered that all letters from Bantam were to be put
together in a book and 'Quoated for future memorie as occasion may
fall out'.[31] The formation of joint-stock adventures after 1613 altered
little in this respect. In December 1614, for example, the Court noted
that a search was to be made for various missing journals which it
was suspected had been lent to outsiders, and the following year, in
August, the Court declared that it had been 'much wronged' by
lending journals before copies had been made.[32] Perhaps the
directors had in mind the journals written by voyage commanders
and its other servants. As has been noted, in January 1615 Saris had
been asked to hand over his journal and provide other information
for Keeling to study.[33]

There were occasional bursts of enthusiasm for putting into order
the vast amount of documentation that accumulated in London. In
the 1630s a volume of abstracts of all letters received from the Indies
since 1619 was compiled and in March 1669 the secretary was
instructed to supervise the indexing of the Court Books (the minutes
of the Court of Committees) from the Company's foundation.
However, in April 1682 it was reported that there were many 'old
books and papers which are in a confused manner layd up in the
garret of the [East India] House'. Some years later it was discovered
that one of the journals of the Surat factory, a factory that was still of
considerable importance to the company – unlike the long since
defunct Hirado one – had been stolen and that 'great quantities of the
Company's packets and other papers were thrown on heaps in the
back warehouse'.[34] Confusion and neglect of documents no longer
judged to be of any worth to operations persisted until the end of the
Company's history.[35]

The Company's attitude towards its records is well illustrated by
the use, or rather lack of use, that was made of them when it tried to
restore direct trade with Japan. The expectation of such a restoration
was central to the Company's strategic thinking in the Indies in the
second half of the seventeenth century and remained so until late in
the century when it finally set its sights on China, which appeared
the more promising market in the directors' calculations.[36]

Nothing had come of the directors' recommendation in 1623 that the southern presidency brave Dutch hostility and attempt to establish an English presence near Amoy. However, the presidency had remained inquisitive about east Asia and in February 1626 wrote enthusiastically about the prospects for profitable trade in the area, including Japan. It was especially optimistic about the possibility of an indirect trade with China from Taiwan and believed that the Chinese were 'hungerie' for trade and would value the English as a counterweight to the Dutch at Zeelandia. As for Japan, the presidency believed, as if it were making a highly original observation, that a combination of Chinese silk and Japanese silver would produce great profits. The equation of silk, silver and profits was correct but it oversimplified and wrongly stated that 'soma and Barr plate' could be carried out freely from Japan and would be accepted as currency throughout the Indies.[37] The following year in a detailed report, the president, Henry Hawley, and his colleagues changed tack and argued that Japan not China should become the Company's goal in east Asia. They urged the Company to obtain letters patent from the new king, Charles I, addressed to the shogun, 'to countenace your first Expendicon' thither. The presidency's plan was conditional upon winning the favour of the 'Emperour' who because of his supreme power would promote the sale of English cloth 'for their is ability in the Buyers and the word of an Emperour may make a will farr more available at one instant in the great Citty of Edo then 40 yeares managing wth Care and industry at the seaside in firando'. To win over the shogun rich presents were not required (because they are 'to him as dust'), but because 'the Japanese are a warlike people' they would be much impressed by displays of European prowess in the art of war.

Hawley recommended that a couple of 'experienced Leaders to shew our manner of Chivalry' and two 'practick Inginers' be sent. He assured the directors that though the Japanese may be warlike 'no Nacon vnder the Sonne observeth more humanety then doth the people of Japaon, their word is a law, their Country is open, they would not have it a prison but all come and goe at pleasure'. Hawley noted that the Dutch shipped silk (which 'yealdeth little less then in Europ'), pepper, spices and Coromandel Coast cloth and brought back copper (for the Coromandel Coast) and silver which they used to buy silk, and suggested that there might be a large market for gold. However, he was confident the Dutch would pose no problem to any English trade in Japan for the VOC imported very little broadcloth and besides, he insisted, in words that echo Cocks's jibes against the Hollanders to the Matsūra, that the English had no grounds to fear Dutch rivalry in Japan for it is the 'Maxim' of the Japanese that 'we have a King and Country of our owne', while they imagine that the Hollanders 'live uppon the spoyle and roame to and againe wth their wives and Children wch they infinitly dislike'. The president concluded, with another echo from the past, that 'this Trade of Japan is the Summum bonum of East India' and boasted that English cloth could sell well. He was confident of a turnover of 'one hundreth thousant cloths' per annum, arguing that while silk was passable in summer, in winter the Japanese had to wear 'tenn Coats one over the other' and that cloth could be traded for Japanese silver. It was was pure, obvious logic, and it was simply nonsense. This incredible assessment was claimed to be based on information obtained from Japanese locally. A similar claim about likely cloth sales in China had been made the previous year. Both claims were contradicted by experience and as recently as December 1623 the presidency, under Thomas Brockeden, had spoken of a market for only 20–30 stammel broadcloths and perpetuanoes in the whole southwards region.[38]

The Batavia presidency's proposal to reopen direct trade with Japan came barely three years after the closure of the Hirado factory. Nevertheless, it is consistent with the presidency's earlier policy that the closure of the factory was an interim measure subject to review. What is astonishing is Hawley's misguided confidence about sales of English cloth. The history of the Hirado factory had demonstrated quite explicitly that English cloth would not sell in any significant quantity. Hawley and his associates were attempting to curry favour in a reckless manner. The assertion that the Company should send its first expedition to Japan appears puzzling at first, especially as Hawley had signed the presidency's report on the closure of the factory in 1624. In fact the presidency had not forgotten about the Hirado factory and had corresponded with Neyenroode concerning the debts outstanding in Japan when the English left. Neyenroode informed the English of the death of Li Tan and that he had left a modest provision for settlement of some of the debts in his will and that these monies, which were not very great, would be sent to Batavia on a Dutch vessel.[39] The monies reached the Batavia presidency on 27 January 1626 and the presidency reported to London that the 'rest of yor debtors in those parts whether dying or living are much alike, for nothing is to be expected only by meere accident whereunto nothing is to be grounded so farr as wee can heare.'[40]

A letter preserved in the Dutch archives and written by Neyenroode on 1 October 1627 (NS), provides evidence that the presidency was serious about the possibility of the Company returning to Japan and had written to the daimyo of Hirado, by way of the Dutch, expecting him to be surprised that the English had remained absent from Hirado for so long. The letter, itself no longer extant, but very flattering, according to Neyenroode, mentioned the accession of Charles I and the English conquest of Ormuz, one of the few recent achievements the Company could boast about. As a token of friendship some cloth was sent. However, the letter erred in assuming that the daimyo had sold off the English property to the Dutch. Neyenroode scornfully dismissed the claim, saying that the VOC had had no need of 'their rotten lodgings' and joked that the Dutch would not have accepted them anyway for 'we can well obtain new wood and don't need their rotten property. Even if the lord of Hirado had presented it to us I woud not have accepted it that the English might not have some reason to talk about us'.[41] Hawley's curious phrasing in February 1627 was obviously intended to mean 'renewed' rather than 'first' contact with Japan.

In spite of Neyenroode's ridicule, the Dutch were in no position to be either patronising or complacent about their own position in Japan. On the contrary, circumstances were favourable for a restoration of direct English trade with Japan at this time. Japan's overseas trade was still expanding, but the Dutch were on the brink of a five year suspension of their trade. This resulted from the so-called 'Taiwan incident'. This was triggered by Japanese resentment of Dutch customs dues on Japanese *shuinsen* trading with Taiwan and culminated in the seizure of the Dutch governor of Taiwan, Pieter Nuyts, by a group of irate Japanese from his quarters in Fort Zeelandia. The incident was not just a simple protest about customs levies. The bakufu still judged Taiwan to lie within Japan's sphere of influence and the nascent Japanese tributary system. The affair fuelled the ambitions of those who sought to dislodge the Dutch from Japan's overseas trade. The issue was finally settled when the Dutch gave in to Japanese demands and delivered Nuyts to the bakufu.[42] The Portuguese suffered a similar suspension from 1628 to 1630 as a result of a Spanish attack on a Japanese *shuinsen* in the Gulf of Siam for which they were held responsible.[43] These developments led to a reduction in imports. Some of the loss was made up by Chinese vessels. The *shuinsen* operators, for reasons which are not entirely clear, were slower to step in.[44]

Meanwhile, in Europe the prospects for the future safety of the Dutch Republic itself were far from auspicious. The Twelve Years' Truce had lapsed in April 1621 and the United Provinces faced renewed warfare with Spain. Militarily the Dutch held their own but the effects of the Spanish embargoes, which were gradually widened and more strictly enforced, began to take their toll on the Dutch economy, especially on what had been its lifeblood, the carrying trade between the Baltic and Iberian and Italian peninsulas. Divisions within Dutch society, especially between advocates of war, including the VOC, and those who preferred peace intensified, but not to the point where they caused the young republic to implode. The Netherlands survived, but it was not at all obvious, at least not until after 1628 when the Mantuan succession crisis in Italy diverted Spanish troops and resources away from the struggle against the United Provinces, that fortune would shine on the young republic.[45] If the external factors were favourable to the English for another try at Japan, the endogenous ones were not. The Company had overextended itself during its first twenty years and regardless of the retrenchment in the early 1620s had yet to resolve the fundamental problem of an inadequate capital base with which to finance and sustain its ambitions, even its more scaled down ones.[46] However, within the broader context of the 'sakoku', or 'closing of the country', debate, if the English Company, and not just its servants at Batavia, had been fully commited to re-establishing its trade with Japan and had made resources available to send a mission, there are solid grounds for believing that the shogunate, still anxious to encourage overseas trade, would have readmitted the English.

In arguing the case for a fresh attempt at Japan, there is no hint in President Hawley's suggestions that a study of the presidency's records had been undertaken. If there had been, the factors would have quickly understood that there was little prospect of a market for English cloth in Japan, certainly nothing approaching 100,000 broadcloths, and that much of what else they seemed to imagine was original in their proposals, especially the connection between silk and silver in Japan's overseas trade, and the importance of securing access to China, had been understood by the Hirado factors even if their efforts in this direction had been unsuccessful. In theory, copies of all 'out' correspondence and the originals of all 'in' letters to the presidency should have been available, even if some of these may have been lost in the brief but disastrous attempt to relocate the presidency in 1624. A more likely scenario is that, as happened in London, papers were not kept systematically but used for immediate purposes, and if not considered important, stored away. In the tropical humidity of Batavia, they were likely to deteriorate. Under these circumstances, what survived, such as a journal of the *Hosiander*'s 1615 voyage to Japan that turned up among the presidency's papers in 1664, was very much a matter of chance.[47]

In London the directors remembered Hirado differently, helped no doubt by Eaton's return to England in late 1626 and by the continuing dispute with Cocks's executors over his will. They did not take Hawley's comments seriously. This did not stop Thomas Smethwick, a freeman of the Company and an adventurer in the third joint-stock, from suggesting to the Court in March 1633 that trade with Japan should be re-established because the market there for English cloth was vast and lucrative. He envisaged profits of 400 per cent and declared that his information was based on a study of Company records, which he submitted for perusal (what these were is unknown), and on the Hawley paper. Smethwick was a frequent critic of the Company with a score to settle, having been passed over for appointment as a factor to Bantam in 1621 because of doubts about his 'soundness in Religion' and various suits in Chancery in which he was involved. But he was far from being the 'troublesome eccentric' Dr Bassett suggests. He enjoyed the backing of the crown and, adopting the same outrageous style that his increasingly desperate royal master was employing to raise money for his government in lieu of calling a parliament, was attempting to extort money from the Company in return for royal protection. The Company gave Smethwick's proposals short shrift, concluding that they were derived from the Hawley paper, which it dismissed as 'ridicualous and the thing impossible'. In their comments the directors drew upon their collective memory, and on some papers from the records, stating that they 'well-remembered the ill success [they] had upon [their] attempt at Japan, having not vented in 22 months above 32 cloathes, and in 5 yeares not above 165, and many of them by retayle'. In fact, during the factory's existence around 120 broadcloths plus a number of bundles ('fardes' and 'bales') of broadcloth, bays and kerseys were imported by the Company into Japan.[48] A second reason for rejecting Smethwick's proposals was that the directors felt that a profitable trade with Japan could only be pursued if it was part of a triangular trade flow with China (to obtain silk) and southeast Asia (also to obtain silk and other commodities). At least the key lessons of the Hirado years had not been forgotten. Smethwick was not unduly put out by the rejection and advanced similar, if not the same proposals in 1635, in which the ghost of Hawley again hangs heavy. Once more the Court threw them out.[49]

The southern presidency made further suggestions for possible trade with Japan and China in a wide-ranging report at the beginning of 1635. There was a recognition of the need to see the Japan trade within its regional context, but there still remained an unshakeable belief that English cloth could become the principal trading commodity. The report appears to indicate an awareness of the Hirado factory, but this is somewhat ambiguous. In their reply the following year, the directors were not as scathing as they had been to Smethwick, and while they recalled the unsuccessful experience in Hirado they showed that their detailed knowledge of these years was fading for they stated that the factory had lasted 'not lesse than 15 or 16 Yeares' (it had lasted almost ten and a half years). The Court generously acknowledged that Robert Coulson, the president, was not simply relying on local hearsay and harbour gossip, as it claimed Hawley had done (although many of the suggestions look like a rehash of Hawley's) and urged Coulson to make further detailed enquiries and to do some research to find out what European commodities could be sold in Japan and what could be exported from there.[50]

In December 1636 Coulson replied, saying that there was not much information to go on concerning the Japan trade because nobody resident at Bantam had been there or was acquainted with it.[51] In reality he does not seem to have bothered himself much to seek out any additional information (the *Hosiander* journal which turned up in 1664 must have been around in the mid 1630s, which adds strength to the argument that by this time whatever papers about Japan had survived in the presidency had been stored away and forgotten about). There is no indication that any effort was made to appraise developments within Japan by consulting the Dutch or members of the Chinese and Japanese diaspora, for there is no mention of the shogunal decrees restricting direct foreign trade by Japanese vessels.

If the Company remained less than enthusiastic about Japan, others were not. John Weddel's voyage to the Indies for the Courteen Association left England in 1635 with instructions to call at Japan and 'proceed to trade according as you shall receive encouragement there'. Weddel was to use Japan as a base to find a northeast passage from the Indies back to England. Alarmed at the implications of the voyage, Weddel received no help from the Company although he carried a pass signed by the king requesting the Dutch to assist him if called upon. There is no indication of any awareness among the members of the Association of the Hirado factory. In January 1637 the voyage reached Macao which had become accessible to the English because of the Anglo-Portuguese Truce signed in Goa in 1635. *En route* they met some Japanese merchants from the *nihonmachi* in Cambodia sailing for Cochinchina, and at Macao they met a few Japanese-Christian exiles whom the voyage's most acute observer, Peter Mundy, described in his lengthy account of the voyage although this was not published until the nineteenth century. However, the Macao authorities were determined not to permit any English trade, refused to allow Weddell to conduct any, and wrote to the Spanish king begging him to exclude Macao from the recent truce.

Despite this setback, Weddel obtained valuable information about Macao's trade with Japan. In particular he learned that the Portuguese were feeling the pinch from Dutch competition and that the VOC was benefiting from the shift in bakufu policy against the Portuguese. He was confident that the Association would be admitted to trade in Japan and even wrote to his superiors that a house had been prepared for the English in Japan (he did not say where). He expected the fruits of the trade to be rich and that in return for silk, quicksilver, coral, broadcloth, sappan wood and deer hides the

Association would receive an excellent return of silver. Weddel was quite misguided about Japanese preparations for a return of the English. The previous year the bakufu had queried the VOC *opperhoofd* in Hirado about why the English had not returned to Japan. He replied because they did not enjoy trade with China. However, if Weddel's ships arrived in Hirado orders had been issued that they were to be kept under surveillance and not permitted to conduct any trade until orders had been received from Edo. The Dutch, on the threshold of success in its Japan trade, were alarmed by the prospect of any renewed English presence in Japan. They kept a close watch on Weddel's movements and noted that even if the Association was different from the East India Company many of its servants were familiar to them from past service in the Indies. However, Weddel's voyage did not proceed to Japan where the previous years' orders had been made more specific: the English ships were to have their rudders, sails and top mast removed and placed in protective custody while Edo pondered any English request. By the time he left the Pearl River estuary Weddel's earlier optimism had evaporated. The Portuguese had been uncooperative and hostile and the Chinese, resentful of the forceful methods Weddel employed to trade at Canton, refused to deal with him. The Association abandoned any hopes of trading with China and Japan.[52]

During the 1630s, as Weddel had noted, Japan's overseas trade was undergoing a major readjustment. In 1633 the number of Japanese merchants permitted to engage in the *shuinsen* trade was limited to seven families, including William Adams's son Joseph.[53] Two years later all Japanese were forbidden to sail overseas, thereby killing off the *shuinsen* trade completely and Japanese were prohibited from leaving or entering the country on pain of death. In 1639 the Portuguese were expelled from Japan following the Christian-millenarian revolt in Shimabara near Nagasaki in 1637–8 in which the Dutch played a small, but indecisive, part in helping to suppress. Finally, in 1641 the Dutch were ordered to move their factory from Hirado to Deshima, the man-made island in Nagasaki harbour which had been constructed to house the Portuguese between 1634 and 1636.

These measures were not woven from an elaborate, carefully planned and systematically implemented policy, rather they evolved from a complex mixture of sometimes incompatible political, economic and strategic considerations, created by the unfolding of events. Crucial to developments in the 1630s was the death of the second shogun, Hidetada, in 1632, and the attainment of full power by Iemitsu, nominal shogun since 1623. Iemitsu and his *rōjū* changed the nature of the bakufu and the structure of its authority, replacing the informal character of power based on personal connection and paternalism, preferred by Ieyasu and Hidetada, with a power structure in which status, defined and regulated by rules and procedures and administered through bureaucratic stricture, took root.[54] By strengthening bakufu power and authority, they were further consolidating Tokugawa rule. Overseas trade did not escape their attention. In particular the bakufu was anxious to restrict the opportunities for *bushi*, as the 'seclusion' decrees described them (that is, daimyo, such as the Matsūra and their retainers) to involve themselves in and benefit from foreign trade. Economic pressure for a restructuring of foreign trade came from the *itowappu* merchants (the 'merchants of the five imperial cities', as the Dutch called them) who resented the fact that the Dutch, and the English in their time, had been free of their fixed prices. In 1633 they appeared to have scored a double victory. Not only was the *shuinsen* trade curbed but Dutch sales of Chinese raw silk were ordered to be made at the price set by the *itowappu*. However, complaints soon followed that the Dutch were circumventing this restriction and selling their silk at higher prices in Hirado, thereby destabilising the market for *itowappu* silk and jeopardising the prosperity of Nagasaki, a matter of great concern to the city elders. From 1636 the *itowappu* merchants requested the *rōjū* to order the removal of the Dutch factory to Nagasaki where the VOC's trade could be more strictly regulated. Their fears were not without foundation. In 1635 and 1636 Dutch imports of silk had increased tremendously to satisfy an increasing demand – the 1635 figure was double that of 1634. The *itowappu* merchants had their sympathisers in Edo but so too had the Dutch and on this occasion the merchants' pleas were ignored. However, they did not give up.[55]

The *shuinsen* merchants, many of whom had enjoyed easy access and close personal relationships with the first two shoguns, were the first to be hurt by the developments of the 1630s. Their direct participation in overseas trade was terminated. Some of their investments were shifted, briefly to the Portuguese, and then to the Dutch, although again not for long. The Portuguese were next. The Shimabara uprising had shown once again that Christianty was a threat to national security. The bakufu refused to distinguish any longer between priest and trader. With a measure of hesitation and reluctance (senior bakufu officials had continued to invest in the Macao voyage even after the Shimabara revolt), and after taking steps to ensure that the Dutch, the Chinese and Satsuma and Tsushima domains could fill any gap, the *rōjū* acted and in 1639 brought to a close almost a century of Luso-Japanese relations. Individual foreign traders such as Melchior van Santvoort and Vincent Romeyn, whom Cocks had described as 'o[u]r fre[nd]', lost out as well. They could not be accommodated within the new structures that governed Japan's overseas trade relations and left Japan accompanied by their families. The wives and offspring of the Dutch and English were ordered out as well (they were judged to be too much tainted by Christianity) and Japanese women were forbidden to associate with the Dutch, even to talk with them.[56] An exception was made of William Adams's Japanese family; they remained in Japan.

The Dutch were elated by the expulsion of the Portuguese and the 10 December 1639 (NS) was proclaimed a day of thanksgiving in Batavia. François Caron, the VOC *opperhoofd* in Hirado, was more cautious, however. Astutely, he noted that 'when it rains on the Portuguese, the company gets splattered too'.[57] He was right. In the autumn of 1640 senior bakufu officials had visited Hirado and after inspecting the recently reconstructed factory, much of it rebuilt in stone and therefore an object of concern, ordered the Dutch to pull down all buildings bearing the inscription 'AD 1640'. All public manifestations of Christianity were forbidden and the Dutch *opperhoofd* was to be permitted to stay in Japan for one year only. Finally, in May 1641 the Dutch were ordered to remove themselves to Nagasaki. Dutch efforts to woo the *rōjū* had proved fruitless. The *itowappu* merchants had emerged as the beneficiaries of the restructuring of foreign trade in the 1630s, although their victory was short lived as the *itowappu* itself was abolished in 1655. The Dutch lost their freedom becoming virtual close prisoners, but at last they were free, although certainly not on terms of their own chosing, of the Matsūra and their incessant demands for loans. In the mid 1630s their debts to the VOC were estimated at *f.* 30,000 (officially they had owed the English 1,524 taels 6 mas 7 candareen when the latter left Hirado). These debts in particular had prompted the Dutch factors in Hirado to advocate removing the factory to Nagasaki on various occasions in the 1630s but they were overruled by Batavia.[58]

The Matsūra and the people of Hirado lost more than the VOC by these developments.[59] In the 1630s a larger number of Hirado people, at the Matsūra's insistence, had been able to participate in the VOC's trade, much to the annoyance of the *itowappu* merchants and the city of Nagasaki. This now ceased and Hirado reverted to being a small, inconsequential island domain, its years of glory in Japan's overseas trade and the much-needed profits it derived from that trade finished. The Sō on Tsushima and the Shimazu in Satsuma, on the other hand, were permitted to retain their trading links with Korea and Ryūkyū respectively and indeed had been ordered promptly to increase their trade by the bakufu after the expulsion of the Portuguese. However, permission for their overseas activities had been made dependent on written authorisation from Edo which had to be renewed at each shogunal or daimyo accession, another indication of Iemitsu's desire to strengthen bakufu power.[60] In addition to trade, which in the case of the Shimazu continued to operate as a safety valve to keep the powerful domain distracted from brooding overmuch about purely domestic considerations, the connections with Korea and Ryūkyū, and the official embassies which continued to come from these kingdoms, further enhanced Tokugawa claims to legitimacy. The missions added weight to the bakufu's pretensions to create a Japan–centered east Asian world order in contradistinction to that of the traditional Chinese one. For example, in 1635 a new title was created for Iemitsu, *Nihon-koku taikun* (Great Prince of Japan).

However, no matter how one choses to interpret the events of the 1630s, Japan did not become a closed country. Indeed the Japanese word to describe this, *sakoku*, was not made up until the beginning of the nineteenth century and was only coined then for a Japanese translation of Kaempher's essay 'An Enquiry whether it be conducive to the good of the Japanese Empire to keep it shut up as it now is, and not to suffer its inhabitants to have any commerce with foreign nations, either at home or abroad', and Japanese continued to live and work at the Japan House, or *wakan*, at Pusan in Korea. Nevertheless, the focus of Japanese international relations reverted to the country's immediate east-Asian setting in which Japan was attempting to assert its status as a great power.[61] Direct contact with people from lands considered peripheral had been cut or strictly limited. The psychological consequences of this phenomenon are still felt today.[62]

By the time that the Dutch were asked by nervous shogunate officials to step in and help fill the vacuum created by the expulsion of the Portuguese, the VOC had already succeeded in transforming its Japan trade from the small-scale activity of the 1610s and 1620s, largely dependent on credit sales to the Matsūra and a few wealthy Kansai merchants (much the same as what the English had been doing), to a highly profitable business. Attacks on Chinese junks to procure silk had also ceased. In the 1630s even in the face of additional restrictions that had further whittled down the free trade privileges of 1609, the Hirado factory had become the major component of the VOC's trade in the Indies. The thirteen Dutch vessels that called at Hirado in 1636 brought almost *f*. 1.6 million worth of goods (80 per cent of which was raw silk and silk fabrics and only 5.5 per cent woolen cloth) and the nine that left that year exported almost *f*. 3.2 million worth of goods. The value of the presents given on the visit to Edo was *f*. 12,561 and the cost of the journey itself *f*. 10,643.[63] The Dutch had come a long way from the days when like the English they had had their share of gallipots and other unsuitable goods cluttering up their godowns in Hirado. The

VOC had quickly re-established their presence in Japan after the five-year suspension over the Taiwan incident. The elimination of Portuguese rivalry in 1639 had appeared to open up an endless vista of increased profits and Dutch imports to Japan in 1640 (f. 6,295,366, the largest ever) reflected this confidence. However, such a prospect was blocked by the removal of their factory to Nagasaki. The Dutch swallowed their pride and the losses incurred in demolishing the Hirado factory and moving to Nagaski, and decided that the trade was worth continuing even if, as the Heren XVII put it, it was necessary to transact their business from the ships' decks to satisfy the requirements of the Japanese.[64]

As for the Portuguese, they made three subsequent efforts to reopen their trade with Japan, all unsuccessful. After the shocking news of their explusion from Japan reached Macao the city authorities decided to send a mission to plead for its repeal. The mission arrived in July 1640 but upon orders from Edo its members were executed, save thirteen who were sent back on a Chinese junk (their own ship was burnt) to bear fearful witness that the Portuguese had indeed been expelled from Japan. An official embassy, in the name of the newly independent Portuguese king, and the first European embassy to Japan, reached Nagasaki in 1647. This time there was no massacre but the mission was not allowed to disembark and present its case and its plea for readmission was rejected. The third request was made in 1685, using the occasion to return some Japanese blown to Macao in a typhoon. It was also turned down.[65]

Meanwhile, England, indeed the British Isles, was otherwise engaged. Whether or not one accepts the view that the unpheaval of civil war and revolution, the first public execution of a European monarch and the establishment of the English republic in 1649 led to the ascendency of a so-called colonial-interloping 'complex' of nouveau merchants successfully challenging the cosy relationship between the crown and the established merchants of the monopoly companies (a Levant–East India 'complex'), there is no question that by the end of the 1640s the East India Company faced a strong and confidently mounted challenge to its monopoly position. The directors were greatly alarmed about the future. When Oliver Cromwell became Lord Protoector in late 1653, they were uncertain as to whether or not the Company would receive a new charter. However, the elevation of Maurice Thompson, perhaps the quintessential 'colonial interloper', to the governorship in December 1657 did not result in the Company losing its monopoly. Reflecting the expansionist mood of the times, partly attributable to the English republic's self-confidence after the defeat of the Royalists at Worcester in 1651, proposals were made for a much fuller participation in the East Indies trade.[66] In September 1658, the

Company decided to send a ship to Japan and one to China. Preparations, including the procuration of a letter from the new protector, Richard Cromwell, to the Japanese shogun and Chinese emperor went ahead at full speed until they were abruptly cancelled on 3 December because of the threat of renewed warfare with the Dutch.[67]

There is little indication about the information on which the Company based its decision. However, one thing is certain, there is no mention in the Court minutes of the directors looking up the Company's records for guidance. Quarles Browne, an able and perceptive man who had gained valuable experience in the East Indies as chief factor at Cambodia from 1651–6 in addition to his service at Bantam, was appointed head of the proposed Japan factory and provided some information about Japan as well as a boundless enthusiasm. In 1661 he presented a paper to the deputy governor, Sir Thomas Chamberlain, outlining prospects for trade in the Far East. He noted that in Cambodia the Japanese merchants were 'the noblest Merchants in those parts, free from baffleinge, constant in his [sic] bargaines and punctuall in his tymes for payments, a ffirme ffriend', another reminder that contacts between British and Japanese continued after 1623.[68] In September 1658 when the project was underway, the Court ordered that the Company's agent at Amsterdam was to be instructed to find out what he could about the 'traffique and custom of Japon' and to obtain any other relevant information. There is also evidence to suggest that the governor himself did his homework. In 1668 when the Company was again seriously considering reopening direct trade with Japan, a special committee set up to investigate the matter heard from Captain Robert Bowen, who had been in Japan in 1622, that he had given the journal of his voyage (a further indication that journals were considered almost as private property) to Maurice Thompson 'about eight years ago'. Since Bowen would have been an old man at the time it would be unreasonable to pin him down to 1660.[69]

In 1663 Browne, who had been appointed agent at Bantam in May of that year, was given permission to attempt a voyage to Japan at his own cost.[70] The adventure never took place, although the enterprising agency sent a voyage to Macao in 1664 where the English finally had access thanks to the concession in Catherine of Braganza's dowry which permitted English trade with Portuguese possessions. The voyage was not successful. Whatever agreements had been concluded in Europe, the Portuguese authorities in Macao still did not welcome the English and refused to allow them to trade. There was no information to be had about Japan because of the long Portuguese absence from there.[71] However, Browne had sparked off a renewed interest within the Company about the prospects for a resumption of trade with Japan and raised hopes for cloth sales in east

Asia. In February 1664, the Court wrote to Bantam sketching some general thoughts about the trade and asked Browne for his views, especially about the most appropriate form of address and language suitable for the 'emperor' of Japan and what presents would be most appreciated. The Court emphasised that if at all possible a letter from Charles II should be avoided because it did not want to trouble the monarch. More to the point, it preferred to see itself as an independent body, and gain recognition as such, able to initiate and conduct trade on its own authority.[72]

Browne's reply repeated the information in his 1661 paper 'which it may be is lost' but nevertheless made some poignant recommendations, the most notable of which was the suggestion that a profitable trade with Japan could only be obtained if intermediate factories were set up either at Ayuthia (the Company had re-established a factory there briefly from 1661 to 1664 although some of the factors stayed on against orders) or Cambodia, to obtain deer hides, sappan wood and other suitable goods for Japan, or at Tongking, where the Chinese and Dutch procured supplies of raw and wrought silk for sale in Japan. Browne added that besides a letter from the Company, one from the king to the Japanese 'emperor' was imperative and that 'What you send the Emperour must bee noble [for] it is the Custome of most kinges to the Northward of the line in these seas to returne at least the vallue of what's sent them and your Agent supposes it's the same here'. He concluded by apologising for not being able to furnish any information about the Hirado factory, declaring that no one present had any recollection of it and that the only written material he could find was the *Hosiander* journal.[73]

From the late 1660s the Company was fully intent on re-establishing a presence in east Asia and a restoration of direct trade with Japan was central to these ambitions. This time the recommendation about establishing an integrated country trade between Japan and southeast Asia, which the Hirado factory had failed to achieve, was given priority. There was also an implicit political calculation in the Company's strategy that if it could play its part, or at least appear to, in the national struggle against the Dutch by driving them out of the Japan trade and developing a market for English cloth there, the directors would be viewed as true patriots in the public eye and be better able to deflect the persistent attacks on the Company's monopoly. Encouraging reports reached London. The recently established factory at Bombay, another jewel in Catherine's dowry, suggested that the Dutch 'company and nation are more hated than feared by the Japanes' while in 1672 the factors at Balasore in Orissa reported: 'This Japan trade by the Dutche's Confession is the best they have in these parts which make them comply with the Japaners in all their demands.'[74]

On 22 May 1668 the Court set up a special committee with a brief 'to consider how a Trade may be had and managed, to the Manylees [the Philippines], Japan, and other parts in the South Seas and to report their Opinions in writeing, what Shipping, Stock, and Comodities will be necessarie and proper for that busines, and what tymes are most seasonable for such a voyage'. The Manila committee, hoping to build on the Anglo-Spanish commercial agreement of 1667 which opened Spanish colonies to English goods, set its sights on establishing a factory at Manila, or at least securing the right to victual and water English ships there. As for Japan and China, the committee members' hopes ran high about the possibility 'for the vent of our Cloth and other Manufactures, those Countries being subject to sharp Winters, where in all probability our Manufacture of Cloth may be proper and after some long time may come to be a common wear'.[75]

There is a strong sense of *déjà vu* about this; little had changed since Hakluyt's time even if reference was to be made over the next few years to the availability of silver, gold and copper in Japan. These were the commodities the VOC exchanged for their silk (from the mid 1650s much of it from Bengal), deer hides and sappan wood, their major imports to Japan. From the 1640s until 1668, when the shogunate, concerned, in much the same way as the critics of the English Company in the early seventeenth century, that the outflow of precious metals was detrimental to the health of the domestic economy, banned the export of silver, the VOC factory at Nagasaki was a major supplier of bullion for Dutch trade in the Indies. For a brief period after 1668 the export of gold kobang flourished, but the most enduring VOC export from Japan was copper. It was immensely profitable in the country trade, especially in India, and was also sent to Europe where it commanded a 2–3 per cent premium over its rival, Swedish copper. Indeed, during the peak years of its export to Europe, Japanese copper greatly affected prices on the Amsterdam market and therefore in Europe generally.[76]

An indication of how the scale of VOC trade with Japan had altered since the closure of the English factory in Hirado can be gained from some comparisons. In 1621–4 the VOC's annual average export of silver, inflated by the windfall from the Manila voyages, was ƒ. 157,924. In 1660–9 it was ƒ. 1,048,821.[77] Copper exports averaged just 369 peculs between 1621 and 1623 and 20,364 between 1670 and 1672.[78] Such activity, especially the copper exports to Amsterdam, could scarcely have escaped the attention of the English company. Yet while the directors may have felt some obligation to emphasise the Company's contribution to the export of English cloth in their public utterances at home, their writings and instructions to their servants in the Indies make it clear that such pronouncements were not hollow propaganda intended for domestic consumption. The true purpose of attempting to restore direct trade with Japan was indeed the sale of cloth; acquiring a share of copper exports from Japan was a secondary consideration. (The directors were ignorant of the bakufu proscription against the import of a number of goods considered unnecessary luxuries at the end of the 1660s; among these was woollen cloth although in practice the ban did not apply to broadcloth.)[79]

The special committee went about its business methodically and vigorously, writing to the English ambassadors in Spain and Portugal to enlist their help, although the hopes of securing trade at Manila came to nothing and the Anglo-Spanish treaty of 1670 excluded Manila from among those Spanish possessions where the English could trade.[80] In October 1668, the committee decided to open hearings and call 'for such persons as have served the Company in India [i.e. the East Indies] & to consult with them what means are most effectual for procuring and opening a way of Commerce & traffique in those parts'. Those summoned included two captains, Robert Bowen and Robert Hackwell who had served in the fleets of defence, although they had not been captains at the time. Hackwell said that 'hee found the Japaoners to be very faithfull treating the English with much kindnesse and Friendship, And he conceives that the Comp may with securitie send a Shipp thither without sending psons first to open the way'. Both men made comments about the goods that could be traded. Bowen said 'Tinkeen [Tongking] and all other silkes' and deer hides were good commodities while Hackwell's memory did not serve him well except that he remembered 'Broad cloth is a good Commoditie being much worne there'. Other men who had been in Japan, but whose names are not recorded, reported to the committee that Ayuthia and Cambodia should not be overlooked in any attempt to trade with Japan. The committee also learned that 'Mr Eaton who was second at Japan is living and dwelleth at Highgate who may be able to give the Company full satisfacon as to the trade there, and of the civilitie of the people.' Unfortunately, he does not appear to have been summoned or even consulted.[81] Perhaps he was in ill health. It is remarkable that the Company was prepared to rely on the recollections of a few old men about events which had taken place some half-century before. This hardly suggests comprehensive or exhaustive research.[82]

One of the witnesses who appeared before the committee reported that when the English had left Hirado they had left debts 'contracted by our last chiefe theire'. It transpired that this story was circulated by the Dutch and it threw the Court into consternation. The committee was ordered to investigate and report back. Eventually it was established that debts were owing to the Company to the tune of 12,000 taels or £2,400. The discovery was made by an examination of the Company records. This could not have been done with any thoroughness for it would have been discovered that there was little chance of recovering what debts remained unpaid. The document confirming that the English were creditors not debtors was a narrative of 'transactions at our coming away' from Hirado which detailed the major transactions of the factory during its last months. It included a copy of the commission left with Neyenroode authorising him to collect the debts. However, there is no mention of the letter from the Dutch about the payment from Li Tan's estate.[83]

The committee had heard strong opinions from some of the witnesses who appeared before it about the importance of an integrated country trade if any factory in Japan was to prove a success. Ayuthia and Cambodia were recommended but Taiwan was also mentioned.[84] The Court took these suggestions seriously and finally in June 1671 sent a newly built ship of 220 tons, the *Advance*, to the Indies with orders to proceed from Bantam to Cambodia, Taiwan and Japan. She carried a cargo valued at £5,342 14s 6d consisting of broadcloth (almost 30 per cent of the value), looking glasses, knives, scissors, glasses, wax figures, 200 Spanish leather skins, India cloth and two chests of reals specifically for Bantam, the sort of unsuitable cargo Cocks and his colleagues had been resigned to receiving. Unfortunately, the *Advance* reached Bantam too late to catch the monsoon for Japan.[85]

The agency had taken its own initiatives regarding the Japan trade. It was encouraged to do so by the sultan of Bantam. In 1670 it sent two ships to Taiwan to explore the possibility of opening trade there. The agency had been encouraged to make this overture on the basis of an invitation from 'Irquow' the 'Principal Potentate of that Island' whose predecessor, 'Coppin', had ousted the Dutch from the island in 1661–2.[86] Whatever the exact nature of this invitation it was not addressed specifically to the English. The English had little idea of whom they were dealing with or that they were about to become entwined in the final act in the Manchu conquest of China that was unfolding around Taiwan, even if the establishment of the Ch'ing dynasty ultimately benefited the East India Company. The Dutch had indeed been expelled from the island in 1662, their men either killed or taken prisoner by the forces of Cheng Ch'eng-kung, known to the Dutch and some of the English as Coxinga. His father Cheng Chih-lung, who had been born in Hirado, had taken control of Li Tan's operations in Japan and on Taiwan and had built them into a formidable commercial and military enterprise, strong enough to become a major player in the dynastic struggles which enveloped southern China from the 1640s as the country passed from Ming to Ch'ing control. Cheng Ch'eng-kung had broken with his father who had switched sides to the Manchus in 1646 after refusing to join the

Prince of T'ang, one of the claimants to the Ming legacy, in an attack on Manchu strongholds inland. Cheng senior lived out the rest of his days in Peking until his execution in 1661 by which time he had outlived his usefulness as bait to effect a settlement with his son. In 1646, realising the source of his power, Cheng Ch'eng-kung retreated to the islands studding the Fukienese coast and continued the struggle against the Manchu. In 1661, determined to find a more secure base for his forces (and setting a precedent for what was to happen some three hundred years later) he crossed to Taiwan and knocked out the Dutch in 1662, a short-lived victory for he himself soon died. For the next twenty years until the Ch'ing conquest of the island in 1683 a delicate balance existed on both sides of the straits. On the death of their leader the Cheng forces splintered. The core held out on Taiwan under Coxinga's son, Cheng Ching, and continued to make forays across to the mainland until they lost control of Amoy in 1680. Other Cheng supporters on the mainland made their peace with the Manchus and helped advance the imposition of Ch'ing rule. Both groups encouraged foreign trade. It had provided money and weapons in the past and continued to do so not only from the sale of goods but from the 'water payments' or protection money exacted from Chinese shipping.[87]

No matter the provenance of the 'invitation', two English ships sailed for Taiwan in 1670. The English obtained an audience with the 'king', that is, Cheng Ching, whom they later called 'Coxin', trading privileges, which at face value appeared favourable, and a list of goods requested by Cheng, in which armaments was well to the top.[88] The Cheng were interested in increasing Taiwan's foreign trade but in their own favour and on their own terms. Access to Taiwan had helped the VOC's trade in Japan to take off in the 1620s but the geopolitical configuration around the island in the 1670s, about which the English were poorly informed, had disrupted trade between China and Japan.

The Japanese had decided to remain aloof from involvement in the dynastic struggle on the mainland, rejecting an appeal from Coxinga's father for help in the 1640s. But the decision had been close and as the struggle developed Japanese sympathies increasingly lay with the Ming who, as Chinese, were infinitely more acceptable to the Japanese than the Manchus whose activities in Korea conjured up a new Mongol threat. Such partiality led the shogunate to discriminate in favour of Ming loyalist traders (essentially the Cheng, who dominated Chinese trade with Japan until their demise). They were made welcome in Japan while trade conducted by Chinese coming from areas already under Manchu control was made difficult. (The distinction was clear because the Manchus had already ordered Chinese to adopt the cue). But Ch'ing policies implemented in the 1660s (sealing off the Chinese coastal provinces, restricting overseas trade and moving the population inland in order to snuff out resistance to Manchu rule) upset trade and reduced the supply of Chinese silk available at Taiwan. The Cheng compensated for this dislocation by obtaining supplies of silk via Manila and Annam and diversifying exports to Japan into sugar, cultivated in Taiwan, and deer hides. The number of Chinese junks visiting Nagasaki from the mainland dropped off markedly after 1662 while those from Taiwan enjoyed a sudden burst which lasted until 1683.[89]

Whatever else, the Dutch expulsion from Taiwan had not upset the VOC's trade with Japan. The origin of its silk imports had already changed. Most now came from Bengal, lesser amounts from Tongking and Persia. In 1647 Bengal silk (first imported in 1640 and exempt from the *itowappu*) amounted to 29 per cent of the VOC's silk imports to Japan; between 1656 and 1672 it averaged 80 per cent, falling back to 75 per cent between 1673 and 1685.[90] It was against this momentous background that the English began to set their sights on Taiwan as one of the co-ordinates in the renewed Japan trade.

The agency in Bantam was pleased with the results of the preliminary visit to Taiwan in 1670 and the following year dispatched another two ships for the island with additional instructions to call at Japan. By then, Bantam was staggeringly ignorant about Japan. In September 1669 the agency, relaying the encouraging opinions it had received from the sultan, had written to London that the Japanese were impatient for the English to come back and resume their former trade which was described as 'a very brave Trade & Advantagious'. It believed that the 'King of Japon effects' the English more than the Dutch and had rejected numerous Dutch overtures (the most recent supposedly made the previous year) to purchase the Company's 'house & Island whereon It stands' because 'he was yearly In Expectation y^t o^r Honble Comp^a would settle their ffactoryes there againe'. The assumption that the former English factory had been on an island confuses a vague awareness of Hirado with the contemporary reality of Deshima where the Dutch were confined and which was, of course, an artificial island. The sultan's purpose in making these comments would seem to have been a desire to sow futher dissension between the two companies. At any rate his comments were not based on first-hand knowledge. More odd were the instructions issued to the *Crown* and *Bantam Merchant*, the two vessels ordered to Taiwan and Japan in 1671. These urged the supercargoes to make discreet inquiries about the Hirado factory in order to find out where it was located (presumably the site) and why it had been removed (whether in the sense of 'physically' or 'closed down' is unclear). There was also a bizarre expectation of finding some Scots and Irish to whom English cloth was to be given in the hope of stimulating demand for future bulk purchases. Even if the edicts in the late 1630s expelling the Japanese consorts of Europeans had not been enforced completely, it is inconceivable that any children who remained in Japan were aware of their Scots or Irish identity! At least the instruction contained reliable information about the strict procedures governing Dutch trade in Nagasaki (the removal of guns, rigging, rudders, the thorough search of ships for Christian artefacts and so forth) and showed that Bantam was fully conscious of the shogunate's detestation of the proselytising nature of Roman Catholicism, by then common knowledge in the Indies anyway.[91]

When it received word from Bantam about the first voyage to Taiwan in 1671, the Court gave its approval in principle even if it suspected that the voyage had also been used as a pretext for private trade.[92] Nevertheless, a revival of the Company's presence in east Asia had become a top priority and the successful overture to Taiwan was deemed opportune even if the directors objected to some of the details of the trade privileges negotiated by the factors. In April 1671 the Court wrote to Bantam informing the agency that it would shortly dispatch ships to follow up the agency's Taiwan initiative and back up any success the *Advance* might have had, although the directors suspected that she had probably missed the monsoon and had been unable to reach Japan. (This was indeed the case and she had been diverted to Persia, a decision which angered the directors when they heard of it.) Three ships left England in September, the *Return* (340 tons), the *Experiment* (260 tons) and the *Zant* (180 tons) with orders to proceed to Japan and to call at Taiwan and Tongking. Factories were to be established in those places, laying the foundations for an annual trade with Japan which would involve three ships, two sailing via Taiwan, one via Tongking, with two returning directly to India, to Fort St George and Surat, the third returning to Bantam. Japan was to be the hub of an integrated country trade furnishing gold, silver and copper. It was an ambitious plan but Dutch experience had shown that direct trade with Japan was both feasible and profitable. Unfortunately, there were flaws in the strategy: broadcloth, not silk, was expected to be the kindling that would fire the exchange; and the structure of Japan's overseas trade was changing yet again.

(iii)   The Return to Japan 1673

The broad contours of the plan for the voyage of the *Return*, the *Experiment* and the *Zant* had been outlined in April and over the next few months the Japan committee of the Court busied itself with preparations for the voyage: assembling the cargo, chosing the factors, drafting the letters from Charles II and the Company to the Japanese 'emperor', and readying the ships. On 2 August William Lymbry, the captain of the *Experiment*, was appointed 'to wear the flag'. The choice of the factors for the new Japan factory took some time. Samuel Baron, a Eurasian born in Tongking where his father had been head of the VOC's factory, was passed over as prospective chief factor. Baron had himself served the Dutch before seeking employment with the English company with a recommendation from the English ambassador in Paris. He was a colourful personality and was reported to be 'well acquainted with Tonqueen, Tywan, Iapan, & China' and had provided the Company with plenty of information for the voyage. But suspicions about the motives for his switch of allegiance were not allayed and besides he had asked for too much money. David Stephens was appointed instead and in the event of his death (which happened on the voyage from Bantam to Taiwan) was to be succeeded by Simon Delboe. Baron was to return to England.[93]

The combined cargo loaded on the three ships amounted to £27,222 5s 4d. All carried similar goods, mainly broadcloth (about 52 per cent of the total value of the goods sent), lead, quicksilver and vermilion. The goods were chosen 'by comparing former proceedings in Iapon wth the pticuler Comodities vsuall sent thither & advising with some experiencd therein' (that is, Quarles Browne's list, the witnesses who appeared before the special committee, and information gleaned from VOC documents captured by the *Slothorne* and the *Phoenix* in 1663).[94] On 6 September the sea captains and factors were ordered to hasten to the ships at Gravesend and shortly before their departure Lymbry received his commission. The detailed instructions for the voyage were set out in a letter to Bantam, dated 21 September. These declared that 'our chiefest end of vndertaking the Iapon trade is the vent of Cloth, and other English Manufacture, and for the procuring of Gold, Silver & Copper for the supply of other our Factories in East India yt wee may not send Gold & Silver from hence'. In addition the Court specifically requested that fifty Japanese kimonos, ten lacquered chests, forty lacquered cabinets, two tons of camphor, ten screens, a 'tub of thea pots of red earth' and some other Japanese goods were to be brought back to England. The factors were to become walking advertisements for their wares, donning 'English Manufacture, as Cloth in the cold season & stuffs in the Somer'. As an inducement, the factors were permitted to buy material at cost from the cargo. English cloth was also to be promoted at Tongking and at Taiwan. The ships were individually furnished with 'copies of seuerall Transactions touching the Iapon trade', 'Copies of the Articles betweene ye Emperor of Iapaon & and the Company in Portuguese & Lattin' and in Japanese, and copies of the king's and Company's letters to the shogun, also with duplicates in Portuguese and Latin.

The first set of documents was the abstract of the consultations held in Hirado from 25 July to 22 December 1623 from which the Court gathered that the English house and godowns had been left in trust with the 'king' of Hirado. Although the ships were to call at Nagasaki enquiries were to be made with 'ye particular persons or their Heires' about the Company's former property in Japan. The documents at least dispelled 'that false report of money owing vs' and the factors were ordered to 'inquire after ye Dutch person that was authorised to receive it for that we find nothing recd in our bookes'. (As much as had been recoverable had been sent to the English presidency at Batavia.) The factors were to use the Japanese copy of the articles between the Company and the shogun, which it took to be the privileges granted to Saris in 1613 giving the Company 'free trade for ever in the Empire of Iapon', as the basis on which to request a resumption of trade. The Court believed that the document, which was in fact a copy of the Japanese document printed in Purchas and therefore a copy of Saris's petition for trade, not of the privileges themselves, would be sufficient 'without being out to send vp to ye Court at Eado or Meacco [Kyoto] for that we haue right therevnto vpon the said Articles & that you need not obteyne it by a New Adresse or Present'. Charles II's letter was to be used as an introduction but if a special address were required the factors were to make one and ensure that the present was chosen 'wth the best husbandry & frugallity that you can'. A number of goods (they included eight bales of broadcloth, knives, scissors, four clocks, drinking glasses, spectacles, magnifying glasses, two brass guns, a mortar piece and carriage, maps and two pictures of Charles II) had been set aside for such a contingency and, if necessary, presents were to be given to other people who might prove influential.

The Company was thoroughly optimistic about the chances of success, mentioning that 'at our retirement [from Hirado] there was much kindness showne from ye greatest to the least that wee had ocasion to correspond wth'. Religion would not be a problem because 'their [the Japanese] disrespect is not so much toward Protestants, as Papists'. The Court even felt that it would be 'dishonorable & vnbecoming' to use false colours and insisted (unlike the Bantam agency's instructions for the 1671 voyage) that the ships enter Nagasaki with the Company's colours, the striped ensign with the Cross of St George in the upper left corner. The Japanese were to be told that 'yt it is but ye Civill distinction or badge of the English Nation, and not such a fforme of a Crosse, as the Papists adore in way of Religion'. The Court felt emboldened enough to order the

factors to refuse to detach the ships' rudders and remove their guns
during their stay as the Dutch had been obliged to do since their
removal to Deshima. Once settled in Japan the chief factor was to
ensure that his subordinates acquainted themselves with the customs
and manners of the country and 'avoid all Drunkenness & disorders
wch are hatefull to Iapaners, they being...a sober people'. (The
directors had not read Cocks's diary). Finally, if need be a pilot and
interpreters were to be hired at Bantam or at Taiwan and a letter
from the king of Taiwan was to be requested testifying to 'our faire
way of trade wth all Nations' which, it was stated, 'is knowne to all
India'. (The *Return*, the only ship from the three to reach Japan relied
on rutters and obtained no such letter of reference at Taiwan.)[95] In
drawing up these instructions there had been no comprehensive
search of Company records – no one thought it worthwhile to wade
through the old papers in the back warehouse – to learn from the
mistakes of the past, nor to establish a clearer picture of the polity
and society the Company's servants would encounter in Japan.
There was no recognition of the value of such an exercise anyway. If
there had been then the Company would have understood from
numerous letters or even from Cocks's diary that the original
privileges had been curtailed in 1616 and that efforts to have them
restored had proven fruitless. In 1671 the Company assumed, with
blithe simplicity, that its request for permission to reopen trade
would prove a mere formality and even hoped its goal could be
achieved cheaply without a visit to the shogun's court.

The *Zant* was the first of the three ships to reach Bantam, on 7
April 1672. The *Return* and the *Experiment* followed almost a month
later. After some deliberation the voyage plan was altered. The
factors to staff the three new factories were chosen: David Stephens
was to head the Japan factory with Baron as his deputy, assisted by
thirteen others, including a steward, a surgeon and a cook; Simon
Delboe was to be chief of the Taiwan factory with nine subordinates;
and William Gifford was appointed chief factor of the six-man
Tongking factory.[96] The *Zant* was sent to Tongking on 27 May and
the *Return* and the *Experiment*, together with a junk, the *Camel*, left
for Taiwan and Japan on 10 June. Before the departure Baron wrote
to the directors informing them that the Dutch had made a profit the
previous year of *f*. 1.5 million in their Japan trade (in fact it was closer
to *f*. 1.9 million). He had been unable to obtain any additional
information about Japan except that the Dutch 'have given us their
thoughts wch wee may call hopes, that we shall not find any good
Recept at Japan'. Baron believed this was only wishful thinking on
their part, for 'they feare the Contrary'.[97]

The voyage to Taiwan went smoothly except that Stephens died
and was succeeded by Delboe as prospective head of the Japan

factory. However, in spite of 'great promises' about trade and the establishment of a factory on Taiwan after their arrival on 16 July, little was achieved there. The road at Tayouan, exposed to the elements, was judged unsafe for the ships, which retreated to the safer haven of Pekou, the Pescadores. There it was decided to transfer all the cargo intended for Japan to the *Return* and let the *Experiment* and the *Camel* return to Bantam. The two ships left on 19 November but failed to reach their goal and were siezed by the Dutch and taken to Batavia, casualties of the third Anglo-Dutch war.[98] The *Return* wintered in the Pescadores, delaying her departure for Japan until 10 June the following year on the grounds that 'the ship is so full [and] cannott use her guns. Besides, in appearing with one Ship the lustre of the designe will be eclipsed'. Also, they had, 'not the copies of the King and Company's Letters' only the originals, which the factors were reluctant to open. One suspects that these were pretexts and that the real reason for the delay was trepidation about what lay in store at Nagasaki. Two ships would have given comfort in numbers but with a redistribution of the cargo the problem of space to manoeuvre the guns could have been overcome. Yet even if it lacked lustre the design had to proceed. There was no valid reason for it not to; fear was an insufficient justification to abort the mission. To defuse possible trouble, the ship's colours were altered, contrary to the Court's orders. The Company's ensign was taken down and a plain striped flag of painted silk hoisted instead. The reason was said to be that the Jesuits had caused much cruelty there 'so that in case cross dollars [i.e. reals bearing a cross] are found amongst the Dutch, ship, goods and life are all forfeited'.[99] The men on the *Return* feared for their lives.

At 11 a.m. on 29 June 1673, a rainy, humid morning, the *Return* sailed into Nagasaki Bay, the first English ship to call at Japan since the *Bull* fifty years before. Japanese officials came aboard almost immediately, posed many niggling questions and ordered the captain to remove the ship's guns and ammunition. All personnel were refused permission to land and were confined to the ship for the duration of the stay and had to signal by waft when they wanted provisions, which they obtained by trading small amounts of weaponry. Communication was mainly in Portuguese, but, according to the factors' account of events, the Japanese interpreters (by then officials not employees of the respective companies as had been the case in the 1610s) also knew Spanish and Dutch. They did not understand English although one of the interpreters claimed that his father had served the English at Hirado. The English handed over what they confidently took to be the copy of the grant of the original privileges. This was immediately recognised by the Japanese as a fake. It was, as has been mentioned, a copy of the abridged petition requesting trade presented by Saris, and bearing his name, in September 1613 – Purchas's 'Japonian Charter'. It had been traced from Purchas on English paper in pen and ink. The Japanese demanded the original privileges themselves but the English replied that these had been handed back when the English left Japan. (This was almost true. The copy of the abridged privileges granted in 1616 had been returned; ironically, the *shuinjō* with the original privileges was either in Oxford, in the Bodleian, or very shortly to be there.) Nevertheless, the first responses to the request for trade conveyed through the interpreters seemed encouraging. The English could only wait impatiently, confined aboard ship, the men increasingly frustrated; the officers, on orders from the Japanese, desisted from exacting corporal punishment.

There were interminable questions to answer, especially about religion, while a reply was awaited from Edo where word had been sent almost immediately after the ship's arrival. One of the first questions the Japanese officials had asked upon learning that the ship was English was whether England was at peace with Portugal and Spain '& how long our king had been Marryed to ye Daughter of Portingall & what Children she had?' Delboe replied that the English were at peace with all nations (he did not know of the renewed warfare with the Dutch but soon would when the Hollanders brought in the captured *Experiment*, on 6 August). He added that the British king had been married for eleven years but without issue and that such marriage compacts were common in Europe for reasons of state. Delboe, pleased with his answer, felt that the Japanese were satisfied with this explanation. According to the Dutch account of this interview (the Dutch had been ordered to have someone in attendance because the English had claimed that they were of the same religion as the Hollanders and to inform the Japanese if nationals other than British were aboard the ship), the Japanese decided to test the English by making them walk on a *fumie*, a plate impressed with a Christian icon which Christian suspects were forced to tread upon to test their faith. Delboe willingly obliged although because it was dark, the Dutch commented, he did not know what he was doing. There is no mention of this incident in the English sources.[100]

Reasons of state may have been sound enough for Englishmen to accept their Protestant monarch's marriage to a Roman Catholic princess, but they seemed neither logical nor desirable to the Japanese. It was over this issue, 'in regard our King was married with the daughter of Portugal, theire enemies...and for no other reason', that the bakufu rejected the English request to reopen direct trade. The *daikan* refused to comply with Delboe's request for a written explanation of the decision to take back to show the directors. On 28 August after a two month stay, the *Return* left Nagasaki harbour having failed in her mission. Assurances had been given that the Dutch would be prevented from following them immediately. Sixty-four boats and over 1,000 men had been assembled in case the ship, which appeared heavily armed to the Japanese, caused any trouble. This was far less than the 50,000-plus men, the elaborate pontoon bridge constructed from small boats to blockade Nagasaki harbour and numerous other small craft which had been assembled in 1647 to ensure that the two galleons of the Portuguese ambassador, Gonçalo de Siqueira de Souza, did not make a run for the open sea. In spite of the show of 'outward curtesy' on the *Return*'s departure and more significantly the 'seeming reluctancy' of the *daikan* 'for our not being admitted to trade here', the English had received little encouragement to try again after Catherine's death, 'for this Emperour's Comands (according to the Iapan saying) were like unto sweat that goeth out of a man's body which never returned again'. Indeed the Dutch reported to their superiors at Batavia that the English were expressly told that if they came back 'ship, crew and cargo' would be burned. If made, the threat was never put to the test for no further English ships reached Japan until the late eighteenth century.[101]

The Japanese had posed the bombshell question about Charles II's marriage to Catherine of Braganza only because the Dutch had wasted no time in informing the bakufu about it after news of the match reached Batavia in 1663. They reminded the Japanese authorities over the summer and autumn of 1672 when news of the English mission and its itinerary reached Japan. (Such tactics were not new. In 1639 two years after their worries that Weddel might show up in Japan, the Dutch had informed the shogunate that English and Danish ships were likely to be used to bring Catholic priests to Japan.)[102] However, while the Dutch had correctly anticipated the bakufu's reaction and the *opperhoofd*, Martinus Caesar, gloated in astonishment that the English 'had not brought a thread of silk with them',[103] the Hollanders were neither acting with unflappable self-confidence nor from a position of strength. The VOC already had strong competition from the Chinese and did not want to face any more from the English. Moreover, they realised, and this had been made apparent on numerous occasions, that they were in Japan on terms dictated by the Japanese. The most recent reminder had occurred in 1672 when the Dutch, and the Chinese, were subjected to the market trade (*shihō baibai:* the Dutch called it *taxatie-handel*, or appraised trade) whereby all imports, not just silk as had been the case with the *itowappu*, were sold at prices fixed by the Nagasaki *daikan* in consultation with representatives of the five major commercial cities (Kyoto, Osaka, Sakai, Edo and Nagasaki). The market trade was an attempt to curb an inflation fuelled when

Japanese demand for imported goods pushed up prices to the benefit of the Dutch and Chinese and fuelled concern in the bakufu about the outflow of specie. The *shihō baibai* cut the profits of the foreign traders and the Dutch reacted by reducing the volume of their imports to Japan as did the Chinese. But no matter how objectionable they found the *shihō baibai* in principle and irksome in practice, the VOC continued to trade with Japan and to make profits, although greatly reduced from previous levels.[104]

As with the restructuring of overseas trade in the 1630s, the *shihō baibai* was not intended to stifle foreign trade but to regulate it. Under these circumstances the shogunate would not have objected to admitting yet another set of traders to trade with Japan, especially if they could supply the Japanese market with those imports greatly in demand, accept Japan's terms of trade, and obey Japanese laws. Increased supply was, after all, another method of taking the sting out of the inflation. Nor would the city of Nagasaki have been adverse to the increased trade and spending the English might have brought. Hence the encouraging words the English heard from the Nagasaki officials after their arrival, the words of regret on their departure and the orders to the Dutch on 11 July (NS) to prepare three houses on Deshima for the English. (The orders were not enforced as the English remained confined to their ship.)[105] The Japanese intended to make up their own minds about the English mission. Other events indicate that the shogunate had no intention of isolating Japan from the outside world. In 1668 the bakufu, anxious about any fall-off in arrivals of Chinese shipping because of the upheavals in the middle kingdom, had ordered the Dutch not to attack Chinese shipping in Japanese waters (the Dutch who had been attacking Cheng shipping in revenge for their expulsion from Taiwan had stopped these assaults in Japanese waters in 1665 because of Japanese protests) and to make the *shihō baibai* more palatable gave the Hollanders permission for their ships to remain an extra month in Nagasaki, something they had long sought.[106] Moreover, trade through the Tsushima and Satsuma domains continued and from the 1660s to the 1680s the shogunate tolerated trade with Siam in the absence of official relations which had been broken off after the attack on the Ayuthia *nihonmachi* in 1630. The Siamese made several unsuccessful attempts to restore diplomatic relations but the trade was cut off abruptly after 1688, although Chinese junks continued to sail from Ayuthia to Nagasaki. Once again the Dutch had intervened to poison the relationship telling the Japanese that the Siamese enjoyed official relations with Portugal and that Catholic missionaries were permitted in the kingdom.[107] The mere whiff of Catholicism was enough to arouse the hostility of the shogunate as the English discovered for themselves.

Had Charles II not been married to a Roman Catholic there is every likelihood that the English would have been readmitted to direct trade with Japan in 1673. How such a development would have altered Japan's subsequent relations with the West is a matter for speculation but there is no doubt that if the English had been permitted to re-establish their trade and were not so worn down by the strict controls over trade and everyday living that they pulled out at some later stage they would have proved themselves at least as serviceable a conduit for the flow of Western learning to Japan in the eighteenth century as the VOC, possibly more so. Just as there was no high road determining that the Dutch would emerge as the only Protestant European power trading with Japan in the 1620s and the only European power after the 1630s, so too there was no guarantee that they would remain the only such European power until the mid nineteenth century. There was no 'special relationship' between the Netherlands and Japan.

The initial response of the factors on the *Return* to their failure was to allege that the Dutch had bribed the Nagasaki officials with £10,000, an assertion absolutely without foundation but one which was duly reported back to London.[108] The Bantam agency was convinced that the *shihō baibai* was part of an elaborate ploy 'to weary them [the Dutch] out of the trade by degrees & not to forbidd them at once. They have an old Prophecy y[t] redd haird men (which they call all that have not black haire) will one time or other do their Land an Injury & from thence also some thinke we were not admitted to trade at Japon'.[109] After it had studied 'the Japan journal' and other papers relevant to the mission, the Court (which had informed Bantam that trade flows with Japan, if established, was to be nurtured despite the difficulties posed by the war with the Dutch) felt miffed about the rebuff, 'w[ch] being in it self a nicety, for that the Dutch are in amity wth the same Nacon wch they declare to haue so great an enmity against'. Discouraged but not despairing, the Court ordered Bantam to try to 'the utmost of yo[r] endeavo[r]' to 'remove this mistake', enlisting the help 'of the King of Bantam or the King of Formosa'. It emphasised that the pursuit of trade with Japan was to be achieved 'in an amicable way for that we like not what yo[u] write to become Robbers or to attempt to p[c]ure our trade by force, although they haue dealt vnkindly w[th] us'.[110]

Taiwan now became central to the ambition to return to Japan. The Court believed that a factory at Taiwan 'may be in effect as if we did trade to China, Japan, & the Manillhaes' and declared 'our affaires there to be of very great concernemt to us, because it must be y[r] Magazine till we can get access directly [i.e. to Japan] and therfore had need to have able & Iudicious persons for the managmt thereof'. The factory was to integrate itself into the existing trade flows with

Japan and Manila to see that English manufactures were included in
that trade and to procure gold and silver from Manila and silver and
copper from Japan, 'wch turnes best to accompt at the Coast [the
Coromandel Coast] and Surratt as also some handsome large Japaon
Chests & Cabinetts'.[111] In other words, there had been no shift in the
Company's policy. Bantam had been thinking along the same lines
anyway and in 1675 was finally able to send a ship to supply the
Taiwan factory which had been languishing since 1672. The factory
failed to live up to expectations.[112]

In pursuing these goals, it was not the economic reality of late
seventeenth-century Japan that influenced the directors, but an
imaginary Japan. To that extent a distorted version of the myth of
Chipangu held sway over their decisions; Japan was no longer seen as
a source of gold and spices but as a lucrative market for English
cloth. The Company's flawed strategy was made all the more
compelling by domestic political considerations. In 1675 the clothiers
of Staines and Coventry petitioned the House of Commons, alleging
that the Company's monopoly over trade from the Cape of Good
Hope to the Straits of Magellan, '1/3 part of the world', blocked the
free export of woollen manufactures to the Indies, including China
and Japan, impoverished woollen manufacture (because the Company was only active in a small part of the area it claimed for its
monopoly), and pushed up the prices of Asian commodities. The
petitioners sought the dissolution of the Company and its replacement by a regulated company. The ritual attack on the Company's
bullion exports was thrown in for good measure. The directors did
not treat the charges lightly and in their reply, before a Commons
committee, listed the efforts that had been made to encourage trade
in the Indies to the advantage of the kingdom. They included Japan
among these, mentioning that they had tried to establish trade there
'to have vented more Cloth and to have procured Gold, Silver and
Copper (which are there in plenty) to have supplied their trade in
other parts of India instead of [exporting] bullion from hence, which
essay cost the Company near £50,000', adding that this was 'too
great a sum for any private person to have hazarded'. The directors
insisted that such efforts and others would continue and that failure
to secure trade in various places stemmed not from lack of effort but
from competition, and because local rulers would not open their
markets to the Company, as was the case in Japan. Seven years later,
the directors wrote to Surat instructing the factors to sell as much
cloth as possible for small profit rather than a little for a greater one.
The directors added that they would be sending greater quantities of
European goods, which 'is very pleasing to the King, as it will be
also to the Parliament when wee have one'.[113]

The Company encouraged its factors in the Indies to use the rulers of Bantam, Siam, Amoy and Taiwan as intermediaries to deliver a letter from the governor and directors to the Japanese 'emperor'. The letter, addressed to 'the most Illustrious, Renowned and Glorious Emperor of the famous empire of Japan' mentioned that the 'sinister informations of some' had lead to the failure of the *Return*'s mission in 1673 but assured the shogun that the Company was long-settled in the Indies and enjoyed just and fair dealings with all rulers. It proudly boasted that 'in fine broadcloth and all other woollen manufactures wee exceed all other nations' and looked forward to selling these goods in Japan.[114] The tactic was poorly conceived. For example, the Tongking factory, under the impression that all had gone well in Japan for the English, asked the master of a Chinese junk to carry letters for its compatriots in Japan; the master refused, fearing that the Japanese would suspect that the letters were from Portuguese and that he would end up in trouble.[115] He was no fool and was fully aware that vessels were searched on arrival in Japan. The Siamese authorities indicated their willingness to co-operate but nothing was done, apparently in order not to complicate the delicate unofficial relations between Siam and Japan. Nevertheless, the Siam factory was able to benefit from these relations, and procure Japanese copper and at least on one occasion invested on a Siamese voyage to Japan.[116] In December 1682 the Tongking factors reported to the directors that they had given the copy of a letter to 'ye Emperor of Japon' to the king. The monarch refused to have anything to do with it; 'he onely says, he had noe correspondence with him, so cannot assist us in that: Neither will any China Jounk adventure to carry it tho' it were to a private Man, much less to the Emperor'.[117]

The directors were no longer prepared to invest more money in direct approaches and decided to play what could have been a trump card, William III's joint accesssion to the British throne, by recommending Madras to consider sending one of the country ships to Japan, reminding the factors there that the Japanese had rejected the 1673 mission only because the king was married to a papist, Portuguese princess.[118] No ships were sent. There was no change in the kind of information on which these recommendations was based, certainly no search of the records. On one occasion, in February 1684, the factors in Madras were informed of an attempt to re-establish contact with Japan by way of Siam and were told to 'gather sufficient instruccon from ye Dutch, their former proceedings; which you may read at large in yᵉ two printed histories of China & the History of Japan'.[119] The latter was probably Montanus's *Atlas Japannensis*. Montanus had based his book on Dutch material, but in keeping with editorial convention had mixed fact and fiction. More confusion was added in the English translation, which appeared in 1670. There is no mention at all of the English factory in Hirado.[120]

Two years later the directors informed their factors in Bengal that they were sending the first part of Purchas, 'a booke very necessary for you thoroughly to peruse at all leisure time' in order to 'arrive at any maturity of understanding in the affairs of India, and of the Dutch wiles & former abuses of our Nation'.[121]

The directors relentlessly pursued the chimera of restoring direct trade with Japan because they believed that 'their [the Dutch] spice and Japan trades are as good as two mines of Gold to the[m]'. In language which resounds with the voice of Cocks, they convinced themselves that the Dutch were 'held in Such great jealousy by ye Japaneers and Generally looked on but very illy' because of their seizure of Bantam in 1682.[122] In fact the VOC's profits from their Japan trade were already in decline. The Dutch had adapted to the *shihō baibai* and to other twists and turns in bakufu policy to overseas trade. But after 1684 when the Ch'ing legalised trade with Japan (official relations between the two empires remained in abeyance) the Chinese became even more formidable competitors. In 1685 new restrictions were imposed on trade at Nagasaki, the *go-jodaka shihō*, or limited trade. The sales value of Dutch goods was limited to *f.* 1.05 million, that of the Chinese to *f.* 2.1 million. The reasons for the enactment of the limited trade are closely related to the continuing debate about the outflow of precious metals through foreign trade and the discussion about the nature of Japan's overseas trade raging within the bakufu. The new resrictions on Dutch and Chinese trade were not anti-foreign, let alone anti-Dutch and did not apply to Tsushima's trade with Korea nor Satsuma's trade with Ryūkyū and they could be circumvented by smuggling, a route more available to the Chinese than the VOC. Indeed, the volume of Japan's overseas trade increased during the late seventeenth century even if trade through Nagasaki itself, which the bakufu could regulate, may have declined. Dutch trade certainly decreased. In 1715 further restrictions were introduced (the Dutch were permitted to have two ships call at Nagasaki yearly, the Chinese thirty) as the Japanese gradually began to place an emphasis on import substitution, for example, developing indigenous sericulture and silk-reeling industries. The Dutch continued to make a profit from the export of copper from Japan but the importance of the Nagasaki factory in the VOC's country trade and Euro-Asia trade had peaked and it was but a shadow of its past glory. Ironically one of the reasons why the factory was not closed in the eighteenth century was a fear that the English might move in and fill the void.[123] By then such apprehensions about English intentions were misplaced. Moreover, Japanese willingness to admit new participants to the country's overseas trade had spent itself.

Arguably it was only a matter of time, until the situation in China stabilised with the consolidation of Manchu control over the south-

ern provinces, before the English shifted their attention away from
Japan. The shift was gradual, not sudden. In 1685 the directors
received a shock when they heard rumours that the Japanese had
banned the import of English cloth, clearly a long-delayed and much
garbled report of the proscription against woollen cloth issued at the
end of the 1660s. This bad news did not deter them from ordering
Madras to send India cloth and reals to Amoy to further any indirect
trade with Japan.[124] By the dawn of the eighteenth century the
Company had given up hopes of attaining a direct trade with Japan
even if some of its servants in the Indies still directed their thoughts
to Japan. In November 1701, Henry Rouse, serving in the Chusan
factory, which operated from 1700 to 1702, reproted his 'pvate
Sentim[ts] of our Intended Trade or Settlem[t] to or at Japan', arguing
that any voyage should be undertaken as part of a more general
reconnaissance of the region, which, if Japan proved unsuccessful,
should take in Ryūkyū (which he referred to only as 'an Island neare
Iapan' but, nevertheless, an interesting suggestion in view of the
Hirado factory's efforts), and possibly Korea, whose tributary
ambassadors the factors had seen passing on their way to Ningpo.[125]
His argument was based on information obtained locally.

The final flourish of the seventeenth-century efforts to restore
English trade with Japan and one of the first chords of the more
aggressive policies the Company's servants were to employ in the
eighteenth century to break into new markets, is contained in an
unsigned letter written around 1701 by one of the Company's factors
en route for Surat. The anonymous author, who reported generally
about the state of the Company's trade in the Indies, had at least read
his Purchas, even if he got the chronology of the Hirado factory
hopelessly confused (he stated that the English had received their
original privileges in 1640), and had studied some of the documents
relating to the *Return*'s voyage. He described the Japan trade as 'one
of the Noblest Comerce...in the whole World'. From his cursory
reading of the papers, he concluded that Japan could supply the
Indies with ready money and that the country 'vends of foreigne
product at least one Million yearly – English manufacturee [i.e.
cloth], Lead & Glass'. If the English were to attempt a restoration of
direct trade, the author recommended sending

at least 4 or 6 Men of Warr (besides Shipps of Comerce) to cruse of[f] and
not goe into Porte [Nagasaki] without they have a kind reception, but
should the Dutch...appear against, the Cheif of this Expedition must be
Impowerd to stop the Dutch as well as the Syam and Chyna Iunks from
going thither unless the two Latter will secure by hostages your Interduc-
tion wch hath when Necessary been made use of by the Dutch in all their
great Settlements in India.

(Siamese junks were of course no longer trading to Japan, only a few from Siam belonging to Chinese.) '[T]his affair', he continued, 'ought to be managed with great secrecy, Prudence and Integrity that neither the Chyneeses or Iapaners be any ways provocked beyound the true Intent of attaining [the] said settlemtent that we may not totally lose this Choise and Unvaluable Flowrs'. He was confident the Japanese would grant permission 'for tis well known the Japaners Cant subsist two years without ye Maijr part of their Usuall Importations, that Country producing Nothing to Manufacture'. He concluded that once the Japanese realised that the English were not Roman Catholics they would have to admit the Company, especially if the English insisted upon adherence to the original privileges 'wch by the Law of Japan can neuer be reversed, it being made perpetuall'.[126] How wrong could one be! Nothing had been learned from the Hirado years.

The directors were no longer interested in such proposals. As had happened to the VOC in the 1620s, a factory on Taiwan had unlocked a door. For the English this was not to Japan but to Amoy, then emerging as a thriving new centre for Chinese overseas trade.[127] Amoy, where a factory was established in 1677, gave the Company the direct access to the China trade which had eluded the Hirado factory. Taiwan and Tongking, the intended co-ordinates of the Japan trade, became superfluous. Taiwan was closed in 1685. The Company remained across the Straits at Amoy and at other places on the China coast before finally securing a factory at Canton where at last it centred its China trade from 1716. The Tongking factory, where for more than twenty years the factors had watched impotently as the Chinese and Dutch drove their trade with Japan, was closed in 1697, its newly found *raison d'être* to supply the rekindled demand for Asian silk in England superseded by supplies from Bengal and, more important for the future, the activity on the China coast.[128]

The Company's east Asian trade was not to be predicated on the exchange of Chinese silk, let alone English cloth, for Japanese silver or copper. It became important to the Company because it furnished a product for which a strong demand in Europe emerged only in the eighteenth century, tea or thea as it was originally called. Until 1690 tea accounted for less than 1 per cent of the Company's imports to England; by 1760 it had reached 40 per cent.[129] After the mid eighteenth century, the China trade became the cornerstone of the East India Company's trade with the Indies. By then the Company was being transformed (no matter how strongly the directors may have attempted to resist the process, just like the Heren XVII with their reservations about Governor General Coen's expansionist proposals) from being primarily a trading organisation, operating on the premise that 'profit not grandeur...is our end in trading', to becoming a major territorial power and its servants the vanguard of empire in the Indies.[130]

The East India Company had travelled a long way in terms of structure, management, accounting practice and profitability from the Hirado days. But so too had England, Europe and, of course, the world. The prelude to the age of empire was already unfolding and Europe's relations with the East Indies, or the Far East as they were to be rechristened eventually (a potent terminology in itself and symbolic of the essence of the new relationship), would have altered radically.

Notes

Abbreviations

ARA KA	Algemen Rijsarchief, Koloniale Archieven, The Hague
BL	British Library, London
CSP	*Calendar of State Papers Colonial, East Indies*, edited by W. Noël Sainsbury, 5 vols, London, 1862–92
Coen: Bescheiden	H. T. Colenbrander and W. Ph. Coolhaas (eds), *Jan Pietersz. Coen: Bescheiden Omtrent zijn Bedrijf in Indie*, 7 vols, The Hague, 1919–53
Diary	Tōkyō Daigaku Shiryō Hensan-jo (ed.), *Nihon kankei kaigai shiryō: Igirisu shōkancho nikki: Diary kept by the Head of the English Factory in Japan (Diary of Richard Cocks, 1615–1622)*, Tokyo, 3 vols, 1978–80
IOL	India Office Library
IOR	India Office Records
Letters Received	William Foster (ed.), *Letters Received by the East India Company from its Servants in the East*, 6 vols, London, 1896–1902
Nachod, *Die Beziehungen*	Oskar Nachod, *Die Beziehungen der Niederländischen Ostindischen Kompagnie zu Japan in siebzehnten Jahrhundert*, Leipzig, 1897
PRO	Public Record Office, London

INTRODUCTION

1 *Indonesian Trade and Society*, The Hague, 1955, p. 261.

2 'The Inequalities of Core and Periphery', in Immanuel Wallerstein, *The Capitalist World Economy*, Cambridge, 1979, pp. 18–19 and passim; and, of course, the *locus classicus, The Modern World System*, 3 vols, New York, 1974, 1980, and San Diego, 1989. For a useful introduction to the 'Modern World System' debate with specific reference to Asia and with excellent bibliography see M. N. Pearson, *Before Colonialism: Theories on Asian-European Relations 1500–1750*, Delhi, 1988.

3 Leonard Blussé, 'Le Modern "World System" et l'extrême Orient: Plaidoyer pour un seizième siècle négligé', in Leonard Blussé, H. L. Wesseling and G. B. Winius (eds), *History and Underde-*

velopment, Leiden, 1980, p. 98. For an unconvincing example of Wallerstein's theory applied to east Asia see Frances V. Moulder, *Japan, China and the Modern World Economy*, Cambridge, 1977.

4   Paul Bairoch, 'Geographical and Trade Balance of European Foreign Trade', *Journal of European Economic History*, III, 1974, pp. 560, 577; Paul Bairoch, 'Le bilan économique du colonialisme: mythes et réalités', in Blussé *et al*, *History and Underdevelopment*, pp. 30–1.

5   Patrick O'Brien, 'European Economic Development: The Contribution of the Periphery', *Economic History Review*, second series, 35:1, 1982, pp. 1–18 esp. pp. 2–3; Patrick O'Brien, 'Europe and the World Economy' in Hedley Bull and Adam Watson (eds), *The Expansion of International Society*, Oxford, 1984, pp. 43–60 esp. pp. 52, 60.

6   See, for example, P. J. Cain and A. G. Hopkins, 'The Political Economy of British Expansion Overseas, 1750–1914', *Economic History Review*, second series, 33:4, 1980, pp. 463–90.

7   *Trade and Civilisation in the Indian Ocean: An Economic History from the Rise of Islam to 1750*, Cambridge, 1985, p. 95. Similarly, Japan's economic success since 1945 owes much to her own extension, even remoulding, of the institutions of capitalism in order to take advantage of new economic and technological opportunities. See Chalmers Johnson, *MITI and the Japanese Miracle*, Stanford, 1983, and Ronald Dore, *Flexible Rigidities*, London, 1987.

8   Niels Steensgaard, 'The Companies as a Specific Institution in the History of European Expansion', in L. Blussé and F. Gaastra (eds), *Companies and Trade*, Leiden, 1981, pp. 245–64, esp. pp. 246–67, 254, 263.

9   On this point see the exploratory article by Woodruff Smith, 'The European–Asian Trade of the Seventeenth Century and the Modernization of Commercial Capitalism', *Itinerario*, 6:2, 1982, pp. 68–90.

10 G. R. Elton, *The History of England*, Cambridge, 1984, p. 30. Professor Elton believes the crop has been harvested and 'insularity is distant' in British historiography. I beg to differ.

11 Edward W. Said, *Orientalism*, New York, 1979 edition. Professor Said's influential book is stimulating. Unfortunately, his reference to the early phase of European expansion is conceptually

flawed and partisan. Until the nineteenth century Asia was not 'a domain with a continuous history of unchallenged Western dominance'. The idea of Asia – and for that matter of Asians – is a Western creation. It is for this reason that I prefer the neutral expression the Indies. Moreover, Said's passing mention of Japan in 1638–9 and to a group of Japanese Christians throwing out the Portuguese (cited as an example of occasional 'native intransigence' to the idyll of European domination) is a nonsense (ibid., p. 73). It may be objected that the idea of Europe and of a European identity were not particularly advanced in the seventeenth century. The concept of Christendom, however, was well defined and is synonymous with the former.

12 G. B. Sansom, *The Western World and Japan*, New York, 1973 edition, p. 66. The view is restated in C. R. Boxer, *The Portuguese Seaborne Empire 1415–1825*, London, 1969, pp. 49–50. It is countered in Chaudhuri, *Trade and Civilisation*, pp. 77–79.

13 Ludwig Riess, 'History of the English Factory at Hirado', *Transactions of the Asiatic Society of Japan*, first series, XXVI, 1898, pp. 1–114, 163–218. On William Adams see, for example, P. C. Rogers, *The First Englishman in Japan*, London, 1956.

14 Quoted in Fritz Stern, *Dreams and Delusions: The Drama of German History*, New York, 1987, p. 237.

15 For the context in which this remark was made see G. E. Aylmer, *The State's Servants: The Civil Service of the English Republic 1649–1660*, London, 1973, p. 167.

CHAPTER 1

1   Henry Yule, *Cathay and the Way Thither*, new edition by Henri Cordier, London, 1915, I, pp. 21–2.

2   J. Innes Miller, *The Spice Trade of the Roman Empire*, Oxford, 1969, p. 244.

3   Yule, *Cathay and the Way Thither*, I, p. 13.

4   J. H. Parry, *The Age of Reconnaissance*, London, 1973 edition, p. 25.

5   Yule, *Cathay and the Way Thither*, I, pp. 11–17, 194–196; Joseph Needham, *Science and Civilisation in China*, Cambridge, 1954, I, pp. 168–9.

6   Yule, *Cathay and the Way Thither*, I, p.

17; Ying-Shih Yu, *Trade and Expansion in Han China*, Berkeley, 1967, pp. 158, 168–9, 198.

7   E. H. Warmington, *The Commerce Between the Roman Empire and India*, London, 1974, pp. 71–2.

8   G. F. Hudson, *Europe and China*, Boston, 1961 edition; Needham, *Science and Civilisation*, I, pp. 170–6; Miller, *Spice Trade*, chs 7 and 8.

9   Yu, *Trade and Expansion*, pp. 156–7; Miller, *Spice Trade*, pp. 193–203, 215.

10 Xinru Liu, *Ancient India and Ancient China: Trade and Religious Exchanges AD1-600*, Delhi, 1988, pp. 18–19, 25–8.

11 Yu, *Trade and Expansion*, p. 159; Yule, *Cathay and the Way Thither*, I, p. 200 and cf. p. 18. Ironically, the Chinese and later the Japanese described the Europeans who arrived on their shores as 'red-haired barbarians'.

12 Charlotte von Verschauer, *Les relations officielles du Japon avec la Chine aux viii^eet ix^esiècles*, Geneva, 1985, p. xiv.

13 Yule, *Cathay and the Way Thither*, I, p. 193.

14 Ibid., pp. 35–57; O. W. Wolters, *Early Indonesian Commerce*, Ithica, 1967, p. 40.

15 Yule, *Cathay and the Way Thither*, I, pp. 52–3; Yu, *Trade and Expansion*, p. 160; Needham, *Science and Civilisation*, I, pp. 191–9; Philip D. Curtin, *Cross-Cultural Trade in World History*, Cambridge, 1984, pp. 99–100.

16 Miller, *Spice Trade*, p. 215; Curtin, *Cross-Cultural Trade*, p. 91.

17 This paragraph is based on Wang Gunwu, 'The Nanhai Trade: A Study of the Early History of the Chinese Trade in the South China Sea', *Journal of the Malayan Branch of the Royal Historical Society*, 31:2, 1958, pp. 3–117; Denis Twitchett (ed.), *The Cambridge History of China*, volume III: *Sui and T'ang China, 589–906*, part 1, Cambridge, 1979; Wolters, *Early Indonesian Commerce*, pp. 75ff, 156; Kenneth R. Hall, *Maritime Trade and State Development in Early Southeast Asia*, Honolulu, 1985, p. 35ff.; Bailey W. Diffie and George D. Winius, *Foundations of the Portuguese Empire 1415–1580*, Minneapolis, 1977, p. 6; Edwin O. Reischauer and John K. Fairbank, *East Asia: The Great Tradition*, Boston, 1960, chs 4, 5, 6.

18 The precise nature of the relationship between trade and state formation remains unclear. Professor Hall's views

(*Maritime Trade*, passim) are controversial. See Pierre-Yves Manguin's review in *Journal of the Economic and Social History of the Orient*, 31:3, 1988, pp. 327–33.

19 George Faldo Hourani, *Arab Seafaring in the Indian Ocean in Ancient and Early Medieval Times*, Princeton, 1951, p. 61; Rita Rose Di Meglio, 'Arab Trade with Indonesia and the Malay Peninsula from the 8th to the 16th Centuries', in D. S. Richards, *Islam and the Trade of Asia: A Coloquium*, Oxford, 1970, p. 108ff; Edwin O. Reischauer, 'Notes on T'Ang Dynasty Sea Routes', *Harvard Journal of Asiatic Studies*, 5, 1940–1, pp. 143–4; Yu, *Trade and Expansion*, p. 178; Robert M. Somers, 'The End of the T'ang', in Twitchett (ed.), *Cambridge History of China*, 3:1, pp. 739–40. See also the elegant account of this trade in Edward H. Schafer, *The Golden Peaches of Samarkand*, Berkeley, 1963.

20 Oskar Nachod, *Geschichte von Japan*, vol. 2, part 2, Leipzig, 1930, pp. 1092, 1094–95; G. Schurhammer, 'O Descobrimento do Japão pelos Portugueses no ano de 1543', *Anais da Academia Portuguesa da História*, second series, I, 1946, reprinted in *Orientalia*, XXI, 1963, pp. 490–4, 524, esp. pp. 490–1.

21 Reischauer and Fairbank, *East Asia: The Great Tradition*, pp. 211–19; Jung-Pang Lo, 'Maritime Commerce and its Relation to the Ming Navy', *Journal of the Economic and Social History of the Orient*, 12, 1969, pp. 57–101; Mark Evlin, *The Pattern of the Chinese Past*, Stanford, 1973; Shiba Yoshinobu, 'Sung Foreign Trade: Its Scope and Origin', in Morris Rossabi (ed.), *China Among Equals: The Middle Kingdom and its Neighbours 10th–14th Centuries*, Berkeley, 1983, pp. 104–8; William H. McNeil, *The Pursuit of Power*, Oxford, 1983, ch. 2; Tapan Raychaudhuri and Habib Irfan (eds), *The Cambridge Economic History of India*, 2 vols, Cambridge, 1982, I, pp. 131–4.

22 The nature and importance of the tributary system is discussed by Wang Gungwu, 'Early Ming Relations with Southeast Asia: Background Essay', in J. K. Fairbank (ed.), *The Chinese World Order*, Cambridge, Massachusetts, 1968, pp. 34–62. The tributary system and the Sung is analysed in Rossabi (ed.), *China Among Equals*, parts 1 and 2. Professor Wills cautions against describing imperial tributary policies as a

system before the Ming dynasty and has some shrewd insights into their operation after 1368 (John E. Wills, Jr, *Embassies & Illusions: Dutch and Portuguese Envoys to K'ang-hsi, 1666–1687*, Cambridge, Massachusetts, 1984, pp. 5–25, esp. p. 14). See also O. W. Wolters, *The Fall of Śrivijaya in Malay History*, Kuala Lumpur, 1975, esp. ch. 3; Hall, *Maritime Trade*, pp. 39–44.

23 Yule, *Cathay and the Way Thither*, i, pp. 149–154; David Morgan, *The Mongols*, Oxford, 1986, pp. 136–41. Shiba, 'Sung Foreign Trade', pp. 94–7.

24 Morgan, *The Mongols*, pp. 73–83, 159–61. The overland route had not ceased to function. It was controlled by the Chin dynasty and continued to serve as a conduit for goods from western Asia although on a much reduced scale from before. The more permanent unity of northern Asia which has survived into our own time was achieved in reverse with the expansion of the Russian empire from the seventeenth century.

25 Yule, *Cathay and the Way Thither*, i, p. 55 ff; William Woodville Rockhill (ed.), *The Journey of William of Rubruck to the Eastern Parts of the World, 1253–5*, London, 1900; Donald F. Lach, *Asia in the Making of Europe*, Chicago, 1965, 1:1, p. 34. Cathay was soon identified as the land of the Seres.

26 This was gradual. His account was dictated to his fellow prisoner in Genoa, Rusticello, in 1298 but it was not printed until 1485 although it enjoyed limited circulation in manuscript, of which 150 are known to exist (Schurhammer, 'O Descobrimento', p. 494).

27 *The Book of Ser Marco Polo*, translated and edited by Sir Henry Yule, 2 vols, London, 1921, ii, pp. 253–4.

28 The following discussion is based on Robert Sabatino Lopez, 'China Silk in Europe in the Yuan Period', *Journal of the American Oriental Society*, 2, 1952, pp. 72–6; Robert-Henri Bauthier, 'Les relations economiques des Occidentaux avec les pays d'Orient, au Moyen Age: points de vue et documents', in Michel Mollat (ed.), *Sociétés et compagnies de commerce en Orient et dans l'océan Indien*, Paris, 1970, pp. 289–308, who plays down the extent of direct contact, esp. p. 292; Eliyahu Ashtor, *Levant Trade in the Later Middle Ages*, Princeton, 1983, pp. 60–3.

29 Robert Sabatino Lopez, 'European Merchants in the Medieval Indies: The evidence of Commercial Documents', *Journal of Economic History*, iii, 1943, p. 166.

30 Needham, *Science and Civilisation*, 5:1, Cambridge, 1985, pp. 23–31; Needham, *Science and Civilisation*, 5:7, *Military Technology: The Gunpowder Epic*, Cambridge, 1986. See Carlo Ginzburg, *The Cheese and the Worms*, Harmondsworth, 1984, pp. 41–49, for the influence of Mandeville on the millar of Montreale, Menochio, at the end of the sixteenth century.

31 Lopez, 'European Merchants in the Medieval Indies', pp. 173–4, 181.

32 *The Book of Ser Marco Polo*, ii, pp. 234–45, 265; G. Ferrand, 'Une navigation européenne dans l'océan Indien au xive siècle', *Journal Asaitique*, 20, 1922, pp. 307–9; Tien-Tse Chang, *Sino-Portuguese Trade from 1514–1644*, Leyden, 1934, pp. 25–8; Jean Richard, 'Les navigations des Occidentaux sur l'océan Indien et la mer Caspienne (xiie-xve siècles)', in Mollat (ed.), *Sociétés et compagnies*, pp. 353–60; G. V. Scammel, *The World Encompassed*, London, 1981, p. 163.

33 Lopez, 'European Merchants in the Medieval Indies', pp. 169–70; Richard, 'Les navigations des Occidentaux sur l'océan Indien et la mer Caspienne', pp. 362–3; Diffie and Winius, *Foundations of the Portuguese Empire*, pp. 24–5; Scammel, *World Encompassed*, pp. 163–4; Felipe Fernández-Armesto, *Before*

33 *Columbus: Explorations and Colonisation from the Mediterranean to the Atlantic, 1229–1492*, London, 1987, pp. 152–3.

34 João de Barros quoted in Diffie and Winius, *Foundations of the Portuguese Empire*, p. 169.

35 The phrase is J. H. Parry's. See *The Age of Reconnaissance*.

36 Richard, 'Les Navigations des Occidentaux sur l'océan Indien et la mer Caspienne', pp. 359–60, 363; C. F. Beckingham, 'The Quest for Prester John', *Bulletin of the John Rylands Library*, 62, 1980, pp. 295–9 reprinted in C. F. Beckingham, *Between Islam and Christendom*, London, 1983.

37 Diffie and Winius, *Foundations of the Portuguese Empire*, pp. 313–17. The institution of the factory had its origins in the Portuguese community in Bruges where a *faitor*, or factor, was the Portuguese king's diplomatic and commercial representative and final arbiter of

disputes among resident Portuguese merchants (ibid., p. 313).

38 G. R. Crone, *Maps and their Makers*, London, 1978 edition, pp. 28–32; Archibald Lewis, 'Maritime Skills in the Indian Ocean 1368–1500', *Journal of the Economic and Social History of the Orient*, XVI, 1973, p. 249n. Needham would like to believe that the boat was Chinese (*Science and Civilisation*, 4:3, pp. 486, 501–2). Heroditus had already described a circumnavigation by the Phoenecians on behalf of the Egyptians sometime between 610 and 595 BC (Miller, *Spice Trade*, pp. 261, 266–7). William Adam also seems to have believed that Africa was circumnavigable (Beckingham, 'The Quest for Prester John', p. 297).

39 Diffie and Winius, *Foundations of the Portuguese Empire*, pp. 175–6; J. H. Parry, *The Discovery of the Sea*, p. 118; C. R. Boxer, *The Portuguese Seaborne Empire*, London, 1977 edition, pp. 35–6.

40 Diffie and Winius, *Foundations of the Portuguese Empire*, p. 180.

41 M. A. P. Meilink-Roelofsz, *Asian Trade and European Influence in the Indonesian Archipelago between 1500 and about 1630*, The Hague, 1962, p. 117; M. N. Pearson, *The New Cambridge History of India: The Portuguese in India*, Cambridge, 1987, pp. 116–30; Luis Vaz de Camões, *The Lusiads*, translated by William C. Atkinson, Harmondsworth, 1952, pp. 161–3.

42 Fernand Bruadel, *Civilization and Capitalism 15th–18th Century*, vol. I, *The Structure of Everyday Life*, London, 1981, pp. 220–1; Mollat (ed.), *Sociétés et compagnies*, pp. 350–1 (comments by Needham and Robert-Henri Bautier); Needham, *Science and Civilisation*, 4:3, Cambridge, 1971, pp. 520–1.

43 Ashtor, *Levant Trade in the Later Middle Ages*, pp. 450–79, esp. pp. 469–78.

44 Lewis, 'Maritime Skills', p. 258.

45 *Asian Trade Revolution*, pp. 91–2.

46 Ibid., pp. 81–95; M. N. Pearson, 'India and the Indian Ocean in the Sixteenth Century' in Ashin Das Gupta and M. N. Pearson (eds), *India and the Indian Ocean*, Calcutta, 1987, p. 91; Geneviève Bouchon, 'Sixteenth, Century Malabar and the Indian Ocean', in ibid., p. 178; K. S. Mathew, 'Trade in the Indian Ocean and the Portuguese System of Cartazes', in Malyn Newitt (ed.), *The First Portuguese Colonial Empire*, Exeter,

1986, pp. 69–83.

47 Curtin, *Cross-Cultural Trade*, pp. 117–19.

48 For the early phase of Portuguese expansion see Boxer, *Portuguese Seaborne Empire*; Diffie and Winius, *Foundations of the Portuguese Empire*. On the economic assumptions of Portugal's maritime empire see Van Leur, *Indonesian Trade and Society*, pp. 117–19; Steensgaard, *Asian Trade Revolution*, pp. 12–21, 81–95 (for the argument that the Estado da Índia was a redistributive enterprise); Das Gupta, 'Introduction II: The Story', in Das Gupta and Pearson (eds), *India and the Indian Ocean*, pp. 28–30; Pearson, 'India and the Indian Ocean in the Sixteenth Century', p. 91; Pearson, *New Cambridge History of India: The Portuguese in India, passim*. See also the important articles by Frederic C. Lane, 'National Wealth and Protection Costs', 'The Economic Meaning of War and Protection', 'Force and Enterprise in the Creation of Oceanic Commerce', 'Economic Consequences of Organised Violence' in Frederic C. Lane, *Venice and History: The Collected Papers of Frederic C. Lane*, Baltimore, 1966, pp. 373–428.

49 Diffie and Winius, *Foundations of the Portuguese Empire*, p. 255.

50 Tomé Pires, *The Suma Oriental of Tomé Pires*, edited and translated by Armando Cortesao, 2 vols, London, 1944, II, p. 226ff. See also Meilink-Roelofsz, *Asian Trade*, chs. 3 and 4.

51 E. G. Ravenstein, *A Journal of the First Voyage of Vasco da Gama (1497–1499)*, London, 1898; Needham, *Science and Civilisation*, 4:3, pp. 507–8.

52 Reischauer and Fairbank, *East Asia: The Great Tradition*, pp. 321–5; Ma Huan, *Ying-yai Sheng-Ian (The Oriental Survey of the Ocean's Shores)*, translated by J. V. G. Mills, Cambridge, 1970; Needham, *Science and Civilisation*, 4:3, pp. 487–94, 524; Tatsuro Yamamoto, 'Chinese Activities in the Indian Ocean before the Coming of the Portuguese', *Diogenes*, 111, 1980, pp. 26–32. For the wakō, see below.

53 Reischauer and Fairbank, *East Asia: The Great Tradition*, pp. 324–5; Mollat (ed.), *Sociétés et compagnies*, pp. 223–5; Needham, *Science and Civilisation*, 4:3, pp. 524–8.

54 C. R. Boxer, *The South China Sea in the Sixteenth Century*, London, 1953, p. xxiv; Chang, *Sino-Portuguese Trade*, pp.

30–1.

55 Chang, *Sino-Portuguese Trade*, pp. 32–3; C. R. Boxer, *The Christian Century in Japan 1549–1650*, Berkeley, 1974 edition, p. 4.

56 Chang, *Sino-Portuguese Trade*, p. 33.

57 Ibid., pp. 33–4; Diffie and Winius, *Foundations of the Portuguese Empire*, pp. 255–9.

58 Professor Boxer argues that the Gores/Ryūkyūans were mainly Japanese (*Christian Century*, pp. 10–14, 453n) and the view is accepted by Meilink-Roelofsz (*Asian Trade*, pp. 78–9, 88, 348n), Professor Lach (*Asia and The Making of Europe*, 1:2, pp. 514, 653) and by Diffie and Winius (*Foundations of the Portuguese Empire*, p. 393). The documentary evidence about the origin of the name and the Portuguese identification is assessed by Shurhammer ('O descobrimento', pp. 510–22). See also A. Kobata and M. Masuda, *Ryukyuan Relations with Korea and South Sea Countries*, Kyoto, 1969, pp. 126–9.

59 Schurhammer, 'O Descobrimento', p. 511.

60 Yule, *Cathay and the Way Thither*, I, pp. 181–2; Chang, *Sino-Portuguese Trade*, pp. 36–7; Boxer, *South China Sea*, pp. xix, xx.

61 Pires, *Suma Oriental*, I, pp. 131, 133–4; Boxer, *Christian Century*, p. 14; Diffie and Winius, *Foundations of the Portuguese Empire*, pp. 380–1, 386, 394.

62 Chang, *Sino-Portuguese Trade*, pp. 55–61; Diffie and Winius, *Foundations of the Portuguese Empire*, pp. 380–1, 394.

63 On their identity see Kwan-wai So, *Japanese Piracy in Ming China during the Sixteenth Century*, Michigan, 1975; Charles O. Hucker, 'Hu Tsung-hsien's Campaign against Hsu Hai, 1556' in Frank A. Kierman Jr and John K. Fairbank (eds), *Chinese Ways in Warfare*, Cambridge, Massachusetts, 1974, pp. 274–80.

64 Boxer, *South China Sea*, pp. xix-xxxvii; Chang, *Sino-Portuguese Trade*, pp. 38–85; Diffie and Winius, *Foundations of the Portuguese Empire*, pp. 383–9; John E. Wills, Jr, *Pepper, Guns & Parleys: The Dutch East India Company and China 1622–1681*, Cambridge, Massachusetts, 1974, p. 8.

65 Boxer, *Christian Century*, p. 16. For Japan's overseas trade see below.

66 Cf. Boxer, *Christian Century*, p. 13; Diffie and Winius, *Foundations of the Portuguese Empire*, p. 383.

67 Cf. Lach, *Asia in the Making of Europe*, 1:2, p. 655. There is also a cover-up explanation for the eight-year hiatus between Bartolmeu Dias's discovery of the Cape of Good Hope and Vasco da Gama's voyage. Diffie and Winius are sceptical about this argument (*Foundations of the Portuguese Empire*, pp. 175–6).

68 Schurhammer, 'O Descobrimento', p. 516.

69 W. E. Dahlgreen, 'A Contribution to the History of the Discovery of Japan', *Transactions of the Asiatic Society of Japan*, first series, XI, 1914, pp. 239–60; Schurhammer, 'O Descobrimento', pp. 526–50; Boxer, *Christian Century*, pp. 14–27. The year was originally believed to be 1542 but 1543 is more likely.

70 Schurhammer, 'O Descobrimento', pp. 538–39; Boxer, *Christian Century*, pp. 24–5. This is the official account by the historian of Portuguese India, Diogo do Couta, written in 1612, not an eyewitness report.

71 Ibid., p. 37.

72 The discussion which follows draws heavily on John Whitney Hall and Jeffrey P. Mass (eds), *Medieval Japan: Essays in Institutional History*, New Haven, 1974; John Whitney Hall and Toyoda Takeshi (eds), *Japan in the Muromachi Age*, Berkeley, 1977; Jeffrey P. Mass (ed.), *Court and Bakufu in Japanese History*, New Haven, 1982; John Whitney Hall, Nagahara Keiji, Kozo Yamamura (eds), *Japan Before Tokugawa*, Princeton, 1981; Peter Judd Arnesen, *The Medieval Japanese Daimyo*, New Haven, 1979; Jeffrey P. Mass and William B. Hauser (eds), *The Bakufu in Japanese History*, Stanford, 1985. Briefer accounts of aspects of the medieval period can be found in Conrad Totman, *Japan Before Perry*, Berkeley, 1981, and Mary Elizabeth Berry, *Hideyoshi*, Cambridge, Massachusetts, 1982.

73 'Epilogue', in Mass (ed.), *Court and Bakufu*, pp. 261–2.

74 *Seiitaishōgun*, 'barbarian subduing generalissimo', a title originally given to military commanders who subdued the 'northern barbarians' or aboriginal inhabitants of Japan and much used in eighth-century Nara.

75 'Epilogue', in Mass (ed.), *Court and Bakufu*, p. 261. The argument that in-

novation was more important than continuity in the Kamakura bakufu is put forward by Jeffrey P. Maas in 'The Emergence of the Kamakura *Bakufu*', in Hall and Maas (eds), *Medieval Japan*, pp. 127–83.

76 John W. Hall, 'The Muromachi Power Structure', in Hall and Toyoda (eds), *Japan in the Muromachi Age*, p. 42.

77 William B. Hauser draws attention to the struggle between centre and locality as a theme in bakufu history ('Afterword' in Hall and Hauser (eds), *Bakufu in Japanese History*, p. 194.

78 The point is well put by Berry, *Hideyoshi*, p. 21.

79 Ibid., p. 22.

80 For an outstanding discussion of the coexistence of *bun* and *bu* see H. Mack Horton, 'Saiokuken Sōcho and the Linked Verse Business', *The Transactions of the Asiatic Society of Japan*, fourth series I, 1986, pp. 45–78.

81 Toyoda Takeshi and Sugiyama Hiroshi, 'Growth of Commerce and the Trades' in Hall and Toyoda (eds), *Japan in the Muromachi Age*, pp. 131–3 which describes other ways in which the Ashikaga tried to make up for the deficiency of their landholdings by involving themselves in commercial activities.

82 Von Verschauer, *Les relations officielles du Japon avec la Chine*, pp. xiv–xv, 1–15.

83 Reischauer, 'Notes on T'ang Dynasty Sea Routes', pp. 142–53.

84 Mori Katsumi, 'The Beginnings of Overseas Advance of Japanese Merchant Ships', *Acta Asiatica*, 23, 1972, p. 4; Reischauer, 'Notes on T'ang Dynasty Sea Routes', p. 160ff; Von Verschauer, *Les relations officieles du Japon avec la Chine*, pp. 132–4, 142–9.

85 Mori, 'Beginnings of Overseas Advance of Japanese Merchant Ships', p. 5; Delmer M. Brown, *Money Economy in Medieval Japan*, New Haven, 1951, p. 9; Von Verschauer, *Les relations officieles du Japon avec la Chine*, pp. 151–2, 161–80.

86 Mori, 'Beginnings of Overseas Advance of Japanese Merchant Ships', pp. 12–13; Shiba, 'Sung Foreign Trade', pp. 105–7.

87 Mori, 'Beginnings of Overseas Advance of Japanese Merchant Ships', pp. 14–15.

88 Ibid. pp. 20–3.

89 *The Book of Ser Marco Polo*, II, pp. 258–63; Wang Gungwu, 'Early Ming Relations with Southeast Asia', pp. 48–9; Yoshi S. Kuno, *Japanese Expansion on the Asiatic Continent*, 2 vols, Berkeley, 1937–40, I, pp. 52–6.

90 Brown, *Money Economy in Medieval Japan*, pp. 12–16, 17; Tanaka Takeo, *Wakō to kango bōeki*, Tokyo, 1961, p. 37; Hayashiya Tatsusaburo, 'Kyoto in the Muromachi Age', in Hall and Toyoda (eds), *Japan in the Muromachi Age*, p. 20.

91 Wang Gungwu, 'Early Ming Relations with Southeast Asia', pp. 49–54; Wolters, *Fall of Śrīvijaya*, chs 3 and 5.

92 Brown, *Money Economy in Medieval Japan*, pp. 17–19; Mori, 'Beginnings of Overseas Advance of Japanese Merchant Ships', p. 17; Benjamin H. Hazard, 'The Formative Years of the *Wakō*, 1223–63', *Monumenta Nipponica*, XXII, 1967, pp. 260–77; Tanaka, *Wakō to kango bōeki*, pp. 1–50; Tanaka, 'Japan's Relations with Overseas Countries', in Hall and Toyoda (eds), *Japan in the Muromachi Age*, pp. 161–3. There is a short introduction to early wakō activity with an excellent map in Tanaka Takeo, 'Wakō no bōeki', in Shūkan Asahi Hyakuka (ed), *Nihon no rekishi*, 15, Tokyo, 1986, pp. 100–4.

93 Wang Yi-T'ung, *Official Relations Between China and Japan 1368–1549*, Cambridge, Massachusetts, 1953, pp. 10–21.

94 Ibid., pp. 22–4.

95 Brown, *Money Economy in Medieval Japan*, pp. 19–20; Wang, *Official Relations*, pp. 4, 37–38; Tanaka, *Wakō to kango bōeki*, pp. 63–67, 89–134; Tanaka, *Chūsei taigai kankei shi*, Tokyo, 1975, pp. 153–65; Tanaka, 'Japan's Relations with Overseas Countries', pp. 166, 169; Wills, *Embassies & Illusions*, pp. 15, 18–19.

96 Quoted in Wang, *Official Relations*, p. 41.

97 The above paragraph is based on Tanaka, 'Japan's Relations with Overseas Countries', pp. 164–5, 178; Kenneth A. Grosberg, *Japan's Renaissance: The Politics of the Muromachi Bakufu*, 1981, pp. 33–7, 49. However, Professor Tanaka emphasises that 'a concept of national authority was not yet fully developed' and that the 'concept of absolute national control over foreign relations and foreign trade' lay very much in the future (Tanaka, 'Japan's Relations with Overseas Countries', p. 178).

98 Wang, *Official Relations*, pp. 60–1; Tanaka, 'Japan's Relations with Overseas Countries', p. 168; Grosberg, *Japan's Renaissance*, p. 49.

99 Toyoda and Sugiyama, 'The Growth of Commerce and the Trades', *passim*; V. Dixon Morris, 'Sakai: From Shoen to Port City', in Hall and Toyoda (eds), *Japan in the Muromachi Age*, pp. 145–58 *passim*; Grosberg, *Japan's Renaissance*, pp. 37–8, 49.

100 Brown, *Money Economy in Medieval Japan*, *passim*; Kobata Atsushi, 'The Production and Uses of Gold and Silver in Sixteenth and Seventeenth Century Japan', *Economic History Review*, second series, 18:2, 1965, pp. 245–66.

101 Wang, *Official Relations*, pp. 89–90, 91, 94–100; Tanaka, *Wakō to kango bōeki*, pp. 121–34; Tanaka, 'Japan's Relations with Overseas Countries', p. 172; Shafer, *Golden Peaches*, p. 211; Dixon Morris, 'Sakai', pp. 154, 156 & n.

102 Wang, *Official Relations*, pp. 100–6; Tanaka, 'Japan's Relations with Overseas Countries', p. 170; Tanaka, *Chūsei taigai kankei*, pp. 160–4.

103 Tanaka, 'Japan's Relations with Overseas Countries', pp. 161–3, 173–4; Arnesen, *Medieval Japanese Daimyo*, pp. 83–6; Lorraine F. Harrington, 'Regional Outposts of Muromachi Bakufu Rule: The Kantō and Kyushu', in Maas and Hauser (eds), *Bakufu in Japanese History*, pp. 85–90, 94–6.

104 Brown, *Money Economy in Medieval Japan*, pp. 26–7; Tanaka, *Wakō to kango bōeki*, pp. 135–68, 187–92; Tanaka, *Chūsei taigai kankei*, pp. 165–94, 300–11; Tanaka, 'Japan's Relations with Overseas Countries', pp. 173, 177; Harrington, 'Regional Outposts of Muromachi Bakufu Rule', p. 94.

105 George Elison, *Deus Destroyed*, Cambridge, Massachusetts, 1973, p. 397 n. 16; Pearson, *New Cambridge History of India: The Portuguese in India*, p. 121.

106 John Critchley, *Feudalism*, London, 1978, ch. 4; John Whitney Hall, 'Japan's Sixteenth Century Revolution', in George Elison and Bardwell L. Smith (eds), *Warlords, Artisans and Commoners*, Honolulu, 1981, pp. 7–21.

107 In time there was an Asian naval response in the eastern Indian Ocean, notably from Achin in Sumatra and from Calicut, which occasionally faced up to the Portuguese, and especially from Asian privateers (Chaudhuri, *Trade and Civilisation in the Indian Ocean*, pp. 156–7; Geoffrey Parker, *The Military Revolution*, Cambridge, 1988, pp. 105–6). But neither the Mughals nor the Chinese, the great powers of the region, developed navies to face up to the Portuguese and other Europeans, nor considered them to be a strategic requirement. This had little to do with technological deficiency. Land-based powers did not view the sea as of major strategic or even commercial importance. In the western Indian Ocean, the Oman navy evolved into a competent naval force which captured Muscat in 1650 and Fort Jesus on Mombassa in 1698 from the Portuguese (Chaudhuri, *Trade and Civilisation in the Indian Ocean*, pp. 77–9, 156–9; Ashin Das Gupta, 'Introduction II: The Story', in Das Gupta and Pearson (eds), *India and the Indian Ocean*, p. 35; M. D. D. Newitt, 'East Africa and Indian Ocean Trade: 1500–1800' in ibid., p. 217; Parker, *Military Revolution*, pp. 105, 112).

108 Jacques Gernet, *China and the Christian Impact*, Cambridge, 1985, p. 88; Keith Thomas, *Religion and the Decline of Magic*, Harmondsworth, 1973, p. 790. See also Jonathan D. Spence, *The Memory Palace of Matteo Ricci*, London, 1984, pp. 20–2.

109 Elison, *Deus Destroyed*, pp. 248–51. Cf. Gernet, *China and the Christian Impact*, pp. 60–1 for the Jesuits in China.

110 Alesandro Valignano, *Sumario de las Cosas de Japon (1583)*, edited by J. L. Alvarez Taladriz, Tokyo, 1954, ch. 9; J. F. Schütte, *Valignano's Mission Principles for Japan*, vol. 1, part 2, *The Solution*, St Louis, 1985, p. 218.

111 José Luis Alvarez Taladriz (ed.), *Documentos Franciscanos de la Christianidad de Japon (1593–1597)*, Osaka, 1973, p. 136.

112 Wang, *Official Relations*, pp. 73–4; Wills, *Embassies & Illusions*, pp. 17–19.

113 Tanaka, 'Japan's Relations with Overseas Countries', p. 178. The importance of overseas trade in stimulating economic activity in south China is discussed in Evelyn Sakakida Rawski, *Agricultural Change and the Peasant Economy of South China*, Cambridge, Massachusetts, 1972, ch. 4.

114 Wang, *Official Relations*, p. 4; Kwanwai So, *Japanese Piracy*, pp. 6, 43.

115 So, *Japanese Piracy*, pp. 5–6 and *passim*; Hucker, 'Hu Tsung-hsien's Campaign against Hsu Hai, 1556', p. 276.

116 Brown, *Money Economy in Medieval*

Japan, chs 5–7; Kobata, 'The Production and Uses of Gold and Silver', pp. 245–6; Robert K. Innes, 'The Door Ajar: Japan's Foreign Relations in the Seventeenth Century', unpublished Ph.D. thesis, University of Michigan, 1980, pp. 21–9; William S. Atwell, 'International Bullion Flows and the Chinese Economy Circa 1530–1650', *Past & Present*, 5, May 1982, pp. 68–90; William S. Atwell, 'Some Observations on the "Seventeenth Century Crisis" in China & Japan', *Journal of Asian Studies*, 45:2, February 1986, p. 227 and sources therein cited. The exact volume of bullion carried between Japan and China, and between the Spanish mines in the New World and Manila, another important source of Chinese silver imports, is a matter of debate. Atwell ('International Bullion Flows', pp. 72–4) provides some words of caution about previous estimates, as does George Brian Souza, *The Survival of Empire: Portuguese Trade and Society in China and the South China Sea 1630–1754*, Cambridge, 1986, pp. 57–8, 84–5. What is not in dispute is that the movement of silver between Japan and China brought about a qualitative and quantitative change in the economic relationship between the two east Asian countries and had important implications for their economies and for anyone participating in their overseas trade.

117 So, *Japanese Piracy*, pp. 132–133; Rawski, *Agricultural Change*, p. 75; Michael Cooper (ed.), *This Island of Japan: João Rodrigues' Account of 16th Century Japan*, Tokyo, 1973, p. 133.
Albert Tscheppe, *Japans Beziehungen zu China seit den ältesten Zeit bis zum Jahre 1600*, Yenchoufou, 1907, pp. 262–3; Okamoto Yoshitomo, *Jūroku seiki Nichi-Ō kōtsū-shi* (A History of Sixteenth Century Contacts Between Japan and Europe), Tokyo, 1936, p. 661 n. 2; Brown, *Money Economy in Medieval Japan*, p. 61; Boxer, *South China Sea*, pp. 313–26 esp. 318–19; Georg Schurhammer, *Francis Xavier: His Life, His Times*, Rome, 1982, p. 123 n. 42; Bodo Wiethoff, *Die Chinesische Seeverbotspolitik und der privat Überseehandel von 1386 bis 1567*, Hamburg, 1963, pp. 24n., 168–9, 175, 201–2; Rawski, *Agricultural Change*, pp. 66–67; Hucker, 'Hu Tsung-hsien's Campaign agianst Hsu Hai, 1556', pp. 276, 280; Innes,

'The Door Ajar', p. 41; Diffie and Winius, *Foundations of the Portuguese Empire*, p. 398; Ng Chin-Keong, *Trade and Society: The Amoy Network on the China Coast 1683–1775*, Singapore, 1983, p. 48.

119 Cf Lach, *Asia in the Making of Europe*, 1:1, p. 655.

120 C. R. Boxer, *Fidalgos in the Far East, 1550–1770*, Oxford 1968, pp. 4–5; Souza, *Survival of Empire*, pp. 19–20.

121 So, *Japanese Piracy*, pp. 94, 110–11.

122 C. R. Boxer, *The Great Ship from Amacon: Annals of Macao and the Old Japan Trade*, Lisbon, 1959, pp. 13, 95; Souza, *Survival of Empire*, p. 40.

123 Paul Aoyama, *Die Missionstätigkeit des hl. Franz Xaver in Japan aus japanische Sicht*, St Augustin/Siegurg, 1967, pp. 83–4; Schurhammer, *Xavier*, p. 123n; Okamoto, *Jūroku seiki Nichi-Ō kōtsū-shi*, pp. 504–8.

124 Diego Pacheo, 'The Founding of the Port of Nagasaki and its Cession to the Society of Jesus', *Monumenta Nipponica*, xxv, 1970, pp. 315, 317, 319–20 and *passim*; Schütte, *Valignano's Mission Principles*, 1:2 pp. 327–34; Elison, *Deus Destroyed*, pp. 94–101.

125 Valignano, *Sumario*, pp. 131–4, esp. p. 132; Pachecho, 'The Founding of the Port of Nagasaki', pp. 319–20; Elison, *Deus Destroyed*, p. 96.

126 Ibid., p. 98.

127 Ibid., pp. 98–9. It was not necessary to build fortifications to create misgivings among the Japanese. The Chinese were concerned about the construction of the Jesuit church in Macao atop a hill (Spence, *Memory Palace*, pp. 53–4). The Chinese had no way of distinguishing between a place of worship and a military structure; nor did the Japanese.

128 Innes, 'The Door Ajar', pp. 47–8.

129 Elison, *Deus Destroyed*, p. 410 n. 43.

130 Michael Cooper, *Rodrigues the Interpreter*, Tokyo, 1974, p. 245.

131 Michael Cooper 'The Mechanics of the Macao Trade', *Monumenta Nipponica*, 27:4, 1974, p. 428. The Jesuits had to pay Macao customs of 3 per cent and freight costs of approximately 10 per cent.

132 Takase Koichiro, 'Unauthorized Commercial Activities by Jesuit Missionaries in Japan', *Acta Asiatica*, 30, 1976, pp. 19–33.

133 C. R. Boxer, *Portuguese India in the Mid-Seventeenth Century*, Delhi, 1980, pp. 48–51, although Professor Boxer's

suggestion that the Company of Jesus was the first multinational is misleading.

134 Antonio de Morga, *Sucesos de las Islas Filipinas*, edited by J. S. Cummins, Cambridge, 1971, p. 196.

135 J. S. Cummins and C. R. Boxer, 'The Dominican Mission in Japan (1602–1622) and Lope de Vega', *Archivuum Fratum Praedicatorum*, XXXIII, 1963, pp. 6–10, reprinted in J. S. Cummins, *Jesuit and Friar in the Spanish Expansion to the East*, London, 1986; Cooper, *Rodrigues*, pp. 245–7.

136 Cooper, 'Mechanics of the Macao Trade', pp. 427–31, especially 430–1.

137 Morga, *Sucesos*, p. 308; Lothar Knauth, *Confrontación Transpacífica: El Japon y el Neuvo Mundo Hispanico 1542–1639*, Mexico, 1972, p. 188; Souza, *Survival of Empire*, pp. 65–70. These Japanese voyages were different from the subsequent *shuinsen* ones (about which see chapter 4 (i) below) and the Portuguese involved were almost certainly those excluded from trade with Japan by the *Armação*. Relations between the Portuguese in Macao and the Spanish in Manila were characterised by rivalry and suspicion stemming from a desire on both sides to protect their own markets and trade. This made strategic cooperation to ward off the threat posed by the arrival of the Dutch – the common enemy – almost impossible. See E. H. Blair and J. A. Robertson (eds), *The Philippine Islands 1493–1898*, 55 vols, Cleveland, Ohio, 1903–5, XVII, p. 226; ibid., XVIII, pp. 194–203; Souza, *Survival of Empire*, pp. 63–86.

138 Shütte, *Valignano's Mission Principles*, I, part 2, pp. 31, 37–8, 41–6, 53.

139 Elison, *Deus Destroyed*, p. 71.

140 Ibid., pp. 72, 131; Elison, 'Cross and Sword', in *Warlords, Artisans and Commoners*, p. 82.

141 M. N. Pearson, 'Goa During the First Century of Portuguese Rule', *Itinerario*, 8:1, 1984, pp. 41–2.

142 Boxer, *Christian Century*, pp. 72–90, 218–26; Boxer, 'European Missionaries and Chinese Clergy 1654–1810', in Blair B. King and M. N. Pearson (eds), *The Age of Partnership: Europeans in Asia before Dominion*, Honolulu, 1979, pp. 97–121; Teontonio R. de Souza, 'The Voiceless in Goa Historiography', in John Correia-Afonso (ed.), *Indo-Portuguese History: Sources and Problems*, Bombay, 1981, pp. 119–20; Stuart B.

Schwartz, 'The Formation of a Colonial Identity in Brazil', in Nicholas Canny and Anthony Pagden (eds), *Colonial Identity in the Atlantic World, 1500–1800*, Princeton, 1985, pp. 41–4. In the South American case the Benedictines were the first to exclude natives and mestizos from holy orders (ibid., p. 41).

143 Elison, *Deus Destroyed*, pp. 42, 81–2, 131–2.

144 Hall 'Japan's Sixteenth Century Revolution', pp. 11–12; Berry, *Hideyoshi*, pp. 85–7; Susser, 'The Toyotomi Regime and the Diamyo', p. 132.

145 Elison (*Deus Destroyed*, pp. 115–33) contains the best analysis of the circumstances surrounding the decree, but see also Boxer, *Christian Century*, pp. 145–52.

146 Elison, *Deus Destroyed*, p. 140 and Berry, *Hideyoshi*, ch. 8 for Hideyoshi's last years.

147 Quoted in Henri Bernard, 'Les debuts des relations diplomatiques entre le Japon et les Espagnols des iles Philippines (1571–1594), *Monumenta Nipponica*, 1, 1938, p. 123.

148 For discussions of the affair see Boxer, *Christian Century*, pp. 163–7, 416–18, 420–4; Elison, *Deus Destroyed*, pp. 135–41; Knauth, *Confrontación Transpacíficoa*, pp. 134–40; Cooper, *Rodrigues*, pp. 132–9, 150–61.

149 For a balanced discussion of Jesuit–friar rivalry see J. S. Cummins, 'Two Missionary Methods in China: Mendicants and Jesuits', *Archivo Ibero-Americano*, XXXVIII, 1978, pp. 33–108 esp. p. 86, reprinted in Cummins, *Jesuit and Friar*. See also C. R. Boxer, 'Friar Juan Pobre of Zamara and His Lost and Found "Ystoria" of 1598–1603', *Indiana University Bookman*, 10, 1969, pp. 25–46, reprinted in C. R. Boxer, *Portuguese Merchants and Missionaries in Feudal Japan, 1543–1640*, London, 1986; Elison, *Deus Destroyed*, p. 479. On the political and cultural implications of missionary activity in China, many of which are relevant to Japan, see Gernet, *China and the Christian Impact, passim*. In India about 60 per cent of converts to Christianity by 1600 belonged to the low caste of fishermen and pearl divers, converted by the Jesuits (Pearson, *New Cambridge History of India: The Portuguese in India*, p. 121).

150 Schütte, *Valignano's Mission Principles for Japan*, vol. I, part 1, *The Problem*, St

Louis, 1980, p. 213; Lach, *Asia in the Making of Europe*, 1:1, pp. 685–6.

151 C. R. Boxer, 'Some Second Thoughts on Indo-Portuguese Historiograhy', in Correia-Afonso (ed.), *Indo-Portuguese History*, pp. 139–40.

152 Schurhammer, 'O Descobrimento', pp. 488, 498.

153 Ibid., p. 529.

154 Ibid., pp. 499–500, 531–2; Boxer, *Christian Century*, p. 454 n. 18.

155 For accounts of the mission see Luís Frois, *La Première ambassade du Japon en Europe, 1582–1592*, edited by J. A. Abranches Pinto *et al.*, Tokyo, 1938; Lach, *Asia in the Making of Europe*, 1:1, pp. 688–706. See also *ibid.*, p. 297.

156 Schurhammer, *Xavier*, pp. 65–6.

157 Richard Hakluyt, *Principal Navigations, Voiages, Traffiques and Discoveries of the English Nation...within the Compase of these 1500 Yeeres*, Glasgow, 12 vols, 1904–5, XI, pp. 324–7.

158 London, 1588, sig.2v.

159 *Principal Navigations*, I, p. xxi.

CHAPTER 2

1 The quotation is from the Milanese ambassador in London, Raimondo de Soncino, written in December 1497 (J. A. Williamson [ed.], *The Cabot Voyages and Bristol Discovery under Henry VII*, Cambridge, 1962, p. 210). See also ibid., pp. 88, 105–6; C. F. Beckingham, 'Some Early European Travellers in Arabia', *Proceedings of the Seminar for Arabian Studies*, 6, 1976, p. 3, reprinted in C. F. Beckingham, *Between Islam and Christendom*, London, 1983; and Kenneth R. Andrews, *Trade, Plunder and Settlement: Maritime Enterprise and the Genesis of the British Empire 1480–1630*, Cambridge, 1984, pp. 49–50. The Spice Islands are technically those islands lying within the arc described by Celebes (Sulawesi), Halmahera, New Guinea and Timor. The English and Dutch, however, referred to the Spice Islands as those islands to the north of Amboina (Ambon) and called them the Moluccas.

2 D. B. Quinn and A. N. Ryan, *England's Sea Empire*, London, 1983, pp. 31–2.

3 Andrews, *Trade, Plunder and Settlement*, pp. 11–12; Quinn and Ryan, *England's Sea Empire*, p. 32.

4 K. R. Andrews, *Elizabethan Privateering: English Privateering during the Spanish War, 1585–1603*, Cambridge, 1963,

pp. 13–14; Pauline Croft, *The Spanish Company*, London, 1973, pp. xiii, xvii.

5 Andrews, *Elizabethan Privateering*, pp. 12–15; Andrews, *Trade Plunder and Settlement*, pp. 141–59; Croft, *The Spanish Company*, pp. xxiii–xxix; Quinn and Ryan, *England's Sea Empire*, pp. 35–8, 82–4.

6 Meilink-Roelofsz, *Asian Trade*, pp. 155–9; Diffie and Winius, *Foundations of the Portuguese Empire*, pp. 360–1, 375–9. Cf. Andrews, *Trade, Plunder and Settlement*, pp. 157–8; Quinn and Ryan, *England's Sea Empire*, p. 37.

7 Sir William Foster, *England's Quest of Eastern Trade*, London, 1933, pp. 65–7; K. R. Andrews, *English Privateering Voyages to the West Indies 1588–95*, Cambridge, 1959, pp. 203–5; Andrews, *Trade, Plunder and Settlement*, pp. 162–4; Elizabeth Story Donno, *An Elizabethan in 1582: The Diary of Richard Madox, Fellow of All Souls*, London, 1976, pp. 16–19 and *passim*. Foster remains of interest but on this and other developments of the quest in the East Indies his interpretations are out of date.

8 Lawrence A. Clayton, 'The Maritime Trade of Peru in the Seventeenth Century', *The Mariners' Mirror*, 72:2, 1986, p. 173.

9 Andrews, *English Privateering Voyages*, pp. 100–23, 216; Andrews, 'Elizabethan Privateering', in Joyce Youings (ed.), *Raleigh in Exeter 1985: Privateering and Colonisation in the Reign of Elizabeth I*, Exeter, 1985, p. 11.

10 Andrews, 'The Elizabethan Seaman', *Mariners' Mirror*, 68:3, 1982, pp. 251–3; Andrews, *English Privateering Voyages*, p. 10; Quinn and Ryan, *England's Sea Empire*, p. 88. Privateering also removed another problem – piracy – which had caused headaches for the Privy Council from the late 1550s, not least because it posed a threat to law and order. The energies of the pirates who had operated from bases around the coasts of England, Wales and Ireland were channelled into privateering (K. R. Andrews, 'The Elizabethan Seaman', p. 250; Andrews, 'Elizabethan Privateering', pp. 3–7).

11 Andrews, *English Privateering Voyages*, p. 34; Andrews, *Trade Plunder and Settlement*, pp. 230–2, 252–3; Andrews, 'Elizabethan Privateering', pp. 12, 17–18.

12 Andrews, *English Privateering Voyages*,

pp. 120, 230–1, ch. 6; *Trade, Plunder and Settlement*, pp. 251–2; Quinn and Ryan, *England's Sea Empire*, pp. 122–3, 126.

13 T. S. Willan, 'Some Aspects of English Trade with the Levant in the Sixteenth Century', *English Historical Review*, LXX, 1955, pp. 390–407; Andrews, *English Privateering Voyages*, p. 218; Andrews, *Trade, Plunder and Settlement*, pp. 87–93.

14 Willan, 'Some Aspects of English Trade with the Levant', pp. 408–10.

15 On the Levant trade see A. C. Wood, *A History of the Levant Company*, London, 1935; T. S. Willan, *Studies in Elizabethan Foreign Trade*, Manchester, 1959, pp. 1–31. See also Niels Steensgaard, 'Consuls and Nations in the Levant from 1570 to 1650', *Scandanavian Economic History Review*, XV, 1967, pp. 13, 55; Derek Massarella, 'The Early Career of Richard Cocks (1566–1624), Head of the English East India Company's Factory in Japan (1613–23), *Transactions of the Asiatic Society of Japan*, third series, XX, 1985, p. 12; Wood, *Levant Company*, pp. 10–14; Andrews, *Trade Plunder and Settlement*, p. 92.

16 The relative weighting of the Cape and caravan routes in supplying Europe with pepper and spices is a matter of controversy. Professor Vitorino Magalhães Godinho argues that the Red Sea and Gulf routes added to supplies but did not replace the Cape route from the 1550s (*L'économie de l'empire portugais aux xv*ᵉ *et xvi*ᵉ *siècles*, 2 vols, Paris 1969, chs 4 and 5, esp. pp. 705–6, 778–80). Professor Steensgaard (*Asian Trade Revolution*, pp. 155–69) argues that the Red Sea and Gulf routes carried the greater volume. This suggestion has been challenged by Professor C. H. H. Wake ('The Changing Pattern of Europe's Pepper Trade and Spice Imports, *ca.* 1400–1700', *Journal of European Economic History*, 2:8, 1979, pp. 361–403) who argues that for most of the sixteenth century, including the 1570s and 1580s, the Portuguese imported around 75 per cent of Europe's pepper and spice needs. See also Eliyahu Ashtor, 'The Changing Pattern of Europe's Recent Research in Levantine Trade', *Journal of European Economic History*, 14:2, 1985, pp. 383–4; C. H. H. Wake, 'The Volume of European Spice Imports at the Beginning and End

of the Fifteenth Century', *Journal of European Economic History*, 15:3, 1986, pp. 621–35. What is not in dispute is the fact that the establishment of the English and Dutch companies sounded the tocsin for the Levant route.

17 *Principal Navigations*, VI, pp. 387–407; Foster, *England's Quest*, pp. 127–35; Andrews, *Elizabethan Privateering*, pp. 214–16.

18 D. B. Quinn (ed.), *The Haklyut Handbook*, 2 vols, London, 1974, p. 345. On Stephens see also Georg Schurhammer, 'Thomas Stephens (1549–1619)', *Orientalia*, XXI, 1963, pp. 367–76; 'Der Marathidichter Thomas Stephens SI: Neue Dokumente', ibid., pp. 377–91.

19 *Principal Navigations*, V, pp. 450–1, 465–505, esp. p. 498.

20 Foster, *England's Quest*, p. 74; John Parker, *Books to Build an Empire*, Amsterdam, 1965, p. 157.

21 Foster, *England's Quest*, pp. 79–109; Andrews, *Trade, Plunder and Settlement*, p. 93–7.

22 *Principal Navigations*, VI, p. 407.

23 Quoted in C. R. Boxer, *The Dutch Seaborne Empire*, p. 5.

24 Violet Barbour, 'Dutch and English Merchant Shipping in the Seventeenth Century', *Economic History Review*, 2, 1929–30, pp. 261–90.

25 Boxer, *Dutch Seaborne Empire*, pp. 5–22; Jan de Vries, *The Economy of Europe in an Age of Crisis, 1600–1750*, Cambridge, 1976, p. 118; Scammel, *World Encompassed*, pp. 373–382; Fernand Braudel, *The Mediterranean and the Mediterranean World in the Age of Philip II*, 2 vols, London, 1975, I, pp. 636–40; Braudel, *Civilization and Capitalism Fifteenth-Eighteenth Century*, III, *The Perspective of the World*, pp. 138–57, 187, 207–10.

26 Lach, *Asia in the Making of Europe*, I:1, pp. 198–204; A. C. Burnell and P. A. Tiele (eds), *The Voyage of Jan Huigen Linschoten to the Indies*, London, 1885, I, p. 151 n.

27 Van Leur, *Indonesian Trade and Society*, pp. 175–80; Andrews, *Trade, Plunder and Settlement*, p. 260; Boxer, *Dutch Seaborne Empire*, pp. 22–4.

28 Anthony Disney, *Twilight of the Pepper Empire: Portuguese Trade in Southwest India in the Early Seventeenth Century*, Cambridge, Massachusetts, 1978, pp. 50–1, 63 and *passim*.

29 William Foster (ed.), *The Travels of John Sanderson in the Levant, 1584–*

1602, London, 1931, pp. 180, 186, 189–90, 212; K. N. Chaudhuri, *The English East India Company*, London, 1966, pp. 11–12. Between 1597 and 1601 a number of pamphlets describing the Dutch voyages were rushed off the presses (C. D. C. Collins, *Handlist of New Pamphlets*, London 1943, xcviii, cxv, cxxxv, p. 112.

30 Henry Stevens and George Birdwood (eds), *The Dawn of British Trade to the East Indies as Recorded in the Court Minutes of the East India Company, 1599–1603*, London, 1886, pp. 1–4, 8.

31 Chaudhuri, *East India Company*, p. 12. Professor Andrews argues that references to the promotion of the common weal by advocates of overseas adventures were generally little more than clichés (*Trade, Plunder and Settlement*, pp. 33–4).

32 Chaudhuri, *East India Company*, p. 12.

33 Stevens and Birdwood (eds), *Dawn of British Trade*, pp. 10–11.

34 These notes are attributed to Richard Hakluyt and are printed in E. G. R. Taylor, *The Original Writings and Correspondence of the Two Richard Hakluyts*, 2 vols, London, 1935, pp. 465–8.

35 Stevens and Birdwood, (eds), *Dawn of Eastern Trade*, pp. 10–11; George Birdwood and William Foster (eds), *The First Letter Book of the East India Company: 1600–1619*, London, 1892, pp. 163–89. Foster, *England's Quest of Eastern Trade*, pp. 146–51; Andrews, *Elizabethan Privateering*, p. 218; Chaudhuri, *East India Company*, p. 12. The brief discussion of the Company's foundation and first two voyages in Quinn and Ryan is inaccurate (*England's Sea Empire*, pp. 151–2). When peace was finally concluded between England and Spain in 1604 (the treaty itself was ratified in 1605) the question of trade in both the Indies was covered by an ambiguous clause which the English chose to interpret as giving them free trade in the Indies. The Spanish rejected such an interpretation but were powerless to do much about it (David B. Quinn, 'James I and the Beginnings of Empire in America', *Journal of Imperial and Commonwealth History*, 2, 1974, pp. 135–52 esp. pp. 139–41; K. R. Andrews, 'Caribbean Rivalry and the Anglo-Spanish Peace of 1604', *History*, 59, 1974, pp. 14–17; Andrews, *Trade, Plunder and Settlement*, pp. 254–5).

36 Chaudhuri, *East India Company*, p. 4.

37 Ibid., pp. 143–44.

38 For introductory discussions of concepts of international law in the early modern period see C. H. Alexandrowicz, *An Introduction to the History of the Law of Nations in the East Indies*, Oxford, 1967; Jörg Fisch, *Die europäische Expansion und das Völkerrecht*, Stuttgart, 1984.

39 Foster, *England's Quest of Eastern Trade*, pp. 170–1; Chaudhuri, *East India Company*, pp. 29–31, 153–4; Steensgaard, *Asian Trade Revolution*, pp. 81–95, 114–20 esp. p. 116; Andrews, *Trade, Plunder and Settlement*, pp. 262, 278. Michelbourne's voyage, comprising one ship and a pinnace, quickly degenerated into one of piracy in southeast Asia and the Company began proceedings in the Admiralty Court against Michelbourne but withdrew them, preferring not to risk running foul of the court. Cunningham's plans failed to materialise. The English Company protested and Cunningham's patent was revoked.

40 Chaudhuri, *East India Company*, p. 140.

41 Birdwood and Foster (eds), *First Letter Book*, pp. 77–80; Foster, *England's Quest of Eastern Trade*, pp. 156–8; Chaudhuri, *East India Company*, pp. 17, 41.

42 S. Arasaratnam, 'India and the Indian Ocean in the Seventeenth Century' in Das Gupta and Pearson (eds), *India and the Indian Ocean*, p. 107. See also Pearson's own study, *Merchants and Rulers in Gujerat*, Berkeley, 1976, and Ashin Das Gupta, 'Gujerati Merchants and the Red Sea Trade, 1700–1723', in Kling and Pearson (eds), *The Age of Partnership*, pp. 123–58.

43 Birdwood and Foster (eds), *First Letter Book*, pp. 363–4.

44 Chaudhuri, *East India Company*, p. 121.

45 Birdwood and Foster (eds), *First Letter Book*, pp. 427–28; W. H. Moreland (ed.), *The Voyage of Peter Floris*, London, 1934, pp. xxxvi–liii; Foster, *England's Quest of Eastern Trade*, pp. 209–10; Chaudhuri, *East India Company*, pp. 40, 42.

46 Birdwood and Foster (eds), *First Letter Book*, p. 387. The letter 'To the highe & Mightie Prince the greate kinge of Iapan' is printed on pp. 426–7.

47 Moreland (ed.), *The Voyage of Peter Floris*, p. 36. See below for their efforts.

48 Hakluyt, *Principal Navigations*, iii, p. 263; v, p. 452; vi, pp. 377–85; Andrews, *Trade, Plunder and Settlement*,

pp. 72–5, 95–6.

49   J. A. Williamson (ed.), *The Observations of Sir Richard Hawkins Knight in his Voyage to the South Seas, Anno Domini 1593*, London, 1933; Scammel, *World Encompassed*, p. 476; Andrews, *Trade, Plunder and Settlement*, p. 257.

50   Foster, *England's Quest of Eastern Trade*, pp. 164–5; T. S. Willan, *The Early History of the Russia Company 1533–1603*, Manchester, 1956, p. 133 and n.

51   Leonard Blussé and George Winius, 'The Origin and Rhythm of Dutch Aggression against the Estado da Índia', in Teotonio R. de Souza (ed.), *Indo-Portuguese History: Old Issues, New Questions*, New Delhi, 1985, p. 75.

52   *Principal Navigations*, VII, pp. 191–203 esp. pp. 191, 195.

53   Richard Willes, *The History of Trauayle in the West and East Indies*, London, 1577; Hakluyt, *Principal Navigations*, VI, pp. 327–47, from which the quotations cited above are taken; *Dictionary of National Biography*; Quinn (ed.), *Hakluyt Handbook*, II, p. 427; Parker, *Books to Build an Empire*, pp. 77–8.

54   *History of the ... kingdome of China*, sig, 2v, 3, pp. 374–81.

55   *The Voyage and Trauaile*, pp. 18–19; Parker, *Books to Build an Empire*, pp. 133–4; Lach, *Asia in the Making of Europe*, 1:1, pp. 469–473. The original Italian edition was published in Venice in 1587.

56   *Principall Navigations*, 1589 edition, pp. 3, 782, 813–15. The map gave a breakdown of the strength of the Chinese army which it estimated with unbelievable precision at 7,923,785 men.

57   *Principal Navigations* (1904–5 edition), V, p. 499.

58   *Principal Navigations*, XI, pp. 422–42.

59   Jan Huygen van Linschoten, *Iohn Hvighen Van Linschoten his Discours of Voyages Into Ye East & West Indies*, f. A3v, 'To the Reader', book 1, pp. 42–8, 142–3; Burnell and Tiele (eds), *The Voyage of Jan Huigen Linschoten*, p. 151 n.3; Van Leur, *Indonesian Trade and Society*, p. 220; Lach, *Asia in the Making of Europe*, 1:1, p. 203.

60   *The travellers breviat*, London, 1601, pp. 128, 155–8. Botero's book sold well and appeared in five editions until 1640 (Parker, *Books to Build an Empire*, pp. 167, 232–3).

61   Linschoten, *Discours*, book 3, pp. 392–6, 400–2; Boxer, *Christian Century*, pp. 130, 406–14; Lach, *Asia in the Making of Europe*, 1:1, pp. 199–200 where Gerritsz is styled a merchant.

62   Stevens and Birdwood (eds), *Dawn of British Trade* pp. 123–4, 143; *Hakluyt Handbook*, I, p. 316. Parker's reference to the money paid is wrong (*Books to Build an Empire*, p. 161). A copy of the *Principal Navigations* was included among the books sent out on the Eighth Voyage and was to be left at Surat or some other appropriate place in the Indies 'to recreate their [i.e. factors'] spirrits wth varietie of historie' (Birdwood and Foster [eds], *First Letter Book*, p. 419). Later in the century Purchas's *Pilgrimes* supplanted Hakluyt.

63   Hakluyt, *Principal Navigations*, VI, p. 333; Linschoten, *Discours*, book 1, p. 44.

64   BL Harleian MS 6249, ff. 1, 106v–110. The section on Japan (cap. 23 of the second book) is printed in Thomas Rundall, *Memorials of the Empire of Japon*, London, 1855, pp. 3–14. On the notion of the scale of social development and the equation of good government with civilisation and the criteria by which these concepts were judged, see Nicholas Canny, 'Edmund Spenser and the Development of an Anglo-Irish Identity', *The Yearbook of English Studies*, 133, 1983, pp. 1–19, esp. pp. 8, 10; Canny, 'Identity Formation in Ireland: The Emergency of the Anglo-Irish', in Canny and Pagden (eds), *Colonial Identity in the Atlantic World*, 1987, p. 173. On Virginia see Loren E. Pennington, 'The Amerindian in English Promotional Literature 1575–1625', in K. R. Andrews et al (eds), *The Westward Enterprise*, Liverpool, 1978, p. 189. Spanish thinkers about worlds beyond Europe also subscribed to the concept of a hierarchy of civilisation. Solorzano Pereira, writing in 1629, divided 'barbarians' into three categories: civilised (the Chinese and Japanese) who were to be treated as equals in international relations; people who had attained a level of civilisation (Peruvians and Mexicans) and who were deemed therefore to have certain rights; and finally, primitive barbarians who enjoyed no rights and could be freely conquered and enslaved (Fisch, *Die europäische Expansion und das Völkerrecht*, p. 258). Such ideas were taken seriously by Spanish policy makers. Philip II was personally concerned about the rights of the Indians toiling in

the Peruvian silver mines (David C. Goodman, *Power and Penury: Government, Technology and Science in Philip II's Spain*, Cambridge, 1988, pp. 174, 177, 185, 186–7).

65 Georg Schurhammer, *Die Zeitgenossische Quellen zur Geschichte Portugeisich-Asiens und seine Nachbarländer...zur Zeit des hl. Franz. Xavier*, Leipzig, 1932, p. 80; G. V. Scammell, 'Manning the English Merchant Service in the Sixteenth Century', *The Mariner's Mirror*, 56, 1970, p. 134.

66 Most of the details of his early life come from a letter written from Japan and dated 23 October 1611 (NS) printed in Thomas Rundall, *Memorials of the Empire of Japon in the xvi and xvii Centuries*, London, 1850, pp. 18–32 (where it is wrongly dated 22 October); Sir William Foster (ed.), *Letters Received by the East India Company from its Servants in the East. 1602–1617*, 6 vols, 1896–1902, I, pp. 142–52 (where it is correctly dated); M. Paske Smith, *Western Barbarians in Japan and Formosa in Tokugawa Days*, New York, reprinted, 1968, pp. 8–15.

67 *Calendar of State Papers Colonial, East Indies...1513–1616.* (CSP) pp. 152, 168, 184, 186, 301, 329; Sir William Foster, *A Supplementary Calendar of documents in the India Office Relating to India or to the Home Affairs of the East India Company*, London, 1928, p. 30; T. Colyer-Fergusson, *The Marriage Register of St Dunstan's Stepney*, 3 vols, London, 1898, I, p. 23.

68 BL Harleian MS 168, f. 178v.

69 Andrews, 'Elizabethan Privateering', p. 7.

70 For a comprehensive discussion of the Morocco trade see Willan, *Studies in Elizabethan Trade*, pp. 92–312.

71 Andrews, *Elizabethan Privateering*, p. 102; Andrews, *Trade, Plunder and Settlement*, p. 102.

72 *Letters Received*, I, p. 142; Diogo do Couto, *Da Asia, Decada XII*, Lisbon, 1788, pp. 447–54. William F. Sinclair and D. Ferguson (trs), *The Travels, of Pedro Teixeira*, London, 1902, p. lxxx, provide an English translation of Do Couto. Do Couto's account of the *voorcompagnie* voyages is garbled although on many points concerning the arrival of the *Liefde* in Japan it is accurate.

73 D. W. Waters, *The Art of Navigation in Elizabethan and Early Stuart Times*, London, 1938, p. 232; Foster, *England's*

Quest of Eastern Trade, p. 149.

74 F. C. Wieder (ed.), *De Reis van Mahu en De Cordes door de Straat van Magalhães naar Zuid-Amerika en Japan 1598–1600*, 3 vols, The Hague, 1923–5, III, pp. 50, 62–7, 69.

75 Ibid., ii, p. 148. Adams recalled the date as 23 or 24 June (*Letters Received*, I, p. 142). However, the date is New Style which Adams used while in the Dutch service.

76 The following account is based on Adams's letter of 23 October 1611 and a fragment of one to his wife which is printed in Samuel Purchas, *Hakluytus Posthumus or Purchas His Pilgrimes*, 20 vols, Glasgow, 1905–6, II, pp. 340–6; Do Couto in Sinclair and Ferguson (trs), *Travels of Pedro Teixeira*, pp. lxxvi–lxxxii; Wieder, *De Reis van Mahu en De Cordes*, I, p. 27, III, p. 8ff. Purchas, the only source for it, prints Adams's letter to his wife after that of the 23 October 1611 which seems most likely. Whether or not it predates the latter is a matter of conjecture but there is no evidence to suggest that it was sent in 1605 (Wieder, *De Reis van Mahu en De Cordes*, III, pp. 53–4. Cf. Riess, 'History of the English Factory at Hirado', p. 11 and Cyril Wild, *Purchas His Pilgrimes in Japan*, Kobe, n.d., p. 85).

77 Adams gives conflicting dates for the day they landed in Japan, 19 April (NS) according to his letter of 23 October 1611 and 12 April (NS) in his letter to his wife. If, as Adams suggests, all his books and instruments were confiscated by the Japanese authorities he was probably writing from memory or piecing together facts from the remembrances of others. In the two letters some dates are accurate others are not including the date of departure from Rotterdam. Wieder, *De Reis van Mahu en De Cordes*, III, p. 13, takes 19 April as the day of arrival.

78 W. Z. Mulder, *Hollanders in Hirado*, Haarlem, n.d. (1986?), pp. 19–23 provides the Japanese references but his interpretation is unconvincing and, alas, not helped by the fact that some of the pages are out of sequence. Boxer, *Great Ship*, p. 60 supplies the only Portuguese reference for De Gouveia's voyage.

79 Hakluyt, *Principal Navigations*, XI, pp. 339–41.

80 These Japanese suspicions are men-

tioned by the Jesuit Fernão Guerreiro in his *Relação Annual* in Sinclair and Ferguson (trs), *Travels of Pedro Teixeira*, p. lxxix n. 5.

81 Herschel Webb, *The Japanese Imperial Institution in the Tokugawa Age*, New York, 1967, pp. 50–1; Berry, *Hideyoshi*, p. 180.

82 Historians are more inclined to stress continuities and see the Toyotomi achievement coming to fruition under the Tokugawa. See the important collection of articles in Hall, Nakamura and Yamamura (eds), *Japan Before Tokugawa*. Foreign policy would appear to be the exception.

83 Don Francisco Tello, 12 July 1599 (NS). (Blair and Robertson [eds], *The Philippine Islands*, x, p. 212).

84 *Nagasaki kungenki* quoted in Seiichi Iwao, 'Jan Joosten', *Bulletin of the Japan-Netherlands Society*, I, 1958, p. 2 and Wieder, *De Reis van Mahu en De Cordes*, III, p. 146; *Letters Received*, I, pp. 148–9. This was the account the English heard on their arrival, Sir E. M. Satow, (ed.), *The Voyage of John Saris to Japan, 1613*, London, 1913, pp. 80, 99.

85 Boxer, *Christian Century*, pp. 286, 487–8 n.21.

86 Morga, *Sucesos de las Islas Filipinas*, pp. 162–4, 194–5; Knauth, *Confrontación Transpacífica*, pp. 132, 140, 180–4, 190–7, 308, which is now the best book on Hispano-Japanese relations. But see also Zelia Nuttall, *The Earliest Historical Relations Betwen Mexico and Japan*, Berkeley, 1906–7 and W. L. Shurz, *The Manila Galleon*, New York, 1939.

87 *Letters Received*, I, pp. 149, 150. The new vessel later saw service in the Philippines. It was the second vessel built under Adams's supervision.

88 Ibid., p. 151; Tōkyō Daigaku Shiryō Hensan-jo (ed.), *Nihon kankei kaigai shiryo... Diary Kept by the Head of the English Factory in Japan*, 3 vols, Tokyo 1978–80 (hereafter cited as *Diary*), I, p. 311.

89 Iwao, 'Jan Joosten', p. 5.

90 *Letters Received*, I, p. 151. The nature of Adams's relations with his Japanese consorts is discussed in Chapter 6 (i) below.

91 Cooper, *Rodrigues*, p. 206.

92 Nuttall, (*Earliest Historical Relations Between Mexico and Japan*, pp. 6–7) accepts the story as does Knauth (*Confrontación Transpacífica*, p. 190 n. 50). The source is in Nakamura Kōya (ed.),

Tokugawa Ieyasu mondo no kenkyū, 4 vols, Tokyo 1956–61, III, p. 543.

93 J. W. Lizermannn (ed.), *De Reis om de Wereld door Olivier van Noort, 1598–1601*, 2 vols, The Hague, 1926, I, pp. 113–15.

94 Morga, *Sucesos de las Islas Filipinas*, pp. 6–7, 164–84, 242 n. 2; Iizermann (ed.), *De Reis om de Wereld door Olivier van Noort*, I, pp. 129–30, 192; Wieder, *De Reis van Mahu en De Cordes*, III, pp. 120–1; Van Leur, *Indonesian Trade and Society*, p. 179. Purchas printed part of this account (*Purchas His Pilgrimes*, II, p. 187).

95 Oskar Nachod, *Die Beziehungen der Niederländischen Ostindischen Kompagnie zu Japan im siebzehnten Jahrhundert*, Leipzig, 1897, Appendix pp. III–IV, VII–VIII; Wieder, *De Reis van Mahu en De Cordes*, III, pp. 36, 81–2, 85–6; Kanai Madoka, 'Nederland en Japan 1602–1680', in M. A. P. Meilink-Roelofsz (ed.), *Die VOC in Azie*, Bussum, 1976, p. 200. The *shuinjō* are described below in Chapter 4 (i).

96 Wieder, *De Reis van Mahu en De Cordes*, III, p. 37.

97 C. R. Boxer, 'The Affair of the "Madre de Deus" (A chapter in the History of the Portuguese in Japan)', *Transactions and Proceedings of the Japan Society of London*, XXVI, 1929, pp. 32–3, 107, reprinted in C. R. Boxer, *Portuguese Merchants and Missionaries in Feudal Japan 1543–1640*, London, 1986; Nachod, *Die Beziehungen*, p. 107.

98 Nachod, *Die Beziehungen*, pp. III–VIII; Wieder, *De Reis van Mahu en De Cordes*, III, pp. 81–6; C. J. Purnell, 'The Log-Book of William Adams, 1614–19', *Transactions and Proceedings of the Japan Society*, London, 13:2, 1915, pp. 270–1.

99 Riess, 'History of the English Factory at Hirado', p. 14; Jonathan I. Israel, *The Dutch Republic and the Hispanic World 1606–1661*, Oxford, 1982, pp. 6–9, 14–15, 20, 35–6. The peace negotiations collapsed in August 1608.

100 The following paragraphs are based on M. E. van Opstall (ed.), *De Reis van de Vloot van Pieter Willemsz. Verehoeff Naar Azie 1607–1612*, The Hague, 1972, pp. 128–31, 147, 328, 328–9, 357, 358–9; Nachod, *Die Beziehungen*, pp. 112–15, IX–XX; Boxer, 'Affair of the "Madre de Deus"', pp. 75–8.

101 Nachod, *Die Beziehungen*, p. x.

102 Boxer ('Affair of the "Madre de Deus"', p. 45 and *Christian Century*, p.

289) gives the wrong date for the arrival of the Dutch in Japan.

103 Conrad Totman, *Politics in the Tokugawa Bakufu, 1600–1843*, Cambridge, Massachusetts, 1967, p. 206.

104 On the Korean embassy see Ronald P. Toby, *State and Diplomacy in Early Modern Japan*, Princeton, 1984, pp. 72–3.

105 Boxer, *Great Ship*, p. 66; Katō Eiichi, 'The Japanese-Dutch Trade in the Formative Period of the Seclusion Policy', *Acta Asiatica*, 30, 1976, p. 47, Innes, 'The Door Ajar', pp. 248–57. Professor Boxer (*Christian Century* p. 289) is wrong to state that freedom from the *itowappu* was a false blessing. In 1612 Japanese merchants paid more for silk brought by the Chinese, Dutch and Spanish than they did for the silk brought from Macao (Nachod, *Die Beziehungen*, p. xxxix) and the disparity between the *itowappu* price and that paid for silk brought by the Dutch was one of the major reasons why the *itowappu* merchants sought to have restrictions imposed on the VOC trade in Japan in the 1630s.

106 Ibid., pp. xi–xii; Tōkyō Daigaku Shiryō Hensan-jo (ed.), *Dai Nihon shiryō*, Tokyo, 1901–, 12:6, pp. 454–5.

107 Opstall (ed.), *De Reis van de Vloot van Pieter Willemsz. Verehoeff Naar Azie*, pp. 147, 148; Katō Eiichi, 'Rengō Oranda Higashi-Indo Kaisha no senryaku kyoten toshite no Hirado shōkan', in Tanaka Takeo (ed.), *Nihon zenkindai no kokka to taigai kankei*, Tokyo, 1987, pp. 431–3.

108 Opstall (ed.), *De Reis van de Vloot van Pieter Willemsz. Verhoeff Naar Azie*, pp. 146, 358–9; Diary, i, p. 311.

109 ARA KA 996, unfoliated, letter of Specx, 3 November 1610 (NS). See also Opstall (ed.), *De Reis van de Vloot van Pieter Willemsz. Verehoeff Naar Azie*, p. 358.

110 Accounts of the Affair of the Madre de Deus as it has become known are contained in Boxer, 'Affair of the "Madre de Deus"', pp. 36–74, 84–7; Boxer, *Christian Century*, pp. 269–85; Boxer *Great Ship*, pp. 70–1, 77–80; Cooper, *Rodrigues*, pp. 261–7. See also Elison, *Deus Destroyed*, p. 435. For Cerqueira's assessment see Katō, 'Rengō Oranda Higashi-Indo Kaisha', pp. 433–5.

111 ARA KA 996, Specx, 3 November 1610 (NS); Nachod, *Die Beziehungen*, p. 143.

112 Ibid., pp. 143–154, xxxi, xxxviii–ix;

Mulder, *Hollanders in Hirado*, pp. 150–2; Katō, 'Rengō Oranda Higashi-Indo Kaisha', p. 443. The Matsūra had interfered with the Dutch voyage to Patani in October 1610 (ARA KA 996).

113 Rundall, *Memorials of the Empire of Japon*, p. 42.

114 Adams to Augustine Spalding in *Letters Received*, i, pp. 209, 210; Moreland (ed.), *Floris*, pp. 33, 35–6.

115 IOR E/3/1, f. 158v; William Foster, *The Journal of John Jourdain 1608–1617*, Cambridge, 1905, pp. 271–2.

CHAPTER 3

1 IOR L/MAR/A/XIV, 14 April 1611; BL Egerton MS 2086, f. 4; Satow (ed.), *Saris*, p. xvii. *Letters Received*, i, pp. 222–4. Cf. ibid., iii, pp. 4, 117, 129.

2 IOR B/3, ff. 3, 3v, 12v, 15, 18, 32v, 34v, 47v, 60, 138, 161, 162. Cf the history of Coree, a black kidnapped from Saldonia Bay by Towerson on his homeward voyage in 1613. It was hoped that after his stay in England Coree would promote mutual understanding between the English and the local people at the Cape and encourage them to provide the English with victuals, a design that met with some success (*Letters Received*, iii, pp. 2, 46, 295–6).

3 C. R. Boxer, *The Tragic History of the Sea*, Cambridge, 1959, p. 4; Boxer, 'The *Carreira da Índia* (Ships, man, cargoes, voyages)', *O cento de Estudas históricos ultramarinos e as començoraões Henriquinas*, 1961, pp. 35–6, reprinted in *From Lisbon to Goa*; Chaudhuri, *East India Company*, pp. 96–7; Niels Steensgaard, 'Freight Costs in the English East Indian Trade 1601–1657', *Scandinavian Historical Review*, xiii, 1965, p. 148. In comparison, Gujarati ships, some of which were massive, generally averaged 300–400 tons (Pearson, *Merchants and Rulers*, p. 8).

4 IOR B/3, ff. 34v, 150, 169v, 170v.

5 Chaudhuri, *East India Company*, pp. 77–8.

6 Willan, *Studies in Elizabethan Foreign Trade*, pp. 1–33; Croft, *Spanish Company*, p. xxx; Croft, 'English Trade with Peninsular Spain 1558–1625', unpublished University of Oxford D. Phil. thesis, 1969, p. 398; Croft, 'Englishmen and the Spanish Inquisition 1558–1625', *English Historical Review*,

LXXXVII, 1972, p. 252.

7 IOR B/3, ff. 148v, 152–152v, 153, 154, 158; Chaudhuri, *East India Company*, pp. 84, 87.

8 Purchas, *Purchas His Pilgrimes*, III, p. 506–16; Satow (ed.), *Saris*, pp. vii, ix, 213–30; *Dictionary of National Biography*; Souza, *Survival of Empire*, p. 67. From internal evidence it is clear that the 'note of requestable commodities vendible in Japan' (Purchas, *Purchas His Pilgrimes*, III, p. 516ff; Satow [ed.], *Saris*, pp. 227–30) dates from after Saris's voyage there. It did not contribute to the Company's decision to open trade with Japan.

9 Chaudhuri, *East India Company*, p. 78. Sometimes a pilot major sailed on voyages (Birdwood and Foster [eds], *First Letter Book*, pp. 297, 329) but generally the master acted as pilot as was the case on other English ships (Andrews, 'Elizabethan Seaman', p. 259).

10 IOR B/5, p. 368; Birdwood and Foster (eds), *First Letter Book*, pp. 396–7, 398–9; *Letters Received*, I, p. 223; Chaudhuri, *East India Company*, pp. 87–8.

11 Birdwood and Foster (eds), *First Letter Book*, pp. 415–16.

12 For a general discussion of recruitment and pay patterns in the merchant navy see Andrews, 'Elizabethan Seaman', pp. 248–62; Chaudhuri, *East India Company*, pp. 105–6; Scammell, 'Manning the English Merchant Service', pp. 131–54. Wages in the VOC were higher, but so too were costs (Steensgaard, 'Freight Costs', p. 149). Private trade is discussed below, Chapter 6 (i).

13 Satow (ed.), *Saris*, pp. 20, 76, 92; Foster, *England's Quest of Eastern Trade*, pp. 165–9. The Company's ships occasionally took out convicted criminals or 'condemned' men, men who were offered the option of servitude to the East India Company or execution, forerunners of the penal settlement convicts. Condemned men sailed with William Keeling's fleet in 1614 and Walter Payton's in 1615 (Keeling Letter Book, p. 29; BL Add. MS 19276, f. 1; *Letters Received*, IV, pp. 122–23. I am most grateful to Professor C. R. Boxer for allowing me to consult the former MS in his possession). Some of those who sailed with Keeling were put ashore at the Cape and left to fend for themselves. Some perished, some sensibly took passage on a Portuguese ship and

three were picked up by an English ship the following year. According to Sir Thomas Roe's chaplain they had no sooner stepped ashore in the Downs when they stole a purse and were executed for their former crimes which had not been pardoned – a fanciful piece of moralising one suspects (Edward Terry, *A Voyage to the East Indies*, London, 1777, pp. 24–7; *Letters Received*, III, pp. 119, 317n).

14 IOR L/MAR/MISC/6, ff. 2–6v. The inventory included some items which were probably not intended for sale such as aqua vitae, biscuit, waistcoats, shirts and shoes. Gunpowder could of course be sold or used by the ships. Some of the broadcloth was disposed of on the voyage to Bantam. The ratio of money to goods in the cargo is typical of the composition of the Company's exports at this time (see Chaudhuri, *East India Company*, p. 115. The figures cited for the money and goods exported by the Company in 1611 include those for the Seventh Voyage).

15 IOR Home Misc. Series 39, ff. 1–6v; Chaudhuri, *East India Company*, p. 139; Eric Kerridge, *Textile Manufactures in Early Modern England*, Manchester, 1985, pp. 5, 21, 216. The shorter length of broadcloth seems to have applied at this time rather than the longer, eighteenth-century length, judging from the Hirado factory's records (Peter Pratt, *History of Japan*, edited by M. Paske Smith, 2 vols, reprinted London, 1972, I, p. 46. Cf. K. N. Chaudhuri, *The Trading World of Asia and the East India Company, 1660–1760*, Cambridge, 1978, p. 222).

16 Chaudhuri, *East India Company*, p. 115; Meilink-Roelofsz, *Asian Trade*, p. 378; Ivo Schöffer and F. S. Gaastra, 'The Import of Bullion and Coin into Asia by the Dutch East India Company in the Seventeenth and Eighteenth Centuries', in Maurice Aymard (ed.), *Dutch Capitalism and World Capitalism*, Cambridge, 1982, pp. 215–33; J. R. Bruijn et al (eds), *Dutch Asiatic Shipping in the Seventeenth and Eighteenth Centuries*, The Hague, 1987, I, pp. 226ff.

17 Chaudhuri, *East India Company*, pp. 13, 111–24 esp. pp. 117–19; Andrews, *Trade Plunder and Settlement*, pp. 34, 263. The symbolic value of cloth as a mark of civilisation which contrasted sharply with the nakedness of savages may have been one of the rationalisa-

tions for cloth exports to English settlements in North America but such considerations were wholly absent from the reasons for exporting cloth to the Indies. On this symbolic value see Michael Zuckerman, 'Identity in British America: Unease in Eden', in Canny and Pagden (eds), *Colonial Identity in the Atlantic World*, p. 149.

18 *Principal Navigations*, I, p. lxxviii (dedication to the third volume of the second edition, 1600); ibid., XI, pp. 422, 441–2; Linschoten, *Discours*, I, p. 44; Birdwood and Stevens, *Dawn of British Trade*, pp. 123–4, 143; Taylor, *Original Writings*, p. 482. An additional reason for Hakluyt's consistent advocacy of sales of cloth other than stouthearted patriotism is the likelihood that he never forgot the debt he owed to the Clothworkers Company, which had made him a pensioner in 1577, and in particular to Richard Staper one of its most influential members and an adventurer in the East India Company. See G. D. Ramsey, 'Clothworkers, Merchant Adventurers and Richard Hakluyt', *English Historical Review*, 92, July 1977, pp. 504–21.

19 Birdwood and Foster (eds), *First Letter Book*, p. 412–13.

20 Ibid., pp. 402–13; Chaudhuri, *East India Company*, pp. 16–17.

21 IOR B/3, ff. 9v. 76v; G/40/2, f. 5; Birdwood and Foster (eds), *First Letter Book*, pp. 397–400, 411; Satow (ed.), *Saris*, p. 188.

22 In February 1607 before the departure of the Third Voyage all captains, masters and two each of their mates were ordered to meet at Sir James Lancaster's house 'for conference wth his wop about neassarie obseruatons in the voyadge' (IOR B/3, f.14v).

23 The details of the pre-departure events are recorded by Saris in his journal. There are two manuscript versions of the journal, one, a fair copy, among the India Office Records (L/MAR/A/XIV) and the other in Tōyō Bunko, Tokyo (D Ser 3, published in transcript and facsimile in an edition by Takanobu Otsuka, *The First Voyage of Captain John Saris to Japan, 1613*, Tokyo, 2 vols, 1941). The latter was compiled by Saris at the instigation of Hakluyt for an edition which failed to materialise and was dedicated in 1617 to Sir Francis Bacon. It was used by Purchas in his account of the Voyage and sup-

plemented by other material provided by Saris. It is much shorter than the India Office version about the voyage to Bantam and self-censors the bitter controversy with Middleton in the Red Sea and at Bantam in order to present the Company in a favourable light but contains more detail about the stay in Japan. However, the hand of the editor, Hakluyt, is evident and it was spiced up to make it more accessible to an English audience. The section of the journal covering the voyage to Japan, based on the India Office version and Purchas, is printed in Satow (ed.), *Saris*. Saris, unlike other commanders, covers the pre-sailing events in some detail. He kept the journal and other papers relating to the voyage in his own possession but on 14 January 1615 the Court requested him to hand over the journal to help the directors with the preparations for William Keeling's voyage (IOR B/5, p. 338). Unfortunately, the original draft of the journal and the other papers published by Purchas are no longer extant.

24 IOR L/MAR/A/XIV, 9 April 1611.

25 Ibid., 7, 11 April 1611.

26 Ibid., 14, 16 April 1611; Andrews, 'Elizabethan Seaman', pp. 246–47.

27 IOR L/MAR/A/XIV, 18 April 1611; *The Lawes or Standing Orders of the East India Company*, London, 1621, pp. 14–15; Chaudhuri, *East India Company*, pp. 100–101, 105.

28 *Letters Received*, I, p. 215.

29 IOR L/MAR/A/XIV, 26 February 1612; Kent Archives Office ON 6713 (fragment of a letter by Richard Dawes, master of the *Thomas*).

30 IOR L/MAR/A/XIV, 1 April 1612.

31 Foster, *England's Quest of Eastern Trade*, pp. 186–193.

32 Kent Archives Office ON 6713.

33 For accounts of events in the Red Sea see Saris's journal IOR L/MAR/A/XIV; L/MAR/MISC/6, ff. 9–20v; Kent Archives Office ON 6713; Sir William Foster (ed.), *The Voyages of Sir James Lancaster to Brazil and the East Indies*, London. 1940; *Letters Received*, I, pp. 162–92, 219–20, 226–30; Foster, (ed.), *Journal of John Jourdain*, pp. 205–18. The version given by Purchas plays fast and free with the facts and amounts to a brazen re-write of history (Purchas, *Purchas His Pilgrimes*, III, pp. 370–401) Dawes reports that Saris refused the Indian merchants' gifts but that Sir Henry helped himself to £3,000–4,000 worth (Kent Archives

Office ON 6713). Middleton was not prudent in his selection from the Cambay cloth. The Company's factor at Macassar wrote to the governor in 1615 complaining that Middleton had chosen 'so many sorts of slight trash' which proved unvendible (*Letters Received*, III, p. 139). Some of the accounting transactions involving the goods acquired in the Red Sea were to haunt Cocks later during his stay in Japan.

34 Kent Archives Office ON 6713. See Foster, *England's Quest of Eastern Trade*, pp. 288–94 for the establishment of Company trade in the Red Sea in the 1620s.

35 Denys Lombard, *Le Sultanat d'Atjeh au temps d'Iskander Muda 1607–1636*, Paris, 1967, *passim*; M. C. Ricklefs, *A History of Modern Indonesia*, London, 1981, pp. 29–32; Arun Das Gupta, 'The Maritime Trade of Indonesia: 1500–1800', in Das Gupta and Pearson (eds), *India and The Indian Ocean*, pp. 257–9; Anthony Reid, 'The Structure of Cities in Southeast Asia, Fifteenth to Seventeenth Centuries', *Journal of Southeast Asian Studies*, 11:3 1980, pp. 240–1; J. Kathirithamby-Wells, 'Forces of Regional and State Integration in the Western Archipelago, c. 1500–1700', *Journal of Southeast Asian Studies*, 18:1, 1987, pp. 32–4.

36 Ibid., p. 33.

37 Foster (ed.), *Journal of John Jourdain*, pp. 231–5.

38 William Foster (ed.), *The Voyage of Sir Henry Middleton to the Mollucas 1604–1606*, London, 1943, pp. 169–70; Van Leur, *Indonesian Trade and Society*, pp. 137–41; Meilink-Roelofsz, *Asian Trade*, pp. 245–7; Ricklefs, *History of Modern Indonesia*, pp. 34–5; Das Gupta, 'Maritime Trade of Indonesia' in Das Gupta and Pearson (eds), *India and the Indian Ocean*, pp. 259–61; Anthony Reid, 'Trade and the Problem of Royal Power in Acheh – Three Stages: c.1550–1700', in Anthony Reid and Lance Castles (eds), *Pre-Colonial State Systems in Southeast Asia*, Kuala Lumpur, 1975, p. 51; Reid, 'The Structure of Cities', pp. 242–3; Kathirithamby-Wells, 'Forces of Regional and State Integration' pp. 34–5.

39 IOR L/MAR/A/XIV, 24–8 October 1612.

40 Ibid., 28 October 1612. The letter is possibly the one referred to in another letter by Adams to Augustin Spalding

in Bantam, dated 12 January 1613 (NS) (*Letters Received*, I, pp. 208–9).

41 IOR L/MAR/A/XIV, 27, 28 October, 6 November 1612; *Letters Received*, II, pp. 278–9; Chaudhuri, *East India Company*, p. 88 n. 4.

42 IOR L/MAR/A/XIV, 30 October, 9 November 1612; Meilink-Roelofsz, *Asian Trade*, p. 248.

43 IOR L/MAR/MISC/6, f. 32v; L/MAR/A/XIV, 27 October 1612; Meilink-Roelofsz, *Asian Trade*, p. 248. Presents were given to other influential people as well, mainly Chinese (IOR L/MAR/MISC/6, ff. 23v–24).

44 IOR L/MAR/A/XIV, 22 December 1612.

45 Ibid., 2 January 1613.

46 Ibid., 12 November 1612.

47 Ibid., 24 November 1612.

48 Ibid., 2 November, 3 December, 9 December 1612, 2 January 1613. The pangeran was not being spiteful. He preferred to see the English accommodated modestly. The English house was already 'verie much bigger and higher than the ordinarie houses'. The same was true of the Dutch one (Foster [ed.], *Voyage of Sir Henry Middleton*, p. 170). Asian potentates had already realised how the Portuguese had become entrenched and impossible to move once they had been allowed to build grander buildings with fortifications. Not all rulers appreciated the danger. The Dutch, who were allowed to build a stone fort in Jacarta, easily took over the city in 1619. At Achin, Iskandar sensed a similar domestic danger and forbade his subjects to build in stone or to have cannon in their houses (Reid, 'The Structure of Cities', p. 246).

49 L/MAR/A/XIV, 18 December; L/MAR/MISC/6, f. 23v; *Letters Received*, I, pp. 221, 229; Foster (ed), *Journal of John Jourdain*, p. 241.

50 IOR Home Misc. 40, f. 36.

51 IOR L/MAR/A/XIV, 8 November 1612.

52 IOR L/MAR/A/XIV, 3, 7, 15, 16 December 1612, 12 January 1613; Satow, (ed.) *Saris*, pp. 84, 87.

53 *Letters Received*, III, p. 276.

54 IOR L/MAR/A/XIV, 7 December 1612; L/MAR/MISC/6, f. 6v.

55 IOR L/MAR/A/XIV, 30 December 1612, 12 January 1613; Satow (ed.) *Saris*, p. 1.

56 Satow (ed.), *Saris*, pp. 10, 12, 15–16; *Letters Received*, I, p. 313. Weldon later

encouraged the English to trade in the Bandas (*Letters Received*, III, p. 308).

57 Meilink-Roelofsz, *Asian Trade*, p. 184.

58 IOR L/MAR/MISC/6, f. 24v; Satow (ed.), *Saris*, pp. 35–7.

59 *Letters Received*, I, p. 314.

60 Satow (ed.), *Saris*, pp. 24, 25.

61 IOR L/MAR/MISC/6, f. 24. The details of the voyage from Bantam to the Spice Islands are in Satow (ed.), *Saris*, pp. 1–63. Not surprisingly, Saris presented his actions in the most favourable light and emphasised the risks he had taken.

62 Wild, *Purchas His Pilgrimes in Japan*, pp. 126–8; Satow (ed.), *Saris*, pp. 63–79, 85.

63 Satow (ed.), *Saris*, p. 93; In Fray Juan Pobre's account of the *San Felipe* incident in 1597, the mendicant refers to Masuda Nagamori, one of Hideyoshi's *bugyō*, persistently questioning about the relationship between Portugal and Spain and why the Spanish king waged war against England. England is specifically mentioned but for Masuda it had no meaning beyond a name (Boxer, *Christian Century*, pp. 420–4).

64 Murakami Naohiro, *Bōekishijō no Hirado*, Tokyo, 1917, pp. 1–5, app. pp. 1–2; Valignano, *Sumario*, pp. 104, 93–6, esp. nn. 94, 97, 102; Knauth, *Confrontación Transpacífica*, pp. 48–9, 100–4; Tanaka, *Chūsei taigai kankei shi*, pp. 198, 212–13, 219, 226, 231. In 1587 a report from Manila claimed that besides offering to put troops at the disposal of the Spanish, the daimyo stood ready to become a vassal of the Spanish king (Knauth, *Confrontación Transpacífica*, p. 122). This seems unlikely. The offer of troops, of which there were many after the pacification of Kyushu and the *sengoku* wars, is plausible but only as a sales pitch to encourage trade between Hirado and Manila. The soldiers were eventually put to use in Korea.

65 [*Aoki Nagashige no ikko*] *Nagasaki konryū narabini shōki kyōyō*, in *Nihon toshi seikatsu shiryō shusei, 6, minato machi hen*, I, Tokyo, 1975 p. 183 (I am grateful to Professor Iwao Seiichi for this reference); Satow (ed.), *Saris*, pp. 81, 83–4, 88, 89–90, 93, 94. Seiichi Iwao, 'Li Tan, Chief of the Chinese Residents at Hirado, Japan in the Last Days of the Ming Dynasty', *Memoirs of the Research Department of the Toyo Bunko*, XVII, 1958, p. 83.

66 Satow, (ed.), *Saris*, p. 89.

67 Nachod, *Die Beziehungen*, pp. 155–6, XXI, XXXV, XXXVII, XL; Eiichi Kato, 'Unification and Adaptation, the Early Shogunate and Dutch Trade Policies', in L. Blussé and F. Gaastra (eds), *Companies and trade: Essays on Overseas Trading Companies during the Ancien Regime*, Leiden, 1981, pp. 220–1.

68 *Letters Received*, I, p. 210; II, p. 114; Satow (ed.), *Saris*, pp. 93, 102–3; Moreland (ed.), *Peter Floris*, p. 74.

69 Meilink-Roelofsz, *Asian Trade*, pp. 263, 265, 398 n. 249; Souza, *Survival of Empire*, p. 84.

70 P. A. Tiele, *De Opkomst van het Nederlandsch gezag in Oost-Indie 1595–1610*, second series, The Hague, 1886, vol. 1, p. 62; Nachod, *Die Beziehungen*, 155–6; Van Opstall, (ed.), *De Reis van de Vloot van Pieter Willemsz. Verhoeff Naar Azie*, p. 359; Katō, 'Rengō Oranda Higashi-Indo Kaisha', pp. 442, 443. Floris was not so convinced and commented on the limited supply of silk at Patani in 1613 estimating it at 150 peculs of raw silk which the Chinese sold at 180 reals the pecul for the best quality. Wrought silk sold for more. However, the Dutch snapped up what was brought by the Chinese (Moreland (ed.), *Peter Floris*, pp. 73, 86).

71 Satow (ed.), *Saris*, p. 103.

72 Ibid., pp. 96, 98–9, 105–6, 206, 211; *Letters Received*, II, pp. 114, 206; III, pp. 154–5, 247–8; *Diary*, I, p. 299.

73 Satow (ed.), *Saris*, p. 83, 85, 86–7, 88–9. Specx had quickly realised that presents were ubiquitous in Japan even on social calls (ARA KA 996, unfoliated, letter of 3 November 1610 [NS]).

74 Satow (ed.), *Saris*, p. 109; *Letters Received*, I, p. 328; Moreland (ed.), *Peter Floris*, p. 86.

75 Satow (ed.), *Saris*, pp. 112–21, 143; *Letters Received*, I, p. 328.

76 Satow (ed.), *Saris*, p. 121.

77 Ibid., pp. 120–9; Constantine Vaporis, 'Post Station and Assisting Villages: Corvée Labour and Peasant Contention', *Monumenta Nipponica*, 41:4, 1986, pp. 379–80.

78 Satow (ed.), *Saris*, pp. 113–15. For the presents that the Dutch gave the ex-shogun and his son on the visit to Sunpu and Edo in 1611, see above p. 86.

79 Satow (ed.), *Saris*, pp. 129–31; *Letters Received*, I, pp. 328–30, 316–17. Saris's account of the audience omits any reference to the squabbling over protocol

(Satow, [ed.], *Saris*, p. 130). The Japanese version of James's letter and Adams's part in translating it is recorded in the *Ikoku nikki* (Register of Foreign Affairs) compiled by Suden, the Rinzai sect Zen priest whose many duties included that of foreign affairs advisor to the bakufu. It is printed in Hayashi Akira (compiler), *Tsūkō ichiran*, 8 vols, Tokyo, 1913, vi, pp. 344–5. James I's letter is printed in Wild (ed.), *Purchas His Pilgrimes in Japan*, pp. 255–6.

80   Satow (ed.), *Saris*, pp. 131–2, 198–9; *Letters Received*, i, p. 329. Although not listed in Saris's inventory, the lead would have been included. The Japanese translation of the abridged petition is in Hayashi (compiler), *Tsūkō ichiran*, vi, pp. 643–4. A version of the English original is in the BL (Cotton Charter, XXVI, 28, f. 67). In the account printed by Purchas (*Purchas His Pilgrimes*, iii, p. 461; Satow (ed.), *Saris*, p. 131) Saris suggests that the principal reason for the court officials demanding that the petition be shortened was a clause in the original requesting permission to bring captured goods from Chinese junks into Japan. The request, Saris alleges, was judged unacceptable by officials after they had consulted 'with the Lieger of China' and was dropped. This is improbable. On the English side the Company had made no formal request to establish trade with China, as Saris suggests, although Saris himself had commented on the ease with which Chinese vessels could be attacked during his stay in Bantam (ibid., p. 227). There is also no mention of the clause in the surviving version of the original petition. On the Japanese side the bakufu did not reach such decisions in consultation with any 'lieger' (that is, liege man) let alone one from China with which the shogunate had no official relations. One suspects that the episode was added later. Nevertheless, the question of the legality of seizing Chinese junks in the China Seas and bringing their goods to Japan was to be raised during the history of the factory.

81   Satow (ed.), *Saris*, pp. 132–3.

82   Satow (ed.), *Saris*, pp. 135–9; Michael Cooper (ed.), *The Southern Barbarians*, Tokyo, 1971, p. 105.

83   *Diary*, i, p. 45.

84   The *shuinjō* containing the privileges, with Ieyasu's vermilion seal is preserved in the Bodleian Library, Oxford (MS JAP b.2 [R]). The document, in excellent condition, was first recorded in the Bodleian's possession in 1680 and was presumed to be Chinese. Its true nature was only realised in 1985. It does not differ from the version in the *Ikoku nikki* (Hayashi [compiler], *Tsūkō ichiran*, vi, p. 346). Two copies of the privileges, dated Keichō 18, 8th month, 28th day (2 October 1613) were given to Saris. The *Ikoku nikki* mentions that one was to be put aboard the ship, the other to be taken to '*Ikara koku*', or *Ikarateira*, one of the Japanese renditions of the Portuguese word for England. Another copy was retained by the bakufu (*Tsūkō ichiran*, vi, p. 346). However, Saris left one copy with Cocks in Hirado. The second copy he took back to England along with a copy of the Japanese version of the abridged petition presented to Ieyasu. The former is the document now in the Bodleian and which Saris kept in his possession after his return home. The latter was eventually given to Purchas who printed it in facsimile as 'The Japonian Charter' granted to the Company together with an alleged translation which is in fact a freely adapted version of Saris's original petition (Purchas, *Purchas His Pilgrimes*, iii, p. 466–8). The Purchas document, the first example of Japanese writing printed in England, claims that the privileges were granted 'in the name of the right honoured knight, Sir Thomas Smith, Governor of the East India Company'. This was for domestic consumption and was intended to boost the Company's prestige. In fact Saris's original petition was made 'in the name of the King's majesty of England' while the privileges themselves bear only the inscription '*Ingirateira*' at the bottom left-hand side. As with the Dutch, the English preferred to maintain the fiction that they were not merely representatives of a commercial organisation. The fraudulent nature of Purchas's 'Japonian Charter' was first pointed out by Ludwig Riess ('History of the English Factory at Hirado', pp. 24, 211–15, who gives the wrong date for the issue of the privileges) and was discussed further by Ernest Satow (*Saris*, pp. lxxxi–ii). For the use to which it was put later in the century see below pp. 359–60. I am preparing an edition of the *shuinjō* in

85 On the manipulation of diplomatic protocol for domestic political purposes see Toby, *State and Diplomacy*, ch. 5, esp. pp. 169–70, 189–95. In 1610 Specx had feared complications might arise from the fact that the VOC was a company and had recommended that appropriate Dutch ships coming to Japan should carry a letter from Prince Maurice and a present in his name 'for they think our government must have a sovereign' (ARA KA 996, unfoliated, 3 November 1610 [NS]).

86 Satow (ed.), *Saris*, p. 130; *Letters Received*, I, pp. 321–2, 328–9, Nuttall, *Earliest Historical Relations Between Mexico and Japan*, p. 17; Michael Cooper (ed.), *They Came to Japan: An Anthology of European Reports on Japan, 1543–1640*, Berkeley, 1965, pp. 116–21, 126; Knauth, *Confrontación Transpacífica*, p. 199.

87 *Letters Received*, I, pp. 321–2, 328–9.

88 BL Add MS 9856, f. 93v; Nuttall, *Earliest Historical Relations Between Mexico and Japan*, pp. 19–22; Knauth, *Confrontación Transpacífica*, pp. 199–220.

89 On this point see Ronald P. Toby, 'Contesting the Centre: International Sources of Japanese National Identity', *International History Review*, 7:3, 1985, p. 357.

90 The Korean embassy of 1607 had been manipulated to make precisely this point (Toby, *State and Diplomacy*, p. 73).

91 Satow (ed.), *Saris*, pp. 140–2. The English were charged for victualling the barque and for the service of the Matsūra official who accompanied them (IOR L/MAR/MISC/6, f. 27v).

92 Ibid., f. 27. It is not wholly clear if this figure includes the cost of the presents given to Ieyasu, Hidetada and Tokugawa officials. Exact figures are no longer extant but Saris records values in the region of 600 reals (Satow, [ed.], Saris, pp. 113–15). Pratt (*History of Japan*, I, p. 40) bases his figure of 1,115 3/8 reals, for presents on Cocks's accounts. Pratt's total seems altogether too high. Cocks's figures are probably comprehensive including the amounts for presents given in Hirado. Cf. Satow (ed.), *Saris*, p. 176.

93 Ibid., pp. 144, 147–8, 159–60, 164–5, 172, 178.

94 Ibid., p. 117; *Letters Received*, II, p. 3.

95 Nachod, *Die Beziehungen*, p. XXIV; Satow, (ed.), *Saris*, pp. 96, 149, 153.

96 Satow (ed.), *Saris*, p. 142. These additional comments, if indeed they were made, should not be taken as an indication of shrewd perception on the part of the Japanese merchants. Rather they were designed to address the debate in England about the nature of the Company's exports.

97 IOR L/MAR/MISC/6, ff. 25, 25v, 26v.

98 Satow (ed.), *Saris*, pp. 151, 153, 157–8, 163, 165, 171, 178.

99 Ibid., p. lxvi and journal *passim*.

100 Ibid., pp. lxviii, lxix.

101 Ibid., pp. 171, 181, 182–3. The date on which the merchandising council was held is uncertain. Saris gives 26 November, but the employment contract with Adams was made on the 24th.

102 Nachod, *Die Beziehungen*, p. XXXIX; Rundall, *Memorials of the Empire of Japon*, p. 43; Satow (ed.), *Saris*, p. 136.

103 Nachod, *Die Beziehungen*, p. xxxix.

104 Opstall (ed), *De Reis van de Vloot van Pieter Willemsz Verhoeff Naar Azie*, II, p. 354.

105 IOR L/MAR/MISC/6, f. 27v; Nachod, *Die Beziehungen*, p. XL; Satow (ed.), *Saris*, pp. 176, 179, 180; *Coen: Bescheiden*, I, pp. 32–33.

106 IOR L/MAR/MISC/6, ff. 26v, 27.

107 IOR B/5, pp. 157–8; Satow (ed.), *Saris*, pp. 182, 183–193.

108 William Foster (ed.), *The Voyages of Thomas Best of the East Indies*, London, 1934, p. 266, Foster (ed.), *Journal of John Jourdain* pp. 304–8, 312. It is likely that the autographed letter of James I 'To the High and Mightie, the Emperor of Japan', dated 10 January 1612 and now in the Bell Collection at the University of Minnesota, was carried on Best's voyage. As Saris had already established a factory at Japan the letter was not forwarded to Japan. Another autographed letter of James I to the 'emperor' of Japan is among the Cotton Charters (BL Cotton Charter XVII. 29). It is dated 11 April 1614 and was probably prepared for David Middleton's voyage which left England in May 1614 although it was not in fact carried to the Indies.

109 Satow (ed.), *Saris*, pp. 193–4, 200; Foster (ed.), *Journal of John Jourdain*, pp. 312–15; *Letters Received*, II, pp. 15–16,

collaboration with Ms Izumi K. Tytler of the Bodleian. This will discuss fully all questions relating to this remarkable discovery.

338.
110 Satow (ed.), *Saris*, pp. 200–3; *Letters Received*, II, p. 144. Cocks received the letter from Saris on 31 August 1615 when the second East India Company ship reached Japan (*Diary*, I, p. 73).
111 IOR B/5, p. 305; Satow (ed.), *Saris*, pp. lix, lx, lxi, lxvi, 197. There is no mention of her having been careened or at least caulked in the surviving records, but this must have been performed somewhere *en route*.
112 IOR B/5, pp. 141, 256; Satow (ed.), *Saris*, pp. lx–lxv, 203–11; *Letters Received*, I, pp. 317, 320–1; II, pp. 3–4. The letter from Wickham is no longer extant.
113 Blair and Robertson (eds), *The Philippine Islands*, XVII, p. 222.
114 IOR B/5, p. 335; Satow, (ed.), *Saris*, pp. lxiii–iv, lxvii–lxviii, lxxiii, 202, 203–11. Saris was correct to emphasise the importance of low shorn cloth. Specx had made the same recommendation to his superiors (Nachod, *Die Beziehungen*, p. XXI, XXIV).
115 Satow (ed.), *Saris*, pp. lxiii–lxiv, 207.
116 Nachod, *Die Beziehungen*, pp. xxiv–xxvii.
117 Ibid., pp. xxv, xxvi, lxv; Kristof Glamann, *Dutch Asiatic Trade 1640–1740*, 2nd edition, The Hauge, 1918, pp. 167–76.
118 *Letters Received*, I, p. 317.
119 Ibid., II, p. 3.
120 IOR B/5, p. 256.
121 Ibid., p. 141; *Letters Received*, I, pp. 320–21, 323.
122 Satow, (ed.), *Saris*, pp. lxxii, lxxiii, lxxiv. In defending the extent of his present-giving by asserting that 'there shalbe noe neede hereafter of giueinge vnto the Emperour', he was taking self-justification too far and creating another falseimpression (ibid., p. lxxii). Presents would still have to be given in Japan; they were expected in lieu of a customs levy.
123 Foster (ed.), *Voyages of Thomas Best*, pp. 287–92. Saris used Best's excessive private trade to justify his own smaller amount (Satow [ed.], *Saris*, p. lxx).
124 Nachod, *Die Beziehungen*, pp. 154–5; Mulder, *Hollanders in Hirado*, pp. 6–7.
125 IOR B/5, p. 304; Satow (ed.), *Saris*, pp. lxiv–v, lxvii, lxx, 208.
126 Nachod, *Die Beziehungen*, pp. 156, XL.
127 Satow (ed.), *Saris*, p. lxii.
128 IOR B/5, pp. 352, 366, 372; Satow (ed.), *Saris*, pp. lxxi–lxxii.

CHAPTER 4

1 Tanaka, *Wakō to kangō bōeki*, pp. 195–7; Berry, *Hideyoshi*, pp. 133–4.
2 Knauth, *Confrontación Transpacífica*, p. 49; Souza, *Survival of Empire*, pp. 184, 196, 199–200, 205; Robert C. Ritchie, *Captain Kidd and the War Against the Pirates*, Cambridge, Massachusetts, 1986; Dian H. Murray, *Pirates of the South China Coast 1790–1810*, Stanford, 1987. On the fleets of defence see below, chapter 7.
3 Purchas, *Purchas His Pilgrimes*, II, pp. 361–4.
4 Morga, *Sucesos*, pp. 114, 158.
5 Giuliana Stramigioli, 'Hideyoshi's Expansionist Policy on the Asiatic Mainland', *Transactions of the Asiatic Society of Japan*, third series, III, 1954, pp. 74–116. On Hideyoshi's foreign policy see also Berry, *Hideyoshi*, pp. 207–17, 232–4.
6 Iwao Seiichi, *Shuinsen bōeki-shi no kenkyū*, new edition, Tokyo, 1985, pp. 41–8.
7 Noël Peri, 'Essai sur les relations du Japon et de l'Indochine aux xvie et xviie siècles', *Bulletin de l'Ecole Française d' Extrême-Orient*, 23, 1923, pp. 49–50.
8 *Diary*, I, p. 310; ibid., II, pp. 175; Peri, pp. 23–30; Iwao, *Shuinsen*, pp. 68–84, 224–6; Innes, 'The Door Ajar', pp. 107–11.
9 Iwao, *Shuinsen*, p. 127 and table following p. 220.
10 Iwao Seiichi, 'Japanese Foreign Trade in the Sixteenth and Seventeenth Centuries', *Acta Asiatica*, 30, 1976, p. 10; Iwao, *Shuinsen*, pp. 288–306.
11 Iwao, *Shuinsen*, pp. 142, 273.
12 Ibid., pp. 156–9.
13 Ibid., pp. 262, 267.
14 Ibid., pp. 269–86.
15 *Coen: Bescheiden*, VII, p. 493. In fact only one *shuinjō* is recorded as having been issued for the Moluccas (Iawo, *Shuinsen*, p. 127).
16 Alessandro Valignano,'Adiciones del Sumario del Japōn (1592)', edited by José Luis Alvarez Taladriz, unpublished, pp. 498–511. (I am most grateful to Dr Michael Cooper for lending me a copy of this rare sequel to Taladriz's edition of the *Sumario*.) I follow Anthony Reid in preferring the term 'bondage' to slavery' (Anthony Reid [ed.], *Slavery, Bondage and Dependency in Southeast Asia*, New York, 1983, pp. 2, 14, 15; Anthony Reid, *Southeast Asia*

in the Age of Commerce 1450–1680, vol. I, *The Lands below the Winds*, New Haven, 1988, pp. 129–36 esp. p. 132). See also Boxer, *Fidalgos in the Far East*, ch. 8; Boxer, *Christian Century*, pp. 226–27; Elison, *Deus Destroyed*, p. 118; J. Fox, '"For Good and Sufficient Reason": An Examination of Early Dutch East India Company Ordinances on Slaves and Slavery', in Reid (ed.), *Slavery, Bondage and Dependency*, pp. 246–62; Spence, *Memory Palace*, p. 192. The Jesuits were concerned about the implications of exporting bondsmen but drew a distinction between Japanese sold into captivity and those sold for domestic service. They kept bonded servants in their own houses, as did the English and Dutch.

17 Curtin, *Cross-Cultural Trade*, ch. 1. For other discussions of diaspora, see Benjamin Braude, 'Venture and Faith in the Commercial Life of the Ottoman Balkans, 1500–1650', *International History Review*, 7:4, 1985, pp. 519–42; Bruce Masters, 'Trading Diasporas and "Nations": The Genesis of National Identities in Ottoman Aleppo', *International History Review*, 9:3, 1987, pp. 345–67.

18 Iwao Seiichi, *Nan'yō Nihonmachi no kenkyū*, Tokyo, 1966, ch 6, the fullest account of the Japanese in Manila; Morga, *Sucesos*, pp. 5, 120–35, 224, 225; Montague Paske-Smith, 'Japanese Trade and Residence in the Philippines before and during the Spanish Occupation', *Transactions of the Asiatic Society of Japan*, first series, XLII, 1914, pp. 685–710.

19 E. M. Satow, 'Notes on the Intercourse Between Japan and Siam in the Seventeenth Century', *Transactions of the Asiatic Society of Japan*, first series, XIII, 1884, pp. 139–210; Iwao, *Nan'yō Nihonmachi*, pp. 148, 207–9 and ch. 5 *passim*; Iwao Seiichi, 'Reopening of the Diplomatic and Commercial Relations between Japan and Siam during Tokugawa Days', *Acta Asiatica*, 4, 1963, pp. 1–31; D. K. Wyatt, *History of Thailand*, New Haven, 1982, pp. 106–8. There is a controversy about whether the powerful head of the Japanese *nihonmachi* at Ayuthia known as Oya Semaphimocq can be identified with Yamada Nagamasa, former retainer of the daimyo of Numazu. The problem is made more vexatious by the propaganda use of the persona of Yamada in the 1930s and early 1940s as a progenitor of

Japanese expansion in Asia. Whether or not one accepts the identification, the head of the Japanese *nihonmachi* in Ayuthia in the 1620s was an individual of immense influence both politically and commercially, in Siam. See Iwao Seiichi's introduction to *Historiael Verhael der Sieckte ende Doot van Pra Interra-Tsia 22^{en} Coninck in Siam, ende den Regherenden Coninck Pra Ongh Srij door Jeremias van Vliet, 1640*, Tokyo 1958, pp. xviii–xxxiii and the documentation in the appendix.

20 For full discussions of the *nihonmachi* and Japanese in southeast Asia see Iwao Seiichi, *Shuinsen to Nihonmachi*, Tokyo, 1966 edition; Iwao, *Nan'yō Nihomachi*; Iwao, *Nan'yō Nihonmachi no kenkyū, zoku*, Tokyo, 1987; Iwao, 'Japanese Emigrants to Batavia', *Acta Asiatica*, 18, 1970, pp. 1–25.

21 No additional buildings were purchased or built. The factors stayed at Japanese inns whose owners helped them find storage for their goods. However, subfactory is a convenient term and the business transacted in the Kinai and at Edo was treated separately for accounting purposes.

22 Satow (ed.), *Saris*, pp. 170–1.

23 *Letters Received*, II, pp. 4–9.

24 Ibid., II, pp. 7–8.

25 The Firando Ledger B runs from 3 December 1613, when the factory was constituted for accounting purposes, to 31 August 1615, the arrival of the *Hosiander*, the Company's second ship to reach Japan which brought news of the establishment of joint-stock voyages. As with so much of the Company's records the ledger was probably lost or sold off as waste paper in the 1850s (see Derek Massarella, '"The Loudest Lies": Knowledge of Japan in Seventeenth Century England', *Itinerario*, 11:2, 1987, pp. 55–6). Ledger A, likewise no longer extant, and not available to Peter Pratt, the Company's servant who completed the unwieldly history of the factory in 1822 (later published as the *History of Japan*, probably covered the accounts of the voyage from Bantam to Japan although Cocks's accounts for this stage of the voyage fill in some of the missing detail.

26 IOR L/MAR/MISC/6, f. 6v; Firando Ledger B in Pratt, *History of Japan*, I, p. 45. The other figure for the total stock left is 22,618 taels 5 mas 3 1/2 candereen

(ibid.). The figures given by Riess ('History of the English Factory at Hirado', p. 34) are wrong.

27 IOR L/MAR/MISC/6, ff. 25–27v; Firando Ledger B in Pratt, *History of Japan*, i, p. 51.

28 Pratt, *History of Japan*, i, pp. 46–49.

29 *Letters Received*, ii, p. 5.

30 IOR L/MAR/A/XIV *passim*; *Letters Received*, i, p. 180.

31 For further details on the Cocks family see Massarella, 'Early Career of Richard Cocks', pp. 4–6.

32 'The State of England, 1600' in Joan Thirsk and J. P. Cooper (eds), *Seventeenth Century Economic Documents*, Oxford, 1972, p. 756.

33 *Diary*, ii, p. 11; ibid., iii, pp. 263, 275; *The Victoria History of the Countries of England, Staffordshire*, vi, London, 1979, p. 207; PRO HCA 13/26, ff 235, 235v; HCA 13/30, f. 129; Foster (ed.), *The Travels of John Sanderson in the Levant 1584–1602*, London, 1931, *passim*; Croft, 'English Trade with Peninsular Spain', p. 154; Barbara Winchester, 'The Johnson Letters, 1542–1552', unpublished University of London Ph.D. thesis, 1953, pp. 112–13.

34 Massarella, 'The Early Career of Richard Cocks', p. 10.

35 Winchester, 'The Johnson Letters', pp. 118–19; M. H. Curtis, 'Education and Apprenticeship', *Shakespeare Survey*, 17, 1964; J[ohn] B[rowne], *The Marchant's Avizo*, edited by Patrick McGrath, Cambridge, Massachusetts, 1957, a good example of the available textbooks on the education of apprentices.

36 PRO SP 94/12, f. 85v; Massarella, 'The Early Career of Richard Cocks', pp. 11–12.

37 J. W. Stoye, *English Travellers Abroad 1604–1667*, London 1952, p. 342; Hartland Taylor, 'Price Revolution or Price Revision? The English and Spanish Trade after 1604', *Renaissance and Modern History*, xii, 1968, p. 10; A. J. Loomie, 'Toleration and Diplomacy: the Religious Issue in Anglo-Spanish Relations, 1603–1605', *Transactions of the American Philosophical Society*, new series, liii, 1963, pp. 3–60.

38 The account of Wilson's life in the *Dictionary of National Biography* does not mention his visit to Bayonne but Cocks refers to it (PRO SP 15/34 p. 136; SP 94/9, ff 11, 12) as does another correspondent (*Historical MSS Commission*,

Calendar of MSS of the Most Hon, The Marquis of Salisbury, xiv, p. 162) and there is a letter by Wilson himself from Bayonne dated 5 March 1603 (PRO SP 15/34, p. 137).

39 PRO SP 94/9, f 161.

40 PRO SP 14/35, f. 37.

41 PRO SP 14/38, f. 106.

42 PRO SP 94/16, f. 226.

43 A fuller account of Cocks's life before he entered the East India Company's service is given in Massarella, 'The Early Career of Richard Cocks', pp. 1–46.

44 IOR L/MAR/A/XIV, 23 November 1612; Foster (ed.), *Journal of John Jourdain*, pp. 226, 232; *Letters Received*, i, p. 208.

45 IOR B/3, ff. 66, 72v; IOR G/12/15, f. 26v; PRO PROB 11/138, ff. 290–91; *Letters Received*, i, pp. 75, 208, 252; iii, p. 293; *C.S.P. Colonial...East Indies...1513–1616*, p. 206; A. Grey (ed.), *The Voyage of François Pyrard of Laval to the East Indies, the Maldives, the Moluccas and Brazil*, vol. i, London, 1887, p. 264; Satow (ed.), *Saris*, pp. 66–7; *Diary*, i, p. 221; Anthony Farrington, 'The Japan Letter Book of Richard Wickham, 1614–1617', *India Office Library and Records Report for the Year*, 1979, p. 37. On his wages see below.

46 IOR G/40/23, f. 10.

47 IOR E/3/5, f. 331 v.

48 *Lawes or Standing Orders*, pp. 46–8.

49 Satow (ed.), *Saris*, pp. 67, 104; *Letters Received*, iv, p. 270.

50 *Letters Received*, ii, pp. 10–13; Pratt, *History of Japan*, i, pp. 65–67. There is a discrepancy of some £27 between the Firando Ledger B figure and that given in the invoice which is probably due to some calicoes marked as missing in the invoice.

51 Firando Ledger B in Pratt, *History of Japan*, i, p. 62.

52 *Letters Received*, ii, pp. 11–12, Chaudhuri, *East India Company*, p. 121.

53 IOR G/12/15, ff. 10, 12v; *Letters Received*, ii, pp. 53–4; Tōkyō Daigaku Shiryō Hensan-jo (ed.), *Nihon kankei kaigai shiryō: Igirisu shōkancho nikki, yakubun hen*, iii, appendix, Tokyo, 1981, pp. 124–5.

54 IOR L/MAR/MISC/6, f. 25.

55 IOR G/12/15, ff. 10, 10v; Purnell, 'Log-Book of William Adams', p. 277; *Letters Received*, ii, p. 47; Firando Ledger B in Pratt, *History of Japan*, i, p. 46. Pratt wrongly describes Mikumoya

as Adams's brother-in-law (ibid., p. 93).

56 IOR G/12/15, ff. 10, 13, 15; Pratt, *History of Japan*, I, p. 47.

57 IOR G/12/15, f. 11v.

58 Ibid., ff. 10v. 16; *Letters Received*, II, pp. 52, 53.

59 Purnell, 'Log-Book of William Adams', p. 277.

60 IOR G/12/15, f. 16; Rundall, *Memorials of the Empire of Japon*, pp. 38–39; *Letters Received*, II, p. 200. Contrary to English conjecture, De Coning appears to have enjoyed good relations with his fellow-Hollanders (Wieder [ed], *De Reis van Mahu en De Cordes*, III, p. 98. In 1616 Cocks turned down a request for employment from another Hollander 'Jacob the Dutch man...a cawker, a pore fellow' (*Diary*, I, p. 298).

61 IOR G/12/15, f. 12. The discrepancy was later discovered to be the result of reckoning the weight according to that marked on the bars in England (Firando Ledger B in Pratt, *History of Japan*, I, p. 94).

62 *Dai Nihon shiryō*, 12:23, pp. 632–48; Wieder, *De Reis van Mahu en De Cordes*, III, pp. 92–115. *Diary*, I, pp. 26, 322, 343; ibid., II, p. 22.

63 IOR G/12/15, ff. 10v, 12; Purnell, 'Log-Book of William Adams', p. 277.

64 IOR G/12/15, f. 12.

65 Ibid., f. 10; *Letters Received*, II, pp. 20, 25, 29, 48, 50.

66 IOR G/12/15, ff. 10v, 12.

67 Ibid., f. 13v; *Letters Received*, II, p. 69.

68 IOR G/12/15, f. 13v.

69 Ibid., ff. 10v, 12, 13, 14, 14v; *Letters Received*, II, pp. 69, 70; Firando Ledger B in Pratt, *History of Japan*, I, pp. 80, 95.

70 IOR G/12/15, f. 15v; Purnell, 'Log-Book of William Adams', p. 277.

71 *Letters Received*, II, p. 69.

72 ARA KA 1000, f. 138v; *Dai Nihon shiryō*, 12:23, p. 635; Katō, 'Japanese-Dutch Trade', pp. 50–1.

73 IOR G/12/15, ff. 15, 15v, 16v; *Letters Received*, II, pp. 69, 74; Firando Ledger B in Pratt, *History of Japan*, I, p. 90. Pratt (ibid., p. 87) gives the wrong date for Wickham's return to Hirado.

74 Firando Ledger B in ibid., p. 96.

75 Ibid., pp. 95–6.

76 Ibid., pp. 90–2, 95–6, 100. The discrepancy of 30 taels 7 mas 5 candereen between the figures given for incidental charges on pp. 90–1 and those on p. 100 can be accounted for by subtracting

30 taels 7 mas 5 candereen, the expenses allowed Adams for travelling from Edo and which were presumably charged to a separate account. Why the 100 taels cash delivered to the factory and included in the original invoice is added to the sales figure is unclear. I have not included it in the sales. Pratt's figures for presents cited on p. 91 are added wrongly. They should amount to 25 taels 1 mas 9 1/4 candereen.

77 Firando Ledger B in Pratt, *History of Japan*, I, pp. 85, 87–8. Eaton's petty expenses did not include the trip back to Hirado and Pratt does not reproduce as detailed a breakdown of his petty expenses as for those of Wickham. There are some slight discrepancies in Pratt's figures but these amount to only fractions of candereens. No figure is given for Eaton's wages.

78 Firando Ledger B in Pratt, *History of Japan*, I, pp. 67, 100–3; *Letters Received*, III, pp. 22, 47. No matter how one interprets the figure's Pratt's profit of 126 taels 7 mas 9 candereen is wrong. It includes presents worth 49 taels 3 candereen given to the Sō but charged to the Hirado factory.

79 Pratt, *History of Japan*, I, pp. 103–4.

80 IOR G/12/15, f. 13v.

81 *Letters Received*, II, p. 201.

82 Ibid.

83 Toby, *State and Diplomacy*, pp. 31, 35, 40, 77.

84 Nachod, *Die Beziehungen*, p. XXIII.

85 *Diary*, I, pp. 138–9, 162–3, 177.

86 *Letters Received*, VI, pp. 4–5.

87 Firando Ledger B in Pratt, *History of Japan*, I, pp. 55–6, 75–8. Pratt's sales figures should be reduced by 1 mas (ibid., p. 78).

88 Ibid., pp. 70–1, 72

89 *Letters Received*, II, pp. 196–7; Hall, *A History of South East Asia*, fourth edition, London, 1981, pp. 217–20. In 1613 six *shuinsen* are recorded as having sailed for Annam and seven in 1614, making it, along with Manila and Ayuthia, one of the most frequented destinations of the *shuinsen* (Iwao, *Shuinsen*, p. 127).

90 *Letters Received*, II, p. 19; Iwao, *Shuinsen*, facing p. 200.

91 Pratt, *History of Japan*, i, p. 55; *Letters Received*, II, p. 197; *Diary*, II, p. 198.

92 *Letters Received*, II, pp. 67–8, 197–8. The Dutch ventured *f.* 8,500 on their voyage in pepper, ivory, cloth and lead and also sent two men (*Coen: Bes-*

cheiden, VII, p. 17). Specx blamed the English for the disaster and for the loss of the VOC's, goods and believed that only one Hollander had been murdered (ibid.). The Dutch visit in 1601 had not been provocative. See W. J. M. Buch, *De Oost-Indische Compagnie en Quinam*, Amsterdam, 1928, pp. 9–10.

93   IOR E/3/5, f. 319v, 336–336v; *Diary*, I, pp. 46–7, 241–2, 262, 303, 309; II, pp. 143, 146; III, pp. 79, 285; N. Murakami (ed.), *The Diary of Richard Cocks Cape-Merchant in the English Factory in Japan, 1615–1622*, 2 vols, Tokyo, 1899, II, pp. 285–6, 296–7; Purnell, 'Log-Book of William Adams', pp. 232, 233, 290–2; Buch, *De Oost-Indische Compagnie en Quinam*, p. 10. The VOC fared no better in trying to recover their goods and were still seeking restitution in 1633 when they sent a voyage to Annam to open a factory (*Coen: Bescheiden*, VII, p. 17; Buch, *De Oost-Indische Compagnie en Quinam*, pp. 11,23).

94   IOR G/12/15, ff. 14, 17; Firando Ledger B in Pratt, *History of Japan*, I, p. 73; *Letters Received*, II, pp. 204–8; Purnell, 'Log-Book of William Adams', p. 283.

95   The most recent discussion of Ryūkyū's status *vis-à-vis* Japan is in Toby, *State and Diplomacy*, pp. 45–52. See also E. S. Crawcour, 'Changes in Japanese Commerce in the Tokugawa Period', *Journal of Asian Sudies*, 22, 1963, pp. 387–400; Robert K. Sakai, 'The Satsuma-Ryūkyū Trade and the Tokugawa Seclusion Policy', *Journal of Asian Studies*, 23, 1964, pp. 391–403.

96   IOR G/12/15, f. 17; Purnell, 'Log-Book of William Adams', pp. 194, 209, 283.

97   Ibid., p. 195; Sakai, 'Satsuma-Ryūkyū Trade', pp. 391–2. The trade conducted by Wickham at Naha implies that the 1611 agreement was not enforced absolutely but the amount of goods involved was minimal.

98   Purnell, 'Log-Book of William Adams', pp. 196–7, 198–9, 201, 202, 206, 207, 283.

99   Ibid., pp. 210, 211, 212.

100 Firando Ledger B in Pratt, *History of Japan*, I, pp. 107–9. The ledger, according to Pratt, gives the profit on sales as 128 taels 5 mas 6 candereen but on the figures he reproduces it could be increased by some 18 taels by including the sale of some gunpowder and Japanese umbrellas at Gotō. Purnell ('Log-Book of William Adams', pp.

213–20) gives Adams's detailed accounts for the voyage including the cost of hiring labour and buying materials.

101 *Diary*, I, p. 19.

102 IOR G/12/15, f. 17; *Letters Received*, III, p. 290; Firando Ledger B in Pratt, *History of Japan*, I, p. 108.

103 *Letters Received*, II, pp. 201, 204; *Diary*, I, p. 26.

104 IOR B/5, pp. 64, 67, 76; B. L. Egerton MS 2121, ff. 15, 23, 29v, 41, 42–43v; Foster (ed.), *The Voyages of Thomas Best*, pp. xii–xiii; *Letters Received*, II, pp. 144, 319, 323, 325, 327, 332, 334, 335, 338, 339; *Diary*, I, pp. 72–3, 74–5, 76.

105 BL Egerton MS 2121, ff. 43–43v; *Diary*, I, pp. 56, 75.

106 The above is based upon Webb, *Japanese Imperial Institution*, pp. 48–57; Asao Naohiro with Marius B. Jansen, 'Shogun and Tenno', in Hall, Nagahara and Yamamura (eds), *Japan Before Tokugawa*, pp. 258–70; B. Susser, 'The Toyotomi Regime and the Daimyo' in Mass and Hauser (eds), *The Bakufu in Japanese History*, pp. 147–52; W. B. Hauser, 'Osaka Castle and Toyotomi Authority in Western Japan', in ibid., pp. 157–8; Totman, *Politics of the Tokugawa Bakufu*, pp. 39–40.

107 Ieyasu's letter in Japanese with a Spanish translation is printed in Knauth, *Confrontación Transpacífica*, facing pp. 242–3. Cf. Nuttall, *Easliest Historical Relations Between Mexico and Japan*, pp. 33–5. The language was less harsh, less direct than the opening words of Hideyoshi's 1587 order: 'Japan is the land of the Gods. Diffusion here from the Kirishitan Country of a pernicious doctrine is most undesireable' (Elison, *Deus Destroyed*, p. 115), but the message was the same.

108 Knauth, *Confrontación Transpacífica*, pp. 197–206. Vizcaíno left Japan with the help of Date Masamune, daimyo of Sendai, who at this time was sympathetic to Christianity. Vizcaíno's own ship was beyond repair. It had been damaged on the voyage from Acapulco and further weakened by Vizcaíno's futile attempt to reach the fabled Isles of Silver and Gold in September and October 1612, another objective of his mission across the Pacific. When the shogunate refused to help, Date came to Vizcaíno's assistance, providing him with a ship and taking advantage of the situation to send envoys to New Spain

in the hope of winning the trade for his own domain (ibid., pp. 203–6).

109 Boxer, *Christian Century*, pp. 314–15; Knauth, *Confrontación Transpacífica*, p. 202.

110 Leon Pagès, *Histoire de la Religion Chrétienne au Japon depuis 1598 jusqu' à 1651*, 2 vols, Paris, 1869–70, II, pp. 239–41; Blair and Robertson, *The Philippine Islands*, XXIX, pp. 80–81; ibid., XXXII, p. 32; Knauth, *Confrontación Transpacífica*, p. 203.

111 BL Add. MS 9856, ff. 93v–94; Nuttall, *Earliest Historical Relations Between Mexico and Japan*, p. 28; Le Père de Charlevoix, *Histoire et description generale du Japon*, II vols, Paris, 1736, II, pp. 119, 134, 144, 145.

112 PRO CO 77/1/42, f. 77.

113 *Letters Received*, II, pp. 26–7; ibid., III, p. 292.

114 BL Cotton Charter, III.13, f. 34; *Letters Received*, II, p. 27.

115 Boxer, *Christian Century*, p. 84.

116 Cf. Boxer, *Christian Century*, pp. 308–9. Boxer's other point about the declining importance of the Jesuits as intermediaries in the silk trade is, however, important (ibid., p. 308). An indication of the importance of Portuguese silk imports in these years can be obtained from Katō, 'Japanese-Dutch Trade', table IV, p. 66.

117 *Letters Received*, II, pp. 19, 20.

118 Ibid., pp. 21–2. Protests to Sunpu through Adams fell on deaf ears (IOR G/12/15, f. 10).

119 *Letters Received*, II, p. 26.

120 IOR G/12/15, f. 15.

121 *Letters Received*, II, pp. 139, 143.

122 Firando Ledger B in Pratt, *History of Japan*, I, pp. 70, 89.

123 BL Cotton Vespasian MS FXVII, f. 79v; *Letters Received*, IV, pp. 44–5, 59; *Diary*, I, p. 211.

124 *Dai Nihon shiryō*, 12:16, pp. 42, 48; ibid., 12:23, pp. 637–9, 640–1; Wieder, *De Reis van Mahu en De Cordes*, III, pp. 95–100.

125 *Diary*, I, pp. 7, 11, 21.

126 *Letters Received*, IV, pp. 78, 98.

127 *Diary*, I, pp. 21, 22, 23, 25, 29, 30, 31. The *Sea Adventure* had heard news of the fall of Osaka castle in Naha in January 1615 although this was clearly news of the start of the winter seige. Nevertheless, on 24 February Adams, himself glad of the reports, reported that the Ryūkyū king held an official thanksgiving (Purnell, 'Log-Book of William Adams', pp. 10, 12).

128 Hauser, 'Osaka Castle', *passim*.

129 Ibid., pp. 117, 119, 189.

130 IOR G/12/15, f. 27v; *Dai Nihon shiryō*, 12:16, pp. 47–8; ibid., 12:23, p. 645; *Letters Received*, II, pp. 78, 98, 99; *Diary*, I, pp. 211, 214–15, 242, 244, 246, 248.

131 BL Egerton MS 2121, ff. 44v., 45–45v.; *Diary* I, pp. 75, 82.

132 IOR G/40/25, pp. 22–3, 27–8; *Letters Received*, III, p. 94; ibid., IV, p. 44.

133 BL Cotton Vespasian MS FXVII, ff. 62v, 63–111v, a contemporary copy written up in England and contained at the back of a 'Diary of Public Events 1509–1521'. There are numerous discrepancies between the figure given in these accounts and those mentioned in other letters. Inadequate accounting by its servants was one of the major headaches which plagued the Company.

134 Ibid., ff. 63–64. The stock included an additional 38 taels 3 mas 7 candereen worth of goods not invoiced at Bantam and there was a discrepancy of 556 taels 4 mas 1 2/3 candereen between the goods unloaded and the amount stated on the inventory drawn up at Bantam, probably a result of pilfering (ibid., ff. 65, 65v.).

135 IOR G/12/15, f. 23v; *Letters Received*, III, p. 255.

136 IOR G/12/15, f. 25v; *Letters Received*, III, pp. 238, 242, 250–1.

137 BL Cotton Vespasian MS FXVII, ff. 66v–67.

138 Ibid., ff. 64, 64v–65, 78v. The figure for the value of the stock sent up to the Kinai includes 133 taels 1 mas 3 candereen not recorded in the invoice sent with the goods.

139 BL Egerton MS 2121, f. 43v; IOR G/12/15, f. 18; *Diary*, I, p. 82.

140 Firando Ledger B in Pratt, *History of Japan*, I, pp. 88, 89–90. His incidentals amounted to 133 taels 4 mas 4 1/2 candereen (ibid., p. 89).

141 IOR G/12/15, f. 17v; Pratt, *History of Japan*, I, p. 90; *Dai Nihon shiryo*, 12:23, pp. 634 (the date of this letter should be 22 April not the 11th), 647; *Diary*, I, pp. 27, 41, 60, 61.

142 Ibid., pp. 74, 82.

143 W. Ph. Coolhaas (ed.), *Generale Missiven van Goeverneurs-General en Raden aan Heren XVII der VOC, deel 1, 1610–1638*, The Hague, 1960, p. 54; *Dai Nihon shiryō*, 12:25, pp. 102–3.

144 IOR G/12/15, f. 20; *Letters Received*, III,

pp. 246–7, 250; *Diary*, I, pp. 74, 82, 122–3, 145–6; Boxer, *Christian Century*, p. 331; Knauth, *Confrontación Transpacífica*, pp. 206–13. On Date's mission to Europe, which did not return to Japan until 1620, see G. Meriwether, 'A Sketch of the Life of Date Masumune and an Account of his Embassy to Rome', *Transactions of the Asiatic Society of Japan*, first series, XXI, pp. 39–105. Some Japanese accompnied the friars back to Acapulco in spite of the shogunate's ban and the declaration in New Spain (Knauth, *Confrontación Transpacífica*, p. 213).

145 *Letters Received*, III, pp. 246, 255, 264; ibid., IV, p. 48.

146 BL Cotton Vespasian MS FXVII, f. 79.

147 Ibid., ff. 69, 79, 95; IOR G/12/15, f. 20; *Letters Received*, III, pp. 241, 244. The goods sent up from Kinai were charged to the subfactory there.

148 IOR G/12/15, ff. 20, 22v; *Letters Received*, III, p. 249; ibid., IV, p. 47; *Diary*, I, pp. 55; Boxer, *Great Ship*, p. 87.

149 IOR G/12/15, ff. 22v, 23; BL Cotton Vespasian MS FXVII, f. 95v; *Letters Received*, III, pp. 207, 209.

150 IOR G/12/15, ff. 20v, 23; BL Cotton Vespasian MS FXVII, ff. 64, 65, 69, 71v, 95v; BL Egerton MS 2121, f. 11v.; *Letters Received*, III, p. 241. The presents given to the Matsūra and at Sunpu amounted to over 10 per cent of the value of the goods brought on the *Hosiander*. Nevertheless, such outlays in Japan bore favourable comparison with rates applicable elsewhere in the Indies. The customs tariff in Achin was 7 per cent, with presents on top of that and at Bantam '5 3/4 per cent and more'. At Patani the English were charged 856 reals for 'anchorage', which was pocketed by senior officials, and they still had to pay a 4 per cent customs levy (Foster [ed.], *The Voyages of Thomas Best*, p. 266; *Letters Received*, II, pp. 39, 79; ibid., III, p. 226; ibid., IV. p. 124. Coen gave similar figures for Patani: 850 reals for anchorage and a 5 per cent customs levy. *Coen: Bescheiden*, I, p. 33). The presents given in Japan were not set at a fixed percentage of a particular ship's cargo. Accordingly, the overheads of presents and the journey to the shogunal court would appear less if the value of the cargo brought to Japan were greater and, more importantly, as Coppindale noted, if sales were better.

151 BL Egerton MS 2121, ff. 51v–53, 54, 55v; BL Cotton Vespasian MS FXVII, ff. 68v, 73, 76v; *Letters Received*, III, pp. 242–3; *Diary*, I, pp. 79–188 *passim*.

152 BL Cotton Vespasian MS FXVII, ff. 75v–76; *Letters Received*, IV, pp. 52–4; *Diary*, I, pp. 178, 183, 186. A marginal note in Osterwick's accounts states that 200 taels in silver were added. Cocks's letter to the Company overlooks this addition (BL Cotton Vespasian MS FXVII, f. 76; *Letters Received*, IV, p. 54). The reals were taken from the *Sea Adventure's* lading (ibid., IV, p. 44). Some of the stones used for ballast were taken out and ebony taken from the Portuguese junk captured by the VOC was loaded on behalf of the Dutch for Bantam (see below p. 257).

153 IOR G/12/15, f. 18; L/MAR/A/XXIII, 25 February 1616; BL Egerton MS 2121, f. 62; *Diary*, I, p. 177; *Letters Received*, III, p. 232; ibid., IV, pp. 45–6, 119. On Eaton's detention see ibid., IV, pp. 103–5, 109, 110, 112, 113; *Diary*, II, pp. 227–8, 229, 230, 231, 233, 235, 239–40. Cocks also sent a letter to the Ōmura daimyo reminding him of the trading privileges granted by the shogun and the clause making the head of the English factory responsible for punishing his own men. The letter would have carried little weight with the Ōmura.

154 *Letters Received*, IV, pp. 48–9 where Cocks mentions Ieyasu's preference that Adams should not venture overseas.

155 IOR G/12/15, f. 23 v.

156 IOR B/5, pp. 18, 58.

157 Ibid., p. 89; G/40/25, p. 29; *CSP Colonial, East Indies...1513–1616*, pp. 290, 291.

158 *Letters Received*, III, p. 246; ibid., IV, p. 44; *Diary*, I, pp. 105, 108.

159 BL Cotton Vespasian MS FXVII, f. 69v. See also *Letters Received*, IV, p. 56; *Diary*, I, pp. 82–145 *passim*.

160 Ibid., pp. 82, 145.

161 BL Cotton Vespasian MS FXVII, ff. 69v, 86; *Letters Received*, III, p. 246. The figures given in BL Cotton Vespasian MS FXVII, f. 69v suggest that the money was originally all in reals. It must have been changed at the last moment. As usual there are discrepancies in the figures. One of Cocks's valuations was made at the time of the junk's departure and another slightly lower figure is mentioned in a letter to the

Company in February 1616 (*Letters Received*, III, p. 246; ibid., IV., p. 56). Osterwick's accounts (BL Cotton Vespasian MS FXVII, f. 86) were drawn up after her return and probably reflect what was discharged and accepted by the Ayuthia factory. The difference between Cocks and Osterwick can be reduced to some 109 taels after writing off goods worth 123 taels 4 mas 1 candereen lost on the voyage (ibid., f. 86v.). The likelihood of pilfering and incomplete records of the presents disbursed explain the remaining difference.

162 *Letters Received*, III, pp. 238, 245; *Diary*, I, p. 123.

163 Purnell, 'Log-Book of William Adams', pp. 98–9.

164 *Letters Received*, III, pp. 153–7. The figures are in Siamese taels which at this time was worth 2.39 reals.

165 *Letters Received*, III, pp. 109–11.

166 Ibid., pp. 178–81. A garbled account of these developments reached Hirado in September 1615 brought by a Japanese who had worked for the English in Siam (*Diary*, I, p. 95).

167 *Letters Received*, III, p. 159; ibid., IV, pp. 87–8.

168 Ibid., III, pp. 158, 178; Tiele, *De Opkomst*, I, pp. 62–3; *Coen: Bescheiden*, I, pp. 33–4, George Vinal Smith, *The Dutch in Seventeenth Century Thailand*, Carbondale, 1977, p. 52. For developments in the Ayuthia kingdom at this time see Wyatt, *Thailand: A Short History*, ch. 5.

169 Purnell, 'Log-Book of William Adams', p. 286.

170 Ibid., pp. 286–7; Katō, 'Rengō Oranda Higashi-Indo Kaisha', pp. 451, 449–50.

171 Purnell, 'Log-Book of William Adams', p. 288; *Letters Received*, IV, pp. 150, 268, 307.

172 BL Cotton Vespasian MS FXVII, ff. 86–86v, 106; *Letters Received*, IV, pp. 88–9, 267–8, 305–7; ibid., V, pp. 18–19. There are discrepancies in the various figures recorded for these transactions. Osterwick, for example, includes the cost of packing and dressing the hides among his figures, Cocks, in his letter to the Company in January 1617, does not. However, the discrepancies are minimal.

173 IOR G/12/15, f. 17v.

174 BL Cotton Vespasian MS FXVII, ff. 69v, 85v–86v, 90v, 91v, 106–106v; IOR G/12/15, f. 17v; *Letters Received*, IV, pp. 259, 267, 354–5; ibid., V, pp. 20–1, 22; *Diary*, I, pp. 335, 369; ibid., II, pp. 3, 6, 13, 42, 43, 46, 50, 51, 101.

175 *Dai Nihon shiryō*, 12:23, p. 644; Coolhaas (ed.), *Generale Missiven*, I, p. 47; Katō, 'Rengō Oranda Higashi-Indo Kaisha', pp. 441, 444, 445; Katō, 'Unification and Adaptation', pp. 220–1.

CHAPTER 5

1 *Letters Received*, III, p. 239.

2 IOR G/12/15, ff. 23v, 24, 40, 41v–42. On this last point the facts were right but the inference wrong. No ships had come in 1611, 1613 nor 1616 (Boxer, *Great Ship from Amacon*, pp. 79, 81, 89), but this had nothing to do with a Chinese desire to oust the Portuguese from the trade.

3 *Letters Received*, II, p. 199.

4 IOR B/5, p. 485; *Letters Received*, II, pp. 189 (which gives the wrong date for its arrival in England), 315.

5 IOR G/12/10, pp. 6–7; B/5, p. 490.

6 IOR G/40/25, p. 25. The voyage carried two letters from James I to the Chinese emperor. If a letter from the British monarch were required for the 'Kinge of Japan' one of the standard blank letters was to be used (ibid., p. 30).

7 *Diary*, I, pp. 47, 51.

8 Ibid., III, p. 28.

9 BL Cotton Vespasian MS FXVII, ff. 66, 67v, 71v, 107v, IOR G/12/15, ff. 41, 41v; *Diary*, I, pp. 42, 115, 196, 374–5; ibid., II, pp. 231; ibid., III, p. 28. My figures for money advanced by the English to the Li differ from those of Professor Iwao ('Li Tan', p. 48). See also ibid., pp. 45–49; Ng Chin-keong, *Trade and Society: The Amoy Network on the China Coast 1683–1735*, Singapore, 1983, pp. 48–9 and cf. John E. Wills Jr, 'Maritime China from Wang Chih to Shih Lang: Themes in Peripheral History' in Jonathan D. Spence and John E. Wills Jr (eds), *From Ming To Ch'ing: Conquest, Region, and Continuity in Seventeenth-Century China*, New Haven, 1979, p. 217 who suggests a more generous interpretation for Li Tan's failure to secure the English a trade in China. Professor Iwao's account of Li Tan is supplemented by the biographical sketch in L. Carrington Goodrich and Chaoying Fang (eds), *Dictionary of Ming Biography 1368–*

1644, 2 vols, New York, 1976, I, pp. 871–74.

10 IOR E/3/5, f. 328v. According to Cocks Li Tan provided loans at 20 per cent per annum without pawn as opposed to the rate of 33 per cent per annum with double pawn set by the Japanese. Cocks was exaggerating the Japanese rates. On other occasions he borrowed money at rates close to Li Tan's without pawn. By international standards the interest charged on loans in Japan was favourable. For rates in the Ottoman Empire see Braude, 'Venture and Faith', pp. 533–4. In England the maximum legal rate of interest was 10 per cent.

11 *Diary*, II, p. 340.

12 IOR G/12/15, ff. 24, 40. *Letters Received*, III, pp. 241, 248, 291; ibid., IV, pp. 258, 266.

13 Nachod, *Die Beziehungen*, pp. XLV–XLVI.

14 IOR G/12/10, p. 10; E/3/5, ff. 256v., 260–260v.; Meilink-Roelofsz, *Asian Trade*, pp. 252, 255.

15 IOR B/5, p. 414.

16 IOR B/5, pp. 479, 539; Chaudhuri, *East India Company*, pp. 203–4. It is interesting to note that the problem of separating the fine from the coarse silk thread cropped up once more in the 1670s when the company was encouraging silk imports from Bengal. The matter surfaced again in the early eighteenth century when the Company finally began to import Chinese raw silk in bulk. However, by the mid-century the skills of Chinese or Japanese weavers were no longer required for the Europeans had invented a machine for reeling silk (K. N. Chaudhuri, *The Trading World of Asia and the English East India Company, 1660–1760*, Cambridge, 1978, pp. 346–7, 349–51), an illustration of the technological gap which had opened between Europe and the Indies since the early seventeenth century.

17 For VOC imports of raw silk from the Indies see Glamann, *Dutch-Asiatic Trade*, ch. 6, esp. pp. 113–14, 116, 117. My conversions differ slightly from Professor Glamann's who takes a pecul to be 120 ponds. I prefer 125 ponds. See also Chaudhuri, *East India Company*, p. 204. In calculating the English sales figure for 1614 I have taken the English pound to be 24 oz, the great pound, in which the Company weighed silk (ibid., p. 203).

18 IOR G/12/15, ff. 39v, 40; *Letters Received*, IV, pp. 260, 267, 268.

19 Smith, *The Dutch in Seventeenth Century Thailand*, p. 52; Mulder, *Hollanders in Hirado*, p. 267–9; Katō, 'Rengō Oranda Higashi-Indo Kaisha', table 6 facing p. 440.

20 PRO CO 77/1/42, ff. 77v–78; CO 77/1/43.

21 *Letters Received*, III, pp. 239, 241.

22 IOR G/12/15, f. 24.

23 BL Cotton Vespasian MS FXVII, f. 81.

24 IOR G/12/15, f. 24; *Diary*, I, p. 53; ibid., III, p. 74; C. R. Boxer, *Jan Compagnie in Japan 1600–1817*, reprinted Tokyo, 1968, p. 27. C. R. Boxer 'Notes on Early European Military Influence in Japan (1543–1853)', *Transactions of the Asiatic Society of Japan*, second series, VIII, 1931 shows its age but remains useful. See also Delmer M. Brown, 'The Impact of Firearms on Japanese Warfare 1543–98', *Far Eastern Quarterly*, 7:3, 1948, pp. 236–53. Professor Parker argues that the massive stone blocks employed in the construction of Japanese castles made them virtually impregnable to attacks by heavy artillery. Consequently, the Japanese (and Chinese) had no strategic need to develop heavy artillery (*Military Revolution*, pp. 142–4). However, the Japanese continued to be intrigued by firepower especially gunnery (Boxer, *Jan Compagnie*, pp. 27–43).

25 Tiele, *De Opkomst*, I, pp. 29, 51, 128, 145, 273; *Coen: Bescheiden*, I, pp. 17, 32; *Diary*, II, p. 186. Seventy-two Japanese appear on the muster role of the VOC at Batavia in January 1620 (*Dai Nihon shiryō*, 12:43, pp. 75–7). See also Katō, 'Rengō Oranda Higashi-Indo Kaisha', p. 456.

26 Thomas Osborne, *A Collection of Voyages and Travels*, 2 vols, London, 1745, II, pp. 326, 328.

27 *Coen: Bescheiden*, VII:1, p. 9; Coolhaas (ed.), *Generale Missiven*. I, p. 47. For details of Dutch food (rice, soybeans, salted fish, sesame oil, vinegar, arrack etc.), construction materials (wood, nails, axes, spades), ship's stores (pulley wheels, anchors) and weaponry (musket, pikes, cannon balls, matchlock etc.) see Katō, 'Rengō Oranda Higashi-Indo Kaisha', pp. 452–3, 454–5, 460, 461, 464. Wickham's comments on the VOC strategy for using Hirado as a supply base were made immediately after the departure of the junk *Fortuijne*

in February 1616 for Bantam whose cargo was made up almost exclusively of these goods (ibid., pp. 454–5).

28 IOR G/12/15, ff. 18, 18v, 20; *Letters Received*, III, pp. 243, 251, 256, 290; ibid., IV, pp. 54, 76; *Diary*, I, pp. 9–10, 122, 205, 255–6, 260, 361, 368–9.

29 IOR B/5, pp. 304, 502–3; PRO CO 77/1/42, f. 78; *Letters Received*, I, pp. 323, 325–7; William Foster (ed.), *Supplementary Calendar*, pp. 35, 38; Foster, *England's Quest of Eastern Trade*, pp. 231–3; Parker, *Books to Build an Empire*, pp. 217–19; Andrews, *Trade, Plunder and Settlement*, pp. 345–53. In his reference to the northwest passage Adams makes no mention of his own alleged service with the Dutch in the quest for a northeast passage. The Company had no official connection with Luke Foxe's voyage in 1631 'for the North West Passage and so by Japan'. The mission failed but contributed to a more profound understanding of the enormity of the undertaking (BL Add. MS 19,302; Andrews, *Trade, Plunder and Settlement*, pp. 353–5). Later in the century, in 1687, the directors informed their servants at Madras that James II personally supported a project to discover a northeast passage to China using a number of small Dutch vessels. The Company was asked to provide some goods but the backers of the voyage could not recruit men for the ships and the project was abandoned (IOR E/3/91, f. 120).

30 IOR G/12/15, f. 18v.

31 Ibid., f. 39v.

32 W. Foster (ed.), *The Voyage of Nicholas Downton to the East Indies, 1614–15*, London, 1939, pp. xii, 208; *Letters Received*, III, p. 173.

33 IOR G/40/25, pp. 129–31; G/12/16, f. 57; Satow (ed.), *Saris*, p. lxv; *Letters Received*, ii, pp. 148, 170, 173–74; ibid., iv, p. 42. There are conflicting figures for the value of the cargo sent on the *Advice* from Bantam and there is a discrepancy between a report the commander, Robert Yowarte, gave of his instructions shortly before his departure and the instructions themselves.

34 IOR G/40/25, pp. 125–28; *Letters Received*, III, p. 113. Money exports from England had indeed dropped in 1614 but they had picked up again the following year (Chaudhuri, *East India Company*, p. 115).

35 *Letters Received*, III, pp. 113, 261–2,

274–5, ibid., IV, pp. 69, 117; Meilink-Roelofsz, *Asian Trade*, pp. 250–3 which gives valuable background information but nevertheless confuses the chronology of events in 1615 and 1616. Dutch attacks on Chinese junks in the Bantam road was the next step in the VOC's efforts to dislodge the Chinese middlemen.

36 BL Cotton Otho MS E.VIII, ff., 254–263, a fragment of the instructions; BL Egerton MS 2086, f. 20; IOR B/5, p. 338 Satow (ed.), *Saris*, p. lxix.

37 IOR B/5, p. 132; Foster (ed.), *The Voyages of Thomas Best*, pp. 270–1; Chaudhuri, *East India Company*, p. 46.

38 See below, Chapter 6 (i).

39 Keeling Letter Book, pp. 20, 21, 23, 31. Walter Payton, the cape merchant on the *Expedition* which Keeling had sent on ahead to Bantam from Surat, had commented after the *Hosiander*'s return from Hirado: 'no newes of any great benefitt there had, or expected futurlye' (BL Add. MS 19,276, p. 61).

40 IOR G/40/24, f. 18v; *Letters Received*, IV, pp. 117, 121; *Diary*, I, pp. 250, 264.

41 BL Cotton Vespasian MS FXVII, ff. 81–83; *Letters Received*, IV, p. 266; Satow (ed.), *Saris*, p. 204. The figures noted by Osterwick do not add up to the total given. There is a shortfall of some 100 taels.

42 *Letters Received*, III, pp. 15, 16, 19, 63, 67–8, 85–6, 91–2. There had been some Western influence on Japanese painting in the sixteenth century largely inspired by pictures, illustrated books and atlases brought back by the mission of the Kyushu boys in 1582, but no distinct genre developed. For a valuable introduction with excellent illustrations to the Western influence on Japanese art see Kobe Shiritsu Bijutsukan (ed.), *Umi no shiruku rodo*, Kobe, 1982. See also Boxer, *Jan Compagnie*, pp. 67–115; Fernando G. Gutérrez S. J., 'A Survey of Nanban Art', in Cooper (ed.), *Southern Barbarians*, pp. 147–206.

43 BL Cotton Vespasian MS FXVII, ff. 84–85v.

44 Ibid., ff. 89–90.

45 IOR G/12/15, ff. 39v–41, 42v; *Letters Received*, IV, pp. 183, 184, 258, 266, 267; ibid., v, pp. 5–8, 7. Gallipots had sold well for a tael in 1613 but in 1616 would be lucky to fetch a mas (*Letters Received*, IV, p. 267). Hirado was not unique in receiving such unsuitable car-

go. Similar complaints were made in Surat and Agra. One factor dismissed them as 'mere idleneses and commodities not fit for your worships to deal in' (ibid., pp. 232, 243).

46 Nachod, *Die Beziehungen*, pp. XLVIII–IX.

47 *Letters Received*, IV, p. 130.

48 Ibid., IV, pp. 129, 131, 133; *Diary*, I, pp. 275–6.

49 BL Cotton Vespasian MS FXVII, ff. 86v–88v; *Diary*, I, p. 281.

50 BL Cotton Vespasian MS FXVII, ff. 96v–98; *Letters Received*, IV, pp. 159–60; *Diary*, I, pp. 276–90.

51 BL Cotton Vespasian MS FXVII ff. 102v–103; *Diary*, I, pp. 295, 296–7; Derek Massarella, 'James I and Japan', *Monumenta Nipponica*, 38:4, 1983, pp. 380–1. A further 13 taels 2 mas of steel was brought up to top up the present. Presumably at some stage Hidetada was shown the pictures, which included the 'King in Parlament', set aside as gifts for bakufu officials (BL Cotton Vespasian MS FXVII, f. 103). If so his reactions are unknown.

52 *Letters Received*, V, p. 9.

53 *Diary*, I, p. 300.

54 Ibid., pp. 302–3.

55 Ibid., pp. 306–7.

56 *Letters Received*, V, p. 9.

57 IOR G/12/15, ff. 34v, 35–35v; *Letters Received*, V, pp. 9, 33; *Diary*, I, p. 314.

58 Ibid., p. 318. Cocks mistakenly called Itakura the 'Lord Cheefe Justice of Japon'. The Japanese version of the curtailed privileges is in the *Ikoku nikki* and is printed in Hayashi (compiler), *Tsūkō ichiran*, VI, p. 346 and Murakami (ed.), *Diary of Richard Cocks*, II, p. 346. An English version is in *Letters Received*, IV, pp. 140–1.

59 Ibid., V, p. 10.

60 Ibid.; *Diary*, I, pp. 315–26; *Dai Nihon shiryō*, 12:25, pp. 105, 109. Adams's account of these events, in a letter to Specx, tallies with Cocks's (ibid., pp. 102–3). The first impression was that the bakufu intended the English and Dutch to trade only in Hirado and the Spanish and Portuguese in Nagasaki but in practice the English and Dutch were allowed to operate in both places although most of their trade was conducted at Hirado (ibid., pp. 103, 104, 109; *Diary*, II, p. 176). Moreover, an order to all the daimyo was issued by the *rōjū* on 8 September informing them that English ships were permitted to call at Hirado or Nagasaki. The *rōjū*'s decree stressed the Christian threat as the reason for imposing the restrictions although bakufu concern to clip the opportunities for daimyo to participate directly in overseas trade is implicit in the decision to curtail the privileges (Hayashi [compiler], *Tsūkō ichiran*, VI, p. 346; Murakami [ed.], *Diary of Richard Cocks*, II, p. 347).

61 BL Cotton Vespasian MS F.XVII, ff., 103v–104. Nothing much was sold during the visit and a small amount of goods was sent back to Hirado (ibid., ff. 102, 104v).

62 Ibid., ff. 87v, 91; *Diary*, I, pp. 340, 341, 343, 345, 348, 349.

63 BL Cotton Vespasian MS F.XVII, f. 101; *Diary*, I, pp. 349, 350–1.

64 IOR G/12/15, f. 39; *Letters Received*, IV, pp. 155, 157; *Diary*, I, pp. 346, 354; Tōkyō Daigaku Shiryō Hensan-jo (ed.), *Igirisu shōkancho nikki, yakubun hen*, III, appendix, pp. 130–1.

65 BL Cotton Vespasian MS F.XVII, ff. 86v–88v, 90v, 91, 96–96v, 98, 101.

66 Ibid., ff. 98v–100v, 101v–102; *Diary*, II, p. 244. The Dutch had their reservations about Kurobe. Van Santvoort in particular believed that Kurobe was a cheat and was greatly distressed when the latter cast aspersions on the Dutchman's honour over some sales in 1615 (Wieder, *De Reis van Mahu en De Cordes*, III, pp. 99–100, 103–4). Nevertheless Kurobe remained one of the VOC's leading customers in Japan and whatever the misgivings of Cocks he tried to remain on good terms with the English (Tōkyō Daigaku Shiryō Hensan-jo (ed.), *Igirisu shōkancho nikki, yakubun hen*, III, appendix, pp. 141–2.

67 *Diary*, I, p. 356.

68 BL Cotton Vespasian MS F.XVII, ff. 105v, 106. Eighty per cent of the money was spent on board and lodging. It is not certain whether the expenses included 336 taels 6 mas advanced to the party when it left Hirado (ibid., f. 88v). Wickham's expenses were separate.

69 Ibid., f. 101; *Letters Received*, V, p. 10; *Diary*, I, pp. 363–4.

70 BL Cotton Vespasian MS FXVII, ff, 109v, 110v.

71 Ibid., ff. 109v–110; *Letters Received*, V, pp. 49–50.

72 BL Cotton Vespasian MS FXVII, ff, 105–105v, 108–108v; Cotton Cart III. 13, f. 17; IOR E/3/5, f. 330; *Letters*

Received, IV, pp. 172, 259–60, 268, 306; *Diary*, I, pp. 272, 366, 368, 370, 371. There are slight discrepancies between the figures given by Osterwick and those given by Cocks for the cost of refitting the junk and the value of her cargo. In the latter case, at least, Osterwick's figures were recorded after Cocks's and are probably more accurate. The differences are minimal but underline the prevalence of sloppy accounting (BL Cotton Vespasian MS FXVII, ff. 108–108v; *Diary*, I p. 368).

73 BL Cotton Vespasian MS FXVII, f. 109v; IOR G/12/15, f. 36v; *Letters Received*, VI, pp. 8–9.

74 *Letters Received*, VI, p. 257. The Dutch got by with fewer men although like the English they employed temporary workers to dress the deer hides (Smith, *The Dutch in Seventeenth Century Thailand*, p. 52).

75 BL Egerton MS 2086, f. 17. A factory was established in Cambodia at the capital Phnom Penh (Lovek), a cosmopolitan city with Chinese, Japanese (it was one of the main destinations for the *shuinsen*), Spanish and Portuguese among its residents, all living in their own quarters. The Cambodian monarchy itself was weak. Savidge wrote to Cocks in May 1617 that there was a good market for India cloth and demand for Japanese silver and that deer hides, wax and other goods vendible in Japan were available. Cocks contemplated a trade with Cambodia using Chinese junks. Unfortunately, the factory got nowhere. Isolation took its toll. Savidge 'fell into a madd humour' and attempted suicide. A factory was re-established in Cambodia in 1651–1656 (*Letters Received*, V, pp. 223–5; ibid, VI, pp. 264, 267; *Diary*, II, p. 309; Iwao, *Nan'yō Nihonmachi*, ch. 4 *passim*; Iwao, *Shuinsen*, p. 127; David P. Chandler, *A History of Cambodia*, Boulder, 1983, esp. p. 85).

76 IOR E/3/5, f. 333; *Letters Received*, IV, p. 306; ibid., V, pp. 263–4, 266–70, 275–6; ibid., VI, pp. 90–1, 256–7, 264.

77 IOR L/MAR/A/XXVI, f. 8v; *Diary*, II, pp. 154, 155, 177–8.

78 IOR L/MAR/A/XXVI, ff. 9–10; *Letters Received*, VI, pp. 256–9, 264–6.

79 *Letters Received*, V, pp. 16–7; Purnell, 'Log-Book of William Adams', p. 290. Coen also reported to the Heren XVII in December 1617 about the good prospects for trade at Cochinchina noting that the port was frequented by Japanese *shuinsen* (he noted that five *shuinsen* had called there with 200,000 taels in silver to procure their cargo) and that the king was anxious to promote overseas trade (*Coen: Bescheiden*, I, p. 295).

80 BL Cotton Cart III.13, ff. 20–33v (Sayers's accounts for the voyage; IOR E/3/5, ff. 318, 319–319v, 336–336v; IOR L/MAR/A/XXVI, ff. 6–6v; *Diary*, II, pp. 45, 46, 47–8; *Letters Received*, V, p. 16; ibid., VI, pp. 259–60; Purnell, 'Log-Book of William Adams', pp. 295–6. As usual there are discrepancies between the figures quoted by Sayers and Cocks, and Sayers's figure for net sales (BL Cotton Cart III.13, f. 20) should be reduced by subtracting the cash brought from Japan which does not count as a sale. The money stolen from Sayers was eventually returned and given over to the custody of the king who refused to hand it over to Sayer's jurebasso preferring to wait for the return of the English and the jurabasso returned to Japan empty-handed (IOR E/3/6, f. 98).

81 See above pp. 156–7.

82 Purnell, 'Log-Book of William Adams', pp. 290–6; Buch, *De Ooste Indische Compagnie en Quinam*, p. 17.

83 Purnell, 'Log-Book of William Adams', p. 297; *Diary*, II, p. 143.

84 Certainly private trade was.

85 *Diary*, II, p. 32.

86 Ibid., pp. 46, 68.

87 Ibid., pp. 53, 54, 72, 73.

88 Ibid., pp. 106–7, 134, 210–11.

89 IOR E/3/5, f. 324v; *Diary*, II, pp. 141, 142, 143, 144, 145, 146, 147–8. Wickham should be credited with persuading Bantam to load the silk. He had previously recommended diverting shipments of silk for England to Japan (IOR G/12/15, f. 38v).

90 *Diary*, II, pp. 151, 153, 154. They had left England in March 1615 in Keeling's fleet (BL Add. MS 19,276, ff., 1, 1v, 4, which gives three of their names, Petter, Michell and Muggett). Unfortunately they kept no record of their stay and the only reference to their presence in England comes just before their departure for home when the Court ordered that gowns were to be bought for the 'Japaneses to shelter them from the extremetie of the weather' (IOR

B/5, p. 347). The Dutch also faced problems over pay with Japanese returning to Hirado after service with the VOC (Mulder, *Hollanders in Hirado*, p. 130). A lack of proper pay-slips compounded by language problems seems to have been at the root of these arguments.

91 *Diary*, II, pp. 148, 149; Pratt, *History of Japan*, I, p. 262. The latter is reproduced from an account book which covered 1617 (OS). Only a fragment was extant when Pratt examined it and even that has now disappeared.

92 Keeling Letter Book, pp. 29, 31, 35.

93 *Letters Received*, VI, p. 13.

94 IOR E/3/5, ff. 328–334v *passim*. Of the two letters sent by Ball, only one has survived. (*Letters Received*, VI, pp. 10–15). The contents of the other, which Cocks termed Ball's 'bitter sweet lett[e]r', can only be surmised from Cocks's reply. Cocks's letter is endorsed 'small matters concerninge ye Compa but questyons between themselues' (IOR E/3/5, f. 335v). This is written in a later hand and is a strange assessment.

95 KA 979, f. 127.

96 BL Cotton Cart III.13, f. 14 *Diary*, II, pp. 154–65; *Dai Nihon shiryō*, 12:27, p. 60 ff. Gifts were also presented to court officials (*Diary*, II, pp. 165–8). The value of the presents is unrecorded by Cocks in the *Diary* but would have formed a large part of the 653 taels 8 mas 9 5/6 candereen Pratt quotes from the fragment account book (Pratt, *History of Japan*, I, pp. 262). On the importance of the embassy see Toby, *State and Diplomacy*, pp. 36, 64–70.

97 BL Cotton Cart III.13, f. 17.

98 IOR E/3/5, f. 333v; BL Cotton Cart III.13, f. 15.

99 IOR E/3/5, ff. 320–320v; 329v–330; E/3/7, f. 126; Murakami (ed.), *Diary of Richard Cocks*, II, pp. 290–5, 297–8; *Diary*, II, pp. 155–72; ibid, III, pp. 287–8, 322.

100 Nagazumi Yōko, 'Itowappu shōnin no seikaku', *Shigaku Zasshi*, 66:1, 1957, pp. 29–39; Nagazumi Yōko, 'Hirado Oranda shōkan nikki o tsūjite mita pancado', *Nihon Rekishi*, 260:1, 1970, pp. 81–96 esp. pp. 93–4; Iwao, *Shuinsen*, pp. 227–8; Katō, 'Japanese–Dutch Trade', pp. 50–63 and Innes, 'The Door Ajar', pp. 262–79.

101 IOR E/3/5, ff. 322–322v; *Diary*, II, pp. 86–120 *passim*. Cocks exaggerates the

fall-out from the restrictions on the English, presumably to impress his superiors. The refusal to restore the original privileges either to the English or Dutch had nothing to do with the activity of Lam's fleet in Manila Bay. For these activities, which decidely lacked deftness in the art of naval warfare, see Tien-Tse Chang, 'The Spanish-Dutch Naval Battle of 1617 Outside Manila Bay', *Philippine Historical Review*, 1, 1965, pp. 68–79. See also C. R. Boxer, 'War and Trade in the Indian Ocean and the South China Sea, 1600–1650', *Mariners Mirror*, 71:4, 1985, p. 424; Ruurdje Laarhoven and Elizabeth Pino Witterman, 'From Blockade to Trade: Early Dutch Relations with Manila, 1600–1750, *Philippine Studies*, 33, 1985, pp. 485–504.

102 IOR E/3/5, f. 322v; BL Cotton Cart III.13, f. 17. *Diary*, II, pp. 163, 164, 176, 177.

103 *Diary*, II, pp. 193, 198–9. The visit had cost at least 584 taels 5 mas 5 candereen (Pratt, *History of Japan*, I, p. 261).

104 IOR E/3/5, f. 325; BL Cotton Cart III.13, f. 15v; *Diary*, II, pp. 170, 171.

105 IOR E/3/5, f. 324v; G/12/15, ff. 38v, 41; BL Cotton Cart III.13, f. 15 *Letters Received*, VI, p. 260, 265; *Diary*, I, p. 339; ibid., II, pp. 168, 169, 173, 194, 199, 203, 209, 218.

106 IOR E/3/5, f. 326.

107 BL Cotton Vespasian F.XVII, ff, 98v–100, 103–4; Pratt, *History of Japan*, I, pp. 269–72; *Diary*, II, pp. 157, 296, 376, 381, 396, 399, 401–2. Pratt's figures on p. 270 do not add up and occasionally do not correspond with Osterwick's.

108 IOR G/12/15, f. 38v.

109 IOR E/3/5, ff. 320v, 329v–330.

110 IOR E/3/5, ff. 318, 320, 320v.

111 IOR E/3/5, ff. 260–260v.

CHAPTER 6

1 Pratt, *History of Japan*, I, p. 54.

2 *Letters Received*, II, p. 200; Firando Ledger B in Pratt, *History of Japan*, I, p. 72. Edmund Scott who had resided in Bantam in 1603 commented that had the word 'fire' been spoken in 'English, Mallayes, Javans, or Chyna' even if he were sound asleep he would have awoken with a start (Foster [ed.], *The Voyage of Sir Henry Middleton*, pp. 97–8, 99).

3 *Diary*, I, p. 20.

4 The figures are derived from Firando

Ledger B in Pratt, *History of Japan*, I, p. 72; BL Cotton Vespasian MS FXVII, ff. 68v, 70v, 71v, 76, 77v, 80, 80v, 81. See also *Diary*, I, pp. 82, 100, 122, 129, 140, 188, 237–38 and March-June 1616, *passim*. The figures given in Pratt, *History of Japan*, I, p. 73 are included in Osterwick's accounts but some of the dates are wrong.

5 Nachod, *Die Beziehungen*, p. CXLIV.

6 Ibid., p. CXLVI; *Letters Received*, V, p. 10.

7 *Diary*, I, pp. 190, 256, 351.

8 Ibid., pp. 190, 366.

9 Ibid., p. 221.

10 Ibid., III, pp. 39, 43, 58.

11 BL Cotton Vespasian MS FXVII, ff. 72v, 108.

12 IOR G/12/15, f. 29; *Diary*, I, pp. 13, 17.

13 BL Cotton Vespasian MS FXVII, ff. 94, 107v, 108; *Diary*, I, pp. 231, 232; 2, p. 247.

14 IOR B/3, ff. 151v–152; Chaudhuri, *East India Company*, pp. 83–4.

15 IOR B/5, p. 4; Chaudhuri, *East India Company*, p. 84.

16 *Letters Received*, II, pp. 6, 8; IV, p. 44. Promotion of junior employees to factors often meant that their original wages fell short of what was required to maintain a man in his new station or to encourage him to forward the Company's business. See Keeling Letter Book, p. 19; *Letters Received*, III, pp. 180–1.

17 IOR B/5, pp. 76, 256, 276; *Letters Received*, I, pp 318–19; Nachod, *Die Beziehvngen*, p. 169; Coolhaas (ed.), *Genereate Missiven*, I, p. 26. Specx's salary was higher than rates set later in the century (Boxer, *Dutch Seaborne Empire*, p. 300). See also Pieter van Dam, *Beschryvinge van de Oostindische Companie* edited by F. W. Stapel and C. W. Th. Baron van Boetzelaar van Asperen en Dubbeldam, 1:1, The Hague, 1927, pp. 575–6.

18 IOR B/5, pp. 256, 276–7 283; *Letters Received*, I, pp. 318–19; ibid., II, pp. 4, 6, 8; ibid., III, pp. 42, 71. The Company had no uniform exchange rate. Although factors' wages were set at 5s to the real the Company set other exchange rates, sometimes as high as 10s, for transactions from which it stood to benefit. The Company bought its reals on the continent at an exchange rate which fluctuated around 4s 6d, about the same rate as the VOC (Chaudhuri,

East India Company, pp. 120 and n., 125–9; Bruijn et al (eds), *Dutch Asiatic Shipping in the Seventeenth and Eighteenth Centuries*, I, p. 227). The fact that the real in Japan was worth 4s meant that, contrary to their special pleading, the factors benefited from a favourable exchange rate. Each £1 of their wages was worth 5 reals, or 40 mas, at 4s as opposed to 4 reals, or 32 mas, at 5s. The factors were reluctant to lose such an advantage and the directors were prepared to make a concession. This was contrary to an admonishment in 1609 to the factors in Bantam to set the exchange rate for wages 'at such an indifferent rate as may be neither too low for us nor too high for you', pointedly reminding their servants that besides buying the reals the Company also carried the risk of the adventure. The fact that Keeling's mission was aborted makes it possible that the concession was never applied. For the 1609 comment see Birdwood and Foster (eds), *First Letter Book*, p. 292; Chaudhuri, *East India Company*, p. 120.

19 Smythe was one of the executors of his will and Wickham sent presents from Japan to the governor and his wife (PRO PROB/11/138, ff. 290–91; IOR G/12/15, f. 42; *Letters Received*, III, pp. 289–93).

20 IOR B/5, p. 256; G/12/15, f. 42; *Letters Received*, II, p. 8. The wages for his three years' service to Christmas 1613 were paid over to his mother according to his instructions in January 1615 after the Court had carefully examined the purser's accounts from the *Clove* and deducted debts outstanding (IOR B/5, pp. 170, 341, 352–4). The money was used to pay off some of Wickham's debts (IOR G/12/15, f. 44v).

21 IOR G/12/15, f. 32; E/3/5, f. 325v *Letters Received*, III, pp. 113, 149, 232; ibid., IV, pp. 44, 45–6, 117, 121; *Diary*, I, p. 177. Osterwick's accounts give figures for factors' allowances but no indication as to what period they cover (BL Cotton Vespasian MS FXVII, ff. 101, 108v–109) and Wickham was given 280 taels 5 mas 5 candereen 'to clear accounts before departing for Bantam in 1617' (ibid., f. 111).

22 *Letters Received*, I, pp. 310–12, 324–7; Wieder, *De Reis von Mahu en De Cordes*, III, p. 44; Opstall, *De Reis van de Vloot van Pieter Willemsz Verhoeff Naar Indie*, p. 148, Katō, 'Rengo Oranda Higashi-

Indo Kaishai p. 432.

23 IOR B/5, p. 107, 212, 412; B/6, p. 282; E/3/5 f. 324v *Coen: Bescheiden*, II, p. 372. On this occasion he sent *f*. 200.

24 IOR B/3, ff. 9v, 76v; Birdwood and Foster (eds), *First Letter Book*, p. 402; Ralph Davis, *The Rise of the English Shipping Industry*, Newton Abbot, 1972, pp. 147–8; Marcus Rediker, *Between the Devil and the Deep Blue Sea*, Cambridge, 1986, p. 130.

25 IOR Home Misc. 41, ff. 107–110v. The sums disbursed by the Company's secretariat were not inconsiderable: 15 September 1615 to 6 October 1615, £3,000; 21 January 1617 to 11 November 1617, £2,500.

26 *Letters Received*, V, pp. 254–55.

27 IOR E/3/5, f. 320, 334v; *Diary*, I, p. 367.

28 For an example of one of the Company's numerous exhortations against private trade see *Letters Received*, III, pp. 327–8.

29 IOR B/5, pp. 339–40, 342–43, 343–44. The goods themselves (worth £286) are interesting as an indication of what factors themselves thought would sell in the Indies: jewels (£15), amber and jet boxes (£2 11s), wrought silk and taffetas (£56 2s), looking glasses (£48 11s), beads (£3 8s), pictures (£20), gloves (£24 18s), broadcloth (£44 13s), knives (£15 11s 6d), hotwaters (£30), and books (£25).

30 Keeling Letter Book, pp. 32, 33.

31 *Letters Received*, V, p. 107.

32 Ibid., VI, p. 131. See also p. 216 and IV, pp. 84, 341, 343.

33 *Letters Received*, V, pp. 118–19.

34 Ibid., pp. 249, 293.

35 IOR G/21/3 pt 2, ff. 7, 7v, 14v, 21v, 24v, 28; Chaudhuri, *East India Company*, pp. 87–8.

36 *Letters Received*, IV, p. 185. Osterwick's distinction between official and private is interesting. Other factors were less circumspect. A perusal of Cocks's diary reveals much about the cape merchant's dealings although he clearly believed that his transactions were within the bounds of the permissible.

37 The inventory of his goods included 417 catties of Nanking silk, pots of musk, assorted cloth, numerous Japanese clothes and artifacts and a library of almost 100 volumes (IOR G/40/23, ff. 4–7).

38 IOR G/12/15, ff. 19, 19v.

39 Wickham had been impressed with Coppindale's own private dealings (Coppindale had brought an adventure in Coromandel cloth, lignum and quicksilver on behalf of Adam Denton at Patani to Japan, but he had failed to sell any) and had written to Nealson that Coppindale had done well 'for a beginner' (IOR G/12/15, f. 21; *Letters Received*, III, p. 244).

40 *Diary*, I, pp. 211–12, 16, 24–25. Wickham does not appear to have done so well in subsequent sales to Benita. See *Letters Received*, IV, pp. 139, 154. Wickham's profits from the Ryūkyū voyage helped fire his enthusiasm for establishing a subfactory at Naha.

41 *Letters Received*, IV, p. 135.

42 IOR G/12/15, f. 38v.

43 IOR G/12/15, f. 20v; *Letters Received*, IV, pp. 150, 176.

44 IOR G/12/15, ff. 20v, 29; *Diary*, II, p. 77.

45 *Diary*, I, p. 190.

46 *Diary*, I, pp. 295, 369, 372, 374.

47 Purnell, 'Log-Book of William Adams', p. 37; *Letters Received*, pp. 93, 104, 126; *Diary*, I, p. 274. The Dutch also invested in this voyage, Specx 600 taels and Leonard Camps 25 taels (Purnell, 'Log-Book of William Adams', p. 37). While Specx's may have been an official investment, Camps's certainly was not.

48 Purnell, 'Log-Book of William Adams', p. 268. Adams records a 200 tael investment by Nealson and a 2 tael one by Hudson but these are crossed out (ibid., pp. 267–68).

49 Keeling Letter Book, p. 31. It is not known whether the coral reached Japan.

50 PRO PROB/11/138, ff. 290–91; IOR B/7, pp. 32–33, 84, 178, 225, 245–6, 270–1, 309, 352–4, 355, 366, 386; B/8, pp. 11, 16–17, 19, 123, 241, 518, 531, 545, 546; B/9, pp. 202, 211; B/10, pp. 63, 66.

51 IOR B/8, p. 401; B/11, pp. 405–6; Chaudhuri, *East India Company*, p. 88.

52 IOR E/3/36, no. 4111. These freemen were modelled on the Dutch free burghers.

53 E/3/84, ff. 115–115v; E/3/92, f. 37; Holden Furber, *John Company*, Cambridge, Massachusetts, 1948, pp. 277–84; Furber *Rival Empires of Trade*, pp. 269–72; Chaudhuri, *East India Company*, p. 88; P. J. Marshall, 'Private British Trade in the Indian Ocean Before 1800', in Das Gupta and Pearson,

(eds), *India and the Indian Ocean*, pp. 276–300; I. B. Watson, *Foundations of Empire: English Private Trade in India 1659–1760*, New Delhi, 1980, pp. 81, 157 and *passim*; Watson, 'Indian Merchants and English Private Interests: 1659–1760', in Das Gupta and Pearson (eds), *India and the Indian Ocean*, pp. 301–16. Professor Chaudhuri suggests (*Trading World*, p. 212) that private trade was highly risky and profits uncertain. This was certainly the early seventeenth-century experience although if factors hit the jackpot the rewards were considerable.

54 Marshall, 'Private British Trade', pp. 278–9.

55 On these last points see Furber, *John Company* and Watson, *Foundations of Empire*.

56 IOR L/MAR/MISC/6, f. 27v; *Diary*, II, p. 129; Pratt, *History of Japan*, I, p. 263.

57 Satow (ed.), *Saris*, p. 22; Meilink-Roelofsz, *Asian Trade*, p. 236; Jean Gelman Taylor, *The Social World of Batavia: European and Eurasian in Dutch Asia*, Madison, 1983, pp. 12–15; Leonard Blussé, 'The Caryatids of Batavia: Reproduction, Religion and Acculturation under the VOC', *Itinerario*, 7:1, 1983, pp. 57–85 esp. pp. 60–5 The Portuguese did not encourage women to travel to the Indies. A small number of orphans were sent on náo from Lisbon but from 1549 to 1750 no governor general of the Estado da Índia left with his wife for Goa. The Portuguese in the Indies preferred concubinage even if this met with the disapproval of the church (C. R. Boxer, *Mary and Misogyny: Women in Iberian Expansion Overseas 1415–1815*, London, 1975, pp. 63–95 esp. pp. 63–8). In Macao, for example, in the 1630s there was only one Portuguese female (Boxer, *Fidalgos*, pp. 127–8).

58 IOR B/5, p. 25. The men's names (Salvador, Samuel and Anthony) were Christian and the phrasing of the language in the Court's rejection of the petition suggests that their wives were English.

59 IOR B/5, pp. 263, 272, 277, 305, 310, 314.

60 IOR B/5, pp. 385, 417, 419–20. The Dutch did things differently. In 1614 the newly appointed governor general, Gerard Reynst, left for the Indies to take up his post accompanied by his wife. She accompanied her husband on voyages to Dutch factories in the Indies (Taylor, *Social World of Batavia*, p. 13). It is not known whether Keeling was aware of Reynst's privilege. That Keeling was deeply in love with Anna can be seen from two of his letters to Anna (Keeling Letter Book, pp. 38, 45). As regards the separation of husband and wife, it was accepted by theologians that this was sanctioned when reasons of state or business were involved (Kathleen M. Davies, 'Continuity and Change in Literary Advice on Marriage', in R. B. Outhwaite (ed.), *Marriage and Society: Studies in the Social History of Marriage*, London, 1981, p. 73).

61 Cooper, *They Came to Japan*, pp. 64–5. This description of the Nagasaki flesh market is virtually identical to Jacob von Neck's description of the situation in Patani (quoted in Reid, *Southeast Asia in the Age of Commerce*, I, p. 155). On prostitution in southeast Asia see ibid., p. 156.

62 Satow (ed.), *Saris*, p. 83. In Burma all foreigners staying for a protracted period were given consorts as a matter of course (D. G. E. Hall, *Early English Intercourse with Burma*, London, 1928, pp. 100–1).

63 IOR G/12/15, ff. 12v, 15v, 27v; *Letters Received*, II, p. 47.

64. *Letters Received*, IV, p. 40; *Diary*, I, p. 195.

65 IOR G/12/15, f. 27; *Letters Received*, IV, pp. 116, 119.

66 *Diary*, I, 149; ibid., II, pp. 9–10, 15, 67, 218.

67 *Letters Received*, III, p. 253; IV, p. 2; *Diary*, II, p. 280.

68 *Letters Received*, II, p. 73; *Diary*, I, pp. 61–2.

69 *Diary*, II, p. 382.

70 Ibid., p. 414.

71 *Diary*, III, p. 184.

72 ARA KA 11,722, p. 61; *Diary*, I. p. 349; II, pp. 180, 401. For young William see below pp. 721–2.

73 *Diary*, III, p. 124.

74 *Coen: Bescheiden*, II, p. 730.

75 Nachod, *Die Beziehungen*, p. LXXII; J. Fox, '"For Good and Sufficient Reasons": An Examination of Early Dutch East India Company Ordinances on Slaves and Slavery', in Anthony Reid (ed.), *Slavery, Bondage and Dependency in Southeast Asia*, New York, 1983, pp. 254–5.

76 ARA KA 1941, f. 345 pr. in Mulder, *Hollanders in Japan*, pp. 258–9; Tōkyō Daigaku Shiryō Hensan-jo (ed.), *Nihon kankei kaigai shiryō: Dagregister gehouden big de Operhoofden van het Nederlandsche Factorij in Japan*, Tokyo, 1974–, II, p. 130; ibid., III, p. 9ff.; ibid., IV, pp. 16–17, 20–1; Iwao, *Nan'yō Nihonmachi, zokū*, p. 347. The decree did not apply to William Adams's children, but Van Santvoort left accompanied by his wife and children. They solemnised their marriage before a Protestant minister in Taiwan.

77 By contrast, in Siam, as in other southeast Asian polities, rulers preferred to acquire or retain population rather than let it go. It was thus more difficult for foreigners to take their offspring out of the kingdom and until 1641 it was forbidden outright. See M. E. van Opstall, 'From Alkammaar to Ayudhya and Back', *Itinerario*, 9:2, 1985, pp. 11–12.

78 *Diary*, I, pp. 300, 305, 311, 317, 327, 331, 354, 355; Tōkyō Daigaku Shiryō Hensan-jo (ed.), *Igirisu shōkancho nikki, yakubun hen*, III, appendix, pp. 146–8. Other caboque parties, an essential feature of Japanese hospitality, on this journey and other ones, are mentioned throughout the diary. The Korean ambassadors were also entertained by whores in 1617 (*Diary*, II, p. 79). Saris's comments on the *kabuki* actresses were added later (Satow [ed.] Saris, pp. 90, 180). Women were finally banned from *kabuki* in 1629, their roles being performed by young boys who maintained the association between *kabuki* and prostitution. See Donald H. Shively, 'Bakufu versus *Kabuki*' in John W. Hall *et al* (eds). *Studies in the Institutional History of Early Modern Japan*, Princeton, 1968, pp. 231–61.

79 *Diary*, I, pp. 147, 280, 282, 307–8. Hawtrey was a bizarre character. On one occasion 'he went & cut his haire after the pagon fation, thinking to turne pagon; w'ch he could not do heare, although he would' (ibid., p. 308).

80 Keith Thomas, 'The Puritans and Adultery: The Act of 1653 Reconsidered' in Donald Pennington and Keith Thomas (eds), *Puritans and Revolutionaries*, Oxford, 1978, pp. 257–82 esp. pp. 259–61; Anthony Fletcher, *Reform in the Provinces: The Government of Stuart England*, New Haven, 1986, pp. 252–62; Keith Wrightson, *English Society 1580–1680*, London, 1982, pp. 99–100;

Martin Ingram, 'The Reform of Popular Culture? Sex and Marriage in Early Modern England', in Barry Reay (ed.), *Popular Culture in Seventeenth Century England*, London, 1988, pp. 141–56.

81 On these attributes see Richard Grassby, 'Social Mobility and Business Enterprise in Seventeenth Century England', in Pennington and Thomas (eds), *Puritans and Revolutionaries*, pp. 370–1.

82 IOR G/40/25, p. 18. Hawkins died on the voyage home from Bantam but his widow remarried with Gabriel Towerson and in 1617 both returned to the Indies, Towerson hoping to do well out of what he imagined was a good connection at the Mughal court. On this voyage the first English women went out to India. Mrs Towerson was accompanied by a maid and the pregnant wife of one of the factors, Richard Steele, who had managed to slip aboard posing as a maid. She gave birth on the voyage. The English women were sent home in August 1619 (*Letters Received*, VI, pp. 121, 141, 147, 167, 222, 223, 227–8, 290–1; Foster (ed.), *Supplementary Calendar*, p. 130).

83 For a study of these later notions in practice see John G. Butcher, *The British in Malaysia 1880–1941*, Kuala Lumpur, 1979, ch. 8 *passim*.

84 Zuckerman, 'Identity in British America: Unease in Eden', pp. 144–7 esp. p. 144.

85 Foster (ed.), *The Voyages of Thomas Best*, pp. 213–14.

86 Ibid., p. 264.

87 IOR B/5, p. 268.

88 Ibid., p. 294; William Foster, *John Company*, London, 1926, pp. 22–4.

89 Pennington, 'The Amerindian in English Promotional Literature 1575–1625', p. 186.

90 On the practice of vassals offering their daughters to a superior monarch see Reid, *Southeast Asia in the Age of Commerce*, I, pp. 151–52. At no stage was such a royal match entertained on the English side.

91 Keeling Letter Book, p. 19; *Letters Received*, III, p. 226; ibid., IV, pp, 167, 125–6; ibid., VI, pp. 29, 69, 72; Foster, *John Company*, p. 24; Ricklefs, *History of Modern Indonesia*, pp. 31–2.

92 IOR B/29, p. 45; B/30, pp. 384, 351; E/3/87, ff. 114–114v; E/3/88, f. 92; E/3/36, no. 4111.

93 *Diary*, II, p. 66.

94 IOR G/21/3 pt 2, p. 15.

95 C. Ernest Fayle (ed.), *Voyage to the East Indies: Christopher Fryke and Christopher Schweilzer*, London, 1929, pp. 113, 177.
96 On this point see Arthur N. Gilbert, 'Buggery and the British Navy', *Journal of Social History*, 10, 1976, pp. 72–98.
97 IOR B/3, ff. 10, 11v, 14v, 17v, 66, 70v, 72v, 117, 165v, 166v: B/5 pp. 21, 27, 28, 61, 68, 78, 85, 96, 255; B/6, pp. 47, 61, 83, 236; *Letters Received*, IV, p. 90; Foster (ed.), *The Voyages of Thomas Best*, pp. xix–xxii; Birdwood and Stevens (eds), *The Dawn of British Trade*, pp. 116, 150, 275–6, 281. Chaplains' wages were fixed at £50, rising for each year's service and preachers could adventure money in the joint-stock. Payment of 1/3 of their wages in the Indies was at the discretion of the voyage commander or chief factors at Surat but was frowned upon by the Company. Preachers were still being paid £50 at the end of the 1660s (IOR B/30, pp. 586, 591).
98 *Letters Received*, v, pp. 36–40, 175–87.
99 This is evident from some jottings in Cocks's diary (*Diary*, II, pp. 111–12 n 196).
100 On the Hellenic ideal see David Constantine, *Early Greek Travellers and the Hellenic Ideal*, Cambridge, 1984.
101 *Rival Empires of Trade*, p. 7. According to one calculation, in 1700 the real standard of living in the future developed world was more or less the same as that of the future Third World. In 1860 the disparity was 1.9:1; in 1913 3.4:1; and in 1950, 5.2:1 (Bairoch, 'Le Bilan économique du colonialisme', p. 33). According to some measures (diet, health, hygiene) the standard of living, certainly the quality of life in the Indies, was if anything higher than in many parts of Europe and Europeans were constantly impressed by the good health and longevity of the people compared with home. See Reid, *Southeast Asia in the Age of Commerce*, I, ch. 2.
102 On this point see Furber, *Rival Empires of Trade*, p. 316. See also p. 324.
103 IOR/G/12/15, f. 44v. In a letter to his mother at the same time he noted that the only letters he had received from England were from friends and the governor of the Company. He feared that one from his mother had been lost or stolen (ibid., *f.* 44).
104 IOR E/3/5, ff. 325v, 326, 338; ARA KA 979, f. 127; *Letters Received*, v, p. 15; Pratt, *History of Japan*, I, p. 263;

Diary, II, p. 139, 251, 253, 319.
105 IOR IOR G/12/15, f. 15.
106 BL Cotton Vespasian FXVII, ff. 73v, 76.
107 Ibid., f. 109v; *Letters Received*, III, p. 246.
108 BL Cotton Vespasian FXVII, ff. 73v, 76, 109v; IOR E/3/5, ff. 329, 330, 332, 338; BL Cotton Cart III:13, f. 15v; Murakami (ed.), *Diary of Richard Cocks*, II, p. 292; *Diary*, II, pp. 212, 214, 217, 233, 234, 237, 239; Pratt, *History of Japan*, I, p. 264; Chaudhuri, *East India Company*, pp. 125–32; Enomoto Sōji, 'Domain Coins in the Early Edo Period', *Acta Asiatica*, 39, 1980, pp. 42–60; Innes, 'The Door Ajar', pp. 578–84; Iwao, *Shuinsen*, pp. 400–6. Cf. Boxer (*Great Ship*, p. 329) who suggests that the Portuguese did not refine their silver for export. This is supported by Peter Mundy's observation in 1637 in Macao that Japanese silver was liable to a 15 per cent surcharge when being rated in reals (R. C. Temple (ed.), *The Travels of Peter Mundy in Europe and Asia, 1608–1667*, III, London, 1919, p. 311).
109 Keeling Letter Book, p. 39.
110 Bruijn *et al* (eds), *Dutch Asiatic Shipping*, I, p. 226; Chaudhuri, *East India Company*, p. 115. Cf. Meilink-Roelofsz, *Asian Trade*, p. 378 n. 149.
111 Keeling Letter Book, pp. 50, 51, 53. His talents were too great to be ignored and he was approached by individuals connected with the proposed Scottish East India Company to which James I granted letters patent in 1618. The letters were soon rescinded after protests from the English Company. To his credit, Keeling declined to help the interlopers (ibid., p. 51; Chaudhuri, *East India Company*, p. 31).
112 IOR B/6, pp. 12, 17–18.
113 Keeling Letter Book, p. 31; IOR E/3/5, f. 201; B/6, p. 12.
114 G. N. Clark, *The Colonial Conferences between England and the Netherlands in 1613 and 1615*, Leydon, 1951, provides a discussion of the background.
115 PRO CO 77/1/43. This was a letter to Sir Thomas Wilson. It is interesting to speculate if this was passed on to the Privy Council as had some of Cocks's earlier letters from Bayonne.
116 *Diary*, II, p. 113; *Letters Received*, IV, pp. 54–5, 86.
117 Ibid., II, p. 86; v, pp. 174–5.
118 Keeling Letter Book, p. 24. See also

ibid., p. 23 and Foster (ed.), *Journal of John Jourdain*, pp. 318–34; *Letters Received*, III, pp. 141, 146, 260, 272.
119 *Letters Received*, III, pp. 136, 140.
120 Quoted in Clark, *Colonial Conferences*, p. 125.
121 Keeling Letter Book, pp. 23–4.
122 IOR B/6, pp. 17–18; Foster (ed.), *Journal of John Jourdain*, p. lxv.
123 IOR B/6, pp. 17–18, 30, 58; Foster (ed.), *The Voyages of Thomas Best*, pp. 294–305; Foster (ed.), *Journal of John Jourdain*, pp. lxv-lxviii, lxxi.
124 IOR E/3/5, f. 250.
125 On the VOC see Meilink-Roelofsz, *Asian Trade*, pp. 194, 196–202; Boxer, *Dutch Seaborne Empire*, pp. 98–9; Glamann, *Dutch Asiatic Trade*, p. 91.
126 Foster, *England's Quest of Eastern Trade*, pp. 263–70; Meilink-Roelofsz, *Asian Trade*, pp. 201–2.
127 *CSP East Indies...1617–1621*, p. 385 *Coen: Bescheiden*, I, pp. 420–1; Chaudhuri, *East India Company*, pp. 60–1.
128 ARA KA 979, f. 127; *Diary*, II, p. 252.
129 IOR E/3/5, f. 326v; *Diary*, II, pp. 216, 217, 221, 222, 224, 225–6, 227, 228.
130 See above p. 177.
131 *Diary*, II, pp. 272, 274, 302, 365; Tōkyō Daigaku Shiryō Hensan-jo (ed.), *Igirisu shōkancho nikki, yakubun hen*, III, appendix, pp. 134–5.
132 IOR E/3/5, ff. 321, 324v, 325, 330, 333v; B/5, p. 125; Chaudhuri, *East India Company*, p. 96; Iwao, *Shuinsen*, p. 117.
133 Smith, *Dutch in Seventeenth Century Thailand*, pp. 52, 79.
134 IOR E/3/5, f. 324; *Diary*, II, pp. 255, 267; Purnell, 'Log-Book of William Adams', p. 242.
135 IOR E/3/5, ff. 325v, 334. The figure was cited by the Dutch as well. Coen, had mentioned it the Heren XVII in his own optimistic assessment of trade prospects in Cochinchina (*Coen: Bescheiden*, I, p. 295).
136 IOR E/3/5, ff. 324, 328; Murakami, *Diary of Richard Cocks*, II, pp. 298–9; *Diary*, II, p. 305.
137 Purnell, 'Log-Book of William Adams', pp. 242–8, 298–302; *Diary*, II, pp. 275, 283, 290, 291.
138 IOR E/3/7, ff. 115–115v; *Diary*, II, pp. 250, 254, 255, 256, 258–9, 290, 291, 304, 305, 311, 327–8; ibid., III, pp. 284–5.
139 Wen-Hsiung Hsu, 'From Aboriginal Island to Chinese Frontier: The Develop-

ment of Taiwan Before 1683', in Ronald G. Knapp (ed.), *China's Island Frontier*, Honolulu, 1980, p. 11; Iwao, *Shuinsen*, pp. 49, 159–60; Knauth, *Confrontación Transpacífica*, pp. 163–4.
140 IOR E/3/5, f. 324; *Diary*, II, p. 322; Pratt, *History of Japan*, I, p. 296; Iwao, 'Li Tan', pp. 40–5.
141 IOR E/3/6, f. 79; Pratt, *History of Japan*, I, p. 296; *Diary*, II, pp. 310, 315, 317; Boxer, *Great Ship*, pp. 95–6. Unfortunately, no figures are available for the Portuguese imports but in 1615 Cocks reported that the náo had brought 900 peculs of Canton silk which was sold at 165 taels per pecul. After the náo had left the price went up to 230 taels for Canton silk and 300 taels per pecul for Nanking (*Letters Received*, III, p. 263; Boxer, *Great Ship*, p. 87). To spread the risk involved in the voyage from Macao to Nagasaki the Portuguese switched from a single náo to a number of galliots from 1618.
142 IOR E/3/6, f. 79v; *Diary*, II, p. 309.
143 *Dai Nihon shiryō*, 12:30, pp. 53–63; *Coen: Bescheiden*, I, 434; ibid., II, pp. 653, 654; ibid., IV, p. 384; Katō, 'Unification and Adaptation', p. 220; Katō, 'Rengō Oranda Higashi-Indo Kaisha', pp. 459–61, 462 (the total in table 25 should be reduced by f. 9), 474–84; Nachod, *Die Beziehungen*, p. XLIX; *Diary*, I, p. 171; Boxer, *Great Ship*, p. 88. The warnings not to attack Portuguese vessels were repeated on subsequent occasions and from 1633 the Dutch were ordered to delay the departure of their ships for twenty days after the galliots had left, a restriction which they tried repeatedly to have removed. By then bakufu and some daimyo were making illegal investments on Dutch and Chinese vessels as well as Portuguese ones. (Nachod, *Die Beziehungen* pp. 275–6; (Boxer, *Great Ship*, pp. 91–3, 134; Nagazumi, 'Japan's Isolationist Policy', pp. 20–1, 33).
144 This argument is based on the estimates for Dutch silk imports to Japan in Katō, 'Japanese-Dutch Trade', p. 66; Katō, 'Rengō Oranda Higashi-Indo Kaisha', pp. 420–1 and the Heren XVII's estimates of demand in Amsterdam in Glamann, *Dutch-Asiatic Trade*, p. 116.
145 IOR E/3/5, ff. 320v, 321.
146 IOR G/12/15, f. 42v; *Letters Received*, VI, p. 10.
147 IOR E/3/5, f. 318.
148 For examples of Cocks's boasts see *Di-*

149 *Diary*, I, pp. 268–9, II, p. 92.
150 IOR E/3/5, ff 328, 329; *Letters Received*, IV, p. 57; v. pp. 15, 41–2. As has been mentioned (above, p. 250), Specx turned down Wickham's offer to carry goods on the *Advice* when she returned to Bantam in February 1618. See also Katō, 'Rengō Oranda Higashi-Indo Kaisha', pp. 452–3.
151 *Diary*, II, p. 106. The point would have been lost on his listener.
152 ARA KA 979, f. 127.
153 IOR E/3/5, f. 323v; Foster, *England's Quest of English Trade*, pp. 263–70; *Diary*, II, p. 103, 113, 119–20. One of the Englishmen serving the Dutch was the scion of a west country gentry family, George Dowriche, son of Robert Dowriche (ibid., p. 132).
154 Ibid., p. 273.
155 Ibid., pp. 333–4.
156 Ibid., pp. 331–2, 334–5.
157 Ibid., pp. 349, 366–70, 380; ibid., III, p. 293; Toby, *State and Diplomacy*, pp. 203–9.
158 *Diary*, II, pp. 368, 369; ibid., III, p. 282.
159 IOR E/3/6, ff. 204–207; Tōkyō Daigaku Shiryō Hensan-jo, (ed.), *Igirisu shōkancho nikki*, III, appendix, pp. 139–40, 143–5; *Diary*, II, pp. 204, 205, 214, 242, 384–5, 386, 389, 399; Peri, 'Essai sur les relations du Japon et de l' Indochine sur xvie et xviie siécles', pp. 62–3.
160 Hayashi (compiler), *Tsukō ichiran*, VI, p. 347; Murakami (ed.), *Diary of Richard Cocks*, II, p. 348.
161 *Diary*, II, pp. 294–5;
162 ARA KA 1006, ff. 123–123v; Nachod, *Die Beziehungen*, p. LXXXI; Nagazumi, 'Japan's Isolationist Policy', pp. 27–8.
163 IOR E/3/5, f. 325; BL Cotton Vespasian MS FXVII, ff. 99v–100; *Diary*, II, pp. 396, 400–1.
164 There are only two letters, both written by Cocks in March 1620, on which to base an account of these events (*Diary*, III, pp. 275ff and 299ff).
165 *Diary*, III, p. 280.
166 IOR E/3/7, f. 34.
167 *Coen: Bescheiden*, I, 434; ibid., II, pp. 654–5; *Dai Nihon shiryō*, 12:32, p. 91.
168 Blair and Robertson (eds), *The Philippine Islands*, XIX, p. 95.
169 IOR E/3/7, f. 115v.
170 Ibid.. Eaton gives the cost in taels of Siam except for the sappan wood.
171 Ibid. f. 116; L/MAR/A/XXVI, f. 22.
172 The Dutch invested 500 taels and

Adams himself 950 taels on this voyage (IOR E/3/7, f. 116; Purnell, 'Log-Book of William Adams', pp. 249–68, esp. p. 268. The English factory also sent some unsaleable stock (Russian hides, damask and cloth) to Manila but it is unknown how this venture turned out (*Diary*, III, p. 289).
173 IOR E/3/7, ff. 115v 116; *Diary*, III, pp. 272; 286–7.
174 *Diary*, III, pp. 287–8.
175 IOR E/3/7, f. 42v.
176 IOR E/3/7, ff. 42, 115v; *Diary*, III, pp. 279–80, 296.
177 IOR E/3/9, f. 145.
178 *Letters Received*, IV, pp. 129–30; ibid., v; pp. 11–12; *Diary*, II, pp. 22–3, 90, 91; ibid, III, pp. 86, 128.
179 Ibid., p. 291. He did not make it home and died on 19 October 1621 after serving in the first Manila voyage (ibid., pp. 122, 125). He was a man of some means. He left his houses at Blackwell to his daughter and 8d to his wife 'for that she should cleame noe p'te of his goods in respect she marryed & plaid the whore in his absence' (ibid., p. 184).
180 IOR E/3/7, f. 116; *Diary*, III, pp. 271, 274, 283–4. As the storage space was bigger than expected, Cocks also sent a private venture of 10 escritoires. Cocks (ibid., p. 284) says the *Godspeed* cost 430 taels; Eaton gives a figure of 2,008 taels (IOR E/3/7, f. 116). The lower figure seems more likely.
181 *Diary*, III, pp. 271, 273, 283–4.
182 *Diary*, II, p. 98; ibid., III, p. 318.
183 BL Cotton Cart. III.13, f. 43; *Diary*, III, pp. 318–19; Pratt, *History of Japan*, II, pp. 283–5.
184 *Diary*, III, p. 321.
185 Ibid.,
186 IOR E/3/7, f. 277.

CHAPTER 7

1 The following two paragraphs are based mainly on Israel, *Dutch Republic*, pp. 61–85; Israel, 'A Conflict of Empires: Spain and the Netherlands 1618–1648', *Past & Present*, 76, August 1977, pp. 34–40; Geoffrey Parker, *The Dutch Revolt*, Harmondsworth, 1979, pp. 261–5; Geoffrey Parker, *The Thirty Years War*, London, 1984, pp. 43, 57, 62, 83.
2 Quoted in Israel, *Dutch Republic*, p. 72.
3 Parker, *Thirty Years War*, pp. 59–61.
4 Thomas Rymer, *Feodera*, London, third edition, 1741, VII, pt III, pp. 115–17;

Clark, *Colonial Conferences*, pp. 132–3.

5 H. T. Colenbrander, *Jan Pietersz. Coen*, The Hague, 1934, pp. 306–8; Disney, *Twilight of the Pepper Trade*, ch. 4; Niels Steensgaard, 'The Dutch East India Company as an Institutional Innovation', in Maurice Aymard (ed.), *Dutch Capitalism and World Capitalism*, Cambridge, 1982, pp. 247–50; Parker, *Military Revolution*, pp. 106–7; Israel, *Dutch Republic*, p. 119; Chaudhuri, *East India Company*, ch. 3.

6 Chaudhuri, *East India Company*, p. 61

7 *Coen: Bescheiden*, I, p. 543 quoted in Clark, *Colonial Conferences*, p. 135.

8 Clark, *Colonial Conferences*, p. 136; *Coen: Bescheiden*, II, p. 750; Meilink-Roelofsz, *Asian Trade*, pp. 202–3.

9 IOR G/21/3, pt 1, f. 316v.

10 Ibid., f. 313. On their return to Java in 1619 the English had removed their factory to Jacarta (recently conquered by the Dutch and renamed Batavia) because of the continued Dutch blockade of Bantam, the latest Dutch tactic in the VOC's ongoing efforts to induce the pangeran to restore the previous arrangement whereby the Dutch, and the English, had bought pepper at prices fixed by themselves. The English were not out of sympathy with Dutch objectives but they soon came to resent their status and treatment as second class citizens in Batavia. In 1627 they returned to Bantam (Meilink-Roelofsz, *Asian Trade*, pp. 254–6). Generally the English continued to refer to Batavia as Jacarta and the Dutch themselves dated their letters from Fort Jacarta. The English had already established a factory there in 1617; the Dutch had maintained a subfactory there since 1611.

11 IOR G/40/1, p. 79; E/3/10, f. 43v. In defence of its acquiesence in Dutch 'greatnesse' and 'soueraign power', which the directors interpreted as shameful cowardice, the presidency noted that if it were staffed by factors who were a match for the Dutch in negotiations the Company's interests would have been better represented. Difficulties and misunderstanding at Batavia could only have been increased by the fact that the English lacked a Dutch dictionary (ibid., ff. 43, 46v).

12 Meilink-Roelofsz, *Asian Trade*, pp. 203–4; Chaudhuri, *East India Company*, pp. 168–72; John Villiers, 'One of the Especiallest Flowers in Our Garden: The English Factory at Macassar 1613–

1667', unpublished paper read at the XXXI International Congress of Human Sciences in Asia and North Africa, Tokyo, 1983; Om Prakash, 'The Dutch East India Company in the Trade of the Indian Ocean', in Das Gupta and Pearson (eds), *India and the Indian Ocean*, p. 193; Om Prakash, *The Dutch East India Company and the Trade of Bengal 1630–1720*, Princeton, 1985, *passim*.

13 Before their departure from Bantam to Masulipatam the English had pillaged four junks to compensate for debts remaining unpaid by various Chinese in Bantam. The Company gained little from this plunder. The men, with Dale's passive acquiesence, helped themselves to the silk from the baskets which were seized (IOR E/3/7, ff. 82–82v).

14 IOR G/40/1, p. 32; Foster (ed.), *Journal of John Jourdain* p. 1xxiv; Andrews, *Elizabethan Privateering*, pp. 196–7.

15 *Diary*, II, p. 329; Pratt, *History of Japan*, I, p. 412; *Coen: Bescheiden*, II, pp. 703, 718.

16 IOR G/40/1, pp. 32, 62; *Diary*, III, p. 120; Pratt, *History of Japan*, I, pp. 412–13; *Coen: Bescheiden*, II, pp. 702, 703; Boxer, *Fidalgos*, p. 100. The maid, Judith, married a mestizo and was still residing there when Peter Mundy visited Malacca in 1637 (ibid.).

17 Pratt, *History of Japan*, I, pp. 330–6, esp. pp. 335–6; Nachod, *Die Beziehungen*, pp. L–LV; *Coen: Bescheiden*, II, pp. 219–20.

18 Pratt, *History of Japan*, I, pp. 336–8, 340–1; *Coen: Bescheiden*, IV, pp. 11–15, 19–21.

19 Tiele, *De Opkomst*, I, p. 180; *Coen: Bescheiden*, I, p. 294; ibid., IV, p. 16.

20 Pratt, *History of Japan*, I, pp. 342–3; Nachod, *Die Beziehungen*, pp. LV–LXI; *Coen: Bescheiden*, II, pp. 653, 731–5 esp. pp. 731, 733.

21 For a full discussion of the VOC's efforts to attract Chinese junks to Batavia see Leonard Blussé, 'The VOC and the Junk Trade to Batavia: A Problem of Administrative Control', in Blussé, *Strange Company: Chinese Settlers, Mestizo, Women and the Dutch in VOC Batavia*, Dordrecht, 1986, pp. 97–155.

22 Nachod, *Die Beziehungen*, p. 156. For the VOC's short-lived expectation of using Siam to intervene on its behalf to secure trade with China between 1604 and 1611 see Smith, *The Dutch in Seventeenth Century Thailand*, pp. 10–13.

23 IOR E/3/7, ff. 277–77v; G/21/2, pt 1, p. 3. The *Expedition* had been captured by the Dutch but returned to the English although she was serving with the Dutch at the time. Her ballast had been removed to make room for rice which she was to carry to Batavia. The daimyo requested the Dutch and English to remove the wreck from the harbour and in September 1621 Cocks agreed to English participation in the salvage operation but referred the costs to Batavia. An inquiry was held later in London (Pratt, *History of Japan*, I, p. 371; *Dai Nihon shiryō*, 12:43, pp. 95–7; *Diary*, III, pp. 167, 171).

24 Nachod, *Die Beziehungen*, p. 176; *Coen: Bescheiden*, II, pp. 729–30. For his eventual departure see below p. 294.

25 IOR E/3/7, ff. 277–77v; G/21/3, pt 1, f. 193; *Diary*, III, pp. 316, 320.

26 IOR G/21/2, pt 1, p. 4; Pratt, *History of Japan*, I, pp. 346–7.

27 IOR G/21/2, pt 1, p. 14; E/3/7, f. 274v. It was the Dutch reaction rather than the Chinese that the English were concerned about. In 1622 a Dutch tribunal in Batavia ruled that the English should pay 40,000 reals for goods seized by the English from Chinese junks with VOC passes bound for Batavia. The English were also requested to pay a fine of 10,500 reals. The presidency was incensed and protested to London (IOR E/3/9, ff. 107–122, 126–139v; *CSP East Indies . . . 1622–1624*, p. 108).

28 IOR G/21/2, pt 1, pp. 1–3, 22; E/3/7, ff. 274v, 277v, 304; *Diary*, III, pp. 13, 317. These sources give the English version of events. The missionary viewpoint is given in Iacinto Orfanel and Diego Collado, *Historia ecclesiástica de los sucessos de la christianidad de Iapón*, Madrid, 1633, chs 16 and 17; Diego Aduarte, *Historia de la provincia del Santo Rosario de la Orden de Predicadores*, Manila, 1640, translated in Blair and Robertson (eds), *The Philippine Islands*, XXXII, pp. 124–9; Joseph Sicardo, *Christianidad del Japon, y dilatada persecvcion que padeció*, Madrid, 1698. The two Dominicans, Orfanel and Collado, were in Japan at the time of the affair (Orfanel was martyred in the Great Martyrdom of 10 September 1622 [NS], and Collado left for Manila at the end of 1622). Aduarte and Sicardo wrote after the event and the latter improvised freely. For example, he states that Hirayama's junk had a *shuinjō*

which it did not (p. 175). Arnulf Hartman's account of the affair (*The Augustinians in Seventeenth Century Japan*, Marylake, King City, Ontario, 1965, pp. 80–104) follows Sicardo and cannot be relied upon either for accuracy or impartiality.

29 IOR G/21/2, pt 1, pp. 6–7; *Dai Nihon shiryō*, 12:43, p. 87ff gives the Dutch version of the resolutions.

30 IOR E/3/7, f. 315.

31 IOR G/21/2, pt 1, pp. 8–11. The Matsūra had received presents after the arrival of the fleet and again in December before the departure of the *Endracht* for the Moluccas and the *James Royal* for Batavia. On the second occasion Takanobu received almost as much silk as the shogun (ARA KA 11,683, 19 and 31 December; *Diary*, III, pp. 6–7)

32 IOR G/21/2, pt 1, pp. 12–13; E/3/7, f. 277v; *Diary*, III, p. 317.

33 In addition to the lead brought by the English, the Dutch had brought 5,000 peculs, some of which Cocks suspected had been seized from English ships during the recent warfare (IOR G/12/2, pt 1, pp. 12–13; *Diary*, III, pp. 217, 322).

34 IOR E/3/7, f. 315. For Takanobu's advice see *Diary*, III, p. 153. He also advised against the recall of Specx to Batavia.

35 *Diary*, III, pp. 66, 70, 79, 119. The principal Japanese backer of this venture, Itamiya Jiemon (Itamiya Migell Dono), took the trouble to obtain an additional pass protecting the junk from attack by the fleet of defence (ibid., p. 69. See also Iwao, *Shuinsen*, pp. 104, 105).

36 IOR G/40/1, pp. 62, 63; E/3/8, f. 98; G/21/3, pt 1, f. 283v. According to the Batavia presidency in January 1619, many of the Company's ships were badly equipped anyway before their departure from England with 'new ropes' made from 'old stuff', powder barrels far short of their alleged weight. (Lennis noted that many of the planks on the *Elizabeth* were 'rought when the stuff was put into her'.) There was a need for rigging ropes, running blocks, powder and shot, anchors, canvas, pitch and tar and sea roles for the smaller vessels which had been sent out for the country trade. The presidency had passed on the problem of supplying and maintaining the Manila fleet to Hirado (IOR E/3/5, ff. 261–261v; G/21/3, pt 1, f. 283). Similar complaints were still being

made in 1649 (IOR E/3/21, f. 76). The Dutch in Hirado also complained about inadequate ship stores and the unseaworthiness of VOC ships (*Coen: Bescheiden*, VII, p. 505; Mulder, *Hollanders in Hirado*, p. 69).

37 IOR G/40/1, pp. 32, 39, 63; E/3/7, f. 277v; *Diary*, III, pp. 166, 317.

38 IOR E/3/7, ff. 277v–78; *Diary* III, p. 317.

39 IOR E/3/7, ff. 275, 314, 315; G/40/1, p. 72; *Diary*, III, pp. 5–6, 8, 14, 17, 36.

40 IOR E/3/5, f. 253. See also *Letters Received*, II, pp. 183, 184, 194 and Chaudhuri, *East India Company*, pp. 79, 105.

41 IOR G/40/1, pp. 63, 71; E/3/8, ff. 86, 103v.

42 IOR E/3/5, f. 261; E/3/8, f. 86.

43 IOR G/40/1, pp. 62, 63, 81.

44 IOR E/3/5, f. 261; G/21/6, f. 310v, 324; G/40/1, p. 81. Cf. the rations laid down for Weddell's fleet in 1624 (*Letters Received*, V, p. 163 n).

45 BL Egerton MS 2123, ff. 166v–167; IOR E/3/10, f. 50. On the supply of victuals for the Company's outward voyages see Chaudhuri, *East India Company*, pp. 103–4, although the use of lemon juice to prevent scurvey was not yet universal at this time. In the Spanish fleets of the *Armada de la Guardia* meat rations were fixed at 6 oz of pork per man. On European voyages, where the possibilities of obtaining additional supplies were greater the allowance was 8 oz (Carla Rahn Phillips, *Six Galleons for the King of Spain*, Baltimore, 1986, pp. 167, 169). Her reconstruction of the nutritional value of the shipboard diet (pp. 167–73) is exemplary but represents the optimum value. It cannot be assumed that the men consistently received their official rations. The same reservation applies to the amounts given in Steensgaard, 'Freight Costs', pp. 149–50. The Dutch factors at Hirado did not share the English presidency's rosy opinion about VOC food supplies and complained about poor victualling and inadequate drink onships coming to Japan (*Coen: Bescheiden*, VII, p. 515; Mulder, *Hollanders in irado*, p. 72).

46 IOR E/3/7, ff 274v–75.

47 *Diary*, III, pp. 161, 164.

48 Ibid., p. 208.

49 Ibid., pp. 18, 19, 48.

50 Ibid., pp. 320–21.

51 Ibid., p. 136.

52 IOR E/3/7, f. 315; G/21/2, pt 1, p. 18; *Diary*, III, pp. 16–17, 22, 23.

53 IOR E/3/8, f. 98; G/21/3, pt 1, ff. 278, 279; Murakami (ed.), *Diary of Richard Cocks*, II, pp. 324–5, 326; *Coen: Bescheiden*, I, pp. 681–2; ibid., VII p. 784. According to a Spanish report, Adams ordered one Chinese junk to be fired, goods and all, because of quarrels over the division of the cargo (Blair and Robertson [eds], *Philippine Islands*, XX, p. 33.

54 For accounts of the voyage see IOR G/21/2, pt 1, pp. 23–35; L/MAR/C/4, ff. 54–60v.

55 Blair and Robertson (eds), *Philippine Islands*, XIX, pp. 117, 164; ibid., XX, pp. 27, 30, 32–3, 46–8, which from internal evidence was written in late 1621 not in July; *Coen: Bescheiden*, VII, p. 790. It was only later that Manila became as solidly fortified as Malacca or Batavia (Parker, *Military Revolution*, p. 122 and n.)

56 *Diary*, III, p. 138; Blair and Robertson (eds), *Philippine Islands*, XX, pp. 20, 33–4; *Coen: Bescheiden*, I, p. 682; ibid., VII, pp. 785, 789, 790. Souza (*Survival of Empire*, pp. 67, 75, 82, 84) provides figures for Chinese and Portuguese shipping arrivals in Manila but data are not available for this year.

57 *Diary*, III, pp. 64–5, 199.

58 *Diary*, III, pp. 3–191 *passim*.

59 *Diary*, III, pp. 30, 41, 59, 67, 69, 71.

60 IOR E/3/5, f 325v, E/3/7, ff. 116, 278, 319; *Diary*, III, p. 323.

61 IOR E/3/8, f. 102; *Diary*, III, pp. 73, 76. Sales worth 731 taels 5 mas 2 candereen were possibly made to Hiranoya as a result of the party (ibid., p. 142).

62 IOR G/21/2, pt 1, pp. 15–18; ARA KA 11,683, 25 September 1620.

63 IOR E/3/7, ff. 278, 319; *Diary*, III, pp. 6, 11, 19, 20, 223, 48, 49, 61, 105, 141, 142, 146–7, 149. Cocks was not exaggerating unduly about the cost of the lead. The lead sent on the *Hosiander* had been rated at 4 taels 8 mas per pecul, the bar lead sent on the *Thomas* in 1616 at 3 taels 6 mas 1 candereen per pecul, and the sheet at 4 taels 8 mas 1 candereen and that on the *Thomas* at 4–5 taels 3 mas (BL Cotton Vespasian MS FXVII, ff. 63v, 81v, 84).

64 IOR G/21/3 pt 1, f. 193. The figures, given by Eaton in February 1622, do not tally; 2 peculs 21 catties are unaccounted for. In addition Eaton reported that a notional 120 peculs were given as presents to Takanobu and

others (i.e. the cash value instead of the goods themselves).

65 *Coen: Bescheiden*, I, p. 682; ibid., VII, p. 789; Boxer, *Great Ship*, p. 100; Souza, *Survival of Empire*, p. 56. There are no complete figures for Portuguese raw silk imports. For an estimate of raw silk imports 1600–1639 see Katō, 'Japanese–Dutch Trade', p. 66 and sources cited, and p. 48. However, this table excludes English imports even if these do not greatly alter the picture. Cf. Innes, 'The Door Ajar', p. 264. Cocks's report of unfounded rumours that the *itowappu* was to be applied to silk piece goods as well as yarn adds additional support to Dr Innes's argument that the Portuguese were switching more to piece goods as a way of circumventing the *itowappu* (*Diary*, III, p. 147; Innes, 'The Door Ajar', pp. 264–7). In 1636 and 1637 Portuguese yarn imports topped 1,500 peculs although this was far surpassed in volume and value by piece goods (Katō, 'Japanese–Dutch Trade', p. 66; Innes, 'The Door Ajar', p. 264).

66 *Diary*, III, p. 137, Cocks omitted this information in his letter to the Company recounting what had happened, preferring instead to blame the Japanese for breach of contract for which 'the Japon Lawes will not take hould on them' (IOR E/3/8, f. 101).

67 Cocks had expected to sell the best Nanking silk at 310 taels, well up on the previous year's price of around 130 taels. However, his suggestion that prices of 400 and 500 taels had been the norm is an exaggeration, perhaps fostered by a belief that if he drew attention to goods that sold well in Japan and fetched high profits but with which the factory had been poorly supplied he could deflect criticism from other aspects of the management of the factory (*Diary*, III, pp. 137, 322). In 1614 prices for Nanking silk were reported at 230 taels per pecul; in 1615, 165–230 taels; in 1616, 250–312 taels; in 1619, 300 taels; and in 1620, 230 taels (IOR G/12/15, ff. 38v, 41; ARA KA 11,722; *Letters Received*, II, p. 203; ibid., III, p. 263; *Diary*, III, p. 286). In the mid 1620s silk prices exceeded 300 taels per pecul and between 1628 and 1632 fluctuated between 550 and 600 taels. This was unusual and in 1636 the Dutch were selling raw silk for 267 taels per pecul (Stapel [ed.], *Beschryvinge*, 2:1, pp. 414,

415, 416; Katō, 'Japanese-Dutch Trade', p. 76 ff. See also Innes, 'The Door Ajar', p. 262).

68 Andrews, *Elizabethan Privateering*, pp. 42–4.

69 IOR E/3/8, ff. 102v–103.

70 IOR G/21/3, pt 1, ff. 189v, 191, 193v, 194v; E/3/8 ff. 121–121v; *Diary*, III, pp. 124, 127, 136, 139, 180, 184.

71 IOR G/21/3, pt 1, f. 194.

72 *Coen: Bescheiden*, I, p. 681; ibid., VII, pp. 789, 793; *Diary*, III, pp. 189–90.

73 IOR G/21/3, pt 1, f. 193v.

74 IOR E/3/8, f. 86.

75 IOR E/3/10, f. 50.

76 *Dairy*, III, pp. 21, 180. It is possible that the pepper in question was for the factory's account.

77 IOR E/3/8, f. 162

78 *Diary*, III, pp. 171, 173–4, 177

79 IOR G/21/3, pt 1, f. 191v.

80 *Diary*, III, pp. 155, 159.

81 *Coen: Bescheiden*, VII, pp. 792, 797–8

82 IOR E/3/8, ff. 102–102v; Murakami (ed.), *Diary of Richard Cocks*, II, p. 328. Generally, however, the English and Dutch shared the same grievances over breaches of the trade privileges (*Coen: Bescheiden*, VII, pp. 792, 797–8; *Diary*, III, p. 131

83 Ibid., pp. 119, 122.

84 Ibid., p. 200.

85 *Diary*, II, pp. 328–9.

86 IOR G/21/3, pt 1, ff. 191v–192; *Diary*, III, pp. 188, 191, 197, 200, 203–4. Eaton's version of these events says only two men were detained, probably a copyist's error for twelve (IOR G/21/3, pt 1, f. 194v).

87 IOR G/21/3, pt 1, ff. 194v–195, 196; *Diary*, III, pp. 206, 228, 229, 237, 238, 256. Cocks claimed that Hasegawa and the daimyo of Hirado supported the demands for the return of the men. This is unlikely; neither men would have involved themselves with such a trivial matter which contravened no Japanese law. Eaton believed the affair soured relations with the Japanese but this is an overstatement.

88 IOR G/21/3, pt 1, ff. 284v–285 (Cocks wrongly inferred that Joosten had been murdered); *Diary*, III, pp. 323, 380; Iwao, 'Jan Joosten', pp. 10–11, 20–2. Cocks was too disparaging in his judgement of Joosten whom he called 'a foule mouthed fellow'. In 1617 the Dutch admiral, Lam, had reported favourably to Batavia about Joosten's work on behalf of the VOC at Hirado. He especial-

ly appreciated Joosten's contacts with influential Japanese (Tiele, *De Opkomst*, I, p. 182). Coen was also impressed by him, recommending him to invest in Chinese silk and silk fabrics rather than camphor if he intended to return home and the governor general offered him a passage back to Europe (*Coen: Bescheiden*, III, p. 197).

89 BL Codex 62–6–18 (91), printed in J. S. Cummins and C. R. Boxer, 'The Dominicam Mission in Japan (1602–1622) and Lope de Vega', *Arcivum Fratrum Praedicatorum*, XXXIII, 1963, pp. 78–91, esp. pp. 78–9 reprinted in J. S. Cummins, *Jesuit and Friar in the Spanish Expansion to the East*, London, 1986; *Diary*, III, pp. 168–9, 179; Boxer, *Great Ship*, p. 104. See also Sicardo, *Christianidad del Japon*, p. 210; Hartman, *Augustinians in Japon*, p. 83.

90 IOR G/21/3, pt 1, ff. 189v, 191v, 195; E/3/8, ff. 110, 122–23; *Diary*, III. pp. 172, 173, 174, 178, 179. There were other cases of attempted desertion (ibid., p. 131).

91 IOR G/21/3, pt 1, f. 195v; *Diary*, III, pp. 125–6, 134, 138.

92 IOR E/3/10, f. 49; E/3/91, ff. 24, 57; G/40/1, p. 31. The Royal Commission (IOR A/1/8) dated 4 February 1623 is, alas, largely illegible.

93 IOR E/3/8, ff. 100, 104; *Coen: Bescheiden*, VII, p. 798. There was a dispute about the valuation of the ships. The Dutch claimed that the *Peppercorn* was an old ship and should be rated less than the *Moyen* even although it was the larger of the two. The rates were fixed at £2,002 for the *Pepppercorn* and *f.* 25,368 for the *Moyen* (ibid., pp. 785–6). The English refused to accept these figures and referred the matter to Batavia (IOR E/3/8, f. 103v).

94 *Diary*, III, pp. 139–40, 141–2.

95 IOR E/3/8, f. 81; *Coen: Bescheiden*, VII, pp. 791, 803; *Diary*, III, p. 159.

96 *Coen: Bescheiden*, III, p. 58.

97 François Valentyn, *Oud en Nieuw Oost-Indien, Vervattende een Naaukeeurige en Uitvoerige Verhandelinge van Nederlands Mogentheyd In die Gewesten*, 5 vols in 8 books, 1724–6, Dordrecht vol. 5, pt 2, book 9, pp. 28–32; Nachod, *Die Beziehungen*, pp. 175–6, LXII; *Coen: Bescheiden*, VII, pp. 785, 801; Iwao Seiichi, *Shuinsen to Nihonmachi*, Tokyo, 1962, pp. 146–7. Cocks had already received an inkling that arms exports were unwelcome to the bakufu in 1617.

The regulations against arms exports, were tightened in 1634 (*Diary*, II, p. 186; Toby, *State and Diplomacy*, p. 123).

98 IOR G/21/3, pt 1, ff. 192, 328; E/3/8, f. 101; *Coen: Bescheiden*, I, pp. 682–3, 738; *Diary*, II, p. 326; ibid., III, p. 160. The Portuguese also had their galliots searched and one was found to be concealing weapons for export (ibid., p. 183). On a more personal note Osterwick asked the president at Batavia to take his servant Samuel into the Company's service, for if the servant were to return to Hirado he would not be able to leave again. Presumably Samuel was in Batavia at this time (IOR G/21/3, pt 1, f. 192).

99 Blair and Robertson [eds], *The Philippine Islands*, XXII, p. 127.

100 BL Egerton MS 2086, f. 63; IOR E/3/9, f. 95; Sicardo, *Christianidad del Japon*, pp. 175–6, 181; Blair and Robertson [eds], *The Philippine Islands*, XXXII, p. 126 ff.

101 *Diary*, III, p. 158.

102 Murakami (ed.), *Diary of Richard Cocks*, II, p. 330.

103 *Diary*, III, pp. 153, 158, 162.

104 Murakami (ed.), *Diary of Richard Cocks*, II, p. 330; *Diary*, III, pp. 162, 177; *Coen: Bescheiden*, VII, p. 784

105 Nachod, *Die Beziehungen*, pp. 176, 178–9 (p. 179 should read De Carpentier as governor general); *Diary*, III, pp. 159–60, 163; Mulder, *Hollanders in Hirado*, p. 59; Katō, 'Unification and Adaptation', pp. 218–19.

106 Ibid., pp. 158, 163.

107 *Diary*, III, p. 205.

108 Murakami (ed.), *Diary of Richard Cocks*, II, p. 325.

109 *Coen: Bescheiden*, VIII, p. 1236.

110 Sicardo, *Christianidad del Japon*, p. 181.

111 *Diary*, III, pp. 193–202

112 IOR E/3/8, f. 101; Murakami (ed.), *Diary of Richard Cocks*, II, p. 325. This was an exaggeration. Other goods were sold in Hirado besides the lead. See *Diary*, III, pp. 150, 157, 186

113 Sicardo, *Christianidad del Japon*, p. 182.

114 IOR G/21/3, pt 1, f. 189.

115 Ibid., f. 193v. See also f. 281.

116 *Diary*, III, p. 200.

117 IOR G/21/3, pt 1, f. 281v. He stated, wrongly, that 'in all neare vpon 100 psons even to Little Children' died.

118 IOR E/3/9, f. 95v; Murakami (ed.), *Diary of Richard Cocks*, II, p. 335.

119 IOR G/21/3, pt 1, ff. 189, 193–193v (Eaton's figures do not tally); *Diary*, III,

pp. 130, 186, 209, 210.

120 IOR G/21/3, pt 1, f. 140, 284v; E/3/9, f. 148.

121 Diary, III, p. 251.

122 IOR E/3/9, f. 95v; Murakami (ed.), Diary of Richard Cocks, II, p. 335.

123 IOR G/21/3, pt 1, f. 283v; Coen: Bescheiden, I, p. 636; ibid., II, pp. 373, 654, 727; ibid., III, p. 164.

124 IOR G/21/3, pt 1, ff. 141v, 194–194v, 195; E/3/8, f. 103v. Eaton gives two sets of figures for the costs but the above is the one from the accounts sent to Batavia. As an indication of how prices could rise when the fleet was in, Cocks records that pitch usually cost 2 taels per pecul but could rise to 7–8 taels when the ships were in port, while Eaton was able to secure a 5 per cent discount on hemp while the fleet was away. The cost of spinning the hemp (12 mas per pecul) and making it into ropes (6 1/2 mas per pecul) was extra (IOR G/21/3, pt 1, f. 194; E/3/8, f. 100v; Folger Library, Washington, D.C., MS X.d.272. The latter is a fragment of Osterwick's accounts. I am grateful to Professor Iwao for drawing this MS to my attention and to Mr A. J. Farrington for supplying me with the precise reference. It confirms the prices recorded by Cocks and Eaton).

125 IOR E/3/8 f. 100v; G/21/3, pt 1, ff. 189–190v; E/3/8, f. 103v; Diary, III, pp. 183, 203.

126 IOR L/MAR/A/XXXV, f. 3ff; E/3/8, f. 103; Pratt, History of Japan, I, p. 443ff.

127 W. P. Groenveldt, De Nederlanders in China, The Hague, 1898, pp. 312–26

128 CSP Colonial, East Indies...1622–1624, p. 25. English protests to Coen about their exclusion from the mission were brushed aside. The Dutch argued that the English had excluded themselves because they had no ships, men, victuals or surgeons available to add to the fleet (Coen: Bescheiden).

129 Groenveldt, De Nederlanders in China, p. 322; Boxer, Fidalgos, p. 72 ff.; Leonard Blussé, 'The Dutch Occupation of the Pescadores (1622–1624)', Transactions of the International Conference of Orientalists in Japan, XVIII, 1973, pp. 32–3.

130 IOR E/3/8, ff. 101v–102; Murakami (ed.), Diary of Richard Cocks, II. p. 327.

131 Iwao, Shuinsen, p. 127; Souza, Survival of Empire, pp. 194–5.

132 Frederich W. Mote and Dennis Twichett (eds), Cambridge History of China, vol. 7, The Ming Dynasty, 1368–1644, pt. 1, Cambridge, 1988, p. 561 n. 25; Gernet, China and the Christian Impact, p. 132; Wills, Embassies & Illusions, p. 70.

133 See Gernet, China and the Christian Impact, passim, and the brief, but perceptive, comments in Cambridge History of China, 7:1, pp. 562–3.

134 Souza, Survival of Empire, pp. 197–8 for the relationship between the Chinese and Portuguese in Canton and Macao.

135 Ibid., p. 196.

136 IOR G/21/3, pt 1, ff. 278v, 283v.

137 Ibid, ff. 283v, 326v; Boxer, Fidalgos in the Far East, pp. 79–83.

138 IOR G/21/3, pt 1, ff. 326v–327.

139 IOR E/3/9, f. 96.

140 Blussé, 'Dutch Occupation of the Pescadores', pp. 36–41.

141 Quoted in Boxer, Fidalgos in the Far East, p. 91. The comment was made by Cornelis van Neyenroode, the Dutch factor at Hirado writing in November 1623, and making the astute parallel with how Hideyoshi's seaborne invasion of Korea had become bogged down on the continent. The Ming authorities saw events in almost the same terms (Wills, Pepper, Guns & Parleys, p. 1).

142 The following is based on Iwao, 'Li Tan', pp. 50–63.

143 Quoted in ibid., pp. 52–3. Camps was writing just before the English closed the Hirado factory.

144 In its heyday, in the late 1640s and early 1650s, Zeelandia had a population of 20,000 Chinese and 1,800 Dutch, most of whom were soldiers. See J. L. Osterhoff, 'Zeelandia, a Dutch Colonial City on Formosa (1624–1662)', in Robert J. Ross and Gerhard J. Telkamp (eds), Colonial Cities, Dordrecht, 1985, p. 55.

145 Quoted in Boxer, Fidalgos in the Far East, p. 92.

146 Blussé, 'Dutch Occupation of the Pescadores', p. 43; Katō, 'Japanese–Dutch Trade', p. 49.

147 IOR E/3/9, f. 94v, G/21/3, pt 1, f. 287.

148 Ibid., ff. 278, 281v, 283v–84.

149 Ibid., ff. 279–79v, 282v; E/3/9, f. 96.

150 Coen: Bescheiden, VII, p. 1038. Camps was restating the views of his superiors. In February 1620 Coen had ordered Specx to send as much raw silk as he could to Batavia for dispatch to the Netherlands. He stressed that better

151 IOR G/21/3, pt 1, ff. 279v–280, 282.

152 Ibid., ff. 279v, 282, 285; E/3/9, f. 95v. Cockram, Osterwick and Cocks called the white silk 'Canton' silk and occasionally Tongking but there is no doubt that the silk off-loaded in Hirado was the top grade silk usually called 'Nanking' silk. In the light of these figures the imports of silk into Japan in 1622 given in Katō, 'Japanese–Dutch Trade', p. 66, is an underestimate.

153 IOR G/21/3, pt 1, ff. 141v, 325v, 326v, 329; E/3/9, ff. 96v, 140, 142. Not all the goods were sold. Some, mostly taffetas, were kept for use as presents (G/21/3, pt 1, f. 285v).

154 IOR G/21/3, pt 1, f. 143.

155 Ibid., ff. 135, 138–38v, 140, 141, 142v, 281v, 282, 326v; E/3/9, ff. 157, 189; Pratt, History of Japan, I, pp. 458–60, esp. p. 459. I have subtracted the cost of exchange (19 per cent for soma, 14 per cent for seda) plus the cost of packing. This amounted to 4,295 taels 9 mas 4 candereen. There are the usual discrepancies in the figures. Batavia reported to London that it had received 156,000 reals from Hirado, which accords with the value of the bullion in reals set in Japan. The directors assumed this was a cash injection. To complicate matters the conversion rate of the real had been set at 4s in Japan which almost tallies with the total invoice value of the bullion at 124,804 taels 4 mas 3 candereen or £31,201 1s 2d. The Company set the real at 5s which raises the sterling rate of 156,000 reals to £39,000. No wonder the directors imagined the voyage had been more profitable than it had been (IOR E/3/9, f. 189; BL Egerton MS 2123, f. 165v. The latter is a fragment of a letter sent from the Court to Batavia. When Pratt examined the document it was still in the Company's archive. Internal evidence makes it clear that the letter was written in the spring of 1623, not the autumn. Cf. Pratt, History of Japan, I, p. 459).

156 IOR G/21/3, pt 1, ff. 135, 138, 140v.

157 Ibid., ff. 141, 282v–283, 285v; E/3/9, ff. 96v, 157; Diary, III, pp. 246–7. At the end of November 1622 Camps wrote to Batavia requesting that broadcloth be sent to Hirado (ARA KA 990, f. 25).

158 IOR G/21/3, pt 1, ff. 326v, 329; CSP Colonial, East Indies...1622–1624, p. 110.

159 IOR E/3/10, f. 52v, G/21/3, pt 2, p. 80.

160 IOR G/21/3, pt 2, p. 129.

161 Murakami (ed.), Diary of Richard Cocks, II, p. 358.

162 Prakash, The Dutch East India Company and the Economy of Bengal, p. 124; Reid, Southeast Asia in the Age of Commerce, I, p. 99. The Spanish also had their problems with assaying silver in their Peruvian mines and had to ensure that strict standards were set and maintained to prevent fraud and waste (Goodman, Power and Penury: Government, Technology and Science in Philip II's Spain, p. 194).

163 IOR E/3/10, f. 49v; IOR Home Misc. 29, p. 1. The latter is a series of extracts from the Court Books listing the 'errors and misdemeanours' of the Company's servants kept by an order of the Court of 8 December 1626 and beginning in September 1624. It was known as the 'Black Book'.

164 IOR G/21/3, pt 1, f. 281v; E/3/8, f. 162.

165 IOR G/21/3, pt 1, ff. 140, 142v, 280, 280v, 282v, 284, 286.

166 CSP Colonial, East Indies...1617–1621, pp. 384, 386; Foster (ed.), Journal of John Jourdain, pp. ixx-ixxi.

167 IOR G/40/1, p. 31.

168 Ibid., pp. 39, 78; E/3/8, f. 162v; CSP Colonial, East Indies...1617–1621, p. 495. Similar comments were made from Bantam in 1649 (IOR E/3/21, f. 73v).

169 IOR G/40/1, pp. 39, 78.

170 IOR G/40/1, p. 65; E/3/8, f. 162v

171 IOR E/3/9, f. 79

172 Ibid., IOR G/21/3, pt 1, f. 325v.

173 Ibid., f. 280.

174 Ibid., f. 282v.

175 Ibid., f. 196.

176 Ibid., f. 192–92v.

177 Ibid., ff. 286v–287. Cocks had already written to the presidency in January 1621 saying that the English had been granted trade in China on the Fukien Coast for two ships annually. He promised that 'the passport' would be sent with the next available ship. It never was; it had never been granted (IOR G/40/1 p. 72).

178 IOR E/3/5, f. 260v.

179 IOR G/21/3, pt 1, ff. 143–143v.

180 *Coen: Bescheiden*, VII, pp. 1038–9. Camps added that the English had delayed their departure because of bad management of their affairs and an inability to balance the accounts (ibid., p. 1039).

181 IOR G/21/3, pt 2, pp. 27, 60; *CSP Colonial, East Indies...1622–1624*, pp. 110–11.

182 IOR G/21/3, pt 2, p. 61.

183 Ibid., pp. 75, 85–7, 90, 92, 103, 104, 112–13.

184 IOR E/3/9, f. 189; *CSP Colonial, East Indies...1622–1624*, p. 110.

185 IOR G/21/3 pt 2, pp. 77, 83–4.

186 IOR G/21/3, pt 1, f. 282v; Pratt, *History of Japan*, I, pp. 468–9; Murakami (ed.), *Diary of Richard Cocks*, II, p. 358. At this time Coen was indeed more interested in exporting camphor from Japan than copper (ARA VOC 1068, f. 397; *Coen: Bescheiden*, II, pp. 727, 748). It soon became apparent that camphor was not much in demand in Amsterdam, hence Coen's advice to Joosten (ibid., III, p. 197).

187 Murakami (ed.), *Diary of Richard Cocks*, II, pp. 355–60.

188 D. K. Bassett, 'The Trade of the English East India Company in the Far East, 1623–84' *Journal of the Royal Asiatic Society*, 1–4, 1960, pp. 34–5.

189 Chaudhuri, *East India Company*, pp. 61–3.

190 BL Egerton Ms 2123, f. 165v. Professor Chaudhuri's figures (*East India Company*, p. 115) need revision in the light of these amounts, which suggest that 1623 was the best year for bullion exports from England since the foundation of the Company.

191 BL Egerton MS 2123, f. 165v.

192 IOR Home Misc. 39, ff. 66–66v. This is a précis of the report which was written by 'Mr Barloe' who had served for eleven years in the Indies. The year of composition, 1622, is tentative. How seriously the directors read the report is impossible to know but their experience with Japanese silver so far belied such a vision.

193 BL Egerton MS 2123, ff. 156v, 157v. There had clearly been a change in attitude regarding Japan from the spring of 1622 when the directors had decided in principle to close 'vnprofitable ffactories at Japan and the like' (IOR B/7, p. 376).

194 Conrad Russell, *Parliaments and English Politics 1621–1629*, Oxford, 1979, pp. 88–9. The embargo started in April 1621 and soon began to bite. See Israel, 'Conflict of Empires', pp. 41–2.

195 The treaty, in Dutch, is found among the Dutch delegation's reports on the negotiations (BL Add. MS 22,866, ff. 467–87v). See also Add MS 22,865, f. 70; *CSP Colonial, East Indies...1622–1624*, pp. 105–7; S. R. Gardiner, *A History of England 1603–1642*, 10 vols, London, 1893, IV, p. 407. Ironically, one of the members of the Dutch negotiating team was Hendrick Brouwer (J. L. Blussé et al. [eds], *De Dagregisters van het Kasteel Zeelandia, Taiwan, 1629–1662*, I, *1629–1641*, The Hague, 1986, p. 259 n. 27). As has been mentioned, the hopes about restitution were in vain. The Dutch haggled over such detail as how much the English should pay for freightage for the pepper the VOC had seized from the English and brought back to Europe (Steensgaard, 'Freight Costs', pp. 143–4). For the English government's foreign policy considerations see Russell, *Parliaments and English Politics*, pp. 130, 145–6. It should be emphasised that the above interpretation is my own and not Professor Russell's.

196 BL Egerton MS 2123, ff. 161–165; IOR E/3/10, f. 43; Gardiner, *A History of England*, IV, p. 408.

197 It could not have been intended for London. As has been mentioned, the Company traded in Persian silk at this time but the silk market was unpredictable and silk imports were opposed by some adventures (Chaudhuri, *East India Company*, pp. 204–206).

198 IOR E/3/10, f. 37.

199 IOR E/3/10, ff. 43, 44v–45; *CSP Colonial, East Indies...1622–1624*, p. 199. Another recommendation in the Court's letter was that the presidency should attempt trade at Tanjore where the Danish East India Company was active. This was acted on but nothing was achieved (BL Egerton MS 2123, f. 165; *CSP Colonial, East Indies...1622–1624*, pp. 205–6; Foster, *England's Quest of Eastern Trade*, pp. 320–1).

200 IOR E/3/10, ff. 7v, 9, 41; Murakami (ed.), *Diary of Richard Cocks*, II, pp. 362–5.

201 IOR E/3/10, ff. 9–9v, 10v; Murakami (ed.), *Diary of Richard Cocks*, II, pp. 265–6; Pratt, *History of Japan*, I, pp.

474–5.

202 IOR E/3/10, f. 10v; Pratt, *History of Japan*, I, p. 475. This was the *shuinjō* issued in 1616, curtailing the factory's privileges.

203 Tōkyō Daigaku Shiryō Hensan-jo (ed.), *Nihon kankei kaigai shiryō: Igirisu shōkancho nikki, yakubun hen*, III, appendix, pp. 166–9.

204 IOR E/3/10, ff. 11–11v; Pratt, *History of Japan*, I, pp. 475–8.

205 IOR E/3/10, ff. 8, 12; Pratt, *History of Japan*, I, pp. 479–80; *Diary*, III, p. 326.

206 The daimyo had repaid the loan exacted after the first Manila voyage in 1622 and after the second had demanded another loan of 4,000 taels which was advanced in cash this time from the proceeds of the sale of silk (IOR G/21/6, f. 140; E/3/9, f. 148). Most of this had been repaid by December 1623.

207 Tōkyō Daigaku Shiryō Hensan-jo (ed.), *Igirisu shōkancho nikki, yakubun hen*, III, appendix, pp. 170–1.

208 IOR E/3/10, f. 12; Murakami (ed.), *Diary of Richard Cocks*, II, pp. 367–71; Pratt, *History of Japan*, I, p. 481.

209 See above, p. 302.

210 KA 992, ff. 386–7.

211 Tōkyō Daigaku Shiryō Hensan-jo, (ed.), *Dagregister...Japan*, I, p. 177.

212 IOR E/3/10, ff. 98–98v; KA 995, ff. 257–60.

213 *Diary*, III, p. 327.

214 In the absence of full accounts it would be hazardous to attempt a guess as to how much the Company had lost in Hirado. The figures produced by Riess in the nineteenth century are wrong. For example, the figure he cites for disbursements in 1617 included not just the money and goods sent on the *Thomas* and the *Advice* (which according to Osterwick's accounts were less than the value of the goods imported) but some of the factory's expenses such as overhauling the *Sea Adventure*. The figure (which should be in taels anyway) does not represent a cash injection for Bantam let alone profit. The figure which he cites as the estimated loss for the factory stems from a misreading of the figure '40^c pounds' as £40,000 instead of £4,000 mentioned when the Court was dealing with John Cocks over his brother's will (BL Cotton Vespasian MS FXVII, ff. 83, 85v, 110; Riess, 'History of the English Factory at Hirado', pp. 112–13). The extract cited by Pratt

from a document no longer extant (*History of Japan*, I, p. 485), which gives a gain of 14,960 (undenominated) for the four years 1620–4, is puzzling. The figures for expenses cited from the same fragment (presents, factory, building and extraordinary charges) appear to be of the right magnitude whether in taels or reals, but the extract omits the Manila voyages. It is unlikely that the gain, whatever it constituted, came from sales in Japan.

215 Tōkyō Daigaku Shiryō Hensan-jo (ed.), *Igirisu shokancho nikki, yakubun hen*, III, appendix, pp. 173–3.

216 Ibid., pp. 178–9. Maria and her daughter, Joan, left Japan in 1639. See above, p. 234.

217 Tōkyō Daigaku Shiryō Hensan-jo (ed.), *Igirisu shokancho nikki, yakubun hen*, III, appendix, pp. 174–6.

218 PRO SP16/4/74, f. 38; SO/3/12, f. 18; C/66/2825 no 35; W. A. Shaw (ed.), 'Letters of Denization and Acts of Naturalization for Aliens in England and Ireland 1603–1700', *Publications of the Huguenot Society of London*, XVIII, 1911, p. 60. Unfortunately, there is no other information about young William and he is not entered in the College records (Trinity College, personal communication). The next Japanese to attend Cambridge did not arrive until 1873, at St Johns (H. J. Edwards, 'Japanese Undergraduates at Cambridge University', *Proceedings of the Japan Society*, London, VII, 1907, pp. 46–58). Some other half-Japanese with Dutch fathers also excelled themselves. See, for example, Iwao Seiichi, 'The Life of Pieter Hartsinck, the Japanner (1637–1680), "Grand Pupil" of Descartes', *Transactions of the Asiatic Society of Japan*, third series, XX, 1985, pp. 145–67.

219 IOR G/21/3, pt 2, p. 13.

220 It is important to stress that the inquest was about the factory's recent business affairs. A full inquiry into its whole operations was never conducted.

221 IOR E/3/10, ff. 98–98v.

222 Ibid., f. 98v.

223 Ibid.

224 IOR G/21/3, pt 2, pp. 51, 52.

225 IOR E/3/10, f. 98v.

226 IOR L/MAR/A/XXXV, f. 15. The exact date is unclear (the MS is now damaged), but it was certainly between 27 and 31 March. I am grateful to Mr John D. Haywood for drawing this to my

attention.

227 *CSP Colonial, East Indies...1625–1629*, p. 300. It is tempting to speculate that it was through this connection that the MSS relating to the Hirado factory in the Cotton Library came into Sir Robert's possession.

228 IOR B/11, 202 p. 228; *CSP Colonial, East Indies...1625–1629*, pp. 114–15, 168, 266. It is possible that Eaton married after his return. A marriage licence was granted to a William Eaton, described as 'marchant and a bachelor aged 38 yeares', to marry Mary Philippes (Guildhall Library, London, London Marriage Licences, MS 10091/11, f. 99v). The age seems right. It is not known whether Eaton saw his son or took any part in his education. One suspects not.

229 IOR B/11 p. 203; Massarella, 'James I and Japan', p. 385.

230 *CSP Colonial East Indies...1625–1629*, pp. 359, 531, 571, 599, 620, 656, 666; ibid. *1630–1634*, p. 32.

231 Ibid., *1625–1629*, pp. 261, 330; ibid. *1630–1634*, p. 337. Although profits from the import of calicoes were high the Company was sensitive to demand and was concerned that too high a level of imports might weaken demand (Chaudhuri, *East India Company*, pp. 194–5).

232 *CSP Colonial East Indies...1625–1629*, pp. 265–6, 278, 300, 309.

233 E. B. Sainsbury (ed.), *A Calendar of the Court Minutes of the East India Company 1635–1679*, II vols, Oxford, 1907–38 [hereafter CCM], *1640–1643*, pp. 68, 70, 162, 172, 177, 189–90, 219, 223, 247, 252, 254, 304, 305, 359, 361, 371; ibid, *1644–1649*, p. 18; William Foster (ed.), *The English Factories in India, 1624–1629*, London, 1906–1912, pp. 6, 41, 99, 147, 149, 283; ibid., *1640–1633*, pp. 202, 203, 242–3; ibid., *1634–1636*, pp. 326, 329; ibid., *1637–1641*, pp. 56, 294; ibid., *1646–1650*, pp. 166, 174–5; Chaudhuri, *East India Company*, pp. 72–3. Clarke, who had acquired a Portuguese mestizo wife was finally dismissed the Company's service in March 1644 for feeding the Courteen Association with information about the Company's activities and quickly found employment with the rival body (Foster, *English Factories in India, 1637–1641*, p. xxxv). Hudson found his way into the Company's 'Black Book', joining his erstwhile colleagues Cocks, Sayers and

Cockram (IOR Home Misc. 29, pp. 4, 5, 6, 53, 55, 56, 58).

CHAPTER 8

1 *Letters Received*, VI, p. 13.

2 C. R. Steele, 'From Hakluyt to Purchas', in Quinn (ed.), *Hakluyt Handbook*, I, p. 76; Lach, *Asia in the Making of Europe*, 2:2, p. 69.

3 PRO SP 14/96, f. 159.

4 PRO SP 14/111, f. 201.

5 For an edition of the letter see Massarella, 'James I and Japan', pp. 377–86.

6 London, 1622.

7 IOR B/7, pp. 348–9.

8 Ibid., p. 348.

9 Lach, *Asia in the Making of Europe*, 1:1, p. 214; Steele, 'From Hakluyt to Purchas', pp. 80–1; G. R. Crone and R. A. Skelton, 'English Collections of Voyages and Travel Writings 1625–1846', in R. Lyman (ed.), *Richard Hakluyt and His Successors*, London, 1946, p. 67. A concern to maintain business secrets is evident at least from 1615 (IOR B/5, p. 468).

10 For Purchas's debt to Hakluyt see Steele, 'From Hakluyt to Purchas', pp. 74–96.

11 Edward Brerewood, *Enquiries touching the diversity of languages, and religions through the chief parts of the world*, London, 1614 (chapter 10 includes a brief mention of the missionary activity in Japan, a fairly accurate estimate of the number of Christians and was reprinted by Purchas); anon., *A briefe relation of the persecution lately made against the Catholike Christians in the kingdome of Japonia*, [St Omer], 1619; anon., *The Theater of Iaponians Constancy in which an hundred & eighteen glorios martyrs suffered death...*, [St Omer], 1624. The two last publications would not have enjoyed much circulation in England. Ironically the martyrs referred to were those who perished in the Great Martyrdom of August 1622 and included Zuñiga and Flores.

12 *Virginia's God be Thanked*, pp. 6–7, 12, 30. Whatever his standing with the Virginia Company, Copland had his detractors in the East India Company. On his return to England, Copland had been welcomed by the Court but was asked to respond to charges that instead of strengthening the men's resolve to fight in the Indies, he had preached to them that the hostilities against the

Dutch were unlawful. Copland refuted the allegations and informed the Court that he had compiled reports about the state of the Company's factories which he promised to turn over. Doubtless these would have included comments about Japan. Unfortunately, the papers have been lost (IOR B/7, pp. 116–17).

13 Parker, *Books to Build an Empire*, p. 184.

14 John C. Appleby, 'An Association For the West Indies? English Plans for a West India Company 1621–29', *Journal of Imperial and Commonwealth History*, 15, May 1987, p. 224.

15 *The Old World and the New*, Cambridge, 1970, p. 29

16 Quoted in P. J. Marshall and Glyndwr Williams, *The Great Map of Mankind*, London, 1982, p. 8.

17 On this point see John Premble's admirable book *The Mediterranean Passion*, Oxford, 1987, esp. p. 259.

18 Parker, *Books to Build an Empire*, pp. 231–3.

19 Royal Society MS CP.19.42; *Philosophical Transactions*, 109, 14 December 1674, pp. 201, 205–6; Robert Boyle, *General heads for the Natural History of a Country great or small*, London, 1692, p. 92. Nachod, *Die Beziehungen*, pp. CLXVII–CLXVIII; W. C. H. Robert (ed.), *Voyage to Cathay, Tartary and the Gold-and-Silver Rich Islands East of Japan*, Amsterdam, 1975.

20 *The Ship of Sulaiman*, translated by John O'Kane, London, 1972, pp. 188–98.

21 Lach, *Asia in the Making of Europe*, 1:1, p. 77; Marshall and Williams, *Great Map of Mankind*, p. 8.

22 Ibid., pp. 24–5; Massarella, 'Loudest Lies', p. 53.

23 Cocks to Wilson, 10 March 1620 printed in Wild (ed.), *Purchas His Pilgrimes in Japan*, p. 228.

24 Canny, 'Edmund Spenser', p. 4.

25 François Caron & Joost Shouten, *A True Description of the Mighty Kingdoms of Japan & Siam, London, 1663*, edited by C. R. Boxer, London, 1935; Arnaldus Montanus, *Atlas Japannensis: being Remarkable Addresses by way of Embassy from the East India Company of the United Provinces to the Emperor of Japan*, translated by John Ogilby, London 1670; Jean de Thevenot, *The Travels of Monsieur de Thevenot into the Levant*, London, 1687; Engelbert Kaempher, *The History of Japan together with a Description of the Kingdom of Siam 1690–1692*, London, 1727. Only Caron and Kaem-

pher had been to Japan. Kaempher's original German manuscript was altered before publication to make it more marketable (Beatrice M. Bodart Bailey, 'Kaempher Restor'd', *Monumenta Nipponica*, 43:1, 1988, pp. 1–33. Kaempher does not mention the English factory in Hirado.

26 *Some Years Travels into Africa and Asia the Great*, London, 1638, pp. 333–6. The first edition appeared in 1634 but contains little about Japan. Other editions followed in 1665 and 1677 and it was translated into Dutch (1658) and French (1663). It was included in John Hamilton Moore's *New & Complete Collection of Voyages & Travels*, London, 1785. The preface is from the 1677 edition.

27 Thomas Salmon, *Modern History: or the Present State of All Nations*, 3 vols, London, 1744, I, p. 46. Other anthologies which draw on the Hirado material published by Purchas include the sixth edition of Pieter Heylyn's *Micrcosmus*, Oxford, 1682, III, p. 220; John Harris, *Navigantium atque Itinerantium Bibliotheca or a Complete Collection of Voyages and Travels*, London, 1744, pp. 860–73; Thomas Astley's *A New General Collection of Voyages and Travels*, London, 1745, I, book 3, pp. 451–531; A. Anderson's *Historical & Chronological Deduction of Commerce from the earliest accounts*, 2 vols, London, 1764, I, pp. 489, 490.

28 Quoted in Crone and Skelton, 'English Collections of Voyages and Travel Writings 1625–1846', p. 91.

29 Chaudhuri, *Trading World*, p. 79. See also K. N. Chaudhuri 'The English East India Company in the 17th and 18th Centuries: A Pre-modern Multinational Organization', in Blussé and Gaastra (eds), *Companies and Trade*, pp. 38–9; Chaudhuri, *Trade and Civilization in the Indian Ocean*, especially pp. 82–3.

30 Joseph Wicki, 'Archives and Libraries in Rome concerning Portuguese India', in John Correia-Afonso (ed.), *Indo-Portuguese History: Sources and Problems*. Bombay, 1981, pp. 37, 38.

31 *Letters Received*, I, pp. xv–xvi; IOR B/3, f. 37v.

32 IOR B/5, pp. 318, 468.

33 See above, p. 193.

34 IOR G/40/1; *CCM, 1668–1670*, pp. 72, 180; William Foster, *A Guide to the India Office Records, 1600–1858*, London, 1919, p. 1 ff; William Foster, *The*

East India House, London, 1924, p. 51 & n.

35 For a fuller discussion of this see Massarella, 'Loudest Lies', *passim*.

36 Bassett, 'Trade of the English East India Company in the Far East', pp. 32–47, 145–56.

37 IOR E/3/11, ff. 87v, 91, 91v, 95–95v. The Spanish were soon to be present on Taiwan. In May 1626 they occupied the northeast portion of the island which they proclaimed a territory of the Spanish king. Attempts to colonise the aboriginal natives met with little success and the Spanish were driven from the island by the Dutch in August 1642 (Hsu, 'From Aboriginal Island to Chinese Frontier. pp. 14–15.

38 IOR E/3/10, f. 50; E/3/11, ff. 87v, 207–210v Pratt, *History of Japan*, ii, pp. 119–26; *CSP Colonial, East Indies...1625–1629*, p. 372.

39 ARA KA 1002, f. 210; KA 11,722, pp. 60–61, 62, 63, 79.

40 IOR E/3/11, f. 99v.

41 ARA KA 11,722, pp. 279–80.

42 Nachod, *Die Beziehungen*, pp. 188–223, 249–53; Caron and Schouten, *A True Description of the Mighty Kingdoms of Japan & Siam*, pp. xvi–xxvi; Knauth, *Confrontación Transpacífica*, pp. 315–18; Nagazumi 'Japan's Isolationist Policy', p. 21. Nuyts spent four years in detention in Japan before being released in 1636.

43 Boxer, *Great Ship*, pp. 115–22.

44 Ibid., pp. 117, 126; Iwao, *Shuinsen*, pp. 127, 381; Innes, 'The Door Ajar', pp. 380, 390, 391–2.

45 Israel, 'A Conflict of Empires', pp. 48–63. See also Jonathan I. Israel, 'The Politics of International Trade Rivalry during the Thirty Years War: Gabreil de Roy and Olivares' Mercantalist Projects, 1621–1645', *The International History Review*, 8:4, 1986, pp. 517–49, especially pp. 520, 539–40.

46 Chaudhuri, *East India Company*, p. 57.

47 Two journals from the *Hosiander* voyage survive, one written by Ralph Coppindale (IOR L/MAR/A/XXIII), the cape merchant, the other by Rowland Thomas, the purser (BL Egerton MS, 2121).

48 BL Cotton Vesp. FXVII, ff. 277–77v; IOR E/3/8, f. 100; *Diary*, ii, pp. 143, 144. In the late 1620s the Dutch did not estimate the market for European cloth in Japan as extensive and had a standing order for fixed amounts of certain kinds

(William Campbell, *Formosa Under the Dutch*, London, 1903, p. 58).

49 IOR B/7, pp. 235, 280, 283–4, 292–93; Pratt, *History of Japan*, ii, pp. 127–9; CCM, *1635–1639*, p. 119; Bassett, 'Trade of the English East India Company in the Far East', p. 40; Chaudhuri, *East India Company*, pp. 58–9; Robert Ashton, *The City and the Court 1603–1643*, Cambridge, 1979, pp. 127–9. Smethwick also gave £100 towards the repairs of St Paul's from his investment in the Company (IOR Home Misc. Series 39, f. 87).

50 Pratt, *History of Japan*, ii, pp. 129–31. Cf. Bassett, 'Trade of the English East India Company in the Far East', p. 40.

51 Pratt, *History of Japan*, ii, p. 131.

52 Temple (ed.), *Travels of Peter Mundy*, iii, pp. 154, 271–2, 294–5, 431, 439, 481, 484, 491, 493, 500, 502ff; Hosea Ballou Morse, *The Chronicles of the East India Company Trading to China 1635–1854*, 5 vols, Oxford, 1926–9, i, pp. 14–30, Tōkyō Daigaku Shiryō Hensan-jo (ed.), *Dagregister...Japan*, ii, pp. 46, 175; iii, pp. 12–13; Blussé et al (eds), *Die Dagregisters van het Kasteel Zeelandia, Taiwan*, i, 1629–1641, p. 346; Chaudhuri, *East India Company*, p. 73; Souza, *Survival of Empire*, p. 214. Morse provides a chronology of events but his interpretation is out of date. Weddel's ship and all aboard perished on the return voyage to England.

53 Iwao, *Shuinsen*, pp. 411–14.

54 John W. Hall, 'Rule by Status in Tokugawa Japan', *Journal of Japanese Studies*, 1:1, 1974, pp. 39–49; Innes, 'The Door Ajar', pp. 153–6, William S. Atwell ('Some Obervations on the "Seventeenth-Century Crisis" in China and Japan,' *Journal of Asian Studies*, 45:2, 1986, pp. 223–44) suggests the possibility of a broader perspective from which to view these events.

55 Nachod, *Die Beziehungen*, p. 226; Nagazumi, 'Japan's Isolationist Policy', pp. 24–5; Katō, 'Japanese-Dutch Trade', p. 66; Innes, 'The Door Ajar', p. 160.

56 Tōkyō Daigaku Shiryō Hensan-jo (ed.), *Dagregister...Japan*, iv, p. 20; Nachod, *Die Beziehungen*, pp. 270–1. The ban on Japanese women associating with the Dutch was eased to the extent that the Dutch were provided with prostitutes to satisfy their bodily needs.

57 Ibid., p. 279.

58 Ibid., pp. 273–6, 279–88, CLI–CLII; Nagazumi, 'Japan's Isolationist Policy', pp. 26–32, 35; Innes 'The Door Ajar', pp. 161–4.

59 Katō, 'Dutch–Japanese Trade', pp. 55–6; Nagazumi, 'Japan's Isolationist Policy', pp. 31–2.

60 Ronald P. Toby, 'Reopening the Question of Sakoku: Diplomacy in the Legitimation of the Tokugawa Bakufu', *Journal of Japanese Studies*, 3:2, 1977, p. 362 n. 120.

61 Toby, *State and Diplomacy, passim*; Toby, 'Contesting the Centre: International Sources of Japanese National Identity', *International History Review*, 7:3, 1985, pp. 347–63. Kaempher's essay is printed as an appendix to the second volume of the *History of Japan*, pp. 52–75.

62 The paranoia about Christianity should not be downplayed among the explanations of bakafu behaviour in the 1630s. As early as 1626 Neyenroode had warned the governor general in Batavia against Dutch ships bringing Japanese back to Japan for fear they might be Roman Catholics, as was the case with Japanese returning from Manila. He urged the governor general to inform Ayuthia of this (ARA KA 1002, f. 210v). In April 1636, the bakufu still insecure about the exact nature of Dutch Christianity asked the *opperhoofd* to explain the difference between the Christianity of the Dutch and that of the Portuguese – exactly the question that Cocks had been asked on numerous occasions during his visits to the shogunal court (Tōkyō Daigaku Shiryō Hensan-jo (ed.), *Dagregister...Japan*, II, p. 45).

63 Nachod, *Die Beziehungen*, pp. CCIV; Katō, 'Japanese–Dutch Trade'. pp. 42–3, 53, 65; Katō, 'Rengō Oranda Higashi-Indo Kaisha', pp. 420–1 (Professor Katō's figures for silk import are more reliable than Nachod's); Prakash, *The Dutch East India and the Economy of Bengal*, p. 119. The dramatic increase in the volume of Dutch trade with Japan after 1624 can be seen from the graph in Katō, 'Rengō Oranda Higashi-Indō Kaisha', p. 504.

64 Nachod, *Die Beziehungen* pp. 288–9, 297; Katō, 'Rengō Oranda Higashi-Indō Kaisha', pp. 420–1.

65 Boxer, *Christian Century*, pp. 384–8. For Macao's own restructuring of its trade after 1639 see Souza, *Survival of Empire, passim*.

66 This is treated more fully in Derek Massarella, 'A World Elsewhere': Aspects of the Overseas Expansioist Mood of the 1650s', in Colin Jones *et al.* (eds.), *Politics and People in Revolutionary England*, Oxford, 1986, pp. 142–6.

67 *CCM, 1655–1659*, pp. 281–3, 286, 290, 300 & n.

68 IOR G/21/4, p. 5 re-printed in D. K. Bassett, 'The Trade of the English East India Company in Cambodia', *Journal of the Royal Asiaitc Society*, April 1962, pp. 55–61, especially p. 57. There are specific references to Scots visiting Japan, on Dutch ships (BL Harleian MS 4254, ff. 21v–22; F. J. Routledge [ed.], *Calendar of the Clarendon State Papers*, Oxford, 1970, v, p. 466). Doubtless other Britons in the VOC's employ did so as well.

69 *CCM, 1655–1659*, pp. 282–5; *1668–1670*, p. 105.

70 Ibid., *1655–1659*, p. 289; Pratt, *History of Japan*, II, p. 133; Bassett, 'Trade of the English East India Company in the Far East', pp. 145–6. From the 1660s Bantam was styled an agency rather than a presidency.

71 IOR G/12/1, pp. 68–76 especially p. 74; Morse, *Chronicles of the East India Company Trading to China*, I, pp. 33–5.

72 Pratt, *History of Japan*, II, pp. 133–4.

73 IOR E/3/28, ff. 191v–193v; G/21/4, p. 2; Pratt, *History of Japan*, II, pp. 135–7.

74 Pratt, *History of Japan*, II, p. 141; Prakash, *Dutch East India Company and the Economy of Bengal*, p. 121 n. 12.

75 IOR B/30, pp. 271, 273; IOL MS Eur D41, pp. 137, 138–41. I agree with Dr Bassett's argument that although there are many references to China and Manila in the sources after 1668 the prize was Japan (Bassett, 'Trade of the English East India Company in the Far East', p. 154). Japan, no matter how unrealistically, was seen as the *sine qua non* of any trade in east Asia.

76 Glamann, *Dutch Asiatic Trade*, pp. 57–9, 63, 173–6; Prakash, *Dutch East India Company and the Economy of Bengal*, pp. 124–30; Henry Roseveare (ed.), *Markets and Merchants in the Late Seventeenth Century: The Marescoe-David Letters 1668–1680*, London, 1987, pp. 46–7, 159. It should be stressed that no matter how profitable the Japan trade was for the VOC, except for odd years the Dutch lagged behind the Chinese as participants in Japan's

overseas trade. See Iwao Seiichi, 'Kinsei Nisshi bōeki ni kansuru sūryōteki kōsatsu', *Shigaku Zasshi*, 62, 1953, p. 28, and the tables in Innes. 'The Door Ajar', pp. 410, 416–17. For a full discussion of Chinese trade through Nagasaki see Yamawaki Teijiro, *Nagasaki no Tōjin bōeki*, Tokyo, 1972.

77 Prakash, *Dutch East India Company and the Economy of Bengal*, p. 20.

78 Derived from Nachod, *Die Beziehungen*, pp. CCVIII–CCIX.

79 Ibid., pp. 355–56, CLXXVII–CXC; C. R. Boxer, 'Jan Compagnie in Japan 1672–1674 or Anglo-Dutch Rivalry in Japan and Formosa', *Transactions of the Asiatic Society of Japan*, second series, VII, 1930, appendix III, p. 185 ff; Innes, 'The Door Ajar', pp. 305–6. Copper does not figure as an East India Company import from the Indies and was in fact exported from Europe (Chaudhuri, *Trading World*, p. 220).

80 IOL MS Eur D41, pp. 138, 144; Serafin D. Quiason, 'The Early Trade of the English East India Company with Manila', *Philippine Historical Review*, 1, 1965, pp. 286–90. My interpretation of events concerning Company policy differs from Professor Quiason's.

81 IOR B/29, p. 62; B/30, p. 319; *CCM, 1668–1670*, pp. 63, 105.

82 In July 1669 a new committee was formed 'to consider further of the Manila trade & how that & Japan may suit together' (IOR B/30, p. 492). The earlier committee concerned itself wholly with Japan and was styled 'the Japan committee', although there was an overlap of personnel.

83 IOR B/29, p. 62; *CCM, 1668–1670*, pp. 105, 111; Pratt, *History of Japan*, I, pp. 469–82; ibid, II, p. 143n; Murakami (ed.), *Diary of Richard Cocks*, II, pp. 361–70.

84 IOR B/29, p. 62.

85 Pratt, *History of Japan*, II, pp. 143–5.

86 IOR E/3/30, no. 3340; Iwao Seiichi (ed.), *Shin-ch'i shih-chi T'ai-wan Ying-kuo mao-i shih-liao* (Sources on English Trade with Taiwan in the Seventeenth Century), Taipei, 1959, p. 76.

87 On these developments see C. R. Boxer, 'The Siege of Fort Zeelandia and the Capture of Formosa from the Dutch, 1661–1662' *Transactions and Proceedings of the Japan Society*, London, XXIV, 1926–7, pp. 16–47; Boxer, 'The Rise and Fall of Nicholas Iquan', *T'ienhsui Monthly*, 11:5, 1941, pp. 401–39;

Donald Keene, *The Battles of Coxinga*, London, 1951, pp. 44–75; Wills, *Pepper, Guns & Parleys*, pp. 25–8; Wills, 'Maritime China from Wang Chih to Shih Lang', pp. 217–29; Lynn A. Struve, *The Southern Ming 1644–1662*, New Haven, 1984, *passim*. The Dutch re-established themselves briefly, from 1664–8, on the northeast of the island. (Wills, *Pepper, Guns & Parleys*, p. 144).

88 Iwao (ed.), *Shih-ch'i shih-chi T'ai-wan Ying-kuo mao-i shih-liao*, pp. 77–9, 131–40. The junk *Camel* did not go on this voyage. It went in 1671 and in 1672 as a pilot ship. Cf Bassett, 'Trade of the English East India Company in the Far East', p. 151.

89 Iwao, 'Kinsei Nisshi bōeki', pp. 12–13, 31; Iwao, 'Japanese Foreign Trade', pp. 12–13; Yamawaki Teijirō, 'The Great Trading Merchant, Cocksinga and His Son', *Acta Asiatica*, 30, 1976, pp. 111–12, 114; Innes, 'The Door Ajar', pp. 174–5; Toby, *State and Diplomacy*, pp. 137–9, 166–7; Struve, *Southern Ming*, pp. 117–20.

90 Prakash, *Dutch East India Company*, pp. 122–3, 125, 131.

91 IOR E/3/30, no. 3340; Pratt, *History of Japan*, II, pp. 140–1, 153–7. Noteworthy is the agency's worry about the sensitive question of why the English had killed their king (Charles I). Concerned lest the Dutch had mentioned this to the bakufu, the factors were instructed to answer any query with the response that the execution had been an act of rebellion and that England was a monarchy, the greatest in Europe. The agency need not have fretted. Such detailed knowledge of English history only became known in Japan in the nineteenth century. Besides, the two ships never made it to Japan and were lost, only the *Camel* returning safely to Bantam (Pratt, *History of Japan*, II, p. 156; Iwao [ed.], *Shih-ch'i shih ch'i Tai'wan Ying-kuo mao-i shih liao*, p. 89, Imai Hiroshi, 'British Influence on Modern Japanese Historiography, *Saeculum*, 38:1, 1987, p. 103).

92 IOR E/3/87, f. 223; Iwao (ed.), *Shih-ch'i shih-chi T'ai-wan Ying-kuo mao-i shih-liao*, pp. 50, 53.

93 IOR B/31, pp. 208, 210, 211, 213, 214, 215, 233, 252, 253, 255, 258, 263, 275, 284, 286, 287, 290, 292, 294, 302, 304, 306–7, 309, 315, 344.

94 IOR E/3/87, ff. 236–37; Pratt, *History*

of Japan, II, pp. 159–60.

95 IOR E/3/87, ff. 235–241v, 241v–243v; Nachod, Die Beziehungen pp. CLXVIII–CLXIX.

96 IOR G/21/6A, p. 16. There were some last minute changes (ibid., pp. 39–40). The pagination refers to the documents beginning with the commission and instructions issued by the agent, Henry Dacres, dated Bantam, 30 June 1671.

97 IOR E/3/33, no 3346; Nachod, Die Beziehungen, p. CCIII.

98 J. A. van der Chijs (ed.), Dagh Register gehouden int Casteel Batavia...1673, Batavia, 1901, pp. 106–7; Iwao (ed.), 'Shih-ch'i shih-chi T'ai-wan Ying-kuo mao-i shih-liao, pp. 140–4; Boxer, 'Jan Compagnie in Japan 1672–1674', appendix II, pp. 182–3.

99 IOL MS Eur D41, p. 162.

100 Van der Chijs (ed.), Dagh Register ...Batavia...1673, p. 328; Boxer, 'Jan Compagnie in Japan 1672–1674', appendix II, pp. 182–83.

101 For the Dutch comment see Van der Chijs, (ed.) Dagh Register...Batavia...1673, p. 328. There are a number of versions of the journal kept by the factors on the Return at Nagasaki, all with minor differences (PRO CO 77/12, ff. 232–47, 250–60v, 262–69; IOR G/21/4, pp. 118–30; Home Misc. Series 456a, pp. 369–422; Bodleian Library, Rawlinson MS A 191, ff. 69–76. Printed versions appear in Kaempher, History of Japan, II, appendix II; Murakami (ed.) Diary of Richard Cocks, II, pp. 374–94; Paske-Smith, Western Barbarians in Japan and Formosa, pp. 70–81; Roger Makin (ed.), Experiment and Return, Kyoto, 1978, which prints three. Murakami (ed.), Diary of Richard Cocks, II, pp. 395–432 and Makin (ed.), Experiment and Return, pp. 1–53 from the back, especially pp. 7, 38–9, 51, 52–3, print valuable documents in Japanese. The ease with which the Japanese officials realised that the document presented to them in Japanese was not the original privileges was noted by Kondō Morishige, who described it in detail, in the early nineteenth century in his compilation Gaiban tsūcho (Kokusho Kankōkai [ed.], Kondō Seisai zenshū, 3 vols, Tokyo, 1906, I, pp. 190–1, separate pagination for each work; Satow [ed.], Saris, pp. lxxxvi-lxxxvii). On the events of 1647 see C. R. Boxer, A Portuguese Embassy to Japan (1644–1647), London, 1928, pp. 27–31; C. R.

Boxer, The Embassy of Captain Gonçalo der Siqueira de Souza to Japan in 1644–1647, Macau, 1938. For the later English voyages to Japan and the attempt by Sir Stamford Raffles to rerestablish a presence in Japan on behalf of the East India Company – to sell woollen cloth and other European manufactures – see M. Paske Smith (ed.), Report on Japan, reprinted London, 1971, pp. 89, 162, 165 and passim; W. G. Beasley, Great Britian and the Opening of Japan 1834–1858, London, 1951, ch. 1. The Dutch surgeon Christopher Frye's statement that several English and French ships lay in Nagasaki harbour in 1683 is a nonsense (Fayle [ed.], Voyages to the East Indies, pp. 98, 101).

102 IOR G/12/1, pp. 154, 157, 158; Van der Chijs (ed.), Dagh Register... Batavia...1663, Batavia, 1891, p. 641; Boxer, 'Jan Compagnie in Japan 1672–1674', pp. 145–6, 162; Tōkyō Daigaku Shiryō Hensan-jo (ed.), Dagregister...Japan, IV, p. 116.

103 Boxer, 'Jan Compagnie in Japan 1672–1674', appendix ii, p. 181. The Return did bring along some Chinese goods but not a significant amount.

104 Nachod, Die Beziehungen, pp. 365–89; Innes, 'The Door Ajar', pp. 306–15; Glamann, Dutch Asiatic Trade, pp. 57–8, 62–3, 68–9, 116–17, 165–82; Prakash, Dutch East India Company and the Economy of Bengal, p. 129.

105 Boxer, 'Jan Compagnie in Japan 1672–1674', p. 164.

106 Nachod, Die Beziehungen, pp. 369, CXC; Wills, Pepper, Guns & Parleys, pp. 34–5, 37.

107 Iwao, 'Kinsei Nisshi-bōeki', pp. 12–13; Iwao, 'Reopening of the Diplomatic and Commercial Relations between Siam and Japan', Acta Asiatica, 4, 1963 pp. 1–31 especially p. 30.

108 PRO CO 77/12, f. 260v; IOR G/12/4, p. 104. Even if the Dutch did give the Japanese officials in Nagasaki a 'sweetner', and this is possible, it would have had no bearing whatsoever on the outcome. Similar unfounded charges were made against the Dutch after Gonçalo de Siqueira de Souza's failure in 1647 (Boxer, A Portuguese Embassy to Japan (1644–1647), p. 5).

109 IOR G/21/4, p. 110. By this time the bakufu made a distinction between the nanban (since the 1630s exclusively identified with the Catholic Portuguese and Spanish) and the Ranjin (Dutch

people) who were referred to less flatteringly as *kōmōjin* (red-haired people). For examples of the distinctions see *Tokugawa Kinreikō*, compiled by Kikuchi Shunsuke, 6 vols, Tokyo, 1931–1932, VI, p. 568; *Tokugawa jikki*, v, p. 403 in *Shintei zōho kokushi taikei*, Tokyo, 1964; Toby, *State and Diplomacy*, p. 195, n. 69.

110 IOR E/3/7, ff. 260v–261; E/3/88, f. 68. The Dutch and Portuguese had concluded a peace treaty in 1662 and traded with each other in the Indies but they had not ceased to be commercial competitors (Souza, *Survival of Empire*, pp. 220–1).

111 IOR E/3/88, ff. 68v–69.

112 IOL MS Eur D41, p. 165; Iwao (ed.), *Shih-ch'i shih-ch'i T'ai-wan Ying-kuo mao-i shih-liao*, pp. 149–50.

113 IOR Home Misc. 392, pp. 295–323 *passim*; E/3/90, f. 14; *CCM, 1674–1676*, pp. xx–xxi; Pratt, *History of Japan*, II, pp. 192–3; Chaudhuri, *Trading World of Asia*, pp. 216–17. In the statement of accounts for the general joint-stock for 1671–1678 the figure was revised to £40,000, but it was stressed that the expenditure was 'not altogether fruitless' for several discoveries had been made and foundations laid which would result in less expenditure in future efforts to obtain trade with Japan, 'which may be very valuable', although no additional funds had been set aside (*CCM, 1677–1679*, p. 340).

114 Pratt, *History of Japan*, II, pp. 195–8.

115 BL Sloane MS 998, f. 45v.

116 Iwao, *Shih-ch'i shih-chi T'ai-wan Ying-kuo mao-i shih-lao*, p. 211; Iwao, 'Reopening Diplomatic and Commercial Relations', pp. 26–8.

117 *Records of Fort St George, Despatches from England 1681–1686*, Madras, 1916, p. 121.

118 *Records of Fort St George, Despatches from England 1686–1692*. Madras, 1929, p. 175.

119 Ibid., *1681–1686*, p. 116

120 See above n. 25. A similar *Atlas Chinensis* which was also translated by Ogilby appeared in 1671. It was erroneously ascribed to Montanus. See Wills, *Guns, Pepper & Parleys*, p. 18n.

121 IOR E/3/91, f. 24.

122 *Records of Fort St George, Despatches from England 1681–1686*, p. 97; *Records of Fort St. George, Letters to Fort St George 1686–1687*, Madras, 1919, p. 107. The Dutch seizure of Bantam, their final triumph in the seventeenth-century struggle against the English and an empty victory, forced the English to withdraw to Sumatra where a factory was established at Bencolen in 1685.

123 Nachod, *Die Beziehungen*, pp. 365–89; Tashiro Kazui, 'Tsushima Han's Korean Trade, 1684–1710', *Acta Asiatica*, 30, 1976, pp. 85–105; Tashiro Kazui, *Nitchō tsuko bōekishi no-kenkyū*, Tokyo, 1981; Tashiro Kazui, 'Foreign Relations During the Edo Period: *Sakoku* Reconsidered', *Journal of Japanese Studies*, 8:2, 1982, pp. 283–306; Innes, 'The Door Ajar', pp. 319–62, 415–518; Glamann, *Dutch Asiatic Trade*, pp. 68–9, 175–82; Prakash, *Dutch East India Company and the Economy of Bengal*, pp. 124–41.

124 *Records of Fort St George, Despatches from England 1681–1686*, p. 148.

125 IOR E/3/62, no. 7765.

126 IOR E/3/56, no. 6988.

127 Ng, *Trade and Society, passim*.

128 Bassett, 'Trade of the English East India Company in the Far East', p. 153; Furber, *Rival Empires of Trade*, p. 127; Chaudhuri, *Trading World*, pp. 345–52, especially pp. 345–6, 388. The court had ordered the Tongking factory's closure in 1695 but as with Hirado the process took longer and the accounts were in a mess (IOR G/12/4, pp. 581, 583).

129 Chaudhuri, *Trading World*, pp. 54–5, 97, 538–9.

130 C. Fawcett (ed.) *English Factories in India*, 4 vols, Oxford, 1936–55, III, p. 237; Chaudhuri, *Trading World*, pp. 55–6.

Bibliographical Essay

What follows is an overview of the primary and secondary sources used in the writing of this book. It is not a comprehensive bibliography but is intended to serve as a guide; the detailed references are contained in the footnotes.

The most important primary sources for the study of the East India Company are contained in the Company's archive located in the India Office Library and Records, now administratively within the British Library. Unfortunately, only a part of the records for the early history of the Company survive. The most important documents are to be found in the Original Correspondence (E/3) and among the Factory Records (G/12, China and Japan, G/21, Java, G/40, miscellaneous, were especially useful). These tell us what the factors in the Indies were thinking and doing. The Court Minutes (B/1 etc.) enable us to understand what policy decisions the directors made but not, alas, how they were reached. The Marine Records (L/MAR) contain useful information about particular voyages.

Some important documents which belong archivally to the Company's records have become displaced. The most important are in the British Library among the Cotton MSS and Charters. These include John Osterwick's accounts from September 1615-January 1617 (BL Cotton Vespasian MS F.XVII, f. 63ff). A few other Company-related documents found their way into other collections; for example, the *shuinjō* granting the English trade privileges in Japan in 1613 and William Adams's log-book are in the Bodleian Library (MS Jap. b.2 [R] and Savil MS 48); letters from Richard Cocks in the Public Record Office (CO 77/1) and the Kent Record Office (ON 6713), and other documents, including Cocks's diary, in the British Library (Add. MSS 31,300; 31301). As is usually the case with research among the archives, relevant material can turn up in unexpected places. The Home Miscellaneous Series in the IOR, for example, contains information about the broadcloth purchased and laden on the *Clove*; BL Egerton MS 2123, an incomplete but important letter from the directors to the Bantam presidency in 1623, the time when the Company was retrenching in the southwards region.

The Dutch East India Company's archive is astonishingly rich. However, the records for the VOC's early trade in Japan do not contain documents with quite the same human element as the English Company's. Nevertheless, it is impossible to understand English activity in Japan and the Indies without reference to the Dutch. The VOC's archive (*Koloniale Archieven Oost-Indie: Archieven van de Vereenigde Oost-Indische Compagnie*) is located in the Algemeen Rijksarchief in The Hague. M. P. H. Rossingh has provided a list of the documents concerning the VOC and Japan (*Het Archief van de Nederlandse Factorij in Japan/The Archive of the Dutch Factory in Japan 1609–1860*, The Hague, n.d.) and the Shiryō Hensan-jo (Historiographical Institute) of the University of Tokyo contains a microfilm collection of the documents relating to Japan which I have used. As a result the references are to the old KA (*Koloniale Archieven*) call numbers rather than the new VOC (*Vereenigde Oost-Indische Compagnie*) ones. The Shiryō Hensan-jo has published a guide to its microfilm holdings from foreign archives (*Historical Documents relating to Japan in Foreign Countries*, Tokyo, 1963–9). Volume 1 deals with the Netherlands.

Japanese source material is contained in the *Ikoku nikki* (Register of Foreign Affairs) compiled by the Zen priest Suden (1579–1633) whose many duties included that of foreign advisor to the shogunate. Relevant documents from this collection and other useful material concerning the English are printed in Hayashi Akira (compiler), *Tsukō ichiran*, 8 vols, Tokyo, 1913, vol. 6. The *Gaiban tsuchō* compiled by Kondō Morishige in the early nineteenth century contains additional information, especially about the abortive attempt to return to Japan in 1673. It has been published in the first volume of an edition of Kondō's writings by Kokusho Kankōkai, *Kondō Seisai zenshu*, 3 vols, Tokyo, 1960. Other Japanese source material relating to the 1673 attempt is printed in volume 2 of Naojiro Murakami, *Diary of Richard Cocks*, 2 vols, Tokyo 1899, and in the Japanese language appendix compiled by Shimizu Hirokazu in Roger Makin (ed.), *Experiment and Return*, Kyoto, 1978. Some letters in Japanese relating to the English factory in Hirado, including some personal ones, survive among the India Office Records and in the British Library. They have been printed as a separate appendix to the third volume of the Japanese translation of Cocks's *Diary* mentioned below. Collections of printed source material in English include Henry Stevens and George Birdwood (eds), *The Dawn of British Trade to the East Indies as recorded in the Court Minutes of the East India*

Company, London, 1886; W. Noël Sainsbury (ed.), *Calendar of State Papers- Colonial, East Indies*, 5 vols, London 1862–92; George Birdwood and William Foster (eds), *The First Letter Book of the East India Company, 1600–1619*, London 1892; William Foster (ed.), *Letters Received by the East India Company from its Servants in the East*, 6 vols, London, 1896–1902; in Dutch, H. T. Colenbrander and W. Ph. Coolhaas (eds), *Jan Pietersz. Coen: Bescheiden Omtrent Zijn Bedrijf in Indie*, 7 vols, The Hague, 1919–53; W. Ph. Coolhaas (ed.), *Generale Missiven van Gouverneurs Generaal en Raden aan Heren XVII der Vereenigde Oost-Indische Compagnie*, 7 vols, The Hague, 1960–79.

The Hakluyt Society and its Dutch counterpart the Linschoten Vereeniging have performed a great service by publishing important editions of source material over the years. Of particular relevance to Japan are Ernest M. Satow (ed.), *The Voyage of Captain John Saris to Japan, 1613*, London, 1900; F. C. Wieder (ed.), *De reis van Mahu en De Cordes door Straat van Magalhães naar Zuid-Amerika en Japan, 1598–1600*, The Hague, 3 vols, 1923–25; M. E. van Opstall (ed.), *De Reis van de Vloot van Pieter Willemsz. Verhoeff naar Azie 1607–1612*, 2 vols, The Hague, 1972. Edward Maunde Thompson's edition of the *Diary of Richard Cocks* for the Hakluyt Society (2 vols, London, 1883) has been superseded by the one edited by Tōkyō Daigaku Shiryō Hensan-jo, *Nihon kankei kaigai shiryō: Igirisu shōkancho nikki (Diary of Richard Cocks, 1615–1622)*. There is an English version (3 vols, Tokyo, 1978–80) and a Japanese translation (3 vols. and Appendix, Tokyo, 1979–82). Naojiro Murakami's edition of Thompson's *Diary of Richard Cocks* (2 vols, Tokyo, 1899) remains useful for the Japanese primary source material it contains in vol. 2. The Shiryō hensan-jo is also editing the *Dagregister* or journal of the Dutch factory in Japan. So far six volumes have appeared covering the period from September 1633 to October 1642 (*Nihon kankei kaigai shiryō: Oranda Shōkancho nikki, Diaries kept by the Heads of the Dutch Factory in Japan, Dagregisters gehouden bij de opperhoofden van het Nederlandsche Factorij in Japan*), Tokyo, 1974–. There is also a Japanese translation.

The secondary source material is vast. One cannot venture far into the study of the Indies, including Japan, without acknowledging a great debt to C. R. Boxer's energetic scholarship. Of Professor Boxer's prodigious writings, *The Portuguese Seaborne Empire: 1415–1825*, London, 1965, and *The Dutch Seaborne Empire*, London, 1965 provide convenient points of departure. K. N. Chaudhuri, *Trade and Civilisation in the Indian Ocean: An Economic History from the Rise of Islam*, Cambridge, 1985, and Philip Curtin, *Cross-Cultural Trade*, Cambridge, 1984, are more ambitious; the former is masterly. There are excellent general accounts of European expansion in B. W. Diffie and George Winius, *Foundations of the Portuguese Empire 1415–1580*,

Minneapolis, 1977; Holden Furber, *Rival Empires of Trade in the Orient 1600–1800*, Minneapolis, 1975; G. V. Scammel, *The World Encompassed*, London, 1981. Geoffrey Parker, *The Military Revolution*, Cambridge, 1988, poses some familiar questions; it answers them in a bold, stimulating manner. J. C. van Leur, *Indonesian Trade and Society*, The Hague, 1955, remains essential reading but should be used in conjunction with M. A. P. Meilink-Roelofsz, *Asian Trade and European Influence in the Indonesian Archipelago, between 1500 and about 1630*, The Hague, 1962, and Niels Steensgaard, *The Asian Trade Revolution*, Chicago, 1974.

The background to England's part in European expansion is given solid coverage in K. R. Andrews, *Trade, Plunder and Settlement*, Cambridge, 1984. The essential starting point for an understanding of the East India Company itself is K. N. Chaudhuri's, *The English East India Company: The Study of an Early Joint-Stock Company 1600–1640*, London, 1965 and his *The Trading World of Asia and the English East India Company, 1660–1760*, Cambridge, 1978. These are thorough economic histories; the latter is a majestic *tour de force*.

The starting point for the VOC's trade in Asia is Kristof Glamann, *Dutch-Asiatic Trade, 1620–1740*, second edition, The Hague, 1981. On Dutch trade in Japan Oskar Nachod's *Die Beziehungen der Niederländischen Ostindischen Kompagnie zu Japan im siebzehnten Jahrhundert*, Leipzig, 1897, remains serviceable especially for the documents in the appendix. Inevitably it shows its age. For the early history of the VOC in Japan Nachod must be supplemented by Katō Eiichi, 'Rengō Oranda Higashi-Indō Kaisha no senryaku kyoten toshite no Hirado shōkan', in Tanaka Takeo (ed.), *Nihon zenkindai no koka to taigai kankei*, Tokyo, 1987; for the later history by Om Prakash, *The Dutch East India Company and the Economy of Bengal 1630–1720*, Princeton, 1985. On the Portuguese in Japan see C. R. Boxer, *The Great Ship from Amacon: Annals of Macao and the Old Japan Trade*, Lisbon, 1959 and on the Portuguese more generally in Asia, A. R. Disney, *Twilight of the Pepper Trade: Portuguese Trade in Southwest India in the Early Seventeenth Century*, Cambridge, Massachusetts, 1978; George Bryan Souza, *The Survival of Empire: Portuguese Trade and Society in China and the South China Sea 1630–1754*, Cambridge, 1986.

Important for the the sixteenth and seventeenth century Japanese background are two collections of essays, John Witney Hall and Toyoda Takeshi (eds), *Japan in the Muromachi Age*, Los Angeles, 1977 and John Witney Hall, Nagahara Kenji and Kozo Yamamura (eds), *Japan Before Tokugawa*, Princeton, 1981. C. R. Boxer, *The Christian Century in Japan, 1549–1650*, Berkeley, 1951, Lothar Knauth, *Confrontación Transpacífica: El Japon y el Nuevo Mundo Hispanico 1542–1639*, Mexico, 1972, George Ellison, *Deus Destroyed,*

Cambridge, Massachusetts, 1973; Robert L. Innes, 'The Door Ajar: Japan's Foreign Relations in the Seventeenth Century', unpublished University of Michigan Ph.D. thesis, 1980, and Ronald P. Toby, *State and Diplomacy in Early Modern Japan*, Princeton, 1983, deal with key aspects of Japan's foreign relations. Among Iwao Seiichi's extensive writings, his books on the *shuinsen* (vermilion seal ships) and the southeast Asian *nihonmachi* (Japanese communities) painstakingly piece together Japan's first major advance into overseas markets, a subject little known about in the West: *Shuinsen bōeki-shi no kenkyū* (A Study of the Vermilion Seal Ship Trade), second edition, Tokyo, 1985; *Nan'yō Nihonmachi no kenkyū* (A Study of the Japanese Communities in the Southern Seas), Tokyo, 1966, *Nan'yō Nihonmachi no kenkyū, zoku* (A Study of the Japanese Communities in the Southern Seas: A Sequel), Tokyo, 1987.

The broader picture of cross–cultural contact is taken up in Donald F. Lach's multi-volume, *Asia in the Making of Europe*, Chicago, 1966-. So far the sixteenth-century volumes have appeared; the seventeenth-century volumes, edited by Lach and Edwin van Kley are in the press and volumes, covering the eighteenth century are planned. This is a monumental study and a labour of love but it confines itself to printed sources. P. J. Marshal and Glyndwyr Williams, *The Great Map of Mankind*, London, 1982, is more modest in ambition, more satisfying in achievement.

Finally, special mention should be made of the numerous publications of the Centre for the History of European Expansion at Leiden University, especially the journal *Itinerario* and the series Comparative Studies in Overseas History of which the first three volumes have been particularly useful: H. L. Wesseling (ed.), *Expansion and Reaction*, Leiden, 1978; P. C. Emmer and H. L. Wessling (eds), *Reappraisals in Overseas History*, Leiden, 1979; Leonard Blussé and Femme Gaastra (eds), *Companies and Trade*, Leiden, 1981. Anyone seeking to remain abreast of the latest research in a field which at last is breaking free of the shadow of empire can ill-afford to ignore the fruits of the Centre's enterprise.

Index

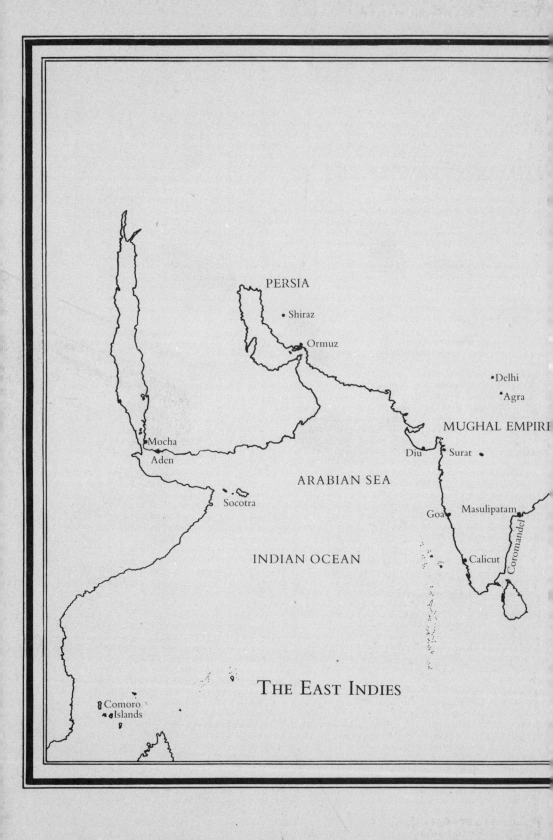

PERSIA

Shiraz

Ormuz

Delhi

Agra

MUGHAL EMPIRE

Mocha

Diu   Surat

Aden

ARABIAN SEA

Socotra

Goa   Masulipatam

Coromandel

INDIAN OCEAN

Calicut

THE EAST INDIES

Comoro
Islands